American Military
Collectibles
Price Guide

American Military Collectibles Price Guide

Collector items of historical interest from the United States of America

Ron Manion

Edited by Eric J. Johansson

Antique Trader Books
P. O. Box 1050
Dubuque, IA 52004

ISBN: 0-930625-47-1
Library of Congress Catalog Card No. 94-79665

Other books and magazines published by Antique Trader Publications:

German Military Collectibles Price Guide
Japanese & Other Foreign Military Collectibles Price Guide
Antiques & Collectibles Annual Price Guide
American Pressed Glass & Bottles Price Guide
American & European Decorative & Art Glass Price Guide
Ceramics Price Guide
American & European Furniture Price Guide
American & European Art Pottery Price Guide
Maloney's Antiques & Collectibles Resource Directory
Comics Values Annual
Rockin' Records Buyers-Sellers Reference Book & Price Guide
The Antique Trader Weekly
Collector Magazine & Price Guide
Toy Trader Magazine
Postcard Collector Magazine
Discoveries Magazine
Big Reel Magazine
Military Trader Magazine
Baby Boomer Collectibles Magazine

To order additional copies of this book
or other publications listed above, contact:
Antique Trader Publications
P. O. Box 1050
Dubuque, IA 52004
Phone: 1-800-334-7165

TABLE OF CONTENTS

FOREWORD. i
HOW TO UTILIZE THIS GUIDE. ii
INTRODUCTION. 1

CHAPTER 1: UNIFORMS & FOOTWEAR
U.S. UNIFORMS & FOOTWEAR
    A. Thru World War I (1919). 7
    B. 1920 - 1945. 12
    C. 1946 - Present. 28

CHAPTER 2: CLOTH INSIGNIA
U.S. ARMY CLOTH INSIGNIA
    A. Thru World War I (1919). 55
    B. 1920 - 1946. 60
    C. 1946 - Present. 80
U.S. AIR FORCE CLOTH INSIGNIA
    A. 1947 - Present. 91
U.S. NAVY & MARINE CORPS CLOTH INSIGNIA
    A. All Periods. 97

CHAPTER 3: METAL INSIGNIA
U.S. ARMY METALLIC INSIGNIA
    A. Thru World War I (1919). 105
    B. 1920 - 1945. 110
    C. 1946 - Present. 114
U.S. NAVY & MARINE CORPS METALLIC INSIGNIA
    A. All Periods. 115
U.S. WINGS
    A. 1913 - 1945. 117
    D. 1946 - Present. 121

CHAPTER 4: HEADGEAR
U.S. VISOR CAPS, SERVICE HATS & CAPS
    A. Thru World War I (1919). 123
    B. 1920 - 1945. 125
    C. 1946 - Present. 133
U.S. HELMETS
    A. Thru World War I (1919). 137
    B. 1920 - 1945. 141
    C. 1946 - Present. 146

CHAPTER 5: INDIVIDUAL EQUIPMENT & FIELD GEAR
U.S. GI FIELD GEAR / INDIVIDUAL EQUIPMENT
    A. Thru World War I (1919). 151
    B. 1920 - 1945. 161
    C. 1946 - Present. 181

CHAPTER 6: EDGED WEAPONS
U.S. KNIVES
    A. Thru World War I (1919). 189
    B. 1920 - 1945. 191
    C. 1946 - Present. 196
U.S. BAYONETS & MACHETES
    A. Thru World War I (1919). 198
    B. 1920 - 1945. 199
    C. 1946 - Present. 200
U.S. SWORDS
    A. All Periods. 201

CHAPTER 7: MEDALS & AWARDS
    U.S. AWARDS & QUALIFICATION BADGES
        A. Thru World War II (1945). 203
        B. 1946 - Present. 205
    U.S. MEDALS
        A. Thru World War I (1919). 206
        B. 1920 - 1945. 208
        C. 1946 - Present. 210

CHAPTER 8: PRINTED MILITARIA
    U.S. MILITARY RELATED BOOKS & MANUALS
        A. Thru World War I (1919). 215
        B. 1920 - 1945. 219
        C. 1946 - Present. 231
    U.S. MILITARY RELATED PHOTOS, POSTCARDS & TRADE CARDS
        A. All Periods. 232
    U.S. MILITARY RELATED POSTERS, MAPS & CHARTS
        A. All Periods. 234
    U.S. NEWSPAPERS, MAGAZINES, BROADSIDES & PERIODICALS
        A. All Periods. 238
    U.S. MILITARY RELATED DOCUMENTS, ASSORTED PAPER
    ITEMS & FRAMED ITEMS
        A. All Periods. 239

CHAPTER 9: MISCELLANEOUS MILITARIA
    U.S. ORDNANCE & FIREARM RELATED PARTS & EQUIPMENT
        A. All Periods. 241
    U.S. MILITARY VEHICLE & AIRCRAFT RELATED ACCESSORIES
        A. All Periods. 244
    U.S. TRENCH ART ITEMS
        A. All Periods. 249
    U.S. MILITARY PLAQUES & TROPHIES
        A. All Periods. 256
    U.S. MILITARY RELATED ARTWORK
        A. All Periods. 258
    U.S. MILITARY RELATED GLASSWARE
        A. All Periods. 259
    U.S. MILITARY SPOTTER MODELS & CARDS & PROMO
    MODELS & KITS
        A. All Periods. 260
    U.S. MILITARY JEWELRY, SWEETHEART ITEMS, CIGARETTE
    LIGHTERS/CASES
        A. All Periods. 263
    U.S. MILITARY RELATED PILLOWCASES & SOUVENIR ITEMS
        A. All Periods. 269
    U.S. MILITARY FLAGS, STREAMERS, GUIDONS, PENNANTS & BANNERS
        A. All Periods. 272

ABBREVIATIONS. 275
GLOSSARY. 277
RESOURCE DIRECTORY. 280
MUSEUMS / LIBRARIES. 283
INDEX. 286

FOREWORD

American Military Collectibles Price Guide covers a wide range of material from cloth to metal insignia, headgear, uniforms, badges, edged weapons, wings and qualification badges.

Within the recent past there has been a steady and healthy increase in the values of such collectibles and this is reflected in this price guide. In an effort to reflect the *current values* of American collectible items, this price guide will center on those items that are considered 'collectible' and command appreciable value.

Fieldgear such as mess tins, canteens, forks, knives, straps, knapsacks, backpacks and the like are *not* covered as they do not reflect a collectors investment opportunity. They are still considerably plentiful and do not appear to be of any substantial interest to collectors. Indeed it is possible to find such articles in Army & Navy Stores and most surplus stores.

American Military Art, though collectable, is so unique that it is virtually impossible to establish a price per item that would apply to all art. Trench art is a case in point—it was a unique art form created by soldiers in the World Wars and there are almost no two items alike.

Another field that is not covered entirely by this value guide is *current* American medals. With recent government changes pertaining to the open sale of these decorations, their prices have plummeted. However, the guide does price the medals of the Civil War to the Second World War as these are still strong in terms of collector prices.

We trust that this guide will prove of interest to collectors in the field of American Militaria.

Ron Manion
Kansas City, Kansas

HOW TO UTILIZE THIS GUIDE

Prices are based on optimum or best condition of an article and any damage to an item or parts missing from it, will devalue the price. Cloth material is assumed to be complete with no mothing or damage and metallic insignia is assumed to have its original finish, pins and all original parts. Any use of reproduction parts, replacement insignia (on uniforms, etc.) will necessarily devalue the worth of an article.

The prices represent current real time values as obtained from Manion's International Auction House catalogs for the past two years. They were gleaned from an examination of a broad range of prices of knockdown items.

It should be noted that American uniforms of the First World War vary widely in value based on the divisional insignia and collar roundels they display. Some units will command more money than others due to scarcity and this is reflected in the price guide. Post-1945 uniforms do not command as much value as those of the First World War, in fact, many can still be purchased for as little as $10 each.

On the other hand, flight helmets of the Army Air Force and US Air Force are very desirable and the helmets associated with High Altitude units now bring prices close to $1000 or over.

There are few surviving examples of Civil War uniforms left on the open market but a sample of the material is given in the price guide for comparative study. No attempt has been made to chronicle the uniforms of the American Revolution, War of 1812 or the Mexican War since they are virtually impossible to find.

It is our hope that the alphabetized format of the price guide with its divisions will make it an easy tool for the American collector who can purchase items with an understanding of the current values of such material.

INTRODUCTION

The extensive item listings in this volume—covering more than 200 years of American military history—can generally be grouped into specific categories. Following are brief descriptions of the areas of primary interest to most collectors of militaria; collecting tips; and references to the applicable chapters.

American Uniforms and Footwear 1776 - Present
(See Chapter 1)

The vast amount of uniform collectors now invest in the cloth apparel of the Spanish-American War period to the Second World War because virtually no uniforms of the Revolutionary War, the War of 1812 nor the Mexican War exist in private collections and few are ever encountered in shows. Civil War uniforms have dried up following the American Civil War Centennial which aroused interest in the garments of that period. Indian War uniforms are equally as scarce.

Because of their lack of ornament, most of the Spanish American War uniforms do not command fair prices despite the recent interest in the period.

The large outpouring of men and divisions in the First World War makes that period of great interest to collectors. Several years ago it was common to purchase a complete enlisted tunic and pants with insignia for $25. Today the same tunics will bring over $200 each!

Although uniforms of the Second World War are not high in value, flight jackets of nylon or leather command prices that approach $1200 if decorated with unit or war art designs. These popular flight jackets transcend the Second World War and even brought attractive prices in the Viet Nam period.

Unfortunately, current American uniforms, with the exception of rare camouflage from Viet Nam, are not considered as highly collectible as those uniforms from the First World War.

United States Cloth and Metallic Insignia 1776 - Present
(See Chapters 2 & 3)

The distinctive insignia worn by the American military has always fascinated collectors and vast amounts of divisional, unit and company patches have been assembled into impressive and very expensive collections.

Insignia from the Civil War to the Indian War period are almost virtually impossible to obtain but those insignia from the era of the Spanish American War to the present are still relatively plentiful.

Cloth insignia has not survived as well as metallic items as it is susceptible to moth damage, wear and soilage. However, what does remain creates an attractive and potentially fine investment opportunity.

Metallic insignia can come in white metal, silver or even gold and with the proper hallmarks and jeweler stamps, can be a good investment for any collector and certain Army and Marine Corps insignia commands very high prices.

United States Wings 1913 - Present
(See Chapter 3)

With their association with the air elements of the Armed Forces, it is not surprising to see that wings in metal, bullion and cloth have long attracted the attention of collectors. These insignia are often of Sterling silver or 1/20 gold fill and are both beautiful and of great intrinsic worth.

Obviously, the earliest wings of the air elements command higher prices than current wings but across their broad spectrum there is great evidence that collector interest exists.

Wings are also identified with elite paratrooper elements in the military and they also command great collector interest. As can be seen by this price guide, there is a wide variety of wings for specialist, assault and all air units and groups affiliated with them.

Prices can range from $5 to over $500 depending on the rarity of the badge and everyone from beginner to advanced collector has the chance to obtain an item for his/her collection.

Maker marks and pin or clutch back arrangements are important in determining value when it comes to wings and this can be seen by the prices and descriptions in the Guide.

United States Helmets 1776 - Present
(See Chapter 4)

The advent of the First World War introduced the steel helmet into American military service. Indeed this seminal war introduced the widest use of steel headgear in the armies of all the belligerent nations. The first American helmets were actually produced by the British on contract until a domestic industry could satisfy the needs of the American army during their campaign in France.

All American M-17 helmets are alike and what establishes collector value is either war art decorations or hand painted unit insignia. As can be clearly seen in the price guide, the rarer unit insignia will bring the value of a helmet to over $100 whereas fairly common insignia will remain in the $35 range. The M-1 helmets of the Second World War are all relatively cheap unless they have some unusual or distinctive insignia. The newest American helmet, the so-called 'Fritz' sells for around $50 with integral cover.

The wide assortment of metallic headgear worn by the Navy and other branches of the military vary widely in prices, this variance being based on unit strength, rarity and function.

In some cases such as with Marine Corps camouflage covers of the Pacific Campaign in the Second World War, the covers are worth more than the price of the helmet.

American Service and Issue Headgear 1776 - Present
(See Chapter 4)

From the Revolutionary War to the Civil War it may be said that there were no standard regulation headgear. Contemporary illustrations show that the men and officers of the earlier armies wore whatever they desired. Even in the Civil War with the ubiquitous kepie and forage caps, there was wide variety of headgear between units. If this was true for the Union, it was more so for the Confederate forces.

Beginning with the Indian Wars there was a movement underway to apply uniformity to headgear. By the Spanish American War period the campaign hat had come into being and was widely worn and could be considered a standard form of headgear.

In the First World War the visored cap with its US federal eagle badge became associated with the Armed Forces. In variations, it still exists today as the official hat of the armed forces. Overseas caps, campaign hats and side caps also appeared during the First World War, many being patterned after British styles. These have since remained in close association with the American Armed Forces.

Berets became popular in the post-World War II period and many from the Viet Nam Campaign will sell for over $400.

The value of headgear lies in its completeness, evident rarity and use by either common or elite units in the military.

American Field Gear and Aircraft/Mechanical Collectibles 1776 - Present
(See Chapters 5 & 9)

Generically speaking, Field Gear covers the range of all those necessary items carried or used by American soldiers during all campaigns. This includes gas masks, mess tins, canteens, webbing, cloth equipment, etc. The value of field gear lies in its rarity and uniqueness. Obviously a metallic cup from the Civil War will bring far more than its equivalent from the 1980s period.

Because of hard use, field gear is often found in severe used or poor condition. The best prices can be realized when unissued equipment is collected or encountered.

However, in relative terms, post-World War II field gear does not command great prices unless it is very unique. Too much was sold through Army-Navy stores and large quantities can still be found on the market.

Aero and war related mechanical parts such as toggle sticks, dash boards, fuel gauges and the like are collectible if they can be identified with a particular aircraft or vehicle. Some items are being purchased in this category in order to complete a vehicle that a collector might own. Others are purchased for display purposes or because they are identified with well known wartime aircraft such as B-17s, B-29s, etc.

Edged Weapons of the USA
(See Chapter 6)

The earliest of American edged weapons were either hand forged by pre-Revolutionary colonists in the form of knives, axes or utility weapons. Swords in the pre-1776 period were of British or French manufacture. It was not until after the Revolutionary War that a native and vibrant sword and edged weapons market developed in the United States with domestic production now supplanting foreign imports.

During the American Civil War, vast quantities of edged weapons were imported both by the Union and Confederate forces. In the case of Union purchases, many were made simply to deny the market to Confederate buyers. The vast assemblage of weapons proved to be a glut on the market after the Civil War and American edged weapon production would not reach a high again until the First World War.

Thereafter it proliferated and a large grouping of specialized knives, bayonets, machetes and swords appeared, particularly during the Second World War and later conflicts. World War II knives are considered highly collectible, but their values are be found more in rare maker marks than in the knives themselves.

As with all items, condition plays a major role in pricing. Moderate age is better than abuse and if an item appears never to have been issued or used, that establishes a higher price. The wide spectrum of edged weapons of all types make them an attractive field for both collecting and investment.

The Award and Qualification Badges of the United States 1776 - Present
(See Chapter 7)

There is a large and broad grouping of insignia that can fall under the heading of Award and Qualification badges. This insignia denotes ratings in the Armed Forces, special skills and qualifications and the presence of awards of a non-medal nature given to individuals or units. Recently there has been a broadening of the field with whole new groupings being introduced by the military.

Under general conditions, the badges of the First World War are considered more desirable than later insignia unless such material is identified with elite Airborne troops or Special Forces. Condition and completeness are elements that also determine prices in this field.

American Military Medals 1776 - Present
(See Chapter 7)

The earliest American medal is the so-called Andre medal, of which three were issued during the Revolutionary War. The Medal of Honor was awarded during the Civil War but at the time was a general medal for valor and did not have the associations of individual heroism that are so closely bound with it today. It would not be until the era of the Spanish American War with its atmosphere of nationalism that medals would be issued for services and campaigns.

By and large medals were not part of the American military tradition but following the First World War there was a surge in the production of medals. This was due to the Second World War, the Korean Campaign, the various Central American interventions and other actions to include Viet Nam and the Gulf War.

The new American Army has introduced a large grouping of medals for new services and achievements that were unknown ten to fifteen years ago and these are still available at low prices for the beginning collector.

Restrictions on the sale and trade of American medals have largely been rescinded, making for the development of a very interesting hobby.

Books, Photo Albums and Printed Material
(See Chapter 8)

The American military has produced literally tens of thousands of field manuals, technical manuals, field books and paper of all types for the instruction of soldiers in virtually every aspect of their military lives.

Books such as regimental histories, command very good prices if they pertain to well known units from the First and Second World Wars. Marine regimental books will sell far better than those of Army units. Naval books have never commanded significant prices. While not all such books have equal value, many become valuable due to their limited or restricted production.

The collection of recruitment posters, war bond posters and the like is an active area for many collectors. These large posters if intact and without disturbing damage, can sell for $70 and up depending on subject matter. Although plentiful at the time of their production, age and time have taken their tole on them and few survive of the thousands printed.

Period postal items associated with the military such as V-Mail, has both a value from a military point of view as well as from a postal perspective.

Old newspapers and magazines pertaining to historic times in the history of the American Republic command significant prices if in well preserved and complete condition. The same applies to historic documents, autographs and photo memorabilia.

American Military and Souvenir War Art Items
(See Chapter 9)

For many collectors, the vast amount of commemorative insignia produced by the armed forces has become a hub of active collecting. Most of the 'war art' material comes from the 1918-present period as there was neither a market nor an interest in such items prior to the First World War.

Plates, glassware, models, jewelry, pillow covers, trench art—all fall into the wide open category of 'war art.' Spotter models are now considered part of this collecting field. These were produced for recognition purposes on the Second World War but are now generically listed as 'war art' because they are collected for purposes other than recognition in today's collector field.

Quality of war art varies widely from the mass produced propaganda material of the 1940s period to hand done trophies created by soldiers in their spare time. Prices as will be seen, also vary widely. Many items in this area are still plentiful and can be obtained for reasonable prices.

U.S. UNIFORMS & FOOTWEAR

A. Thru World War I (1919)

BLOUSE, ARMY EM, 3RD INF DIV., WWI: 1917-pattern, in dark OD wool w/full dark tan cotton lining + nice multi-piece felt 3rd Div. patch on left shoulder + discharge stripe + 3 bullion o/seas stripes + Pfc./engr. chevron on rt. sleeve + US & "B/Engr." collar discs + 2 Pb. ribbon bars-includes WWI Victory w/5 large campaign stars + Pb. Marksman badge. Above avg. cond...$128.00

BLOUSE, ARMY EM, 3RD INF DIV., WWI: 1917-pattern in OD wool w/dark tan cotton lining + French cord stitched on felt 3rd Army patch on left shoulder + discharge & bullion o/seas stripes + corporal chevron on rt. sleeve + US & Am collar discs. Above avg. cond............................$61.00

BLOUSE, ARMY EM, 4TH CORPS, WWI: 1917-pattern medium-shade OD wool blouse. Fully lined. Has French silk machine embr. on lt. OD felt 4th Corps patch on left shoulder + embr. on it. OD felt o/seas stripe cross-stitched to left cuff + US & Qm collar discs. Avg. cond..$65.00

BLOUSE, ARMY EM, 33RD DIV., WWI: 1917 pattern OD wool serge blouse w/full dark tan cotton lining. Gold bullion tape on felt 33rd Div. patch on left shoulder + discharge stripe + 2 bullion o/seas stripes + corp. chevron + US & "Arty/C" (has '124' scratched above crossed cannon design) collar discs. Avg. cond....................$65.00

BLOUSE, ARMY EM, 40TH DIV., WWI: 1917-pattern in dark OD wool serge w/full cotton lining. Cord stitched on felt 40th Div. patch (star burst design) + discharge patch + bullion o/seas stripe + nice Qm corporal chevron on rt. sleeve w/dark tan felt stripes & branch design stitched in white & dark yellow on lt. OD wool base + US & Transport collar discs. Avg. cond..$145.00

BLOUSE, ARMY EM, AERO SERVICE, WWI: Yellow-tan wool 1912-pattern blouse w/OD cotton lining + 3 bullion o/seas stripes + silk embr. on dark blue felt "69" above 3-bladed prop patch on rt. shoulder. Above avg. cond............................$175.00

BLOUSE, ARMY EM, WWI: 1912-pattern in OD wool. Fully lined in tan cotton w/2 bullion o/seas stripes + sgt. chevron on rt. sleeve. USNA & 302/Inf collar discs. Above avg. cond............................$40.00

BLOUSE, ARMY EM, WWI: 1917-pattern in OD wool. Unlined. Has discharge stripe +#3 bullion o/seas stripes + sgt. chevron on rt. sleeve + US & Signal collar discs. Above avg. cond............................$38.00

BLOUSE, ARMY EM, WWI: Size 44 4-pocket blouse in OD wool w/tan cotton lining + paper size label in standing collar + dark bronze eagle buttons + stitch grommet holes for collar discs-none attached. Above avg. cond............................$182.00

BLOUSE, ARMY EM, WWI

BLOUSE, ARMY OFFICER, WWI: Lt. OD whipcord w/full dark tan cotton lining, woven Boston tailor's label in neck, brown "vegetable" eagle buttons& dark tan woven cuff braid. Has one-piece felt 5th Div. patch hand stitched to left shoulder, pair French-made Pb. major leaves, 3 o/seas stripes&US & Inf collar devices. Lacks one pocket flap button. About size 38. Avg. cond..................................$80.00

BLOUSE, ARMY OFFICER, WWI: Nice quality. Tailored in lt. OD wool serge & fully lined in dark tan ribbed cotton w/woven clothier's label, brown "vegetable" eagle buttons, dark tan woven cuff braid, pair U.S. collar devices & three bullion o/seas stripes. About size 40/42. Avg. cond. $80.00

BLOUSE, ARMY OFFICER, WWI: Nice quality in lt. OD wool serge w/full cotton lining + woven NY tailor's label in neck + lt. OD woven cuff braid. Named & 1918 dated. Has pair Pb. 2nd lieut. bars, U.S. & Arty collar devices, & 2 bullion o/seas stripes. Has had 1930s era 1st Army patch w/arty insert stitched to left shoulder. Avg. cond........................$51.00

BLOUSE, SUMMER, ARMY EM, WWI: 1912 pattern in dark tan cotton w/set of 1902-pattern dark bronze removable buttons. Avg. cond......................................$20.00

BLOUSE, SUMMER, ARMY EM, WWI: 1917-pattern in dark tan twill w/removable dark bronze eagle buttons. Smallish size. Exc. cond..$30.00

BLOUSE, SUMMER, ARMY OFFICER, WWI: Dark tan cotton w/lt. OD woven cuff braid, set of removable "vegetable" eagle buttons, pair Pb. Cavalry & U.S.R. collar devices, pair 2nd lieut. bars. Above avg. cond...$45.00

BLOUSE, SUMMER, ARMY OFFICER, WWI: Tailor-made in lt. OD cotton twill w/ removable eagle buttons. Named & 1917 dated. Has single nice Pb. Qm collar device w/pierced design. Above avg. cond...$80.00

BLOUSE, SUMMER, ARMY OFFICER, WWI

BLOUSE, USMC EM BANDSMAN: Size 2-L scarlet red melton wool blouse w/white piping + 1912-1913 dated USMC Qm markings + white & black cotton lining + gilt brass USMC buttons (one replacement) + golden-yellow woven trim on standing collar & cuffs. Average cond...$133.00

BLOUSE, USMC EM DRESS BLUE: Size 1-L in navy blue wool serge w/scarlet red epaulettes, faced standing collar & trim + 1909-1910 USMC Qm markings + white & black cotton lining & gilt brass USMC buttons. Leather tab still intact in collar. Exc. cond.......................................$229.00

BREECHES, ARMY EM, WWI: Brown-shade wool w/zinc US Army button fly + lace calves. Medium size. Avg. cond......$26.00

BREECHES, ARMY OFFICER, WWI: Lt. OD whipcord w/button calves & fly. Includes dark tan cotton belt. Approx. 30" waist. Avg. cond.......................................$16.00

CUT-AWAY COAT, RHODE ISLAND MILITIA OFFICER, CIVIL WAR: Dark red wool with

Rhode Island crest button by D. Evans, Attleboro. Gold litzen or bars on white stand up collar. Gold & white dress litzen on tails. Full liner, white cuffs with stand up vertical gold trim. Lacks one button. Double-breasted. Above avg. cond. $200.00

FIELD BOOTS, ARMY OFFICER, WWI: Approx. 14" tall in medium shade brown leather w/rawhide lace fronts, cap toes, leather soles & rubber soles. Above avg. cond. $76.00

FIELD BOOTS, "PERSHING" STYLE, WWI: Ankle-high in brown leather w/leather bluchers, lace fronts, leather soles & heels w/hob nails. Large size. Avg. cond. $591.00

FLYING COAT, ARMY OFFICER, AERO SERVICE, WWI: 3/4 length in brown leather w/large vegetable buttons on double-breasted front + brown wool lining + slash pockets + matching belt + button tabs at cuffs. "Classic" pattern associated with WWI flyer's. Avg. cond..........$375.00

FORAGE CAP RAIN COVER, ARMY, INDIAN WARS ERA: Black oilcloth. Fabric still pliable. Above avg. cond..........$54.00

FROCK COAT, ARMY OFFICER, 1872: Navy blue melton wool body w/gilt brass 1872-pattern buttons on double-breasted front + black cotton lining + short standing collar + nice pair sew-on shoulder boards w/heavy gold bullion borders, dark velveteen inserts & bullion lt. col. rank. About size 36. Above avg. cond..$500.00

JACKET AND VEST, ZOUAVE, CIVIL WAR: Dark blue rough wool body with red trim & fancy red scroll work on body. Matching dark blue vest with red tape piping. Near mint cond.................$195.00

LEGGINGS, LEATHER, ARMY OFFICER, WWI: 12" tall in semi-soft black leather w/ buckle adj. strap at top of each. Avg. cond...$30.00

LEGGINGS, LEATHER, ARMY OFFICER, WWI: 12" tall in semi-soft dark brown leather w/spiral wrap straps. Above avg. cond...$12.00

LEGGINGS, USMC, WWI: 12.75" tall in lt. olive canvas w/lace sides & leather insteps w/nickel buckles. USMC marked. Above avg. cond............................$24.00

MITTENS, FLYING, ARMY, AERO SERVICE, WWI: Black leather bodies w/ adj. strap across wrist of each & 6.5" dark brown leather gauntlets. Above avg. cond...$93.00

OVERCOAT, ARMY EM, 76TH DIV., WWI: Lt. OD wool coat w/large bronze eagle buttons on double-breasted front + adj. tab on each cuff + dark tan cotton lining.

Has nice oversize multi-piece 76th Div. patch on left shoulder + corporal chevron on rt. sleeve & 2 bullion o/seas stripes. Avg. cond..$49.00

OVERCOAT, ARMY EM, AERO SERVICE, WWI: Heavy OD wool body w/large eagle double-breasted front + button tab at each cuff + slash pockets. Has discharge stripe + 2 bullion o/seas stripes. Silk embr. on dark blue felt circular 4-bladed prop design patch. Above avg. cond......$27.00

OVERCOAT, ARMY EM, WWI: Heavy OD wool w/dark bronze eagle buttons on double-breasted front + button tab on each cuff. Avg. cond.......................$20.00

OVERCOAT, ARMY OFFICER, WWI: Private purchase in lt. OD melton wool w/double-breasted front + woven clothier's label. Fully lined in cotton. Has 2 rows of black woven quatrefoil rank on each cuff. Above avg. cond..$45.00

PEACOAT, NAVY, WWI: Heavy navy blue serge wool-double breasted front. Named. Medium size. Avg. cond.................$43.00

SACK COAT, ARMY BANDSMAN, 1895: Navy blue melton wool w/standing collar + black woven trim & braid on cuffs + concealed button front. Lined in black cotton. Each side of collar has sew-on "simulated bullion" gilt brass lyre device. Above avg. cond.............................$40.00

SACK COAT, ARMY EM, 1872: Navy blue melton wool body w/white felt trim & faced standing collar, cuffs, tail & epaulettes + gilt brass 1855-pattern buttons + 9-button front. Fully lined. Name ink stamped on lining. Above avg. cond..$328.00

SACK COAT, ARMY EM, 1872/1902: Private-purchase in navy blue melton wool w/fold-over collar + 6-button blouse front + gilt brass rimless eagle buttons + black cotton lining w/fancy stitching & large initials + fancy red trim on inner flap. Has red-on-blue sgt. chevron + gunner 1st class insignia + 2 hashmarks on each sleeve. Good shape & large size for period. Very unusual in that it is a 1874 pattern w/fold-over collar & no epaulettes but has no piping & features 1902 buttons & insignia. Above avg. cond...........$90.00

SACK COAT, ARMY EM, 1889: Navy blue melton wool body w/fold-over collar + 5 button front w/brass 1855 pattern buttons. Inside edge of button front w/ornate red felt trim. Black lining w/fancy red stitching & man's name. Ornate black stitching on each cuff. Has 1902 felt 1st class gunner chevron on rt. sleeve. Avg. cond...$75.00

SACK COAT, ARMY EM, 1895: Navy blue melton wool body w/black mohair trimmed standing collar & front. Lined in black cotton. Each cuff is covered in black melton wool w/ornate black woven trim. Woven clothier's label. Named. Average cond...$59.00

SACK COAT, ARMY EM, 1902: Navy blue melton wool body w/6-button front + red piped standing collar, cuffs & epaulettes + rimless gilt brass eagle buttons + black cotton lining. Each sleeve has red-on-blue sgt. 1st class chevron. Woven clothier's label in neck. Avg. cond.................$57.50

SACK COAT, ARMY EM DRESS, 1902: Navy blue melton wool blouse w/standing collar + lt. blue piping & belt hooks at waist. Fully lined in black cotton. Has 1921 gilt brass eagle button front + gilt brass type I "US/3" & "Inf/A" collar discs. Above avg. cond....................................$145.00

SACK COAT, ARMY EM DRESS, 1902

SACK COAT, ARMY OFFICER, 1895: Navy blue melton wool body w/black woven mohair trim on standing collar, concealed button front & cuffs. Lined in black cotton. Woven clothier's label. Has nice pair open-catch Pb. Signal Corps. Each shoulder has black cloth covered metal buttons. Avg. cond...........................$49.00

Inside lining has "U.S./24 INF./107/B" stenciled in white. Above avg. cond...$90.00

SACK COAT, ARMY, SPANISH-AMERICAN-WAR: Navy blue melton wool coat w/five 1855-pattern button front + fold over collar. Fully lined. Also, Mills pattern belt in black web w/metal fittings & many stitched bullet loops. Avg. cond.................$345.00

SAM BROWNE BELT, ARMY OFFICER, WWI: 2.25" wide stitched brown leather belt w/cross-strap & brass fittings. Avg. cond..$20.00

SAM BROWNE BELT, ARMY OFFICER, WWI: Stitched brown leather belt w/brass fittings, matching cross strap & leather sword hanger w/brass snap hooks. Belt & cross-strap are named to a 1st lieut. in 305th Inf, Co. L. About size 30. Avg. cond...$41.00

SERVICE SHOES, ARMY, 1900s: Smooth brown leather ankle-high bodies w/lace insteps + cap toes + leather soles. Size 7 E. Contract markings. Avg. cond. $318.00

SERVICE SHOES, ARMY, 1900s

SHAKO & DRESS COAT, 7TH NEW YORK STATE N.G., 1872: Model 1872 black wool covered shako w/black trim & chin strap + thick oilcloth visor + gilt brass crossed cannon side buttons + leather sweatband + black trim circular top w/ printed paper Military Goods Store's label inside + white pompom + stamped brass plate on front of crown w/ 7" numeral. Front is 4 1/2" high. Back is 5 1/2" high. Also, large size blue-gray waist-length dress coat w/long tails + gold wire trim & black woven trimmed standing collar, cuffs, tail & triple-breasted front + domed gilt brass NY N.G. buttons + New York maker's label in neck + provisions for removable shoulder boards-none included + 2 gold wire stripes on each sleeve & bullion flaming bomb device on each tail. Named to man in Co. C. Avg. cond..$387.00

SHELL JACKET, UNION CAVALRY, CIVIL WAR: Dark blue wool serge body w/1855 pattern buttons + single breasted button front + yellow piped cuffs & standing collar. Poor cond...........................$840.00

SHIRT, ARMY, WWI: OD wool pull-over w/ button neck & cuffs + reinforced elbows. Large size. Above avg. cond..........$50.00

SHIRT, ARMY, WWI: In OD wool w/button front, printed maker's label in neck, button

cuffs & patch chest pockets. 15 1/2" neck. Avg. cond..............................$21.00

SWEETHEART JUMPER, NAVY, WWI: USN style in navy blue wool w/bright white piping on cuffs & collar, woven "Paul Jones" label in neck, white trim on left chest pocket, Quartermaster style patch at neck. Avg. cond. $20.00

SWORD BELT, NAVY OFFICER, WWI: 1.5" wide stitched black leather belt w/circular dull gilt brass buckle & fittings + hanger straps. Approx. size 30" waist. Above avg. cond..$87.00

SWORD SASH, OFFICER, CIVIL WAR: Maroon wool sash w/knots & tassels, worn w/dress uniform & sword. Near mint cond...$225.00

UNIFORM, ARMY EM, 3RD INF DIV., WWI: 1917-pattern OD wool serge blouse w/ dark tan cotton lining + neat patch on left shoulder-3rd Div. design w/cord stitched stripes on dark blue velveteen base w/ small 3rd Army patch inset in felt, cord & bullion stitched construction + discharge stripe + 3 bullion o/seas stripes + inf/Pfc. chevron on rt. sleeve + "7/Inf/C" collar disc + 4 ribbons including WWI Victory w/6 campaign stars. Includes OD wool breeches w/plastic button fly & calves. Neat theater-made o/seas cap in lt. OD wool serge w/campaigns & unit handwritten on cotton lining. OD wool puttees. Nice WWI Victory medal on long drape wrap brooch ribbon w/Aisne, Champagne-Marne, St. Mihiel, Meuse-Argonne & clasps. Avg. cond.......$177.00

UNIFORM, ARMY EM, 3RD INF DIV., WWI

UNIFORM, ARMY EM RAILWAY, WWI: Nice quality private purchase blouse in lt. OD wool serge w/dark tan cotton lining, type I "IOWA" & Arty collar discs, large 2-piece felt & French cord stitched Railway patch on left shoulder & sgt. chevron on each sleeve. Includes pair dark tan wool serge breeches w/button calves & fly + lt. OD wool o/seas cap w/dark tan cotton sweatband. Avg. cond. $85.00

UNIFORM, ARMY EM, WWI: 1917-pattern dark-shade OD wool blouse w/dark tan cotton lining + clear 1917 dated Qm label + nice silk mach. embr. on OD wool base 1st Army patch w/silk machine embr. "P" insert + discharge patch + bullion o/seas stripe + corp. chevron on rt. sleeve + "US/4" & "Inf/PC" collar discs. Includes matching wool breeches w/zinc US Army button fly + puttees. Above avg. cond. $143.00

UNIFORM, ARMY EM, WWI: 1918-pattern blouse in lt. olive wool serge w/nice set of dark brown "vegetable" eagle buttons + paper size label still intact in standing collar + full dark tan cotton lining + nice French silk mach. embr. on OD wool 37th Div. patch on left shoulder + discharge stripe + bullion o/seas stripe + 2 "US" collar discs. Size 36. Includes matching breeches w/zinc US Army button fly & lace calves. Above avg. cond. $100.00

UNIFORM, ARMY NCO, WWI: Officer's quality, tailor made blouse has silk GHQ patch w/OD wool border on left shoulder, has discharge stripe, 4 bullion o/seas stripes, sgt's chevron, 2 US collar discs + WWI Victory medal w/"France" bar, WWI NY state medal-both on ribbons & pinned to the left chest. Includes cloth Chau-Chau clip bag & 1930s era Sam Brown belt in black leather w/cross strap & brass fittings. Avg. cond. $149.00

UNIFORM, ARMY OFFICER FIELD GRADE MESS DRESS, 1905: 1905 dated tailor-made tailcoat in navy blue melton wool w/satin lapels + gold wire lieut. col. grade quatrefoil + gold wire braid w/ribbed arty insert & sew-on arty device on each cuff + nice pair detachable braided gold epaulettes. Named. Has 4-place minimedal dress Pb. bar on left lapel, includes Philippine Congressional, Spanish War Service, Philippine Campaign & WWI Victory medals. Coat has latter era gilt brass eagle buttons. Includes matching trousers w/gold wire stripe w/ribbed arty insert down each leg & adj. strap across rear. Above avg. cond...$244.00

UNIFORM, ARMY OFFICER FULL DRESS, 1902: Navy blue melton wool frock coat w/1912-pattern eagle buttons on double-breasted front + gold wire trimmed

standing collar w/red & black inserts. Each cuff has 2 rows quatrefoil, direct embr. artillery (flaming bomb) & gold wire braid. Also, ornate heavy gold wire shoulder boards. Includes matching trousers. Large size. Above avg. cond..................$390.00

UNIFORM, NAVY CPO DRESS BLUE, WWI: Private purchase jumper in navy blue wool w/woven maker's label in neck + unusual all white insignia cross-stitched into place; CPO Quartermaster rate on rt. sleeve, apprentice knot at neck, & hashmark on left sleeve. Unusual. Includes pair issue 13-button trousers. Also, WWI era dark brown leather Sam Browne belt + navy blue woolen knit sleeveless undershirt + gray/white woolen knit thermal underwear set. Avg. cond................................$35.00

UNIFORM, NAVY EM DRESS BLUE, WWI: Navy blue wool jumper w/red stripe around left shoulder & 2 bullion o/seas stripes on left cuff. Named. Includes nice pair 13-button trousers w/woven clothier's label & neckerchief. Avg. cond.......$33.00

UNIFORM, NAVY EM UNDRESS WHITE, WWI: White cotton jumper, trousers, sailor cap & neckerchief. Avg. cond...$26.00

UNIFORM, USMC EM, WWI: Forest green wool blouse w/standing collar never pierced for collar discs, wool-on-felt corporal chevron cross-stitched to each sleeve, 3 bullion o/seas stripes & bullion wound stripe on rt. cuff. About size 38. Includes size 3-M forest green wool trousers w/1918-1919 dated USMC Qm markings + zinc USMC button fly + adj. strap across rear of waist. Above avg. cond..$368.00

UNIFORM, USMC EM, WWI

WINTER HOOD (MODEL 1884), ARMY, INDIAN WARS ERA: Dark tan (almost brown) cotton body w/brown trim, red chintz wool lining & button flap at neck.

Remains of paper label still attached to body. 1894-95 dated Qm markings inside on lining. Exc. cond.........................$80.00

B. 1920 - 1945

BELT, ARMY OFFICER, WWII: 36" long lt. OD web belt w/gilt tip. In Gemsco maker's box marked "U.S. Officers Web Belt" on lift-off lid. Above avg. cond.............$38.00

BLOUSE (MODEL 1921), ARMY EM: Tailor-made lt. OD wool body w/woven Honolulu tailor's label, full dark tan cotton lining gilt brass eagle buttons, nice oversize multi-piece felt 24th Div. patch on left shoulder, bullion o/seas stripe, type II "US/21" & "Inf/I" collar discs. WWI Victory medal pinned to left chest pocket flap & FOB pendant w/ design of Great Seal of America design on white satin ribbon on rt. chest pocket. Above avg. cond.........................$139.00

BLOUSE (MODEL 1926), ARMY EM: Nice quality private purchase item in lt. OD wool serge w/brass eagle buttons, dark tan cotton lining, woven clothier's label, stitch grommet holes in collar for insignia (none included), belt hooks at waist, silk machine embr. on lt. OD felt 27th Div. patch on left shoulder. Felt corporal chevrons & 4 hashmarks. Named. Size 36 1/2. Above avg. cond. $40.00

BLOUSE, AAF EM, WWII: Size 39L in OD wool serge w/20th A/F patch on left shoulder, AAF patch on rt. shoulder, woven s/sgt. chevrons, 2 o/seas bars, one hashmark, US & AAF collar discs, 3" Cb sterling Aerial Gunner wing w/nice patina, 4 place ribbon group & discharge patch. Above avg. cond..........................$100.00

BLOUSE, AAF EM, WWII

BLOUSE, AAF EM, WWII: 36R in OD wool serge w/belt hooks at waist. Has 7th A/F patch on left + sgt. chevrons + 4 o/seas bars + one hashmark + US & AAF collar discs + ribbon bar. Above avg. cond...$34.00

BLOUSE, AAF OFFICER, WWII: In dark OD gabardine w/matching belt & woven Ellington Field Exchange label. Named. Has embr. felt AAF patch on left shoulder. About size 38L. Above avg. cond...$26.00

BLOUSE, AAF OFFICER, WWII: Private purchase in dark OD gabardine w/ matching belt (lacks buckle). Woven maker's label. Named & dated 1944. Has machine silk embr. felt 8th A/F patch on left shoulder. About size 37............$37.00

BLOUSE, ARMY EM, WWII: 37R in OD wool serge w/belt hooks at waist, embr. felt 8th Corps patch on left shoulder, sgt. chevrons, hashmark, U.S. collar disc, & 2-place Pb. ribbon bar. Above avg. cond. $20.00

BLOUSE, ARMY EM, WWII: Size 44L in OD wool serge, 1942 dated Qm label, & 4th Serv. Cmd. patch on left shoulder. Above avg. cond...$66.00

BLOUSE, ARMY EM CBI, WWII: Early WWII era 4-pocket OD wool serge blouse w/ removable rimless gilt brass eagle buttons, Army Serv. Forces patch on left shoulder, theater made hand embr. twill CBI patch on rt. shoulder, first sgt. chevrons & 2 o/seas bars & one hashmark. Avg. cond......................$25.00

BLOUSE, ARMY OFFICER, WWII: Size 46R in dark OD gabardine w/1945 dated Qm label, matching belt, 32nd Div. patch on left shoulder, bullion o/seas bars, pair Pb. w/o bars, US & w/o collar devices, & 4-place ribbon group. Avg. cond........$30.00

BLOUSE, ARMY OFFICER, WWII: Dark OD gabardine w/gilt brass Engr. buttons, matching belt w/ribbed brass buckle, woven Wichita, KS clothier's label, 5th Army patch on left shoulder, Pb. 1st lieut. bars, US & Engr. (pierced design) collar devices. Size 39. Above avg. cond...$20.00

BLOUSE, ARMY OFFICER, WWII: Dark OD gabardine w/matching belt w/ribbed gilt brass buckle, woven clothier's label & 5th Army patch on left shoulder. About size 38. Above avg. cond......................$21.00

BLOUSE, NAVY AVIATION OFFICER, WWII: Private purchase in gabardine w/black woven lieut. rank braid & line officer star on each cuff. Avg. cond..................$20.00

BLOUSE, NAVY AVIATION OFFICER, WWII: Tailor made in green gabardine. Size 44 XL w/bronze NAVY buttons, black woven lieut. rank & line officer star on each cuff. Avg. cond......................................$37.00

BLOUSE, NAVY CPO, WWII: With athletic instructor rate. Dark tan cotton twill blouse w/removable gilt NAVY buttons & rate on left sleeve. Size 38.........................$35.00

BLOUSE, NAVY OFFICER DRESS WHITE, WWII: White cotton w/standing collar & gilt buttons. Has WWII wool covered shoulder boards w/gold tape ensign rank & line stars. Med. size. Above avg. cond...$22.00

BLOUSE, SERVICE, COAST GUARD PO, WWII: Private purchase, 4 pocket blouse in navy blue melton wool w/gilt buttons, PO2 Boatswain's Mate rate & cuff shield on rt. sleeve, Shore Est. PO collar devices & WWI Victory ribbon bar. Size 39. .... $20.00

BLOUSE, SERVICE, NAVY OFFICER, WWII: Private purchase in dark tan gabardine w/detachable gilt NAVY buttons, detachable ensign grade line officer shoulder boards. Outline of naval aviator wing on left chest (not included). Size 40. Avg. cond.........................$20.00

BLOUSE, SERVICE, USMC OFFICER, WWII. Tailor made in forest green gabardine. Collar stitch grommeted for devices (not included). Named & 1945 dated. Med. size. Quantico, Va. tailor label inside. No belt. Above avg. cond..$21.00

BLOUSE, SUMMER, MARITIME SERVICE OFFICER, WWII: Dark tan cotton blouse w/removable gilt brass USMS buttons, removable lieut. jg. grade line officer shoulder boards & Atlantic War Zone ribbon bar on left chest. About size 38...$50.00

BLOUSE, SUMMER, USMC EM, 1920s: Size 1-M, dark tan twill body w/pointed cuffs & standing collar w/stitch grommet hole. Removable set of dark bronze finish USMC buttons + pleated chest pockets. Above avg. cond.............................$90.00

BLOUSE, USMC EM DRESS BLUE, 1930s: Size 4-L pocketless body in navy blue melton wool w/standing collar stitch grommeted for devices (not included), red piping & 1933-1934 dated USMC Qm markings. Avg. cond......................$35.00

BLOUSE, USMC EM, WWII: Size 1-L in forest green wool w/1942-43 dated USMC Qm markings, 1937-pattern EG&A collar devices, 2nd Marine Div. patch on left shoulder, corp. chevrons. Lacks belt. Avg. cond...$39.00

BLOUSE, USMC EM, WWII: Size 2-L in forest green wool w/1941-1942 dated USMC Qm markings. Has 1st Marine Div. patch on left shoulder, woven PFC.

chevrons & Gemsco hmkd. 1937 pattern EG&A collar devices. No belt. Above avg. cond..$66.00

BLOUSE, USMC EM, WWII: Size 6-S in forest green wool w/1941-42 dated USMC Qm markings. Has fully embr. 6th Marine Div. patch on left shoulder, woven PFC. chevrons & wide plastic coated Purple Heart ribbon bar. No belt. Avg. cond...$45.00

BLOUSE, USMC OFFICER, WWII: Forest green gabardine w/woven Quantico uniform shop label & belt hooks at waist. Size 39/40. W/belt. Named & 1943 dated. Above avg. cond............................$25.00

BOOTS, CAVALRY, ARMY, 1930s: 17" tall brown leather bodies w/2 leg-strap closures + lace insteps + cap toes. Top of each have had 2.75" tall section of russet brown leather added w/top strap restitched in place. About size 8/9. Avg. cond...$75.00

BOOTS, CAVALRY, ARMY, 1930s: Smooth russet brown leather w/cap toes, completely laced fronts, leather soles, & rubber heels. Faint ink stamp markings inside. Size 8 1/2F. Above avg cond...$133.00

BOOTS, COMBAT 2 BUCKLE, ARMY, WWII: Dubbed brown roughout leather bodies w/ lace insteps & smooth leather 2-buckle uppers. 1944 dated. Avg. cond.......$65.00

BOOTS, COMBAT 2 BUCKLE, ARMY, WWII: Size 12A. Roughout brown leather bodies w/rawhide lace insteps & smooth leather 2-buckle uppers. Faint Qm markings. Show little use. Above avg. cond. $171.00

BOOTS, COMBAT 2 BUCKLE, ARMY, WWII

BOOTS, FIELD (1931 PATTERN), ARMY: Approx. 17" tall in russet brown leather w/

UNIFORMS

full lace fronts + corded rubber soles & heels. Avg. cond. $90.00

BOOTS, FIELD, ARMY, WWII: 17" tall in smooth brown leather w/cap toes, lace insteps & three leg-strap tops. 1941 dated Qm markings. Size 9D. Includes pair US marked nickel spurs. $145.00

BOOTS, FIELD, ARMY, WWII

BOOTS, FLIGHT (A-6), AAF, WWII: Fleece lined. Large-size in dark brown leather w/ molded black rubber soles + woven AAF marked spec. labels. Avg. cond. ... $50.00

BOOTS, FLIGHT (A-6), AAF, WWII: Dark brown leather bodies w/fleece lining, woven AC marked spec. labels, good original zipper fronts, leather retaining straps across front & molded black rubber soles. Medium size. Above avg. cond. $187.00

BOOTS, FLIGHT (A-10), AAF, WWII: Molded black rubber corded soles natural color roughout hightop bodies w/brown leather trim & fleece lining + woven spec. labels. Size large. Avg. cond. $282.00

BOOTS, FLIGHT, HEATED INSERTS, AAF, WWII: OD w/woven AAF spec. labels & snap fasteners. Size medium. Near mint cond. $20.00

BOOTS, FLIGHT, NAVY, WWII: Fleece lined. Size x-large. Dark brown leather bodies w/ black molded rubber soles, original dual zipper front to each, woven BuAero marked spec. label & lace panel in back. Above avg. cond. $40.00

BOOTS, "JUMP", ARMY AIRBORNE, WWII: Dark brown leather w/cap toes & lace fronts. About size 8. Avg. cond. .. $125.00

BOOTS, "JUMP", ARMY AIRBORNE, WWII: Russet brown leather w/cap toes, beveled heels, & rawhide lace fronts. Lacks most of woven maker's label but have

embossed Corcoran markings. Size 9D. Avg. cond. $210.00

BOOTS, MOUNTAIN, ARMY, WWII: Dark brown leather w/square toes, lace fronts, heavily cleated soles & 1943 dated issue markings. Exc. cond. $65.00

BOOTS, RIDING, ARMY OFFICER, 1920s: Approx. 18" tall smooth russet brown leather bodies w/leather soles & heels + stitched web pull loops inside of each. Nocona Boot Co. marked. Includes pair nickel spurs w/leather retaining straps. About size 9. Above avg. cond. .. $140.00

BREECHES, ARMY OFFICER, 1930s: Lt. OD gabardine w/button front, lace calves, & reinforced thigh areas. Faint 1930s dated. Avg. cond. $24.00

BREECHES, "PINK", ARMY OFFICER, 1930s: Private purchase in "pink" gabardine w/button fly, lace calves, & stitched thigh panels. About size 28" waist. Avg. cond. $20.00

BREECHES, SUMMER, ARMY, 1930s: 35x23" in dark tan cotton w/lace valves, zinc US Army buttons & 1937 dated Qm label. Paper Qm inspector tags still stapled to body. Exc. cond. $40.00

CAPE, NURSE, ARMY, WWII: Navy blue melton wool body w/dark maroon lining, fold-over collar & button neck. Size "S" label in neck. Also, white cotton cap in protective storage bag & pair US & Med/N collar devices. Above avg. cond. .. $44.50

CAPE, NURSE, NAVY, WWII: Navy blue melton wool w/red wool lining, two tabs on front w/gilt brass NAVY buttons, standing collar w/bullion "S.U.S.N." direct embr. into left side of collar. Woven nurse's apparel maker's label in neck. Initials in woven letters inside. Above avg. cond. $55.00

COAT, FOUL WEATHER DECK, NAVY OFFICER, WWII: Size 42. Dark OD impregnated body w/black trim, large fold-over collar, shearling lining, printed naval contract label in neck & double breasted front. Above avg. cond. $223.00

COAT, LEATHER, NAVY AVIATION OFFICER, WWII: Transport pilot. 3/4 length in dark brown leather, large real fur collar, double breasted front, satin & alpaca lining, woven BuAero marked spec. label in neck, matching belt & slash pockets. Size 40. Exc. cond. $237.00

COVERALLS, CAMO HBT JUNGLE, ARMY, WWII: Reversible from green to tan spot pattern camo HBT w/zipper front, pleated cargo pockets on chest & each thigh w/ good metal snaps & metal star & wreath adj. tab at each cuff. Size 36R. Suspenders intact. Above avg. cond. $279.00

COVERALLS, CAMO HBT JUNGLE, ARMY, WWII: Reversible from green to tan spot pattern camo HBT w/zipper front, button adj. tabs at sleeve cuffs & snap closures on pleated pockets. Suspenders removed. Size 40R. Above avg. cond. $180.00

COVERALLS, HBT (M1938), ARMY, WWII: Lt. OD HBT w/metal star buttons & attached belt & several pockets. Medium size. Avg. cond. $25.00

COVERALLS, HBT (M1943), ARMY, WWII: 38R in dark OD HBT w/matching belt, several pockets, metal star buttons & gas flap. Above avg. cond. $36.00

COVERALLS, HBT (M1943), ARMY, WWII: Size 36R in dark OD HBT w/metal star button front, matching belt, several pockets, gas flap & button adj. cuffs. Near mint cond. $93.00

COVERALLS, HBT (M1943), ARMY, WWII

COVERALLS, HBT, USMC PARATROOPER, WWII: Lt. OD HBT body has replacement full zipper front, EG&A stencil on left chest over small pocket w/ USMC stencil on snap closure flap, larger pocket on rt. chest & large pocket on back. No pads on sleeves (are in different shade OD as body). Lower zippered pockets are canvas faced. HBT sections on lower body have been shortened approx. 8" in front & back. Avg. cond. $322.00

DRESS, SERVICE, WAC OFFICER, WWII: Lightweight finely textured light tan cotton body w/matching belt, zip front, pleated chest pockets & pleated waist. Size 12. Has pair curve form Pb. captains bars & US & AAF collar devices. Above avg. cond. $93.00

FLAK BODY ARMOR SET, AAF, WWII: Dark OD canvas covered manganese steel plates. Inner sides lined w/corduroy. Have printed spec. labels. Includes front, rear & abdomen pieces. Avg. cond. $400.00

FLIGHT SUIT (A-4), AAF, WWII: Size 36 in OD gabardine w/woven AAF marked spec. label in neck, zipper front, matching belt, several pockets & embossed brown leather name tag stitched to left chest. Above avg. cond. $368.00

FLIGHT SUIT (A-4), AAF, WWII

FLIGHT SUIT (A-4), AAF, WWII: Size 38 in OD gabardine w/woven AAF marked spec. label in neck, zipper front, several pockets & matching belt. Avg. cond. $40.00

FLIGHT SUIT (AN-6550), AAF, WWII: OD gabardine w/zipper front, woven spec. label, matching belt, several pockets, & faint AAF ink stamp markings in neck. Size 42. Avg. cond. $50.00

FLIGHT SUIT (AN-S-31), AAF, WWII: Size 36-M in dark OD gabardine w/woven spec. label, matching belt & several pockets. Above avg. cond. $50.00

FLIGHT SUIT (AN-S-31), NAVY, WWII: Size 36-S in tan cotton w/woven spec. label, matching belt, zipper front & several pockets. USN marked below spec. label. Avg. cond. $70.00

FLIGHT SUIT (F-3A), AAF, WWII: Electrically heated. Includes medium size jacket in issue carton, med./long trousers in issue envelope. Both w/AAF marked contract labels. Above avg. cond. $118.00

FLIGHT SUIT (K-1), AAF, WWII: Size med./ reg. in dark tan cotton w/woven spec. label, AAF ink stamp markings in neck, zipper front, several pockets & color AAF patch design printed on left shoulder. Above avg. cond. $177.00

FLIGHT SUIT (L-1), AAF, WWII: Med./reg. in OD gabardine w/woven spec. label in neck, zipper front & several pockets. Above avg. cond. $52.00

FLIGHT SUIT (L-1), AAF, WWII: Size med./ long in light gabardine. In issue cardboard carton w/AAF contract markings. Near mint cond. $177.00

FLIGHT SUIT (M-426A), NAVY, WWII: Dark tan cotton body w/woven BuAero/US Navy marked woven spec. label in neck, zipper front & matching belt. Above avg. cond. $225.00

FLIGHT SUIT OUTER JACKET (F-2), AAF, WWII: Size 40 in dark OD barathea w/ woven AAF marked spec. label, concealed button front, patch chest pockets w/ scalloped flaps, concealed pocket on lower rt. front, button cuffs, adj. waist tabs & nice heavy bullion on felt AAF patch on left shoulder. Above avg. cond. .. $177.00

GLOVES, 1935 ISSUE, ARMY: Dark tan roughout leather 5-finger bodies w/dark tan leather palms & snap adjustment at wrists. Well marked. Medium size. Avg. cond. $24.00

GLOVES, ARMY AIRBORNE, WWII: Off white smooth & roughout horsehide 5-finger bodies w/adj. web strap across each wrist. Above avg. cond. $145.00

GLOVES, DRESS WAC, WWII: White doeskin. Exc. cond. $55.00

GLOVES, FLIGHT, AAF, WWII: For type F-2 & F-3 flight suits. Electrically heated. Dark brown leather. 5-finger design. Woven AAF marked spec. labels. Size 11. Above avg. cond. $116.00

GLOVES, FLIGHT (B-3A), AAF, WWII: Dark brown leather. 5-finger design. Size 11. Faint AAF ink stamp markings. Printed spec. label inside left glove. Near mint. $108.00

GLOVES, FLIGHT (D-2), AAF, WWII: Yellow-tan leather 5-finger bodies w/dark OD knit wrists + printed AAF marked spec. labels. Size 10. Above avg. cond. $160.00

GLOVES, FOUL WEATHER DECK, NAVY, WWII: navy blue knit wool bodies w/ gauntlets that cover much of forearm. Exc. cond. $40.00

GLOVES, LEATHER, USMC, WWII: Rough-out tan leather 5-finger bodies & gauntlets w/machine stitched smooth dark tan leather palms. Well marked. Above avg. cond. $25.00

GLOVES, WOOL, ARMY EM, WWII: Dark OD wool 5-finger bodies w/dark brown leather faced palms. Size 8. Woven Qm tag in each. Near mint cond. $50.00

HELMET COVER, CAMO HBT M-1, USMC, WWII: Reversible from green to tan spot pattern camo w/EG&A stencil on each side. Above avg. cond. $82.00

INVASION VEST, ARMY, WWII: Dark OD canvas body w/dark OD trim. Web strap closure front w/many pockets that cover

front & backsides + dark finish metal fittings. US marked on large rear top pocket. "Medium" size stenciled in neck. US manufactured version. Near mint cond. $2,260.00

JACKET, COLD WEATHER (N-1), NAVY AVIATION OFFICER, WWII: Lt. OD ribbed cotton w/alpaca collar & lining, zipper/ button front, slash pockets. NAVY marked. Size 40. Spec. label intact. Some wash fading. Avg. cond. $55.00

JACKET, FIELD (M1941), ARMY, WWII: Lt. OD poplin body lined in OD wool, good original zipper/button front, 1942 dated Qm tag, button tabs at cuffs & waist, slash pockets & epaulettes. Exc. cond. $65.00

JACKET, FIELD (M1941), ARMY, WWII: Lt. OD poplin body w/OD wool lining, epaulettes, zipper/button front & button tabs at cuffs & waist. Size 38R. Above avg. cond. $269.00

JACKET, FIELD (M1941), ARMY, WWII

JACKET, FIELD (M1941), ARMY, WWII: Lt. OD poplin w/OD wool lining, zipper/button front, epaulettes, slash pockets & button tabs at cuffs & waist. Small size. Avg. cond. $28.00

JACKET, FIELD (M1941), NAVY, WWII: Dark OD poplin w/OD wool lining, zipper/button front & slash pockets. NAVY marked. Faint name ink stamped on left chest w/ very faint signs of removed name tape in same area. Large size. Above avg. cond. $103.00

JACKET, FIELD (M1941), USMC FEMALE, WWII: Lt. OD poplin w/OD wool lining, epaulettes, zipper/button front, slash pockets & button tabs at cuffs & waist. Solid medium size. Above avg. cond. $84.00

JACKET, FIELD (M1941), WAC, WWII: Lt. OD poplin body w/OD wool lining, good original zipper/button front, slash pockets, epaulettes & button tabs at cuffs & waist. Faint size label. Has WAC's name label stitched inside neck. Medium female size. Above avg. cond............................$140.00

JACKET, FIELD (M1941), WAC, WWII

JACKET, FIELD (M1943), AAF, WWII: Size 36L in dark OD cotton w/button front, 1945 dated Qm label, 8th Air Force patch on left shoulder, pair Pb. 2nd lieut. bars & name in small ink stamped letters above left chest pocket. Above avg. cond.....$120.00

JACKET, FIELD (M1943), ARMY, WWII: Size 36R in dark OD cotton w/button front & 1944 dated Qm label. All labels intact. Above avg. cond $145.00

JACKET, FIELD (M1943), ARMY, WWII

JACKET, FIELD (M1943), ARMY AIRBORNE, WWII: Size 40R in dark OD cotton w/button front & faint 1945 dated Qm label. Has 11th A/B Div. patch w/ attached tab cross-stitched in white thread to left shoulder & woven s/sgt. chevrons. Above avg. cond. $105.00

JACKET, FIELD (M1943), WAC, WWII: Size 10R in dark OD cotton w/button front. 1944 dated Qm label. Above avg. cond. $45.00

JACKET, FLIGHT (A-2), AAF, WWII: 414TH Bomb Squadron. Medium brown leather-size 40 w/AAF spec. label in neck. Good lining, original zipper & waistband-original cuffs. Has 5" dia. tooled & painted leather patch on left chest w/comical likeness of Donald Duck in sailor suit-standing on left tailplane of B-17, just the tail of the B-17 is visible-"414th" tooled into leather along lower edge. Back of jacket painted w/12" long likeness of OD finish B-17 in flight among the clouds-fairly simple-in muted tones but fills up the back of the jacket. Above avg. cond. $2,638.00

JACKET, FLIGHT (A-2), AAF, WWII: Brown leather body w/period replacement "Talon" zipper front + dark tan cotton lining + original knit cuffs & waistband. About size 40. Above avg. cond. $683.00

JACKET, FLIGHT (A-2), AAF, WWII: Size 42 in clean dark brown leather w/woven AAF marked spec. label in neck. Zipper front, original knit cuffs & waistband & incised brown leather name tag stitched to left chest. Above avg. cond. $1,630.00

JACKET, FLIGHT (A-2), AAF, WWII

JACKET, FLIGHT (A-2 "WAR ART"), AAF, WWII: Size 38 w/large Rough Wear AAF spec. label in neck. Couple nips in waistband-old replacement cuffs (correct color) & zipper. Has 6" dia. patch on left chest "Alone - Unarmed - Unafraid?" Blackbirds" around the edge-likeness of comical Magpie in center-star & moon in background - bomb in 1 hand & camera in the other-he wears a red bowler & smokes a cigar. Avg. cond. $1,150.00

JACKET, FLIGHT (A-2 "WAR ART"), AAF, WWII: 40R in dark brown leather w/woven spec. label in neck. Has 8th AF patch on left shoulder, 6" dia. squadron patch on left chest-comical likeness of wolf in flight clothing riding a camouflage bomber w/bomb under his arm-back has large likeness of same wolf riding bomber w/eight ball under his arm-"Section Eight"w/clouds-31 bombs below. Man was a sgt. in the 729 B.S. 452 B.G. on the B-17 "Section Eight". Exc. cond. $1,575.00

JACKET, FLIGHT (A-2 "WAR ART"), AAF, WWII: 8th Air Force. Light brown leather-size 42 w/woven Aero Leather spec. label in neck. Good original zipper-excellent cuffs & waistband. Has gold leaf impressed name tag on left chest-silver painted leather lieut.'s bars on shoulder straps + 11" dia. painted rendition of the 8th Air Force patch in center of back w/30 large painted silver mission bombs superimposed over the 8th air force patch design. Avg. cond. $1,650.00

JACKET, FLIGHT (A-2 "WAR ART"), AAF, WWII: Dark brown leather-size 40 w/ woven Spiewak AAF spec. label in neck. Has large likeness of pin-up girl wearing Uncle Sam top hat & red, white & blue bikini "Miss Fortune" in red & white letters across top-35 red bombs painted below. Avg. cond. $1,250.00

JACKET, FLIGHT (A-2 "WAR ART"), AAF, WWII: Dark brown leather w/5" dia., English made felt Bomb squadron patch on left chest-has stylized view of B-17 in flight w/falling bombs, flak guns shooting back & small, stylized geometric caricature of Hitler's face-motto "Potestas Accuratioque." Has large red & white block letters "Yank" on right chest. Size 40 w/woven Rough Wear AAF spec. label in neck. Above avg. cond. $2,330.00

JACKET, FLIGHT (A-9), AAF, WWII: Size 40 in dark OD cotton w/fur lined built-in hood + AAF marked woven spec. label in neck + quilted OD satin lining + zipper/button front + several pockets + knit cuffs. Above avg. cond. $175.00

JACKET, FLIGHT (A-11), AAF, WWII: Size 34 in dark OD cotton w/woven AAF marked spec. label in neck, fur lined built-in hood w/real fur trim, alpaca lining, zipper/button front, several pockets, adj. tab at cuffs, epaulettes, color printed AAF patch design decal on left shoulder & AAF ink stamp markings. Exc. cond. .. $643.00

JACKET, FLIGHT (AL-1), NAVY, WWII: OD cotton body w/woven BuAero marked spec.label, alpaca lining, zipper/button front, several pockets & zippered expansion panels at cuffs. Size 38/40. Above avg. cond. $223.20

JACKET, FLIGHT (AN-J-3A), NAVY, WWII: Size 36 in dark brown leather w/good original zipper front, good original waistband, real fur collar, good satin lining w/worn woven BuAero spec. label. Never had any insignia. Leather soft. Spec. label is marked as "Spec. AN-J-3A" jacket. Avg. cond. $397.00

JACKET, FLIGHT (AN-J-4), AAF, WWII: Fleece lined. Size 38 in dark brown leather w/large fleece collar, woven AAF marked spec. label, good original zipper front, adj. leather tabs at waist. Above avg. cond. $1,420.00

JACKET, FLIGHT (AN-J-4), AAF, WWII

JACKET, FLIGHT (AN-J-4), AAF, WWII: Fleece lined. Size 40 in dark brown leather w/large fleece collar, good original zipper front, AAF marked woven spec. label, color AAF patch design decal on left shoulder, adj. leather tabs at waist. Well marked. Above avg. cond. $380.00

JACKET, FLIGHT (B-3), AAF, WWII: Fleece lined. Size 38 in dark brown leather w/AAF marked spec. label in neck, corroded original zipper front, large fleece collar, blank leather rank tab on each shoulder & adj. waist straps. Avg. cond. $559.00

JACKET, FLIGHT (B-5), AAF, WWII: Fleece lined in dark brown finish w/large fleece collar & fleece cuff trim. Size 38R w/ woven spec. label in neck & AAF decal on left shoulder. Near mint cond. .. $3,160.00

JACKET, FLIGHT (B-10), AAF, WWII: Size 36 in dark OD cotton w/real fur collar, good original zipper woven AAF marked spec. label in neck, front epaulettes, color AAF patch design decal on left shoulder & original knit cuffs & waistband. Avg. cond. $935.00

JACKET, FLIGHT (B-10), AAF, WWII: Size 40. Dark OD cotton body w/large real fur collar, alpaca lining, AAF marked woven spec. label in neck, good original zipper front, epaulettes, lower patch pockets, & knit cuffs & waistband. Above avg. cond. $1,194.00

JACKET, FLIGHT (B-10 "WAR ART"), AAF, WWII: Size 34 in dark OD cotton w/real fur collar, woven AAF marked spec. label in neck, period "Conmar" replacement zipper front, original knit waistband & replacement knit cuffs & epaulettes & color AAF patch design printed on left shoulder. Has "USA" painted in large red letters above left pocket & sgt. chevron inked on left sleeve. Avg. cond. .. $525.00

JACKET, FLIGHT (B-13), AAF, WWII: Size 40 in dark OD gabardine w/woven AAF marked spec. label in neck, satin lining, concealed chest pockets w/buttoned flaps, slash pockets below, concealed button front, button adj. cuffs & waist tabs & 9th Air Force patch on left shoulder. Above avg. cond. $384.00

JACKET, FLIGHT (B-13), AAF, WWII

JACKET, FLIGHT (B-15), AAF, WWII: OD cotton body w/large real fur collar, alpaca lining, good original knit cuffs & waistband, snap closure slash pockets & pocket on left sleeve. About size 40. Above avg. cond. $310.00

JACKET, FLIGHT (D-1), AAF, WWII: Fleece lined. Dark brown leather w/large fleece collar & replacement zipper front. Chain on outside of neck for hanging-up. Medium size. Avg. cond. $292.00

JACKET, FLIGHT (G-1), NAVY, WWII: Dark brown leather body w/good original zipper front, real fur collar, original knit cuffs & waistband, reddish brown satin lining. Faint trace of spec. label long since removed. Size 40. Left chest has embr. on twill sqdn. patch w/design of Warner Bros. "Bugs Bunny" character holding movie

camera & eating carrot-is riding atop diving B-17 w/camera on each wing tip & nickname "Sweet Sixteen." Above avg. cond. $1,000.00

JACKET, FLIGHT (G-1), NAVY, WWII

JACKET, FLIGHT (G-1), NAVY, WWII: Soft dark brown leather body w/real fur collar, original zipper front, original knit cuffs & waistband. Has unusual woven spec. label marked "Model G-1/Flying Jacket" w/ contract number below. Large size. Avg. cond. $156.00

JACKET, FLIGHT (M-422A/G-1), NAVY, WWII: "JOLLY ROGER'S" Size 38 dark brown leather jacket w/real fur collar, woven BuAero marked spec. label, good original zipper front, period replacement cuffs & waistband, good satin lining. Has 4.75x5" mach. stitched on black felt VF-17 patch stitched to rt. chest. Avg. cond. $591.00

JACKET, FULL DRESS MESS, USMC OFFICER, WWII: Short black wool body w/16-gold eagle buttons, gold plated sleeve designs & darkening to gold brocade stand-up collar. Red satin lining. Above avg. cond. $75.00

JACKET, IKE, AAF EM, WWII: 36S in OD wool serge w/theater-made machine embr. on felt Airborne Troop Carrier patch on left shoulder, corps chevrons, 4 o/seas bars, one hashmark, Sb. US & AAF collar discs & 3" wide Pb. sterling AAF Aircrew wing. Has 4-place ribbon bar w/Army Good conduct w/4 knots. Above avg. cond. $79.00

JACKET, IKE, AAF EM, WWII: Size 34R in OD wool serge w/theater-made silk machine embr. on blue felt Airborne Troop Carrier patch on left shoulder, felt-on-felt sgt. chevrons, 2 o/seas bars, US & AAF collar discs & 3" wide Cb sterling AAF Aircrew wing on left chest. Above avg. cond. $55.00

JACKET, IKE, AAF EM, WWII: 36L in OD wool serge w/9th Air Force patch on left shoulder, 12th Air Force patch on rt. shoulder, corporal chevrons, 6 o/seas bars, one hashmark, AF Engr. Spec. patch on rt. cuff, & discharge patch. Includes tan cotton necktie & AAF piped OD wool o/seas cap-top fold stitched closed to give "cocky" look. Above avg. cond. ... $175.00

JACKET, IKE, AAF OFFICER, WWII: OD gabardine body has been cut-down from a tailor made blouse. Has pleated chest pockets w/concealed buttons. AAF patch on left shoulder. Officer's US & AAF collar devices. Size approx. 38. Exc. cond. $33.00

JACKET, IKE, AAF OFFICER, WWII: Private purchase in dark OD gabardine w/2" wide waistband & adj. tabs. Green satin lining. Has fully embr. 9th AF patch on left shoulder, pair Pb. 1st lieut. bars, US & AAF collar devices & 3" wide Pb. sterling AAF pilot wing on left chest. About size 38. Above avg. cond. $124.00

JACKET, IKE, ARMY AIRBORNE EM, WWII: Size 38R in OD wool serge w/11th AB Div. patch w/separate tab on left shoulder, 27th Div. patch on rt. shoulder & 3 cord stitched on OD wool serge o/seas bars. Above avg. cond. $40.00

JACKET, IKE, ARMY OFFICER, WWII: OD wool w/tan cotton lining. Has exposed plastic buttons, 1st lieut. bars, felt AAF patch on left, felt 9th AF patch on right, 1 ribbon bar, discharge patch, 4 bullion o/seas bars & meritorious unit sleeve wreath. Above avg. cond. $30.00

JACKET, IKE, ARMY OFFICER, WWII: Size 42R in OD wool serge w/satin lining & 1945 dated Qm label. Has 6 o/seas bars on left cuff. Above avg. cond. $93.00

JACKET, IKE, ARMY OFFICER, WWII

JACKET, IKE, USMC EM, WWII: Custom made from cut down issue size 6-L forest green wool blouse. 1944 dated USMC Qm markings. Has pleated chest pockets, concealed button front & button adj. cuffs & tab on each side of waist. Above avg. cond. $27.00

JACKET, IKE, WAC, WWII: English made. Size 10 S OD wool waist length jacket w/ 1944 dated spec. label, buckled waist belt, fully embr. SHAEF patch on left shoulder, theater made embr. on felt ETO Adv. Base patch on rt. shoulder, 2 o/seas bars, T-corporal chevrons, US & Signal collar discs, & 2 ribbon bars. Includes size 14R OD wool skirt w/broad arrow marked & 1944 dated spec. label. Above avg. cond. $70.00

JACKET, "JUMP" (M1942), ARMY AIRBORNE, WWII: Lt. OD cotton body w/ good original zipper front, zippered pocket in neck, gray metal snaps on angled chest pocket flaps & lower pocket flaps, matching belt & epaulettes. About size 38. Above avg. cond. $400.00

JACKET, "JUMP" (M1942), ARMY AIRBORNE, WWII: Lt. OD cotton body w/ replacement "Talon" zipper front, zippered pocket in neck, brass snap closures, four pleated front pockets w/angled chest pockets & matching belt. Canvas reinforcement added to each elbow & lower pocket edges. About size 38. Avg. cond. $185.00

JACKET, "JUMP" (M1942), ARMY AIRBORNE, WWII: Lt. OD cotton w/button fly & large pleated cargo pocket on each thigh w/gray metal snap closure flaps. About size 32" waist. Exc. cond. $500.00

JACKET, "JUMP" (M1943), ARMY AIRBORNE, WWII: Modified M-1943 pattern trousers in dark OD cotton w/large pleated dark OD canvas pocket stitched to each thigh w/metal snap closure flaps & dark OD web tie straps. Faint Qm label. Include detachable suspenders. Medium size. Above avg. cond. $244.00

JACKET, MOUNTAIN, ARMY, WWII: Lt. OD poplin body w/four large front pockets, large pocket on back, zipper/button closure front & button tab at cuffs. Suspenders have been removed & lacks waist belt. Medium size. Avg. cond. $164.00

JACKET, REEFER, COAST GUARD CPO, WWII: Size 36R w/woven US Navy label, gilt brass USCG buttons on double breasted front, bullion CPO Boatswain's mate rate (applied stripes) & 3 hashmarks (embr. stripes) on lt. sleeve, bullion USCG shield on rt. cuff. Above avg. cond. $25.00

JACKET, REEFER, NAVY AVIATION
OFFICER, WWII: Tailor-made in navy blue
wool serge w/woven tailor's label, heavy
bullion on wool backing naval aviator wing
on left chest, gold wire ensign rank & line
officer star on each cuff. Size 38. .. $42.00

JACKET, REEFER, NAVY MEDICAL
OFFICER, WWII: Navy blue wool serge
w/woven clothier's label, double-breasted
front, gold wire comm. rank & med. device
on each cuff, 3-place plastic-coated wide
ribbon bar. Large size. Above avg. cond.
.... $24.00

JACKET, REEFER, NAVY OFFICER, WWII:
Navy blue wool serge w/gilt NAVY buttons
on double breasted front, gold wire
commander rank & line officer star on
each cuff. Woven clothier's & NAVY Reg.
uniform labels. Size 38. Above avg. cond.
.... $25.00

JACKET, REEFER, NAVY OFFICER, WWII:
Tailor-made in navy blue gabardine w/gilt
brass buttons on double breasted front,
woven tailor's label & gold wire lieut. rank
& line officer star on each cuff. Left chest
has nice full size Pb. naval aviator wing
that is LGB/G.F. hmkd. over nice wide 3
place plastic coated ribbon bar for Pacific
Serv. Large size. Exc. cond. $73.00

JACKET, REEFER, NAVY WARRANT
OFFICER, WWII: Private-purchase in
navy blue whipcord w/woven Pettibone
clothier's label, gold wire CWO rank &
bullion carpenter device on each cuff.
Named. About size 38. Lacks removable
buttons. Above avg. cond. $20.00

JACKET, SERVICE, NAVY WOMEN
RESERVE OFFICER, WWII: Reserve
blue wool serge, w/satin lining, gilt NAVY
buttons, lt. blue woven lieut. jg. rank & line
officer star on each cuff & correct collar
patches. Small size. Above avg. cond.
.... $16.00

JACKET, STEWARD, ARMY TRANSPORT
SERVICE (ATS), 1930s: Short white
cotton body w/woven "Army Navy Tailors
Panama, rt.P." label in neck, epaulettes, 2-
button front, button cuffs & smooth gilt
metal buttons. Small size. Above avg.
cond. $40.00

MACKINAW (M1938), ARMY, WWII: Lt. OD
canvas body w/OD wool faced collar &
lining + large OD plastic buttons on
double-breasted front + matching belt +
lower concealed pockets & button adj.
tabs at cuffs. Still has paper inspector tag
attached. Qm tag. Large size. Exc. cond.
.... $177.00

MACKINAW (M1938), ARMY, WWII: OD
canvas body w/matching belt + OD wool
lining & large collar & button tabs at cuffs.
Above avg. cond. $30.00

MACKINAW (M1943 "JEEP COAT"), ARMY,
WWII: Size 38 in dark OD cotton w/large
OD plastic buttons on double-breasted
front + 1945 dated Qm label. Above avg.
cond. $74.00

MACKINAW (M1943 "JEEP COAT"), ARMY,
WWII: Size 40 in dark-shade olive cotton
w/tan lining + 1945 dated Qm tag &
double-breasted front. Above avg. cond.
.... $27.00

MITTENS, FLIGHT, AAF, WWII: Fleece lined.
Dark brown leather bodies w/separate
"trigger" finger. Above avg. cond. .. $50.00

MITTENS, FLIGHT, AAF, WWII

MITTENS, FLIGHT, NAVY, WWII: With
trigger finger. Dark brown leather w/fleece
lining & faint NAVY markings. Above avg.
cond. $72.00

MITTENS, NAVY, WWII: Dark tan leather w/
adj. strap across wrist. USN marked.
Includes OD knit liners. Above avg. cond.
.... $20.00

NURSE'S CAPE, NAVY, 1930s: Navy blue
melton wool body w/short standing collar
+ scarlet red wool lining + twin strap
closure front w/gilt brass buttons w/design
of anchor. Avg. cond. $30.00

OVERALLS, USMC FEMALE, WWII: Size 14
in lt. OD cotton w/USMC marked spec.
tag, built-in suspenders & patch pockets.
Many paper Qm inspector tags still
stamped to body. Near mint cond.
.... $55.00

OVERCOAT, ARMY EM, WWII: Size 42R in
heavy OD wool, large gilt eagle buttons on
double-breasted front & 1941 dated Qm
label. Theater made 1st Allied Airborne
Patch on left shoulder. Above avg. cond.
.... $41.00

OVERCOAT, ARMY OFFICER, WWII: Size
37R in lt. OD poplin w/double-breasted
front, matching belt & 1943 date Qm label.
Includes correct button-in liner + matching

hood. Above avg. cond.
.... $70.00

OVERCOAT, SHORT LENGTH, ARMY OFFICER, WWII: Size 42R in OD melton wool w/horn buttons on double breasted front & 1942 dated Qm label. Avg. cond.
.... $34.00

OVERCOAT, USMC EM, WWII: Size 2-L in forest green wool w/large bronze USMC buttons, double breasted front & 1942-43 dated USMC Qm markings. Above avg. cond. $40.00

OVERCOAT, USMC EM, WWII: Size 4-S in forest green gabardine, w/large dark bronze plastic USMC buttons & 1942-43 dated USMC Qm markings. Above avg. cond. $20.00

OVERCOAT, USMC OFFICER, WWII: Private purchase in forest green melton wool w/bronze USMC buttons on double breasted front, woven Quantico, Va. Post Exchange label. Named & 1944 dated. Med. size. Above avg. cond. $35.00

OVERCOAT, WAC OFFICER, WWII: Lt. OD poplin w/double breasted front. Named. No belt. Med. size. Above avg. cond.
.... $28.00

OVERSHOES, ARMY ARCTIC, WWII: Black canvas covered bodies w/molded rubber soles, metal latch closure fronts & dated 1944. Size 10. Above avg. cond. .. $27.00

PARKA, FLIGHT (A-9), AAF, WWII: Dark OD cotton w/built-in collar, lined in real fur, quilted lining, woven spec. label in neck, button & original zipper front, knit cuffs, epaulettes & 4 front pockets. About size 38. Avg. cond. $300.00

PARKA, FLIGHT (B-9), AAF, WWII: Dark OD cotton body w/fur lined built-in hood, zipper/button front, woven spec. label in neck, quilted green satin lining, several pockets, adj. tabs at cuffs. Small size 14 tag in neck. Near mint cond. $185.00

PARKA, FLIGHT (B-9), AAF, WWII: OD cotton body w/quilted satin lining, AAF marked woven spec. label in neck, built-in fur lined hood, good original zipper/button, several pockets, knit cuffs & epaulettes. Size 40. Above avg. cond. $177.00

PARKA, FLIGHT (B-11), AAF, WWII: Size 40 in dark OD cotton w/real fur lined built-in collar, woven AAF marked spec. label in neck, epaulettes, good original zipper/ button front, several pockets, adj. tab at each cuff. Above avg. cond. $538.00

PARKA, FLIGHT (D-2), AAF, WWII: Dark OD poplin pullover body w/full alpaca lining, AAF marked woven spec. label in neck, alpaca lined built-in hood trimmed w/real fur, zipper neck & several pockets. Size medium. Above avg. cond. $630.00

PARKA, FLIGHT (D-2), AAF, WWII: Large size w/lt. OD poplin body w/alpaca lining, built-in hood trimmed in real fur, zipper neck, drawcord at neck & slash chest pockets w/lower patch pockets. Above avg. cond. $500.00

PARKA, OVERCOAT TYPE W/LINER, ARMY, WWII: Size 42. Reversible from lt. OD to white w/1942 dated Qm label + zipper/button front + built-in hood + several pockets + button tab at each cuff & built-in web waistbelt. Includes correct dark brown pile liner. Above avg. cond.
.... $240.00

PARKA, OVERCOAT TYPE W/LINER, ARMY, WWII

PEACOAT, NAVY, WWII: Navy blue melton wool w/double-breasted front. About size 38. Above avg. cond. $21.00

PURSE, NAVY WAVE, WWII: Black leather w/2 black, 1 blue scarf, change purse, & mirror all inside. Snap flap w/black leather carry strap. Avg. cond. $55.00

RAINCOAT, ARMY, 1930s: 54" length body in dark tan cotton w/large brown finish metal buttons, snap adj. cuffs, fold-over collar, slash pockets & printed label in neck. Large size. U.S.A. marked. Lower front has stenciled unit markings. Above avg. cond. $29.00

RAINCOAT (DISMOUNTED MODEL), ARMY, WWII: Medium size in lt. OD w/ button front & 1945 dated Qm label. Fabric pliable. Above avg. cond. . .$30.00

RAINCOAT (DISMOUNTED MODEL), ARMY, WWII: Medium size in resin coated lt. OD material w/button front. Qm label faint but good shape. $53.00

SAM BROWNE BELT, ARMY OFFICER, 1920s: Stitched brown leather belt w/brass fittings. No cross-strap. Includes brown leather pistol clip ammo pouch & equip. slide. All pieces are Qm Corps marked & 1922 dated. Above avg. cond. $23.00

SAM BROWNE BELT, ARMY OFFICER, 1930s: 2.25" wide stitched dark tan leather belt w/matching cross-strap + gilt brass fittings. Size 32. Avg. cond. . $22.00

SAM BROWNE BELT, ARMY OFFICER, 1930s: Handsome brown leather belt w/ brass fittings & cross belt + sword hanger w/nickel silver chain. Near mint cond. $97.00

SCARF, COLD WEATHER, USMC, WWII: 8" wide x 6' long scarf in marine green, serge wool, fringed on ends & stitch bound edges. Near mint cond. $20.00

SERVICE COAT, ARMY NURSE, WWII: Size 16R in navy blue wool w/maroon trim on epaulettes, woven cuff braid, 1942 dated Qm tag, matching belt, gilt brass eagle buttons, pair Pb. 2nd lieut. bars & US & Med/N collar devices. Above avg. cond. .... ,$76.00

SERVICE COAT, ARMY NURSE, WWII

SERVICE DRESS, ARMY NURSE, WWII: Textured dark OD cotton w/piped epaulettes + woven cuff braid + matching belt + removable eagle buttons + pair US collar devices. Fitted w/pair Cb 1st lieut. bars. Medium size. Above avg. cond. $80.00

SHIRT, AAF OFFICER, WWII: Dark OD gabardine w/woven tailor's label in neck & nice embr. felt AAF patch on left shoulder. Named. About size 38. Above avg. cond. $25.00

SHIRT, ARMY AIRBORNE EM, WWII: Size 14 1/2/32 lt. OD wool shirt w/gas flap. Has 11th Airborne Div. patch, matching separate tab cross-stitched in heavy white

thread to left shoulder & woven T-corporal chevrons. Above avg. cond. $38.00

SHIRT, ARMY EM, WWII: 15-32" lt. OD wool serge shirt w/US Army, Pacific patch on left shoulder, Army Amph. units patch on rt. & woven T-sgt. chevrons. Above avg. cond. $20.00

SHIRT, ARMY OFFICER, WWII: Issue in worsted OD wool w/woven Reg. Army Officer's Shirt label in neck & faint Qm tag. Size 15-32. Above avg. cond. $27.00

SHIRT, CAMO HBT FATIGUE, ARMY, WWII: Reversible from green to tan spot pattern HBT w/concealed button front, button adj. cuffs & deep billow chest pockets. About size 40. Above avg. cond. $216.00

SHIRT, CAMO HBT UTILITY, USMC, WWII: Reversible from green to tan spot pattern HBT w/metal USMC buttons, button front & cuffs & large internal pocket on each side of chest. Man's name & other info. stenciled on back. About size 38. Has Hollywood costumer's label. Avg. cond. $190.00

SHIRT, CAMO HBT UTILITY, USMC, WWII

SHIRT, CAMO HBT UTILITY, USMC, WWII: Reversible green to tan spot pattern HBT w/metal USMC buttons, large internal chest pockets. Back stenciled w/man's name & unit designation (311 in half-circle). Size 38/40. Above avg. cond. $265.00

SHIRT, DENIM FATIGUE, ARMY, 1930s: Blue denim w/button front + fold-over collar + patch lower pockets. Name stenciled in lower waist. About size 36. Avg. cond. $61.00

SHIRT, DENIM FATIGUE, ARMY, 1930s: Dark blue denim w/US Army marked zinc buttons front + lower patch pockets w/ button closure flaps + straight cuffs. About size 36-38. Above avg. cond. $217.00

UNIFORMS

SHIRT, DENIM FATIGUE, NAVY, 1930s: Dark blue denim body w/fold-over collar, lower patch pockets, straight cuffs, & removable metal buttons. Name label stitched into neck. About size 36. Above avg. cond. $50.00

SHIRT, DENIM UTILITY, NAVY, 1930s: Dark blue denim body w/fold-over collar, lower patch-type pockets, straight cuffs, & removable blue plastic NAVY buttons. About size 36. Exc. cond. $29.00

SHIRT, HBT FATIGUE, ARMY, WWII: Dark OD HBT w/metal star buttons, deep billow chest pockets & pair woven s/sgt. chevrons. Size 38. Above avg. cond. $25.00

SHIRT, HBT FATIGUE, WAC, WWII: Medium size in dark OD HBT w/OD plastic button front, gas flap, patch chest pockets & 1943 dated Qm tag. Exc. cond. $37.00

SHIRT, HBT UTILITY, NAVY, WWII: Size 36 in dark OD HBT w/3-pocket front (USN stencil on chest pocket), metal star & wreath buttons & naval contract markings in neck. Near mint cond. $23.00

SHIRT, HBT UTILITY, USMC FEMALE, WWII: 3 pocket. Lt. OD HBT w/metal USMC buttons & EG&A stencil on chest pocket. Size 36/38. Avg. cond. $25.00

SHIRT, HBT UTILITY, USMC, WWII: Lt. OD HBT w/black finish buttons w/brass USMC buttons, EG&A stencil on chest pocket. large internal pocket on each side of chest & gas flap. About size 42. Above avg. cond. $66.00

SHIRT, HBT UTILITY, USMC, WWII: Lt. OD HBT body w/OD plastic button front & cuffs, 3 pockets & EG&A stencil on chest pocket. About size 38. Above avg. cond. $30.00

SHIRT, SUMMER, WAC, WWII: Lightweight tan cotton w/pleated chest pockets & button front, Pb. 1st lieut. bar & Med/N officer insignia. Name label. Size 12. Above avg. cond. $25.00

SHIRT, USMC EM, WWII: Dark tan worsted wool w/scalloped pocket flaps, fully embr. 3rd Amph. Corps patch on left shoulder, forest green wool on tan twill PFC. chevrons, discharge patch & pair 1937-pattern EG&A collar devices. Medium size. Above avg. cond. $40.00

SHIRT, USMC EM, WWII: Distinctive mustard tan wool shirt w/button front & 1942 dated spec. tag. Size 3. Still has paper Qm spec. tag attached. Above avg. cond. $30.00

SHIRT, UTILITY, USMC FEMALE, WWII: Lt. OD cotton w/3 pocket, button front & cuffs, & EG&A stencil. Medium size. Above avg. cond. $28.00

SHIRT, WAAC, WWII: In tan w/matching tie. Near mint cond. $31.00

SHOES, ATHLETIC, ARMY, WWII: Lt. OD canvas high ankle top canvas bodies w/ molded rubber soles & lace insteps. Converse brand. Size 8. Avg. cond. $20.00

SHOES, JUNGLE ANKLE HIGH, ARMY, WWII: Dark OD canvas w/lace insteps + molded black rubber soles. Size 9 1/2. Faint Qm markings. Above avg. cond. $80.00

SHOES, SERVICE ANKLE HIGH, ARMY, WWII: Size 9D. Dark brown leather w/cap toes, lace fronts, comp. soles. Avg. cond. $62.00

SHOES, SERVICE ANKLE HIGH, ARMY, WWII: Smooth russet brown leather w/cap toes, lace fronts, faint 1942 dated Qm markings & composite leather & rubber soles. Size 8C. Exc. cond. $187.00

SHOES, SERVICE ANKLE-HIGH, USMC, WWII: Dark tan roughout leather w/corded rubber soles & lace fronts. 1944 dated contract markings. Size 7D. Above avg. cond. $98.00

SHOES, SERVICE ANKLE-HIGH, USMC, WWII

SHOES, SERVICE ANKLE-HIGH, USMC, WWII: Size 14E in roughout brown leather w/lace insteps & corded rubber soles. 1945 dated markings & USMC inspector marked. Exc. cond. $85.00

SHOES, SERVICE LOW QUARTER, ARMY OFFICER, WWII: Size 7 1/2D in smooth russet brown leather w/lace insteps, leather soles & rubber heels. Well marked. Near mint cond. $103.00

SHOES, SERVICE LOW QUARTER, ARMY OFFICER, WWII: Smooth brown leather bodies, lace insteps, leather soles, & rubber heels. Qm inspector marked. About size 9 1/2. Above avg. cond. $53.00

SKI BOOTS, ARMY, WWII: Dark brown leather ankle-high bodies w/square toes, rawhide lace insteps & heavily cleated soles. Size 7 EE. Above avg. cond. $50.00

SKI BOOTS, Size 8 1/2E in dark brown leather w/heavily cleated soles & lace insteps. Faint Qm markings. Above avg. cond. $135.00

SKI PARKA, ARMY, WWII: Reversible. Lt. OD to white poplin w/built-in hood, 3-button neck, button tab on each cuff, slash pockets, 1942 dated Qm tag. Med. size. Hood was fur trimmed but trim neatly removed. Lt. OD color shows some "bleeding" through to white side. .. $35.00

SKI PARKA, ARMY, WWII: Reversible. Medium size. Lt. OD to white poplin w/fur trimmed built-in hood, button neck, slash chest pockets, 1942 dated Qm tag & button tabs on cuffs. Above avg. cond. $87.00

SKIRT, SUMMER, WAC, WWII: Dark tan worsted wool. Zipper fly. Washed out size label. Medium size. Avg. cond. $14.00

SKIRT, WINTER, WAAC, WWII: Size 14 in OD baranthea w/1943 dated Qm tag & zip fly. Near mint cond. $32.00

SURVIVAL VEST (C-1), AAF, WWII: Dark OD nylon body w/button front, AAF marked woven spec. label, many pockets labeled to contain various survival items (none included), built-in holster & faint color AAF patch design printed on left chest. Above avg. cond. $150.00

SURVIVAL VEST (C-1), AAF, WWII: Dark OD nylon w/button front, AAF marked woven spec. label, many pockets labeled to contain various survival items (none included), built-in holster & color AAF patch design printed on left chest. Above avg. cond. $252.00

SWEATER, FLIGHT (C-2), AAF, WWII: OD knit wool sweater w/zipper front. Size 36 w/woven spec. label in neck. Above avg. cond. $300.00

SWEATER, HIGH NECK, ARMY, WWII: Lt. OD wool knit w/5 OD plastic button neck. Medium size. Above avg. cond. $39.00

SWORD BELT, ARMY AIR CORPS OFFICER FULL DRESS, 1930s: Black leather body covered in gold wire w/ribbed ultramarine blue inserts, matching hanger straps & brass fittings. Includes 1851 pattern buckle that is maker hmkd. Avg. cond. $282.00

SWORD BELT, NAVY OFFICER DRESS, 1930s: Folded & stitched black leather belt w/gilt brass fittings + hanger straps. Avg. cond. $35.00

TAILCOAT, NAVY OFFICER DRESS, 1930s: Navy blue melton wool w/double breasted front, gold wire lieut. cuff braid & line stars. Has provisions for shoulder boards. Avg. cond. $27.00

TROUSERS, ARMY, 1930s: Size 36x35" in OD wool w/1937 dated Qm label + button fly. Above avg. cond. $36.00

TROUSERS, ARMY OFFICER, WWII: 30" waist in dark OD gabardine w/1944 dated Qm label. $36.00

TROUSERS, CAMO HBT FATIGUE, ARMY, WWII: Reversible from green to tan spot pattern HBT w/OD plastic button fly & large cargo pocket on each thigh. Washed-out Qm label. Medium waist size. $248.00

TROUSERS, CAMO HBT FATIGUE, ARMY, WWII: Reversible from green to tan spot pattern camo HBT, 1943 dated Qm label, OD plastic button fly, & large cargo pocket on each thigh. Size 32x33". Still has paper inspector tags attached. Near mint cond. $156.00

TROUSERS, CAMO HBT UTILITY, USMC, WWII: Reversible from green to tan spot pattern camo w/snap closure fly & conventional cut pockets. Size 30" waist. Avg. cond. $133.00

TROUSERS, COLD WEATHER, ARMY TANKER, WWII: Lt. OD cotton body w/ "bib" front, OD wool lining, built-in suspenders & good zippers. Small/medium size. Above avg. cond. .. $100.00

TROUSERS, COLD WEATHER, NAVY, WWII: Bib front. Dark blue ribbed cotton w/dark blue wool lining, built-in suspenders & woven contract label. Med. size. Above avg. cond. $11.00

TROUSERS, COLD WEATHER, NAVY, WWII: Dark blue ribbed cotton body w/ metal latch closure "bib" front + suspenders + navy blue wool lining + printed naval contract label. U.S. Navy marked across front. $65.00

TROUSERS, DRESS (1937 PATTERN), ARMY OFFICER: Tailor made in navy blue melton wool w/button fly & gold wire stripe down each leg w/ribbed red insert. Named & 1937 dated. Exc. cond. $49.00

TROUSERS, FIELD, ARMY, WWII: Size 38x33" in lt. OD wool serge. 1943 dated Qm label marked "Special". Above avg. cond. $32.00

TROUSERS, FIELD, ARMY, WWII: 32x31 in OD wool serge w/1944 dated Qm label. Above avg. cond. $19.00

TROUSERS, FIELD, ARMY, WWII: Size 36x32 in dark OD cotton w/OD plastic button fly + 1945 dated Qm label. Near mint cond. $74.00

TROUSERS, FIELD, WAC, WWII: Size 18R in unusual dark green shade cotton w/ button fly + 1943 dated Qm label & elastic insteps. Still has paper spec. tags stapled to body. Near mint cond. $21.00

TROUSERS, FLIGHT (A-3), AAF, WWII: Dark brown leather w/AAF marked woven spec. label & built-in suspenders. Zipper front needs some repair. Fleece lined. Avg. cond. $40.00

TROUSERS, FLIGHT (A-5), AAF, WWII: Size 42R in dark brown leather w/AAF marked woven spec. label. Built-in suspenders & good original zippers. Fleece lined. Above avg. cond. .. $129.00

TROUSERS, FLIGHT (A-8), AAF, WWII: Dark OD cotton w/quilted lining, zipper fly, adj. strap across rear & 2 front patch pockets. Simple printed label marked "A-8 Type/Size Small". Above avg. cond. $25.00

TROUSERS, FLIGHT (A-8), AAF, WWII: Size 38 in dark OD cotton w/quilted lt. OD cotton lining, woven AAF marked label & detachable suspenders. AAF ink stamp markings. Above avg. cond. $72.00

TROUSERS, FLIGHT (A-9), AAF, WWII: Dark OD cotton w/alpaca lining, zipper fly, 2 front patch pockets, knit cuffs, simple label printed "A-9 Type/Size Small." Exc. cond. $27.00

TROUSERS, FLIGHT (A-11), AAF, WWII: Dark OD cotton w/alpaca lining, woven AAF marked spec. label, good zippers & detachable suspenders. Size 38. Well marked. Above avg. cond. $51.00

TROUSERS, FLIGHT (A-11), AAF, WWII: Size 34" waist in dark OD cotton w/alpaca lining, woven AAF marked spec. label, correct detachable suspenders & large AAF ink stamp markings. Avg. cond. $22.00

TROUSERS, FLIGHT (B-1), AAF, WWII: Fleece lined. Dark brown leather w/built-in suspenders, AAF patch design decal & Air Corp. marked woven spec. label. Size small. Above avg. cond. $34.00

TROUSERS, FLIGHT (B-1), AAF, WWII: Fleece lined. Medium size dark brown leather w/good original zippers, built-in zippers, AAF marked woven spec. label. Above avg. cond. $80.00

TROUSERS, FLIGHT (B-1), AAF, WWII: Fleece lined. Medium size dark brown leather w/good original zippers, built-in zippers, embossed spec. markings. AAF patch design decal on front. Above avg. cond. $142.00

TROUSERS, FLIGHT (F-1), AAF, WWII: Size 38 in dark OD nylon w/woven AAF marked spec. label & detachable suspenders. Above avg. cond. $21.00

TROUSERS, FLIGHT (F-3A), AAF, WWII: Electrically heated. Size medium/reg. In original paper envelope w/GE marked spec. label. Above avg. cond. $36.00

TROUSERS, FLIGHT (M-446A), NAVY, WWII: Fleece lined. Size 38. Dark brown leather, built-in suspenders, BuAero marked woven spec. label, leather insteps. NAVY marked. Above avg. cond. $70.00

TROUSERS, HBT FATIGUE, ARMY, WWII: 34x32" in dark OD HBT w/OD plastic button fly & 1944 dated Qm label. Exc. cond. $66.00

TROUSERS, HBT FATIGUE, WAC, WWII: XL size in dark OD HBT w/button fly & 2 button flap hip pockets. 1943 dated Qm label. Near mint cond. $51.00

TROUSERS, HBT UTILITY, USMC, WWII: Lt. OD HBT. Conventional cut w/metal USMC button fly. About size 32" waist. Avg. cond. $45.00

TROUSERS, HBT UTILITY, USMC, WWII: Lt. OD HBT w/metal USMC buttons & conventional cut pockets. Approx. 34" waist. Exc. cond. $145.00

TROUSERS, (KERSEY-LINED), ARMY, WWII: Size 32x30" in lt. OD cotton twill w/ button fly & 1942 dated Qm label. Avg. cond. $72.00

TROUSERS, MOUNTAIN, ARMY, WWII: 34x31 in lt. OD poplin w/1942 dated spec.label, 2-button waistband w/zip fly, large pleated cargo pocket on each thigh, concealed zip closure waist pockets, 2 rear pockets & elastic insteps. Near mint cond. $282.00

TROUSERS, "PINK", ARMY OFFICER, WWII: Private purchase in "pink" gabardine. About size 44" waist. Above avg. cond. $30.00

TROUSERS, USMC EM, WWII: Size 5-M in forest green wool. Have several Qm inspector tags still stapled to body. Exc. cond. $28.00

TROUSERS, USMC EM, WWII: Size 6S in forest green wool. Well marked. Named. Clean. Above avg. cond. $45.00

TROUSERS, WINTER, NAVY, WWII: In dark blue ribbon cotton w/navy blue wool lining, attached suspenders & metal latch closure "bib" front. USN marked. Woven contract label. Size medium. Above avg. cond. $40.00

UNIFORM, (1937 PATTERN), ARMY OFFICER MESS DRESS: Navy blue melton wool waist-length jacket w/red satin faced lapels, removable gilt eagle buttons on double-breasted front, arty. piped gold wire braid & direct embr. bullion arty device above on each cuff. Includes ornate heavy gold braid shoulder boards. Woven maker's label. About size 36/38. Includes ribbed white cotton vest & medium blue melton wool trousers w/red stripe down each leg. Same maker's label as jacket. Above avg. cond. $145.00

UNIFORM, (1937 PATTERN), ARMY OFFICER MESS DRESS

UNIFORM, ARMY AIR CORPS EM SUMMER, 1930s: M-1926 pattern tan cotton blouse w/removable gilt buttons, belt hooks at waist, Cb US & AAF collar discs. Small size. Includes tan cotton breeches w/zinc US Army button fly, lace calves, AAF piped tan cotton o/seas cap, necktie & US marked & 1931 dated brown leather garrison belt. Also, dark tan cotton mackinaw belt w/plastic buckle. Avg. cond. $74.00

UNIFORM, ARMY OFFICER, 1930s: Whipcord OD tunic, dated 1934(inside pocket) w/embr. Army Service forces patch, matching breeches, Sam Browne belt w/sword chains, spurs & leggings. OD canvas B-4 w/officers name & rank on sides. Avg. cond. $72.00

UNIFORM, COAST GUARD OFFICER GRAY SERVICE, WWII: Private purchase gray gabardine blouse w/removable black plastic USCG buttons, removable gray USCG ensign shoulder boards. Named & 1943 dated. Woven maker's label. Size 38. With mismatched trousers, gray cotton shirt w/maker's label, o/seas cap w/satin lining & maker markings on leather sweatband. Above avg. cond. $56.00

UNIFORM, NAVY OFFICER DRESS, 1920s: Navy blue melton wool overcoat w/gilt

USN buttons on double-breasted front, gold wire lieut. rank & Dental Corps device on each cuff. Provisions for shoulder boards. Naval Uniform Shop label in neck. Named & 1922 dated. Includes trousers. Above avg. cond. $20.00

UNIFORM, NAVY OFFICER EVENING DRESS, 1920s: Tailor-made waist length jacket w/long tails in navy blue melton & Annapolis, Md. tailor's label in neck. Removable gilt USN buttons on double-breasted front, gold wire lieut. jg. rank & line officer on each cuff & provisions for removable shoulder boards. Named & 1923 dated. Includes trousers in navy blue melton wool. Above avg. cond. $21.00

UNIFORM, NAVY PO1 UNDRESS WHITE, NAVY, WWII: White cotton jumper w/PO1 Radioman rate on left sleeve. W/trousers. Avg. cond. $22.00

UNIFORM, NAVY PO2 DRESS BLUE, WWII: Navy blue wool jumper w/PO2 Radioman rate on left sleeve. Large size. w/13-button trousers. Above avg. cond. $11.00

UNIFORM, NAVY PO2 UNDRESS BLUE, WWII: Navy blue wool jumper w/PO2 Aviation Machinist Mate rate on left sleeve, w/13-button trousers. Named. Above avg. cond. $11.00

UNIFORM, NAVY PO2 UNDRESS WHITE, WWII: White cotton jumper w/PO2 Aviation Machinist Mate rate on left sleeve & discharge patch, w/trousers. Named. Above avg. cond. $11.00

UNIFORM, NAVY SEABEE DRESS BLUE, WWII: Med./long size navy blue wool jumper w/Seabees patch on left shoulder, PO1 Carpenter's Mate rate & 2-place wide ribbon bar, w/13-button trousers. Above avg. cond. $20.00

UNIFORM, USMC EM DRESS BLUE, 1920s: Size 2-M pocketless blouse in navy blue melton wool w/standing collar, red piping, pair 1921-pattern EG&A dress collar devices, PFC./infantry chevron cross stitched to each sleeve, gun pointer first class mark on rt. cuff. USMC Good Conduct medal engraved to man, numbered, 1st enlistment & 1923-1926 on reverse & sterling sharpshooter badge pinned to left chest. Lining in each armpit shows alterations. Includes correct size 3-M medium blue wool trousers w/1921-1922 dated USMC Qm markings + zinc USMC button fly. Above avg. cond. $302.00

UNIFORM, USMC EM, WWII: 1943 dated forest green wool blouse w/USMC Qm markings, forest green wool on scarlet felt PFC chevron & one hashmark on each sleeve. No belt. Size 38. Also, 4-pocket navy blue wool dress blouse w/red piping, 1937-pattern dress EG&A devices & gold tape on scarlet felt PFC. chevron & hashmark on each sleeve. W/correct medium blue wool trousers. All named to same man. Above avg. cond. $38.00

UNIFORM, USMC EM, WWII: 5-L forest green wool blouse, w/1941-1942 dated USMC Qm markings, Aircraft Fuselage 4th Wing patch on left shoulder, wool on felt corporal chevrons, 1937 pattern EG&A devices & discharge patch. No belt. Also, dark tan worsted wool shirt & forest green wool trousers. Above avg. cond. .. $55.00

UNIFORM, USMC FEMALE SERVICE, WWII: Nice quality forest green wool serge jacket w/satin lining, bronze plastic USMC buttons, pair 1937 pattern collar devices, wool on felt corps chevrons, discharge patch. Medium size. Includes matching skirt & tan worsted necktie. Above avg. cond. $93.00

UNIFORM, USMC FEMALE SUMMER, WWII: Green seersucker short sleeve jacket w/correct corps chevrons & matching skirt. Lacks removable buttons. Above avg. cond. $59.00

UNIFORM, USMC OFFICER EVENING MESS DRESS, WWII: Tailor made waist length jacket in navy blue melton wool w/ quilted ribbed red satin lining, single breasted on "false" button front, bullion & cord trimmed standing collar, epaulettes & cuffs. Each epaulette has sew-on bullion one-star general's device. Named to lieut. & 1940 dated. W/correct trousers w/gold wire stripe & red insert stripe down each leg. Above avg. cond. $100.00

UNIFORM, USMC OFFICER EVENING
MESS DRESS, WWII

UNIFORM, WAAC, WWII: Tunic & skirt w/ label in the pocket & ink stamped name &

service number on collar. Has large brown buttons on front & skirt. Above avg. cond. $72.00

UNIFORM, WAC HBT FATIGUE, WWII: Medium size dark OD HBT shirt w/metal star buttons, gas flap & patch chest pockets. Medium size dark OD HBT fatigue trousers w/1943 dated Qm tag & OD plastic buttons. Exc. cond. $37.00

UNIFORM, WAC OFFICER SUMMER SERVICE, WWII: Dark tan gabardine jacket w/woven tailor's label, machine embr. on felt AAF patch on left shoulder. Named & 1945 dated. Med. size. W/dark tan worsted wool skirt. Above avg. cond. $72.00

UNIFORM, WAC SUMMER SERVICE, WWII: Lightweight tan cotton shirt w/ button front, small pleated chest pockets & 9th Corps patch on left shoulder. Size 12. W/good tan cotton twill skirt. Avg. cond. $28.00

UNIFORM, WAVES OFFICER, WWII: Includes jacket & short-sleeve dress in gray seersucker. Jacket w/removable navy blue plastic NAVY buttons, reserve blue woven ensign rank & embr. on white felt supply corps device on each cuff. Both have woven Women's Naval Reserve labels. About size 21. Above avg. cond. $50.00

UNIFORM, WAVES OFFICER, WWII: Reserve blue wool serge jacket w/woven clothier's label, lt. blue woven lieut. jg. rank & supply corps device on each cuff, & collar patches. Includes matching skirt & lightweight medium blue cotton blouse. All pieces w/WAVES' name label. Above avg. cond. $47.00

UNIFORM, WAVES, WWII: Gray seersucker jacket w/single blue plastic NAVY button on front, WAVE collar patches, name label stitched in neck & garment care labels. Smallish size. Includes pleated skirt made from similar material as neckerchiefs, service hat w/stitched brim & removable gray seersucker top. Avg. cond. ... $54.00

C. 1946 - Present

BLOUSE, ARMY OFFICER: Dark OD gabardine w/matching belt w/ribbed buckle, woven clothier's label, Meyer hmkd. Pb. captain's bars, US & Arty collar devices, 8th Army patch on left shoulder & 5th Army on rt. Above avg. cond. ..$35.00

BLOUSE, (CLASS "A"), ARMY AIRBORNE EM: 36R in AG worsted w/1981 dated spec. label, white on blue Airborne tab over 6th Div. patch on left shoulder, sgt.

chevrons, 2 hashmarks & padded Canadian para wing on rt. chest. Lacks pocket flap buttons. Above avg. cond. $28.00

BLOUSE, DRESS BLUE, ARMY FEMALE OFFICER: Size 16 tall in lightweight blue worsted material w/gilt buttons, silk woven cuff braid w/ribbed buff inserts. Exc. cond. $11.00

BLOUSE, DRESS BLUE, ARMY OFFICER: Size 43R in navy blue gabardine w/silk woven cuff braid w/burgundy piped inserts. $11.00

BLOUSE, SUMMER, ARMY OFFICER: Size 40S. Tailor made in tan gabardine w/U.S. Army, Europe patch on left shoulder, "U.S." & Gen. Staff Corps collar devices, Pb. major leaves, DUC ribbon. Avg. cond. $10.00

BLOUSE, SUMMER ARMY OFFICER: Size 39L in dark tan worsted wool w/1952 dated Qm label, OD border 3rd Armor Div. patch w/"Spearhead" tab on left shoulder, pair 1st lieut. bars, US & Armor collar devices. Above avg. cond. $22.00

BODY ARMOR, AVIATOR, ARMY: Vietnam era. Includes both sections; armored vest (T64) & apron (T65). All w/printed spec. labels. Includes correct bag marked to contain this type of vest. Above avg. cond. $400.00

BODY ARMOR, AVIATOR, ARMY

BOOTS, ARCTIC: Ex-large size w/white felt bodies, thick composition soles, 2-buckle canvas & leather uppers & lace insteps. Above avg. cond. $20.00

BOOTS, ARCTIC: Heavy molded white rubber bodies w/cleated soles, lace fronts. US marked. Size 9R. Exc. cond. .. $40.00

BOOTS, COMBAT, ARMY: "Speed Lace". Size 11 1/2W in black leather w/molded rubber soles. 1989 dated. W/instructional tag. Near mint cond. $35.00

BOOTS, COMBAT, ARMY: 1950s. Russet brown leather w/cap toes, lace fronts, neoprene soles. In original issue box. Size 8 1/2. Near mint cond. $49.00

BOOTS, COMBAT, ARMY: 1950s. Russet brown leather w/cap toes, lace fronts, neoprene soles. Markings faint-about size 10. Exc. cond. $35.00

BOOTS, COMBAT, ARMY: Size 10R in black leather w/cap toes, lace fronts, neoprene soles. 1956 dated Qm $52.00

BOOTS, COMBAT, ARMY: Size 12XN in all black leather w/lace fronts "tire tread" molded rubber soles. 1982 dated. Near mint cond. $35.00

BOOTS, COMBAT, ARMY: Size 8 1/2R black leather w/cap toes & lace-in zipper fronts. 1962 dated. Above avg. cond. $40.00

BOOTS, COMBAT FEMALE, ARMY: Size 3XW black leather bodies w/lace fronts, "tire tread" soles. 1980 dated. Near mint cond. $20.00

BOOTS, COMBAT FEMALE, ARMY: Size 4N black leather bodies w/lace fronts, "tire tread" soles. 1977 dated. Near mint cond. $20.00

BOOTS, "JUMP", ARMY AIRBORNE: Size 8 E, black leather w/beveled heels, cap toes, lace fronts & woven Corcoran label. Avg. cond. $31.00

BOOTS, JUNGLE, ARMY: Patterned after Vietnam issue but w/black nylon canvas uppers, black leather bodies, "speed lace fronts", cleated soles & drain vents. Size 8W. Instructional card still attached. Last of the jungle boots. Near mint cond. $35.00

BOOTS, JUNGLE, ARMY: Size 10 1/2W. Dark OD canvas uppers, black leather bodies, cleated soles. 1988 dated. Spike protective marked. Near mint cond. $40.00

COVERALLS, ARMY: Med. size in OD sateen w/1970 dated spec. label. Exc. cond. $11.00

COVERALLS, HBT, ARMY: Immediate post-WWII in dark OD HBT w/OD plastic buttons, belt, several pockets & gas flap. Size 38. Exc. cond. $16.00

COVERALLS, HBT, ARMY: OD w/metal star buttons, matching belt, several pockets, gas flap, 1948 dated Qm label. Size "S" tag. Black printed on white web name tape on rt. chest. Above avg. cond. $30.00

FLAK VEST (KEVLAR), ARMY: Lightweight, OD cotton vest has large pockets for 8 different slip-on Kevlar type armor plates. Tie strings in front. Well made but very light. No markings. Above avg. cond. $144.00

UNIFORMS

FLAK VEST (KEVLAR), ARMY: Woodland camo nylon covered body w/velcro closure front, large instructional label. Size medium. 1984 dated. Exc. cond. $143.00

GRENADE CARRIER VEST, ARMY: Dark OD mesh & nylon body w/many individual ammo pockets, snap/velcro front. US marked & 1973 dated. Mint cond.
.... $35.00

JACKET, FATIGUE, ARMY DESERT STORM CAMO BDU: Size large/long in 6-color desert camo. Has color 22nd Field Arty. Support Cmd. patch on left shoulder & US flag patch on rt. shoulder. Left chest pocket has color novelty Op. Desert Storm 1991 patch & embr. on tan twill Op. Desert Storm patch on rt. chest pocket. Has brown embr. on tan US Army pocket tape & name tape in Arabic letters. Exc. cond.
.... $38.00

JACKET, FATIGUE, ARMY DESERT STORM CAMO BDU: Small/regular size in 6-color desert camo w/subdued 32nd Arty. patch on each shoulder w/color US flag patch below on rt. Brown embr. on tan web pocket tapes. Exc. cond. $28.00

JACKET, FIELD, ARMY CAMO TIGER STRIPE: Lightweight cotton body w/zipper & button closure front, 4 patch-type pockets on front w/single exposed button closure flaps, pocket on left sleeve, button cuffs, epaulettes & black cotton lining. Size 38. Near mint cond. $75.00

JACKET, FIELD, ARMY CAMO TIGER STRIPE

JACKET, FIELD (M1951), ARMY: Dark OD cotton body w/zipper & snap closure front, faint printed Qm markings. Size med./reg. Has OD border 7th Div. patch on left shoulder, OD embr. on blue twill master sgt. chevrons, yellow-on-black woven US Army pocket tape, theater made fully machine embr. name tape w/attached unit crest design along top edge. Above avg. cond. $50.00

JACKET, FIELD (M1951), ARMY: Reg./small in dark OD cotton w/zipper front, 1952 dated Qm markings. Above avg. cond.
.... $37.00

JACKET, FIELD (M1951), ARMY: Size reg./med. in dark OD cotton w/zipper & snap closure front & all labels intact. 1962 dated. Above avg. cond. $34.00

JACKET, FIELD (M1951), ARMY: Size reg./small in dark OD cotton w/all labels intact, zipper/snap closure front. 1960 dated. Has subdued name tapes. Above avg. cond.
.... $24.00

JACKET, FIELD (M1951), ARMY: Size small-short in dark OD cotton w/zipper & snap closure front, all labels intact. 1961 dated. Has 7th Army patch on left shoulder, yellow-on-AG master sgt. chevrons, yellow-on-black woven US Army tape, embr. on white web name tape. Near mint cond. $66.00

JACKET, FIELD (M1965), ARMY: In dark OD cotton w/color insignia-fully 4th Missile Cmd. patch on left shoulder, theater-made Korean 1st Div. patch on specl. 4 chevrons, yellow-on-black US Army tape & white web name tape. Size med./reg. Avg. cond. $16.00

JACKET, FIELD (M1965), ARMY: Size short-small in dark OD cotton w/zipper & snap closure front. 1967 dated. Has color sgt. chevrons, para wing, subdued 3rd Army patch & pocket tapes. Above avg. cond.
.... $24.00

JACKET, FIELD (M1965), ARMY: Size small-reg. solid black cotton. Above avg. cond.
.... $20.00

JACKET, FLIGHT, ARMY AVIATOR: Medium/short in OD aramid w/zipper front, knit cuffs & waistband, several pockets, 1974 dated spec. label. Has color insignia; fully embr. 1st Cav. Div. patch on rt. shoulder, embr. on twill "Mohawk/OV-1B" patch on left chest & embr. on twill "CH-47/Chinook" patch on rt. chest & Aviation School patch on left shoulder, subdued captains rank patches. Above avg. cond. $164.00

JACKET, FLIGHT, ARMY AVIATOR: OD aramid body w/zipper front, several pockets, knit cuffs & waistband, velcro panel on left chest & 1976 dated label. Has embr. on twill "Desert Storm '91" patch on left chest, embr. on twill "Fighting Sixth/Second Squadron" Air Cav. patch on rt. chest. Above avg. cond. $40.00

JACKET, FLIGHT, ARMY AVIATOR: Size large/long in OD aramid w/zipper front, several pockets, knit cuffs & waistband. 1989 dated spec. label. Near mint cond.
.... $75.00

JACKET, FLIGHT, ARMY AVIATOR: Size large/reg. in OD non-melting nylon w/ zipper front, 1990 dated spec. label, knit cuffs & waistband & several pockets. Has color embr. on twill B Co. 101-Avn/ Regt(AH)/101 Abn Div(Asslt)/Kingsman patch on rt. chest, "Desert Storm '91" patch on left chest over velcro attached name tag w/silver embossed pilot wing & para wing designs, subdued 101st A/B Div patch & tab on left shoulder, 1st Cav. Div. patch on rt. shoulder, 1st lieut. rank patches. Above avg. cond. $165.00

JACKET, FLIGHT, ARMY AVIATOR: Size medium/short in dark OD non-melting nylon w/1980 dated spec. label, knit cuffs & waistband, slash pockets w/velcro closure flaps, pocket on left sleeve. Near mint cond. $67.00

JACKET, FLIGHT, ARMY AVIATOR: Size small/long in non-melting OD aramid w/ quilted lining, 1977 dated spec. label, zipper front, slash pockets, pocket on left sleeve, knit cuffs & waistband. Exc. cond. $50.00

JACKET, FLIGHT, ARMY AVIATOR. Size small/long, non-melting OD nylon w/ quilted lining, 1984 dated spec. label, zipper front, slash pockets, pocket on left sleeve, knit cuffs & waistband. Mint cond. $85.00

JACKET, FLIGHT, ARMY AVIATOR

JACKET, FLIGHT, ARMY AVIATOR: Size medium/long in OD Aramid w/1976 dated spec. label, zipper front, pocket on left sleeve, slash pockets, knit cuffs & waistband. Exc. cond. $70.00

FLIGHT JACKET (B-15C) W/TROUSERS, USAF: Dark blue nylon insulated body w/ dark blue nylon lining, dark blue fur collar, woven spec. label, good original zipper front, faded original knit cuffs & waistband, small closure slash pockets w/snap tab above each, pocket on left sleeve. Size 38. Early USAF patch design decal on left shoulder. W/type D-1A trousers insulated dark blue nylon w/good original zippers, several pockets. Above avg. cond. $1,350.00

JACKET, FLIGHT (CWU-36P), COAST GUARD: Sage green fire resistant material w/zipper front, 1980 dated spec. label, several pockets, knit cuffs & waistband. Has plastic sealed commander leaves, large embr. on cotton USCG Aviation Medical Officer patch on rt. chest, velcro attached gold embossed name tag on left chest, w/design of Flight Surgeon Badge over commander's name & USCG. Near mint cond. $180.00

JACKET, FLIGHT (G-1), COAST GUARD: Size 40 in dark brown leather w/simulated fur collar, 1976 dated spec. label, original zipper front, original knit cuffs & waistband, good lining. Has large embr. on twill USCG Search & Rescue, CGAS Elizabeth City, N.C. patch on rt. chest, gold leaf on black leather name tag on left chest w/design of Naval Aircrew wing over name & "AD USCG." Above avg. cond. $265.00

JACKET, FLIGHT (G-1), NAVY: Dark brown leather body w/real fur collar, satin lining, good original zipper front, replacement knit cuffs & waistband. Large size. Avg. cond. $150.00

JACKET, FLIGHT (G-1), USMC: 1960s era jacket w/real fur collar, replacement zipper front, BuAero marked woven spec. label, replacement knit cuffs & waistband. Size 42. Has embr. on twill HMT 204 patch on rt. chest, velcro attached name tag on left chest, gold embossed naval aviator wing over name & "Capt USMC", merrowed edge 4th Marine Air Wing patch on rt. sleeve & US flag patch on left sleeve. Avg. cond. $302.00

JACKET, IKE (M1946), ARMY EM: Size 36R in OD wool serge w/1948 dated Qm label, Supreme HQ Allied Powers, Europe patch cross-stitched to left shoulder. Corporal chevrons. Above avg. cond. $20.00

JACKET, IKE (M1946), ARMY EM: Size 38R in OD wool serge w/2nd Army patch on left shoulder, US Army Forces Western Pacific patch on rt. shoulder, small yellow-on-blue corporal chevrons, 5 embr. on dark OD gabardine o/seas bars & 2 hashmarks. Exc. cond. $18.00

JACKET, IKE (M1946), ARMY EM: Size 38R in OD wool serge. Exc. cond. $25.00

JACKET, IKE (M1950), ARMY EM: Size 38R in OD wool serge w/1951 dated Qm tag. Has been converted to zipper front. Has bevo style weave 1st Div. patch on left

UNIFORMS

shoulder, corporal chevrons, & single Sb. Inf collar device. Above avg. cond. $20.00

JACKET, IKE (M1950), ARMY EM: Size 38R in OD wool serge w/40th Div. patch on left shoulder, China H.Q. patch on rt. shoulder, woven s/sgt. chevrons & multi-piece Cb US & Qm collar discs. Above avg. cond. $35.00

JACKET, IKE (M1950), ARMY EM: Size 40R in OD wool serge w/large Qm tag, 1st Army patch on left shoulder, US Army Forces Western Pacific (sewn on reverse) on rt. shoulder, OD embr. on felt master sgt. chevrons, 8 hashmarks, 2 o/seas bars, 10-place cord stitched ribbon group on OD wool serge lt. backing on left chest. Above avg. cond. $17.00

JACKET, MESS DRESS, ARMY OFFICER: White cotton waist length w/removable gilt buttons, full colonel cuff braid & removable gold wire dress shoulder boards. Woven clothier's label. Size 38. Above avg. cond. $40.00

KOREAN WAR ERA FLIGHT JACKET (B-15 "WAR ART"): Commercial copy in light OD cotton w/simulated OD fur collar, knit cuffs & waist band, zipper front & chest pocket-slash style waist pockets. Back has large, heart shape design w/girl in see-through bathing suit holding fencing foil-a red heart on her left breast-flowery initials "K G"-fancy names along lower edge-for 4 cities in Korea/Japan-scroll below-"Japan-Korea 55-56". Faint letters above "Return From Hell," faint names "Bob" & "Bea" painted on chest. Avg. cond. $400.00

KOREAN WAR ERA NAVY FLIGHT SUIT (Z-2 ANTI-BLACKOUT): Lightweight OD nylon w/woven spec. label, diagonal zipper front, several pockets. Size 40S. Above avg. cond. $32.00

KOREAN WAR ERA NAVY FLIGHT SUIT (Z-2 ANTI-BLACKOUT): Size 36L in OD nylon w/woven spec. label, diagonal zipper front, several pockets, pressure hose. Above avg. cond. $93.00

KOREAN WAR ERA PARKA & LINER: Large size dark OD M1951 parka w/1951 dated Qm markings, built-in hood, zipper/snap closure front, correct button-in liner w/1951 dated Qm markings. Above avg. cond. $20.00

KOREAN WAR ERA USAF FLIGHT JACKET (B-15C): Size 38 in dark blue nylon w/large fur collar, woven spec. label, good original zipper front, small pocket on left sleeve, slash pockets w/snap tab above each, knit cuffs & waistband. Above avg. cond. $979.00

KOREAN WAR ERA USAF FLIGHT JACKET (B-15C): Size 40 in dark blue nylon w/large fur collar, woven spec. label, zipper front, knit cuffs & waistband, pocket on left sleeve, slash pockets w/snap tab above each. Above avg. cond. $1,840.00

KOREAN WAR ERA USAF FLIGHT JACKET (B-15D): Dark blue nylon body w/dark blue nylon lining, woven spec. label (some wear to lettering), good original zipper front, large fold over fur collar, good navy blue knit cuffs & waistband, pocket on left sleeve, slash pockets w/snap nylon tab above each, faint color printed early USAF patch design on left shoulder. Size 38. Avg. cond. $1,155.00

KOREAN WAR ERA USAF FLIGHT JACKET (L-2A): Dark blue nylon body & lining w/woven spec. label, slash pockets w/snap closure flaps, pocket on left sleeve, epaulettes, original knit collar & waistband w/snap tab. Replacement zipper & cuffs. Avg. cond. $1,168.00

KOREAN WAR ERA USAF FLIGHT JACKET (N-2A): Size large in dark blue nylon w/woven spec. label, built-in hood trimmed in real fur ruff, good original zipper button/zipper front, snap closure slash pockets, pocket on left sleeve, knit cuffs & waistband, faint color early USAF patch design printed on left shoulder. Exc. cond. $696.00

KOREAN WAR ERA USAF FLIGHT JACKET (N-2A): Size large in dark blue nylon w/woven spec. label, built-in hood trimmed in real fur, zipper/button front, dark color patch design on left shoulder, pocket on left sleeve, slash pockets w/snap tab above each, knit cuffs & waistband. Above avg. cond. $525.00

KOREAN WAR ERA USAF FLIGHT JACKET (N-2A): dark blue nylon lining w/woven spec. label, real fur trimmed built-in hood, dark color early USAF patch design decal on left shoulder (near 100%), zipper/button closure front, several pockets, blue knit cuffs & waistband. Name & "19th BSA 22 BWG" inked. Med. size. Above avg. cond. $1,420.00

KOREAN WAR ERA USAF FLIGHT JACKET (N-3): Dark blue nylon body w/real fur ruff trimmed built-in hood, zipper/button front, several pockets, faint color early USAF patch design on left shoulder. Med. size. Avg. cond. .. $368.00

KOREAN WAR ERA USAF FLIGHT JACKET (N-3B): Dark blue nylon w/built-in hood trimmed in real fur, "Talon" replacement zipper front, several pockets, faint USAF decal on left shoulder, woven spec. label. Size small. Avg. cond. $380.00

KOREAN WAR ERA USAF FLIGHT SUIT (G-4A ANTI-G PNEUMATIC): Dark blue nylon body w/woven spec. label, color printed early USAF patch design on left chest, zipper front w/brown leather tab along edge left edge, several pockets, pressure hose. Size small/short. Above avg. cond. $154.00

KOREAN WAR ERA USAF FLIGHT SUIT (G-4A ANTI-G PNEUMATIC)

KOREAN WAR ERA USAF FLIGHT SUIT (G-4A ANTI-G PNEUMATIC): Size small/ long in dark blue nylon w/woven spec. label & ink stamp markings, zipper front, color printed early USAF patch design on left shoulder. Above avg. cond. $84.00

KOREAN WAR ERA USAF FLIGHT SUIT (K-2): Size small-reg. in light weight OD nylon w/woven spec. label, zipper front. Zippers show some light corrosion but are operable. Avg. cond. $25.00

KOREAN WAR ERA USAF FLIGHT SUIT (K-2A): Size med./short in dark blue nylon w/woven spec. label, zipper front, several pockets. Near mint cond. $59.00

KOREAN WAR ERA USAF FLIGHT SUIT (K-2A): Size med./long in dark blue nylon w/woven spec. label, zipper front & several pockets. Above avg. cond. $139.00

KOREAN WAR ERA USAF FLIGHT SUIT (K-2A): Size med./short in dark blue nylon w/woven spec. label & ink stamp markings, dark (near 100%) patch design decal on left shoulder, zipper front, several pockets. Exc. cond. $161.00

KOREAN WAR ERA USAF FLIGHT SUIT (L-1A): Med./reg. in dark blue gabardine w/ woven spec. label & ink stamp markings, zipper front, faint color printed USAF patch design on left shoulder, several pockets. Avg. cond. $75.00

KOREAN WAR ERA USAF FLIGHT SUIT (L-1A): Size xlarge/reg. dark blue gabardine w/woven spec. label, zipper front, several pockets. left chest has 4 female snap ends for name tag (not included). Avg. cond. $125.00

KOREAN WAR ERA USAF FLIGHT SUIT (L-1A): Size large/long in dark blue gabardine w/woven spec. label, zipper front, several pockets. Left chest has 4 female snap ends for name tag (not included), 2 female snap ends on each shoulder. Above avg. cond. $125.00

KOREAN WAR ERA USAF FLIGHT SUIT (L-1A): Size large/reg. in dark blue gabardine w/woven spec. label & faint USAF ink stamp markings, zipper front, several pockets. Above avg. cond. $49.00

KOREAN WAR ERA USAF FLIGHT SUIT (L-1A): Size med./short in dark blue gabardine w/zipper front, woven spec. label & USAF ink stamp markings, several pockets. Has 4.5" dia. embr. on black twill sqdn. patch on left chest w/comical half hawk/half sabre jet fighter design. Above avg. cond. $187.00

KOREAN WAR ERA USAF FLIGHT SUIT (L-1A): Size small-reg. in dark blue gabardine w/zipper front, woven spec. label, several pockets. Well marked. Avg. cond. $35.00

KOREAN WAR ERA USAF FLIGHT SUIT (L-2A): Size 38 in dark blue nylon w/ epaulettes, woven spec. label, zipper front w/snap closure waist tab, knit collar, cuffs & waistband, pocket on left sleeve, slash pockets. Avg. cond. $815.00

KOREAN WAR ERA USAF FLIGHT TROUSERS (A-11C): Dark blue nylon w/ woven spec. label, knit cuffs. Good zippers. Size 32. Above avg. cond. $80.00

KOREAN WAR ERA USAF FLIGHT TROUSERS (A-11C): Size 32 in dark blue nylon w/woven spec. label, USAF ink stamp markings, well marked, correct detachable suspenders. Above avg. cond. $72.00

KOREAN WAR ERA USAF FLIGHT TROUSERS (D-1A): Dark blue nylon body w/dark blue nylon lining, woven spec. label, correct detachable suspenders, good original zippers, early USAF patch design ink stamp markings & blue knit cuffs. Size 38. Above avg. cond. .. $75.00

KOREAN WAR ERA USAF FLIGHT TROUSERS (D-1A): Dark blue nylon w/ woven spec. label, detachable suspenders, knit cuffs. Well marked. Size 32. Above avg. cond. $45.00

UNIFORMS

KOREAN WAR ERA USAF FLIGHT TROUSERS (F-1A): Dark blue nylon w/ woven spec. label. Size 28. Above avg. cond. $45.00

KOREAN WAR ERA USAF PARKA & LINER: Size large in dark OD cotton w/ 1951 dated USAF/Qm marked spec. label (1947 pattern dated), zipper/button front, built-in hood intact web waistbelt, matching pile liner. Exc. cond. $74.00

KOREAN WAR ERA USAF RADIO CARRIER VEST (E-1): Blue nylon body w/ zipper front, woven spec. label & USAF ink stamp, color early USAF patch design printed on left chest. Above avg. cond. $177.00

KOREAN WAR ERA USAF RADIO CARRIER VEST: Dark blue nylon w/zipper front, color printed USAF patch design on left chest, worn woven spec. label & faint USAF ink stamp design. Above avg. cond. $205.00

KOREAN WAR ERA USAF SOUVENIR JACKET 58TH FTR. BOMBER. WG.: Reversible w/zipper front, knit collar, cuffs & waistband & slash pockets. One side in black & silver-gray satin w/4.5" dia. 5th Air Force patch design direct silk mach. embr. into rt. chest, simulated "blood" chit embr. into center of back w/US, UN & S. Korean flag designs over message below in Oriental characters, "58th Ftr. Bmr. Wg" above & "Japan-Korea" below. Reverse in quilted silver satin w/black stripes, prowling tiger & eagle designs on chest, "Japan," Mt. Fuji, map of Japanese Islands & locations & dragon on back. Medium size. Near mint cond. $722.00

KOREAN WAR ERA USMC EM DRESS BLUE BLOUSE: Navy blue melton wool 4-pocket blouse w/standing collar & red piping, gilt USMC buttons. 1937-pattern dress collar devices. Stamped size 2-M inside lining. Has bright silver finish Rifle Marksman badge on left chest. Above avg. cond. $38.00

KOREAN WAR ERA USMC EM DRESS BLUE BLOUSE: Navy blue melton wool w/ standing collar, red piping, embr. on felt dress corporal chevrons (w/o cross rifles). Size 36. Above avg. cond. $20.00

KOREAN WAR ERA USMC EM UNIFORM: Tan worsted wool shirt-about size 38, 31x33L dark tan cotton twill trousers w/ button fly & 1951 dated markings. Above avg. cond. $34.00

KOREAN WAR ERA USMC FLIGHT JACKET (G-1): WWII era jacket. Size 38 in dark brown leather w/real fur collar, woven BuAero/NAVY marked spec. label, good original zipper front, original knit cuffs & waistband, satin lining. Zipper pull

has Korean coin attached. Has 5" dia. fully embr. VMF(N) 513 sqdn. patch stitched to rt. chest. Above avg. cond. $1,210.00

KOREAN WAR ERA USMC FLIGHT JACKET (G-1)

KOREAN WAR ERA USMC FLIGHT JACKET (A-2): Dark brown leather-size 40 w/woven maker's label. Has Asian made "Marine Aircraft Group 11" on left shoulder, large Asian made, red & yellow name tag on left chest w/winged USMC device over name, serial number & USMC. Has 5x7" USMC VMJ-1 squadron patch on rt. chest, diamond shaped USMC 1st Marine Air Wing patch on rt. shoulder, red & yellow tabs above & below-Japan, Korea, Philippines & Okinawa. Size 40. Above avg. cond. $500.00

MITTENS, ARCTIC: Dark OD cotton w/lt. brown leather palms w/alpaca facing & adj. straps on wrists & gauntlets. Korean war era. Medium size. Avg. cond. $20.00

NAVY AVIATOR FIELD JACKET (M1941): W/USS Nautilus insignia. Dark OD poplin body w/OD wool lining, zipper/button front, slash pockets. Has large embr. on twill USS Nautilus patch on rt. chest & gold embossed on black leather tag on left chest w/faint likeness of submarine badge & "USS Nautilus SSN 571." Back stenciled in black "SSN 571/101." Large size. Avg. cond. $328.00

NAVY FLIGHT JACKET (CWU-36/P): Med. size in sage green nomex w/1987 dated spec. label, zipper front, knit cuffs & waistband, several pockets. Above avg. cond. $136.00

NAVY FLIGHT JACKET (CWU-36/P): Sage green flame resistant jacket w/zipper front, 1980 dated spec. label, pocket on left sleeve, slash pockets, knit cuffs & waistband. Velcro attached US flag patch on left chest. Plastic sealed Capt. bars. Med. size. Avg. cond. $164.00

NAVY AVIATOR FLIGHT JACKET (CWU-36/ P): Large size in sage green polyamide w/ 1991 dated spec. label, zipper front, several pockets, knit cuffs & waistband, velcro panel on left chest. Has velcro attached USCG lieut.'s name tag w/ embossed design of naval aviation wing, large embr. on twill USCG Search & Rescue, CGAS Elizabeth City, NC patch on rt. chest. Above avg. cond. $150.00

NAVY AVIATOR FLIGHT JACKET (CWU-36/ P): Sage green polyamide w/zipper front, knit cuffs & waistband, several pockets. Has US flag patch on left shoulder, Tomcat "Grim Reapers" patch on rt. shoulder, velcro attached brown vinyl name tag on left chest w/gold embossed naval aviator wing over man's name & "LT. USN." Lacks spec. label. Above avg. cond. $160.00

NAVY FLIGHT JACKET (CWU-45/P): Sage green polyamide body w/zipper front, several pockets, good knit cuffs & waistband, velcro panel on left chest, large 1987 dated spec. label. Size large. Above avg. cond. $129.00

NAVY AVIATOR FLIGHT JACKET (CWU-45/ P): Large size in sage green nylon w/ zipper front, 1980 dated spec. label, slash pockets, pocket on left sleeve, velcro panel on left chest, knit cuffs & waistband. Has twill Attack Sqdn. 216 patch on left chest, fully embr. "Strike Fighter/NAVY Hornet" patch on rt. chest, fully embr. "Corsair II" patch on left chest. Exc. cond. $240.00

NAVY AVIATOR FLIGHT JACKET (CWU-45/ P): Sage green polyamide w/zipper front, 1984 dated spec. label, knit cuffs & waistband, several pockets, velcro panel on left chest. Has color US flag patch on left shoulder, Naval Air Station Norfolk, Va. patch on left chest & HM-18 sqdn. patch on rt. chest. Above avg. cond. $164.00

NAVY AVIATOR FLIGHT JACKET (CWU-45/ P): Sage green polyamide w/zipper front, large 1986 dated spec. label, knit cuffs & waistband, several pockets. Has classic "Tomcat" patch on left shoulder, embr. on twill, "F-14" patch on rt. shoulder, twill Navy Fighter Weapons School patch on left chest & USS Midway patch on rt. chest. Above avg. cond. $100.00

NAVY AVIATOR FLIGHT JACKET (CWU-45/ P): Sage green polyamide w/zipper front, large 1986 dated spec. label, several pockets, knit cuffs & waistband. Has US flag patch on left shoulder, twill "Intruder" patch on rt. shoulder + large USS George Washington CV-73 patch on rt. chest,

velcro panel on left chest. Exc. cond. $166.00

NAVY AVIATOR FLIGHT JACKET (CWU-45/ P): Sage green polymide body w/zipper front, knit cuffs & waistband, slash pockets w/velcro closure flaps, pocket on left sleeve. Has large embr. on cotton AWACS "Hawkeye" patch stitched to left chest, large embr. on twill Miramar Naval Air Station patch stitched to rt. chest. Lacks spec. label. Med. size. Above avg. cond. $402.00

NAVY AVIATOR FLIGHT JACKET (CWU-45P)

NAVY AVIATOR FLIGHT JACKET (G-1): 1950s. Size 42, dark brown leather w/real fur collar, worn woven spec. label, replacement Conmar zipper front, original knit cuffs & waistband, satin lining. Has large embr. on felt sqdn. patch w/design of eagle clutching aerial bomb & mine in talons. Avg. cond. $264.00

NAVY AVIATOR FLIGHT JACKET (G-1): 1950s. Dark brown body w/real fur collar, woven BuAero marked spec. label, good original zipper front, original knit cuffs & waistband, good lining. Size 36. Faint trace of name tag on lower left chest. Has had section of zipper flap removed. Avg. cond. $376.00

NAVY AVIATOR FLIGHT JACKET (G-1): 1950s. Dark brown leather w/real fur collar, original zipper front, satin lining, original knit cuffs & waistband. Lacks spec. label. Size 40. Avg. cond. . $106.00

NAVY AVIATOR FLIGHT JACKET (G-1): 1950s. Size 38, dark brown leather w/ period replacement zipper front, woven BuAero marked spec. label, woven knit cuffs & waistband, satin lining. Fur collar has been neatly removed & replaced by fold over knit collar in similar size & shape. Avg. cond $72.00

NAVY AVIATOR FLIGHT JACKET (G-1): 1960s. Size 40 in dark brown leather w/ real fur collar, 1962 dated BuAero marked spec. label, good original zipper front, original knit cuffs & waistband & satin lining. Avg. cond. $185.00

NAVY AVIATOR FLIGHT JACKET (G-1): 1970s. Dark brown leather w/simulated fur collar, good original zipper front, good nylon lining, original knit waistband. Has velcro attached name tag on left chest, gold embossed naval aviator wing design on dark red vinyl w/name & "LT. USMC." Replacement cuffs. Lacks spec. label. Avg. cond. $125.00

NAVY AVIATOR FLIGHT JACKET (G-1): 1970s. Dark brown leather w/simulated fur collar, nylon lining, original zipper front. knit waistband. Lacks cuffs. Size 40. Avg. cond. $48.00

NAVY AVIATOR FLIGHT JACKET (G-1): Dark brown leather w/simulated fur collar, good original zipper front, good knit cuffs & waistband, nylon lining. Lacks spec. label. Appears current issue & about size 42. Has large F-14 patch on rt. shoulder, US flag patch on left shoulder, VS-27 patch on rt. chest & velcro attached pilot's name tag on left chest w/"U.S. Navy 'The Cats Night Out'" patch below. Above avg. cond. $180.00

NAVY AVIATOR FLIGHT JACKET (G-1): Size 38 in dark brown leather w/simulated fur collar, good original zipper front, original knit cuffs & waistband, good lining. Printed 1977 dated spec. label. Above avg. cond. $145.00

NAVY AVIATOR FLIGHT JACKET (G-1)

NAVY AVIATOR FLIGHT JACKET (G-1): Size 40 in dark brown leather w/Wep marked 1962 dated spec. label, real fur collar, good original zipper front, knit cuffs & waistband, good satin lining. Exc. cond. $331.00

NAVY AVIATOR FLIGHT JACKET (G-1): Size 40 in dark brown leather w/real fur collar, 1962 dated woven spec. label, good original zipper front, good original knit cuffs & waistband & satin lining. Fully embr. "Task Force Bravo" patch on left shoulder, "USS Wasp" patch on rt. shoulder + gold embossed on black leather NAVY aviator's name tag over "Traron-25" patch on left chest, sqdn. patch on rt. chest. Above avg. cond. $685.00

NAVY AVIATOR FLIGHT JACKET (G-1): Size 40 in dark brown leather w/simulated fur collar, printed 1986 dated spec. label, good original zipper front, good nylon lining, original knit cuffs & waistband. Above avg. cond. $171.00

NAVY AVIATOR FLIGHT JACKET (G-1): Size 42 in dark brown leather w/real fur collar, woven BuAero marked spec. label, good original zipper front, good original knit cuffs & waistband, good satin lining. Has embr. on black felt US Navy patch on left shoulder, large Patrol 60 patch on rt. chest. Above avg. cond. $387.00

NAVY AVIATOR FLIGHT JACKET (G-1): Size 44 in dark brown leather w/1967 dated woven spec. label, real fur collar, good original zipper front + original knit cuffs & waistband. Avg. cond. $115.00

NAVY AVIATOR FLIGHT JACKET (G-1): Size 44 in dark brown leather w/simulated fur collar, 1976 dated spec. label, replacement zipper front, replacement knit cuffs & waistband. Above avg. cond. $159.00

NAVY AVIATOR FLIGHT JACKET (G-1): Size 46 in dark brown leather w/simulated fur collar, 1975 dated printed spec. label, good original zipper front, good original knit cuffs & waistband, good lining. Exc. cond. $198.00

NAVY FLIGHT JACKET (L-2B): Med. size in sage green nylon w/orange nylon lining, zipper front, knit collar, cuffs & waistband, several pockets. MIL/Alpha Industries marked contract spec. label. Above avg. cond. $61.00

NAVY FLIGHT JACKET (N-2B): Size Med. in sage green nylon. Has 1983 dated military contract marked spec. label, simulated fur ruff trimmed built-in hood, zipper/button front, several pockets, knit cuffs & waistband. Avg. cond. $23.00

NAVY FLIGHT JACKET (N-2B): Size large w/sage green nylon body + printed 1982 dated spec. label, built-in collar trimmed in real fur ruff, zipper/button front, several pockets, good knit cuffs & waistband. Exc. cond. $59.00

NAVY AVIATOR FLIGHT SUIT (ANTI-G TYPE II): OD nylon-1 piece w/diagonal zipper across front-pressure tube off left waist. Has woven spec. label. Size 36. Exc. cond. $40.00

NAVY AVIATOR FLIGHT SUIT (NOMEX): sage green-zipper front-38R. Has direct embr. lieut.'s bars on shoulders w/ "Groucho"-flight officer wing & real name direct embr. into left chest w/likeness of black bird in flight on green "V" w/"Black Ravens" on rt. chest. Appears to be 1980 dated. Avg. cond. $35.00

NAVY AVIATOR FLIGHT SUIT JACKET: Size 42R in OD nylon w/good original zipper front, 1963 dated BuWep/NAVY marked woven spec.label, knit collar & cuffs, deep billow chest pockets. Has gold embossed on black leather NAVY Cdr.'s name tag stitched to left chest w/likeness of Naval Aviator wing. Avg. cond. $650.00

NAVY AVIATOR FLIGHT SUIT: Lightweight tan cotton w/zipper front, woven 1958 dated BuAer spec.label w/"Mil-C-5390-D (Aer)" specs, zipper front, several pockets. Exc. cond. $40.00

NAVY AVIATOR FLIGHT SUIT: Size 40L in bright orange cotton w/1959 dated navy Dept. marked woven spec. label, zipper front, several pockets. Above avg. cond. $25.00

NAVY AVIATOR FLIGHT SUIT: Size 40L in orange cotton w/zipper front, several pockets. Has printed Wep spec. label. Name Inked above left chest pocket. Avg. cond. $20.00

NAVY AVIATOR FLIGHT SUIT: Size 40R in bright. orange cotton w/printed Wep spec. label, zipper front, several pockets. Sleeves neatly finished short. Has dark blue stenciled on wide white web "Cdr. O'Neill" tape on left chest & "CO VT 25" tape on rt. chest. Large sage green nylon pocket neatly added to rt. leg w/snap closure flap that also has 2 small pockets. Above avg. cond. $55.00

NAVY AVIATOR PARTY SUIT: Dark green cotton body w/yellow "racing" stripes down left front, zipper front, small zippered pocket on each sleeve, zippered sleeve cuffs & zippered bolero leg cuffs. Has concealed left chest pocket w/large velcro closure flap that has patch likeness of naval aviation wing w/"Hawkeye" direct embr. below. Size 40. Exc. cond. .. $91.00

NAVY CAMO DESERT UTILITY JACKET: Med./long in 3-color desert camo ripstop. Has brown embr. on tan poplin US Navy tape in English & Arabic on left Exc. cond. $27.00

NAVY CAMO WOODLAND FATIGUE UNIFORM LOT: Med.-long ripstop shirt w/ "US Navy" iron-on stencil on left chest. W/ matching small-long ripstop trousers + size small ripstop utility cap. Exc. cond. $20.00

NAVY COLD WEATHER DECK JACKET: Dark OD cotton w/"fuzzy" lining, zip front & several pockets. Size small. 1981 dated. Has "Go Navy," HC-8, USS Kalamazoo AOR-6 & Helsuppron-Eight patches. "KZOO/327/1st Ft" stenciled on back. Above avg. cond. $40.00

NAVY COLD WEATHER DECK JACKET: Dark OD cotton w/synthetic "fuzzy" lining, zipper/button front. 1980 dated. Size small. Above avg. cond. $20.00

NAVY COLD WEATHER DECK JACKET: Size Med. in OD cotton w/zipper & button front & several pockets. 1983 dated. Name stenciled on left chest. "LSD 38/ 065" stenciled on back. Small tear to left shoulder but clean otherwise. Above avg. cond. $20.00

NAVY COLD WEATHER JACKET (A-1): Dark green nylon w/synthetic lining, zipper/snap front, large 1963 dated spec. label, slash pockets. NAVY marked. Size small. Above avg. cond. $49.00

NAVY COLD WEATHER TROUSERS: Dark OD nylon insulated bodies. Med. size. Printed naval contract tag. Above avg. cond. $25.00

NAVY CPO BLOUSE: 1950s. Size 42. Private purchase in dark tan gabardine w/ bullion CPO Qm rate & 6 hashmarks on left sleeve. Above avg. cond. $20.00

NAVY CPO REEFER JACKET: Size 40XL in navy blue wool serge w/gilt brass NAVY buttons on double-breasted front. 1976 dated. Above avg. cond. $20.00

NAVY DECK JACKET: Med. weight garment in OD nylon w/patch chest pockets, zipper/button front, NAVY marked on left chest, collar facing & lining in fuzzy OD material, button adj. tab at each cuffs & faint naval contract label. Size small. Avg. cond. $45.00

NAVY FLIGHT DECK LIFE PRESERVER (MARK I VEST TYPE): Dark red cotton body w/OD trim, reflective panel on each shoulder, snap front, manual inflation tube, 1981 dated spec. label. Med. size. Has strobe light pouch on left chest-includes 1991 dated SDU-5/E light-includes battery unit & works, US marked OD plastic whistle-both attached to pouch w/white parachute cord, sea dye marker pouch on lower left front w/dye marker. Above avg. cond. $55.00

UNIFORMS

NAVY FLIGHT DECK LIFE PRESERVER (MARK I VEST TYPE): Green cotton body w/snap closure front, reflective panels on shoulders, manual inflation tube, strobe light pouch on left chest (no light included), unused sea dye marker in sage green dye marker pouch on lower left front. Has "HMH-461" stenciled on back. Size large & 1977 dated. Avg. cond. $38.00

NAVY FLIGHT DECK LIFE PRESERVER (MARK I VEST TYPE): Pale dark red cotton w/OD trim, snap front, 1991 dated spec. label, several pockets, manual inflation tube, reflective strips on shoulders & back. Large size. Near mint cond. $28.00

NAVY MIDSHIPMAN DRESS UNIFORM LOT: Waist-length navy blue melton wool jacket w/gilt NAVY buttons on double-breasted front, gold wire trim on standing collar & cuffs, "Annapolis Dress Collar" marked "false" collar insert. Named & 1950 dated. W/matching trousers. Above avg. cond. $38.00

NAVY NURSE DRESS WHITE UNIFORM: White cotton jacket w/gilt NAVY buttons, gold wire ensign rank & bullion Med. Corps device on each cuff, woven Naval Uniform Shop label. Named & 1971 dated. 3-place ribbon bar for Korean Service. affixed to left chest. W/matching skirt named to same Nurse. Med. size. Above avg. cond. $32.00

NAVY OFFICER BLOUSE: WWII era tan cotton blouse w/removable gilt NAVY buttons. Has removable lieut. cdr. line officer shoulder boards. Size 38. Above avg. cond. $20.00

NAVY OFFICER DRESS OVERCOAT: Navy blue melton wool double-breasted coat w/ woven clothier's label marked "Tailored for the United States Naval Academy," curve-form line officer ensign grade shoulder boards. Size 38. Above avg. cond. $55.00

NAVY OFFICER OVERCOAT: Long-length in navy blue melton wool w/gilt buttons on double-breasted front, 1974 dated spec. label, provisions for removable shoulder boards-none included. Size 36R. Above avg. cond. $34.00

NAVY OFFICER UNIFORM: Tailored tan worsted wool blouse w/gilt navy buttons, provision for removable shoulder boards-none included, woven "Navy Exchange" label. Size 40. W/trousers. Exc. cond. $20.00

NAVY OFFICER UNIFORM: W/navy blue wool serge reefer jacket w/goldwire lt. rank & line officer star on each cuff. Has woven "Tailored for the United States Naval Academy" label. Named. Size 42. Also, tan worsted wool summer service blouse w/gilt navy buttons. Size 38. Above avg. cond. $25.00

NAVY OFFICER UNIFORM: Navy blue gabardine overcoat w/matching belt, double-breasted front. W/green gabardine officer blouse w/black woven lieut. jg. rank & line officer star on each cuff. Size 38. Avg. cond. $34.00

NAVY SCPO UNIFORM : Private-purchase reefer jacket in navy blue wool serge. Size 40R. Has SCPO Boatswain's Mate rate & 5 hashmarks on left sleeve. All stripes in gold wire. Has 11-place sew-on ribbon group for WWII thru Korea service. Bullion shows some tarnish. W/trousers. Avg. cond. $32.00

NAVY SEABEE CAMO DESERT BDU FATIGUE JACKET: Small-reg. in six-color desert camo. Has brown embr. on tan cotton US Navy & name pocket tapes, "Seabees" patch design direct embr. in brown on left chest pocket, embr. on tan twill "Amphibious Construction Battalion Two" patch on rt. shoulder. Exc. cond. $40.00

NAVY SEABEE CAMO DESERT BDU FATIGUE UNIFORM : Small-reg. jacket in six-color desert camo w/brown embr. on tan cotton US Navy & name pocket tapes, Seabee's patch design direct embr. into left chest pocket, embr. on twill Amph. Constr. Bn. Two patch (in desert colors) on rt. shoulder. W/matching small-reg. trousers w/man's name tape above rear pocket. Above avg. cond. $51.00

NAVY SOUVENIR JACKET: 1950s "Baseball" styled in dark blue wool w/lt. blue trim, snap closure front, striped knit collar, cuffs & waistband, slash pockets. Has large chenille United States Naval Communications Unit 3 patch on left chest, applied felt "US Navy Asmara Eritrea East Africa" letters on back. Size 38. Avg. cond. $145.00

NAVY SOUVENIR JACKET: Black wool body w/black satin lining, knit collar, cuffs & waistband, patch chest pockets w/slash lower pockets, zipper front. Has button stitched to each side of shoulder. has "Jaybo" direct embr. into left chest pocket flap, patch on rt. chest pocket w/Personnel mans rating design, US flag patch on rt. sleeve, Aquarius birth sign patch on left sleeve. Has "USS. Saipan (LHA-2)/ 'Arkansas, Ohio," likeness of US eagle & flag, various ports-of-call & "Med. Cruise/ 1985" direct embr. into back. Med. size. Above avg. cond. $75.00

NAVY SOUVENIR JACKET: Black wool body w/black satin lining, zipper front, button cuffs, patch chest pockets, lower slash pockets. Has Scorpio birth sign patch on rt. shoulder. 6 colorful nationality flags on left chest. Rt. chest has NAVY "I Crossed the Line of Death" patch. Name direct embr. into left chest pocket flap w/large 6th Fleet patch above. Has "USS. Trenton (LPD-14)/'Maryland'," large design of eagle & US flag, various ports-of-call & "Med. Cruise/1986" on back. Med. size. Exc. cond. $86.00

NAVY SOUVENIR JACKET: Black wool body w/black satin lining, zipper front, knit collar & cuffs, patch chest pockets, lower slash pockets. Has "Rich" direct embr. into left chest pocket flap & Multinational Peacekeeping Force Beruit, Lebanon patch above, U.S. 6th Fleet patch on rt. chest. Back has direct embr. "USS. Barnstable County (LST-1197)/'New York City'" above design of eagle clutching US flag, various ports-of-call, "Lebanon/Med. Cruise/1985" below. Size 38. Above avg. cond. $86.00

NAVY SOUVENIR JACKET

NAVY SOUVENIR JACKET: Black wool body w/black satin lining, zipper front, printed Chinese maker's label, snap cuffs, slash lower pockets & elastic waistband. Has name patch on left chest, colorful design of S. America & Africa continents w/ locations on back w/"USS Barnstable Cty LST-1197/WATC-87" above & "Unitas XXVIII 1987" below. Size 38. Exc. cond. $91.00

NAVY SOUVENIR JACKET: Black wool body w/zipper front, black satin lining, striped knit collar & cuffs, patch chest pockets w/ lower slash pockets. Has NC state flag patch on left shoulder, US & Confederate flag patches on rt. shoulder, large US Navy patch on left chest w/"Foresta" direct embr. into left chest pocket flap, Electronicsman rating design patch on rt. chest. Back has "USS. Nashville (LPD-13)/'North Carolina" over large eagle/US flag design in center, various ports-of-call & "Med. Cruise/1990-91." Size 42. Exc. cond. $93.00

NAVY SOUVENIR JACKET: Large-size sports-style jacket-blue nylon body w/snap closure front, striped knit collar, cuffs & waistband, slash pockets. Has large transfer design of ship in center w/"LCC-20" above & "USS Mount Whitney LCC-20" below. Above avg. cond. $38.00

NAVY SOUVENIR JACKET: Med. weight in green satin w/quilted lining, snap closure front, striped knit collar, cuffs & waistband, slash pockets. Size large. Large transfer design on back of Arab atop a camel in cross-hairs, ship's crest design & reads "U.S.S. Conyngham/DDG-17/Persian Gulf Yacht Club/MEF-2-87." Above avg. cond. $49.00

NAVY SUBMARINE UTILITY COVERALLS: Size 44R in dark blue poly/cotton blend w/ 1991 dated spec. label. Near mint cond. $40.00

NAVY WARRANT OFFICER UNIFORM: Navy blue wool serge reefer jacket w/gold wire rank & crossed anchors on each cuff, 12-place sew-on ribbon group for WWII thru Korean Service, woven Naval Uniform Shop label. Named & 1955 dated. Med. size. W/trousers, necktie, long-length dress overcoat w/provisions for removable shoulder boards-none. Service overcoat w/liner. Above avg. cond. $45.00

OVERCOAT, ARMY: Size 36R AG gabardine w/matching belt & button-in liner. Above avg. cond. $20.00

OVERCOAT, ARMY: Reg./medium in dark OD cotton w/double breasted front, matching belt, matching button in liner. 1953 dated. Exc. cond. $51.00

SCARF, PARADE, ARMY: Dark red cotton w/ embr. on twill patch stitched to 1 side w/ motto "On The Line." Exc. cond. .. $20.00

SHIRT, FATIGUE, ARMY CAMO TIGER STRIPE: Dark pattern on ripstop w/button front, straight cuffs, lower patch pockets w/single exposed button flaps. Size 38. Above avg. cond. $20.00

SHIRT, FATIGUE, ARMY DESERT STORM CAMO BDU: Size small/short in 6-color desert camo pattern w/subdued 3rd Army patch on left shoulder, 22nd Field Army Support Cmd. patch on rt. Brown embr. on tan US Army & name pocket tapes. Exc. cond. $22.00

SHIRT, FLIGHT (NOMEX), ARMY AVIATOR: Size medium/long in OD nomex w/zipper front, 1971 dated spec. label, epaulette added to each shoulder in matching material. Has subdued insignia-direct machine embr. senior pilot & basic para wing & U.S. Army on left chest, name on rt. chest, major & Aviation (winged prop device) collar devices. Also, 7th Div. patch w/Ranger tab above on left shoulder. Above avg. cond. $25.00

SHIRT, HBT FATIGUE, ARMY: In dark OD HBT w/metal star & wreath buttons, patch chest pockets, straight cuffs, 1949 dated printed issue markings. Size small. Near mint cond. $11.00

SHIRT, WOOL, ARMY: Lt. OD wool serge w/ epaulettes & 1951 dated Qm markings. Size 38. Above avg. cond. $20.00

SURVIVAL VEST (SRU-21), ARMY AVIATOR: Green nylon mesh body w/ several attached pockets & pistol holster that never been sewn in includes odd survival type radio painted red. Lacks spec. label. Avg. cond. $118.00

SURVIVAL VEST (SRU-21/P), ARMY AVIATOR: Size large in sage green mesh w/many sage green pockets for survival items, 1970 dated spec. label, zipper front, velcro/lace adj. back panel. Contents include 2 dressings, package of trioxane heating fuel, tourniquet, distress marker light, green marker, flashlight & strobe light battery. Accessories are 1980s era. All unused & in packages. Above avg. cond. $124.00

TROUSERS, FATIGUE, ARMY CAMO TIGER STRIPE: Dark pattern on ripstop. Conventional cut w/zip fly. Avg. cond. $30.00

TROUSERS, FATIGUE, ARMY CAMO TIGER STRIPE: Dark pattern camo on loose weave medium weight cotton w/ zipper fly, conv. cut pockets. Size 42" waist. Above avg. cond. $59.00

TROUSERS, FIELD (M1951), ARMY: Reg./ large in dark OD cotton w/1952 dated Qm markings. Near mint cond. $20.00

UNIFORM, ARMY CAMO DESERT BDU FATIGUE: 3-color desert camo pattern size small/x-short ripstop jacket w/ subdued 3rd Army patch on left shoulder, color U.S. flag patch on rt. shoulder. W/ matching x-small/short trousers. Above avg. cond. $20.00

UNIFORM, ARMY CAMO FATIGUE: Panamanian made. Cotton shirt w/spot pattern camo in dark green shades on dark tan w/button front, woven Panama Army-Navy Store's label, patch chest

pockets, button cuffs, & epaulettes. Medium size. W/matching trousers. Exc. cond. $61.00

UNIFORM, ARMY CAMO NIGHT DESERT: Parka w/printed grid design, built-in hood, button front. Medium size. W/button-in liner for jacket, trousers. Exc. cond. $40.00

UNIFORM, ARMY CAMO TIGER STRIPE FATIGUE : Dark pattern tiger pattern printed on loose weave cotton shirt w/ button front, straight cuffs & lower patch pockets. Med. size. W/conventional cut trousers w/zipper fly in similar pattern as shirt. Boonie hat in similar fabric but darker pattern camo. Above avg. cond. $107.00

UNIFORM, ARMY CAMO TIGER STRIPE FATIGUE: Med. weight cotton w/dark pattern design w/button front, patch chest pockets & lower pleated pockets w/single exposed button closure flaps. Size 38. W/ trousers. Exc. cond. $45.00

UNIFORM, ARMY EM DRESS BLUE: Private purchase worsted wool blouse w/ yellow trim, s/sgt. chevron & 2 hashmarks on each sleeve, US & Cavalry collar discs, 3-place ribbon bar for Vietnam service, expert shooting badge w/2 qualification bars, & DUC ribbon. Size 39, matching trousers w/detachable suspenders, 2 bow ties, complete size 7 1/4 visor cap w/ worsted blue top & gilt brass device. Exc. cond. $56.00

UNIFORM, ARMY EM KOREAN WAR ERA: 38XL OD wool serge Ike jacket w/1944 dated Qm label, 2nd Div. patch on left shoulder, embr. on felt s/sgt. chevrons, US & Arty collar discs, theater made 2 place plastic coated ribbon bar-Korean Serv. w/2 camp. stars & UN Korean Serv. Also, 33x33 OD wool serge field trousers, lt. OD web trousers w/friction buckle, dark OD worsted wool tie, OD wool o/seas cap w/ arty piping, purple-shade satin lining & simulated leather sweatband. Above avg. cond. $20.00

UNIFORM, ARMY FEMALE SUMMER: W/ long sleeve summer wrap jacket in lt. green poly/knit (AG-388) w/gilt eagle buttons & 1979 dated spec. label. Size 8R. W/skirt in matching material. Above avg. cond. $30.00

UNIFORM, ARMY OFFICER: Size 42L dark OD gabardine blouse w/1950 dated Qm label, matching belt w/ribbed buckle, embr. on twill 71st Div. patch on left shoulder, unusual wide green & red felt loop on each epaulette. Also, dark tan worsted wool shirt w/fully embr. 71st Div. patch, pair "pink" trousers, 2 dark OD worsted ties. Above avg. cond. $55.00

UNIFORM, ARMY OFFICER (CLASS "A"): 1961 dated. Size 44R blouse in AG wool serge w/major oak leaves & US & Engr. collar devices. Trousers w/black web belt, necktie. Above avg. cond. $24.00

UNIFORM, ARMY OFFICER DRESS BLUE: Private purchase blouse in navy blue gabardine w/gold wire woven cuff braid w/ ribbed orange insert, gilt eagle buttons, sew-on 2nd lieut. of signal corps shoulder boards w/heavy bullion trim. Named & 1957 dated. Size 40. Matching trousers. Above avg. cond. $45.00

UNIFORM, ARMY SPECIAL FORCES EM (CLASS "A"): 1986 dated. Size 42R blouse w/Special Forces patch & Airborne tab on left shoulder, USARV patch on rt. W/trousers, Bancroft brand rifle green beret w/Special Forces School flash on front. Exc. cond. $55.00

UNIFORM, COAST GUARD OFFICER: Private purchase navy blue gabardine reefer jacket w/gilt buttons, gold wire & CG shield on each cuff, woven Naval Outfitter's label. Size 40L. W/trousers, removable lieut. grade USCG shoulder boards. Above avg. cond. $19.00

USAF COLD WEATHER BOOTS: Molded black rubber bodies & soles w/lace fronts, early USAF patch design ink stamp on each. Size 12D. Above avg. cond. $20.00

USAF COLD WEATHER JACKET: Flight jacket style in navy blue nylon w/quilted lining, "Timber King" label, large "fur" collar, epaulettes, several pockets, zip front & knit cuffs & waistband. Left chest has tinsel USAF crest patch w/"Tyson" direct embr. above, 3701 MTS patch & Honor Flight tab on rt. chest w/"Flt 142" below. Left shoulder has Desert Shield patch, Calif. & Ohio patches on rt. sleeve. "U.S. Air Force - You Can Handle It!" on back w/Desert Shield & POW patches in center. Large size. Above avg. cond. $55.00

USAF COLD WEATHER PARKA (N-3B MODIFIED): Sage green cotton body w/ real fur trimmed built-in hood, sage green oxford lining w/printed "Type N3B Modified" marked spec. label, zipper/ button front, several pockets. Exc. cond. $220.00

USAF COLD WEATHER PARKA (N-3B): Sage green cotton w/1981 dated spec. label, simulated fur ruff trimmed built-in hood, zipper/button front, several pockets. Avg. cond. $32.00

USAF COLD WEATHER PARKA (N-3B): Sage green cotton w/built-in simulated fur ruff trimmed hood, 1986 dated spec. label,

zipper/button front & several pockets. Size small. Above avg. cond. $21.00

USAF COLD WEATHER PARKA (N-3B): Sage green nylon body w/sage green nylon lining, built-in hood trimmed in real fur, zipper/button front, several pockets & color printed early USAF patch design on left shoulder. Woven spec. label. Above avg. cond. $200.00

USAF COLD WEATHER PARKA (N-3B)

USAF COLD WEATHER PARKA (N-3B): Sage green nylon body w/sage green nylon lining, real fur trimmed built-in hood, zipper/button front, several pockets, dark color printed early USAF patch design on left shoulder. M. size. Above avg. cond. $286.00

USAF COLD WEATHER PARKA (N-3B): Sage green nylon w/woven spec. label, zipper/button front, several pockets, real fur trimmed built-in hood & sage green satin lining. Faint color early USAF patch design printed on left shoulder. Above avg. cond. $145.00

USAF COLD WEATHER PARKA (N-3B): Size large in sage green nylon w/sage green nylon lining, built-in hood trimmed in real wolf fur, woven spec. label, zipper/ button front, color printed patch design decal on left shoulder, several pockets. Exc. cond. $450.00

USAF EM FATIGUE UNIFORM: Blue poly/ cotton shirt. W/color insignia-large 321st SMS patch on rt. shoulder, 1st lieut. collar patches, para wing, pocket tapes, "Combat Crew" badge, Missleman qual. badge on left chest pocket & SAC patch on rt. W/trousers. Above avg. cond. $30.00

USAF EM UNIFORM: Complete size 6 7/8 visor cap w/worsted top, frosted device. 1977 dated. Medium size worsted USAF shade blue shirt. W/senior m/sgt. chev. +

size 40R lightweight cotton jacket w/zipper front, raincoat. Above avg. cond. .. $22.00

USAF FATIGUE SHIRT: 14 1/2x31" OD durapress shirt. w/subdued insignia s/sgt. chevrons, pocket tapes, trans. qual. badge, TAC pocket patch, color printed 4450th Tac. Grp. pocket patch. Above avg. cond. $20.00

USAF FEMALE EM UNIFORM: Private purchase USAF shade blue knit jacket. Size 18 tall w/s/sgt.chevrons. Also, lt. blue shirt. w/slip on capt. rank loops, necktie, flight nurse badge, plastic name tag, skirt. Exc. cond. $27.00

USAF FLIGHT BOOTS (A-1): Size XXL Dark brown leather w/fleece lining, molded black rubber soles, good original zipper fronts w/leather retaining straps across front, woven spec. labels & early USAF decal on side of each. Above avg. cond. $52.00

USAF FLIGHT COVERALLS (CWU-62/P): 1988 dated. Size med./reg. w/built-in booties. Near mint cond. $45.00

USAF FLIGHT GLOVES (B-3A): Pair dark brown leather, B-3A 5 finger gloves well marked. Size 10. W/knit inserts, w/some snags. Well marked leather mittens w/ sage green knit inserts. Avg. cond. $21.00

USAF FLIGHT JACKET (B-15C): Size 42 in sage green nylon w/woven spec. label, large fur collar, color printed early USAF patch design on left shoulder, good original zipper front, original knit cuffs & waistband (couple snags but good), pocket on left sleeve, snap closure slash pockets w/small snap tab above each. Above avg. cond. $735.00

USAF FLIGHT JACKET (B-15C)

USAF FLIGHT JACKET (B-15D): Sage green nylon body w/sage green nylon lining, large fur collar, woven spec. label w/ink stamp markings below, good original zipper front, nylon tab along zipper front,

slash pockets w/snap tab above each, color patch design decal on left shoulder, pocket on left sleeve, original knit cuffs & waistband. Size 42. Name inked. Avg. cond. $760.00

USAF FLIGHT JACKET (B-15D): Size 38 in sage green nylon w/sage green nylon lining, fur collar, woven USAF spec. label, good original zipper front, original knit cuffs & waistband, snap closure slash pockets w/snap tab above on each side, pocket on left sleeve, color printed early USAF patch design on left shoulder. Above avg. cond. $1,001.00

USAF FLIGHT JACKET (B-15D): Size 42, sage green nylon w/sage green nylon lining, woven spec. label, large fur collar, zipper front, knit cuffs & waistband, printed color early USAF patch design on left shoulder, pocket on left sleeve, slash pockets w/small snap tab above each. Has faint gold embossed on black leather rank tabs. Above avg. cond. $825.00

USAF FLIGHT JACKET (B-15D)

USAF FLIGHT JACKET (B-15D): Size 42, sage green nylon w/woven spec. label, large fur collar, sage green nylon lining, good original zipper front, knit cuffs & waistband, faint color patch design decal on left shoulder, pocket on left sleeve, slash pockets. Avg. cond. $685.00

USAF FLIGHT JACKET (B-15D): dark sage green nylon body & lining w/zipper front, large fur collar, knit cuffs & waistband, snap closure slash pockets w/snap tab above each. Lacks spec. label & oxygen mask tab. Has large embr. on twill patch on left shoulder w/design of bloody dagger through skull, large twill TAC patch rt. chest. Med. size. Above avg. cond. $374.00

USAF FLIGHT JACKET (CWU-36/P): Sage green polyamide w/zipper front, knit cuffs & waistband, several pockets, several

velcro attachment panels on shoulders &
chest, 196 dated spec. label. Size x-large.
Good shape. Above avg. cond. .. $145.00
USAF FLIGHT JACKET (CWU-36/P): Sage
green polyamide w/zipper front, several
pockets, knit cuffs & waistband & 1980
dated spec. label. Has unusual velcro
attached name tag (unused) on left chest
w/embr. naval style aviator wing, US flag
patch on left shoulder. Size small. Above
avg. cond. $160.00
USAF FLIGHT JACKET (CWU-45/P): Sage
green polyamide body w/zipper front,
large 1986 dated spec. label, knit cuffs &
waistband, several pockets, velcro panel
on each shoulder, velcro attached senior
pilot's name tag on left chest, velcro
attached embr. on black vinyl USAF Air
Combat Cmd. patch on rt. chest, blue
embr. on OD cluster rank patch on each
shoulder. Exc. cond. $139.00
USAF FLIGHT JACKET (CWU-45/P): Sage
green polyamide w/zipper front, printed
spec. label, knit cuffs & waistband, pocket
on left sleeve, slash pockets & velcro
panel on left chest. Has plastic sealed
capt. bars & several velcro attachment
panels w/US flag & Mil. Airlift Cmd.
patches. Size 38-40. Above avg. cond.
.... $189.00
USAF FLIGHT JACKET (CWU-45/P): Size
x-large in sage green polyamide w/1980
dated spec. label, zipper front, several
pockets, knit cuffs & waistband. Has
velcro attached theater made subdued
name tag on left chest mach. embr. design
of master aircrew wing & msgt's name,
color US made patches 4950th Maint.
Sqdn. patch on left shoulder, 4950th Test
Wing patch on rt. shoulder & AF Systems
Cmd. patch on rt. chest. Avg. cond.
.... $160.00
USAF FLIGHT JACKET (EXPERIMENTAL):
Dark blue cotton jacket in similar design to
type L-2A jacket w/knit collar, cuffs &
waistband, epaulettes, zipper front w/snap
waistband, slash pockets, pocket on left
sleeve & dark blue satin. Has woven
"Experimental Test Sample - Clothing
Branch" label. Has closely trimmed lieut.
col. leaf on each epaulet, Strategic Air
Cmd. patch on rt. chest, "Casteel" direct
embr. into left chest. Med. size. Above
avg. cond. $1,995.00
USAF FLIGHT JACKET (EXPERIMENTAL):
L-2 style. Dark blue cotton shell w/dark
blue nylon lining, zipper front w/blue knit
collar, cuffs & waist band, slash pockets
w/snaps flaps & snap tab at waistband-
just like L-2. Has early SAC patch on rt.
chest, made w/no scroll below, plastic
sealed major leaves sewn to shoulders.
Size 38. Near mint cond. $2,200.00

USAF FLIGHT JACKET (EXPERIMENTAL)

USAF FLIGHT JACKET (L-2B): Sage green
nylon body w/orange nylon lining, zipper
front, epaulettes, 1961 dated spec. label,
knit collar, cuffs & waistband, several
pockets & color printed early USAF patch
design on left shoulder. Size medium. Avg.
cond. $263.00
USAF FLIGHT JACKET (L-2B): Sage green
nylon w/orange nylon lining, 1976 dated
spec. label, zipper front, several pockets,
knit collar, cuffs & waistband, velcro panel
on left chest, fully embr. SAC patch on rt.
chest. Above avg. cond. $171.00
USAF FLIGHT JACKET (L-2B): Size x-large
in sage green nylon w/orange nylon lining,
zipper front, 1961 dated printed spec.
label, epaulettes w/plastic sealed lieut. col.
leaf on each, knit collar, cuffs & waistband,
several pockets. Has US flag patch on left
shoulder, twill 9th MAS patch on rt.
shoulder, fully embr. Mil. Airlift Cmd. patch
on rt. chest, velcro attached sage green
nylon panel on left chest has color pilot
wing stitched to panel over web name
tape. Above avg. cond. $450.00
USAF FLIGHT JACKET (L-2B): Size large in
sage green nylon w/orange nylon lining,
good original zipper front, 1960 dated
printed spec. label, knit collar, cuffs &
waistband, slash pockets w/snap closure
flaps, pocket on left sleeve, epaulettes &
color printed early USAF patch design on
left shoulder. Has faint silver embossed on
black leather name tag on left chest traces
of other removed insignia. Above avg.
cond. $774.00
USAF FLIGHT JACKET (MA-1): Size x-
large, sage green nylon w/orange nylon
lining, good original zipper front, 1961
dated printed spec. label, knit collar, cuffs
& waistband, several pockets. Has plastic
sealed col. eagles, large fully embr. Mil.

Airlift Cmd. patch on rt. chest, silver embossed on black leather name tag in clear plastic pocket on left chest w/ likeness of cmd. pilot wing, name & USAF. Above avg. cond. $425.00

USAF FLIGHT JACKET (MA-1)

USAF FLIGHT JACKET (MA-1): Dark-shade sage green nylon body w/orange nylon lining, zipper front, several pockets, knit collar, cuffs & waistband. Printed USAF marked spec. label. Med. size. Above avg. cond. $118.00

USAF FLIGHT JACKET (MA-1): Med. size in sage green cotton w/1958 dated woven spec. label. Zipper front, pocket on left sleeve, slash pockets w/snap tab above each, knit collar, cuffs & waistband. Above avg. cond. $1,473.00

USAF FLIGHT JACKET (MA-1): Sage green nylon body w/sage green nylon lining, zipper front, knit collar, cuffs & waistband, several pockets & velcro panel on left chest. Large size. Above avg. cond. $374.00

"USAF FLIGHT JACKET (N-2): Size XL in OD nylon w/real fur trimmed & lined built-in hood, woven spec. label, zipper/button front, good original knit cuffs & waistband, small pocket on left sleeve, snap closure slash pockets w/snap tab above each, leather tab along zipper on left front. Above avg. cond. $1,315.00

USAF FLIGHT JACKET (N-2A): Size Med. in sage green nylon w/1963 dated woven spec. label, real fur trimmed built-in hood, good original zipper/button, several pockets, original knit cuffs & waistband. Above avg. cond. $409.00

USAF FLIGHT JACKET (N-2B): Large size in sage green nylon w/sage green nylon lining, real fur trimmed built-in hood, good original zipper/button front, several pockets, 1961 dated woven spec. label, knit cuffs & waistband. Above avg. cond. $387.00

USAF FLIGHT JACKET (N-2B): Sage green nylon body w/sage green nylon lining, zipper/button front, built-in hood trimmed in simulated fur ruff, 1977 dated spec. label, several pockets, knit cuffs & waistband. Above avg. cond. $60.00

USAF FLIGHT JACKET (N-2B): Sage green nylon w/real fur trimmed built-in hood, zipper/button front, knit cuffs & waistband, several pockets. Lacks spec. label from neck. Large size. Above avg. cond. $155.00

USAF FLIGHT JACKET (N-3B MODIFIED): Sage green cotton body w/real fur trimmed attached hood, 1972 dated spec. label marked "Modified," ERDL pattern camo cotton lining, zipper/button front, several pockets. Med. size. Avg. cond. $177.00

USAF FLIGHT JACKET (N-3B): Size large in sage green nylon w/real fur trimmed built-in hood, printed 1962 dated spec. label, dark (near 100%) patch design decal on left shoulder, zipper/button front, several pockets. Near mint cond..............$369.00

USAF FLIGHT MITTENS (N-2): Dark brown leather w/early USAF ink stamp markings on each. Above avg. cond..............$25.00

USAF FLIGHT MITTENS (N-4B): Sage green nylon w/tan leather palms & alpaca facings, tri-strap adj. gauntlets & woven spec. labels. W/OD wool liners w/woven spec. labels. Both well marked. Exc. cond. $35.00

USAF FLIGHT SHIRT (A-1A): Size x-large. In early USAF shade blue wool serge w/ woven spec. label. Button front & 4 front pockets. Above avg. cond............ $48.00

USAF FLIGHT SHIRT (A-1B): Coat style body shirt. in issue package. Size Med. in sage green wool serge w/woven spec. label visible. Clear bag contains large spec. label. Near mint cond. $100.00

USAF FLIGHT SHIRT (A-1B): Sage green serge w/woven spec. label, button front, faint color early USAF patch design printed on rt. chest, 4 pocket front. Med. size. Above avg. cond. $38.00

USAF FLIGHT SUIT (27/P): Size 38S in sage green aramid w/zipper front, several pockets, 1985 dated spec. label. Some traces of removed insignia. Avg. cond. $30.00

USAF FLIGHT SUIT (27/P): Size 44L in sage green aramid w/zipper front, several pockets, several velcro attachment panels. Above avg. cond. $35.00

USAF FLIGHT SUIT (ANTI-G PRESSURE): 1950s. Sage green nylon body w/zipper front, lace panels, pressure hose, color printed early USAF patch design on left chest. Above avg. cond. $100.00

USAF FLIGHT SUIT (CWU-1/P): Early example in sage green nylon w/1958 dated woven spec. label, hood in zippered collar, zip front, several pockets. Size med./reg. Above avg. cond. $93.00

USAF FLIGHT SUIT (CWU-1/P): Insulated sage green nylon body w/1960 dated woven spec. label, zipper front, several pockets, hood in zippered collar. Size small-reg. Above avg. cond. $97.00

USAF FLIGHT SUIT (CWU-21/P): Sage green fire resistant material w/zipper front & several pockets. Lacks spec. label. Has color cloth 2nd lieut. bars on shoulders, signs of other removed insignia. Avg. cond. $20.00

USAF FLIGHT SUIT (CWU-28/P): Size 42L orange fire resistant nylon w/1971 dated spec. label, zipper front, several pockets, velcro panel on each shoulder & left chest. Rt. chest has 2 thin velcro strips running parallel to pocket. Above avg. cond. $33.00

USAF FLIGHT SUIT (EXPERIMENTAL): Dark blue fine cotton twill w/matching belt, has silver metal USAF buttons on shoulders, pockets & cuffs, zipper front, 4" dia. 303rd bomb squadron patch on rt. chest pocket. Approx. size 40 w/color woven Experimental Test Sample label inside. Near mint cond. $387.00

USAF FLIGHT SUIT (EXPERIMENTAL ABOVE)

USAF FLIGHT SUIT (EXPERIMENTAL): Type K-2B pattern suit in sage green cotton w/woven Aero Medical Labratory label, zipper front, several pockets. Approx. size small-reg. Trace of removed name tag from left chest. Above avg. cond. $1,073.00

USAF FLIGHT SUIT (K-2A): Size med./short in lightweight dark blue nylon w/woven spec. label, zipper front, several pockets. Above avg. cond. $91.00

USAF FLIGHT SUIT (K-2B): Size M. reg. in sage green cotton w/woven spec. label & USAF ink stamp markings, zipper front, many pockets, good color printed early USAF patch design on left shoulder. Avg. cond. $66.00

USAF FLIGHT SUIT (K-2B): Size small-reg. in sage green cotton w/woven spec. label & USAF ink stamp markings, zipper front, many pockets & dark early USAF patch design printed on leftshoulder. Above avg. cond. $164.00

USAF FLIGHT TROUSERS (A-11B): Dark blue nylon w/knit cuffs & detachable suspenders. Med. size. Above avg. cond. $118.00

USAF FLIGHT TROUSERS (D-1B): Size 30 in sage green nylon w/woven spec. label, detachable suspenders. Zippers intact. Avg. cond. $55.00

USAF FLIGHT TROUSERS (E-1): Size 38 in olive wool serge w/woven spec. label, zip fly & knit cuffs. Exc. cond. $50.00

USAF FLIGHT TROUSERS (E-1A): Size 42 in USAF shade blue wool serge w/woven spec. label, USAF ink stamp markings. Still has paper Qm inspector tag stapled to body. Near mint cond. $28.00

USAF FLIGHT TROUSERS (E-1B): Size 32 in sage green wool serge w/woven spec. label. Well marked. In sealed issue bag. Near mint cond. $40.00

USAF FLIGHT TROUSERS (F-1B): Size 32 in insulated sage green nylon w/woven spec. label, ink stamp markings, correct detachable suspenders. Above avg. cond. $40.00

USAF OFFICER BLOUSE: Size 43R in worsted USAF shade blue. Frosted silver USAF buttons. 1961 dated woven spec. label. Avg. cond. $12.00

USAF OFFICER FATIGUE SHIRT: Vietnam era. Size 116 1/2x36 in dark OD sateen w/ color insignia; major collar patches, pilot wing, woven nylon USAF pocket tape, neat blue web name tape w/"chain stitched" white letters, Mil. Airlift Cmd & 305th ARR Sq. pocket patches. Exc. cond. $25.00

USAF OFFICER IKE JACKET (M1951): Size 37R in USAF shade blue wool serge w/ 1951 dated Qm label. Converted to zipper front. Has US collar devices & sew-on bullion major leaves. Above avg. cond. $30.00

USAF OFFICER MESS DRESS UNIFORM: Waist length white worsted jacket w/ frosted silver USAF buttons, removable major grade shoulder boards, bowtie. Med. size. Also, matching black worsted jacket w/trousers, suspenders in maker carton. Above avg. cond. $37.00

USAF OFFICER UNIFORM: Tailor made in early shade USAF blue gabardine w/ woven labels. 8th Army patch on left shoulder, 3 frosted silver bullion o/seas bars on matching blue gabardine background on left cuff. Med. size. w/ matching trousers. Above avg. cond. $30.00

USAF PARTY SUIT: Dark green cotton body w/zipper front, short sleeves, several concealed zippered pockets. Has direct hand embr. likeness of senior pilot wing on left chest w/"Pete" below. Has Thai color mach. made 13th Air Force patch on rt. chest & "13th Air Force/Flight Examiner/C-130" patch on rt. shoulder. Size 38. Exc. cond. $76.00

USAF PARTY SUIT: Dark green knit body w/ zipper front, short. sleeves, several pockets, epaulettes, white knit bolero leg cuff inserts & expansion panels in back w/ white knit inserts. Has Theater made color insignia, U.S. flag patch on left shoulder, S. Korean flag patch on rt. shoulder. Rt. chest has embr. on knit twill 6151st CAM Sqdn "Combat Ready" w/direct embr. likeness of 'Warthog' plane & "Assam Draggings" above. Left chest has frontal view of 'Warthog' & reads "Korean Air National Guard/Warthog Warrior" in English & Korean w/design of master grade Transportation badge & name above. Each thigh has large direct embr. dragon design. Large size. Exc. cond. $164.00

USAF PARTY SUIT

USAF RADIO CARRIER VEST (E-1): 1950s. OD nylon body w/woven spec. label,

zipper front, color printed early USAF patch design on left chest. Size small. Near mint cond. $115.00

USAF RADIO CARRIER VEST (E-1): Dark OD nylon body w/zipper front, woven spec. label & early USAF patch design ink stamp, color printed early USAF patch design on left chest. Near mint cond. $100.00

USAF RADIO CARRIER VEST (E-1): In original sealed cardboard box. Remains of paper spec. label on one end. Large size. Near mint cond. $76.00

USAF RADIO CARRIER VEST (E-1): Vest is still in sealed issue carton w/remains of spec. label on one end. Near mint cond. $145.00

USAF SGT.IKE JACKET: Size 38R jacket is private Japanese maker made in USAF shade blue wool serge w/satin lining, woven Osaka clothier's label, oversize heavy bullion on felt 8th Air Force patch on left shoulder, master sgt. chevrons, 5 o/seas bars, 7 hashmarks, US collar discs, custom made 6 place ribbon group for WWII serv./occupation serv. w/2" wide bullion Aircrew wing above on left chest, all on single USAF shade blue wool backing. Above avg. cond. $160.00

USAF SURVIVAL VEST: Size large in sage green mesh w/zipper front & sage green nylon pockets for survival items (not included). 1976 dated spec. label. Avg. cond. $16.00

USAF WOMAN FLIGHT JACKET (B-17B): Sage green nylon body w/large fur collar, sage green nylon lining, good original zipper front, original knit cuffs & waistband printed spec. label pocket on left sleeve, slash pockets, sew on 1st lieut. bars (embr. on sage green cotton), Tac. Air Cmd. patch on rt. chest. Avg. cond. $576.00

USAF/AAF TRANSITION FLIGHT JACKET (B-15D): Sage green nylon body w/sage green nylon lining, printed spec. label, knit collar (replaced fur collar), cuffs & waist band zipper front, faint color printed early USAF patch design on left shoulder, pocket on left sleeve, slash pockets w/ snap tab above each. Size 40. Above avg. cond. $812.00

USMC AVIATOR FLIGHT JACKET (G-1): Size 40 in dark brown leather w/fur collar, 1961 dated woven BuAero marked spec. label, good zipper front, knit cuffs & waistband, satin lining. Has theater made machine embr. on cotton "Viet-Nam 1969-70" tab over fully embr. Tonkin Gulf Yacht Club patch on left shoulder, embr. on twill F-4 Phantom patch on rt. shoulder, fully embr. USS America & embr. on twill

VMAQ-2 "Can Do Easy" patches on rt. chest, theater made machine embr. on cotton Viet Cong Hunting Club patch on left chest over gold embossed on black leather USMC lieut.'s name tag. Back has large US Marine Corps patch. Above avg. cond. $518.00

USMC BODY ARMOR (M-53 LOWER TORSO): Dark OD nylon covered flexible body w/expansion panels & zip sides. Large USMC marked instructional label. Above avg. cond. $44.00

USMC DRUM & BUGLE CORPS UNIFORM: Scarlet worsted pocketless blouse w/navy blue trimmed standing collar & epaulettes, removable gilt brass USMC buttons, 1962-pattern EG&A collar devices, dress aiguilette w/brass tip. Size 36L. Named & 1962 dated on Marine Corps Depot of Supplies label. W/white vinyl dress belt w/ smooth gilt buckle & fittings, medium blue gabardine dress trousers w/red stripe down each leg. Above avg. cond. $155.00

USMC DRUM & BUGLE CORPS UNIFORM

USMC EM DRESS BLUE UNIFORM: Navy blue gabardine blouse w/standing collar, red piping, removable gilt buttons, corp. chevrons (w/crossed rifles), wide white web belt w/smooth gilt brass buckle & fittings. Size 38. W/32x31" medium blue gabardine w/red stripe down each leg, 1957 dated spec. tag, tan web trouser belt, complete size 7 visor cap w/white cotton top, 1962 pattern device. Above avg. cond. $76.00

USMC FLIGHT JACKET (MA-1): Sage green nylon w/orange nylon lining, zipper front, several pockets, knit collar, cuffs & waistband, printed spec. label. Has name direct embr. into left chest, USMC patch on rt. chest, US flag patch on left shoulder, Asian made Marine Avn. Training Support. Grp. 90/Memphis, Tenn. patch on rt. shoulder, large embr. on felt EG&A patch

on back w/United States Marines direct embr. Size small. Above avg. cond. $160.00

USMC OFFICER DRESS BLUE UNIFORM: Private purchase in navy blue gabardine size 39 w/"false" collar insert. Matching belt, woven clothier's label. W/correct dress blue gabardine trousers w/red stripe down each leg, web trouser belt. Above avg. cond. $45.00

USMC OFFICER DRESS WHITE UNIFORM: Private purchase in white cotton w/set removable buttons, standing collar stitch grommeted for collar devices (not included), pointed cuffs. Size 38. W/ trousers. W/protective garment bag. Above avg. cond. $38.00

USMC OFFICER EVENING DRESS UNIFORM: 1950s. Navy blue melton wool waist length jacket w/single row of gilt buttons on "false" button front, standing collar, red satin lining, woven maker's label. Has bullion & cord trim on collar, cuffs & epaulettes & insert in collar. Named & 1958 dated. W/dress shirt, red satin cummerbund, trousers w/gold wire stripe down each leg w/ribbed red satin insert. Med. size. Above avg. cond. $196.00

USMC OFFICER IKE JACKET: 1950s. Forest green gabardine w/satin lining. Named & 1956 dated on USMC Depot of Supplies label. Size 42R. Above avg. cond. $37.00

USMC OFFICER SUMMER UNIFORM: Private purchase tan gabardine blouse w/ pointed cuffs & set bronze USMC buttons. Named. W/matching belt. Med. size. W/ trousers, dark tan worsted wool shirt. Has woven USMC approved labels. Exc. cond. $20.00

USMC SGT. DRESS BLUE UNIFORM: Navy blue melton wool blouse w/standing collar, red piping, removable brass buttons, sgt. dress chevron on each sleeve w/crossed rifles below, 1962 pattern collar devices. Size 40. W/medium blue wool trousers w/ red felt "blood" stripe down each leg. Above avg. cond. $35.00

USMC SHOOTING JACKET: OD sateen w/ button front, pads on rt. shoulder & each arm. Avg. cond. $10.00

USMC SOUVENIR JACKET: Custom made tour jacket made from splotch camo pattern material with full collar & upper pockets with zippers. Front zipper marked "YKK." Gold & black bevo (woven) "Star Eagle Okinawa" tailor label. Machine sewn color winged skull patch to left shoulder. Japanese made 3 Marine Division full color patch tort. Shoulder with San Diego,

Alaska, 79-80, Okinawa, Japan, 3rd MarDiv, & CP Hansen red & gold machine sewn arcs below. To the rear is a large 10" full color machine-sewn patch with Eagle, Globe & anchor & "United States Marine Corps." Small adult size. Exc. cond. $69.00

USMC UTILITY SHIRT (SPECIAL PATTERN): In white cotton w/concealed button front, patch chest pocket w/iron on USMC EG&A stencil on chest pocket & fold back cuffs. Size 36. Mint cond. $20.00

USMC UTILITY TROUSERS: Dark OD HBT w/OD plastic buttons. Conv. cut. Type used w/special pattern utility shirt. About 30" waist. Above avg. cond. $20.00

VIETNAM ERA ARMY AVIATOR COVERALLS: 1972 dated OD sateen coveralls w/Nam made hand embr. color 2nd Field Force, Vietnam patch on left shoulder, hand embr. color pilot wing on left chest & subdued US made 1st Cav. Div. patch on rt. shoulder. Appears to be size small. Avg. cond. $28.00

VIETNAM ERA ARMY AVIATOR FLIGHT JACKET (L-2B): Size large in sage green nylon w/orange nylon lining, 1970 dated spec. label, zipper front, several pockets, knit collar, cuffs & waistband. Has US made subdued insignia, Ranger tab on left shoulder, 101st Airborne patch w/tab on rt. shoulder, major leaves, CIB, pilot wing, para wing & US Army tape on left chest, name tape on rt. chest. Avg. cond. $433.00

VIETNAM ERA ARMY AVIATOR FLIGHT JACKET (L-2B)

VIETNAM ERA ARMY AVIATOR FLIGHT JACKET (L-2B): Size large in sage green nylon w/orange nylon lining, zipper front, knit collar, cuffs & waistband, several pockets, 1970 dated spec. label. Has subdued insignia, plastic sealed capt. bars, Air Def. Center & School patch on left shoulder, Americal Div. patch on rt. shoulder, CIB, aviator wing & US Army & name pocket tapes. Above avg. cond. $250.00

VIETNAM ERA ARMY AVIATOR FLIGHT JACKET (MA-1 USAF TYPE): Size med. Sage green nylon w/orange nylon lining. 1963 dated printed spec. label, zipper front, knit collar, cuffs & waistband (cuffs are replacements). Has subdued US made 1st Avn. Bde. patch on rt. shoulder, Delware N.G. patch on left shoulder, senior pilot wing, nylon US Army & name pocket tapes, embr. on twill 198th Avn. Co. Weapons Platoon "Ghost Riders" patch on rt. chest, subdued metal w/o bars. Above avg. cond. $535.00

VIETNAM ERA ARMY AVIATOR FLIGHT JACKET (MA-1): Sage green nylon w/ orange nylon lining, zipper front, knit collar, cuffs & waistband, several pockets, 1968 dated spec. label. Has subdued 7th Corps patch on left shoulder, subdued pilot wing & name tape on left chest, color capt. rank patches. Size small. Above avg. cond. $485.00

VIETNAM ERA ARMY AVIATOR FLIGHT SHIRT (NOMEX): Small/long in OD nomex w/zipper front, US made color 101st Airborne Div. patch on left shoulder, woven nylon US Army subdued pocket tape. Above avg. cond. $23.00

VIETNAM ERA ARMY AVIATOR JUNGLE JACKET: Small-long in OD poplin. Has subdued insignia, hand embr. 1st Avn. Bde. patch on left shoulder, hand embr. senior pilot & para wings, printed on web US Army pocket tape, hand embr. name tape. Exc. cond. $43.00

VIETNAM ERA ARMY CAMO JUNGLE FATIGUE UNIFORM: Jungle jacket w/US made embr. on twill 196th Inf Bde. patch on left shoulder, fully embr. Americal Div. patch on rt., subdued pocket tapes (small size), small-reg. trousers. W/boonie hat-about size 65/8. All in ERDL pattern camo ripstop. Above avg. cond. $157.00

VIETNAM ERA ARMY EM BLOUSE (CLASS "A"): Size 37R in AG wool serge. 1964 dated w/4th Div patch on left shoulder, pfc chevrons. Above avg. cond. $24.00

VIETNAM ERA ARMY EM JUNGLE JACKET: Small-reg., 3rd pattern in OD rip stop material. Has Nam made subdued twill 25th division patch on left shoulder, Nam made subdued cloth combat inf. badge & "US Army" tape on left chest. Avg. cond. $60.00

VIETNAM ERA ARMY FIELD JACKET (M1965): Dark OD cotton w/zipper & snap closure front. Has color US made 173rd Airborne Div. patch & tab on left shoulder w/theater made subdued "Ammo" tab above, early color US made Special Forces patch & tab on rt. shoulder, US embr. on twill subdued sgt. chevrons, theater made para wing, yellow on black US Army tape & theater made subdued name tape. Small size. Avg. cond. $38.00

VIETNAM ERA ARMY FIELD JACKET (M1965): Size small-reg. OD cotton. 1971 dated. Above avg. cond. $37.00

VIETNAM ERA ARMY FLAK JACKET: Size Med. in OD nylon, 1968 dated on spec. tag. From 5th Special forces master sgt. Above avg. cond. $45.00

VIETNAM ERA ARMY JUNGLE FATIGUE JACKET (1ST PATTERN): Med. size in OD poplin w/color US made insignia, early color Special Forces patch & tab on left shoulder, s/sgt. chevrons, combat medic badge, para wing, yellow woven on black US Army tape, bevo SVN para wing, printed on white web name tape, bevo ARVN Special Forces patch on rt. chest pocket. Avg. cond. $138.00

VIETNAM ERA ARMY JUNGLE FATIGUE JACKET (1ST PATTERN): Med. size, OD poplin w/all color U.S. made insignia, early Special Forces patch & tab on left shoulder, yellow embr. on AG master sgt. chevrons, basic para wing over yellow woven on black US Army pocket tape, printed on white web name tape. Avg. cond. $125.00

VIETNAM ERA ARMY JUNGLE FATIGUE JACKET (1ST PATTERN): Short/small in OD poplin. All tags. Has color insignia that appears to be added after the fact; US made early Special Forces patch & tab on left shoulder, s/sgt. chevrons, green felt loop on each epaulet, US made CIB & senior para wing, mach. embr. on black cotton US Army pocket tape, bevo SVN para wing on rt. chest, bevo ARVN Special Forces patch on left chest, printed on OD web name tape. Above avg. cond. $408.00

VIETNAM ERA ARMY JUNGLE FATIGUE JACKET (2ND PATTERN): OD poplin, size small/short. Has black & yellow "U.S. Army" & black on white name tape, color spec. 4 chevrons on twill &, color hand embr. "528 Medical Det. Mobile Lab" pocket patch on rt. chest. Avg. cond. $105.00

VIETNAM ERA ARMY JUNGLE FATIGUE JACKET (2ND PATTERN): Size reg./small in OD poplin. Above avg. cond. $59.00

VIETNAM ERA ARMY JUNGLE FATIGUE JACKET (3RD PATTERN): Med./reg. OD poplin. 1967 dated. Has subdued insignia, tropical pattern embr. on twill 1st Cav. Div.

patch on left shoulder & 25th Div. patch on rt. shoulder, s/sgt.chevrons. Also, expert infantryman badge, aircrew wing & ARVN para wing badges, Nam mach. made US Army & name pocket tapes. Above avg. cond. $74.00

VIETNAM ERA ARMY JUNGLE FATIGUE JACKET (3RD PATTERN): OD poplin. 1967 dated. Size med./reg. Name inked. Never had any insignia. Above avg. cond. $32.00

VIETNAM ERA ARMY JUNGLE FATIGUE SHIRT: Lightweight OD cotton shirt. w/A-L ink stamp. Button front w/patch type chest pockets w/single exposed button flaps. Has woven nylon US Army subdued pocket tape & subdued Nam mach. embr. on OD nylon name tape. Above avg. cond. $28.00

VIETNAM ERA ARMY JUNGLE FATIGUE SHIRT: Lightweight dark OD poplin fatigue shirt. w/naval contract markings. 15" neck. Has had original chest pockets neatly replaced w/closely matching pleated OD poplin pockets w/single exposed button closure flaps w/stitch grommet drain holes. Left shoulder has rare subdued iron on Special Forces patch design & Airborne tab on left shoulder, iron on master para wing & "US Army" on left chest. Trace of removed pocket tape from rt. chest. Iron on insignia used for only short time during Vietnam era. Above avg. cond. $114.00

VIETNAM ERA ARMY JUNGLE FATIGUE SHIRT

VIETNAM ERA ARMY JUNGLE FATIGUE TROUSERS (1ST PATTERN): Size x-small/reg. in OD poplin. All tags intact. Near mint cond. $177.00

VIETNAM ERA ARMY JUNGLE FATIGUE TROUSERS (2ND PATTERN): In OD poplin. Drawstrings in cuffs intact. Large size. Avg. cond. $48.00

VIETNAM ERA ARMY JUNGLE FATIGUE TROUSERS (2ND PATTERN): Size med./

reg. in OD poplin. All tags intact. Above avg. cond. $66.00

VIETNAM ERA ARMY JUNGLE FATIGUE UNIFORM: Med./long jacket & long/med. trousers both in OD ripstop. Near mint cond. $35.00

VIETNAM ERA ARMY NURSE JUNGLE FATIGUE SHIRT: Size 12 in OD poplin w/ patch chest pockets & 1967 dated spec. label. Has color US made lieut. col. & Medical Serv. Corps collar patches, subdued mach. embr. on OD cotton 44th Med. Bde. patch on left shoulder, crude subdued mach. embr. on cotton name & US Army pocket tapes, color Nam hand embr. on dark maroon cotton 93 Evac Hosp-Vietnam patch on rt. chest pocket. Above avg. cond. $133.00

VIETNAM ERA CAMO DUCK HUNTER FATIGUE SHIRT: Med. weight cotton w/ spot pattern camo on dark tan background, black finish metal star buttons, lower patch pockets w/single exposed button closure flaps, button front, straight cuffs. Med. size. Above avg. cond. $34.00

VIETNAM ERA CAMO DUCK HUNTER FATIGUE UNIFORM: Heavy cotton shirt. w/spot pattern camo on natural background w/metal star buttons, button front & cuffs, billow chest pockets. Washed out size tag. Size 38, matching trousers w/metal star buttons, button fly, several pockets. Above avg. cond. $387.00

VIETNAM ERA CAMO ERDL PATTERN FATIGUE TROUSERS: On poplin. Size large/reg. Exc. cond. $101.00

VIETNAM ERA CAMO JUNGLE FATIGUE JACKET: Size large/short. in ERDL pattern camo ripstop. 1968 dated. Mint cond. $50.00

VIETNAM ERA CAMO JUNGLE FATIGUE JACKET: Size small/reg. in ERDL pattern camo ripstop. Has theater made subdued insignia, hand embr. CIB & SVN para wing, inf branch collar patch & pocket tapes on ERDL camo material. Also, US made subdued Sp. Forces patch & tab, hand embr. color para wing (appears Korean made) & capt. rank patch. Above avg. cond. $164.00

VIETNAM ERA CAMO JUNGLE FATIGUE TROUSERS: Med./reg. in ERDL pattern camo ripstop. Mint cond. $55.00

VIETNAM ERA CAMO JUNGLE FATIGUE TROUSERS: Size reg./med. in ERDL pattern camo ripstop. 1969 dated. More brown shades in camo. Above avg. cond. $42.00

VIETNAM ERA CAMO JUNGLE FATIGUE UNIFORM: Med./short. ERDL pattern

jacket. Never had any insignia. W/med./ long ERDL pattern camo poplin trousers. Above avg. cond. $101.00

VIETNAM ERA CAMO TIGER STRIPE FATIGUE SHIRT: Heavy cotton w/billow chest pockets w/single exposed button closure flaps & button cuffs. Qm marked size tag. Exc. cond. $196.00

VIETNAM ERA CAMO TIGER STRIPE FATIGUE TROUSERS: Heavyweight tiger stripe cotton camo w/zipper fly & button waistband, slash concealed front pockets, billow rear pockets & lower billow pocket on each thigh w/twin exposed button closure flaps, small pocket below on left leg. Size "S." Mint cond. $237.00

VIETNAM ERA CAMO TIGER STRIPE JUNGLE FATIGUE UNIFORM: Heavy weight tiger stripe cotton shirt w/black plastic buttons, button front, straight cuffs, billow chest pockets w/twin exposed button closure flaps. Qm marked. W/Qm marked heavy weight tiger stripe cotton trousers w/button fly, several pockets, heavy tiger stripe cotton boonie hat w/ wide stitched brim, short crown w/bullet loop band & light weight tiger stripe cotton liner. Medium size. Exc. cond. $460.00

VIETNAM ERA CAMO TIGER STRIPE JUNGLE FATIGUE UNIFORM

VIETNAM ERA F-4 PHANTOM PILOT ASCOT: Black nylon body w/silk embr. likeness of F-4 in yellow thread center most. Near mint cond. $200.00

VIETNAM ERA FLAK VEST: Dark OD nylon covered flexible body w/3/4 collar, zipper/ snap closure front, lace adj. sides, labels intact. Size medium. 1968 dated. Above avg. cond. $72.00

VIETNAM ERA FLAK VEST: Size large. Dark OD nylon covered soft vest w/lace adj. sides, snap/zipper closure front, 3/4 collar, 1968 dated spec. & instruction labels. Above avg. cond. $55.00

VIETNAM ERA FLIGHT BOOTS (JET PILOT): Black leather bodies w/lace fronts, rubber soles w/beveled heels & 1974 dated spec. markings. Size 8 1/2 rt. Above avg. cond. $40.00

VIETNAM ERA GRENADE CARRIER VEST (M-79): Dark OD nylon & mesh w/many indiv. pockets for ammo, velcro/snap closure front. 1968 dated. Size large. Appears unissued. Exc. cond. $139.00

VIETNAM ERA GRENADE CARRYING VEST (M-79): Dark OD mesh & nylon w/ many individual ammo pockets, snap/ velcro closure front. US marked & 1974 dated. Med. size. Near mint cond. $37.00

VIETNAM ERA JUNGLE BOOTS: Size 10W. Black leather bodies w/OD canvas uppers, lace fronts, cleated soles. 1969 dated. Spike protective marked. Exc. cond. $66.00

VIETNAM ERA JUNGLE BOOTS: Size 10XN. Black leather bodies w/OD canvas uppers, cleated soles, lace fronts. Spike Protective marked & 1968 dated. Near mint cond. $25.00

VIETNAM ERA NAVY AVIATOR FLIGHT JACKET (G-1): Dark brown leather & real fur collar, unissued w/excellent original zipper, cuffs & waistband, woven spec. label is 1971 dated. Size 36. Exc. cond. $292.00

VIETNAM ERA NAVY AVIATOR FLIGHT JACKET (G-1): Size 36 in dark brown leather w/fur collar, 1967 dated spec. label, good lining, good original zipper front & original knit waistband. Above avg. cond. $184.00

VIETNAM ERA NAVY AVIATOR FLIGHT JACKET (G-1): Size 38 in dark brown leather w/fur collar, 1964 dated woven spec. label, good satin lining, good original zipper front, good original knit cuffs & waistband. Has large embr. on twill VAN 12 patch stitched to left chest. Above avg. cond. $471.00

VIETNAM ERA NAVY AVIATOR FLIGHT JACKET (G-1): Size 44 in dark brown leather w/1972 dated woven spec. label, simulated fur collar, good original zipper front, original knit cuffs & waistband, good lining. Exc. cond. $178.00

VIETNAM ERA NAVY AVIATOR FLIGHT JACKET (G-8): Dark OD nylon body w/ 1969 dated spec. label, zipper front, knit collar & cuffs, several pockets, elastic charged waistband. Size 40R. Above avg. cond. $400.00

VIETNAM ERA NAVY AVIATOR FLIGHT SUIT (CS/FRP-1): Size 44R in dark OD polyamide w/zipper front, printed spec. label, zipper front, several pockets & velcro panel on left chest. Has mach. embr. on twill "U.S.N.T.P.S." patch on left shoulder. Above avg. cond. $24.00

VIETNAM ERA NAVY AVIATOR SUMMER FLIGHT SUIT: Size 42-R in lightweight tan cotton w/woven spec. label marked Mil-C-5390-D (Aer), zipper front, several pockets w/angled chest pockets. Above avg. cond. $50.00

VIETNAM ERA NAVY FLIGHT DECK ID VEST: Green jersey silk body w/snap closure front, lace adj. sides, printed 1969 dated spec. label. Size large/x-large. Exc. cond. $28.00

VIETNAM ERA NECKERCHIEF: Dark OD cotton knit. Well marked & 1969 dated. Near mint cond. $15.00

VIETNAM ERA SOUVENIR CAMO JACKET: Made from quilted camo poncho liner w/lt. blue silk-like lining, zipper front, straight cuffs, slash pockets. Has unusual "chain stitched" direct mach. embr. dragon on left chest, dragon head on rt. chest, dragon on each sleeve. Back has famous quote "When I Die...," "Duc Pho," "69 70," map of Nam & locations & "Viet Nam." Size 38. Exc. cond. $177.00

VIETNAM ERA SOUVENIR CAMO JACKET

VIETNAM ERA SOUVENIR JACKET: Black cotton body w/white silk-like lining, zipper front, slash pockets, button cuffs. Has color direct hand embr. designs, tiger head & Oriental character on chest, dragon on each sleeve, quote "Fighter by Day Lover by Night Drunkard by Choice Ready to Flight," map of Nam & locations, "Viet*Nam 68 69" on back. Size 38. Above avg. cond. $145.00

VIETNAM ERA SOUVENIR JACKET: Black cotton body w/zipper front, white silk-like lining, button cuffs, slash pockets & elastic panel at each side of waist. Has all color direct hand embr. designs, Oriental character on rt. chest, tiger head on left chest, dragon on each sleeve, "Chu*Lai," map of Nam & surrounding areas w/ locations, "Viet*Nam" & "66*67" on back. Size 34. Above avg. cond. $100.00

VIETNAM ERA SOUVENIR JACKET: Maroon velveteen body w/white silk-like lining, zipper front, button cuffs & slash pockets. Has Asian mach. embr. on twill CCS Mike Facs patch on rt. chest w/silver tinsel bullion details, silver tinsel Oriental characters direct embr. into left chest, large dragon design on each sleeve. Back has direct embr., "Fighters by Day Love[r]s by Night," "Ban Me-Thuot," map of Nam & locations, "Drunkard by Choice Ready to War," "Viet-Nam" & "72-73." Size 38. Above avg. cond. $549.00

VIETNAM ERA SOUVENIR JACKET
(FRONT VIEW)

VIETNAM ERA SOUVENIR JACKET
(REAR VIEW)

VIETNAM ERA USAF FLIGHT JACKET (L-2B): Sage green nylon body w/orange nylon lining, 1966 dated spec. label, zipper front, knit cuffs & waistband, several pockets. Replacement cuffs. Capt.'s name inked. Above avg. cond. $180.00

VIETNAM ERA USAF FLIGHT JACKET (L-2B): Sage green nylon w/orange nylon lining, zipper front, 1966 dated printed spec. label, several pockets, knit collar, cuffs & waistband. Has plastic sealed major leaves, fully embr. Mil. Airlift Cmd. patch on rt. chest, fully Asian mach. embr. Aerospace Rescue & Recovery Serv. patch on left shoulder, clear plastic pocket on left chest for name tag. Above avg. cond. $229.00

VIETNAM ERA USAF FLIGHT JACKET (L-2B): Size medium, in sage green nylon w/ orange nylon lining, zipper front, knit collar, cuffs & waistband, several pockets, 1976 dated spec. label. Has color insignia, plastic sealed capt. bars, fully embr. 833d Air Div. patch on rt. shoulder, 49th Tac. Ftr. Wg. patch on left shoulder, TAC patch on rt. chest, velcro attached USAF Capt.'s name tag on left chest w/embossed senior wing design. Above avg. cond. ... $200.00

VIETNAM ERA USAF FLIGHT JACKET
(L-2B)

VIETNAM ERA USAF FLIGHT JACKET (L-2B): Size x-large in sage green nylon w/ bright orange lining. 1966 dated printed spec. label, zipper front, knit collar, cuffs & waistband. Avg. cond. $138.00

VIETNAM ERA USAF FLIGHT JACKET (MA-1): Large size in sage green nylon w/ orange nylon lining, zipper front, knit collar, cuffs & waistband, several pockets. Has color insignia embr. on twill 363d Tac. Recon Wg patch on left shoulder, embr. on twill TAC patch on rt. chest, fully embr. 16 TAC. Recon Sqdn. patch on rt.

shoulder, stenciled on white web name tape on left chest. Above avg. cond. $387.00

VIETNAM ERA USAF FLIGHT JACKET (MA-1): Sage green nylon body w/orange nylon lining, zipper front, knit collar, cuffs & waistband, 1967 dated spec. label, several pockets. Size small. Above avg. cond. $225.00

VIETNAM ERA USAF FLIGHT JACKET (MA-1): Sage green nylon body w/orange nylon lining, zipper front, 1968 dated spec. label, knit collar, cuffs & waistband, several pockets. Medium size. Above avg. cond. $241.00

VIETNAM ERA USAF FLIGHT JACKET (MA-1): Size small in sage green nylon w/ orange lining, zipper front, knit collar, cuffs & waistband, pocket on left sleeve, slash pockets & 1970 dated printed spec. label. Avg. cond. $138.00

VIETNAM ERA USAF FLIGHT JACKET (MA-1): Size x-large in sage green nylon w/orange lining, zipper front, knit collar, cuffs & waistband, pocket on left sleeve, slash pockets & 1969 dated printed spec. label. Above avg. cond. $201.00

VIETNAM ERA USAF FLIGHT JACKET (MA-1): Size large in sage green nylon w/ orange lining, zipper front, knit collar, cuffs & waistband, slash pockets & 1972 dated printed spec. label. Above avg. cond. $84.00

VIETNAM ERA USAF FLIGHT JACKET (MA-1): Size x-large in sage green nylon w/orange lining, zipper front, knit collar, cuffs & waistband, pocket on left sleeve, slash pockets & 1969 dated printed spec. label. Above avg. cond. $305.00

VIETNAM ERA USAF FLIGHT SUIT (K-2B): Med./reg. in sage green cotton w/zipper front, many pockets, 1968 dated spec. label. Above avg. cond. $35.00

VIETNAM ERA USAF FLIGHT SUIT (K-2B): Size med./reg. in sage green cotton w/ 1965 dated spec. label, zipper front, many pockets, plastic sealed capt. bars. Above avg. cond. $20.00

VIETNAM ERA USAF FLIGHT SUIT (K-2B): Size med./reg. in sage green cotton w/ 1969 dated spec. label, zipper front, several pockets. Has color US flag patch on left shoulder, embr. on twill USAF Aux. CAP patch on rt. chest, plastic sealed cmd. pilot's name tag on left chest, subdued lieut. col. leaves. Mint cond. $93.00

VIETNAM ERA USAF FLIGHT SUIT (FRU-21/P): OD flame resistant material w/ zipper front, several pockets velcro panel on left chest. Lacks spec. label but good

shape & strong color. Med. size. Above avg. cond. $20.00

VIETNAM ERA USAF JUNGLE FATIGUE JACKET: Large/reg. in OD ripstop w/ subdued mach. embr. on twill Air borne Spec A-220 patch on left shoulder, US made color "A-220 Air Borne" patch on left chest pocket, theater made subdued pocket tapes. Sleeves neatly finished short. Faint trace of removed chevrons. Above avg. cond. $35.00

VIETNAM ERA USAF JUNGLE FATIGUE JACKET: Med./reg. in OD ripstop w/ subdued Nam mach. made capt. collar patches, USAF pocket tape. Above avg. cond. $20.00

VIETNAM ERA USAF JUNGLE FATIGUE JACKET: Small-short. in OD poplin. Has subdued Nam hand embr. insignia, major leaf collar patches outlined in golden-yellow thread, senior pilot wing, US Air Force & name pocket tapes. Exc. cond. $40.00

VIETNAM ERA USAF JUNGLE FATIGUE SHIRT: Private purchase in dark OD poplin w/button front, patch chest pockets, pocket added to each sleeve in matching material, sleeves neatly finished short. Has hand embr. subdued insignia, lieut. col. leaf on each collar outlined in white thread, cmd. pilot wing on left chest, all direct embr., hand embr. on cotton USAF & name pocket tapes. Med. size. Above avg. cond. $45.00

VIETNAM ERA USAF OFFICER JUNGLE FATIGUE JACKET: Med./reg. OD poplin 3rd pattern jacket w/sleeves neatly finished short. Has subdued Nam hand embr., major leaf on each collar outlined in yellow thread, senior pilot wing, USAF & name. Above avg. cond. $40.00

IETNAM ERA USAF OFFICER UNIFORM: 39S tropical weight jacket in worsted USAF shade blue w/1970 dated spec. label, Meyer hmkd lieut. col. leaves. W/ 1971 dated trousers. Above avg. cond. $12.50

VIETNAM ERA USAF PARTY SUIT & ASCOT: black cotton w/Thai tailor's label has Capt.'s bars, pilot wing & name all direct embr. Hand made USA flag patch on left, machine made patches include Thai shield on rt. shoulder, "Dragon Flight 55" unit patch on left chest pocket. Has neat yellow dragon design direct embr. in to rt. chest-breathing fire w/missiles in hands & bombs in his feet. includes bright yellow nylon ascot w/same dragon design direct embr. into it. Exc. cond. $170.00

VIETNAM ERA USAF PARTY SUIT: 1 pc., blue cotton & zipper front w/short sleeves. Has Thai color machine made patches-US flag on left shoulder, "Vietnam 1010 Missions EC-47" patch on rt. shoulder, "Southeast Asia War Games Participant" patch on left chest, "Yankee Air Pirates" & "Vietnam-Old Tiger-Antique Airlines" patches on rt. chest. Has direct embr. command pilot wing & name "Dick" on left chest. Near mint cond. $283.00

VIETNAM ERA USAF SURVIVAL VEST: Sage green nylon & mesh w/many pockets for survival items (not included), zip front sew-on revolver holster & faint spec. label. Has been dyed in black. Avg. cond. $35.00

VIETNAM ERA USMC AVIATOR FLIGHT JACKET (G-1): Size 38 in dark brown leather w/1971 dated woven spec. label, good original zipper front, knit cuffs & waistband, fur collar. Has large Tonkin Gulf Yacht Club patch over leather USMC Lt.'s (pilot) name tag on left chest, VMA-223 sqdn patch on rt. chest, theater made "Viet-Nam 1969-70" tab over U.S. flag patch on left shoulder. Above avg. cond. $387.00

VIETNAM ERA USMC AVIATOR FLIGHT JACKET (G-1)

VIETNAM ERA USMC CAMO JUNGLE FATIGUE JACKET: Med./reg. in ERDL pattern camo ripstop. 1968 dated. Stencil on left chest pocket. Above avg. cond. $59.00

VIETNAM ERA USMC CAMO JUNGLE FATIGUE JACKET: Size med./long 3rd pattern jacket in ERDL pattern camo poplin w/iron on USMC stencil on left chest pocket. 1968 dated. All tags. Avg. cond. $100.00

VIETNAM ERA USMC CAMO JUNGLE FATIGUE JACKET

VIETNAM ERA USMC EM SERVICE BLOUSE: 37R in forest green wool. 1968 dated. W/belt. Has lance Cpl. chevrons, 3 place bar for Nam serv., shooting badge & 1962 pattern collar devices. Above avg. cond. $16.00

VIETNAM ERA USMC FLAK VEST (M1955): Dark OD nylon covered ballistic plates w/ zipper/snap closure front, large USMC marked 1967 dated label. Med. size. Avg. cond. $84.00

VIETNAM ERA USMC FLAK VEST: OD nylon covered ballistic plates, w/large label. Avg. cond. $45.00

VIETNAM ERA USMC JUNGLE FATIGUE JACKET: Size med./reg. in OD poplin w/ USMC EG&A iron on stencil on left chest pocket. Above avg. cond. $25.00

WAC SUMMER DRESS: Size 10S in taupe shade cotton w/correct removable buttons, short. sleeves, matching belt, 1951 dated Qm tag. Near mint cond. $11.00

WARM-UP JACKET, ARMY: Dark blue flannel jacket w/golden-yellow stripes on sleeves, knit cuffs & waistband, slash pockets. Back has large machine embr. (appears Korean) Intelligence Branch design in center w/"102d Military Intelligence Bn" above & "Bravo Company" below. Rt. chest has embr. design of what appears to be spy satellite. Size 36. Above avg. cond. $24.00

U.S. ARMY CLOTH INSIGNIA

A. Thru World War I (1919)

ARMY 1902 MEDICAL CHEVRONS: Rect. dark tan cotton twill bases w/burgundy & white felt inserts. Near mint cond. $19.00

ARMY 2ND CHEMICAL BATTALION PATCH: 2" w/embr. emblem in brown, red & blue. Above avg. cond. $108.00

ARMY 57TH REGT., 31ST CA BDE.PATCH: OD wool field w/embr. blue triangle in center. Near mint cond. $40.00

ARMY BAKER CHEVRONS (1902): Rect. dark tan twill bases w/dark tan felt appliques. Above avg. cond. $11.00

ARMY BAKER CHEVRONS (1902): Red felt appliques on rect. white cotton bases. Above avg. cond. $11.00

ARMY C. ARTY CHEVRON (1902): Rect. dark tan cotton twill base w/applied red felt arty shell design. Exc. cond. ... $10.00

ARMY CAVALRY FERRIER CHEVRON (1902): Rect. white cotton base w/applied yellow felt specialty design. Rare. Exc. cond. $13.00

ARMY CAVALRY FERRIER CHEVRON (1902): Rect. white cotton base w/applied yellow felt specialty design. Rare. Above avg. cond. $16.00

ARMY CAVALRY SADDLER CHEVRON (1902): Rect. white cotton base w/applied yellow felt specialty design. Above avg. cond. $12.00

ARMY CAVALRY SADDLER CHEVRON (1902): Rect. white cotton base w/applied yellow felt specialty design. Above avg. cond. $24.00

ARMY CAVALRY SADDLER CHEVRON (1902): Rect. white cotton base w/applied yellow felt specialty design. Unused. Only light soiling. Above avg. cond. $11.00

ARMY CORP. OF CAVALRY CHEVRONS (1902): Applied yellow felt stripes on white cotton bases. Above avg. cond. $15.00

ARMY CORP. OF CAVALRY CHEVRONS (1902): Applied yellow felt stripes on white cotton bases. Off uniform but good. Above avg. cond. $14.00

ARMY CORP. OF ORDNANCE CHEVRONS (1902): Lt. OD wool bases w/applied black felt stripes w/red cord borders + cord stitched flaming bomb device. Above avg. cond. $34.00

ARMY ENGINEER CHEVRONS (1902): Red felt branch design on rect. white cotton bases. Above avg. cond. $12.00

ARMY EXPERIMENTAL CHEVRONS FOR SGT. 1ST CLASS OF SIGNAL CORPS (1902): Matched pair. White felt stripes w/ white cord trim + cord stitched branch device on back felt backings. Above avg. cond. $25.00

ARMY FIRST SGT. OF CAVALRY CHEVRONS (1902): Applied yellow felt stripes on white cotton bases. Avg. cond. $17.00

ARMY FIRST SGT. OF CAVALRY CHEVRONS (1902): Applied yellow felt stripes on white cotton bases. Off uniform but good. Above avg. cond. $16.00

ARMY MECHANIC CHEVRONS (1902): Dark tan felt appliques on brown cotton rect. bases. Exc. cond.....................$11.00

ARMY MECHANIC CHEVRONS (1902): Lt. blue felt appliques on white cotton rect. bases. Above avg. cond. $10.00

ARMY MECHANIC CHEVRONS (1902): Rect. white cotton bodies w/applied red felt specialty design. Above avg. cond...$10.00

ARMY MECHANIC CHEVRONS (1902): White felt appliques on dark tan cotton twill rect. bases. Exc. cond. $11.00

ARMY MEDICAL CHEVRONS (1902): Dark blue felt rect. bases w/white & green felt appliques. Exc. cond.....................$11.00

ARMY MEDICAL CHEVRONS (1902): Maroon felt branch design on rect. white cotton bases. Above avg. cond. $19.00

ARMY MEDICAL CHEVRONS (1902): Rect. dark tan twill bases w/dark tan stitched devices. Exc. cond..........................$13.00

ARMY SIGNAL CORPS CHEVRONS (1902): Rect. dark tan twill base w/cord stitched devices. Exc. cond.............$10.00

ARMY ARTY CHEVRONS (1902): Dark blue rect. felt bases w/red felt appliques w/ black embr. details. Above avg. $16.00

ARMY MEDICAL CHEVRONS (1902): Rect. lt. OD wool serge bases w/burgundy & white felt inserts. Above avg. cond..$11.00

ARMY MINE PLANTER PLOTTER DRESS CHEVRON (1902): 2.75" dia navy blue felt base w/golden-yellow felt border & red felt design. Exc. cond...........................$20.00

ARMY OFFICER SHOULDER BOARDS (1872): Navy blue melton wool covered "banjo" shaped bodies w/thick red & white cord trim + white fringe + 1872-pattern button on each. Brass slider backed. Good shape for great age. Above avg. cond. $125.00

ARMY ORDNANCE CHEVRONS (1902): Red felt appliques on rect. white cotton bases. Above avg. cond..................$12.00

ARMY SGT OF Q.M.C. CHEVRONS (1902): White linen bases w/applied buff felt stripes + cord stitched branch design. Above avg. cond.............................$34.00

ARMY SGT. Q.M.C. CHEVRON (1902): Buff felt chevrons on OD wool base w/cord stitched branch design. Exc. cond. $19.00

ARMY SGT. Q.M.C. CHEVRON (1902): Buff felt chevrons on OD wool base w/cord stitched branch design. Above avg. cond. $17.00

ARMY SIGNAL CHEVRONS (1902): Dark tan cotton twill rect. bodies w/cord stitched Corps devices. Near mint cond. $11.00

ARMY SIGNAL CORPS ELECTRICIAN CHEVRON (1902): 2.75" dia navy blue felt base w/silk mach. embr. design & chain-stitched border. Exc. cond. $19.00

CAVALRY 1ST SGT. CHEVRONS (1872): Pair of chevrons, 3 gold felt stripes w/ twisted black thread to outline. Between arms is black wool piece w/gold diamond centered. Above avg. cond. $51.00

CAVALRY CORPORAL CHEVRON (1872): Pair of chevrons, two gold felt stripes outlined by black twisted thread. Avg. cond. $29.00

CAVALRY LANCE CORPORAL DRESS CHEVRON (1899): Pair of chevrons, gold felt stripe w/gold brocade cover. Above avg. cond. $55.00

CAVALRY STABLE SGT. CHEVRON (1872): Single chevron. Three gold felt stripes outlined by Black twisted Thread. Black center & Gold horse's head. Above avg. cond. $56.00

CIVIL WAR 3RD CORPS (3RD DIV) CLOTH PATCH: Blue/gray diamond w/silver wire trim. Some moth damage. Below avg. cond. $90.00

CIVIL WAR ARTY. HAT CORD: Braided red cord w/tassels & slide. Tassels still have original string ties. Exc. cond. $20.00

CIVIL WAR MILITIA SGT. CHEVRON: Single chevron. Sewn gold braid on black cloth in curved 'V' style. 3 stripes, showing some darkening & wear on finish. Avg. cond. $55.00

CIVIL WAR SHOULDER BOARDS: From Schuyler, Hartey & Graham catalogue - for 2nd Lieut. Bullion trimmed & checked brocade center. Appear unused but bullion

has darkened. Above avg. cond. $250.00

CIVIL WAR SHOULDER BOARDS

COASTAL ARTY BRIGADE PATCH: Red embr. triangle on OD wool triangle- 4" a side. For 55th Coast Arty Regiment, 31st Brigade. Exc. cond. $40.00

COASTAL ARTY BRIGADE PATCH: White embr. triangle on OD wool triangle- 4" a side. For 59th Coast Arty Regiment, 31st Brigade. Exc. cond. $45.00

GENERAL INTERMEDIATE SUPPLY DEPOT PATCH: Yellow & red on black diamond shaped. Includes xerox reference copy of letter that demonstrates existence of at least one such center. Exc. cond. $75.00

GENERAL INTERMEDIATE SUPPLY DEPOT PATCH

HOSPITAL CORPS CHEVRON (1872): Pair of chevrons. Three green felt stripes outlined by white twisted thread + Black center & green over white patee cross. Above avg. cond. $32.00

HOSPITAL STEWARD COLLAR TABS: 1898-1902 SB Patee crosses in metal. Shows age & tarnish. Avg. cond. .. $16.00

INFANTRY 1ST SGT. CHEVRON (1885): Pair of chevrons, three White felt stripes outlined by black twisted thread + white diamond outlined in black wool field between arms of chevron. Above avg. cond. $61.00

INFANTRY COLOR SGT. CHEVRON (1899): Single chevron. 3 white twill stripes separated by black twist thread w/ tan insert & sewn circle in center. For the field service blouse. Avg. cond. $20.00

INFANTRY FIRST SGT. CHEVRON (1899): Single chevron. 3 white twill stripes separated by black twist thread w/Tan insert & sewn diamond in center. For the field service blouse. Avg. cond. $20.00

PIONEER SPECIALTY CHEVRONS (1872): Dark blue wool w/crossed axes cutout filled from white wool. Near mint cond. $20.00

SPANISH AMERICAN WAR CAVALRY SERVICE STRIPES: Gold wool w/white wool stripe in center. Defined SAW service. Exc. cond. $28.00

SPANISH AMERICAN WAR INFANTRY SERVICE STRIPES: Blue wool w/white wool stripe in center. Defined SAW service. Exc. cond. $28.00

WWI 3RD ARMY PATCH: Overseas cap size. 1" dia. blue felt w/French silk cord stitched design. Above avg. cond. . $20.00

WWI AEF SIBERIAN PATCH & COLLAR DISC: Multi-piece felt on cotton base patch w/design of bear. Approx. 2 3/4x 3 3/4". Some light soiling. Includes "27/Inf/B" type I collar disc w/dark bronze finish. Above avg. cond. $225.00

WWI AEF SIBERIAN PATCH & COLLAR DISC

WWI ARMY 12TH DIV. PATCH: 3.25x4" red felt rectangle base w/applied black felt crescent of tree (?) design in center, Muslin backed. Exc. cond. $51.00

WWI ARMY 14TH ENGINEER REGIMENT PATCH: 3" square of OD wool likely hand embr. in diamond pattern w/winged disk in center. Mint. Near mint cond. $68.00

WWI ARMY 1ST ARMY ENGINEER PATCH: 2.5x3.5" silk mach. embr. "A" design w/ embr. engr. castle insert. On uncut lt. OD felt base. Exc. cond. $36.00

WWI ARMY 1ST ARMY ENGINEER PATCH: 3.25x4.25" OD wool base w/mach. Silk

embr. black "A" & red engr. castle design. Above avg. cond. $35.00

WWI ARMY 1ST ARMY ENGINEER PATCH: Approx. 3.25x4" lt. OD felt base w/silk mach. embr. "A" design w/engr. castle insert. cond. Above avg. cond. $45.00

WWI ARMY 1ST ARMY ENGINEER PATCH: Approx. 3x4" lt. OD felt base w/silk mach. embr. large "A" design w/red engr. castle insert. Exc. cond. $20.00

WWI ARMY 1ST ARMY PATCH: Multi-piece const. in felt on OD wool. 4x3" dim. Above avg. cond. $24.00

WWI ARMY 1ST ARMY PATCH: Three piece construction. Black wool 'A' w/red & white bars between legs. Above avg. cond. $15.00

WWI ARMY 1ST CORPS PATCH: Black wool disc w/embr. white ring . Some moth nips. Above avg. cond. $30.00

WWI ARMY 1ST CORPS SCHOOL PATCH: 2 5/8" wide. 5-piece felt constr. Above avg. cond. 20.00

WWI ARMY 1ST INF DIV. PATCI I: red felt '1' on OD wool. 2.25" wide. Some damage to the '1.' Exc. cond. $11.00

WWI ARMY 1ST INF DIV. PATCH: 2.25x3.75" OD wool base w/1.75" tall red felt "1" applique. Above avg. cond. $20.00

WWI ARMY 27TH DIV. "LIBERTY LOAN" PATCH: Bevo woven. Edges folded & off uniform but clean. Above avg. cond. $20.00

WWI ARMY 28TH DIV. PATCH: Yellow felt keystone in 28th Div. shape & size. Above avg. cond. $28.00

WWI ARMY 29TH DIV. PATCH: Machine embr. on OD wool w/minor moth nips. Above avg. cond. $20.00

WWI ARMY 2ND DIV. PATCH: Large 3.75" wide orange felt base w/5-point white felt star applique w/cord stitched Indian head design. Off uniform-some fading to orange color but good overall shape. Avg. cond. $90.00

WWI ARMY 2ND DIV. PATCH

WWI ARMY 2ND DIV. PATCH: Large square blue felt base measures approx. 4". Has multi-piece felt applique 5-point star & Indian head design. Shows moth damage but original example. Below avg. cond. $66.00

WWI ARMY 2ND DIVISION PATCH: Three part construction on black wool. Hand sewn feathers on warriors headdress. Great condition for age. Exc. cond. $100.00

WWI ARMY 32ND DIV. PATCH: 1 5/8x5" lt. OD wool base w/applied dark red felt design. Off uniform. Above avg. cond. $13.00

WWI ARMY 33RD DIV. PATCH: 2.75" dia. Multi-piece design. Above avg. cond. $22.00

WWI ARMY 33RD DIV. PATCH: 2.75" dia. black felt disk w/applied felt design. Lot includes gilt wire o/seas stripe. 2 piece on OD wool. Different design from above 33rd Div. patch. Above avg. cond. $25.00

WWI ARMY 35TH DIV. PATCH: 2.75" dia. Multi-piece felt constr. w/2 red & 2 yellow quadrants on brown-shade felt base w/ yellow felt backing. Avg. cond. $47.00

WWI ARMY 3RD ARMY PATCH: 1.5" dia. blue felt base w/2-piece felt applique design. Several small nips. Avg. cond. $30.00

WWI ARMY 3RD INFANTRY DIVISION SLEEVE PATCH: 3x3" faded blue wool with white embr. stripes. Postcard photo 1923, overseas stripe & 2 alum ID discs on string. Avg. cond. $40.00

WWI ARMY 42ND DIV. PATCH: 2.75" wide. 3-piece felt "rainbow" design on OD wool base. Above avg. cond. $24.00

WWI ARMY 63RD CAVALRY DIV. PATCH: red embr. 'X' on yellow felt square 2.25" wide. Avg. cond. $11.00

WWI ARMY 81ST DIV. PATCH: Dark red silk mach. embr. design & border on uncut lt. OD felt. Above avg. cond. $45.00

WWI ARMY 83RD DIV. PATCH: 3" wide black felt triangular base w/silk mach. embr. design. Off uniform. Avg. cond. $38.00

WWI ARMY 89TH DIV. PATCH: 2.75" dia. dark tan felt base w/black silk mach. embr. 4-quadrant border w/"W" in center w/blue insert. Couple nips but good. Above avg. cond. $55.00

WWI ARMY AERO SQDN. 404 & 473 PATCH: Silk cord stitched & 404 & 473" over four-blade prop design on uncut navy blue felt. Exc. cond. $20.00

WWI ARMY ARMOR CHEVRON (2ND DESIGN): Tan embr. on OD wool base. Above avg. cond. $30.00

WWI ARMY ARMOR SENIOR SGT CHEVRON (1ST DESIGN): OD embr. on OD felt base. Above avg. cond. $30.00

WWI ARMY ELECTRICIAN SPECIALTY CHEVRON: OD wool base w/applied OD felt border + embr. sparks design. Exc. cond. $19.00

WWI ARMY ENGINEER C. A. C. CHEVRON: Embr. on OD wool. Exc. cond. $25.00

WWI ARMY GUNNER 1ST CLASS C. A. C. F. A. CHEVRON: Tan twill base w/applied dark tan felt design. Exc. cond. $10.00

WWI ARMY GUNNER 1ST CLASS MINE CO. C. A. C. CHEVRON: Tan twill base w/ applied dark tan felt design. Exc. cond. $10.00

WWI ARMY GUNNER 2ND CLASS MINE CO. C. A. C. CHEVRON: Tan twill base w/ applied dark tan felt design. Near mint cond. $10.00

WWI ARMY INF/CAVALRY CHEVRON: Lt. OD wool base w/applied dark tan felt crossed saber design. Exc. cond. . $23.00

WWI ARMY JUNIOR GRADE HOSPITAL CHEVRON: OD embr. caduesus above wreath design on dark OD wool. Above avg. cond. $21.00

WWI ARMY MASTER HOSPITAL SGT. MED. DEPT. CHEVRON: Brown embr. on OD wool. Unused. Above avg. cond. $18.00

WWI ARMY MASTER QM CHEVRON: Color embr. design on lt. OD wool base. Rare. Exc. cond. $35.00

WWI ARMY MASTER SIGNAL ELECTRICIAN CHEVRON: OD embr. on dark tan twill. Exc. cond. $18.00

WWI ARMY MUSICIAN SENIOR SGT. CHEVRON: OD wool base w/embr. lyre design in center w/5-point star above & wreath below. Above avg. cond. ... $20.00

WWI ARMY PFC MEDICAL CORPS CHEVRONS: Applied dark tan felt stripes w/cord stitched design on dark tan twill. Exc. cond. $23.00

WWI ARMY PFC/ARMOR CHEVRONS: Both embr. on OD wool bases. 1st & 2nd designs. Above avg. cond. $24.00

WWI ARMY PFC/ARMORED FORCES CHEVRON: 1st design embr. in OD on OD wool base. Exc. cond. $10.00

WWI ARMY Q.M. SGT. Q.M.C. CHEVRONS: Applied felt stripes & embr. design on OD wool. Exc. cond. $10.00

WWI ARMY RADIO SGT. C. A. C. CHEVRON: OD wool base w/applied stripes & embr. design. Above avg. cond. $17.00

WWI ARMY RAILWAY PATCH: four color background & red spoked wheel in center w/white wings. Patch is balloon shaped. Above avg. cond. $58.00

WWI ARMY RAILWAY PATCH

WWI ARMY SENIOR SGT. ARMOR CHEVRON (2ND DESIGN): Tan embr. design on OD wool base. Above avg. cond. $34.00

WWI ARMY SENIOR SGT. BAND CHEVRON: OD embr. design of lyre w/5-point star above & wreath below on OD wool. Exc. cond. $20.00

WWI ARMY SENIOR SGT. BAND CHEVRON: OD embr. on dark tan twill. Exc. cond. $10.00

WWI ARMY SENIOR SGT. TRANSPORTATION CHEVRON: Brown embr. on OD wool base. Avg. cond. $40.00

WWI ARMY SERVICE OF SUPPLY PATCH: Rhomboid of Black felt w/Red embr. 'S S' logo. Unused. Exc. cond. $20.00

WWI ARMY SGT. Q.M.C. CHEVRONS: applied felt stripes & embr. design on lt. OD wool bases. Exc. cond. $10.00

WWI ARMY SGT. SIGNAL CORPS CHEVRON: Dark tan applied felt stripes + brown hand stitched branch device on tan twill. Exc. cond. $11.00

WWI ARMY UNIT PATCH: Blue wool field 65mm sq. w/red swastika in center & 13mm white disc in center of swastika wreathed in gold wire. Possible variant on old 45th Div. patch. Above avg. cond. $133.00

WWI ARMY UNIT PATCH

WWI AVIATION OFFICER COLLAR TABS: Pair on OD twill w/bullion embr. 'US' over bullion winged prop. Mint. Near mint cond. $102.00

WWI AVIATION OFFICER COLLAR TABS

WWI C. ARTY FIREMAN CHEVRONS. Applied dark tan felt on dark tan twill. Near mint cond. $40.00

WWI DISTRICT OF PARIS PATCH: Bullion design on approx. 3x4.5" black felt section. Above avg. cond. $27.00

WWI ENGINEER C. A. C. CHEVRON: Stitched on OD wool base. Exc. cond. $25.00

WWI RAILHEAD & REGULATING STATION PERSONNEL PATCH: 3" black felt diamond w/embr. red border & embr. white 'R' in center. Exc. cond. $40.00

WWI RED CROSS MEDICAL PROCTOR BADGE: 2" disk w/red cross in center & tan border. Avg. cond. $40.00

WWI USMC DRESS BLUE SGT CHEVRONS: pair w/applied golden-yellow tape stripes on red felt. 3 chevrons w/3 curved rockers. Exc. cond. $28.00

WWI USMC M. G. BN. PATCH: 4" purple felt square w/white felt 5-point star applique w/mach. silk embr. Indian head design in center. Exc. cond. $164.00

WWI USMC PATCH: 4.75" wide dark red felt base w/folded under edges. Has applied white felt 5-point star design & mach. silk embr. Indian head design. Off uniform. Original. Above avg. cond. $229.00

WWI USNA INSIGNIA LOT: 2 type I "USNA" Em collar discs + red printed "N. A." on dark tan cotton armband + 2 felt-on-felt sgt chevrons. Above avg. cond. ... $20.00

B. 1920 - 1945

AMERICAN FIELD SERVICE HALF MOON PATCH: Tan wool background embr. w/ blue trim & numeral '1' & red 'AMERICAN FIELD Service arcs over top & 'A A S' at bottom. Exc. cond. $34.00

AMERICAN MILITARY RESERVE 10 SQDN. PATCH: Design embr. on powder blue wool. Mint cond. $26.00

ARMY 10TH CORPS PATCH: German made. 2.75" dia. Heavy silver bullion design on blue felt base. Felt section of "X" design shows some mothing but very little tarnishing. Above avg. cond. $26.00

ARMY 11TH AIRBORNE DIV. PATCH: Japanese made. 2.75x4" blue felt base w/ heavy silver bullion design & attached Airborne tab. Some light tarnish & age. Above avg. cond. $105.00

ARMY 12TH DIV. JACKET PATCH: 9x7" shield of blue felt w/sewn gold bulls head. For Philippines Div. Mint. Near mint cond. $75.00

ARMY 1ST CAV. DIV. PATCH: Pre-WWII. 3-piece felt constr. Approx. 3.5x5" size. Off uniform but good. Above avg. cond. $72.00

ARMY 1ST CAV. DIV. PATCH: Pre-WWII. 3.25x4.5" yellow cotton base w/black felt applique design. Avg. cond. $37.00

ARMY 1ST DIV. PATCH: 1930s. 2.75" wide tan twill base w/applied red felt "1." Near mint cond. $19.00

ARMY 1ST DIV. PATCH: Pre-WWII. 2x3.75" dark tan twill base w/silk mach. embr. "1." Exc. cond. $20.00

ARMY 24TH DIV. PATCH: Pre-WWII. 2.25" dia. Multi-piece felt constr. w/stitched black cotton border. Above avg. cond. $19.00

ARMY 24TH DIV. PATCH: Pre-WWII. Multi-piece felt design. Approx. 2.5" dia. Exc. cond. $11.00

ARMY 28TH DIV. PATCH: Pre-WWII. 2.5" dia. OD wool base w/silk mach. embr. "keystone" design. Above avg. cond. $20.00

ARMY 2ND CAV. PATCH: Pre-WWII. Shield in yellow felt w/blue chevron & two 8 point stars. Above avg. cond. $19.00

ARMY 2ND CORPS PATCH: Pre-WWII. 2.5" wide. Mach. embr. design on OD wool base-some nips to base. Avg. cond. $28.00

ARMY 2ND DIV. PATCH: Pre-WWII. 3.25x3.75" size. 2-piece felt w/embr. Indian head design. Off uniform but good. Above avg. cond. $24.00

ARMY 2ND DIV. PATCH: Pre-WWII. 3.25x4" black felt body w/applied white felt star & mach. embr. Indian head design. Off uniform but good. Above avg. cond. $20.00

ARMY 2ND DIV. PATCH: Pre-WWII. Approx. 3 3/8x4 3/8" black felt base w/applique white felt star w/silk mach. embr. Indian head design. Off uniform. Above avg. cond. $35.00

ARMY 30TH DIV. PATCH: Machine embr. on uncut OD wool section. Exc. cond. $12.00

ARMY 30TH DIV. PATCH: Pre-WWII. 41x60mm silk mach. embr. design on uncut OD wool base. Above avg. cond. $11.00

ARMY 36TH DIV. PATCH: Pre-WWII. 2.5" dia. dark tan twill base w/lt. OD embr. border + applied lt. blue felt design. Exc. cond. $20.00

ARMY 36TH DIV. PATCH: Pre-WWII. 2.75" dia. tan twill base w/silk mach. embr. design. Above avg. cond. $25.00

ARMY 36TH DIV. PATCH: Pre-WWII. 3" dia. dark-shade OD wool serge base w/lt. blue silk mach. embr. design. Has one nip-near mint otherwise. Exc. cond. $24.00

ARMY 37TH DIV. PATCH: Pre-WWII. 2.5" dia. Two-piece felt constr. Near mint cond. $12.00

ARMY 3RD ARMY PATCH: Beautifully embr. on OD wool. Really. Mint w/paper tag. Mint cond. $20.00

ARMY 3RD ARMY PATCH: German made. 2.25" dia. blue felt base w/cord stitched border & silver bullion "A." Nip to edge. Above avg. cond. $18.00

ARMY 3RD ARMY PATCH: German made. 2.25" dia. Silver bullion "A" & cord stitched border on blue felt. Couple small nips to edge. Exc. cond. $20.00

ARMY 3RD ARMY PATCH: German made. 2.25" dia. Silver bullion "A" & cord stitched border on felt base. Above avg. cond. $18.00

ARMY 3RD ARMY PATCH: German made. 2.5" dia. Fully embr. in bevo style weave w/OD border. Near mint cond. $13.00

ARMY 3RD CORPS PATCH: Pre WWII. Silk mach. embr. design on 4.25" wide OD wool base. Exc. cond. $20.00

ARMY 41ST DIV. PATCH: Pre-WWII. Silk mach. embr. design on 3.5" wide navy blue felt base. Above avg. cond. .. $20.00

ARMY 43RD DIV. PATCH: 1920s. fully embr. patch design on brown felt. Has been removed from uniform and has some light wear and soiling from use. 3.25" wide. Above avg. cond. $26.00

ARMY 45TH DIV. PATCH: Pre-WWII. 3" wide dark red felt base w/mach. embr. golden yellow swastika design. Exc. cond. $27.00

ARMY 45TH DIV. PATCH: Pre-WWII. 3.25" wide red felt base w/applique felt design. Old-design. Couple small nips but good appearance. Above avg. cond. $41.00

ARMY 45TH DIV. PATCH: Pre-WWII. Old-design in 2-piece felt constr. w/applique swastika-pattern design. Above avg. cond. $38.00

ARMY 4TH DIV. PATCH: Fully embr. US made patch that has had "ivy" design bordered in bullion. Above avg. cond. $16.00

ARMY 4TH DIV. PATCH: German made. 2 1/8" square dark olive felt base w/green cord stitched ivy design. Exc. cond. $16.00

ARMY 4TH DIV. PATCH: German made. 2 3/8" lt. OD felt base w/cord stitched "ivy" design w/bullion trim & border. Exc. cond. $20.00

ARMY 56TH CAV. BDE. PATCH: Pre-WWII. 2.75" dia. dark tan twill base w/silk mach. embr. design. Exc. cond. $45.00

ARMY 5TH DIV. PATCH: German made. 2.75x4.75" red felt base w/heavy silver bullion design & attached '5th Div. Germany' "tab." bullion & bright. Near mint cond. $20.00

ARMY 64TH CAVALRY DIV. PATCH: Pre-WWII. 2.5" wide black felt base w/mach. embr. design. Avg. cond. $28.00

ARMY 71ST DIV. PATCH: German made. 2.75" dia.OD wool base w/bullion & cord stitched design. Above avg. cond. $35.00

ARMY 78TH DIV. PATCH: German made. 3.5" wide red felt base w/silver bullion design & border. Above avg. cond. $25.00

ARMY 7TH ARMY PATCH: German made. Gold bullion design w/red felt insert on blue felt base. Exc. cond. $20.00

ARMY 80TH DIV. PATCH: German made. 2" wide silver bullion & cord stitched design on section of uncut OD wool serge. Above avg. cond. $32.00

ARMY 82ND AIRBORNE DIV. PATCH: German made. Bevo weave w/attached tab. Mint cond. $20.00

ARMY 84TH DIV. PATCH: German made. 2.5" dia. silver bullion design & border on red felt base. Above avg. cond. $40.00

ARMY 89TH DIV. PATCH: Pre-WWII. 2.25" dia. OD wool base w/applied yellow felt sunflower design & mach. embr. center. Glue/paper remains on back but front . Above avg. cond. $24.00

ARMY 96TH DIV. PATCH: German made. 3" wide. Fully embr. Near mint cond. $11.00

ARMY 96TH DIV. PATCH: German made. 3.25" wide OD wool base w/silver bullion border & cord stitched design. Exc. cond. $41.00

ARMY 9TH CORPS PATCH: Pre-WWII. 2.5" dia. blue felt base w/3-piece dark red felt design. Exc. cond. $25.00

ARMY 9TH ENG. CMD. PATCH: German made. 2.75" wide blue felt base w/heavy bullion design. Off uniform. Above avg. cond. $36.00

ARMY 9TH ENGR. CMD. PATCH: German made. 2.5" wide. Fully embr. Bevo style. Above avg. cond. $25.00

ARMY AAA CMD. EASTERN PATCH: Pre-WWII. 2.5" wide dark red felt base w/silk mach. embr. design. Above avg. cond. $20.00

ARMY AIR CORPS PATCH: 2 5/8" dia. felt base w/applied felt "pinwheel" design. Near mint cond. $21.00

ARMY AIR CORPS PATCH: 2 5/8" dia. yellow-orange felt base w/applied blue felt pinwheel design. Exc. cond. $12.00

ARMY AIR CORPS PATCH: 86mm dia. disk fully embr. on white felt. White star w/red center centered on dark blue circle. Bordered by red, white & blue arcs forming a complete circle. The red arc w/ white letters 'UNITED,' White arc w/ 'STATES' in blue & Blue arc w/'AIR CORPS' in white letters. Exc. cond. $36.00

ARMY ARMOR 710 TRIANGLE PATCH: German made. 3.5" wide. Bevo style fully embr. w/OD border. Off uniform. Avg. cond. $20.00

ARMY ARMOR PATCH: Pre-WWII. 7" chenille patch of a knights helmet in maroon & gray. Exc. cond. $20.00

ARMY EMBLEM SHOULDER PATCH: Embr. in gold on light blue, Mint-quite handsome 2" disc. Exc. cond. $20.00

ARMY EUROPE PATCH W/ATTACHED "BERLIN" TAB: Theater made. 2 3/4x 4 1/8" blue felt base w/bullion & cord stitched design. Exc. cond. $52.00

ARMY EUROPE PATCH: Embr. on blue velour & features an orange band at top.

Well done German made. Mint cond. $20.00

ARMY EUROPE PATCH: German made. 2 3/8x3 1/4" fully mach. embr. w/bullion details & border. Above avg. cond. $20.00

ARMY EUROPE PATCH: German made. 2 5/8x3 1/2" w/blue wool base w/cord stitched design + bullion border. Avg. cond. $20.00

ARMY EUROPE PATCH: German made. 2 7/8x3 3/4" w/blue wool serge base w/cord stitched design w/bullion trimmed border. Avg. cond. $20.00

ARMY EUROPE PATCH: German made. 2.5" wide blue felt base w/bullion & cord stitched design. Also, fully embr. Armor School patch w/OD border. Above avg. cond. $20.00

ARMY EUROPE PATCH: Theater made. 2.75x3.5" dark blue felt base w/bullion & cord stitched design. Remains of paper backing. Off uniform. Avg. cond. ... $20.00

ARMY EUROPE PATCH: Theater made. 3 1/8" wide blue felt base w/bullion & cord stitched design. Some tarnish but appearance. Above avg. cond. $20.00

ARMY FORCES WESTERN PACIFIC PATCH: German made. 2.5" dia.Red felt base w/bullion & cord stitched design. Above avg. cond. $25.00

ARMY GLIDER AIRBORNE CAP INSIGNIA: Japanese made. 56mm dia. dark blue felt base w/heavy silver bullion design. Glider faces to left. Above avg. cond. $40.00

ARMY HAWAIIAN DEPT. PATCH: Pre-WWII. Approx. 2 1/2x2 1/8" red felt backing w/ applied felt design. Has 4 male snap ends on back. Above avg. cond. $19.00

ARMY II CORPS PATCH: Handsome rendition of II Corps, embr. in white on blue wool & all sewn to Oblong yellow felt. Sharp looking. Exc. cond. $95.00

ARMY II CORPS PATCH

ARMY MECHANIC 6TH CLASS SPEC CHEVRON: 1930s. Lt. OD felt on black felt base. Above avg. cond. $19.00

ARMY MUSICIAN CHEVRONS: Pair. Corp. grade. OD embr. on black felt w/lyre design in center. Near mint cond. $24.00

ARMY MUSICIAN CHEVRONS: Pair. Sgt. grade. OD embr. on black felt w/lyre design in center. Exc. cond. $34.00

ARMY SPEC. 7 CHEVRON FOR SUMMER UNIFORM: OD embr. on tan twill. Near mint cond. $37.00

ARMY SPEC. 7 CHEVRON: OD embr. on dark felt. Exc. cond. $30.00

ARMY SPECIALIST 1ST CLASS CHEVRON: Pre-WWII. OD embr. on black felt. Near mint cond. $30.00

ARMY SPECIALIST 1ST CLASS CHEVRON: Pre-WWII. OD embr. on tan twill. Near mint cond. $25.00

ARMY UNIVERSITY FACULTY PATCH: 3.5x2" rect. blue felt base w/silk mach. embr. lettering. Exc. cond. $20.00

BATTY GENERAL HOSPITAL PATCH: 2.75x3.75" shield shape maroon cotton body w/white mach. embr. border & letters. Exc. cond. $21.00

CALIFORNIA STATE GUARD PATCH: 2.75" dia. Fully embr. Near mint cond. ... $10.00

INDIANA STATE GUARD PATCH: Fully embr. on tan twill. Mint cond. $27.00

MASSACHUSETTS STATE GUARD PATCH: 2.5" dia. Fully embr. w/thin OD border. Near mint. $20.00

MASSACHUSETTS STATE GUARD PATCH: 5" wide. Silver-gray embr. lettering & border on dark green wool serge oval-shaped base. Exc. cond. $44.00

PENN. 213TH C. ARTY REGT. PATCH: 2 1/8" wide. Fully mach. embr. Off uniform. Above avg. cond. $55.00

PENN. STATE UNIT PATCH: 2.25x2.75" "keystone" shape patch in half red/half blue. Reads "U.S./55/C." Fully mach. embr. Above avg. cond. $24.00

TENNESSEE STATE GUARD PATCH: 3" dia. Embr. on dark red cotton. Above avg. cond. $20.00

WWII ARMY 505TH PARACHUTE ENG. REGT. OVAL: British made. Silk embr. white border on 2" wide black felt base. Exc. cond. $37.00

WWII ARMY 102ND DIVISION PATCH: Hand made. 65mm dia. dark blue wool base w/border & design stitched in heavy, gold tone nylon. Avg. cond. $32.00

WWII "AIR POLICE" ARMBAND: Supermarine blue wool body w/applied golden-yellow letters. Above avg. cond. $36.00

WWII AACS PATCH: Army Airways & Communications Service showing world w/plane circling it on red ribbon of Morse code. Exc. cond. $20.00

WWII AAF 10TH AIR FORCE PATCH: CBI made. 2.75" dia. Mach. embr. design on cotton. Cotton backed. Exc. cond. $25.00

WWII AAF 10TH AIR FORCE PATCH: Color cord stitched & gold wire on stiff blue background 40mm dia. Mint cond. $27.00

WWII AAF 10TH AIR FORCE SHOULDER PATCH: 10 part leather construction of 3" patch. Good detail. Exc. cond. $118.00

WWII AAF ATC FLIGHT JACKET PATCH: 5" dia. brown leather disc w/applied ATC patch design decal. Off jacket but shows little age. Above avg. cond. $96.00

WWII AAF 12TH AF PATCH: Triangular. 4" sides on leather w/hand painted image. Above avg. cond. $60.00

WWII AAF 12TH AIR FORCE PATCH: Theater made. 3 1/8" wide blue felt base w/heavy bullion design. Above avg. cond. $39.00

WWII AAF 12TH AIR FORCE SHOULDER PATCH: 4" triangle w/wings of gold bullion & gold ribbon + star of silver bullion Silver bullion has darkened. Above avg. cond. $145.00

WWII AAF 13TH AIR FORCE JACKET PATCH: 5" dia. leather disc w/hand painted 13th AF design. Shows age from wear. Avg. cond. $64.00

WWII AAF 13TH BOMB SQUADRON PATCH: 3.5x5" blue felt oval w/simple stitched likeness of Grim Reaper w/blood dripping scythe in center. Australian made-rare-shows light age. Above avg. cond. $160.00

WWII AAF 13TH BOMB SQUADRON PATCH: 4" oval in dark blue felt w/embr. white skeleton carrying a bloody scythe. Exc. cond. $45.00

WWII AAF 15TH AIR FORCE PATCH: Gold bullion for trim, wings & '15' at top Silver bullion for star. All on blue wool field. Near mint cond. $35.00

WWII AAF 15TH AIR FORCE PATCH: Gold bullion on blue velvet. Detailing, slight darkening of bullion. Above avg. cond. $40.00

WWII AAF 15TH AIR FORCE PATCH: Italian made. 2.5" dia. black felt base w/heavy bullion design. Some tarnish. Avg. cond. $35.00

WWII AAF 15TH AIR FORCE PATCH: Italian made. 2.5" dia. Heavy bullion design on blue satin. Some tarnish but much gilt still visible. Avg. cond. $36.00

WWII AAF 15TH AIR FORCE PATCH: Italian made. Heavy bullion on dark felt w/three female snap ends on back for attachment to uniform. Some tarnish. Avg. cond. $40.00

WWII AAF 15TH AIR FORCE PATCH: Theater made. 2 7/8x3 5/8" size. Multi-piece felt body w/heavy bullion design. Avg. cond. $276.00

WWII AAF 15TH AIR FORCE PATCH: gold and silver bullion design with pink embr. center to the star. 2.5" diam., some wear and patina to the bullion. Above avg. cond. $24.00

WWII AAF 1ST AIR COMMANDO JACKET PATCH: 5" dia. multi-color machine embr. on navy blue wool. Very colorful-rare unit! Exc. cond. $689.00

WWII AAF 1ST AIR COMMANDO JACKET PATCH

WWII AAF 1ST COMPOSITE SQDN. PATCH: 5" w/gold trim enclosing winged skull w/cobra at top & bomb below. Very clean. Exc. cond. $37.00

WWII AAF 20TH AIR FORCE JACKET PATCH: 5.5" dia. brown leatherette border w/ribbed cotton center-heavy cord stitched center design. Mint cond. $45.00

WWII AAF 20TH AIR FORCE PATCH: Embr. patch design on blue felt. 3" dia. Above avg. cond. $24.00

WWII AAF 2ND AIR FORCE PATCH: Approx. 2.25x2.75" blue felt base w/heavy bullion design. Above avg. cond. .. $34.00

WWII AAF 307TH BOMB GRP. JACKET PATCH: 5" dia. grain leather disc in blue w/yellow border & off-white stylized letters "LR"-neatly hand painted-shows age toning but has never been worn. Near mint cond. $150.00

WWII AAF 367TH FIGHTER SQDN. PATCH: Embr. design of screaming monkey wearing flight helmet & goggles on yellow felt. 3.25" dia. Unissued. Mint cond. $76.00

CLOTH INSIGNIA

WWII AAF 35TH FIGHTER GRP. JACKET PATCH: 5x6" gray felt base w/finely embr. silk thread design-"Attack to Defend." Quality-shows little age. Near mint cond. $258.00

WWII AAF 35TH FIGHTER GRP. JACKET PATCH

WWII AAF 3RD AIR FORCE PATCH: Variant. 2.5" dia. embr. on felt. Above avg. cond. $13.00

WWII AAF 401ST FIGHTER GRP. JACKET PATCH: 5" shield w/3 crossed pikes, a band of b/w checks & curved diagonal of red, yellow & blue bands. Exc. cond. $20.00

WWII AAF 424TH BOMB SQDN. PATCH: 5" white felt disk w/hand embr. black border and emblem. Shows black bomb w/red sun & blue sea. For 307th Bomb Grp & 424 bomb Squadron. Near mint cond. $213.00

WWII AAF 429TH BOMB SQDN. PATCH: Design embr. on yellow felt. Gauze back. Above avg. cond. $45.00

WWII AAF 429TH BOMBER SQDN. PATCH: Embr. design of Indian w/bow & arrow drawn on 4 lobed orange felt. 3.5" wide. Mint cond. $177.00

WWII AAF 449TH BS CLOTH DI: Rare gold wire on blue cloth 1" tall DI. Avg. cond. $93.00

WWII AAF 470TH BOMB SQDN. UNIT PATCH: A replacement training unit, 6" chenille patch w/silk thread on green wool felt. Features sitting bear juggling 4 orange & white bombs. Above avg. cond. $237.00

WWII AAF 4TH AIR FORCE PATCH: 2.75x3" blue felt base w/heavy bullion design & embr. border. Above avg. cond. $38.00

WWII AAF 534TH BS PATCH: 4" disc hand painted on leather, removed from a jacket. Shows winged cartoon dinosaur w/bombs in hands & snorting smoke. Dinosaur red, wings black. Avg. cond. $315.00

WWII AAF 553 BOMB SQDN., 386 BOMB GRP. PATCH: 4.5" dia. brown leather disc applied decal design. Off flight jacket.

Approx. 65% of decal design remains. Avg. cond. $124.00

WWII AAF 58TH BOMB WING "BIKINI ATOLL" JACKET PATCH: 5" dia. Color machine embr. on blue twill w/mushroom cloud w/"58th Wing" across top-"509" below. Lot includes 2 photo copied likenesses of the comical "Joint Task Force One Short Snorter"-also photo copy of crew photo posed by B-29 w/same insignia as patch painted on front. Exc. cond. $214.00

WWII AAF 5TH AIR FORCE PATCH: 3" Gold & silver bullion on blue wool backing. Well done. Exc. cond. $44.00

WWII AAF 5TH AIR FORCE PATCH: 3" diam.-Australian machine embr. in silk on blue cotton. Near mint cond. $20.00

WWII AAF 5TH AIR FORCE PATCH: Theater made. 2.75" dia. dark blue felt base w/ hand embr. design. Off uniform. Above avg. cond. $20.00

WWII AAF 5TH AIR FORCE PATCH: Theater made. Approx. 2.75" dia. w/mach. embr. design on purple-blue felt. Above avg. cond. $27.00

WWII AAF 5TH AIR FORCE PATCH: Theater made. Silk mach. embr. on 3" dia. dark blue felt base. Off uniform. Above avg. cond. $20.00

WWII AAF 601ST PHOTO FLT JACKET PATCH: 2.75 x 4" Blue twill w/white thread embr. Arced '601ST PHOTO FLT' over embr. aircrew wing. Avg. cond. $35.00

WWII AAF 60TH SERV. GP. SQDN. PATCH: Mach. embr. on 4" wide dark OD felt base. Exc. cond. $40.00

WWII AAF 614TH BOMBARDMENT SQDN. JACKET PATCH: 5" disc, fully embr. w/red devils face w/gold wings & green bomb below. Blue field. Sharp one. Exc. cond. $87.00

WWII AAF 614TH BOMBARDMENT SQDN. JACKET PATCH

WWII AAF 661 HELLCATS T.D. SCROLL: 3 3/8" wide orange felt base w/black embr. lettering & border. Light paper/glue

remains on back from display. Exc. cond.
.... $50.00

WWII AAF 77TH FIGHTER SQUADRON PATCH: 5" jacket patch embr. on twill showing card hand of two pair of 7's split by Ace. Red background w/black trim. Exc. cond. $145.00

WWII AAF 79TH FIGHTER GRP. "SKULL" SQUADRON PATCH: 6 piece leather construction w/blue background. Shows Full face view w/missing face & smaller skull in space looking up & lightning bolts from eyes. 5" long. Above avg. cond. $132.00

WWII AAF 828TH BOMB SQDN. JACKET PATCH: embr. design of covered wagon on white felt. 4.75" dia. Mint cond. $76.00

WWII AAF 84TH BOMBARDMENT SQDN. PATCH: Embr. design of Devil with bomb on orange twill. 4" dia. Mint cond. $75.00

WWII AAF 862ND TANK DESTROYER BN. PATCH: 3x4.75" tan felt base w/silk mach embr. design of winged black skull over lightning bolt. shape. Above avg. cond. $177.00

WWII AAF 8TH AIR FORCE PATCH: Bulllon on blue wool field. Bullion is darkening from age, otherwise excellent piece. Above avg. cond. $145.00

WWII AAF 8TH AIR FORCE PATCH

WWII AAF 8TH AIR FORCE PATCH: English made on dark blue wool-upswept wings w/ some tarnish. Removed from uniform. Above avg. cond. $114.00

WWII AAF 8TH AIR FORCE PATCH: English made. 2 5/8" dia. blue felt base w/silk mach. embr. design. Near mint cond. $38.00

WWII AAF 8TH AIR FORCE PATCH: English made. 2.5" dia. Silk mach. embr. on felt. Exc. cond. $24.00

WWII AAF 8TH AIR FORCE PATCH: English made. 2.75" dia. Mach. silk embr. on felt base. Exc. cond. $35.00

WWII AAF 8TH AIR FORCE PATCH: English made. Hand stitched cord design on 2.75" dia. blue felt base. Above avg. cond. $35.00

WWII AAF 8TH AIR FORCE PATCH: Fully embr. WWII patch that has had bullion trim added to design-bullion work not WWII. Exc. cond. $12.00

WWII AAF 8TH AIR FORCE PATCH: Std fully embr. patch w/design overlayed in heavy bullion. Exc. cond. $28.00

WWII AAF 8TH AIR FORCE PATCH: Theater made beautifully embr. patch in blue w/ Winged 8 in soft yellow. Near mint cond. $37.00

WWII AAF 8TH AIR FORCE PATCH: Theater made. 2 5/8" dia. Silk mach. embr. on felt base. Above avg. cond. $19.00

WWII AAF 8TH AIR FORCE PATCH: Theater made. 2.5" dia. blue felt base w/silk mach. embr. design w/short, stubby wings. Some light soiling & fading. Avg. cond. ... $20.00

WWII AAF 8TH AIR FORCE PATCH: Theater made. 2.5" dia. w/silk mach. embr. design. Above avg. cond. $11.00

WWII AAF 8TH AIR FORCE PATCH: Theater made. Approx. 2.5" dia. w/silk mach. embr. design. Near mint cond. $20.00

WWII AAF 8TH AIR FORCE PATCH: Theater made. Approx. 2.5" dia. Fully silk mach. embr. w/stubby wing design. Off uniform. Above avg. cond. $40.00

WWII AAF 8TH AIR FORCE PATCH: hand stitched, short wing on blue felt. Avg. cond. $30.00

WWII AAF 8TH AIR FORCE PATCI I: silk cord stitched on blue wool. Above avg. cond. $20.00

WWII AAF 9TH AIR FORCE PATCH: 5 piece construction w/silver bullion wings & star on blue wool background light tarnish on wings. Above avg. cond. $32.00

WWII AAF 9TH AIR FORCE PATCH: English made. 2.5x2.75" blue felt base w/silk mach. Embr. design. Couple nips to edge but piece. Above avg. cond. $20.00

WWII AAF 9TH AIR FORCE PATCH: Gold & silver bullion to form image w/red embroidery to give contrast. Above avg. cond. $44.00

WWII AAF 9TH AIR FORCE PATCH: Theater made. 2 3/8" wide dark blue felt base w/ heavy bullion design. Off uniform. Avg. cond. $45.00

WWII AAF 9TH AIR FORCE PATCH: Theater made. 2 5/8" wide dark blue felt w/silk mach. embr. design. Exc. cond. $11.00

WWII AAF 9TH AIR FORCE PATCH: Theater made. 2.5" wide dark blue felt base w/

hand embr. design. Above avg. cond.
.... $20.00
WWII AAF 9TH AIR FORCE PATCH: Theater made. Heavy bullion, cord & applique design on 2.5x3" blue satin base. Light age. Above avg. cond. $33.00
WWII AAF 9TH ENGINEERING COMMAND: Near Mint fully embr. patch. Exc. cond.
.... $20.00
WWII AAF AAD PATCH: 2.75" wide. "Arrowhead" shape patch w/blue mach. embr. on white cotton. Exc. cond.
.... $20.00
WWII AAF AIR FERRY COMMAND FLIGHT JACKET PATCH: 5" dia. color machine embr. design on medium brown wool-felt. Has been removed from jacket-some light nips around the edge. Avg. cond.
.... $19.00
WWII AAF AIR GUNNERY SCHOOL PATCH: 5" leather circle w/decal in center. Shows demon riding .50 cal. gun w/wings. Very good condition. Exc. cond.
.... $145.00
WWII AAF AIR TRAINING COMMAND PATCH: gold and silver bullion design on blue felt. 2.5" diam., unissued. Mint cond.
.... $22.00
WWII AAF AIR TRANSPORT COMMAND PATCH: 4" painted patch on 5" leather disk. Shows some crazing & chip on one side. Leather has gentle fold crease. Avg. cond. $49.00
WWII AAF ATC FLIGHT JACKET PATCH: 5" dia. brown leather disc w/ATC decal patch design. Some storage age but never been applied to jacket. Avg. cond. $34.00
WWII AAF ATC FLIGHT JACKET PATCH: 5" dia. brown leather disc w/applied ATC patch-design decal. Above avg. cond.
.... $91.00
WWII AAF ATC FLIGHT JACKET PATCH: 5" dia. dark brown leather disc w/decal ATC patch-design. Exc. cond. $82.00
WWII AAF BLOOD CHIT: Printed US flag at top & Foreign language phrases. Many Island languages used. Exc. cond.
.... $135.00
WWII AAF BLOOD CHIT: Used by US bomber crews on shuttle missions. Has American flag at top & Russian phrases + phonetic pronunciation. Folded as pamphlet undated. Exc. cond. $150.00
WWII AAF BOMB SQDN. PATCH: full embr. triangle of pirate on white twill disc. Exc. cond. $45.00
WWII AAF BOMBER UNIT JACKET PATCH: 4" disc w/embr. red dinosaur w/Alley Oop astride & throwing yellow bombs. Exc. cond. $68.00

WWII AAF BRF #1 PATCH: Embr. design on blue felt. Has flying stork carrying baby airplane in sling over outline of the U.S. 4" dia. Mint cond. $75.00
WWII AAF CIMMARON OR MUSTANG FIELD PATCH: One or the other used this as flying school insignia. Full color embr. on white felt. Big red wings w/shield. Exc. cond. $34.00
WWII AAF COMMUNICATIONS SPEC. CUFF PATCH: 2.75" wide black wool base w/gold bullion design. Above avg. cond.
.... $16.00
WWII AAF DESERT AIR FORCE PATCH: Mach. embr. on felt. Back has glue/paper residue from display but front. Above avg. cond. $20.00
WWII AAF ENGR. SPEC. TRIANGLE CUFF PATCH: English made. 2.5" wide. Silk mach. embr. on blue felt. Exc. cond.
.... $34.00
WWII AAF FAR EAST AIR FORCE PATCH: 2.5" diamond w/gold & silver bullion on blue felt background. Some signs of aging on bullion & minor wear on border. Above avg. cond. $44.00
WWII AAF FERRY CMD FLIGHT JACKET PATCH: 4.25" fully embr. design on 5" dia. brown-shade OD wool disc. Some mothing to wool border. Avg. cond.
.... $80.00
WWII AAF FERRY COMMAND PATCH GROUPING: Includes design in 3 7/8, 2 1/2 & 1 3/8" dia. All fully embr. on golden yellow base shape. Exc. cond. $80.00
WWII AAF FERRY COMMAND PATCH: 3.75" dia. Fully embr. Mint cond. .. $38.00
WWII AAF FLIGHT JACKET FLAG BLOOD CHIT: 9x7" 9 piece leather construction US flag design on white background near mint. Near mint cond. $121.00
WWII AAF JACKET PATCH 527TH BOMB SQDN. PATCH: 4.5" dia. on thin-soft leather. Painted skull & crossed bombs design. Avg. cond. $80.00

WWII AAF JACKET PATCH 527TH BOMB
SQDN. PATCH

WWII AAF JACKET PATCH 67TH TROOP CARRIER 433rd TRP GRP: 5" powder blue felt with embr. wings over eagle over fire & parachute w/box. Has been sewn on & edges are uneven. Avg. cond. $200.00

WWII AAF JACKET PATCH: 5" dia. fully machine embr. likeness of two globes being circled by 4 engine plane in figure eight pattern. Above avg. cond. $75.00

WWII AAF JACKET PATCH: Hand painted on leatherette, 5" disc w/58th wing at top & 509 at bottom + Atomic explosion in center. Above avg. cond. $49.00

WWII AAF LEATHER SQUADRON PATCH: 5" disc of leather w/4" painted emblem. Shows red bird carrying bombs in its feet over stylized globe. Likely squadron Identifier. Above avg. cond. $72.00

WWII AAF PATCH W/AIR TRANSPORT COMMAND TAB: Italian made. Heavy bullion on cloth AAF patch design w/ attached tab. Approx. 3x3.25" o/a size. Avg. cond. $23.00

WWII AAF PATCH: 2 5/8" dia. blue felt base w/tinsel bullion design. Near mint cond. $20.00

WWII AAF PATCH: 2 7/8" dia. blue wool base w/heavy bullion design. Backed in black cotton. Off uniform but good. Above avg. cond. $20.00

WWII AAF PATCH: 3" dia. in heavy gold bullion on dark blue wool-CBI hand made-unusual variation. Avg. cond. $37.00

WWII AAF PATCH: Blue felt body is somewhat oval-shaped (approx. 2.75" tall & 2.5" wide) w/heavy bullion design. Off uniform but good. Above avg. cond. $25.00

WWII AAF PATCH: Blue wool back w/gold thread border. Gold bullion for wings & silver for star. Handsome. Exc. cond. $72.00

WWII AAF PATCH: Blue wool field w/gold wire wings & silver bullion star in center + embr. red center. Clean looking. One moth nip. CBI patch w/gold wire & silver bullion. Very clean. Above avg. cond. $28.00

WWII AAF PATCH: CBI made. 2 3/8" dia. Dark blue wool base w/folded under edges-cotton backed w/4 male-end snaps. Design in heavy bullion. Above avg. cond. $28.00

WWII AAF PATCH: CBI made. 2.5" dia. Blue velveteen base w/heavy bullion design. Lt. blue cotton backed w/4 male snap ends. Above avg. cond. $16.00

WWII AAF PATCH: CBI made. 2.5" dia. Dark blue wool base w/cord stitched border &

design. Has 3 male snap ends on back. Some surface mothing but neat example. Avg. cond. $20.00

WWII AAF PATCH: CBI made. 2.75" dia. dark blue wool base w/heavy bullion design. Back covered in black smooth cotton w/4 male snap ends. Above avg. cond. $20.00

WWII AAF PATCH: CBI made. 3" dia. Heavy bullion design on dark blue velvet. Ink stamp markings on reverse. Light tarnish. Above avg. cond. $36.00

WWII AAF PATCH: CBI made. 3" dia. Heavy bullion design on blue felt. Paper & cotton backed. Above avg. cond. $32.00

WWII AAF PATCH: CBI made. Approx. 2.75" dia. dark blue velveteen base w/heavy bullion design. Off uniform-light tarnish. Avg. cond. $36.00

WWII AAF PATCH: Gold & silver bullion for emblem on purple silk backing. Very interesting. Above avg. cond. $44.00

WWII AAF PATCH: Gold & silver bullion to form wing & star w/red cloth center. Center is fading & gold bullion is darkening slightly. Above avg. cond. $26.00

WWII AAF PATCH: Italian made. 2.5" dia. dark wool base w/heavy bullion design. Wrapped in cellophane. Above avg. cond. $25.00

WWII AAF PATCH: Printed variant. 2.75" dia. Backed in white cotton. Off uniform. Avg. cond. $37.00

WWII AAF PATCH: Theater made. 2.75" dia. blue felt base w/heavy bullion design. Couple nips & some light even tarnish. Backed in black cotton. Off uniform. Avg. cond. $25.00

WWII AAF PATCH: Variant. 2.75" yellow-orange felt base w/mach. embr. standard AAF patch ensign w/blue wings + white star w/red insert. Near mint cond. $196.00

WWII AAF PATCH: Variant. Based on standard AAF design. 2.75" dia. Mach. embr. on twill-has no red circle in center. Exc. cond. $12.00

WWII AAF PHILIPPINE AIR FORCE PATCH: Fully embr. Original. Above avg. cond. $27.00

WWII AAF S/SGT. CHEVRONS: Matched pair. Unofficial. Olive embr. on dark felt w/ winged prop design. Above avg. cond. $24.00

WWII AAF SGT. CHEVRONS: Pair. Unofficial. Woven on dark twill w/winged prop design in center. Off uniform bit good. Avg. cond. $23.00

WWII AAF SQUADRON PATCH: 4.5" dia. machine embr. design w/likeness of tiny man atop eagle in flight -eagle is clutching bomb in his talons. Soiled. Above avg. cond. $140.00

WWII AAF SQUADRON PATCH: 4.5" dia. machine embr. on white twill likeness of smiling flyboy in helmet & goggles clutching bomb falling downward. Avg. cond. $90.00

WWII AAF SQUADRON PATCH: 4.75" dia. blue twill disc w/likeness of snow man in top hat clutching giant 8 ball atop the globe. Above avg. cond. $50.00

WWII AAF SQUADRON PATCH

WWII AAF SQUADRON PATCH: 5" dia. hand painted on brown leather disc. Shield w/2 upright swords and 6 bees w/ scroll below "Surgam." Unused. Exc. cond. $150.00

WWII AAF SQUADRON PATCH: 5" diam.- color machine embr. on white felt-comical rendition of Bugs Bunny style rabbit swinging boxing glove that leaves streaks in form of the US flag in its wake. Soiled w/age-believe this was a 90th Bomb grp. unit. Above avg. cond. $89.00

WWII AAF TECH. TRAINING CMD. INSTRUCTOR PATCH: 3x2" embr. on medium blue cotton w/winged prop design embr. in center. Near mint cond. .. $60.00

WWII AAF TRAINING SCHOOL INSIGNIA PATCH: For either Cimmarron or Mustang field, Okla. 5" white felt wing w/US shield in center & red silk thread wings embr. Near mint cond. $17.00

WWII AAF US TECH REP PATCH: scarce fully embr. patch design, 2.75" dia. Unissued. Mint cond. $26.00

WWII AAF WINGED BOOT NOVELTY PATCH: 2x2" stiffened black felt base w/ fine silver wire embr. winged boot design. Near mint cond. $100.00

WWII AAF YUMA ARMY AIR FIELD JACKET PATCH: 4" dia. thin brown leather disc w/comical decal design applied-Fox standing atop Cactus w/6 gun

at his side-firing Aerial style .50 cal. M. G. Exc. cond. $160.00

WWII AF FLIGHT TRAINING PATCH: 70mm dia. tan twill w/3 blade prop on red ball in center of 5 point star-letters "TWFWO" around star. Mint. Mint cond. $151.00

WWII ALASKA TERRITORIAL STATE GUARD PATCH: Approx. 3.5" square blue felt base w/silk mach. embr. design. Above avg. cond. $20.00

WWII ALASKAN DEFENSE CMD PATCH 1ST TYPE: 2.5" dia. Fully embr. w/OD border. Seal design w/Northern Lights & "ADC" in background. Above avg. cond. $38.00

WWII ARMY 100TH DIV. PATCH: 2.25x2.5" blue felt base w/bullion design & border. Above avg. cond. $25.00

WWII ARMY 101ST AIRBORNE PATCH: Foreign made w/full color embroidery & attached airborne arc. Avg. cond. $72.00

WWII ARMY 101ST AIRBORNE DIV. PATCH: English made. 2.5" wide w/mach. embr. design on black felt. Includes matching Airborne tab w/hand embr. letters on black felt. Exc. cond. $35.00

WWII ARMY 101ST AIRBORNE PATCH & TAB: Full embr. on black wool w/black border. Full color eagle w/airborne tab in yellow on black. Exc. cond. $90.00

WWII ARMY 101ST AIRBORNE PATCH & TAB

WWII ARMY 101ST AIRBORNE PATCH: Gold bullion w/'AIRBORNE' TAB. Gold wire for beak, red thread for tongue. On black wool. Exc. cond. $80.00

WWII ARMY 101ST AIRBORNE PATCH: British made, fully embr. w/white tongued eagle. One piece incl. the airborne tab at top. Dulled w/age. Above avg. cond. $185.00

WWII ARMY 101ST AIRBORNE PATCH: Famous screaming eagle patch w/ airborne tab. This variant has the white tongue vs. the usual red tongue. Fully embr. Exc. cond. $60.00

WWII ARMY 101ST AIRBORNE PATCH

WWII ARMY 101ST AIRBORNE PATCH

WWII ARMY 10TH DIV. PATCH: Mint patch embr. & unattached Tab reading 'MOUNTAIN.' Above avg. cond. ... $20.00

WWII ARMY 113TH CAVALRY REGT.PATCH: 2.5" wide. Bevo style. Yellow background w/red horse & two fleur-de-leis one red & one green. Above avg. cond. $100.00

WWII ARMY 113TH CAVALRY REGT.PATCH

WWII ARMY 119TH "GHOST" DIV. PATCH: 2.25" dia. Fully embr. Near mint cond. $20.00

WWII ARMY 127TH AIRBORNE ENGR. BN. PATCH: 3" dia. Fully embr. Near mint cond. $45.00

WWII ARMY 12TH ARMY GRP. PATCH: Fully embr. Near mint cond. $12.00

WWII ARMY 12TH ARMY GRP. PATCH: Theater made. 2 1/8" wide OD wool serge

base w/cord stitched design. Exc. cond. $25.00

WWII ARMY 12TH DIV. (PHILIPPINE) PATCH: Fully embr. Avg. cond. $30.00

WWII ARMY 14TH "GHOST" DIV. PATCH: Fully embr. w/OD border. Exc. cond. $23.00

WWII ARMY 14TH AAA CMD. PATCH: Approx. 3" dia. Fully embr. off uniform but good. Above avg. cond. $24.00

WWII ARMY 158TH RCT PATCH: 3" wide blue felt base w/silk mach. embr. design. Above avg. cond. $48.00

WWII ARMY 163RD RCT PATCH: shield w/ blue & diag. red stripe. Cattle skull over all in center. Near mint cond. $75.00

WWII ARMY 163RD RCT PATCH

WWII ARMY 1778TH ENGINEERS PATCH: Full embr. w/'17' over dice & eight ball. Above avg. cond. $24.00

WWII ARMY 17TH AIRBORNE DIV. PATCH W/TAB: Fully embr. w/OD trim. Shows Gold eagle claws in center. Arch mated to patch w/tan fabric. Above avg. cond. $20.00

WWII ARMY 17TH AIRBORNE DIV. PATCH W/TAB: OD border patch w/matching tab fully embr. on blue cotton base. Exc. cond. $20.00

WWII ARMY 17TH AIRBORNE DIV. PATCH: English made. 2.25" dia. patch w/pale OD border. Fully mach. embr. Includes hand embr. on felt Airborne tab. Mint cond. $45.00

WWII ARMY 17TH AIRBORNE DIV. PATCH: English made. Approx. 2.25" dia. Fully mach. embr. w/lt. OD border. Includes English-made Airborne tab w/embr. lettering on black felt base. set. Exc. cond. $30.00

WWII ARMY 17TH AIRBORNE DIV. PATCH: thin OD border-machine embr. Above avg. cond. $42.00

WWII ARMY 17TH CAV. REGT. PATCH: Fully embr. patch design, square shield shaped, 3" wide, unissued cond. Remains of glue and paper to back. Near mint cond. $25.00

WWII ARMY 17TH CAVALRY SQDN. PATCH: 2 7/8x3 1/2" size. Fully embr. Exc. cond. $22.00

WWII ARMY 187TH AIRBORNE RCT PATCH: Bullion on blue & red felt, cotton backed & foreign made. Avg. cond. $108.00

WWII ARMY 187TH AIRBORNE REGT. PATCH: Oversized patch w/winged chute over flames. Exc. cond. $35.00

WWII ARMY 18TH INFANTRY REGT. PATCH: Bevo style. Unit emblem w/motto on thin silk cloth. Above avg. cond. $27.00

WWII ARMY 1ST ALLIED AIRBORNE ARMY PATCH: Theater-made. Mach. embr. on lt. blue cotton. Only lettering is attached "Airborne" tab. "Link" bullion border. Above avg. cond. $77.00

WWII ARMY 1ST ALLIED AIRBORNE PATCH: English made embr. on blue wool, Mint. Near mint cond. $30.00

WWII ARMY 1ST ALLIED AIRBORNE PATCH: Theater made. 2.25x3.25" o/a size. Mach. embr. design on medium blue felt w/attached matching tab. Near mint cond. $28.00

WWII ARMY 1ST ARMY COMPONENT PATCH: Fully embr. w/golden yellow insert. Exc. cond. $50.00

WWII ARMY 1ST ARMY COMPONENT PATCH: Fully embr. w/green & yellow insert. Near mint cond. $16.00

WWII ARMY 1ST ARMY COMPONENT PATCH: Fully embr. w/lt. blue insert. Near mint cond. $11.00

WWII ARMY 1ST ARMY SHOULDER PATCH: Black & red felt on OD gabardine. Off uniform. Near mint cond. $55.00

WWII ARMY 1ST FILIPINO BN. PATCH: fully embr. patch with OD border. 3" dia. Mint cond. $12.00

WWII ARMY 1ST SPEC SERV. FORCES PATCH: Red Indian arrowhead w/white trim & USA across tip + Canada down the center. Avg. cond. $34.00

WWII ARMY 1ST SPECIAL SERVICE FORCE PATCH: Fully embr. Near mint cond. $28.00

WWII ARMY 1ST SPECIAL SERVICE FORCE PATCH: Red arrow shoulder patch w/USA horiz. Across tip & Canada vert. down center. Exc. cond. $37.00

WWII ARMY 1ST SPECIAL SERVICE FORCE SHOULDER PATCH: Red bevo style embr. arrow head w/USA in white across tip & Canada vertically below. Near mint cond. $185.00

WWII ARMY 1ST SPECIAL SERVICE FORCE SHOULDER PATCH

WWII ARMY 1ST SPECIAL SERVICES FORCES PATCH: Gold bullion trimmed & lettered arrowhead of red wool. Avg. cond. $229.00

WWII ARMY 1ST SPECIAL SERVICES FORCES PATCH

WWII ARMY 21ST CORPS PATCH: Variant. 2.5" square. Embr. on blue cotton. Off uniform. Avg. cond. $28.00

WWII ARMY 25TH DIV. PATCH: Theater made. 2 1/8x3" tan felt base w/red felt applique & heavy gold bullion design. White satin backed. Off uniform. Above avg. cond. $25.00

WWII ARMY 26TH DIV. PATCH: Variant. 3.5" wide medium-shade olive green twill base w/blue mach. embr. design. Exc. cond. $28.00

WWII ARMY 28TH BASE HOSPITAL ICELAND PATCH: 55x73mm shield-shaped dark blue felt base w/red felt applique main applique panel w/gold bullion trim. Has applique & bullion trimmed design of island in corner w/ bullion "41" inside this design & bullion "28" to its side. Avg. cond. $90.00

WWII ARMY 28TH DIV. PATCH: OD border. Fully embr. Exc. cond. $12.00

WWII ARMY 2ND AIRBORNE INF BDE.WITH TAB: fully embr. patch design with attached tab in gold on black. Shows some age and use soiling, evidence of prior display from slight staple mark. 2" wide. Exc. cond. $28.00

WWII ARMY 2ND CHEMICAL MORTAR PATCH: Italian made. Cord stitched design on silk base. Approx. 42x51mm size. Above avg. cond. $150.00

WWII ARMY 2ND DIV. PATCH: Fully embr. OD border. Off uniform but good. Avg. cond. $35.00

WWII ARMY 2ND DIV. PATCH: Variant. 1 7/8x2 1/4" black felt base w/silk embr. Indian head over 5-point star. Off uniform w/some light soiling but good. Avg. cond. $25.00

WWII ARMY 2ND DIV. PATCH: Variant. Standard size but w/mach. embr. design on black felt. Some age. Avg. cond. $24.00

WWII ARMY 30TH DIV. PATCH: English made. 1.5x2.25" Fully silk mach. embr. Near mint cond. $20.00

WWII ARMY 30TH DIV. PATCH: Theater made. 1 3/4x2 3/8" dark red felt base w/ cord stitched w/thin bullion border design. Above avg. cond. $20.00

WWII ARMY 30TH DIV. PATCH: Theater made. 2.25x1.5" size. Fully mach. embr. Near mint cond. $30.00

WWII ARMY 317TH ENG REGT. POCKET PATCH: Red & white 4" shield w/motto in banner at bottom. Exc. cond. $26.00

WWII ARMY 31ST DIV. PATCH: Theater made. 2 3/8" dia. white felt base w/cord stitched design. Exc. cond. $20.00

WWII ARMY 325TH INF PATCH: 4" narrow shield & embr. Has eagle standing in front of parachute. Motto 'Lets Go,' at bottom is "1st ABN BAT GP." Above avg. cond. $20.00

WWII ARMY 327TH INF AIRBORNE RECON: Unusual patch -embr. on blue cloth & shows angry bird dressed in GI helmet, rifle & shirt but Samurai sword, Jap wide leg trousers & jungle clogs. Above avg. cond. $125.00

WWII ARMY 34TH DIV. PATCH: Fully embr. w/pale OD border + black thread back. Above avg. cond. $12.00

WWII ARMY 368TH F. A. CLOTH DI: 1 3/8x 1 3/4" fully embr. crest design. Above avg. cond. $20.00

WWII ARMY 36TH DIV. PATCH: Italian made. 36th Division Fully embr. w/tan colored T in center. Above avg. cond. $39.00

WWII ARMY 36TH DIV. PATCH: Theater made. 1.75x2.5" size. Fully mach. embr. w/dark blue background. Exc. cond. $35.50

WWII ARMY 36TH DIV. PATCH: Theater made. 2x2.75" OD wool serge base w/ quilted design w/bullion border. Above avg. cond. $38.00

WWII ARMY 38TH AIR DEPOT GRP. PATCH: 3.5" wide design is felt panel & cord stitch const. on black wool backing. Above avg. cond. $76.00

WWII ARMY 3RD ACR PATCH: 2.75" dia. w/ heavy bullion design on blue cloth base. Above avg. cond. $12.00

WWII ARMY 3RD RANGER BN. SCROLL: 3.75" wide. Embr. on felt. Off uniform. Avg. cond. $20.00

WWII ARMY 41ST DIV. PATCH: 2.75" wide. Multi-piece felt & heavy gold bullion constr. Above avg. cond. $25.00

WWII ARMY 43RD DIV. PATCH: Variant. 3x2.25" wide fully embr. Based on standard design w/OD border-has lt. blue embr. "43" in center. Exc. cond. $20.00

WWII ARMY 442ND RCT PATCH (2ND DESIGN): Fully embr. Above avg. cond. $20.00

WWII ARMY 442ND RCT PATCH(1 D DESIGN): 2.5" dia. Fully embr. Near mint cond. $34.00

WWII ARMY 442ND RCT PATCH 1ST TYPE: fully embr. patch design, 2.5" diam., appears unissued with some remains of glue and paper to the back. Near mint cond. $29.00

WWII ARMY 442ND RCT PATCH: 2.5" dia. Fully embr. Near mint cond. $36.00

WWII ARMY 442ND RCT PATCH: 2.5" dia. Fully embr. Near mint cond. $45.00

WWII ARMY 44TH DIV. PATCH: OD border. Fully embr. Above avg. cond. $11.00

WWII ARMY 44TH DIV. PATCH: Std. issue fully embr. patch w/orange center covered in heavy bullion. Some even tarnish. Above avg. cond. $25.00

WWII ARMY 45TH DIV. PATCH: Variant. 2.25" square of pink wool w/coarse weave & hand embr. gold thunderbird w/gold border. Piece of work. Exc. cond. $40.00

WWII ARMY 45TH DIV. PATCH: 55x55mm red felt base w/heavy gold bullion embr. Thunderbird design. Above avg. cond. $72.00

WWII ARMY 45TH DIV. PATCH: OD border. 3.75" wide. Fully embr. on dark OD cotton base w/OD border. Near mint cond. $40.00

WWII ARMY 45TH DIVISION PATCH: 60x60mm red felt base w/thunderbird design woven in fine gold wire. European made. Above avg. cond. $68.00

WWII ARMY 474TH AAA BN. SHOULDER PATCH: Foreign made. Fully embr. in red yellow & green. Incl. document in support of piece. Above avg. cond. $244.00

WWII ARMY 475TH INFANTRY PATCH: Full embr. w/star upper left & sun lower right split by red lightning. Clean patch. Exc. cond. $150.00

WWII ARMY 49TH AAA BDE. PATCH: Fully embr. Approx. 2.75x3.25". Near mint cond. $25.00

WWII ARMY 49TH AAA BDE. PATCH: Fully embr. Near mint cond. $23.00

WWII ARMY 49TH AAA BDE. PATCH: Mach. silk embr. on lt. blue felt base. Near mint cond. $12.00

WWII ARMY 501ST PARACHUTE OVAL: soiled red cotton w/thick embr. light blue border. Avg. cond. $32.00

WWII ARMY 502ND AIRBORNE INF REGT. JACKET PATCH: Features winged death's head on shrouds against black field. Blue white & red rings form rim. Avg. cond. $150.00

WWII ARMY 502ND AIRBORNE INF REGT. JACKET PATCH

WWII ARMY 502ND AIRBORNE INFANTRY POCKET PATCH: 3.75" dia. Mach. embr. design on black twill. Exc. cond. $200.00

WWII ARMY 503RD AIRBORNE INF REGT. PATCH.: Fully embr. shows chute above eagles wings & eagle carrying the rock. Above avg. cond. $20.00

WWII ARMY 504TH AIRBORNE PATCH: Bib scarf size mint. Exc. cond. $14.00

WWII ARMY 505TH PARACHUTE INF REGT. OVAL: English made. 2" wide black felt base w/silk embr. white border. Slight nip to side but . Above avg. cond. $35.00

WWII ARMY 505TH PARACHUTE INF REGT. PARA OVAL: English made. 2" wide black felt base w/mach. embr. white border. Exc. cond. $45.00

WWII ARMY 506TH AIRBORNE INF BDE.PATCH: Nicely embr. w/gold eagle in

center & dice on either side to ID unit. Above avg. cond. $171.00

WWII ARMY 506TH AIRBORNE INF BDE.PATCH

WWII ARMY 507TH AIRBORNE INF REGT. BERET FLASH: Well done British made embr. flash w/orange rim & black field. Near mint cond. $61.00

WWII ARMY 507TH AIRBORNE INF REGT. PATCH: 5" disc w/orange field & spider in harness carrying rifle & bomb in arms. Hourglass emblem on spider's stomach. Some use signs. Avg. cond.

.... $244.00

WWII ARMY 507TH AIRBORNE INF REGT. PATCH

WWII ARMY 508TH AIRBORNE INF REGT. PATCH: Shows red devil parachuting & carrying Tommy gun. Above avg. cond.

.... $23.00

WWII ARMY 508TH AIRBORNE INF REGT. PATCH: 2.75" dia. Embr. design of parachuting red devil on twill. Off uniform. Avg. cond. $20.00

WWII ARMY 509TH AIRBORNE INF PATCH: Fully embr. w/famous 509th emblem in center incl. 'GERONIMO' w/4 parachute troops coming down on each side + rim reads '509TH PARACHUTE INFANTRY BATTALION.' Avg. cond. $39.00

WWII ARMY 509TH AIRBORNE INF BERET BADGE: Gold bullion on black wool, has

509 at top over jump man & 'GERONIMO' Italian made. Above avg. cond. .. $251.00

WWII ARMY 509TH AIRBORNE INF BERET BADGE

WWII ARMY 5307TH COMPOSITE UNIT "MERRILL'S MARAUDERS" PATCH: Fully embr. Variant w/large lettering. Above avg. cond. $30.00

WWII ARMY 5307TH COMPOSITE UNIT PATCH: Fully embr. Variant w/small lettering. Near mint cond. $30.00

WWII ARMY 551ST AIRBORNE INF REGT. REUNION PATCH: 5x4" gold bullion & wire on black wool. Bullion forms large eagle w/embr. shield & banner on chest. Shows palm tree over crossed sword & lightoning i motto 'ATERRICE YATAQUE.' Minor darkening of bullion. Above avg. cond. $72.00

WWII ARMY 555TH PIR SHOULDER PATCH: Fully embr. + tab. Red background w/white glider & chute, tab reads 'AIRBORNE.' Exc. cond. $27.00

WWII ARMY 5TH ARMY PATCH: Italian made. Felt base w/bullion border. Has bullion design on applied blue satin panel. Off uniform. Avg. cond. $25.00

WWII ARMY 5TH DIV. PATCH: OD border. Fully embr. Near mint cond. $11.00

WWII ARMY 5TH DIV. PATCH: Variant. 2.25" wide. Fully embr. on tan twill w/thin white border. Above avg. cond. $23.00

WWII ARMY 60TH SERV. GRP. PATCH: mach. embr. design on OD wool. 3.75" wide. Exc. cond. $15.50

WWII ARMY 66TH DIV. PATCH: 2.75" dia. Fully embr. Near mint cond. $37.00

WWII ARMY 6TH "GHOST" AIRBORNE DIV. PATCH: Fully embr. w/OD border. Exc. cond. $22.00

WWII ARMY 6TH ARMOR DIV. PATCH: British made. Silk mach. embr. design on

3.75" wide OD wool base. Exc. cond. $20.00

WWII ARMY 6TH ARMY PATCH: Standard fully embr. patch on tan twill w/heavy silver bullion & stitched applied over original design. Exc. cond. $37.00

WWII ARMY 6TH ARMY PATCH: Standard fully embr. patch on tan twill w/heavy silver bullion & stitched applied over original design. Above avg. cond. $11.00

WWII ARMY 6TH CAV. GRP. PATCH: Theater made. Embr. on 2 7/8x3 1/2" blue felt base. Also, OD border 14th Armor Div. patch. Above avg. cond. $13.00

WWII ARMY 70TH DIV. PATCH: OD border. Fully embr. Exc. cond. $11.00

WWII ARMY 77TH DIVISION PATCH: cut & folded & has sewn on. Above avg. cond. $28.00

WWII ARMY 78TH DIV. PATCH: 3" wide red felt base w/silver bullion design & border. Theater made. Avg. cond. $20.00

WWII ARMY 799TH TANK BATL. PATCH: Embr. on herringbone twill. Above avg. cond. $28.00

WWII ARMY 7TH ARMY PATCH: Theater made. 4.25" wide. Bevo style weave + separate fully embr. "Seven Steps to Hell" tab. Exc. cond. $11.00

WWII ARMY 7TH CORPS PATCH: OD wool disc w/purple wool polygram & white embr. 7. Exc. cond. $20.00

WWII ARMY 82ND AIRBORNE SNIPER PATCH: Foreign made & embr. on red field, has 82nd A/B emblem in center w/ sniper rifle in front. 'SNIPER' is at top & '2/ 505 INF' at bottom. 2.5 x 2.5 sq. Above avg. cond. $177.00

WWII ARMY 82ND AIRBORNE SNIPER PATCH

WWII ARMY 82ND AIRBORNE PATCH: Airborne tab at top. On coarse twill cloth. Exc. cond. $21.00

WWII ARMY 82ND AIRBORNE SIGNAL BN. PATCH: orange background w/a parachuting telephone & 'THE COMMANDERS VOICE' at bottom. Above avg. cond. $20.00

WWII ARMY 83RD DIV. PATCH: 3" triangle w/black background, orange emblem & OD border. W/original paper tag. Mint cond. $72.00

WWII ARMY 85TH INF REGT. PATCH: Shows age but is excellent embr. Used, slight soiling. Avg. cond. $36.50

WWII ARMY 88TH DIV. PATCH: Theater made. 2 3/8" wide blue felt base w/gold bullion border. Above avg. cond. .. $37.00

WWII ARMY 8TH DIV. PATCH: Theater made. Mach. embr. "wavy" design on OD wool base. Above avg. cond. $15.00

WWII ARMY 91ST CHEMICAL MORTAR BN.. TAB: 4.25" wide. Fully embr. Yellow lettering & border on blue background. Above avg. cond. $40.00

WWII ARMY 94TH DIV. PATCH: Theater made. 3" dia. Mach. silk embr. on gray felt. Black cotton backed. Near mint cond. $40.00

WWII ARMY 99TH DIV. PATCH: Theater made. 2.75x3" OD wool base w/multi-piece felt applique & cord stitched design. Above avg. cond. $66.00

WWII ARMY 9TH ENG COMMAND PATCH: Gold bullion on blue wool shield. Feathers AAF winged star framing red disc w/three runways in gold bullion + 'IX' above. Quality job good color and preservation. Exc. cond. $50.00

WWII ARMY 9TH ENG COMMAND PATCH

WWII ARMY 9TH ENG. CMD. PATCH: Fully embr. Exc. cond. $20.00

WWII ARMY 9TH SERV. CMD. PATCH: 2.25" dia. embr. on dark tan twill. Above avg. cond. $37.00

WWII ARMY AIRBORNE CAP INSIGNIA: Italian made. 1.75" dia. Heavy bullion chute design & border on faded lt. blue satin. Avg. cond. $37.00

WWII ARMY AIRBORNE COMMAND PATCH: Fully embr. incl. airborne tab at top. Used. Avg. cond. $20.00

WWII ARMY AIRBORNE GLIDER CAP DEVICE: Cloth patch-embr. glider on blue field- for overseas cap. Above avg. cond. $11.00

WWII ARMY AIRBORNE PATHFINDER PATCH: embr. w/yellow torch & wing + red flames. Exc. cond. $227.00

WWII ARMY AIRBORNE PATHFINDER PATCH

WWII ARMY AIRBORNE TRAINING CENTER SICILY PATCH: 4" dia. red felt base w/mach. silk embr. design. Small nip to one edge but very example. Exc. cond. $155.00

WWII ARMY AIRBORNE TROOP CARRIER PATCH: 2.75" wide w/mach. embr. design on blue felt. Off uniform. Above avg. cond. $20.00

WWII ARMY AIRBORNE TROOP CARRIER PATCH: Theater made. 2.5x3.25" dark blue felt base w/silk mach. embr. design. Off uniform-some age. Avg. cond. $25.00

WWII ARMY AIRBORNE TROOP CARRIER PATCH: Fully embr. Off uniform but clean. Above avg. cond. $22.00

WWII ARMY ALASKAN DEF. CMD. PATCH: 2.5" dia. Fully embr. w/OD border. Near mint cond. $30.00

WWII ARMY ALASKAN DEF. CMD. PATCH: Mach. embr. design on white felt. Early style w/seal design & "ADC" above. Near mint cond. $32.00

WWII ARMY ALASKAN DEF. CMD. PATCH: Old design embr. on white twill w/black

border. 2.75" dia. Exc. cond.
.... $35.00

WWII ARMY ALASKAN DEFENSE COMMAND PATCH: Orange background w/embr. polar bear under big dipper & 'ALASKA.' This is one that doesn't show up often. Near mint cond. $150.00

WWII ARMY ALASKAN DEFENSE
COMMAND PATCH

WWII ARMY ALASKAN DEF. CMD. PATCH: 2.25" dia. Fully embr. w/OD border. Near mint cond. $20.00

WWII ARMY ALEUTIAN ISLANDS CMD. PATCH: 3" dia. w/mach. embr. design on blue twill. Exc. cond. $30.00

WWII ARMY ALLIED AIRBORNE PATCH: shield fully embr. w/enclosed tab. Full color but light soiling. Avg. cond. .. $20.00

WWII ARMY ALLIED FORCES H.Q. PATCH: Theater made. 2.5" dia. w/cord stitched design on blue felt. Above avg. cond.
.... $22.00

WWII ARMY ALLIED FORCES H.Q. PATCH: Theater made. 2.5" w/hand embr. design. Some nips but interesting variant. Avg. cond. $20.00

WWII ARMY ANTI-AIRCRAFT UNIT PATCH: full color target ring w/yellow center & black aircraft being shot down. Avg. cond.
.... $28.00

WWII ARMY ARMOR FORCES "714" PATCH: Fully embr. w/OD border. Exc. cond. $14.00

WWII ARMY ARMOR FORCES PATCH W/ ATTACHED "112TH ARMORED CAVALRY" TAB: Patch w/OD border. Fully embr. on tan twill. Mint cond. $45.00

WWII ARMY ARMORED PATCH: Bullion on black wool w/crossed swords & 'A' above cross + motto in banner below, 'BOUTES EN AVANT.' Some color fade on gold bullion. Avg. cond. $17.00

WWII ARMY COMM PATCH: 3" w/gold sun in center w/headset riding lightning bolt. There is a transmit tower at one end & lines at bottom. near mint. Exc. cond.
.... $20.00

WWII ARMY D-DAY ARMBAND: Reflective material for US flag on armband. Intended to improve night ID. Incl. printed Survival chit for airmen (Not the flagged blood chit.). Above avg. cond. $90.00

WWII ARMY D-DAY PATCH DISPLAY: 18x22" oak frame has OD wool background & contains 28 different Army sleeve patches for units active on the D-day operation. Brass army blouse button on strip of WWII Victory ribbon in each corner. display. All patches are WWII designs but 5 are post-war origin. looking display. Above avg. cond. $210.00

WWII ARMY ENGINEER PATCH: Engineer special brigade patch w/no blue, only red & white images. Above avg. cond.
.... $40.00

WWII ARMY ENGINEERING INTELLIGENCE PATCH: fully embr. patch design, 2.5" wide oval. Unissued cond. Mint cond. $28.00

WWII ARMY ETO ADV BASE SLEEVE PATCH: Padded cloth & bullion trim + embroidery. Some fading of colors. Above avg. cond. $22.00

WWII ARMY ETO ADV. BASE PATCH: English made. 2.25" wide dark blue felt base w/cord stitched design. Avg. cond.
.... $16.00

WWII ARMY ETO ADV. BASE PATCH: Printed on canvas. Theater made. 2 3/8x3 1/4". Exc. cond. $20.00

WWII ARMY ETO ADV. BASE PATCH: Theater made. 2 3/8x3 1/4" blue felt base w/bullion & cord stitched design. Above avg. cond. $20.00

WWII ARMY ETO ADV. BASE PATCH: Theater made. 2.25x3.25" size medium blue cotton oval base w/applique cotton panel & cord stitched design. Exc. cond.
.... $20.00

WWII ARMY ETO ADVANCED BASE PATCH W/SEPARATE OISE TAB: Theater made. Both fully mach. embr. Off uniform but clean. Above avg. cond. $20.00

WWII ARMY EUROPEAN CIVIL AFFAIRS PATCH: Theater made. 2.25x3" fully mach. embr. Off uniform but good. Above avg. cond. $10.00

WWII ARMY FIRST FILIPINO BN. PATCH & MORE: Fully embr. Also, theater made bullion on felt 7th Div. patch + Jungle Expert patch. Exc. cond. $24.00

WWII ARMY FORCES FAR EAST PATCH: 50mm dia. disk w/red embr. & silver wire trim. Shows silk mountain w/silver wire

snow & embr. blue sky. Avg. cond.
....$20.00

WWII ARMY FORCES PACIFIC PATCH: Nicely done on blue velour w/silver bullion & heavy red thread. Slight signs of aging. Above avg. cond. $45.00

WWII ARMY FORCES WESTERN PACIFIC PATCH: Theater made. Approx. 2 3/8" dia. Silver bullion base w/red cord stitched border, blue bullion stars & gold bullion lightning bolt. On red felt base. Avg. cond. $45.00

WWII ARMY HEADQUARTERS ALLIED FORCES SOUTHEAST EUROPE PATCH: 2.5" wide. Shield-shaped. Fully embr. bevo style weave. Near mint cond. $58.00

WWII ARMY HONOR GUARD SCROLL: 3.75" wide w/hand embr. lettering & border on blue satin on tan cotton base. Exc. cond. $30.00

WWII ARMY HOSTESSES PATCH: Fully embr. Near mint cond. $20.00

WWII ARMY HUNGARIAN OCCUPATION FORCES PATCH: 2 7/8" wide. Fully embr. Exc. cond. $20.00

WWII ARMY INVASION ARMBAND: White oilcloth body w/printed U.S. flag design. Safety pin adj. back (pins still intact). Unissued cond. Near mint cond. .. $61.00

WWII ARMY JACKET PATCH UNITED STATES AIR-CORPS: 2.75" dia. Fully embr. on white felt base w/"wavy" cut border. Exc. cond. $20.00

WWII ARMY JACKET PATCH UNITED STATES PARATROOPS: 3.75" dia. White embr. chute design & lettering on lt. blue felt. Exc. cond. $20.00

WWII ARMY KISKA TASK FORCE PATCH LOT: 3 examples-machine embr. in silver gray shade-2 show age from wear. Lot includes 2 PFC chevrons-gray on black. Above avg. cond. $33.00

WWII ARMY LEDO ROAD PATCH: CBI made. 3" wide. Fully mach. embr. off uniform some soiling. Avg. cond. .. $40.00

WWII ARMY LEDO ROAD PATCH: Fully embr. Near mint cond. $14.00

WWII ARMY LEDO ROAD PATCH: 6 part construction in leather. Good details. Exc. cond. $52.00

WWII ARMY LEDO ROAD PATCH: Theater made. 2 3/4x3 1/8" fully embr. Exc. cond. $40.00

WWII ARMY LEDO ROAD PATCH: Theater made. 67x80mm size. Fully mach. embr. CBI-made. Exc. cond. $60.00

WWII ARMY LEDO ROAD PATCH: Used patch, intact, fully embr. & showing some fading. Avg. cond. $40.00

WWII ARMY LEDO ROAD PATCH: Multi piece leather patch, 2.75" wide. Some light wear. Near mint cond. $44.00

WWII ARMY MAAF PATCH: Theater made. 3.5x2 dark blue felt base w/silk mach. embr. design. Couple nips. Above avg. cond. $30.00

WWII ARMY MAAG CHINA PATCH: CBI style embr. w/China kumontang sun & 'MAAG' white on red all over stripes. Above avg. cond. $20.00

WWII ARMY MEDICAL UNIT SHOULDER PATCH: Shield w/tricolor field & gold embr. Fleur de Leis over banner 'AID TO THE WOUNDED.' Exc. cond. $40.00

WWII ARMY MISSION TO IRAN PATCH: 2 1/8x2 3/4" size. Heavy gold bullion design on black wool base. Above avg. cond. $32.00

WWII ARMY MISSION TO IRAN SHOULDER PATCH: Black vert. oval w/ white embr. showing Crown over lion w/ raised sword. Above avg. cond. ... $55.00

WWII ARMY MISSION TO IRAN SLEEVE PATCH: Black wool w/gold bullion outlining design & forming design. Four snaps on back to mount to shoulder. Above avg. cond. $40.00

WWII ARMY MISSION TO MOSCOW PATCH: Fully embr. Avg. cond. $28.00

WWII ARMY MISSION TO MOSCOW PATCH: Well done. Full embr. triangular patch w/Russian spelling of America at top. Very clean. U.S. machine made. Exc. cond. $20.00

WWII ARMY MISSION TO SAUDI ARABIA PATCH: 2 3/8" dia. embr. on green twill. example. Mint cond. $70.00

WWII ARMY OF OCCUPATION AVIATOR PATCH: R/W/B 3" disc w/small R/W/B disc & white A in center. Felt multi piece. Exc. cond. $26.00

WWII ARMY OFFICER 1ST LT. BULLION INSIGNIA: Two pair embr. on OD winter gabardine. Exc. cond. $25.00

WWII ARMY OFFICER MAJOR FULL DRESS SHOULDER BOARDS: Boxed by Vangard & cellophane sealed inside. Color coded for field arty. Near mint cond. $20.00

WWII ARMY PANAMA HELLGATE PATCH: Silk mach. embr. design on dark red felt base. Exc. cond. $11.00

WWII ARMY PERSIAN GULF CMD. PATCH: Theater made. 2 1/2x2 7/8" dark green felt base w/mach. & cord stitched design. variant. Above avg. cond. $25.00

WWII ARMY PHILIPPINE GENDARMES PATCH: Elongated oval with Knights head at top & ornate battle ax in center. Above avg. cond. $20.00

WWII ARMY PHILIPPINE GENERAL STAFF PATCH: 2.75x3.5" w/fully embr. design on lt. OD twill. Mint cond. $20.00

WWII ARMY PHILIPPINE GENERAL STAFF PATCH: Fully embr. on OD twill w/OD border. Exc. cond. $15.00

WWII ARMY PHOTOGRAPHER PATCH: 4x1 3/8" black felt base w/hand embr. lettering & border in thick orange thread. Near mint cond. $76.00

WWII ARMY RANGER TAB: White embr. on black wool. 7th RANGER Bn. w/red border. Above avg. cond. $20.00

WWII ARMY SERVICE FORCES PATCH: padded & embr. w/silver wire & red/blue thread. Four snaps on back for attaching to blouse sleeve. Silver darkening. Above avg. cond. $20.00

WWII ARMY SHAEF PATCH: bullion and heavy cord embr. patch on blue twill with paper backing. Shows some soiling and wear and has been removed from uniform. 2.75" wide. Avg. cond. $13.00

WWII ARMY SIGNAL UNIT PATCH: Embr. on blue cloth, Signal corps emblem w/ 123rd Sig. Bn. bracketing. Above avg. cond. $23.00

WWII ARMY SOUTH EAST ASIA CMD. PATCH: color design printed on 2.5" dia. dark blue canvas base. Eagle head faces to rt. Exc. cond. $20.00

WWII ARMY SPECIAL RECON CLOTH TAB: Black wool w/embr. red letters & trim. Reads 'SPECIAL RECON. BN..' Above avg. cond. $110.00

WWII ARMY TANK BATTALION PATCH: 4" embr. shield for 62nd tank Bn. Exc. cond. $40.00

WWII ARMY TANK DESTROYER PATCH: 8 cog tank design. embr. design on chiffon-like material, gauze backed. 2.75" dia. Exc. cond. $40.00

WWII ARMY TANKER DIAMOND-SHAPED SLEEVE PATCH: 4" wide. Fully embr. Near mint cond. $25.00

WWII ARMY TRANSPORT CORP RED BALL EXPRESS PATCH: 2x2.25" mustard yellow cotton base w/mach. embr. design. Clean. Exc. cond. $38.00

WWII ARMY TRANSPORT CORP RED BALL EXPRESS PATCH: 2x2.25" yellow cotton base w/mach. embr. design. Some soiling & age. Avg. cond. $45.00

WWII ARMY TRIESTE FORCES PATCH W/ TAB: Fully embr. patch on blue cotton backing. Includes theater-made "Trust" tab hand embr. on felt. Off uniform. Above avg. cond. $25.00

WWII ARMY TROOP CARRIER COMMAND PATCH: Well embr. in gold on blue-shows eagle carrying soldier. Near mint cond. $32.00

WWII ARMY TROOP CARRIER COMMAND PATCH: 4.5" black w/gold embr. Used & slightly soiled. Above avg. cond. .. $37.00

WWII ARMY UNIT PATCH: Fragrant Legion 5, featuring skunk sitting up holding sign w/title & 5 in wreath. Nicely done. Above avg. cond. 20.00

WWII ARMY UNIT PATCH: yellow cotton w/ Green dragon on tracked undercarriage in center. Reads 'RECON PLATOON.' Above avg. cond. $40.00

WWII ARMY US FORCES IN WESTERN PACIFIC PATCH: Two piece construction w/bullion trim. Theater made. Avg. cond. $20.00

WWII ARMY V ARMOR CORPS PATCH: Armor triangle shaped patch is fully embr. w/OD border. Exc. cond. $48.00

WWII ATC FLIGHT JACKET PATCH: 4.75" dia. brown leather disc w/applied decal patch design. Avg. cond. $45.00

WWII ATC PATCH: Flight jacket size w/decal patch-design applied to 5" brown leather disc. Avg. cond. $38.00

WWII BATTY GENERAL HOSPITAL PATCH: 2 7/8x3 7/8" maroon cotton body w/mach. embr. white lettering & border. Exc. cond. $40.00

WWII CALIF. STATE MILITIA PATCH: 4 1/8" wide. Yellow embr. on thick black felt base. Above avg. cond. $34.00

WWII CBI BLOOD CHIT FIRST TYPE: Chinese flag at top + Chinese characters below. Kumontang stamp visible on front & back. Series #404 stamped on lower left. Sewn to cloth, may have been removed from uniform. Worn but presentable. Avg. cond. $387.00

WWII CBI BLOOD CHIT: 7x9.5" hand embr. silk on white silk panel w/Chinese flag cross stitched above several black embr. characters. Near mint cond. 121.00

WWII CBI BLOOD CHIT: 8x10" color printed on white silk w/Burma peacock flag over several rows of Burmese characters. White muslin backing. Rare. Near mint cond. $379.00

WWII CBI BLOOD CHIT: 8x10" printed rayon chit w/Chinese flag over several rows of characters. Serial numbered w/large red chop mark. Avg. cond. $150.00

WWII CBI BLOOD CHIT: 9.5" sq. leather 16 piece construction w/US & china Flag + CBI emblem & Chinese characters. Some small stains on leather. Above avg. cond. $195.00

WWII CBI BLOOD CHIT: All leather construction, multi piece using 16 pieces. Has US, Chinese flags & CBI emblem + Chinese characters. Taken from jacket, two minor tears on side. Above avg. cond. $282.00

WWII CBI BLOOD CHIT

WWII CBI BLOOD CHIT: 9x11" with US & Chinese flags in 12 piece construction across top & several black ink Chinese characters below. Avg. cond. $165.00

WWII CBI BLOOD CHIT: 9x9" white silk body backed in off-white muslin. Color printed w/US flag across the top-small blue serial number stamped below w/5 language plea below-none of them in English. Avg. cond. $100.00

WWII CBI BLOOD CHIT: CBI made. Blood chit w/o languages. US flag on silk - 10x6" on 13.5x8" silk panel backed by coarse cloth. Avg. cond. $120.00

WWII CBI BLOOD CHIT: Has Chinese flag at top & Chinese characters below + Kumontang stamp at bottom. Silk 10x8.5" one side. Exc. cond. $150.00

WWII CBI BLOOD CHIT: Serial #91194, w/ US flag at top & 7 languages shown below. On rayon w/some discoloration on edges. Avg. cond. $79.00

WWII CBI BLOOD CHIT: Unusual cardboard blood chit for Chinese pilots. Red & blue Chinese flag w/Kumontang sun + Chinese characters at bottom. Some damage along edges. Avg. cond. $145.00

WWII CBI CHINA HQ PATCH: fully embr. patch is 2.75" wide. Mint cond. $49.00

WWII CBI CHINESE AVIATION TRAINING PATCH "ARIZONA": 3" orange felt disc w/ winged china rising sun embr. in center. Near mint cond. $55.00

WWII CBI CHINESE COMBAT COMMAND SLEEVE PATCH: 1 pc. white cotton body w/color printed design-OD cotton backed. Exc. cond. $129.00

WWII CBI CHINESE COMBAT COMMAND SLEEVE PATCH: CBI made. 60x85mm color printed on cotton w/thin OD cotton backing. Exc. cond. $50.00

WWII CBI CHINESE COMBAT COMMAND SLEEVE PATCH

WWII CBI CHINESE COMBAT TRAINING COMMAND PATCH.: Shield w/hand embr. on twill & silk. slight color fade. Above avg. cond. 38.00

WWII CBI GHQ SLEEVE PATCH: theater made embr. w/blue velvet field & white chain stitch & backs w/tan cloth. Off uniform. Avg. cond. $136.00

WWII CBI PATCH: 4 piece construction w/ hand sewn sunburst & star. Snaps installed on back. Above avg. cond. $40.00

WWII CBI PATCH: 7 piece leather construction w/crudely cut out star & sun. Brown leather trim. Avg. cond. $59.00

WWII CBI PATCH: 7x9" shield design in 7 pc. leather construction. Has soiled spot in center but has never been sewn to anything. Above avg. cond. $82.00

WWII CBI PATCH: CBI made. 2 1/4x3 1/8" size. Multi-piece red/white cotton & wool field constr. w/hand embr. suns. Tan cloth backed & some glue remains on back. Avg. cond. $24.00

WWII CBI PATCH: CBI made. 2 1/8x2 3/4" size. Thick cord hand embr. in "wavy" pattern. Off uniform but good. Above avg. cond. $20.00

WWII CBI PATCH: CBI made. 2.5x3.5" dark blue wool base w/heavy silver bullion suns + cord & wire stitched stripe field. shape w/little tarnish. Above avg. cond. .. $25.00

WWII CBI PATCH: CBI made. 2.5x3.5". Bullion suns on blue wool w/cord stitched bullion stripe field. Cotton backed. Above avg. cond. $28.00

WWII CBI PATCH: CBI made. 2.75x3.5". Heavy silver bullion suns on blue satin + heavy wire & cord woven stripe field. On trimmed tan cotton base. CBI made. Above avg. cond. $20.00

WWII CBI PATCH: CBI made. 2x2.75". Bullion suns on dark blue velvet w/cord stitched & bullion stripe field. Black cotton backed. Some light tarnish. Above avg. cond. $24.00

WWII CBI PATCH: CBI made. Approx. 2 3/8x3 3/8" w/cord stitched suns on blue wool + ribbed one-piece stripe field. Tan cotton backed. Off uniform. Avg. cond. $30.00

WWII CBI PATCH: Hand embr. 70x80mm blue wool base w/silver bullion stripes & design-sequin border. Near mint cond. $30.00

WWII CBI PATCH: Silver bullion w/silver wire 5 piece construction. Avg. cond. ... $28.00

WWII CBI PATCH: Small size. Theater made. 33x40mm blue velveteen base w/ bullion suns + cord & wire stitched stripe field. Above avg. cond. $28.00

WWII CBI PATCH: Theater made. 2 1/2x 3 1/8" design w/bullion suns + cord & wire stitched stripe field on uncut dark blue wool base. CBI made. Above avg. cond. $20.00

WWII CBI PATCH: Two piece cloth construction, faded. Avg. cond. $22.00

WWII CBI SHOULDER PATCH: Blue field w/ white sun & white star. Red & white stripes below. Shield shaped. Above avg. cond. $20.00

WWII CBI SLEEVE PATCH: Embr. stripes & blue velvet w/chain stitch wording & tan cloth lined. Avg. cond. $131.00

WWII CBI SLEEVE PATCH

WWII CHINESE AVIATION CADET TNG. (INSTRUCTOR) PATCH: 3" dia. embr. on dark tan twill. Light glue remains on back from display. Exc. cond. $22.00

WWII CIVILIAN MIL GOV. OFFICER COLLAR TABS: Pair. Slip-on green felt bodies w/lt. OD cotton loops on back. Have yellow embr. borders & lettering. Exc. cond. $50.00

WWII D-DAY INVASION ARMBAND: Printed U.S. flag design in color on white oilcloth base. Adj. holes at ends. Above avg. cond. $75.00

WWII FLYING TIGER SQUADRON PATCH ON LEATHER: Embr. on brown wool & attached to leather jacket. This portion preserved. Shows tiger jumping thru Chinese star hoop/wearing Uncle Sam top hat & ripping Japanese flag. Avg. cond. $315.00

WWII JAPAN MILITARY TRIALS STAFF PATCH: 68x80mm size. Fully mach. embr. Exc. cond. $381.00

WWII KEEP EM FLYING PATCH: Black wool w/red lettering & silver airplane in center. Avg. cond. $61.00

WWII MAAF POCKET PATCH: Silver bullion wings in center w/gold bullion trim. Below wing is 'MAAF.' Avg. cond. $20.00

WWII MAINE STATE GUARD PATCH: Embr. on felt. Off uniform but good. Above avg. cond. $20.00

WWII MEDIC ARMBAND: White cotton twill body w/red cotton red cross applique. Marked w/maker proof. Light yellowing but unused. Above avg. cond. $23.00

WWII NORMANDY INVASION ARMBAND: Red band w/'SLT' for 'SHORE LANDING TRAFFIC' used by Beach forces directing equipment landing & loading. Above avg. cond. $55.00

WWII NORMANDY INVASION ARMBAND: Red band w/'SLT' for 'SHORE LANDING TRAFFIC.' Used by Beach forces directing equipment landing & loading. Above avg. cond. $72.00

WWII OSS SLEEVE PATCH: English made example of yellow-gold cord stitched design on 2.5x3.5 oval black wool disc. A very rare patch to find an original example of. Avg. cond. $145.00

WWII PACIFIC COMMAND BLAZER PATCH: Approx. 3 1/8x3 1/2" bullion & embr. on satin panel constr. on pocket-shape dark blue felt base. Backed in blue cotton w/several male snap end attachments. Above avg. cond. $20.00

WWII RED CROSS ARMBAND: white cloth w/sew-on red cross & not sewn together in back. Near mint cond. $24.00

WWII TENNESSEE STATE GUARD PATCH: 3" dia. Embr. on dark red cotton. Avg. cond. $20.00

CLOTH INSIGNIA

WWII TEXAS DEFENSE GUARD PATCH: 3.5" dia. Embr. on twill. Some yellowing. Avg. cond. $25.00

WWII TEXAS DEFENSE GUARD PATCH: Approx. 3.25" dia. embr. on white twill. Avg. cond. $40.00

WWII TEXAS NAT GUARD PATCH: Blue embr. shield w/single white star & red T. Avg. cond. $23.00

WWII U.S. MISSION TO IRAN PATCH: 2.25x3" black wool base w/heavy bullion design. Has 4 female snap-end attachments on back-original. Above avg. cond. $45.00

WWII US FLAG SHOULDER PATCH: Hand embr. possible English made. Above avg. cond. $34.00

C. 1946 - PRESENT

ARMY 101ST AIRBORNE DIV. PATCH: Bevo style embr. w/red tongued eagle & airborne tab at top. Near mint cond. $37.00

ARMY 127TH AIRBORNE ENGR. BN. POCKET PATCH: 3" dia. Fully embr. Mint cond. $65.00

ARMY 127TH ENGR. BN. POCKET PATCH: 3" dia. Fully embr. w/cut-edge. Mint cond. $135.00

ARMY 13TH INF REGT. "FIRST AT VICKSBURG" POCKET PATCH: Fully embr. on dark olive twill. Near mint cond. $15.00

ARMY 141ST F. A. BN. PATCH: 3 1/8x4 7/8" dark red felt base w/mach. silk embr. design. Near mint cond. $50.00

ARMY 141ST F. A. BN. POCKET PATCH: 3x4.75" mach. embr. on red felt. Some spots of glue remains on back from display but front very . Exc. cond. . $28.00

ARMY 15TH CAV. REGT. POCKET PATCH: Variant. Fully embr. in bevo style weave w/ motto. Near mint cond. $20.00

ARMY 15TH CAVALRY REGT. POCKET PATCH: German made. 3x3.5" size. Fully embr. Mint cond. $20.00

ARMY 163RD R.C.T. PATCH: 2" wide. Fully embr. Non-merrowed edge. Near mint cond. $48.00

ARMY 16TH INFANTRY REGT. POCKET PATCH: German made. 3x3.5" flat bevo. Near mint cond. $15.00

ARMY 187TH AIRBORNE INF REGT. PATCH: 2 3/8" dia. German-made fully mach. embr. Design of skull & crossbones over 24th Div. patch design. Mint cond. $45.00

ARMY 187TH AIRBORNE INF REGT. POCKET PATCH: 3x3.75" fully embr. w/ gray background color. Above avg. cond. $20.00

ARMY 187TH R.C.T. PATCH: Fully embr. w/ cut-edge. White border variant. Exc. cond. $20.00

ARMY 188TH ABN INF 'WINGED ATTACK' POCKET PATCH: fully embr. patch with scroll at bottom. 3.75" wide. Mint cond. $46.00

ARMY 188TH AIRBORNE "WINGED ATTACK" POCKET PATCH: 3 3/4x3 7/8" size. Fully embr. w/non-merrowed edge. Some glue/paper remains on back from display but front very clean. Exc. cond. $80.00

ARMY 1ST CAV. BLAZER PATCH: 2.75x4" w/woven gold wire shield + cord stitched horse head & border + black velveteen band. Cb. Texas maker marked on reverse. Near mint cond. $12.00

ARMY 1ST CAV. DIV. "AERIAL ARTILLERY" PATCH: 3 3/8x4 1/2" black cotton base w/ US embr. design of winged mythical character grasping lightning bolt over 1st Cav. patch design. Above avg. cond. $20.00

ARMY 1ST CAV. DIV. PATCH: Reverse design. Std. size. Fully embr. w/black border. Mint cond. $20.00

ARMY 24TH DIV. PATCH: Theater made. 2.25" dia. black felt base w/felt, green satin & bullion design. White cotton backed. Off uniform but good. Above avg. cond. $25.00

ARMY 25H DIV. PATCH: Theater made. 1 7/8x2 3/4" dark red felt base w/heavy bullion design. Above avg. cond. .. $25.00

ARMY 25TH DIV. PATCH: Theater made. 2.25x3" red felt base w/yellow stitched design & gold bullion borders. Exc. cond. $20.00

ARMY 2ND INF BDGE PATCH W/ ATTACHED AIRBORNE TAB: Fully embr. w/attached Airborne tab. Off uniform but clean. Exc. cond. $20.00

ARMY 2ND LOG CMD. PATCH 1ST TYPE: Fully mach. embr. Exc. cond. $60.00

ARMY 2ND LOGISTICAL COMMAND PATCH: 1st type. 55x85mm oval shaped design w/red "2" on map of Korea in center. Above avg. cond. $64.00

ARMY 2ND RANGER CO. CAMP FRANK D. MERRILL PATCH: 4" dia. Fully embr. w/Inf School & Ranger tab design. Mint cond. $10.00

ARMY 351ST RCT 'AX HEAD' STYLE PATCH: fully embr. patch design, 2" wide, shaped like ax head. Unissued. Mint cond. $40.00

ARMY 3RD ARTY PATCH: bullion batch German made 4" shield. Motto at bottom. some darkening of wire. Above avg. cond. $35.00

ARMY 3RD F. A. BN. POCKET PATCH: 2 5/8x4 1/4" fully mach. embr. w/cut-edge. Mint cond. $20.00

ARMY 40TH ARMOR CO. F BERLIN TANK CREW PATCH: 1950s/60s. embr. design on black twill, has been removed from a uniform but is in very cond. 3" wide. Near mint cond. $20.00

ARMY 40TH DIV. PATCH: Theater made. 2.25" square red felt base w/heavy gold bullion design. Above avg. cond. $40.00

ARMY 40TH DIV. PATCH: Theater made. 3.5" wide blue felt base w/heavy bullion sunburst design. Above avg. cond $38.00

ARMY 40TH DIV. PATCH: Theater made. Approx. 3.25" square uncut blue felt section w/heavy bullion sunburst design. Near mint cond. $32.00

ARMY 45TH DIV. PATCH: Theater made. 3.5" wide red felt base w/heavy bullion design. Above avg. cond. $81.00

ARMY 502ND AIRBORNE INFANTRY POCKET PATCH: 2.5" wide. Fully embr. on lt. blue cotton w/motto "Strike." Exc. cond. $25.00

ARMY 503RD AIRBORNE INF REGT. POCKET PATCH: 1950s. 2.25x3.75" size. Embr. on twill w/attached yellow-on-black Airborne tab. Above avg. cond. $20.00

ARMY 504TH AIRBORNE INF REGT. POCKET PATCH: 2x3" size. Fully embr. Exc. cond.. $20.00

ARMY 504TH AIRBORNE INF REGT. POCKET PATCH: Embr. design on yellow twill. Shield reads "504 Devils C." 2x3" size. Mint cond. $20.00

ARMY 504TH AIRBORNE INF REGT. POCKET PATCH: Fully embr. Reads "Airborne/504 Devils/E." Near mint cond. $14.00

ARMY 504TH PARACHUTE INF REGT. PATCH: 1950s. 4 1/8" dia. gray felt disc w/ mach. embr. design of red devil over chute. Paper/glue remains on reverse from display but front very clean. Exc. cond. $45.00

ARMY 505TH AIRBORNE INF REGT. POCKET PATCH: 2 5/8x3 7/8". Fully

embr. w/non-merrowed edge. Mint cond. $75.00

ARMY 505TH AIRBORNE INF REGT. POCKET PATCH: 2 5/8x4" w/embr. design on white twill. Some glue residue on reverse from display but frontal appearance is. Above avg. cond. $20.00

ARMY 508TH R.C.T. PATCH: Fully embr. w/ attached Airborne tab. Above avg. cond. $20.00

ARMY 5TH F. A. BN. POCKET PATCH: Fully embr. Above avg. cond. $14.00

ARMY 65TH RCT PATCH: 68x65mm Japanese machine made shield design in black w/white Maltese cross in center. No scrolls, etc.-plain shield. Near mint cond. $38.00

ARMY 716TH MILITARY POLICE BN.PATCH: Bevo weave. Uncut. Exc. cond. $36.00

ARMY 8TH ARMY PATCH: Theater made. 2 3/8" wide. Heavy silver bullion on red felt. Above avg. cond. $20.00

ARMY 8TH RECON CO. PATCH: 2.75" wide. Fully embr. w/cut-edge. Near mint cond. $49.00

ARMY 94TH HELICOPTER SQDN. PATCH: Rare 1950s patch for an early pioneer in Army aviation. Red field w/winged chopper & '94' above. Above avg. cond. $51.00

ARMY AVIATION PATCH: Partially embr. on blue cloth showing twin prop aircraft, sword w/eagle on guard & 'CAC.' Banner reads 'LONG TRIP.' Above avg. cond. $33.00

ARMY CARIBBEAN DEF. CMD. PATCH W/ ATTACHED 33RD INFANTRY TAB: Fully embr. on tan twill. Exc. cond. $13.00

ARMY CHOPPER PATCH: 498th Dust-Off, fully embr. Above avg. cond. $20.00

ARMY DRUM & BUGLE CORPS TAB: Theater made. 4.5" wide w/cord stitched lettering & 1st Div. patch design on dark red felt. Exc. cond........................... $24.00

ARMY FIELD ARTILLERY SCHOOL BLAZER PATCH: heavy bullion & ribbed red applique design is approx. 3x3.75" size on uncut scarlet red wool base. In original Gemsco packaging. Older piece. Exc. cond. $22.00

ARMY FORCES FAR EAST PATCH W/ ATTACHED "JOINT HQ FEC" TAB: 2x2.25" overall size. Fully mach embr. Near mint cond. $48.00

ARMY HHD 58TH TRANS BN. PATCH: red background w/Viking girl & HHD 58TH / TRANS BN. embr. on bottom. Above avg. cond. $22.00

ARMY JOINT HQ FEC PATCH: Fully embr. w/attached tab. Near mint cond. ... $35.00

ARMY JUNGLE EXPERT PATCHES W/ ATTACHED "BALBOA" TABS & 1967 DATE: Includes color & subdued version. Fully embr. Mint cond. $22.00

ARMY RYUKYUS CMD. PATCH: Theater made. 2.25" dia. heavy gold bullion on felt. Above avg. cond. $25.00

ARMY SPEC FORCES PATCH: Black w/ white sword & yellow edge. May be SVN made. Above avg. cond. $32.00

ARMY SUPREME HQ ALLIED POWERS, EUROPE PATCH: German made. 2.25x3" black felt base w/bevo design. Exc. cond. $40.00

ARMY TAIWAN DEFENSE COMMAND PATCH: Theater mach. embr. on 2.75x3.75" blue twill base. Off uniform but shape. Above avg. cond. $38.00

CONNECTICUT G.F.C. 1ST CO PATCH: Fully embr. w/cut-edge. Exc. cond. $20.00

DESERT STORM ARMY 1ST CAV. DIV. NOVELTY PATCH: 4x6" golden-yellow twill body w/attached "Desert Storm" tab + black horse head + orange & white striped band + "313" at bottom. Mint cond. $15.00

DESERT STORM BLOOD CHIT: 10x15" white rayon body w/US flag at top-5 languages below. Quality suggests that this is a privately made, rather than issue item. Near mint cond. $23.00

JAPANESE WAR CRIMES TRIALS PATCH: ID patch in black w/gold lettering reads "WAR CRIMES TRIALS/IMTFE/ TOKYO JAPAN." Gilt wire trim. Mint. Near mint cond. $230.00

JAPANESE WAR CRIMES TRIALS PATCH

KOREAN WAR ARMY 187TH AIRBORNE COMBAT LEADERSHIP SCHOOL PATCH: 2.75" diam., Japanese machine made w/likeness of temple gate over winged parcel w/crude likeness of chute canopy in center-"Leadership by Example" in scroll below. Mint cond. $64.00

KOREAN WAR ARMY 1ST CORPS PATCH: Korean made. 2 3/8" dia. black felt base w/heavy bullion design. Above avg. cond. $20.00

KOREAN WAR ARMY 2ND BN, 9 INF WEAPONS "CHARLIE MANCHU/KEEP UP THE FIRE" PATCH: Korean made. 3.5" dia. black twill w/green applique panel & mach. embr. constr. Exc. cond. $20.00

KOREAN WAR ARMY 2ND DIV. PATCH: Korean made. embr. shows arrowhead w/ 2nd Div. mascot inside astride the Korean DMZ. Soiled. Incl. Philippine army shoulder tab embr. blue on tan twill. Above avg. cond. $25.00

KOREAN WAR ARMY 30TH HM. CO./1ST IN US ARMY/1ST IN KOREA PATCH: Korean made. 2.75x3" size. Fully mach. embr. Near mint cond. $22.00

KOREAN WAR ARMY 40TH DIV. PATCH: Theater made. 2.5" square blue felt base w/heavy bullion sunburst design. Back Has 8 female snap ends. Some sporadic nips. Avg. cond. $25.00

KOREAN WAR ARMY 8TH ARMY PATCH: Korean made. 2.75" wide. Pinkish-red felt base w/heavy silver bullion design. Light even tarnish. Off uniform. Avg. cond. $20.00

KOREAN WAR ARMY 97TH AAA HONOR GUARD PATCH: fully embr. patch design, Japanese made, in unissued cond. Has tab at top. 3" wide. Mint cond. $27.00

KOREAN WAR ARMY ARMORED CAV. OFFICERS COLLAR DEVICES: Asian made. Brass CB crossed sabers behind tank & w/37 above turret. One pair. Exc. cond. $20.00

KOREAN WAR ARMY AVIATOR BLOOD CHIT: Printed on white rayon w/large U.S. flag printed at top & message in 10 different languages below. 1951 dated & serial numbered. Avg. cond. $25.00

KOREAN WAR ARMY C. BTRY 1/92 'RED DEVILS' POCKET PATCH: Korean made. Approx. 3x3.75" black twill base w/ applique panel & mach. embr. design. Exc. cond. $20.00

KOREAN WAR ARMY KOREAN COMM. ZONE PATCH: 65x73mm dark green base w/mach. embr. design. Cloth backed. Exc. cond. $66.00

KOREAN WAR ARMY KOREAN COMM. ZONE PATCH: Korean made. 2.75x3.25" size. Green felt body w/bullion design. Off uniform. Bullion is dark from age but still decent. Above avg. cond. $48.00

KOREAN WAR ARMY MIL GOVT. OF KOREA PATCH: Red blue swirl done on early polyester fabric, some bleed where colors meet. Avg. cond. $75.00

KOREAN WAR ARMY MILITARY GOVT. OF KOREA PATCH: 2" disc w/red & blue swirl pattern. Fully embr. Above avg. cond. $60.00

KOREAN WAR ARMY RADAR/NONE SO SILENT WE CANNOT DETECT/EYES OF NIGHT PATCH: Korean made. Subdued. 3 5/8" dia. mach. embr. on OD cotton. Exc. cond. $20.00

KOREAN WAR ARMY SECURITY AGENCY CLOTH WINGS: Black wool two piece w/ gold bullion feathers & bullion letters 'A-S-A' Minor moth nips. Above avg. cond. $76.00

KOREAN WAR CIVIL ASSISTANCE COMMISSION PATCH: Shield w/silver bullion & hand stitched silk on full color felt. Removed from Vet's uniform. Above avg. cond. $240.00

KOREAN WAR ERA SOUVENIR JACKET PATCH: 'Returned from Hell.' Korean made. has embr. designs of Japanese, US, UN and Korean flags with map of Korea and Japan flanked by patch designs for US Forces Far East and 8th Army. On black wool, shield shaped, 9" wide. Above avg. cond. $24.00

KOREAN WAR KOREAN SERVICE SOUVENIR PATCH: Korean made 7" disk w/US & Korean flag bracketing a shield w/ nested nested hearts. above shield is 'XXIV/216QM.' Reads 'I SPENT MY TIME IN HELL/SEOUL KOREA' & '1948.' Above avg. cond. $29.00

TERRITORIAL GUARD PATCH: 3.5" Blue field w/big dipper, north star & initials A T G. For Alaska Territorial Guard. Exc. cond. $37.00

TEXAS STATE GUARD PATCH: 2" wide. Fully embr. patch has star embr. over in heavy silver bullion & "T" trimmed w/ bullion. Above avg. cond. $25.00

VIETNAM ERA ARMY 8TH CAC GUNNERS TAB: Vietnamese made red trim, black background, White lettering reads "18th 2ND FLT/GUNNER CAC." Avg. cond. $20.00

VIETNAM ERA ARMY 92 ASSAULT HEL. AVIATION UNIT POCKET PATCH: Vietnam made. Hand embr. color design on OD cotton w/motto "We Bow To No One." Off uniform. Avg. cond. $40.00

VIETNAM ERA 1ST BDE.1ST CAV. SCOUTS PATCH: Vietnam made. 5" dia. white cotton base w/mach. embr. design. Backed in paper & loose weave cloth material. Some glue/paper remains on reverse from display. Exc. cond. $44.00

VIETNAM ERA 254 HEL. AMB. "DUST OFF" POCKET PATCH: Vietnam made. 2.75x4" w/hand embr. design on blue cotton. Traces of glue/paper remains on back from display but near mint otherwise. Exc. cond. $40.00

VIETNAM ERA 557TH Q.M. AERIAL SUPPLY CO. PATCH: 2.5x3". Fully embr. Mint cond. $48.00

VIETNAM ERA ARMY 1/11 RECON KILLER TEAMS PATCH: Vietnam made. 3.75" dia. w/mach embr. design on blue cotton. Near mint cond. $32.00

VIETNAM ERA ARMY 1/4 CAVALRY POCKET PATCH: Vietnam made. 4" dia. Color-machine embr. on red cotton. Near mint cond. $48.00

VIETNAM ERA ARMY 101ST AIRBORNE DIV. GUNNER/A/377 ARTY POCKET PATCH: Vietnam made. 3.75" dia. Hand & cord embr. design. Exc. cond. $45.00

VIETNAM ERA ARMY 101ST AIRBORNE DIV. PATCH: Vietnam made. 2.5x3" black twill w/hand embr. design & attached Airborne tab. Exc. cond. $40.00

VIETNAM ERA ARMY 101ST AIRBORNE DIV. PATCH: Vietnam made. 2.5x3.5" o/a size. Black cotton base w/applique design & mach. embr. attached "Airborne" tab. Paper backed. Exc. cond. $35.00

VIETNAM ERA ARMY 101ST AIRBORNE DIV. PATCH: Vietnam made. 2.75x3.25" size. Mach. embr. design on black twill w/ attached "Vietnam" tab. Paper backed. Near mint cond. $26.00

VIETNAM ERA ARMY 101ST AIRBORNE DIV. PATCH: Vietnam made. 2.75x3.25" w/mach. embr. design on black cotton & attached tab. Cloth backed. Above avg. cond. $30.00

VIETNAM ERA ARMY 11TH ACR PATCH: Vietnam made. Subdued. 2.5x3.25" w/ hand embr. design on OD twill. Above avg. cond. $10.00

VIETNAM ERA ARMY 11TH INF REGT. POCKET PATCH: Vietnam made. 3.25x3.5" multi piece cotton & mach. embr. contr. Light age. Above avg. cond. $20.00

VIETNAM ERA ARMY 128TH AVIATION TOMAHAWK POCKET PATCH: 3.5x4" Vietnam made. multi piece cotton & mach. embr. design. Exc. cond. $19.00

VIETNAM ERA ARMY 134TH AVN. CO. POCKET PATCH: Vietnam made. 4" dia. Multi-piece cotton w/mach. embr. comical design. Avg. cond. $75.00

VIETNAM ERA ARMY 138TH ASA AVN. CO. "LEFT JAB" POCKET PATCH: Japanese mach. embr. on 3" blue twill base. Near mint cond. $20.00

VIETNAM ERA ARMY 138TH RADIO RESEARCH AVN. CO. POCKET PATCH: 3.25x3.75". Japanese-made w/mach. embr. & applique design on blue twill. Near mint cond. $30.00

VIETNAM ERA ARMY 13TH AIRBORNE/ PATHFINDER DET. SCROLL: Vietnam made. 5 1/8" wide. Mach. embr. design on black cotton. Mint cond. $26.00

VIETNAM ERA ARMY 14TH INF SCROLL: "E CO/GOLDEN DRAGONS/14TH INF." 5.75" wide. Golden-yellow border & lettering on black cotton. Remains of paper backing. Above avg. cond. $27.00

VIETNAM ERA ARMY 156TH AVN CO/ STALKING GROUNDS POCKET PATCH: 3.75" dia. Japanese mach. embr. on blue cotton twill. Mint cond. $25.00

VIETNAM ERA ARMY 156TH AVN. CO. "STALKING GROUNDS" PATCH: Asian made. 3.75" dia. Mach. embr. on blue satin. Exc. cond. $28.00

VIETNAM ERA ARMY 15TH AVN BDE. PATCH: Vietnam made. black design on OD twill. 2.25" wide. Exc. cond. $20.00

VIETNAM ERA ARMY 15TH SUPPORT CMD. PATCH: Vietnam made. 2.75" wide. Mach. embr. design on yellow satin. Avg. cond. $35.00

VIETNAM ERA ARMY 168TH ENGR. BN. POCKET PATCH: Vietnam made. 2.75x2.75" OD twill base w/applique & mach. embr. design. Above avg. cond. $34.00

VIETNAM ERA ARMY 16TH INF REGT. POCKET PATCH: Vietnam made. 2.75x3.25" cotton base w/hand embr. design. Above avg. cond. $20.00

VIETNAM ERA ARMY 16TH INF REGT. POCKET PATCH: Vietnam made. approx. 2.75x3.25". Hand embr. on cotton. Off uniform-some age. Avg. cond. $20.00

VIETNAM ERA ARMY 173RD AIRBORNE BDE. SHOULDER PATCH: Thailand made. Subdued Black on OD fatigue cloth. Shows Winged knife. Above avg. cond. $20.00

VIETNAM ERA ARMY 173RD AIRBORNE DIV. PATCH: Vietnam made. Approx. 2x3.5" size. Blue cotton base w/mach. embr. design & attached tab. On the crude side. Exc. cond. $34.00

VIETNAM ERA ARMY 174TH A.H.C. "SHARK" POCKET PATCH: Vietnam

made. 4.5x3" w/mach. embr. design on red cotton. Near mint cond. $18.00

VIETNAM ERA ARMY 178TH AVN. CO. "CHINOOK" PATCH: Vietnam era. 1 7/8" dia. blue cotton base w/hand embr. design. Above avg. cond. $32.00

VIETNAM ERA ARMY 17TH SPEC OPS SQDN. PATCH: Fully embr. Above avg. cond. $22.00

VIETNAM ERA ARMY 187TH ABN. INF MORTAR BATTERY "RED LEGS" PATCH: Vietnam era. 3x4.25" white twill base w/ mach. embr. comical design. Exc. cond. $112.00

VIETNAM ERA ARMY 189TH ASLT. HEL. CO. "GHOST RIDERS" POCKET PATCH: Vietnam made. 3.75" dia. Hand embr. design on cotton. Exc. cond. $40.00

VIETNAM ERA ARMY 189TH GUNS "AVENGERS" AVN. POCKET PATCH: Vietnam made. 3.25x3.75" black cotton base w/hand embr. design of Grim Reaper. Exc. cond. $35.00

VIETNAM ERA ARMY 18TH AVIATION COMPANY PATCH: Theater made. 3.5" dia. Mach. embr. design w/hand embr. lettering. Avg. cond. $32.00

VIETNAM ERA ARMY 18TH ENGR. BDE. PATCH: Vietnam made. Subdued. 2.75" wide. Mach. embr. design on dark OD cotton. Paper backed. Off uniform. Above avg. cond. $20.00

VIETNAM ERA ARMY 18TH M.P. BRIGADE BRASSARD: Vietnam made. 9" tall glossy black vinyl body w/applied white vinyl "MP" letters & mach. made color patch above. Snap closures at back. Avg. cond. $80.00

VIETNAM ERA ARMY 195TH AHC GUN PLATOON/THUNDER CHICKENS POCKET PATCH: Vietnam made. 3.5x4" lt. blue cotton shield-shaped base w/hand embr. design. Above avg. cond. ... $91.00

VIETNAM ERA ARMY 195TH AHC GUN PLATOON/THUNDER CHICKENS POCKET PATCH

VIETNAM ERA ARMY 196TH A.S.H.C. "WE HAUL IT ALL" POCKET PATCH: Vietnam made. 4" wide multi piece cotton & mach. embr. design. Gauze/paper backed. Near mint cond. $22.00

VIETNAM ERA ARMY 196TH INF BDE. PATCH ON POCKET HANGER TAB: Fully mach. embr. (appears Japanese made). Sealed in clear plastic w/brown vinyl pocket tab. Near mint cond. $30.00

VIETNAM ERA ARMY 198TH MED. POCKET PATCH: Vietnam made. 3.75" wide shield-shaped red cotton base w/ mach. embr. design. Backed in Vietnamese paper. Exc. cond. $40.00

VIETNAM ERA ARMY 199TH INF BDE. PATCH: Vietnam made. Subdued. 2x3" OD poplin base w/mach. embr. design that has red embr. heart design. Remains of paper backing. On the crude side. Above avg. cond. $35.00

VIETNAM ERA ARMY 199TH INF BDE. PATCH: Vietnam made. Subdued. Hand embr. design on OD cotton base. Off uniform. Avg. cond. $30.00

VIETNAM ERA ARMY 1ST AVIATION BDE. PATCH ON POCKET HANGER: Vietnam made. 2.25x3.25" w/embr. on dark blue twill. Sealed in plastic & on lt. green vinyl pocket tab. Near mint cond. $24.00

VIETNAM ERA ARMY 1ST AVIATION BDE. PATCH: Vietnam made. Hand embr. on blue cotton twill. Off uniform. Approx. 2x3 1/8" size. Avg. cond. $10.00

VIETNAM ERA ARMY 1ST AVIATION BRIGADE PATCH: Color embr. on blue w/ "25th Avn. Co." tab attached. small flaw in top border-Asian made. Above avg. cond. $18.00

VIETNAM ERA ARMY 1ST AVN. BDE. PATCH: Japanese made. 2x3". Fully mach. embr. Off uniform. Above avg. cond. $20.00

VIETNAM ERA ARMY 1ST AVN. BDE. PATCH: Vietnam made. Subdued. 2.25x3.25" OD cotton base w/mach. embr. design. Off uniform but good shape. Above avg. cond. $20.00

VIETNAM ERA ARMY 1ST BRIGADE AVIATION PLT PATCH: Vietnam made. 3.5" dia. Multi-piece cotton w/mach. embr. design. Above avg. cond. $20.00

VIETNAM ERA ARMY 1ST CAV. POCKET PATCH: Shows civil war era soldier in gear w/"FIRST REGIMENT OF DRAGOONS/ORGANIZED 1833." Above avg. cond. $37.00

VIETNAM ERA ARMY 1ST CAV. SHOULDER PATCH: Vietnam made. For D troop, 2nd squadron, 1st cav. regiment. Removed from another source. shaped

like MSGT chevron w/"BLACK HAWK" at top over crossed M.G.'s & black chopper. Next is "AERO RIFLE" over unit designators. Vertical rifles frame image. Above avg. cond. $48.00

VIETNAM ERA ARMY 1ST CAV. SNIPER PATCH: Subdued 1st Cav. patch w/sniper ring & weapon emblem in center. Weapon embr. in blue. Above avg. cond. ... 139.00

VIETNAM ERA ARMY 1ST CAV. DIV. "TUNNEL RAT" SUBDUED PATCH: Vietnam era. 4x5.5" OD poplin base w/ black mach. embr. horse head & border + applied black cotton band w/mach. embr. in white "Tunnel Rat" letters. Exc. cond. $94.00

VIETNAM ERA ARMY 1ST CAV. DIV. 41ST SCOUT DOG PLT. PATCH: Asian made. approx. 3.75x6.25". Fully mach. embr. w/ attach unit scroll + lt. OD border. Post-Nam. Near mint cond. $25.00

VIETNAM ERA ARMY 1ST CAV. DIV. PATCH W/ATTACHED "DIVISION BAND" SCROLL: Vietnam made. 4x5.75" yellow cotton base w/mach. embr. horse head & applied cotton band. Glue/paper remains on back from display. Above avg. cond. $40.00

VIETNAM ERA ARMY 1ST CAV. DIV. PATCH W/ATTACHED "FLYING HORSEMEN" SCROLL: Vietnam made. 3.75x5.75" golden-yellow cotton base w/ embr. horsehead + applied band & scroll. Exc. cond. $35.00

VIETNAM ERA ARMY 1ST CAV. DIV. PATCH W/ATTACHED HONOR GUARD SCROLL: Vietnam made. 4.25x5.75" yellow cotton base w/mach. embr. horsehead + applied band. Backed in Vietnamese paper & gauze. Above avg. cond. $45.00

VIETNAM ERA ARMY 1ST CAV. DIV. PATCH: Subdue. US made patch mach. embr. on OD cotton w/"8th Engr. Bn." direct embr. in red into band. Above avg. cond. $20.00

VIETNAM ERA ARMY 1ST CAV. DIV. PATCH: Vietnam made. 2 1/4x2 7/8" yellow cotton base w/black velveteen horse head & band & direct embr. "Liaison Team." Backed in purple cotton. Exc. cond. $30.00

VIETNAM ERA ARMY 1ST CAV. DIV. PATCH: Vietnam made. 4x5.75" golden-yellow cotton base w/mach. embr. horsehead + applied band w/"Vietnam" direct embr. + large attached Airborne tab. Backed in Vietnamese paper. Near mint cond. $39.00

VIETNAM ERA ARMY 1ST CAV. M.P. PATCH: Vietnam made. Approx. 3.5x5 3/

8" size. Golden-yellow cotton base w/ attached "Military Police" tab + mach. embr. horse head & applied black cotton band. Remains of paper backing. Above avg. cond. $38.00

VIETNAM ERA ARMY 1ST CAV. PARACHUTE OVAL: Vietnam made. Approx. 2" wide. Hand embr. on white cotton w/folded-under edges. Above avg. cond. .,.................................... $40.00

VIETNAM ERA ARMY 1ST CAVALRY LRRP PATCH: Theater made, machine made patch w/embr. design on yellow twill. 3" wide. Avg. cond. $40.00

VIETNAM ERA ARMY 1ST DIV. "VIET NAM" PATCH: Vietnam made. 2 1/8x3.25" lt. olive cotton base w/red mach. embr. "1" & "Viet Nam." Remains of paper backing. Above avg. cond. $32.00

VIETNAM ERA ARMY 1ST DIV. PATCH: Vietnam made. 2x3.75" OD cotton base w/"chain" stitched red "1" design & attached "Vietnam" tab w/mach. embr. letters. Paper backed. Exc. cond. ... $25.00

VIETNAM ERA ARMY 1ST PLT 'WIDOW MAKERS' PATCH: embr. design on black twill, spade shaped patch, 3.5" wide, unissued. In cond. Mint cond. $42.00

VIETNAM ERA ARMY 1ST RAIDER FORCE BDE.SCROLL: Vietnam made. 4.5" wide. Mach. embr. on black cotton. Exc. cond. $26.00

VIETNAM ERA ARMY 1ST TRANSPORTATION REPAIR BN. PATCH: Featuring yellow jacket w/tools & gold '1.' Exc. cond. $20.00

VIETNAM ERA ARMY 201ST AVN CO PATCH: The Red Barons Air Support unit. shows yellow map of Vietnam in center. Exc. cond. $40.00

VIETNAM ERA ARMY 20TH ARTY. AERIAL ROCKET 1ST CAV. DIV. PATCH: Vietnam made. 3.5x4.75" w/hand embr. design on black cotton base. Above avg. cond. $75.00

VIETNAM ERA ARMY 20TH ARTY. AERIAL ROCKET 1ST CAV. DIV. PATCH

VIETNAM ERA ARMY 20TH ENGINEER BDE. PATCH: Vietnam made. 3" wide white twill base w/applied red velveteen & mach. embr. design. Above avg. cond. $20.00

VIETNAM ERA ARMY 20TH SPECIAL OPS SQDN. PATCH: "ILLIGETIMUS NON CARBORUNDUM." Embr. on blue cloth. Exc. cond. $22.00

VIETNAM ERA ARMY 21ST VIETNAMESE RANGER BN. SCROLL: Vietnam made. 3.5" wide. Hand embr. on black cotton. Exc. cond. $49.00

VIETNAM ERA ARMY 235TH ARMED HELICOPTER COMPANY-ORDNANCE DETACHMENT PATCH: Vietnam made. 5" wide black twill triangular base w/mach. embr. design. Exc. cond. $32.00

VIETNAM ERA ARMY 24TH CORPS PATCH: Vietnam made. 2 5/8" wide. Multi-piece constr. paper backed. Exc. cond. $20.00

VIETNAM ERA ARMY 25TH AVN. BN. A CO "LITTLE BEARS" POCKET PATCH: Vietnam made. Approx. 3.25" dia. lt. blue cotton base w/hand embr. design. Off uniform. Avg. cond. $68.00

VIETNAM ERA ARMY 25TH DIV. PATCH: Asian made. 2x3" w/mach. embr. design on red cotton. Exc. cond. $20.00

VIETNAM ERA ARMY 25TH DIV. RECONDO POCKET PATCH: Subdued. 3" wide. US made. Embr. on dark OD cotton. Mint cond. $25.00

VIETNAM ERA ARMY 269TH ORDNANCE DETACHMENT PATCH: Machine embr. on red cloth. Mint cond. $22.00

VIETNAM ERA ARMY 294TH CAVALIERS AVIATION POCKET PATCH: Vietnam made. 4" dia. multi piece cotton base w/ applique & mach. embr. design. Remains of paper backing. Above avg. cond. $30.00

VIETNAM ERA ARMY 29TH RCT PATCH W/ "JOINT HQ. FEC" TAB: 2" dia. standard fully embr. patch. Has had fully Asian mach embr. tab attached to top. Exc. cond. $32.00

VIETNAM ERA ARMY 2ND FIELD FORCE VIETNAM PATCH W/ATTACHED AIRBORNE TAB: Vietnam made. 2.5x4" w/mach. embr. design on OD cotton. Exc. cond. $30.00

VIETNAM ERA ARMY 2ND FIELD FORCE VIETNAM PATCH: Vietnam made. 2.25x3.25" w/applied velvet panels on blue cotton & hand embr. sword design. Off uniform. Avg. cond. $20.00

VIETNAM ERA ARMY 2ND FIELD FORCE VIETNAM PATCH: Vietnam made.

2.25x3.5" w/hand embr. design on blue twill. Avg. cond. $10.00

VIETNAM ERA ARMY 2ND INF REGT. POCKET PATCH: Vietnam made. 2.25x3.75" cotton base w/hand embr. design. Mint cond. $25.00

VIETNAM ERA ARMY 2ND VIETNAMESE RANGER GP. SCROLL: Vietnam made. White hand embr. lettering on black cotton w/red hand embr. border. Exc. cond. $40.00

VIETNAM ERA ARMY 32ND MEDICAL DEPOT VIETNAM POCKET PATCH: Vietnam made. large 4x4.75" maroon cotton base w/hand embr. design. Patch is paper backed & sealed in clear plastic pocket hanger w/button hanger tab. Above avg. cond. $160.00

VIETNAM ERA ARMY 330TH RADIO RESEARCH CO. 8TH DET PATCH: Machine embr. design on black cloth. Black cut edge. Mint cond. $34.00

VIETNAM ERA ARMY 33RD F. A. POCKET PATCH: Vietnam made. 2.25x3.25" w/ hand embr. design on red cotton. Avg. cond. $20.00

VIETNAM ERA ARMY 345TH GEN. MEDICAL DISPENSARY POCKET PATCH: Vietnam made. 2 7/8x3 3/4" red cotton base w/hand embr. design. Off uniform. Above avg. cond. $45.00

VIETNAM ERA ARMY 351ST RCT PATCH: 1 7/8x1 3/4" size. Fully embr. Non-merrowed edge. Exc. cond. $32.00

VIETNAM ERA ARMY 35TH VIETNAMESE RANGER BN. SCROLL: Vietnam made. 3.5" dia. Hand embr. on ERDL pattern camo poplin. Exc. cond. $26.00

VIETNAM ERA ARMY 36TH VIETNAMESE RANGER BN. SCROLL: Vietnam made. 3.5" dia. Hand embr. on black cotton. Exc. cond. $40.00

VIETNAM ERA ARMY 37TH VIETNAMESE RANGER BN. SCROLL: Vietnam made. 3.5" dia. Hand embr. on black cotton. Exc. cond. $40.00

VIETNAM ERA ARMY 38TH INF SCOUT DOG ARC: Vietnam made. 3.5" wide on large piece of uncut black twill-machine stitched design w/hand embr. letters-"38th Inf-Scout Dog-Follow Us." $20.00

VIETNAM ERA ARMY 39TH MED. DET. POCKET PATCH: Vietnam made. 3.25x3.75" maroon cotton base w/hand embr. design. Exc. cond. $40.00

VIETNAM ERA ARMY 39TH SIGNAL POCKET PATCH: Vietnam made. 4" square gray cotton base w/hand embr.

MACV-patch design based design. Near mint cond. $20.00

VIETNAM ERA ARMY 3D BN/RANGER AIRBORNE/75TH INF SCROLL: Vietnam made. 4" wide. Mach. embr. on black nylon material. Above avg. cond. .. $50.00

VIETNAM ERA ARMY 40TH ARTY BDE.PATCH: Fully embr. on tan twill w/ non-merrowed edge. Exc. cond. .. $25.00

VIETNAM ERA ARMY 41ST ARTY BATRY E SHOULDER PATCH: Asian made. OD green background w/subdued lettering. Says at top 'QUAD 50'S.' Shows blue cartoon Quad mount with all guns blazing. Above avg. cond. $20.00

VIETNAM ERA ARMY 42ND VIETNAMESE RANGER BN. SCROLL: Vietnam made. 3.5" dia. Hand embr. on ERDL pattern camo ripstop. Exc. cond. $40.00

VIETNAM ERA ARMY 43RD VIETNAMESE RANGER BN. SCROLL: Vietnam made. 3.5" dia. Hand embr. on ERDL pattern camo ripstop. Exc. cond. $40.00

VIETNAM ERA ARMY 4TH DIV. POCKET PATCH: Theater made. Hand made w/ green stars on white background + leather hanger w/button slot. Above avg. cond. $20.00

VIETNAM ERA ARMY 506TH ABN INF ARC: Asian made. Subdue. 4.25" wide. Mach. embr. on OD cotton. Back has glue/paper remains from display. Above avg. cond. $25.00

VIETNAM ERA ARMY 52ND VIETNAMESE RANGER BN. SCROLL: Vietnam made. 3.5" wide. Hand embr. on black cotton. Exc. cond. $40.00

VIETNAM ERA ARMY 544TH CORPS-THE PUSHERS-CHU LAI RVN PATCH: Vietnam made. Approx. 3.5" dia. Mach. embr. & cotton applique constr. Above avg. cond. $65.50

VIETNAM ERA ARMY 544TH CORPS/CHU LAI RVN/THE PUSHERS PATCH: Vietnam made. 3.5" dia. w/multi piece cotton & mach. embr. design. Exc. cond. $38.00

VIETNAM ERA ARMY 54TH AVIATION CO./ AIR MOBILE "BLAZER" PATCH: 3.75x4" size. Red felt base w/ribbed satin applique panels & hand embr. design of Otter in native straw hat & Vietnamese characteristics & MACV patch design w/ motto "Otter Air Service." quality-appears to be made for reunion, etc. Exc. cond. $16.00

VIETNAM ERA ARMY 5TH DIV. LRRP PATCH: Vietnam made. 3x3.5" multi piece cotton base w/mach. embr. design. Near mint cond. $21.00

VIETNAM ERA ARMY 5TH SPECIAL FORCES GRP BERET FLASH: Vietnam made. Red & yellow stripes on black field for 5th Spec Forces Grp. Avg. cond. $40.00

VIETNAM ERA ARMY 68TH ARMED HELICOPTER CO PATCH: machine embr. design on light blue twill. 2.75" wide. Mint cond. $24.00

VIETNAM ERA ARMY 6TH VIETNAMESE RANGER GP SCROLL: Vietnam made. 3.5" dia. Hand embr. on black cotton. Exc. cond. $40.00

VIETNAM ERA ARMY 755TH MED. DET. POCKET PATCH: Vietnam made. 3.5x3.5" shield-shaped blue cotton shield w/hand embr. design. Some traces of glue remains on back from display but . Exc. cond. $72.00

VIETNAM ERA ARMY 75TH INF 1ST BDE.RANGER AIRBORNE SCROLL: 3 1/8" wide. Embr. on black twill. Off uniform. Avg. cond. $34.00

VIETNAM ERA ARMY 75TH RANGER BERET FLASH: Vietnam made. 2x2.25" size. Applied cotton panel & hand embr. color design on OD ripstop base. Exc. cond. $55.00

VIETNAM ERA ARMY 82ND AIRBORNE DIV. PATCH W/VARIANT TAB: Vietnam made. Multi-piece cotton w/attached tab & mach. embr. design. Has red "B" on tab. Remains of paper backing. Exc. cond. $32.00

VIETNAM ERA ARMY 82ND AIRBORNE DIV. PATCH: Vietnam made. Approx. 2.25x3.5". Hand embr. design on red twill w/attached tab. Exc. cond. $35.00

VIETNAM ERA ARMY 82ND AIRBORNE PATCH: Fully embr. w/Vietnam tab & closed arc. Red velour field w/'AA' emblem in center. good looking. Exc. cond. $50.00

VIETNAM ERA ARMY 82ND AIRBORNE PATCH

VIETNAM ERA ARMY 87TH INF SCROLL :"CO C/WE CONQUER/87TH INF." Vietnam made. 5" wide black cotton base

w/lt. blue mach. embr. Above avg. cond. $24.00

VIETNAM ERA ARMY 8TH RADIO RESEARCH FIELD STATION POCKET PATCH: Japanese-mach. embr. on blue cotton twill w/design of truck w/M.G.s & reads "God is our Shotgun/Babysitter/ Mac's Marauders." Near mint cond. $35.00

VIETNAM ERA ARMY 91ST EVAC. HOSPITAL, VIETNAM POCKET PATCH: Vietnam made. Approx. 3x3.37" size. multi piece cotton constr w/mach. embr. design. Exc. cond. $25.00

VIETNAM ERA ARMY 93RD EVAC. HOSP. PATCH: Fully embr. U.S. made example w/merrowed edge. In matching clear plastic pocket hanger w/button tab. Exc. cond. $20.00

VIETNAM ERA ARMY 94TH MED. DET. "DRINK TO YOUR HEALTH" POCKET PATCH: Vietnam made. 3.75" dia. Hand embr. design on green cotton. Exc. cond. $36.00

VIETNAM ERA ARMY 9TH DIV. PATCH: Vietnam made. 2.75" dia. dark OD cotton base w/3-piece velveteen & cotton panel design. Off uniform. Above avg. cond. $25.00

VIETNAM ERA ARMY 9TH DIV. PATCH: Vietnam made. Subdued. 2.5" dia. w/ applied velvet panel on OD cotton. Still attached to section of OD ripstop cloth directly cut from jungle jacket. Avg. cond. $30.00

VIETNAM ERA ARMY A TROOP 7/17 KNIGHT AVIATION POCKET PATCH: Vietnam made. 4" dia. red cotton base w/ hand embr. & applied cotton panel design of Cobra Gunship over chess knight design. Near mint cond. $35.00

VIETNAM ERA ARMY A/377 ARTY/ANV MAINT. POCKET PATCH: 4.5" dia. orange cotton base w/comical mach. embr. design. Japanese-made. Near mint cond. $31.00

VIETNAM ERA ARMY ADVISORY TEAM 73 "CHUONG-THIEN/CO VAN MY" PATCH: Vietnam made. 3.25x3.5". Multi-piece cotton base w/mach. embr. design. Exc. cond. $36.00

VIETNAM ERA ARMY AIRBORNE SCROLL: "CO F/Ranger Airborne/425." Subdued. 4.75" wide. Embr. on cotton. Off uniform but very clean. Exc. cond. $24.00

VIETNAM ERA ARMY AIRBORNE PATCH: Vietnam made. 4" disc w/Eagle in jump suit, equip & weapon + '1ST BRIGADE' at bottom. Above avg. cond. $60.00

VIETNAM ERA ARMY AIRBORNE PATCH: Vietnam made. A/B wings of destiny -4" shield w/black eagle holding chute. motto at bottom. Above avg. cond. $118.00

VIETNAM ERA ARMY AIRBORNE PATCH

VIETNAM ERA ARMY AIRBORNE/LONG RANGE PATROL TAB: Vietnam made. 3.75" wide white cotton base w/green mach. embr. border & lettering. Exc. cond. $20.00

VIETNAM ERA ARMY ARMORED WHISPERING DEATH NOVELTY POCKET PATCH: Vietnam made. 4" disk two piece construction depicting cartoon tank w/grin firing all guns. Above avg. cond. ...., $20.00

VIETNAM ERA ARMY AVIATION "CAC LONG TRIP" PATCH: Vietnam made. 4.5x4.25" size. Has hand embr. design of 1st Av Bde patch design in upper left corner, likeness of twin engine Army plane & "CAC" in lower rt. corner. Attached scroll at bottom reads "Long Trip." Exc. cond. $32.00

VIETNAM ERA ARMY AVIATION "RATTLER" POCKET PATCH: approx. 4x4" OD cotton section w/color mach. embr. design. Above avg. cond. ... $40.00

VIETNAM ERA ARMY AVIATION "RATTLER" UNIT POCKET PATCH: Vietnam made. 4x4.25" OD twill base w/ mach. embr. color design of chopper over coiled rattlesnake. Above avg. cond. $25.00

VIETNAM ERA ARMY AVIATION "THE ROYAL COACHMAN" POCKET PATCH: 4.5" wide diamond-shaped yellow cotton base w/mach. embr. design of old-time carriage. Remains of paper backing. Appears Japanese-made. Above avg. cond. $35.00

VIETNAM ERA ARMY AVIATION COBRA UNIT PATCH: Shows cobra on cobra chopper in center + 'Mustangs' at top & 'Death rides a dark horse" at bottom. Likely Asian made. Above avg. cond. $29.00

VIETNAM ERA ARMY AVIATION ELECTRONIC SUPPORT CO NORTH (PROV) PATCH: Vietnam hand embr.

design on orange twill with wide red embr. edges. 3.5" wide. Unissued. Mint cond. $22.00

VIETNAM ERA ARMY AVIATION MATERIAL MANAGEMENT CENTER PATCH: Design hand embr. on green material. Mint cond. $20.00

VIETNAM ERA ARMY AVIATION PATCH: Dark blue triangle w/large Black widow spider & 'C Co' at top & 101AHB / black / widow at bottom. Neat patch. Exc. cond. $20.00

VIETNAM ERA ARMY AVIATION PATCH: OD green w/Black embr. chopper on top & O-2 aircraft below. For 611th Transco (ADS). Above avg. cond. $20.00

VIETNAM ERA ARMY AVIATION PATCH: machine embr. design on white twill with winged shield bearing a '2' at center and a sword piercing the shield. 4" dia. Exc. cond. $26.00

VIETNAM ERA ARMY AVIATION UNIT POCKET PATCH: Vietnam made. 3.25" dia. white cotton disc w/mach. embr. comical design of aviator atop Huey & reads "Cowboys." Above avg. cond. $22.00

VIETNAM ERA ARMY AVIATION UNIT POCKET PATCH: Vietnam made. 3x3.5" white cotton twill base w/mach. embr. design of dragon w/gunship armament & reads "Dragon 30." Above avg. cond. $22.00

VIETNAM ERA ARMY AVIATION UNIT POCKET PATCH: Vietnam made. Reads "220/We Observe." Multi-piece & mach. embr. constr. Near mint cond. $220.00

VIETNAM ERA ARMY AVIATION UNIT POCKET PATCH: Vietnam made. Reads "Wings of the Iron Horseman Pegasus." Multi-piece & mach. embr. constr. Remains of paper backing. Exc. cond. $40.00

VIETNAM ERA ARMY BLACK TIGER COMMANDO TEAM 98 POCKET PATCH: Vietnam made. 4" dia. dark yellow cotton base w/hand embr. design. Above avg. cond. $145.00

VIETNAM ERA ARMY BRAVO 3/17 HUNTER KILLER STOGIE PATCH: embr. design on red twill, 3.5" diam., some age soiling to the piece. Unissued. Exc. cond. $42.00

VIETNAM ERA ARMY BUCCANEER POCKET PATCH: 4" dia. black cotton disc w/applied white cotton skull & cross bones - "Buccaneer" across the top. Near mint cond. $21.00

VIETNAM ERA ARMY C/16 DARKHORSE/ GUNSMITH POCKET PATCH: Vietnam made. 3.75x2.75" swallow-tail guidon-shaped multi piece cotton base w/mach. embr. lettering. Exc. cond. $25.00

VIETNAM ERA ARMY CAV. BLUE GHOST POCKET PATCH: Vietnam made. 4.25" dia. Multi-piece cotton base w/mach. embr. design. Above avg. cond. ... $36.00

VIETNAM ERA ARMY CAV. CS BELT BUCKLE: Asian made, stamped brass copy of the oval buckle w/"CS" in center-lead backed. Comes in the typical, flimsy blue & white cardboard carton. Near mint cond. $31.00

VIETNAM ERA ARMY CAVALRY RECON PATCH: Vietnam made. embr. design on red twill. 3" wide. Mint cond. $26.00

VIETNAM ERA ARMY FILTHY FIVE FLYING DEATH PATCH: embr. design on black twill, spade shaped, 5" wide, unissued. Some light age wear. Near mint cond. $48.00

VIETNAM ERA ARMY HELICOPTER UNIT PATCH: 2.5x3.5" silk stitched confederate flag design on red cotton-"Rebels." Mint cond. $21.00

VIETNAM ERA ARMY HELICOPTER UNIT PATCH: 3.5 x 4" rect. patch for 335th AHC 'RAMRODS.' Has Mustached man smoking pipe & wearing western hat w/1st PLT over it. Above avg. cond. $29.00

VIETNAM ERA ARMY HELO PATCH: Vietnam made. for co. Wm. Tell, heart shaped patch w/diagonal band & mountaineer hat on one side & cross on the other. In plastic container w/button tab. Above avg. cond. $40.00

VIETNAM ERA ARMY JUNGLE EXPERT PATCH: Asian made. Subdue. Approx. 3x2.75" mach. embr. on dark OD twill w/ attached tab. Semi-crude. Exc. cond. $18.00

VIETNAM ERA ARMY KIT CARSON SCOUT SHOULDER TAB: Yellow trim on black background & orange letters for comment. Above avg. cond. $40.00

VIETNAM ERA ARMY LAOTIAN EXPEDITIONARY FORCE PATCH: Vietnam made. 4.5" dia. loose weave cotton disc w/hand embr. Huey chopper design. Exc. cond. $68.00

VIETNAM ERA ARMY LONG RANGE PATROL TAB: Black w/yellow embr., reads 9th/long range patrol/div. Appears Asian made. Above avg. cond. $72.00

VIETNAM ERA ARMY LRRP PATCH: Theater made. Subdued. black embr. design on heavy OD canvas. Has been removed from a uniform, 2" wide. Above avg. cond. $28.00

VIETNAM ERA ARMY MAAG LAOS SHOULDER PATCH: Theater made hand embr. w/title at top & three headed elephant on red field. Exc. cond. .. $70.00

VIETNAM ERA ARMY MAAG VIETNAM TAB: 3.25" wide camo parachute silk base w/hand embr. border & lettering in green/yellow-shade thread. Backed in paper w/ Thai characters. Above avg. cond. $99.00

VIETNAM ERA ARMY MACV PATCH W/ ATTACHED AIRBORNE TAB: Vietnam made. 2 1/8x3 1/2" red cotton base w/ hand embr. design. Paper backed. Above avg. cond. $25.00

VIETNAM ERA ARMY MASTER SGT. CHEVRONS: Vietnam made. Subdued. Hand embr. stripes on OD cotton bases. Off uniform but in good shape. Avg. cond. $20.00

VIETNAM ERA ARMY MED UNIT PATCH: Theater made 198th Med patch w/Medical staff in center & cobra wrapped around it. Exc. cond. $32.00

VIETNAM ERA ARMY PATCH: Black poplin background w/cow skull in center - reads '3RD HERD'/'GUN SQUAD.' Characters in yellow. Above avg. cond. $26.00

VIETNAM ERA ARMY PATCH: OD Green twill w/'FORWAR' at top + 2 images of horse operating stick separated by diagonal bar. Above avg. cond. $20.00

VIETNAM ERA ARMY PATCH: Shows to red cowboy hat resting on black boots w/ 'SHORT' below piece. Exc. cond. . $24.00

VIETNAM ERA ARMY PATROL DOGS PATCH: Vietnam made. 3.5x4" w/mach. embr. design of fierce K-9's head on shield-shaped brown cotton base. Scroll below reads "Insure/Protect/Defend." Above avg. cond. $60.00

VIETNAM ERA ARMY PATROL DOGS PATCH

VIETNAM ERA ARMY RECON SCROLL: Vietnam made. "2/Recon/500." 4.25" wide w/mach embr. yellow lettering & border on black twill. Exc. cond. $29.00

VIETNAM ERA ARMY RECON TEAM ILLINOIS SHOULDER PATCH: 5" flat top shield in red w/"airborne"/on canopy of winged skull & crossbones. Below is "CCC"/ILLINOIS/RECON." Theater made. Exc. cond. $80.00

VIETNAM ERA ARMY RECONDO POCKET PATCH: Asian-made. White cotton "arrowhead" w/mach. embr. "V" & "Recondo." Backed in ERDL pattern camo ripstop. Avg. cond. $55.00

VIETNAM ERA ARMY RECONDO TAB: Asian made. Subdue. 2 1/8" wide. Mach. embr. on OD cotton. Exc. cond. ... $25.00

VIETNAM ERA ARMY RT ALABAMA CCC RECON PATCH: Vietnam made. 3.5x2" white cotton base w/hand embr. color design. Exc. cond. $146.00

VIETNAM ERA ARMY SCOUTS POCKET PATCH: 3x5" red/white oval w/color machine embr. OH-6 in center-"Scouts-Eyes With Teeth." Near mint cond. $26.00

VIETNAM ERA ARMY SECURITY FORCE VIETNAM POCKET PATCH: Vietnam made. 3x3.5" w/hand embr. design on lt. blue cotton base. Near mint cond. ...., $54.00

VIETNAM ERA ARMY SECURITY DETACHMENT TAB: Vietnam made. 3.75" wide, semi-circular curved black body w/ machine stitched border & letters. Removed from uniform. Above avg. cond. $20.00

VIETNAM ERA ARMY SHOULDER TAB: Nam made subdued tab reads 'LRRP' black on OD green. Avg. cond. $50.00

VIETNAM ERA ARMY STRATCOM PHULAM POCKET PATCH: Vietnam made. 3x4" w/hand embr. design + motto "Communications For Defens." Near mint cond. $38.00

VIETNAM ERA ARMY SUPERIOR DRIVER POCKET PATCH: Vietnam made. 3.5x3.5" yellow cotton shield w/hand embr. green cross on striped Vietnam flag background-"Superior Driver" in scroll below. Shows age & wear. Avg. cond. $32.00

VIETNAM ERA ARMY THE LONG KNIVES PATCH: Vietnam made. 4" square w/"THE LONG KNIVES" over Cavalry man holding bloody sword & "D TRP 3/5 CAV." at bottom. Above avg. cond. $52.00

VIETNAM ERA ARMY UNIT PATCH: "271-361 INNKEEPER." Shows Black embr. Pegasus w/a small 'DELTA' by wings. Left side has '271-361' & top has 'INNKEEPER.' Above avg. cond. ..$72.00

VIETNAM ERA ARMY USARV PATCH IN POCKET HANGER: Vietnam made. Multi-piece cotton body w/mach. embr. sword. Sealed in clear plastic pocket hanger w/ tab. Exc. cond. $24.00

VIETNAM ERA ARMY USARV PATCH: Subdue. US made version mach. embr. on OD twill. Off uniform. Avg. cond. $11.00

VIETNAM ERA ARMY USARV PATCH: Vietnam made. Subdued. 1 7/8x3" size. OD cotton base w/applied velvet panels & hand embr. sword. Off uniform. Avg. cond. $12.00

VIETNAM ERA ARMY USARV PATCH: Vietnam made. Subdued. 2x3" size. OD cotton base w/applied velvet panels + mach. embr. sword design. Off uniform. Above avg. cond. $11.00

VIETNAM ERA ARMY VIET CONG HUNTING CLUB PATCH: Nam made. 3.5" dia. w/mach embr. design on yellow cotton w/OD ripstop backing. Off uniform. Avg. cond. $24.00

VIETNAM ERA NOVELTY PATCH: 5" dia. Embr. Rabbit hunters lodge w/Bugs Bunny & Elmer Fudd. Exc. cond. $65.00

VIETNAM ERA USMC NOVELTY JACKET PATCH. 5x9" Asian machine embr. likeness of a sinister eyed helicopter-"HMM-163-Marines." Near mint cond. $38.00

VIETNAM MADE ARMY 1ST CAV. DIV. PATCH: Subdue. Vietnam made. Approx. 4x6 1/8" PD cotton base w/attached mach. embr. "Vietnam/1968 1969" scroll w/applied black velveteen horse head & band. Remains of paper backing. Above avg. cond. $40.00

VIETNAM ERA ARMY 121ST AVN. CO. POCKET PATCH: Vietnam made. 3.5x3.75" black cotton base w/hand embr. design & mach. embr. border. Off uniform. Avg. cond. $64.00

U.S. AIR FORCE CLOTH INSIGNIA

A. 1947 - Present

KOREAN WAR USAF 335TH FIGHTER SQDN. PATCH: 3.75x4" fully embr. shape. Above avg. cond. $402.00

KOREAN WAR USAF BLOOD CHIT 1ST TYPE: 9x12" color printed rayon body w/ US, UN, British & S. Korean flags at top & 4 language message at bottom. Serial numbered. Very scarce official issue. Avg. cond. $395.00

KOREAN WAR USAF BLOOD CHIT: 1951 dated w/US flag at top & 6 oriental + 4

European languages below. Exc. cond.
.... $28.00
KOREAN WAR USAF BLOOD CHIT: Near
mint & good condition. 1951 dated &
carrying restricted tags at top & bottom.
Message in ten languages beneath the
US Flag. Exc. $26.00
KOREAN WAR USAF BLOOD CHIT: Printed
on nylon cloth. American 48 star flag at
top & 10 language message printed
below. Exc. cond. $40.00
KOREAN WAR USAF BLOOD CHIT: Printed
on nylon cloth. American 48 star flag at
top & 13 language message printed
below. 'Restricted' at top & bottom
masked out. Exc. cond. $30.00
KOREAN WAR USAF BLOOD CHIT: Printed
on nylon cloth. American 48 star flag at
top & 13 language message printed
below. 'Restricted' at top & bottom
masked out. Exc. cond. $30.00

KOREAN WAR USAF 335TH FIGHTER
SQDN. PATCH

KOREAN WAR USAF DET PATCH: 2" embr.
for 618th AC & W SQDN., has red cross in
center, title at top & Det 7/DOC at bottom.
Above avg. cond. $24.00
USAF 101ST FIS PATCH: quality embr. w/
great gull & spread wings outside of patch.
Near mint cond. $20.50
USAF 13TH FIS PATCH: 1950s. embr.
design on orange twill with scroll at
bottom. 3.75" wide. Unissued. Mint cond.
.... $42.00
USAF 13TH FIS PATCH: 1950s/60s.
Triangle in orange & black w/Voodoo
across top & Airplane w/13 on bottom
passing over. Mint patch. Near mint cond.
.... $25.00
USAF 166TH FIS PATCH: 4" w/banner - has
crow firing MG tied to snake. Banner
reads '166 Ftr Intcp Sqdn.' Exc. cond.
....$21.00
USAF 179TH FIS "CAVE CANUM" PATCH:
8" dia. Fully embr. w/comical design. Mint
cond. $30.00

USAF 179TH FIS NOVELTY PATCH: 1960s.
8" disc in bevo style embr. w/'179TH FIS
CAVE CANUM' on rim & large mean bull
dog in center w/machine gun. Mint-sharp.
Exc. cond. $20.00
USAF 17TH BOMBARDMENT WING
PATCH: 4x5.5" size. Embr. on gray twill.
Near mint cond. $20.00
USAF 19TH TFS PATCH: 1950s. 4.75" dia.
embr. design on black felt. Exc. cond.
.... $25.00
USAF 20TH FIGHTER BOMBER WING
PATCH: 1950s. 5" dia. Fully embr. Exc.
cond. $44.00
USAF 20TH FIGHTER BOMBER WING
PATCH: embr. design on black felt. 3"
wide. Unissued. Mint cond. $25.00
USAF 23RD TOW TARGET SQDN. PATCH:
3.75x5.25" fully embr. w/comical pelican
based design. Near mint cond. $32.00
USAF 26TH BOMB GRP. PATCH: 3.5x4"
Embr. on twill. Off uniform but still good.
Avg. cond. $20.00
USAF 27TH AIR DIV. PATCH: 4x4" embr. on
twill. Above avg. cond. $20.00
USAF 306TH BOMB WING PATCH (F-111):
Sac shield style w/weapon piercing cloud.
Used. Avg. cond. $21.00
USAF 309TH AIR COMMANDO PATCH:
partial embr. 4" & shows sword w/winged
blade over cloud w/parachute below.
reads on rim '309 AIR COMMANDO
SQUADRON PRIMUM.' Above avg. cond.
.... $50.00
USAF 313TH TAC FTR SQDN. LUCKY
PATCH: 4.75x4.25" embr. on orange twill.
Mint cond. $11.00
USAF 322ND BOMB SQDN. PATCH:
2.75x4" size. Fully embr. w/comical design
of "Uncle Sam" dropping aerial bombs.
Mint cond. $24.00
USAF 327TH TROOP CARRIER
SQUADRON JACKET PATCH: 5.5" blue
poplin w/machine embr. '5 deuces' logo &
tag reading '327th TROOP CARRIER
SQDN.' Exc. cond. $22.00
USAF 3305TH PTG AAA PATCH: golden-
yellow mach. embr. on 2" dia.
supermarine blue twill base. Near mint
cond. $20.00
USAF 331ST FIS PATCH: Approx. 3 7/8" dia.
w/mach. embr. design on black twill. Exc.
cond. $60.00
USAF 343RD FIGHTER GRP. (AIR
DEFENSE) PATCH: 3.75x4". Fully embr.
Near mint cond. $25.00
USAF 347TH TROOP CARRIER SQDN.
PATCH: 4x5.5" diamond-shaped patch w/
embr. comical design on white twill. Some
light soiling. Above avg. cond. $20.00

USAF 3505TH PILOT TRAINING GRP. PATCH: 1950s. embr. design on light blue felt. 4.25" dia. Unissued. Mint cond. $22.00

USAF 354TH FIGHTER INTERCEPTOR SQDN. PATCH: 1950s. 3 3/4" dia. embr. on twill. Exc. cond. $45.00

USAF 355TH FIGHTER GRP. PATCH: 3x3" embr. on twill. 1950s/1960s era. Exc. cond. $21.00

USAF 356TH FTR DAY SQDN. PATCH: 1950s. 5x5.75" size. Fully embr. Exc. cond...$42.00

USAF 38TH MUNITIONS MAINTENANCE SQDN. PATCH.: Mint on plastic sealed card from NS Meyer Inc. Embr. missile emblems on blue twill background. Near mint cond. $20.00

USAF 3RD AIR POSTAL SQDN. PATCH: Multi-piece cotton constr. body w/mach. embr. comical design. 5x4.5" size. Also, embr. on twill "Weapons Loading Team" & "Turn Around Director" patches. Near mint cond. $24.00

USAF 401ST FIGHTER WING PATCH: 3.75x4.5" fully embr. Exc. cond. ... $25.00

USAF 414TH FIGHTER GRP. PATCH: 3.75x4" fully embr. Mint cond. $21.00

USAF 417TH FTR BMR SQDN. PATCH: 1950s. 4x5 3/4" embr. on twill. Exc. cond. $48.00

USAF 417TH FTR BMR SQDN. PATCH: Approx. 6x4.25" embr. on red cotton. Near mint cond. $34.00

USAF 417TH FTR BMR SQDN. PATCH: 1950s. Approx. 6x4.25" size. Embr. on twill. Exc. cond. $32.00

USAF 42ND BOMB WING (SAC) UNIT PATCH: Squared shield in blue w/a yellow diagonal band containing four 'O.' There is a red bomb in each blue field. Banner at bottom reads 'AETH NOBIS.' Fully embr. Above avg. cond. $20.00

USAF 42ND BOMBARDMENT WING PATCH: 4x4". Fully embr. on dark tan twill. Near mint cond. $32.00

USAF 43RD BW UNIT PATCH: embr. blue & yellow w/motto at bottom. Exc. cond. $20.00

USAF 44TH BOMB SQDN. PATCH: 3.5x4.5" fully embr. Exc. cond. $42.00

USAF 460TH FIS 'CAVE TIGRIM' PATCH: 1960s. fully embr. patch design with scroll across bottom. 3.75" wide. Unissued. Mint cond. $26.00

USAF 460TH FIS PATCH: 1950s. fully embr. 7.5 x 6" w/banner across lower 1/3. reads CAVE TIGRIM. Large Tigers head at top. Nicely done. Exc. cond. $38.00

USAF 460TH FTR. INTECP. SQDN. PATCH: 3.75x3". Fully embr. Slight embr. flaw on background-hardly noticeable because

has black embr. on black twill backing. Above avg. cond. $21.00

USAF 482ND FIS PATCH: 50s/60s triangle w/bird carrying red missiles & title at bottom. Exc. cond. $20.00

USAF 48TH FIS F-106 DEVILS PATCH: 4x6" triangular-shaped. Fully embr. Mint cond. $42.00

USAF 49TH F.I.S. PATCH: 3.5x4.5" fully embr. Exc. cond. $20.00

USAF 49TH FIS PATCH: 1950s. Old design. Fully embr. 3 1/4x6". Near mint cond. $50.00

USAF 4TH FIGHTER BOMBER GRP. PATCH: 1950s. 2.75x5.5" size. Fully embr. Near mint cond. $34.00

USAF 4TH FIGHTER WING PATCH: fully embr. shield design. Near mint cond. $23.00

USAF 507TH FIGHTER GRP. PATCH: 3.75x4.25" embr. on twill. 1950s/1960s era. Exc. cond. $23.00

USAF 511TH FTR. BMB. SQDN. PATCH: 1950s. 4x4 1/2" embr. on twill. Exc. cond. $42.00

USAF 524TH BOMB SQDN. PATCH: 4" embr. disc. Motto 'Vigilance for peace.' Above avg. cond. $30.00

USAF 528 BOMB SQDN. PATCH: 4" dia. Fully embr. w/comical design. Near mint cond. $24.00

USAF 53RD WEATHER RECONNAISSANCE SQDN. PATCH: 4x4.5". Fully embr. Some glue/paper remains on back from display but unused cond. Exc. cond. $20.00

USAF 56TH FIS PATCH: 4.5" disc full color w/embr. gamecock w/constabulary uniform & billy club. 5 star brackets on each side & '56th' at bottom. Sharp patch for a history filled unit. Exc. cond. $243.00

USAF 56TH WRS PATCH: 1950s. 3" dia. Embr. on twill. Near mint cond. $20.00

USAF 585TH TMG BLAZER PATCH: Black felt w/gold & silver wire trim, modeling & motto. Shield w/4 part heraldic emblem & motto reading '585TH TACTICAL MISSILE GRP.' Avg. cond. $20.00

USAF 5TH FIS PATCH: 5" embr. w/bobcat in center. Avg. cond. $30.00

USAF 60TH FTR INCEPT. SQDN. PATCH: 4" dia. Embr. on twill w/comical design of black crow in flight helmet & scarf. Exc. cond. $20.00

USAF 6171ST AIR BASE SQDN. PATCH: Theater made. 3.75x3.75" w/comical "Garfield the Cat" design mach. embr. on blue cotton. Above avg. cond. $20.00

USAF 6431ST AIR BASE GRP. PATCH: 4" shield w/title in banner at bottom. Silver bullion for image of aircraft climbing from field thru stars to clouds. Above avg. cond. $59.00

USAF 64TH FTR INTCP SQDN. PATCH: 5" full embr. disc w/scorpion on yellow wing & banner with unit name. Exc. cond. $49.00

USAF 64TH FTR. INTCP. SQDN. PATCH: 4.75x5.5" fully embr. Mint cond. ... $40.00

USAF 687TH A C & W SQDN. PATCH: 4.75" dia. Fully embr. w/attached scroll at bottom. Mint cond. $22.00

USAF 733RD TROOP CARRIER SQDN. "THE ONLY WAY TO FLY" PATCH: 5x5.25" fully embr. Near mint cond. $30.00

USAF 73RD AIR DIVISION PATCH: 3.75x4" size. Fully embr. w/attached scroll. Mint cond. $20.00

USAF 76TH FTR. INTCP. SQDN. PATCH: 4x4.75" size. Mach. embr. design on twill. Off uniform. Above avg. cond. $42.00

USAF 777TH TROOP CARRIER SQDN. PATCH: 4x4.5" embr. on twill. Near mint cond. $34.00

USAF 80TH FBS HEADHUNTERS PATCH: Hand embr. silk on medium green felt. Colorful & details. Has mis-spelling "Headhunters." Neat looking. Approx. 2 1/8x2 1/2". Above avg. cond. $48.00

USAF 81ST FTR. BMR. SQDN. PATCH: embr. design on light lavender twill with tab at bottom. 4" dia. Unissued cond. Mint cond. $30.00

USAF 873RD TAC MISSILE SQDN. PATCH: Embr. 5" disc w/banner, Japanese embr. Exc. cond. $35.00

USAF 8TH AERIAL PORT SQUADRON PATCH: Playboy bunny in black at center w/'DELTA PLAYBOYS' at bottom. Above avg. cond. $22.00

USAF 93RD FIGHTER INTERCEPTOR SQDN. PATCH: 5x5.25" w/comical design embr. on dark blue twill. Near mint cond. $40.00

USAF 93RD FIS PATCH: 4" orange background w/bucking bronco w/rider in center. Above avg. cond. $30.00

USAF 95TH BOMB WING PATCH: Full embr. shield w/white cross on blue field - motto Justice w/victory. Above avg. cond. $30.00

USAF 95TH FTR. INTCP. SQDN. PATCH: 1950s/1960s. 5x5.75" size. Design of skull in top hat & holding cane in hand on twill. Exc. cond. $32.00

USAF 97TH FIGHTER SQDN. "THUNDERBIRD" PATCH: 3.75" dia. Fully embr. Exc. cond. $23.00

USAF 9TH AIR COMMANDO SQDN. "'C' FLT." PATCH: Asian mach. embr. comical flying "Snoopy" design on twill. 4" wide. Post-Nam. Mint cond. $27.00

USAF ADC ROCKET MEET PATCH: 1958. 3x2.5" fully embr. Exc. cond. $32.00

USAF ADC ROCKET MEET PATCH: 1959. 3x2.5" fully embr. Above avg. cond. $32.00

USAF AEROCLUB PATCH FROM NOUASEUR AFB, MOROCCO: 8" long w/ stars at top & w/light plane sticking thru tower. Base name at top. Above avg. cond. $60.00

USAF ANG FIGHTER PATCH: Colorful Indian & headdress in center for 171st FIS 5". Exc. cond. $21.00

USAF ATOMIC TEST GRP. PATCH: USAF type shield w/unit emblem & 4925th test grp. A(atomic). Avg. cond. $25.00

USAF F-111 BOMB SQDN. PATCH: 1960s. Shows Angry tiger head on Atomic blast w/arrow pointing forward. Now related to B-2 Bomb Squadron at Whitman AFB, MO. Above avg. cond. $20.00

USAF BIG GOOSE BAY PATCH: 9.5" disc Partially embr. in color w/fish leaping over outline of Labrador. Rim reads '95TH STRAT WING GOOSE BAY, LABRADOR/ THE FLYING FISHERMEN.' Above avg. cond. $22.00

USAF BITBURG AFB GERMANY 23rd TFS UNIT PATCH: Shows hawk w/red-white-blue wings & boxing gloves on talons in a dive. Exc. cond. $20.00

USAF BLOOD CHIT: 1961 dated w/US flag at top & language phrases below. Appear to be for European operations. Sealed in cellophane. Near mint cond. $30.00

USAF BLUE FOXES PATCH: Mint embr. w/ blue fox holding MG. Banner reads '18TH FIGHTER SQUADRON.' Near mint cond. $20.50

USAF CAPTAIN NAME TAG: Subdued mach. embr. design of pilot wing over name & "CAPT. USAF" on uncut OD cotton backed in newspaper w/Oriental printing. Exc. cond. $20.00

USAF CLEVER NOVELTY PATCH: 4" w/Wily Coyote holding the Road Runner, reads 'BEEP BEEP YOUR ASS' I TEAM DBOG. Avg. cond. $37.00

USAF DET 1, 84TH FIS PATCH: 4x4.5" embr. on orange twill. Exc. cond. ..$21.00

USAF F-101 PILOTS "VOODOO ONE-O-WONDER" PATCH: 4" dia. Embr. on twill. Mint cond. $30.00

USAF F-101 UNITS FLIGHT SURGEONS "VOODOO WITCH DOCTOR" PATCH: 4" dia. Embr. on twill. Mint cond. $16.00

USAF F-101 WEAPONS SYSTEMS OFFICER "VOODOO SCOPE WIZARD" PATCH: 4" dia. Embr. on twill. Mint cond. $24.00

USAF F-106 49TH FIS PATCH: 4x4.75" embr. on twill. Near mint cond. ... $200.00

USAF F-106/5TH FIS AIRCRAFT PATCH: 1960s. orange embr. design on blue triangle, has been removed from a uniform, 3" wide. Exc. cond. $200.00

USAF F-15 DEMO TEAM JACKET PATCH: Bevo style embr. w/F-15 in center & 'F-15' over + 'EAGLE' under + 'DEMONSTRATION TEAM' on tab. Exc. cond. $12.00

USAF F-4G BACK OF JACKET PATCH: 8" fully embr. disc w/weasel dressed in Little phantom costume & rim 'F-4G PHANTOM II ADVANCED WILD WEASEL.' Near mint cond. $20.00

USAF FIGHTER GRP. PATCH: Full embr. multi-colored shield for 114th Fighter Grp.. Near mint cond. $20.00

USAF FIGHTER SQDN. 21 PATCH: 3.75x4.5" w/embr. design on twill. Off uniform w/some soiling. Avg. cond. $40.00

USAF FIGHTER UNIT PATCH: 79th TFS w/ tiger & claws in center of 5" shield. Exc. cond. $12.00

USAF FIGHTER UNIT PATCH: Nicely embr. in green & white 49th FIS patch. Exc. cond. $20.00

USAF FIGHTER WEAPONS SCHOOL: 4.5" shield w/target in center & red weapon aimed for center. Above avg. cond. $32.00

USAF GENERAL GRADE SLIP-ON SHOULDER RANK TABS: USAF-shade blue knit w/silver tinsel embr. stars. Includes 1, 2, 3 & 4-star gen. pairs. Near mint cond. $24.00

USAF INTERCEPTOR SQDN. PATCH: 1950s. 5" felt flocking on nylon patch for 132nd Ftr Intcp Sq. Above avg. cond. $50.00

USAF J79 'TIGER BY THE TAIL' OVER 2000 HOURS FLIGHT TIME: fully embr. patch with outer ring in gold tinsel. 5" dia. Mint cond. $20.00

USAF JACKET PATCH: 5" dia. fully embr. w/ Angry turbaned Arab carrying scimitar over his head in center. Above avg. cond. $20.00

USAF JACKET PATCH: From Kadena Transient alert. 9.5" disc fully embr. w/

cartoon cobra in center & 'FOLLOW ME' on his hood. Near mint cond. $20.00

USAF KOMAKI AIRDROME - BASE COMM PATCH: Fully embr. w/alligator operating teletype. Rim reads at top 'BASE COMMUNICATIONS/KOMAKI AIR DROME' & at bottom 'APO 710/6019TH AB SQDN. Exc. cond. $20.00

USAF MASTER AIR DEFENSE PATCH: 3.75" dia. Fully embr. Near mint cond. $32.00

USAF MULTI-NATIONAL TIGER MEET PATCH: 1992. Bevo style 4" disc w/sabre tooth tiger centered on 4 pt star w/flags of participants on rim. Exc. cond. $12.00

USAF NAVIGATOR FLIGHT SUIT NAME TAG: Theater made. 4 1/2x2 7/8" golden-yellow cotton base w/black cotton border + mach. embr. design in black of navg. wing over name & "Capt. USAF." Avg. cond. $100.00

USAF NOVELTY PATCH: Post-WWII. Shows camel in desert w/'WHEELUS GOLF CLUB' at top & 'TRIPOLI, LIBYA' below. Avg. cond. $10.00

USAF PATCH W/MOTTO "OUR EYES NEVER CLOSE": Approx. 2x1.5" size. Fully embr. Near mint cond. $20.00

USAF PHOTO RECON PATCH: Blunt diamond w/Owl over flaming 'HOT STUFF' & 'an/aad-5' between wings. Near mint cond. $25.00

USAF PHOTO SQDN. PATCH: 3.75" dia. black twill base w/comical embr. design of bee-like caricature w/"glowing" tail & holding aerial camera. Avg. cond. $20.00

USAF RAMSUN THAILAND '7' PATCH: theater made, machine embr. design on red twill. 2.75" wide, has been worn but is in cond. Near mint cond. $25.00

USAF SAC PATCH: Fully embr., great detail. Above avg. cond. $20.00

USAF SECURITY SERVICE PATCH: Blazer style w/'64 E-SK COMMANDERS 66' at top & 'USAF SECURITY SERVICE' in banner at bottom. 4 panels in center show aspects of Service. Above avg. cond. $25.00

USAF SQUADRON PATCH: 5" triangle fully embr. w/Pegasus rising above clouds and sword on pillow. Banner below reads '5th SQDN.' Above avg. cond. $20.00

USAF STRATEGIC AIR CMD. PATCH: 3.75x4.25" embr. on white twill. Off uniform but clean. Above avg. cond. $20.00

USAF THUNDERBIRDS JACKET SIZED PATCH: 5" machine embr. w/vivid color on

Thunderbird emblem & 'THUNDERBIRDS' at bottom. One sharp AF patch. Exc. cond. $96.00

USAF TRAINING SQDN. PATCH: Design of lightweight plane & nuclear mushroom cloud. Reads "59-5/The Fallouts." Fully embr. Exc. cond. $19.00

USAF TRANSITION CONTINENTAL AIR CMD. PATCH: Fully embr. Mint cond. $26.00

USAF U-2 PATCH W/UNIT IDENTIFIED: Dragon lady Lockheed U-2 w/banner reading "349th Strat. Recon Squadron." Fully embr. 4" shield. Important Nam era Patch. Exc. cond. $41.00

USAF UNIT PATCH: 1960s. 21st Special Operations Grp./knife. Theater made, fully embr. Exc. cond. $20.00

USAF VOODOO F-101 PATCH LOT: 1. Voodoo one-o-wonder-Winged witch doctor mask 2. Voodoo Scopewizard - Lightning bolts around mask 3. Voodoo Medicine man- crossed tools behind mask. Exc. cond. $30.00

USAF VOODOO ONE-O-WONDER PATCH: 4" dia. w/colorful mach. embr. design on black velveteen. Exc. cond. $20.00

USAF WILLIAM TELL WEAPONS MEET PATCH: 1980. 3.75" dia. Embr. on white twill. Above avg. cond. $20.00

USAF WILLIAM TELL WEAPONS MEET PATCH: 1982. 4" dia. Fully embr. Near mint cond. $10.00

USAF/NATO JOINT PATCH: 1970 TAC WEAPONS TEAM w/German, Canadian & American flag at top. Near mint cond. $20.00

VIETNAM ERA USAF "EAGLE INSTRUCTOR" PATCH: Asian made. 3 7/8" dia. Mach. embr. on navy blue twill. Off uniform. Avg. cond. $20.00

VIETNAM ERA USAF 133RD EOD 'MINI ARC LIGHT SQUAD' PATCH: 3.5" yellow felt disk w/black edge trim & showing the grim reaper w/scythe raised against a 'Huey' chopper. Unit & motto on perimeter. Avg. cond. $50.00

VIETNAM ERA USAF 1ST OPTIONS SQDN. PATCH: Asian made. 4.25x4.25" mach. embr. on yellow twill. Off uniform. Above avg. cond. $32.00

VIETNAM ERA USAF 315TH SPS PANTHER/SECURITY SECURITY PATCH: Vietnam made. 2.75" dia. Mach. embr. on red cotton. Near mint cond. $72.00

VIETNAM ERA USAF 497TH FIS WILD WEASEL: 4" diam.-fully embr.-US made. Near mint cond. $42.00

VIETNAM ERA USAF 5TH AIR FORCE SEA SURVIVAL PATCH: 3x4.75" Japanese color machine made w/seahorses flanking life ring, lettering in center + "Numazu, Japan" on life ring. Mint cond. $24.00

VIETNAM ERA USAF 6912TH SECURITY SQDN. PATCH: 3.75x3.75" embr. on scarlet felt. Near mint cond. $25.00

VIETNAM ERA USAF 8TH AERIAL PORT SQDN. PATCH: 4x4" size. Hand embr. on dark blue cotton. Above avg. cond. $28.00

VIETNAM ERA USAF 8TH AERIAL PORT SQDN. PATCH: Vietnam made. 3.25" dia. blue cotton body w/hand embr. design + attached tab at bottom. Off uniform. Avg. cond. $22.00

VIETNAM ERA USAF 9TH OPS SQUADRON CHIEU HOI NOVELTY PATCH: Vietnam made. 3.75" dia. blue cotton base w/mach. embr. & applique cotton panel constr. w/comical design of "flying Snoopy." Exc. cond. $60.00

VIETNAM ERA USAF ARC LIGHT 70 WUR E-41 'JUST DOING OUR THING' PATCH: embr. design on red twill. Comes with neat note giving background of the design written by pilot. In unissued cond. 3.75" wide, appears Asian made. Mint cond. $32.00

VIETNAM ERA USAF B-52 NOVELTY PATCH: North Vietnam SAM bait featuring B-52 in large fishhook. Exc. cond. $20.00

VIETNAM ERA USAF B-52 NOVELTY PATCH: Vietnam made. Green B-52 in Center & 'PEACE HELL/BOMB HANOI' on border. 4" disc. Above avg. cond. $21.00

VIETNAM ERA USAF BLOOD CHIT: 1962 dated w/50 star flag at top & message displayed in 14 languages. Nylon cloth. Exc. cond. $35.00

VIETNAM ERA USAF BLOOD CHIT: nylon material w/American flag at top & language phrases below. Exc. cond. $20.00

VIETNAM ERA USAF CRASH CREW PATCH: Embr. 4" w/tab. Shows Crash crewman chopping thru flames w/rim reading 'MABS-36 CRASH CREW KY HA RS VIET NAM' & tab reads '1965-66.' Exc. cond. $60.00

VIETNAM ERA USAF F-4 TWO HUNDRED MISSION PATCH: White twill ace of spades w/center spade made of '2 hundred missions' and stem saying 'F-4/ Vietnam.' Dead center is the little phantom caricature. Avg. cond. $63.00

VIETNAM ERA USAF F-5 PATCH: Vietnam made. White embr. on blue twill showing outline of aircraft & red F-5 on wings. Avg. cond. $35.00

VIETNAM ERA USAF FLIGHT EXAMINER/ C-123 PATCH: Vietnam made. 2.75x3" size. Multi-piece cotton base w/mach. embr. lettering. Exc. cond. $30.00

VIETNAM ERA USAF FREQUENT WIND- SAIGON 1975 POCKET PATCH: 4" diam.- hand embr. design-frontal view of C-130 superimposed over map of Nam. Above avg. cond. $26.00

VIETNAM ERA USAF HOTSHOT RF-4C RECON 100 MISSION PATCH: 7x4" triangle w/yellow 'RF-4C' over '100' w/ cartoon RF-4C imposed & 'COMBAT MISSIONS/NORTH VIETNAM.' Avg. cond. $119.00

VIETNAM ERA USAF MISSION PATCH: Shield for 200 missions in an A-37 VNAF. (not USAF). Nam made patch embr. but low quality. Above avg. cond. $70.00

VIETNAM ERA USAF NAIL PATCH: Sewn on black cloth, embr. top view of OV-10 w/ red nail passing thru & 'NAIL' at top + 'FAC' & 'PHOTO.' US flag embr. on black cloth. 50 star flag. Avg. cond. $87.00

VIETNAM ERA USAF NOUASSEUR AERO CLUB JACKET PATCH: Asian made 4.5x8.5" bullet shaped design w/likeness of mailed fist clutching small airplane in flight-field of stars above. Above avg. cond. $52.00

VIETNAM ERA USAF NOVELTY PATCH: 3.5" dia. white cotton disc w/machine embr. design of Snoopy + 1st Annual Danang Vietnam Rocket City Ballye." Near mint cond. $35.00

VIETNAM ERA USAF NOVELTY PATCH: Vietnam made. 3x4" shield-shape patch w/hand embr. & applied cotton panel design on white loose woven cotton. Has comical bird design w/"United States Air Force" below US flag field. Exc. cond. $26.00

VIETNAM ERA USAF PARTY SUIT PATCH: 2.5x4" white cotton 1/2 circle w/red border-likeness of black "Spooky" in center w/"Fabulous Four Engine Fighters" around it. Near mint cond. $100.00

VIETNAM ERA USAF SOUTHEAST ASIA WAR GAMES PARTICIPANT PATCH: w/ peace symbol-US flag-Nam & Thai

symbols all in center. Above avg. cond. $20.00

VIETNAM ERA USAF TANKER OPS PATCH FOR FREQUENT WIND & MAYAGUEZ: Thailand made. 6" w/tanker boom diagonally across center & Eagle w/US shield on chest at bottom tabs read 'THAILAND/CAMBODIA VIETNAM.' Above avg. cond. $20.00

VIETNAM ERA USAF UNIT NOVELTY PATCHES: 3" disc w/peace emblem & 'SOUTH EAST ASIA WAR GAMES PARTICIPANT' + 3" disc w/target rings centered over the Thai, Cambodian, Vietnam area. Above avg. cond. .. $21.00

U.S. NAVY & MARINE CORPS CLOTH INSIGNIA

A. All Periods

CIVIL WAR NAVY PO SLEEVE RANK: Shows eagle perched on fouled anchor, perimeter outlined in dots. Above avg. cond. $35.00

CIVIL WAR SHIP SHOOTER CAP DEVICE: Very rare Naval item, Oval of black wool w/gold bullion wreath & 'U. S. S. S.' inside. Gold wire trim. Wool shows light soiling but no signs of wear/damage. Avg. cond. $685.00

CIVIL WAR SHIP SHOOTER CAP DEVICE

COAST GUARD AVDET 131/ARCTIC '93' JACKET PATCH: 5" dia. Fully embr. w/ comical design of polar bear grabbing for helicopter + motto "If I Could Catch a Dauphin I'd Eat It To." Colorful. Mint cond. $10.00

COAST GUARD AVDET-130/DEEP FREEZE 1993/SAC M10 JACKET PATCH: 5x5.5" shield-shaped body. Fully embr. Near mint cond. $20.00

COAST GUARD BASE TERMINAL IS. PATCH: 4 3/8" wide embr. on twill. Interesting design. Exc. cond. $25.00

COAST GUARD LORAN STATION FALLON, NEVADA "MASTER 9940" JACKET

PATCH: 4.5" dia. Fully embr. Colorful. Mint cond. $10.00

COAST GUARD SAN DIEGO ASM'S/SAR DOGS JACKET PATCH: Approx. 5.25x5" size. Fully embr. w/comical design & motto "We Don't Need No Stinkin' Chutes." Colorful. Mint cond. $10.00

COAST GUARD STATION CHANNEL IS. HARBOR SEARCH & RESCUE/FED. LAW ENFORCEMENT PATCH: 5" dia. Fully embr. Colorful. Mint cond. $10.00

COAST GUARD STATION GRAYS HARBOR SEARCH & RESCUE JACKET PATCH: Approx. 4.5x5". Fully embr. Mint cond. $10.00

COAST GUARD WMEC 620 RESOLUTE ASTORIA, OREGON JACKET PATCH: 4.5x5.75" size. Fully embr. W/design & reads "SAR/MLE/Fisheries Conservation." Mint cond. $10.00

DESERT SHIELD NAVY USS DWIGHT D. EISENHOWER OP. "WE DID THE DITCH" PATCH: 5" dia. Embr. novelty design on twill w/gold tinsel detail. Near mint cond. $20.00

DESERT STORM USMC PATCH: 5" shield full color & embr. bevo style w/USMC emblem on bannered US flag + saber on sun. Has 'WEAPONS CO/BLT 1/4/HEAVY GUNS' below. Near mint cond. $14.00

DESERT STORM USMC PATCH: 5th Marine expeditionary brigade- red background w/ winged sword & '5' encircling hilt. Bevo style embr. Exc. cond. $16.50

MARINE BANJO BOARDS: Late 1800s. Red knotted cord board w/Bright metal USMC emblems on red wool field & brass trim. Very clean. Pair of col.'s bullion dress shoulder pieces w/gold trim & dark green background. Exc. cond. $43.00

MARINE DRESS CHEVRON: Late 1800s. Gold braid on red felt-3 stripes of chevron w/3 matching horizontal stripes. For Quartermaster Sgt. Very good condition. Exc. cond. $30.00

NAVY 100 OMS PATCH: Theater made. embr. design on white twill. 3" square, black merrowed border. Mint cond. $20.00

NAVY ACADEMY CADET CLOTH RANK INSIGNIA: Gold bullion Star on black wool. Mfg. Label says 'BOS Cadet' & dated 1973. Above avg. cond. $20.00

NAVY AIR STATION NEW YORK JACKET PATCH: embr. design on light blue twill with tab at bottom. 5" dia. Mint cond. $16.00

NAVY AVIATOR NAS SOUTH WEYMOUTH PATCH: Gold bullion pilot wings at top over outline of bay area. Title in banner. Above avg. cond. $20.00

NAVY AVIATOR AIR-ANTI-SUBRON 83 PATCH: 4.75x5.25" fully embr. w/ merrowed edge. Near mint cond. $15.00

NAVY AVIATOR BLUE ANGELS PHANTOMS PATCH: 1960s. 4x4.75" embr. on white cotton twill. From Blue Angel pilot collection. Near mint cond. $77.00

NAVY AVIATOR CORSAIR II PATCH: 3.5x4.25" shield-shaped. Red & white base colors. Fully embr. Mint cond. $20.00

NAVY AVIATOR EA-3B DOUGLAS SKYWARRIOR "THE WHALE" PATCH: 4.5" dia. Fully embr. Mint cond. $21.00

NAVY AVIATOR F3H DEMON FIGHTER PATCH: 90mm white w/narrow black bulls eye rings & red devil in center. Text at top reads 'Demon Driver.' Above avg. cond. $44.00

NAVY AVIATOR FIGHTING 20 SQUADRON PATCH: 4x5" heavy stitched skull design-some soiling. Above avg. cond. $60.00

NAVY AVIATOR FIGHTING 31 PATCH: Japanese made. 3.25x4" fully embr. Woven Tokyo maker's label on back. Mint cond. $40.00

NAVY AVIATOR FIGHTING 33 SQDN. PATCH: approx. 6.5x5.5" size w/mach. embr. design on black twill. Exc. cond. $35.00

NAVY AVIATOR HMM-261 SQDN. PATCH: Japanese made. 4.5x5" fully mach. embr. Near mint cond. $28.00

NAVY AVIATOR HS-1 SQDN. PATCH: 3.75x4.5" embr. on white twill. A bit stiff. Above avg. cond. $20.00

NAVY AVIATOR MWWU-2 SQDN. PATCH: Japanese made. 4.25x4.75" size. Fully mach. embr. Mint cond. $20.00

NAVY AVIATOR OUTFIT PATCH: 6" embr. w/banner at bottom for VRC-50 featuring a black embr. devil dog w/red ball on blue field. Mint. Near mint cond. $25.00

NAVY AVIATOR PATCH: 3" color & embr. for VF 725 & shows winged dog riding rocket. Above avg. cond. $28.00

NAVY AVIATOR PATCH: 6" disc + upper & lower tabs. Fully embr. w/weasel riding pair of missiles like ski's & carrying thunderbolt. Upper tab reads 'NAS CUBI POINT PHILIPPINES,' Lower reads 'MOBILE MISSILE MAINTENANCE FACILITY.' Exc. cond. $75.00

NAVY AVIATOR TACRON ELEVEN SQDN. PATCH: 4x5" embr. on twill. Mint cond. $28.00

NAVY AVIATOR VAP 62 SQDN. PATCH: 3.75x4.25" fully embr. w/comical design. Near mint cond. $27.00

NAVY AVIATOR VAP 62 SQDN. PATCH: Approx. 4x4.25" size. Fully embr. Near mint cond. $23.00

NAVY AVIATOR VMT-18 "DEVIL PUPS" SQDN. PATCH: 5x5.5" size. Embr. comical design on lt. blue twill. Exc. cond. $35.00

NAVY AVIATOR VR-773 PATCH: Japanese made. 4.5x4.5" size. Fully mach. embr. Off uniform. Avg. cond. $25.00

NAVY AVIATOR PATCH

NAVY BASE PATCH: 5" triangle bullion patch featuring the statute of Liberty, for New York NAS. Near mint cond. ..$20.00

NAVY BLAZER PATCH: Modern. Bullion 3" disc w/Pb, shows scenes from Naples area + Bullion rampant lion & Aircraft carrier. Rim reads in bullion, 'UNITED STATES NAVY SUPPORT ACTIVITY, NAPLES, ITALY.' Above avg. cond. $12.00

NAVY CAP RIBBON: U.S.S WORDEN. Full-length black ribbon w/gold wire letters. Some light even tarnish. Above avg. cond. $45.00

NAVY CAP RIBBON: U.S.S. DENVER. Full-length black ribbon w/wire woven letters. Only some light tarnish. Above avg. cond. $21.00

NAVY CAP RIBBON: U.S.S. MIANTONOMAH. Full length black ribbon w/wire woven letters. Some light tarnish but letters still & bright. Above avg. cond. $25.00

NAVY CAP RIBBON: U.S.S. OHIO. Black ribbon w/wire woven letters. Some even tarnish. Appears to have been removed from a display. Avg. cond. $40.00

NAVY CAP RIBBON: U.S.S. PEORIA. Full-length black ribbon w/gold wire woven lettering. Avg. cond. $22.00

NAVY CARRIER PATCH: 3" full color & embr. w/tabs, USS Kearsarge CVS-33 in lower & 'IN OMNIBUS PINNACULUM' in upper, Ship in front of mountains at center. Exc. cond. $37.00

NAVY COMBAT SWIMMER PATCH: Mint embr. w/gold jump wing Mine & torpedoes & Scuba diver passing thru. Exc. cond. $40.00

NAVY CPO SHOULDER RATE: Right shoulder 1918 period CPO Quartermaster rate. Above avg. cond. $17.00

NAVY CPO SHOULDER RATE: Sharp WWII Black on tan PO1 turret Capt. rate, right shoulder. Exc. cond. $27.00

NAVY HELANTISUBRON TWELVE PATCH: Japanese made. 4.5x4". Fully mach. embr. Has Tokyo maker's label on back. Mint cond. $27.50

NAVY INTELLIGENCE PATCH: 4" color showing eagle w/earphones & all seeing eye in chest. motto reads In God We Trust, all others we monitor. Exc. cond. $16.00

NAVY LIBERTY JUMPER CUFFS: green & gray woven design of submarine "dolphin" badge. Current but . Mint cond. $11.00

NAVY MIDSHIPMAN'S RATE: Pre-1920s. BULLION & GOLD BRAID. Shows darkening. Avg. cond. $14.00

NAVY MILITARY SEA TRANSPORTATION SERVICE PATCH: gold embr. design on black felt. 3" dia. Appears to be unissued. Exc. cond. $20.00

NAVY NATTC MEMPHIS PATCH: 4.5" wide triangular-shaped patch. Off uniform but clean. Above avg. cond. $20.00

NAVY PATRON 90 JACKET PATCH: Fully embr. 5" showing full face of lion in stylized pose. Above avg. cond. ... $20.00

NAVY PETTY 2ND RATE: Winter red chevrons on black wool w/embr. eagle & crossed anchors for Boatswains mate. Above avg. cond. $24.00

NAVY RECRUITING SERVICE ARMBAND: White embr. on navy blue felt body. Exc. cond. $20.00

NAVY SUBMARINE SQDN. FIVE "DETECT*ATTACK*DESTROY" PATCH: 5x5.25" fully embr. Mint cond. $12.00

NAVY U.S. NAVAL STATION, KEFLAVIK, ICELAND JACKET PATCH: 4" dia. Embr. on twill. Mint cond. $23.00

NAVY USS FORRESTAL (AIRCRAFT CARRIER) JACKET PATCH: 4x4.75". Embr. on twill. Avg. cond. $12.00

NAVY USS GALVESTON PATCH: 4" dia. Mach. embr. on twill. Exc. cond. ... $16.00

NAVY USS GEORGE CLYMER JACKET PATCH: Shield shaped w/ship emblem in

center & title at top. Embr. on cream B/G.
Above avg. cond. $20.00
NAVY USS HALEAKALA JACKET PATCH:
5" disc w/image of volcano erupting. Title
on perimeter. Above avg. cond. $20.00
NAVY USS RANDOLPH MED CRUISE
JACKET PATCH: 1957-58. Silver bullion
on black wool. 6" dia. w/ship in center w/
CVA above & 1957 '15' 1958 below. Rim
reads Med -USS- Cruise /RANDOLPH.
Avg. cond. $50.00

NAVY USS RANDOLPH MED CRUISE
JACKET PATCH

NAVY USS ROBERT E. LEE (SSBN-601)
JACKET PATCH: 4.25x4.75" fully embr.
Above avg. cond. $12.00
NAVY USS SARATOGA PATCH: 1958 Med
Cruise, 5" fully embr. Above avg. cond.
.... $200.00
NAVY USS SILVERSIDES PATCH: 4" shield
w/Nuclear Sub in center for SSN-679.
Exc. cond. $10.00
NAVY CAP TALLY: Full-length black ribbon
is approx. 1 1/16" wide. Has wire woven
"Minnesota" lettering. Some light even
tarnish. Above avg. cond. $49.00
USMC 13TH DEF. BN. PATCH: 3" wide
white felt base w/mach. embr. design.
Exc. cond. $12.00
USMC 2ND DIV. PATCH: Standard 2nd Div.
patch but in rare kidney shape w/yellow
hand and torch . Above avg. cond.
.... $165.00

USMC 2ND DIV. PATCH

USMC 3RD MARINE 2ND BDE. DIV.
PATCH: Gold 3 on red shield, in black
shield w/sword piercing all & second BN.
banner at top. Exc. cond. $12.00
USMC 704TH MARINE RAIDER BN.
PATCH: 3" wide. Mach. embr. on blue felt.
Off uniform. Above avg. cond. $55.00
USMC AVIATOR 1ST MARINE AIR WING
PATCH: Japanese made. 4.25" wide. Fully
mach. embr. Exc. cond. $24.00
USMC AVIATOR 2ND MARINE DIV.
AVIATION UNIT PATCH: Fully embr. patch
in traditional 2nd Div. patch-design but has
design of "Bronco" twin-engine airplane
over white hand grasping yellow torch +
attached "Eyes of the Division" tab at
bottom. Approx. 3x5" size. Exc. cond.
.... $34.00
USMC AVIATOR HMH-777 SQDN. PATCH:
Japanese made. 4x4.25" fully mach.
embr. Off uniform. Above avg. cond.
.... $20.00
USMC AVIATOR HMM 362 "UGLY ANGELS"
SQDN. PATCH: Japanese made. 4.5x5.5"
size. Fully mach. embr. Near mint cond.
.... $45.00
USMC AVIATOR HMM-163 "RIDGE
RUNNERS" SQDN. PATCH: Japanese
made. 4.5x5.25" fully mach. embr. Exc.
cond. $20.00
USMC AVIATOR MAG-14 PATCH: 4x4.75"
size. Embr. on lt. blue twill. Exc. cond.
....$30.00
USMC AVIATOR MAG-41 PATCH: 4 5/8"
wide triangular-shape lt. blue twill base w/
embr. design. Near mint cond. $20.00
USMC AVIATOR MALS-12 "MARAUDERS"
SQDN. PATCH: 4x4.25" embr. on maroon
cotton. Near mint cond. $20.00
USMC AVIATOR MWSG-12 PATCH:
Japanese made. 5.5" wide triangular-
shaped patch w/comical design. Fully
mach. embr. Near mint cond. $23.00
USMC AVIATOR PATCH: HMM-773 6" disc
w/bottom banner, embr. black w/red
lightning & yellow strike point. Exc. cond.
.... $20.00
USMC AVIATOR PATCH: MAG-39, Embr. 5"
triangle w/eagle perched on globe. Exc.
cond. $20.00
USMC AVIATOR SE-MADE HMR-L-162
PATCH: Japanese made. 4.25x4.75" w/
mach. embr. design on cotton. Remains of
paper backing. Exc. cond. $25.00
USMC AVIATOR VMA-214 "BLACKSHEEP"
SQDN. PATCH: 4x5 1/8" size. Fully embr.
Near mint cond. $45.00

USMC AVIATOR VMAQ-2 "CAN DO EASY" SQDN. PATCH: Japanese made. 4.25x5.5" size. Fully mach. embr. w/ "Playboy" bunny head design. Near mint cond. $25.00

USMC AVIATOR ATTACK SQUADRON 215 PATCH: 5" disc w/green/white check rim & Knight's helmet framed in wings. Avg. cond. $66.00

USMC AVIATOR MFA 333 SQDN. PATCH: Japanese made. 4.75x5" size. Fully mach. embr. Near mint cond. $20.00

USMC CHEVRONS: 1890s. Pair of Sgt. chevrons w/paymaster's emblem in center. Gold ribbed ribbon on red felt, shows light wear. Exc. cond. $134.00

USMC CO "A" MARINE BARRACKS INFANTRY SMALL UNIT JUNGLE PATROL SCHOOL PATCH: Philippine fully mach. embr. 4x3.75" size. Near mint cond. $19.00

USMC EMBLEM PATCH: 6" embr. in brown & white on white felt. Some aging evident. Above avg. cond. $25.00

USMC EMBLEM PATCH: R/W/B embr. 6" patch. Near mint cond. $25.00

USMC INFANTRY SCHOOL UNIT JUNGLE PATROL SCHOOL, SUBIC BAY, P. I. PATCH: For Co. "B" Marine Barracks. Fully mach. embr. Theater-made. Mint cond. $12.00

USMC LOGISTICS COMMAND PATCH: Fully embr. red field 6" pentagon shaped jacket patch. Has Blue gauntlet w/Marine emblem at wrist gripping arrows & wheat stalks. At top is title & motto reads, 'COPIAS/SUSTINIMUS.' THIS IS A GOOD ONE. Near mint cond. $50.00

USMC PATCH: MASS-2, 6" shield w/bar at top. Okinawa based, shows embr. antenna unit in center over Okinawa map. Exc. cond. $20.00

USMC QM SGT. CHEVRONS: 1800s. Scarlet field w/three rows of yellow gold braid separated to show red between rows & includes 3 horizontal stripes to close inverted 'V.' Avg. cond. $10.00

USMC QM SGT. FULL DRESS CHEVRONS: Used. Above avg. cond. $20.00

USMC RECRUIT DEPOT SAN DIEGO EDSON TO SAN ONOFRE 15 MILE RUN JACKET PATCH: 5.75" dia. Embr. on twill. Mint cond. $21.00

USMC RECRUITING ARMBAND: Navy blue felt body w/thick white flocked "RECRUITING SERVICE U.S. MARINES" lettering. Above avg. cond. $37.00

USMC SGT. MAJOR OF THE MARINE CORPS CHEVRONS: Forest green embr. on tan twill. Exc. cond. $20.00

USMC SGT. MAJOR OF THE MARINE CORPS DRESS BLUE UNIFORM CHEVRONS: Golden-yellow embr. on red felt. Scarce. Mint cond. $12.00

USMC TRANSPORT SGT. CHEVRONS: Have 3 chevrons above & 3 flat rockers. Forest green wool on dark tan twill. Off uniform-couple moth nips. Avg. cond. $72.00

USN AVIATOR VP 11 AVIONICS-72 JACKET PATCH: 5" diam.-Philippine made w/scene of winged horse's ass in the center. Above avg. cond. $21.00

VIETNAM ERA NAVY 7TH FLEET JACKET PATCH: Japanese made. 4x6.5" rect. body w/fully mach. embr. design of flaming upright sword & "Playboy" bunny head. Off jacket but is clean. Above avg. cond. $125.00

VIETNAM ERA NAVY 7TH FLEET JACKET PATCH

VIETNAM ERA NAVY AVIATOR PATROL SQDN. 31 PATCH: 4.75x4.75" size. Fully mach. embr. Off uniform. Above avg. cond. $17.00

VIETNAM ERA NAVY AVIATOR VA-212 "RAMPANT RAIDERS" SQDN. PATCH: Japanese made. fully mach. embr. 4 3/ 8x5 1/2" size. Exc. cond. $55.00

VIETNAM ERA NAVY FAR EAST CRUISE JACKET PATCH: Japanese made. Approx. 5x3.5" size. Fully mach. embr. w/ 6-flag design background including US, UN, Japan, Hong Kong & SVN. Off jacket but good cond. Above avg. cond. $30.00

VIETNAM ERA NAVY NAS 21 SAIGON VIETNAM PATCH: Vietnam made. 3x3.75" size w/mach. embr. & applique design on dark blue cotton base. Exc. cond. $129.50

VIETNAM ERA NAVY PATCH: Vietnam made. Blue shield w/red/white bars in center & crossed anchors inside wreath. 'Viet nam' at bottom + 'TECHNICAL

CLOTH INSIGNIA

ADVISORY TEAM' at top. Above avg. cond. $75.00

VIETNAM ERA NAVY PATCH: partial embr. w/Blue wolf w/trident in center & 'US NAVY VIET NAM' on rim. tabs 'SEA WOLF' at top & 'HELATK LT. RON-3' at bottom. Above avg. cond. $75.00

VIETNAM ERA NAVY PROLIBERTATE/ HARBOR SECURITY/CHU LAI RVN/SAT CONG PATCH: Vietnam made. 4" dia. Mach. embr. & applique panel constr. Exc. cond. $100.00

VIETNAM ERA NAVY TONKIN GULF YACHT CLUB PATCH: 2.75" dia. Fully mach. embr. Near mint cond. $17.00

VIETNAM ERA NAVY TONKIN GULF YACHT CLUB PATCH: 3x3". Fully Japanese mach. embr. Exc. cond. $25.00

VIETNAM ERA NAVY USS LANSING DER-388 EARLY WARNING PATCH: 3" dia. Embr. on twill. Above avg. cond. $20.00

VIETNAM ERA NAVY USS JUNEAU LPD-10 PATCH: Asian made. 4" dia. Fully mach. embr. Near mint cond. $11.00

VIETNAM ERA USMC 1ST MARINES NOVELTY PATCH: Has skull & crossbones in center of 1st Marine patch w/tabs 'DEATH BEFORE DISHONOR' & ''LANDING FORCE' & 'SOUTHEAST ASIA VIETNAM 1967-68.' Exc. cond. $11.00

VIETNAM ERA USMC 3RD RECON BN. NOVELTY PATCH: Asian made. 3x3 3/8". Fully mach. embr. Exc. cond. $30.00

VIETNAM ERA USMC AVIATOR HMM 161 SQDN. PATCH: Asian made. 4.5x5.25" size. Mach. embr. design on white cotton. Remains of paper backing. Exc. cond. $23.00

VIETNAM ERA USMC AVIATOR HMM 261 PATCH: Asian made. 5.5x5" w/mach. embr. design on yellow cotton. Near mint cond. $25.00

VIETNAM ERA USMC AVIATOR HMM 364 VIETNAM/PURPLE FOXES SQDN. PATCH: Asian made. 5" dia. Mach. embr. design in lt. shade purple on white cotton. Exc. cond. $48.00

VIETNAM ERA USMC AVIATOR UNIT PATCH: fully embr. 5" dia. + two tabs. Shows ugly angel w/thunderbolt & 'UGLY ANGELS' below. Upper tab 'KY HA VIETNAM,' Lower 'HMM-362.' Above avg. cond. $177.00

VIETNAM ERA USMC AVIATOR VMA (AW) 121 SQDN. PATCH: Asian made. 4x4" mach. embr. on twill. Exc. cond. ... $20.00

VIETNAM ERA USMC AVIATOR VMA(AW) 533 SQDN. PATCH: Japanese made.

4.5x5.25" fully mach. embr. Off uniform. Exc. cond. $40.00

VIETNAM ERA USMC AVIATOR VMA-223 "BULLDOGS" PATCH: Asian made. 4.5x5.75" size. Fully mach. embr. Near mint cond. $37.00

VIETNAM ERA USMC AVIATOR VMA-231 SQDN. PATCH: Asian made. Approx. 4.5x5" size. Fully mach. embr. Near mint cond. $34.00

VIETNAM ERA USMC AVIATOR VMFA (AW) 242 PATCH: Asian made. 3.25x4" w/ mach. embr. "Bad Boys Club" design on black twill & reads "Bad Boys Asian Tour-94/Badoer Than Ever." Near mint cond. $20.00

VIETNAM ERA USMC AVIATOR VMFA-112 "COWBOYS" SQDN. PATCH: Asian made. 4.75x5.25" size. Fully mach. embr. Above avg. cond. $30.00

VIETNAM ERA USMC AVIATOR VMGR-152 SQDN. PATCH: Asian made. 4.25x4.5" size. Mach. embr. on white twill. Near mint cond. $20.00

VIETNAM ERA USMC MAW TU-PAC WEAPONS & TACTICS INSTRUCTOR PATCH: Asian made. 4.25x4.5" size. Fully mach. embr. Exc. cond. $24.00

VIETNAM ERA USMC P.B.R. MOBILE BASE/MEKONG DELTA/REP. OF VIETNAM PATCH: Vietnam made. 4x4.25" shield-shaped blue cotton base w/ mach. embr. & applique design. Near mint cond. $139.00

VIETNAM ERA USMC P.B.R. MOBILE BASE/MEKONG DELTA/REP. OF VIETNAM PATCH

VIETNAM ERA USMC PATCH: Appears Asian made, Inverted arrowhead in embr. red w/Deaths head on 3rd Marine Div. emblem. At bottom is '3rd mar div' & at top in banner is 'RECON CO.' soiled. Above avg. cond. $34.00

VIETNAM ERA USMC WES-17 "PRIMO ET OPTIMO" PATCH: Asian made. 5.25x5.5" size. Fully mach. embr. Near mint cond. $28.00

WWI NAVY PO1 CORPSMAN ATTACHED TO MARINES RATE W/ADD-ON STRIPES: Forest green wool base w/ green embr. crow, red embr. red cross design & applied felt stripes. Above avg. cond. $45.00

WWI USMC MSGT DRESS CHEVRONS: Pair w/yellow tape on red wool 8" w/ horizontal rockers. Exc. cond. $22.00

WWI USS JERSEY NAVAL RESERVE RATES: Pr embr. on white twill 2nd & 3rd class QM. Above avg. cond. $20.00

WWII NAVY AMPH. FORCES PATCH: 2.75" dia. Fully embr. Design of tanks dislodging from alligators mouth. Near mint cond. $30.00

WWII NAVY AMPH. FORCES PATCH: 2.75" dia. Fully embr. Above avg. cond. $23.00

WWII NAVY AMPHIBIOUS FORCES PATCH: 2nd design. Fully embr. Above avg. cond. $10.00

WWII NAVY AMPHIBIOUS FORCES STRIKER PATCH: Embr. on uncut navy blue felt. Design of tanks dislodging from alligator's mouth. Exc. cond. $10.00

WWII NAVY AVIATOR PATCH: White Felt w/ USN/Aviation in red on rim & blue wing w/ gold anchor & US shield in center. Good looking. Exc. cond. $20.00

WWII NAVY BLOOD CHIT: 8.5x10" white leather w/color printed likeness of US and Chinese flags over black ink Chinese characters and anchor design. Very unusual. Above avg. cond. $161.00

WWII NAVY CAP RIBBON: For USS Indiana, ribbon uncut & gold color on words darkening. Avg. cond. $55.00

WWII NAVY CAP RIBBON: USS PEORIA. Black taffeta material w/gold bevo wire letters 'USS PEORIA.' 34" has been sewn on liberty cap. Avg. cond. $22.00

WWII NAVY COMMISSARY STEWARD BULLION RATE: heavy gold wire design of crescent with 2 bars beneath on navy gabardine. In uncut, unissued cond. Mint cond. $20.00

WWII NAVY CORPSMAN ATTACHED TO MARINES PO1 RATE: Forest green wool base w/OD embr. crow + red embr. red cross design + applied forest green wool stripes on scarlet red felt base. Exc. cond. $30.00

WWII NAVY CORPSMAN ATTACHED TO MARINES PO2 RATE: Forest green wool base w/OD embr. crow + red embr. red cross design + applied forest green wool stripes on scarlet red felt base. Above avg. cond. $25.00

WWII NAVY CPO RATE W/INITIALS: Winter rate w/red on black for CPO. Additionally has 'NHNSG' in place of specialty code. Means 'NEW HAMPSHIRE NAVAL STATE GUARD.' Avg. cond. $60.00

WWII NAVY MOSQUITO PT BOAT PATCH: 2.5" dia. w/mach silk embr. design of mosquito atop torpedo on black felt. Exc. cond. $20.00

WWII NAVY MTB PATCH: Embr. on dark felt w/"PT" & torpedo running through waves design. Above avg. cond. $20.00

WWII NAVY PO1 ATHLETIC INSTRUCTOR RATE: Australian made. 1943 dated. Bevo woven. Navy blue on white. Exc. cond. $20.00

WWII NAVY PO2 CHEMICAL WARFAREMAN RATE: Navy blue wool serge w/applied red felt stripes. Some sporadic nips but scarce. Avg. cond. $12.00

WWII NAVY PT BOAT PATCH: 2.75" dia. Fully embr. w/design of torpedo running through waves. Exc. cond. $28.00

WWII NAVY SUBMARINE PATCH: painted on canvas patch. Shows angry fish w/'373' across back & torpedoes launching from each '3.' For SS-373. Above avg. cond. $160.00

WWII NAVY USS FRANKLIN SHIP'S PATCH: Aircraft Carrier USS Franklin's patch. 5" white felt outline of Ben Franklin w/details embr. in blue. Exc. cond. $94.00

WWII NAVY V-5 PROGRAM PATCH: 2.5" wide wing over shield design. Fully embr. Near mint cond. $20.00

WWII USMC 18TH DEFENSE BN. PATCH: Fully embr. Above avg. cond. $20.00

WWII USMC 1ST M. A. C. PARATROOPS PATCH: Fully embr. Exc. cond. $40.00

WWII USMC 1ST MAC SERVICE OF SUPPLY BN. PATCH: Fully embr. Near mint cond. $34.00

WWII USMC 1ST MAR. DIV. PATCH: Unofficial. Fully embr. Design of coiled snake. Above avg. cond. 20.00

WWII USMC 1ST MARINE DIV. SHOULDER PATCH: Australian made on bevo silk embr. w/burlap backing. Superior example. Near mint cond. $159.00

WWII USMC 1ST MARINE DIV. PATCH:
Bevo weave design on cloth base. Backed
in white cotton. Exc. cond. $40.00
WWII USMC 1ST MARINE DIV. PATCH:
Unofficial. Fully embr. w/coiled snake
design. Exc. cond. $20.00
WWII USMC 1ST MARINE DIV. PATCH:
Hand stitched & bullion diamond shaped
patch on black wool. Avg. cond.
.... $145.00

WWII USMC 1ST MARINE DIV. PATCH

WWII USMC 2ND DIV. PATCH: "Pear"
shaped design. Fully embr. Approx. 3"
wide. Exc. cond. $150.00
WWII USMC 2ND MARINE DIV. PATCH:
Arrowhead of red wool w/gold bullion fist
holding torch upright w/'2' below flames.
Above avg. cond. $28.00
WWII USMC 2ND MARINE DIV. PATCH:
Fully embr. Exc. cond. $25.00
WWII USMC 3RD AMPH. CORPS PATCH:
Fully embr. Near mint cond. $27.00
WWII USMC 4TH DEF. BN. PATCH: Fully
embr. Avg. cond. $20.00
WWII USMC AVIATOR 1ST MARINE AIR
WG. PATCH: Fully embr. Off uniform but .
Above avg. cond. $20.00
WWII USMC AVIATOR 2ND MARINE AIR
WING PATCH: Fully embr. Off uniform but
clean. Above avg. cond. $19.00
WWII USMC AVIATOR 3RD MARINE AIR
WING SLEEVE PATCH: Near Mint, shows
Wings on USMC crest over III. Exc. cond.
....$20.00
WWII USMC AVIATOR PATCH: Fully embr.
1st MAC engineers patch. sharp. Exc.
cond. $12.00
WWII USMC AVIATOR VMJ-352 SQDN.
PATCH: Approx. 4 1/8" dia. Fully embr.
Clean. Exc. cond. $200.00
WWII USMC FMF-PAC ANTI-AIRCRAFT
ARTY. PATCH: Fully embr. Exc. cond.
.... $42.00
WWII USMC FMF-PAC DOG PLATOONS
PATCH: Fully embr. Exc. cond. $20.00
WWII USMC FMF-PAC DUKW COMPANIES
PATCH: Fully embr. Exc. cond. $20.00
WWII USMC FMF-PAC SUPPLY PATCH:
Fully embr. Off uniform-light soiling but
good. Avg. cond. $28.00

WWII USMC ICELAND DETACHMENT
SHOULDER PATCH: white cord embr.
design of polar bear on ice flow on black
elastic. Uncut and unissued. Above avg.
cond. $45.00
WWII USMC ICELANDIC PATROL
PATCHES: Two patches- white paint
stenciled on black wool. For uniform
shoulder. Above avg. cond. $87.00

WWII USMC ICELANDIC PATROL
PATCHES

WWII USMC MARINE RAIDER BN. PATCH:
Shield fully embr. w/deaths head on red
diamond in center, for 704th BN. Avg.
cond. $19.00
WWII USMC SHIP DETACHMENT PATCH:
Fully embr. Off uniform but good. Above
avg. cond. $20.00

U.S. ARMY METAL INSIGNIA

A. Thru World War I (1919)

1872 "US" BELT PLATE: 55x85mm cast brass rectangular plate w/US in oval center most. Above avg. cond. $78.00

ARMY 7TH CAVALRY DEVICE: 2.75" wide. Gilt brass. Open-catch Pb. Some corrosion. Avg. cond. $45.00

ARMY ARMOR INFANTRY COLLAR DISC TYPE II: Type II Sb. (missing screw) for Company A. Bronze finish shows wear. Above avg. cond. $40.00

ARMY BELT BUCKLE (1851-1874 DRESS): Stamped brass w/fittings on rear. gilded figures on face. Light wear signs. Above avg. cond. $60.00

ARMY BELT BUCKLE
(1851-1874 DRESS)

ARMY BELT PLATE (1872): Heavy brass rectangular body w/US in oval design. Avg. cond. $70.50

ARMY CAV. CAP DEVICE (1898): Bronze. Crossed sabers w/safety pin type fastener. Above avg. cond. $36.00

ARMY CAV. DEVICE (1902): "1/Cav/L." 2.25" wide. Gilt bras. Pb. Above avg. cond. $27.00

ARMY CAVALRY OFFICERS HAT DEVICE: Appears 1880 period, S/B brass, crossed sabers w/5 above & F below cross. Above avg. cond. $62.00

ARMY COLONEL SHOULDER EAGLE: Silver gilt over brass w/open catch P/B. Shoulder size. Avg. cond. $30.00

ARMY COMMISSARY SGT. DEVICE (1903): 1 7/8" wide. Multi-piece. Gilt wreath w/ nickel crescent moon design. Sb. Above avg. cond. $39.00

ARMY DEVICE (1874): "8/Cav/D." Gilt brass. Sb. Above avg. cond. $52.00

ARMY EM COLLAR DISC (ENGR/301) TYPE I: Dark bronze. Has applique "301" numbers on castle design. Sb. Above avg. cond. $25.00

ARMY EM COLLAR DISC (MG/INF/B) TYPE I: dark bronze finish. Sb. Above avg. cond. $20.00

ARMY EM COLLAR DISC TYPE I: Bronze finish. Sb. Small "NA" in rectangle over US + applied "323" numerals. Exc. cond. $72.00

ARMY ENGR OFFICER DEVICE (1895): "1/Engr." Large 48mm wide dark bronze finish engr. castle design. Sb. Exc. cond. $166.00

ARMY GENERAL'S AIDE BRONZE STAR DEVICE: Army eagle on 5-pt bronze star. PB. Collar size. Has nice age patina. Near mint cond. $14.00

ARMY HELMET EAGLE FRONT PLATE (1881): Stamped brass. Crossed rifles design w/applied nickel "11" numerals to shield. Wire attachment loops on rear. Above avg. cond. $23.00

ARMY HELMET INF FRONT PLATE (1872): Stamped brass. Has "2" applique to shield. Above avg. cond. $28.00

ARMY INF DEVICE (1874): "2/Inf/I I" design w/"46" in circle in center. Gilt brass. Sb. Above avg. cond. $25.00

ARMY INF DEVICE (1874): Gilt brass. Sb. Basic "3/Inf/M" design w/center having circle w/"2" in center. Avg. cond. $22.00

ARMY INF DEVICE (1895): "25/Inf/M." Gilt brass. Sb. Above avg. cond. $20.00

ARMY INF DEVICE (1895): "I I/Inf/2." stamped brass inf. bugle design. Sb. Above avg. cond. $13.00

ARMY INF OFFICERS COLLAR DEVICES (1890s): Infantry crossed rifles w/19 over & K under cross. Pb.w/open clasp. Nice finish. Above avg. cond. $20.00

ARMY INF HELMET FRONT PLATE (1881): stamped brass in gilt plating. Sb post. Above avg. cond. $13.00

ARMY OFFICER WINGED EAGLES COLLAR BRASS (1930s): matched set with screw backs, only worn for a short period. Avg. cond. $100.00

ARMY OFFICERS BELT BUCKLE (1851): Post-CW Period. Brass. Complete w/Nice gilding on face. Above avg. cond. ..$45.00

ARMY ORDNANCE EM CAP BADGE (1905): Sb. Dark bronze finish. Flaming bomb within wreath design. Above avg. cond. $25.00

ARMY QM COLLAR INSIGNIA (1896): Quill & Key. Gilded brass. Wire prong back. Obsolete in 1900. Above avg. cond. $32.00

ARMY QUARTERMASTER CHEVRON BADGE (1902): Large 68mm wide Qm branch design w/pierced design. Several lug fasteners on reverse. Dark bronze finish. Exc. cond. $76.00

ARMY SANITATION OFFICER COLLAR DEVICE: 28mm high dark bronze pierced design w/applique "S." Pb. "Fire Bronze" hmkd. Above avg. cond. $30.00

CARTRIDGE BOX PLATE (1840s): Brass. Lug back 3.5" wide oval w/US in center. Filled back & shows light wear. Above avg. cond. $111.00

CARTRIDGE BOX PLATE (1840s)

CARTRIDGE BOX PLATE: 50x75mm cast brass plate-loops on reverse-a cipher which includes the letters "NG" -possibly an "A" in center. Unusual. Avg. cond. $20.00

CAVALRY DEVICE (1874): 2 3/8" wide. Sb. Has "8" above crossed design-below hashed designation but now removed. Clean cond. Above avg. cond. $23.00

CAVALRY INSIGNIA (1872): 2.75" wide. Stamped brass. Wire loop attachments. Exc. cond. $20.00

CIVIL WAR CAVALRY CAP DEVICE: Large stamped brass crossed saber design w/ four wire loop attachments on back. Has been finished in matte black. Avg. cond. $72.00

CIVIL WAR CAVALRY CAP DEVICE

CIVIL WAR CAVALRY FLAT BUTTON: Shows crossed sabers w/'A' above cross. Some light surface spotting. Above avg. cond. $20.00

CIVIL WAR CAVALRY SHAKO PLATE: 68mm wide. Stamped brass. Crossed saber design over "bursting" rays. Some corrosion. Avg. cond. $59.00

CIVIL WAR ENLISTED "HARDEE" HAT EAGLE SIDEPLATE: 48x68mm size. Stamped brass body. Lacks prong attachments. Avg. cond. $60.00

CIVIL WAR INFANTRY CAP BADGE: Brass w/lug backs. Nice detailing. Exc. cond. $40.00

CIVIL WAR INFANTRY CAP INSIGNIA: 3 3/8" wide stamped brass inf. horn design w/wire attachment loops on reverse. Above avg. cond. $24.00

CIVIL WAR INFANTRY KEPI DEVICE: Stamped brass inf. horn device. 88mm wide. Lacks one of two wire loop attachments on back. Above avg. cond. $32.50

CIVIL WAR INFANTRY KEPI DEVICE: Gilt finished brass horn for kepi with 2 soldered loops for mounting. Above avg. cond. $37.00

CIVIL WAR INFANTRY SHAKO DEVICE: Bugle brass. For Infantry shako, lug back & some wear evident. Above avg. cond. $27.00

CIVIL WAR IX TH CORPS PIN: Multi piece const. w/red felt insert. Features US shield on perimeter + crossed cannon & anchor in center w/rope '9' imposed. Pb. Metal shows some age. Exc. cond. $292.00

CIVIL WAR MASS 3RD MILITIA BELT BUCKLE: curved brass plate w/ metal '3' attached. Typical condition for age. Above avg. cond. $114.00

CIVIL WAR OHIO 7TH INF INSIGNIA: Stamped brass image of rooster for 7th Ohio Inf. Prong mounted on cap or coat. Excellent detail. Above avg. cond. $195.00

CIVIL WAR PIN: Pb. shows rifle & saber crossed behind knapsack w/'NMA' on back. Bed roll at top & eagle resting on that. Red & blue enamel give color. Above avg. cond. $28.00

CIVIL WAR RHODE ISLAND CORPS METAL INSIGNIA: US shield w/Rhode Island Corps Anchor & 'BAND OF HOPE' diagonally across shield. Stamped metal & PB. Above avg. cond. $60.00

CIVIL WAR SHAKO SIDE BUTTON (1851 PATTERN): 41mm dia. stamped brass body w/design of early spread wing eagle & wreath border. Prong back. Exc. cond. $30.00

CIVIL WAR UNION "US" BELT BUCKLE: 83mm wide oval-shaped stamped brass body w/lead filled back + circular studs for attachment to belt. Avg. cond. $108.00

CIVIL WAR UNION "US" BELT BUCKLE

CIVIL WAR UNION POUCH PLATE: 86mm wide stamped brass oval body w/ embossed "US." Reverse is lead filled w/2 wire loops for attachment. Above avg. cond. $107.00

CIVIL WAR UNION POUCH PLATE

CO. K WASHINGTON GREYS BUCKLE: 72x56mm brass body w/black finish lettering. "776/S&K/Prussia" hmkd. on reverse. Avg. cond. $50.00

CONFEDERATE VETERANS REUNION BADGE (1919): 33x40mm stamped bronze badge-spread wing eagle over scene of Gen. J. B. Gordon on horseback-shield that is half Confederate flag & half union shield. PB. Mint cond. $145.00

HELMET FRONT PLATE (1812 - 1830): Brass 3.25x2" plate w/ American eagle carrying banner 'OLD RELIABLE' over montage of cannon, flags & gear. At bottom reads 'FEDERAL GOVERNMENT' Pierced for sewing to cap. Avg. cond. $135.00

HOSPITAL STEWARD DEVICE (1904): 1 7/8" wide. Dark bronze finish. Sb. Avg. cond. $40.00

INDIAN AFFAIRS OFFICER COLLAR DEVICES (1900): Pb. Winged sheaf of arrows. Above avg. cond. $76.00

INDIAN WAR ARMY SCOUT BADGE: Brass Crossed arrows on domed & decorated oval. Mount missing. Avg. cond. ... $45.00

INDIAN WAR ARMY SCOUT CAP DEVICE: Handsome silver crossed arrows w/USS in upper cross + 4 wire loops LB. Great detail on feathers. Classic piece of Indian war's history. Exc. cond. $250.00

INDIAN WARS ARMY OFFICER BELT BUCKLE (1851 PATTERN): 77x52mm brass body. Design of eagle surrounded by wreath. Includes keeper. Avg. cond. $60.00

INDIAN WARS ARMY OFFICER BELT BUCKLE (1851 PATTERN)

INDIAN WARS CAVALRY DEVICE (1/CAV/ L): 60mm wide. Gilt brass. Has had Cb fasteners soldered to saber tips. Avg. cond. $40.00

INDIAN WARS CAVALRY DEVICE: Large 85mm wide stamped brass device w/ prong backing. Unused. Exc. cond. $30.00

INDIAN WARS CAVALRY HAT DEVICE: Brass & lead filled crossed sabers for officers full brimmed hat. Need some polishing. Above avg. cond. $58.00

INDIAN WARS CAVALRY HAT DEVICE

INDIAN WARS CAVALRY KEPI CAP DEVICE: Lug back brass crossed sabers in gilded brass. Appear mint. Exc. cond. $32.00

NCO CAP WREATH (1902): 48mm wide gilt wreath w/nickel "DKH" in center. Sb. Above avg. cond. $20.00

NEW YORK GUARD CROSS STRAP PLATE: brass sheet w/7 attached by wire, early turn of the century NY guard. Avg. cond. $23.00

METAL INSIGNIA

NEW YORK GUARD HELMET FRONT
PLATE (1881): Gilt plated stamped brass
body. Applied nickel "4" numeral on shield.
Above avg. cond. $13.50

NEW YORK GUARD HELMET FRONT
PLATE (1881): Stamped brass body.
Applied nickel "2" numeral on shield. Avg.
cond. $14.50

NEW YORK MILITIA BELT BUCKLE: Buckle
& keeper in brass w/ oval center & "NY" in
center of oval. Above avg. cond. $45.00

NEW YORK MILITIA BELT BUCKLE: 1850
pattern recovered item w/damage to two
sides. all fitting on back intact. Initials SNY
clear. Avg. cond. $171.00

NEW YORK MILITIA BELT BUCKLE

NEW YORK MILITIA POUCH PLATE:
Approx. 56mm wide. Stamped brass. Lug
back. Avg. cond. $27.00

NEW YORK NATIONAL GUARD 23 REGT.
UNIT BADGE: 25mm white enamel cross
w/circular blue enamel beltlet "Vigilantia
NGNY" + "23" in center-small "B" pendant
hanging below. Pb. w/latch type safety on
open catch. Jeweler hmkd. Appears to be
at least 10K gold. Near mint cond.
.... $75.00

NEW YORK STATE CARTRIDGE BOX
PLATE (1881): Stamped brass. Wire loop
attachments on reverse. 57mm wide. Exc.
cond. $23.00

PENNSYLVANIA NATIONAL GUARD
KEYSTONE COLLAR DEVICE: Bronze
keystone device w/crossed sabers & GT
below. SB & for Governors Troops
(Pennsylvania NG). Above avg. cond.
.... $72.00

RECRUITING SERVICE BADGE: 1 7/8"
wide gilt wreath w/"RS" letters in center.
Open-catch Pb. Above avg. cond.
.... $25.00

SPANISH AMERICAN WAR ARMY COL.'S
RANK DEVICE: Pb. dress full col.'s bar w/
raised eagle on black background & gold
trim. Above avg. cond. $29.00

USR COLLAR DEVICES: P/B bronze finish
& on orig. 'Liberty Bronze' sales cards.
Near mint cond. $37.00

WWI ADJ. GEN. FIELD CLERK OFFICER
COLLAR DEVICE: Open-catch Pb.
Bronze finish. Above avg. cond. ... $10.00

WWI AIR SERVICE OFFICER COLLAR
INSIGNIA: Winged prop. Pb. Obverse
matches, but reverse has diff. sized rivets
& colored pins. Above avg. cond.
.... $133.00

WWI AIR SERVICE SIGNAL CORPS
OFFICER COLLAR DEVICE: French
made, bronze finish, Pb. Signal corps
device w/small brass winged globe
applied to center. Near mint cond.
.... $53.00

WWI ARMY ADJUTANT GENERAL DEPT.
OFFICER COLLAR DEVICES: Dark
bronze finish. Open-catch Pb. Exc. cond.
.... $37.00

WWI ARMY AIR SERVICE EM COLLAR
DISC TYPE I: Dark bronze finish w/
winged prop design w/wide wings & short,
stubby prop. Has horizontal line
background. Sb. Above avg. cond.
.... $20.00

WWI ARMY AIR SERVICE EM COLLAR
DISC TYPE I: Dark bronze. Sb. Stubby,
short prop design. Above avg. cond.
.... $45.00

WWI ARMY AIR SERVICE OFFICER
COLLAR DEVICE: bronze signal corps
officer's collar device-PB w/small silver
wing device riveted to center. PB. Near
mint cond. $40.00

WWI ARMY ARMOR COLLAR DISC: SB
bronze post 1918 version showing Mark
VIII tank over dragons. Appears to French
made. Avg. cond. $52.00

WWI ARMY EM COLLAR DISC TYPE I: "5/
Arty/D." Bronze finish. Sb. Nice shape.
Above avg. cond. $23.00

WWI ARMY ARTY EM COLLAR DISC TYPE
I: "18/Arty/A." Dark bronze finish. Sb.
Above avg. cond. $39.00

WWI ARMY ARTY EM COLLAR DISC TYPE
I: "324/Arty/E." Bronze finish. Sb. Above
avg. cond. $24.00

WWI ARMY ARTY OFFICER COLLAR
DEVICES: C/B pair, Arty w/brass crossed
cannon showing some tarnish & 456 at
cross on each. Avg. cond. $34.00

WWI ARMY BAND OFFICER COLLAR
DEVICE: Bronze finish lyre design w/
applique "6" in center. Open-catch Pb.
Above avg. cond. $20.00

WWI ARMY BRIG. GEN. STARS: 30mm
wide. Textured surface. Loop on reverse
of each for attachment. Some wear to

silver finish but nice. Above avg. cond. $49.00

WWI ARMY BRIG. GEN. STARS: Pair. 26mm wide. Dark bronze finish. Open-catch Pb. Above avg. cond. $51.00

WWI ARMY C. ARTY OFFICER COLLAR DEVICE: Dark bronze finish. Open-catch Pb. Above avg. cond. $30.00

WWI ARMY CAV. EM COLLAR DISC TYPE I: "1/Cav/E." Bronze finish. Sb. Above avg. cond. $82.00

WWI ARMY CAV. OFFICER COLLAR DEVICE: "1/Cav." Shirt size. 30mm wide. Open-catch Pb. Exc. cond. $20.00

WWI ARMY CAV. OFFICER COLLAR DEVICE: "3/Cav." Shirt size. 30mm wide. Dark bronze. Open-catch Pb. Above avg. cond. $22.00

WWI ARMY CAVALRY OFFICERS COLLAR DEVICE: 4th Cav. Bronze. Exc. cond. $23.00

WWI ARMY CHEMICAL CORPS OFFICER COLLAR DEVICES: Pb. Bronze finished officer shirt collar devices w/'1' on top of benzene ring. Exc. cond. $82.00

WWI ARMY CHEMICAL CORPS OFFICER
COLLAR DEVICES

WWI ARMY COMMISSARY OFFICER COLLAR DEVICE: dark finished bronze, Pb. with simple catch. Appears unissued. Mint cond. $26.00

WWI ARMY COMMISSARY OFFICER COLLAR DEVICES: Pr. bronze toned Pb. commissary officer collar devices. Above avg. cond. $20.00

WWI ARMY DENTAL CORPS OFFICER COLLAR DEVICES: Dark bronze [pierced design w/gilt brass "DC" appliques. Slightly mis-matched pair. Open-catch Pb. Above avg. cond. $45.00

WWI ARMY EM COLLAR DISC TYPE I: "T." Sb. Above avg. cond. $20.00

WWI ARMY ENGINEER CORPS OFFICER COLLAR DEVICES: 32mm wide. Pierced design. Nice detail. Dark bronze finish. Open-catch Pb. Exc. cond. $37.00

WWI ARMY FIELD CLERK ADJ. OFFICER COLLAR DEVICES: Dark bronze finish. Open-catch Pb. Above avg. cond. $30.00

WWI ARMY GEN. FIELD CLERK OFFICER COLLAR DEVICE: Open-catch Pb. Dull gilt finish. Above avg. cond. $13.00

WWI ARMY GENERAL STAFF OFFICER COLLAR DEVICES: Multi-piece constr. in dark bronze finish. Open-catch Pb. Nice examples. Exc. cond. $55.00

WWI ARMY GHQ EM COLLAR DISC TYPE I: Dark bronze finish. Sb. Above avg. cond. $50.00

WWI ARMY INF EM COLLAR DISC TYPE I: "26/Inf/D." Nice bronze finish. Sb. Above avg. cond. $38.00

WWI ARMY INF EM COLLAR DISC TYPE I: "332/Inv." Dark bronze finish. Numerals are applique . Sb. Avg. cond. $66.00

WWI ARMY INF EM COLLAR DISC: "27/Inf/B." SB excellent condition. Exc. cond. $60.00

WWI ARMY INF EM COLLAR DISC: "27/Inf/M." SB bronze. Exc. cond. 60.00

WWI ARMY INF MG EM COLLAR DISC TYPE I: "MG/Inf/A." Bronze finish. Sb. Above avg. cond. $12.00

WWI ARMY INF MG EM COLLAR DISC TYPE I: "MG/Inf/A." Dark bronze finish. Sb. Above avg. cond. $25.00

WWI ARMY INF OFFICER COLLAR DEVICE: "14/Inf." Bronze finish. Pb. Above avg. cond. $51.00

WWI ARMY INF OFFICER COLLAR DEVICES: "382/Inf." Dark bronze. Open-catch Pb. Above avg. cond. $20.00

WWI ARMY INF OFFICER COLLAR DEVICES: Dark bronze. Open catch Pb. Above avg. cond. $20.00

WWI ARMY MEDICAL EM COLLAR DISC TYPE I: "Med/PC." Even dark bronze pendant w/applique "P" & "C" numerals. Sb. Exc. cond. $213.00

WWI ARMY OFFICER 2ND LT. BARS: Textured "coffin lid" bodies w/ open-catch Pb. Matched. Above avg. cond. $25.00

WWI ARMY OFFICER 2ND LT. BARS: stamped brass-appear French made-simulated bullion design. Full size for blouse. Above avg. cond. $19.00

WWI ARMY OFFICER CAP DEVICE: Heavy cast bronze design-SB-Tiffany Hmkd. Standard design & size, fair detail. Near mint cond. $50.00

WWI ARMY QM BADGE: Bronze finish on brass w/Pb. initials 'QMC' across top. Above avg. cond. 40.00

METAL INSIGNIA

WWI ARMY QM CORPS OFFICER COLLAR DEVICES: One sew-on with loops to back and a Pb type, all in dark finished bronze. Near mint cond. $20.00

WWI ARMY OFFICER CAP DEVICE

WWI ARMY SGT. ID BRACELET: 35x25mm curve form silver metal body mach. engraved to sgt, serv. number & "U.S.A." On linked wrist chain. Avg. cond. $30.00

WWI ARMY SIBERIAN EXP. INF EM COLLAR DISC TYPE I: "27/Inf." Dark bronze finish. Applique "2" & "7" numbers over crossed rifles. Sb. Above avg. cond. $50.00

WWI ARMY SIGNAL CORPS OFFICER COLLAR DEVICES: French made. Bonze finish. Open catch Pb. Above avg. cond. $24.00

WWI ARMY TRANSPORTATION EM COLLAR DISC: Dark bronze finish. Non-pierced design w/simulated tire tread around edge. Sb. Exc. cond. $20.00

WWI ARMY USV EM COLLAR DISC TYPE I: Dark bronze finish disc w/applique "V" device in rectangle design over "US." Sb. Above avg. cond. $135.00

WWI CHEMICAL CORPS COLLAR DEVICES: Pb. Bronze finished officer Blouse collar devices. Nice set. Exc. cond. $50.00

WWI DOGTAGS: Two tags for same indiv., both show wear. Kept on shoelace cord w/key. Avg. cond. $21.00

WWI FIELD CLERK EM COLLAR DISC TYPE I: Gilt. Exc. cond. $30.00

WWI IOWA HAT DEVICE: S/B Brass eagle w/Collar device (type I style) containing "IOWA." Exc. cond. $16.00

WWI MAJOR LEAVES: Pair. Open-catch Pb. Above avg. cond. $27.00

WWI OFFICER COLLAR DEVICE: Brass w/wearing bronze finish Pb. & 'SDSC' above crossed rifles. Above avg. cond. ... $27.00

WWI OFFICER INFANTRY COLLAR DEVICES: Both P/B bronze or bronze finish. One has 304 in cross. Avg. cond. $26.00

WWI PHILIPPINE FORCES COLLAR DEVICE: Pb. metal shows wear & loss of finish. Has US eagle in center w/special shield on breast. Avg. cond. $30.00

WWI TRANSPORTATION CORPS PIN: Pb. metal wheel w/brass mercury's hat in center. 1" dia. Above avg. cond. $11.00

WWI USNA 329 EM COLLAR DISC TYPE I: Dark bronze finish. Sb. Small "NA" in rectangle over US. Above avg. cond. $27.00

B. 1920 - 1945

ARMY AIR CORP FLYING CADETS US AIR CORPS COLLAR DEVICE: 82x45mm nickel plated brass w/large winged propeller (WWI style) in oval center w/raised letters and date. Above avg. cond. $135.00

ARMY AIR CORP OFFICER COLLAR DEVICE: 1920-30s. Winged prop Pb. brass collar device. Mint. Near mint cond. $30.00

ARMY AIR CORPS OFFICER'S COLLAR DEVICE: 1920-30s. 30mm size in gilt & silver metal w/twin screw post fasteners. Mint cond. $40.00

ARMY ARTY EM COLLAR DISC TYPE II: 1930s experimental. Pale red enamel finish. Avg. cond. $20.00

ARMY EM COLLAR DISC TYPE II: "C. Arty/A." Gilt brass. Sb. Lot includes Arty chevron embr. in red on OD wool base w/red border. Avg. cond. $20.00

ARMY EM COLLAR DISC TYPE II: "US/NY/174." Gilt brass. Sb. Above avg. cond. $23.00

ARMY INF BANDSMAN COLLAR DISC TYPE II: "Inf/Musician." Gilt brass. Sb. Design of crossed rifles w/lyre design below. Sb. Above avg. cond. $22.00

ARMY OFFICER 1ST LT. OF ARTY DRESS SHOULDER BOARDS: 1938. Curve-form. Heavy gold bullion trim + rank w/ribbed red insert. Above avg. cond. $40.00

ARMY OFFICER COLLAR DEVICES: "104/Cav." Gilt brass. Cb. Above avg. cond. $20.00

ARMY OFFICER COLLAR DEVICES: "128/Arty." Pb w/"fall-in" catch. Gilt brass. Above avg. cond. $45.00

ARMY OFFICER MAJOR LEAVES RANK INSIGNIA: Shirt size. Gilt. Pb. BB&B/Bronze hmkd. Avg. cond. $30.00

ARMY QM EM COLLAR DISC TYPE II:
1930s experimental. Buff enamel finish.
Above avg. cond. $20.00

ARMY SIGNAL CORPS AVIATION
OFFICER COLLAR DEVICE: Bronze satin
finish signal corps pattern device w/
applique silver-colored spread wing
design in center. Open-catch Pb. Exc.
cond. $45.00

NEW YORK S. G. COLLAR DISC TYPE II:
Clear plastic covered silver-colored body.
Pb. Exc. cond. $20.00

NEW YORK STATE GUARD HELMET
PLATE.: Die struck gilded brass w/eagle
over state emblem & '14' imposed on
front. Exc. cond. $20.00

USMC EM CAP DEVICE: 1937 pattern.
bronze SB design shows some wear to
the finish. Above avg. cond. $12.00

USMC OFFICER COLLAR DEVICE: 1937
PATTERN. Gilt on silver device for left
side. For use on Officer's dress blues. PB,
hmkd. Near mint cond. $45.00

USMC OFFICER QUARTERMASTER
DEPT. COLLAR DEVICE: Dark bronze
finish. Open-catch Pb. Exc. cond.
.... $29.00

WEST POINT CUFF LINKS: Well hmkd.
Gold filled. Have crest design & reads
"USMA - Duty Honor Country." Exc. cond.
.... $34.00

WWII AAF 10TH TROOP CARRIER GROUP
DI: Sterling marked. Pb w/safety catch.
Red & blue enameled. Above avg. cond.
.... $28.00

WWII AAF 12TH OBSERVATION GROUP
DI: Multi-piece. Pb. Above avg. cond.
.... $30.00

WWII AAF 12TH RECON. SQDN. DI: Pb.
Gilt brass & enamel. Dondero hmkd.
Above avg. cond. $19.00

WWII AAF 14TH FIGHTER GRP. DI: Sb.
Nickel & enamel. Meyer hmkd. Above avg.
cond. $45.00

WWII AAF 15 AIR FORCE DI'S: matched
pair-PB-maker marked. sterling-scarce.
Above avg. cond. $25.00

WWII AAF 153TH OBSERVATION SQDN.
DI: gilt brass & enamel. Pb. Exc. cond.
.... $34.00

WWII AAF 15TH AIR FORCE PATCH-TYPE
DI: brass & enamel. Pb. Above avg. cond.
.... $20.00

WWII AAF 15TH AIR FORCE STICKPIN:
16mm dia. in brass & enamel. Above avg.
cond. $23.00

WWII AAF 16TH FTR. GRP. DI'S: Pair. Pb.
enameled metal one is for 16th Ftr. Grp.
w/mail fist & lightning. Other has motto

'PURGAMOUS COELUM.' Above avg.
cond. $22.00

WWII AAF 16TH FTR. GRP. DI: Gilt brass &
enamel. Sb. Above avg. cond. $30.00

WWII AAF 17TH BOMB GROUP DI: Sb. Gilt
brass & enamel. Meyer hmkd. Exc. cond.
.... $44.00

WWII AAF 19TH BOMB GROUP DI: Gilt
brass & enamel. Pb. Meyer hmkd. Exc.
cond. $40.00

WWII AAF 19TH BOMB GROUP DI: Sb. Gilt
brass & enamel. Meyer hmkd. Nice shape.
Above avg. cond. $30.00

WWII AAF 1ST FIGHTER GROUP DI: Sb.
Gilt brass & enamel. Am. Metal Crafts,
Attleboro hmkd. Above avg. cond.
.... $30.00

WWII AAF 20TH FIGHTER GRP DI: Pb. Gilt
brass & enamel. Gemsco hmkd. Above
avg. cond. $16.00

WWII AAF 22ND BOMB GROUP DI: Sb. Gilt
brass & enamel. Meyer hmkd. Above avg.
cond. $20.00

WWII AAF 27TH BOMB GROUP DI: hmkd.
NS Meyer on back, Metal & enamel shield
w/orange & blue diagonal field + closed
fist & flower. Motto-'INTELLIGENCE
STRENGTH.' Exc. cond. $20.00

WWII AAF 2ND BOMB GROUP DI: Pb. Gilt
brass & enamel. Meyer hmkd. Above avg.
cond. $14.00

WWII AAF 31ST FTR. GRP. DI: Pb. Gilt
brass & enamel. Meyer hmkd. Above avg.
cond. $19.00

WWII AAF 33RD FIGHTER GRP. DI: Pb. Gilt
brass & enamel. Meyer hmkd. Above avg.
cond. $28.00

WWII AAF 34TH BOMBARDMENT GROUP
DI: Sterling hmkd. Gilt & enamel finish.
Pb. Above avg. cond. $49.00

WWII AAF 3RD BOMB GRP. DI: Brass &
enamel. Pb. Above avg. cond. $23.00

WWII AAF 3RD STAFF SQDN. DI: Gilt &
enamel. Pb. Above avg. cond. $27.00

WWII AAF 3RD WING DI: Pb. Gilt brass &
nice enamel finish. Gemsco hmkd. Above
avg. cond. $13.00

WWII AAF 4TH AIR BASE SQDN. DI: Gilt
brass & enamel. Pb. Metal Arts Co. hmkd.
Above avg. cond. $30.00

WWII AAF 57TH FIGHTER GRP DI: Pb. Gilt
brass & enamel. Meyer hmkd. Above avg.
cond. $20.00

WWII AAF 5TH BOMB GROUP DI: Multi-
piece constr. Pb. Meyer hmkd. Above avg.
cond. $40.00

WWII AAF 5TH BOMB GROUP DI: Pb.
Brass winged silver skull w/motto 'KIAIO
KAIEWA' at bottom. Exc. cond. $18.00

WWII AAF 6TH AIR FORCE PATCH-TYPE DI'S: 3/4" wide. Enamel detail. Pb w/"fall-in" catch. Above avg. cond. $28.00

WWII AAF 7TH BOMB GROUP DI: Sb. Gilt brass & enamel. Meyer hmkd. Above avg. cond. $20.00

WWII AAF 88TH RECON SQDN. DI: Sb. Gilt brass & enamel. Above avg. cond. $30.00

WWII AAF 8TH AIR FORCE PATCH-TYPE COLLAR DISC: English made. Gilt brass & enamel. Open-catch Pb. From group of insignia. Exc. cond. $28.00

WWII AAF 8TH FIGHTER GRP. DI: Sb. Gilt brass & enamel. Above avg. cond. $18.00

WWII AAF 91ST OBSERVATION SQDN. DI: Brass & enamel P/B on card. Shows knight chasing the devil. Near mint cond. $20.00

WWII AAF 91ST RECON SQUADRON DI: Pb diamond shaped brass & enamel DI showing knight on horse back chasing devil. Hmkd. NS Meyer. Exc. cond. $34.00

WWII AAF 9TH BOMB GRP. DI: Pb. Gilt brass & enamel. Above avg. cond. $19.00

WWII AAF 9TH BOMB GROUP DI: Mint in plastic & on card. Pb. enameled brass. Near mint cond. $28.00

WWII AAF 9TH BOMB GROUP DI: Pb enameled brass shield w/band of iron crosses in center & coiled snake at top. Motto 'SEMPER PARATUS.' Exc. cond. $14.00

WWII AAF AIR FERRY CMD. DI: Pb. gilt metal w/ enameled emblem. Displayed in box w/clear lid. Exc. cond. $65.00

WWII AAF AIR SERVICE CMD. DI: 3-blade design. Pb. LeVelle/sterling hmkd. Some tarnish. Avg. cond. $20.00

WWII AAF AIR SERVICE CMD. DI: 4-blade design. Pb. Metal Arts/sterling hmkd. Some even tarnish. Above avg. cond. $20.00

WWII AAF AIR SERVICE CMD. DI'S: 3-blade variation. Pb. Enamel detail. LeVelle/sterling hmkd. Avg. cond. $28.00

WWII AAF AIR TRANSPORT COMMAND DI'S: matched pair-30mm dia. in sterling & enamel CB, LeVelle hmkd. Above avg. cond. $27.00

WWII AAF AIR TRANSPORT SERVICE OFFICER LAPEL DEVICES: appear sterling but not marked, drop in Pb, some patina to the metal. Above avg. cond. $38.00

WWII AAF ATC DI'S: Enameled details. Pb. LeVelle & Co./sterling hmkd. On maker card. Avg. cond. $23.00

WWII AAF ATC PATCH TYPE DI: 29mm dia. Painted details. LaVelle/sterling hmkd. Cb. Some tarnish. Also, Cb Di w/motto "Mobile Might." Above avg. cond. $24.00

WWII AAF BOMB UNIT DI: Pb. enameled metal w/winged bomb in center & motto "ALAE SUPRA CANALEM." Above avg. cond. $35.00

WWII AAF CIVILIAN FLIGHT INSTRUCTOR VISOR CAP DEVICE: 60mm wide. Sterling hmkd. Heavy Pb. Above avg. cond. $125.00

WWII AAF COMPOSITE GROUP PATCH-TYPE DI: Theater made. 24x29mm. Open-catch wire Pb. Avg. cond. ... $75.00

WWII AAF FIGHTER UNIT DI: SB enameled brass w/ motto "VICTORY BY VALOR." Exc. cond. $23.00

WWII AAF GULF COAST TRAINING CENTER DI'S: SB 1.25" enameled shields. Exc. cond. $20.00

WWII AAF INSTRUCTOR PIN: Pb. enamel on brass w/winged prop fixed to center & "INSTRUCTOR" at top & "AAF TTC" at bottom. Some tarnish on brass, nearly flawless. Exc. cond. $95.00

WWII AAF RONDEL PIN: Enameled. Pb. Blue field w/white 5 pt star & red circle center. Exc. cond. $20.00

WWII AAF TRAINING SERVICE ENAMELED BADGE: PB, enameled background with applied winged prop in gilt with white enamel prop. 1.75" wide, in nice condition. Exc. cond. $34.00

WWII AIR CADET CAP BADGE: Winged prop. Gilt finish on wing. Sb. Sterling marked. Above avg. cond. $35.00

WWII AMERICAN WOMEN VOLUNTARY SERVICES PIN: 19x30mm size. Enameled details. Pb. Serial numbered B104 & Robbins hmkd. in reverse. Avg. cond. $20.00

WWII ARMY 11TH CAV. REGT. DI'S: Gilt brass & enamel finish pierced bodies. Pb. Meyer hmkd. Above avg. cond. $19.00

WWII ARMY 12TH C. ARTY REGT. DI: Sb. Pierced design. Gilt brass & enamel. Dondero hmkd. Above avg. cond. $28.00

WWII ARMY 142ND ENGR. BN. DI'S: Screwback. Meyer hmkd. Gilt brass & enamel. Above avg. cond. $16.00

WWII ARMY 16TH INFANTRY REGIMENT DI: SB metal & enamel w/blue & white inverted turret design. Avg. cond. .. $20.00

WWII ARMY 175TH F. A. DI'S: Enamel details. Pb. Dondero/sterling hmkd. Avg. cond. $30.00

WWII ARMY 180TH INF REGT. DI'S: Nickel & enamel. Pb w/unusual roller catch. Above avg. cond. $18.00

WWII ARMY 181ST ARTY DI: Multi-piece. Gilt brass & enamel. Above avg. cond. $25.00

WWII ARMY 235TH ARTY OBSERVER CO BADGE: full color enameled Pb. badge. Shows crossed cannon w/235 above & observ. below. Above avg. cond. .. $27.00

WWII ARMY 252ND ARTY DI'S: Gilt brass & enamel. Open-catch Pb. Above avg. cond. $12.00

WWII ARMY 260TH F. A. BN. DI: 33x35mm. Australian made. Gilt brass w/enameled design. Open-catch Pb. Bishop/Brisbane hmkd. Above avg. cond. $25.00

WWII ARMY 290 ENGINEER BN.DI: Sb. Nickel & enamel. Dondero/sterling hmkd. Above avg. cond. $20.00

WWII ARMY 301ST ORD. REGT. DI: Niokol & enamel. Pb. Balfour/sterling hmkd. Above avg. cond. $20.00

WWII ARMY 302ND ORD. REGT. DI: Multi-piece. Brass & enamel. Pb. Dieces & clust hmkd. Avg. cond. $25.00

WWII ARMY 310TH ENGR. DI: Pb. Gilt & enamel. Dondero/sterling hmkd. Above avg. cond. $12.50

WWII ARMY 310TH INF REGT. DI. Plastic Pb. w/Blue shield & cross + tree separated by lightning flash. Motto at bottom reads "ALLONS MESENFANTS." Exc. cond. $30.00

WWII ARMY 323RD INF DI: Gilt brass & enamel. Pb. Sterling hmkd. Avg. cond. $27.00

WWII ARMY 399TH INF REGT. DI: Pb. Sterling hmkd. Light age. Above avg. cond. $20.00

WWII ARMY 4TH CAVALRY OFFICER COLLAR DEVICE: nice even finished bronze metal crossed swords with "4" above. Pb. with simple catch. Near mint cond. $20.00

WWII ARMY 54TH CAVALRY BDE. DI: Multi-piece constr. Sb. Meyer hmkd. Above avg. cond. $36.00

WWII ARMY 5TH ARMY BELT BUCKLE: Unofficial buckle in gilded brass & enamel. Minor chipping to the enamel. Unmarked. Above avg. cond. $32.00

WWII ARMY 65TH A. F. A. BN. DI: Gilt brass & enamel. Open-catch Pb. S. E. Eby hmkd. Above avg. cond. $10.00

WWII ARMY 746TH AIR DEFENSE LOT: Pr 746th Pb. DI's, Pr Domed white gold brass US w/746 & Coast arty w/A on makers card + Panama defense patch & E for excellence coast Arty patch- all unissued. Exc. cond. $21.00

WWII ARMY 96TH SIGNAL BATTALION DI: Sterling w/enamel face & Horse & rider in metal. PB. Said to have supported Merrill's Marauders. Exc. cond. $40.00

WWII ARMY ARMOR FORCES OFFICER COLLAR DEVICES: Gilt brass. Cb. WWI tank design. Above avg. cond. $13.00

WWII ARMY ARMOR SCHOOL DI: Enamel details. Pb. Sterling hmkd. Avg. cond. $20.00

WWII ARMY ARTY OFFICER COLLAR DEVICES: "816/Arty." Gilt brass. Cb. On maker card. Above avg. cond. $20.00

WWII ARMY CHEMICAL CORPS EM COLLAR DISCS: All C/B & on orig. Gemsco card. All type IV polished brass. Near mint cond. $20.00

WWII ARMY COMMAND & STAFF COLLEGE DI: Sterling hmkd. Pb. Above avg. cond. $30.00

WWII ARMY EM TANK DESTROYER COLLAR BRASS: round stamped brass of armored half track & bar back w/Cb. Hard to find. Near mint cond. $17.00

WWII ARMY G-2 INTELLIGENCE DI'S: CB brass w/sphinx in center. Good detail & near mint. Exc. cond. $27.00

WWII ARMY INF OFFICER COLLAR DEVICE: "AA/Inf": Has applique "A. A." over crossed rifles. Cb. Meyer hmkd. Above avg. cond. $30.00

WWII ARMY INF OFFICER COLLAR DEVICES: Australian made. Smooth brass bodies are Luke/Melbourne hmkd. Cb. Above avg. cond. $20.00

WWII ARMY INFANTRY DI: Pb. Sterling w/ enamel & motto "FORTIOR EXASPERIS." Exc. cond. $20.00

WWII ARMY OFFICER CAP BADGE: gilt finish, SB, Luxembourg maker marked. Some wear to the finish. Avg. cond. $31.00

WWII ARMY OFFICER COL.'S EAGLE RANK INSIGNIA: 50mm size-matched pair-curve formed-PB-"Luxembourg" hmkd. Nice-oversize pair. Some light tarnish. Above avg. cond. $67.00

WWII ARMY OFFICER COLLAR DEVICE: "8/Cav/E." Gilt brass. Twin Sb posts. Wear to gilt. Avg. cond. $27.00

WWII ARMY OFFICER COLLAR DEVICES: "187/Arty/Obsn." Gilt brass. Cb. Above avg. cond. $21.50

METAL INSIGNIA

WWII ARMY OFFICER COLLAR DEVICES: "320/Arty." Gilt. Cb. In maker carton. Above avg. cond. $39.00

WWII ARMY OFFICER COLONEL EAGLE RANK INSIGNIA: Pb. Frosted finish. Pb. Curve-form. "Shold-R-Form/Meyer/ sterling." hmkd. Above avg. cond. $32.00

WWII ARMY OFFICER COLONEL EAGLE RANK INSIGNIA

WWII ARMY OFFICER GENERAL 3 STAR BAR RANK INSIGNIA: Appear to be stainless steel, shows some tarnish to patina. Above avg. cond. $28.00

WWII ARMY OFFICER GENERAL STAR RANK INSIGNIA: 30mm-heavy sterling-CB-Luxembourg maker marked. Above avg. cond. $48.00

WWII ARMY OFFICER VISOR CAP DEVICE: English made. 50mm wide. Sb. J. R. Gaunt, Made in England hmkd. Above avg. cond. $30.00

WWII ARMY OFFICER VISOR CAP DEVICE: Gilt brass. Sb. On Smilo Co. maker card. Above avg. cond. $18.00

WWII ARMY OFFICER VISOR CAP DEVICE: Luxembourg. Dull gilt finished brass w/single Sb post. Hmkd. on reverse on star field. Above avg. cond. $42.00

WWII ARMY OFFICER VISOR CAP DEVICE: Luxembourg. Gilt brass. Hmkd. Sb. Above avg. cond. $40.00

WWII ARMY TANK DESTROYER FORCES EM COLLAR DISC: English made. Gilt brass. Sb. Design of half-track mounting anti-tank weapon. Avg. cond. $20.00

WWII ARMY TANK DESTROYER FORCES EM COLLAR DISC: English made. Mutli-piece. Sb. Exc. cond. $40.00

WWII ARMY TRANSPORTATION DI: SB enameled brass w/globe over train engine. Motto "DILIGENTER." Exc. cond. $20.00

WWII ARMY TROOP CARRIER DI'S: C/B Brass w/enamel & gilt finish. Face shows gilt eagle carrying rifleman in talons. Motto at bottom. Above avg. cond. $25.00

WWII ARMY UNIT DI: Enameled design w/ motto "Junto Servimos." Pb. Dondero/ sterling hmkd. Above avg. cond. .. $21.00

WWII ARMY UNIT DI: Green & blue enamel, PB, & motto "SIC ETUR AS ASTRA." Above avg. cond. $20.00

WWII CALIFORNIA STATE GUARD "2" COLLAR DISC: Gilt brass. Multi-piece. Sb. Above avg. cond. $23.50

WWII CIVIL AIR PATROL 'DUCK CLUB' LAPEL PIN: Stamped brass w/PB & image of Duck in the water. Nice luster. Above avg. cond. $82.00

WWII MAINE STATE GUARD PLASTIC DI: Pb. Nice shape. Scarce. Near mint cond. $20.00

WWII MO. STATE GUARD 3RD REGT. DI: Sb. Maker hmkd. Nice shape. Above avg. cond. $11.00

WWII N. Y. GUARD DI'S: Motto "Fidelis Et Constans." Sb. Gilt brass & enamel. Robbins hmkd. Above avg. cond. .. $11.00

WWII USMC QM OFFICER COLLAR DEVICES: In bronze finish. Pb. Imperial hmkd on reverse. Above avg. cond. $38.00

WWII WAAC CAP DEVICE: Gilt brass. Multi-piece. Sb. Above avg. cond. $30.00

WWII WAC BELT BUCKLE: Experimental. Similar to std brass buckle but w/dark brown finish & national emblem on front. Exc. cond. $20.00

C. 1946 - Present

ARMY AIRBORNE DOMED EM COLLAR DISC: Domed brass body w/miniature applied likeness of basic para wing over "U.S." Cb. Above avg. cond. $34.00

ARMY AIRBORNE/ARTY DOMED EM COLLAR DISC: Gilt brass. Has crossed cannon over basic para wing design. Multi-piece. Cb. Scarce. Above avg. cond. $20.00

ARMY AIRBORNE/ENGR. DOMED EM COLLAR DISC: Gilt brass. Has engr. castle over basic para wing design. Multi-piece. Cb. Scarce. Above avg. cond. $20.00

ARMY GENERAL INTERLOCK PATTERN BUCKLE: Silvered images on brass base, eagle interlocking to wreath on main piece. Above avg. cond. $35.00

ARMY GENERAL STAFF BREAST BADGE: 2-piece construction, gilt & enameled

design. Meyer marked to back, CB. Mint
cond. $28.00

ARMY GENERAL STAR RANK INSIGNIA:
Pair of blackened metal three star insignia
attributed to Gen. Westmoreland in 1969.
Above avg. cond. $99.00

ARMY OFFICER COLONEL EAGLE RANK
INSIGNIA: Full-size. Cb. Hmkd "HLP
STER./G-I." Exc. cond. $20.00

ARMY SGT. COLLAR INSIGNIA: Gold filled.
CB. Above avg. cond. $20.00

ARMY SGT. MAJOR COLLAR BRASS:
Multi-piece Cb. Includes beautiful disc w/
enamel & gilt design + U.S. disc. Exc.
cond. $107.00

ARMY TANK DESTROYER FORCES EM
COLLAR DISCS: Are multi-piece Cb. Gilt
brass. Meyer hmkd. Come on Meyer card
that shows age. Exc. cond. $25.00

JOINT CHIEFS OF STAFF METAL BADGE:
Alloy wreath w/gilt Joint chiefs emblem in
center & labeled. Three prong clutch back.
Uncommon & impressive. Exc. cond.
.... $23.00

MILITARY SEALIFT COMMAND OFFICER
VISOR CAP BADGE: 2 separate piece
design. Gilt & nickel w/enamel detail. Near
mint cond $32.00

MILITARY SEALIFT COMMAND VISOR
CAP BADGE: Multi-piece design in gilt,
nickel & enamel. On black woven cap
band-ends never stitched together. Near
mint cond $20.00

TEXAS STATE GUARD 104TH M. P. BN.
BEERCAN DI: Thin stamped metal body
w/painted design. Cb. Above avg. cond.
.... $35.00

USAF SGT. MAJOR COLLAR BRASS:
Frosted silver finish. Multi-piece. Cb. Near
mint cond. $129.00

VIETNAM ERA ARMY 114TH AVIATION
"KNIGHTS OF THE AIR" BEERCAN DI:
Vietnam made. 26mm wide. Thin stamped
metal body w/painted design. Cb. Above
avg. cond. $28.00

VIETNAM ERA ARMY 145TH AVIATION BN.
BEERCAN DI: Vietnam made. 22x31mm
thin stamped metal body. Cb. Painted
design. Above avg. cond. $28.00

VIETNAM ERA ARMY 173RD ABN
BRIGADE BEERCAN DI: Vietnam made.
CB enameled w/Casper the Ghost
standing in front of chopper & unit
particulars below. Above avg. cond.
.... $32.00

VIETNAM ERA ARMY 1ST FIELD FORCE
PATCH-TYPE BEERCAN DI'S: 25x31mm
thin stamped metal bodies w/painted
design. Pb. Above avg. cond. $30.00

VIETNAM ERA ARMY 29TH F. A. BEERCAN
DI: Vietnam made. Thin stamped body w/
painted detail. Cb. Above avg. cond.
.... $21.50

VIETNAM ERA ARMY 32ND F. A.
BEERCAN DI: Vietnam made. Thin
stamped metal body w/painted details. Cb.
Above avg. cond. $21.50

VIETNAM ERA ARMY 5TH MECH. DIV. DI:
CB Beer can DI w/red diamond crest +
small SVN flag lapel pin. Above avg. cond.
.... $20.00

VIETNAM ERA ARMY 5TH SPEC FORCES
GROUP TAG: Brass tag 1" across
engraved for Nha Trang base + "REL TO
CONUS"/170. Above avg. cond. $11.00

VIETNAM ERA ARMY 93RD EVAC HOSP
PATCH-TYPE DI ON POCKET HANGER
TAB: 43x69mm thick nickel metal w/nice
enameled design. Exc. cond. $20.00

VIETNAM ERA ARMY ENGINEER CMD.
PATCH-TYPE BEERCAN DI: 22x32mm
thin stamped metal body w/painted
design. Cb. Couple chips to paint but
good. Above avg. cond. $20.00

VIETNAM ERA USAF 3RD TACTICAL
FIGHTER WING BEERCAN DI: 27mm
wide. Thin stamped metal body w/painted
detail. Cb. Above avg. cond. $17.00

U.S. NAVY & MARINE CORPS METAL INSIGNIA

A. All Periods

COAST GUARD RESERVE VISOR CAP
DEVICE: Gilt finish w/blue enamel detail.
Sb. Exc. cond. $20.00

COAST GUARD SHORE ESTABLISHMENT
PO VISOR CAP DEVICE: Stamped brass.
Sb. Gilt finish. Above avg. cond. ... $13.00

COMM. IN CHIEF PACIFIC BREAST
BADGE: CB brass 1.75" badge w/
enameled 8 pt compass rose & brass
eagle over globe & 4 star banner in center.
Rim reads "COMMANDER IN CHIEF
PACIFIC." Above avg. cond. $50.00

MARITIME SERVICE CPO VISOR CAP
BADGE: Gilt. Multi-piece. Sb. Near mint
cond. $33.00

MARITIME SERVICE OFFICER VISOR CAP
DEVICE: Multi-piece. Rhodium & gilt
finish. Sb. Mint cond. $30.00

NAVAL ACADEMY CUFF LINKS: Post Civil
War Era. Brass links w/old naval academy
emblem on face. Stored in small black box

leatherette finish & velvet interior. Above avg. cond. $47.00

NAVAL CAP EMBLEM: 1890's era stamped brass emblem 2.25x2", comprised of leafed wreath w/diagonal fouled anchor in center. Prong back for mounting. Exc. cond. $90.00

NAVAL MILITIA BUCKLE: Circular wreath around anchor w/shield. In shield is apparently state emblem w/horns of plenty & Naval stocking cap. Gilded brass w/loop. Above avg. cond. $25.00

NAVY WARRANT OFFICER BOATSWAIN SHIRT-SIZE DEVICES: Sterling hmkd. Cb. Exc. cond. $16.00

USMC DRESS HELMET EG&A DEVICE: 1880s. Massive stamped design has approx. 86mm wide wingspan. Silver plated finish. Loop attachment to back. Rare. Avg. cond. $290.00

USMC EAGLE EMBLEM: S/B 3x3.5" dimensions, nicely done gilded eagle, globe & anchor. Suitable for helmet wear, Likely enlisted helmet 1900 era. Exc. cond. $177.00

USMC EG&A DEVICE: 1898. Cap size in silver-colored finish. Prong back. Exc. cond. $28.00

USMC EG&A DEVICE: 1898. Thin stamped body in nickel finish w/prong back. Exc. cond. $24.00

USMC EM COLLAR DEVICE: 1921 pattern. For rt. side of color. In bronze finish. Sb. Avg. cond. $25.00

USMC OFFICER ADJ. GEN. DEPT. COLLAR DEVICE: Pierced design. Dark bronze finish. Open-catch Pb. Above avg. cond. $37.00

USMC OFFICER COLLAR DEVICES: 1937 pattern. Sterling, H-H hmkd. Sb. In copper colored finish. Above avg. cond. ... $40.00

USMC OFFICER DRESS COLLAR EG&A DEVICES: 1937 pattern. Sb. Meyer/210 hmkd. on reverse. In Meyer package. Exc. cond. $72.00

USMC OFFICER VISOR CAP DEVICE: 1937 pattern, 1950s era. Multi-piece. Sb. 211 hmkd. Exc. cond. $45.00

USMC OFFICER VISOR CAP DEVICE: 1937 pattern. Multi-piece. Sb. Pb. H&H/sterling/1/20 10K hmkd. "Fall-in" catch. Above avg. cond. $49.50

WWI NAVY CPO VISOR CAP DEVICE: Multi-piece. Open-catch Pb. Above avg. cond. $20.00

WWI NAVY OFFICER VISOR CAP DEVICE: Heavy bullion on dark felt sew on backing. Some tarnish. Avg. cond. $25.00

WWI USMC EM CAP DEVICE: S/B bronze E/G/A + letter of documentation for orig. owner of device. In use 1918-1919 Parris Island, SC. Exc. cond. $40.00

WWI USMC EM DRESS VISOR CAP EG&A DEVICE: Sb. Wear to gilt finish. Avg. cond. $32.00

WWI USMC EM EG&A VISOR CAP DEVICE: Dark bronze finish. Sb. Comes w/locking nut. Avg. cond. $33.00

WWI USMC EM VISOR CAP DEVICE: Gilt finish. Sb. Some wear to finish at highlights. Avg. cond. $35.00

WWI USMC EM VISOR CAP EG&A DEVICE: Natural brass finish. Sb. Some age. Avg. cond. $35.00

WWI USMC EM VISOR CAP EG&A DEVICE: Sb. Bronze finish over gilt. Avg. cond. $27.00

WWI USMC OFFICER CAMPAIGN HAT CORD: Bullion wire body w/matching acorns & slide. Above avg. cond. .. $65.00

WWI USMC OFFICER CAMPAIGN HAT CORD: Gold wire w/acorns & slide w/scarlet striping. Above avg. cond. .. $62.00

WWII COAST GUARD CPO VISOR CAP DEVICE: Multi-piece. Pb. Above avg. cond. $14.00

WWII COAST GUARD OVERSEAS CAP SIZE DEVICE: Multi-piece. Has three Sb posts. "1/20 10k on Sterling" hmkd. On V. H. Blackington & Co. maker card. Above avg. cond. $34.00

WWII COAST GUARD WARRANT OFFICER VISOR CAP DEVICE: Multi-piece. Sb. Meyer hmkd. On Meyer maker card. Above avg. cond. $24.00

WWII MARITIME SERVICE OFFICER'S VISOR CAP BAND: Direct embr. bullion radio sparks inside wreath on black woven band. Above avg. cond. $23.00

WWII MARITIME SERVICE PETTY OFFICER VISOR CAP DEVICE: Red enameled details. Sb. A. C. Co. hmkd. Some tarnish. Sterling. Avg. cond $16.00

WWII MERCHANT MARINE BADGE. Gilded brass P/B w/eagle over USNR banner. Near mint cond. $75.00

WWII NAVY MIDSHIPMAN SHIRT-SIZE ANCHORS: Cb. Gilt finish. Show some tarnish. In maker carton. Above avg. cond. $30.00

WWII NAVY NURSE CORPS BULLION DEVICES: Heavy bullion devices direct embr. into uncut section of navy blue felt. Exc. cond. $25.00

WWII NAVY OFFICER COLLAR BRASS:
Pair Pb. gilded brass USN pins for uniform
collar. Exc. cond. $22.00

WWII NAVY OFFICERS GARRISON CAP
DEVICE: PB-closed clasp, sterling silver
two piece device 23mm high. Exc. cond.
.... $56.00

WWII NAVY SUBMARINERS DOLPHIN
CAP DEVICE: Gold filled PB, nice finish.
Above avg. cond. $20.00

WWII NAVY V-5 PROGRAM PIN: 36mm
wide. Pb w/"fall-in" catch. Sterling/B. B.
Co. hmkd. Avg. cond. $30.00

WWII USMC EM WAR ECONOMY EG&A
COLLAR DEVICE: 1937 pattern. Dark
bronze plastic. Above avg. cond. .. $16.00

WWII USMC OFFICER QM DEPARTMENT
SERVICE COLLAR DEVICE: Dark bronze
finish. Pierced design. Pb w/"fall-in" catch.
H-H/Imperial hmkd. Exc. cond. $28.00

WWII USMC QUARTERMASTER'S DEPT.
COLLAR DEVICE: Pierced design in dark
bronze finish. "Fall-in" catch Pb. Imperial
hmkd. Exc. cond. $28.00

U.S. WINGS

A. 1913 - 1945

AAF PILOT WING: Pre WWII, unmarked,
Pb., 73mm w/unusual curved & bowed
wing. Above avg. cond. $145.00

ARMY AVIATOR PILOT WING: 1932 pattern.
3 1/8" size. Pb w/safety catch. Sterling
marked. Has nice age patina highlights to
the sterling. Exc. cond. $112.00

ARMY AVIATOR PILOT WING: 1921 pattern.
77mm in massive, solid back sterling
struck design. Standard pattern worn
through 1920-30-40s but has early, heavy
brass pin & catch. Unmarked but tests
sterling-typical issue pattern. Above avg.
cond. $50.00

ARMY AVIATOR PILOT WING: Pb. open
catch 68mm, S/S, HMKD. B-B on back.
1921 pattern. Compares to Campbell's
#48. Exc. cond. $100.00

NATIONAL ASSOC. AIR FORCE WOMEN
WING: 2". Enameled center. 1 piece. Pb.
Sterling/LeVelle hmkd. Avg. cond.
.... $22.00

NAVAL AVIATOR WING: 2 13/16" wide. Gilt.
Orber hmkd. Open catch Pb. Exc. cond.
.... $67.00

NAVY PILOT WING: Heavy gold bullion on
white twill. Above avg. cond. $16.00

NAVY V-5 ENAMELED PIN: 3/4" size. Pb.
Sterling & maker marked. Blue enameled.
Shield shaped w/Navy, wings in center &
V-5 below. Avg. cond. $48.00

TRENCH ART STYLIZED WING PIN: 2"
heavy brass w/rounded wings & round
shield. Name engraved across wing w/
design around it. Pb. Avg. cond. ... $32.00

WWI ARMY PILOT WING: 1.25" gilt brass
spread wing w/enameled "US" on red,
white & blue shield design. Open-catch
Pb. Exc. cond. $100.00

WWI INSTRUCTOR PILOT WING: For US
instructor at French airfields in WWI 1917-
1918. 88mm gilt wing S/B w/square nuts.
Exc. cond. $250.00

WWI NAVAL AVIATOR WING: 2.75" wide
heavy bullion wing on navy blue felt
backing. Avg. cond. $75.00

WWI NAVY PILOT WING: Bullion embr. on
black wool. Wing w/shield over anchor.
Exc. cond. $195.00

WWI NAVY PILOT WING: Heavy gold
bullion design. 2.75". 3" black felt base.
Above avg. cond. $189.00

WWI NAVY PILOT WING: Heavy gold
bullion design. 3 1/8", 3.75" wide black felt
base. Above avg. cond. $200.00

WWI PILOT WING: Pb.-closed clasp on
cloth wrapped brass. 3 part wing, left &
right wing & center US shield. Shield cast
w/letters US centered. Unusual rope like
edge borders inside shoulder of each
wing. Near mint cond. $1,160.00

WWI PILOT WING: Unusual variant of 1918
pattern. Pb. hmkd. 'Meyer rolled plate'
silver 3" wing w/interesting patina & great
detail. The US normally on shield is
omitted. Matches Campbell's #32 less the
US. Exc. cond. $192.00

WWI PILOT WING

WWII AAF AERIAL GUNNER WING: 2".
Multi-piece. Pb. Sterling/Meyer hmkd.
Above avg. cond. $25.00

WWII AAF AERIAL GUNNER WING: 2". Pb.
Multi-piece design. Amico/sterling hmkd.
Avg. cond. $23.00

WWII AAF AERIAL GUNNER WING: 3 1/8".
Multi-piece. Pb. Sterling hmkd. Above
avg. cond. $55.00
WWII AAF AERIAL GUNNER WING: Moody
Bros./sterling hmkd. Multi-piece. 3". Pb.
Avg. cond. 171.00
WWII AAF AIR GUNNER WING (VARIANT):
3" size-1 pc., die struck-PB, sterling. Made
w/no target design behind central design.
Exc. cond. $50.00
WWII AAF AIRCREW WING: 2", PB-sterling-
1 pc. Near mint cond. $50.00
WWII AAF AIRCREW WING: 2". Amico/
sterling hmkd. Pb. Avg. cond. $25.00
WWII AAF AIRCREW WING: 3 1/8". Multi-
piece. Gemsco/sterling hmkd. Pb. Above
avg. cond. $35.00
WWII AAF AIRCREW WING: 3 1/8". Pb.
Gemsco/sterling hmkd. Above avg. cond.
.... $75.00
WWII AAF AIRCREW WING: 3", PB-sterling.
Avg. cond. $30.00
WWII AAF AIRCREW WING: 3", frosted
sterling-CB-"Amico" hmkd. Above avg.
cond. $20.00
WWII AAF AIRCREW WING: 3"-PB-Sterling
w/hmkd. Gemsco, NY. Die struck. Above
avg. cond. $72.00
WWII AAF AIRCREW WING: 3.25". PB.
Juarez Mexico Sterling marked. 1 pc.
Above avg. cond. $100.00

WWII AAF AIRCREW WING

WWII AAF AIRCREW WING: English made.
Bullion 3" design on uncut dark blue felt
base. Avg. cond. $38.00
WWII AAF BOMBARDIER WING: 2". Multi-
piece. Pb. Amico/sterling hmkd. Above
avg. cond. $36.00

WWII AAF BOMBARDIER WING

WWII AAF BOMBARDIER WING: 2". Multi-
piece. Pb. Meyer/sterling hmkd. Above
avg. cond. $28.00
WWII AAF BOMBARDIER WING: 3 1/8"
wide heavy silver bullion design on uncut
dark OD gabardine base. Near mint cond
.... $42.50
WWII AAF BOMBARDIER WING: 3 1/8". 1
piece. Pb. Sterling/A. E. Co. hmkd. Avg.
cond. $145.00
WWII AAF BOMBARDIER WING: 3 1/8".
Multi-pc. PB. Gemsco/sterling marked.
Above avg. cond. $70.00
WWII AAF BOMBARDIER WING: 3". 1
piece. Cb. Sterling hmkd. Avg. cond.
.... $36.00
WWII AAF BOMBARDIER WING: 3". Multi-
pc. Pb. Meyer/sterling marked. Avg. cond.
.... $82.00
WWII AAF BOMBARDIER WING: Australian
made. Multi-piece design. Open-catch. "C
Luke, Melbourne, Australia" hmkd. Above
avg. cond. $325.00
WWII AAF BOMBARDIER WING: English
made. 3.5x1.5" blue felt padded
rectangular base w/3" wide hand embr.
design. Exc. cond. $61.00
WWII AAF BOMBARDIER WING: 3 1/8"
wide in heavy silver bullion. On uncut dark
OD gabardine. Exc. cond. $21.00
WWII AAF COMMAND PILOT WING: 2". PB.
hmkd. "N S MEYER." Exc. cond. .. $20.00
WWII AAF COMMAND PILOT WING: 3 1/8".
Pb. Amico/sterling hmkd. Avg. cond.
.... $95.00
WWII AAF COMMAND PILOT WING: 3".
PB. Sterling. Near mint cond. $195.00
WWII AAF COMMAND PILOT WING: 3".
CB. Marked 'JOSTENS/STERLING.' Exc.
cond. $135.00
WWII AAF COMMAND PILOT WING: 3". Pb
Hmkd. 'N S Meyer.' Heavy die struck. Exc.
cond. $53.00

WWII AAF COMMAND PILOT WING

WWII AAF COMMAND PILOT WING: 3". PB.
Josten Hmkd. Sterling. Above avg. cond.
.... $165.00
WWII AAF CREWMEMBER WING: English
made. 3 1/8" wide. Silver finished brass.

Multi-piece constr. Open-catch Pb. "J.R. Gaunt/London" hmkd on reverse. Above avg. cond. $74.00

WWII AAF FLIGHT NURSE WING: 2". PB. Sterling. 'AMICO' hmkd. Above avg. cond. $170.00

WWII AAF GLIDER PILOT WING: 3". PB. English made (J. Gaunt) silver plated wing w/large "G" imposed on shield in center. Excellent detail. Exc. cond. $136.00

WWII AAF GLIDER PILOT WING: 3". Pb. 1 piece. Amcraft/sterling hmkd. Above avg. cond. $177.00

WWII AAF LIAISON PILOT WING: 3". PB. Meyer marked. Exc. cond. $118.00

WWII AAF NAVIGATOR WING: 2". Pb. Sterling hmkd. Nice even patina. Above avg. cond. $30.00

WWII AAF NAVIGATOR WING: 3 1/8". Pb. A.E. Co./sterling hmkd. Above avg. cond. $122.00

WWII AAF NAVIGATOR WING

WWII AAF NAVIGATOR WING: 3". PB. Meyer/sterling hmkd. Above avg. cond. $45.00

WWII AAF NAVIGATOR WING: 3". Pb. Amico/sterling hmkd. Above avg. cond. $139.00

WWII AAF NAVIGATOR WING: 3". Sterling hmkd. PB. Avg. cond. $33.00

WWII AAF NAVIGATOR WING: CBI made. 2 7/8" hand embr. in white cord on uncut dark tan cotton twill base. Above avg. cond. $27.00

WWII AAF OBSERVER WING: 2". 1 piece. Pb. Meyer/sterling hmkd. Above avg. cond. $35.00

WWII AAF OBSERVER WING: 2". 1 piece. Pb. Meyer/sterling hmkd. Above avg. cond. $40.00

WWII AAF OBSERVER WING: 2". Sterling. Luxembourg. PB-pivot hinge & closed clasp. Exc. cond. $82.00

WWII AAF OBSERVER WING: 3 1/8". 1 piece. CB. Gemsco pattern. Sterling Hmkd. Above avg. cond. $45.00

WWII AAF OBSERVER WING: 3 1/8". Pb. Gemsco/sterling hmkd. Avg. cond. $93.00

WWII AAF OBSERVER WING

WWII AAF OBSERVER WING: 3" wide in heavy silver bullion on 4x1.75" blue felt base. Exc. cond. $55.00

WWII AAF OBSERVER WING: 3" wide in heavy silver bullion on uncut dark OD gabardine. Above avg. cond. $40.00

WWII AAF OBSERVER WING: 3". 'Sterling' & 'NS Meyer' marked. Exc. cond. $61.00

WWII AAF OBSERVER WING: 3". CB. Sterling. Luxembourg marked. Exc. cond. $180.00

WWII AAF OBSERVER WING: 3". PB. Sterling marked. Amico marked. Solid die stamped design. Avg. cond. $80.00

WWII AAF PILOT WING 3RD PATTERN: CB, 3" Sterling Luxembourg 3rd pattern wing w/crisp features. Hmkd. on back. Exc. cond. $175.00

WWII AAF PILOT WING: 1 3/8". Open catch Pb. 1 piece. Sterling hmkd. Above avg. cond. $22.00

WWII AAF PILOT WING: 1.5". PB. Sterling AAF style pilot wing w/star on embossed on shield-"SB" on 1 wing & "AD" on the other wing. Above avg. cond. $20.00

WWII AAF PILOT WING: 2". 1 piece. Pb w/ "fall-in" catch. Amico/sterling hmkd. Avg. cond. $25.00

WWII AAF PILOT WING: 2". 1 piece. Pb. Amico/sterling hmkd. Above avg. cond. $20.00

WWII AAF PILOT WING: 2.75". PB. Unmarked sterling. Above avg. cond. $95.00

WWII AAF PILOT WING: 3 1/16" wide. Cb. Sterling hmkd. Feather detail. Above avg. cond. $61.00

WWII AAF PILOT WING: 3" wide. Feather detail. PB. Sterling hmkd. Exc. cond. $135.00

WWII AAF PILOT WING: 3", Pb. in scarce Orber style pattern. Straight entry safety catch. Avg. cond. $37.50

WWII AAF PILOT WING: 3". CB.
Luxembourg 3rd pattern in A. E. Co. style.
Sterling. Above avg. cond. $125.00
WWII AAF PILOT WING: 3". Cb. Amcraft/
sterling hmkd. Avg. cond. $32.00
WWII AAF PILOT WING: 3". Cb. Sterling
hmkd. Avg. cond. $27.00
WWII AAF PILOT WING: 3". LGB/sterling
hmkd. Pb. Avg. cond. $55.00
WWII AAF PILOT WING: 3". Meyer/sterling
hmkd. Pb. Above avg. cond. $25.00
WWII AAF PILOT WING: 3". PB. Sterling.
Gemsco hmkd. In maroon velour lined
box. Exc. cond. $135.00
WWII AAF PILOT WING: 3". PB. Unmarked
sterling. Avg. cond. $30.00
WWII AAF PILOT WING: 3". PB. Unmarked.
Exc. cond. $34.00
WWII AAF PILOT WING: 3". Sterling. CB.
Luxembourg hmkd. Exc. cond. ... $134.00
WWII AAF PILOT WING: 3.25". Bullion/glitter
wire on dark blue wool field. Black thread
for detail outlines. Exc. cond. $65.00
WWII AAF PILOT WING: Australian made.
3". Silver finish. Open-catch. Hmkd
"Angus & Coote Stg. Sil." Above avg.
cond. $125.00
WWII AAF PILOT WING: CB. Sterling w/
Amcraft hallmark & sunburst pattern on
back. Exc. cond. $80.00
WWII AAF PILOT WING: Dark green twill w/
embr. edge & silk backing, multi-color
bullion & theater made. Rarer than
sterling. Above avg. cond. $50.00
WWII AAF PILOT WING: English made. 3".
PB. Sterling. "Angus & Coote" marked.
Near mint cond. $180.00
WWII AAF SR PILOT WING FOR FLIGHT
JACKET: 3 1/2x1 3/8" dark brown leather
base w/hand stitched 3 1/8" wide wing
design. Never applied to jacket. CBI
made. Exc. cond. $74.00
WWII AAF SR PILOT WING: 2". CB,
Unmarked sterling. Above avg. cond.
.... $24.00
WWII AAF SR PILOT WING: 2". PB. Hmkd.
"LUXEMBURG, NY." Sterling. Exc. cond.
.... $195.00
WWII AAF SR PILOT WING: 2". PB.
Sterling. Avg. cond. $25.00
WWII AAF SR PILOT WING: 3". Cb.
Jostens/sterling marked. Above avg. cond.
.... $125.00
WWII AAF SR PILOT WING: 3". PB.
Sterling, Amcraft Hmkd. Above avg. cond.
.... $177.00

WWII AAF SR PILOT WING: 3". PB. Sterling
LGB Hmkd. 1 pc. Exc. cond. $195.00
WWII AAF SR PILOT WING: 3". Pb. Hmkd
Amcraft Attleboro Mass Sterling. Above
avg. cond. $117.50

WWII AAF SR PILOT WING

WWII AAF TECHNICAL OBSERVER WING:
One of the rarest WWII AAF wings. 3".
Solid back w/pierced "O" & superimposed
"T." Pb. Sterling. No maker's mark. Exc.
cond. $189.00
WWII AIR TRANSPORT COMMAND CAP
BADGE: 47x50mm winged kittyhawk
design on shield w/"ATC" in letters across
wing tips. Twin screwpost fasteners. Near
mint cond. $145.00
WWII AIR TRANSPORT COMMAND
FLIGHT ENGINEER HALF WING: 55mm.
Dark bronze, fine feathered 1/2 wing on
disc w/3 blade prop in center. Pb. w/safety
catch. Above avg. cond. $240.00
WWII AIRBORNE PARA WING ON PARA
OVAL: English made. Sterling wing is
Gaunt/London hmkd. w/open-catch Pb +
2 combat stars & one arrowhead devices.
On rare 507th British-made para oval w/
silk embr. border on black felt base. Above
avg. cond. $142.00
WWII AIRBORNE CHAPLAIN JUMP WING:
English Made. 1.5". PB. Sterling. Marked
"JR Gaunt/London." Exc. cond. $80.00
WWII AIRBORNE CHAPLAIN PARA WING:
English made. Open-catch Pb. Has cross,
arrowhead & star appliques. London
maker/sterling hmkd. Above avg. cond.
.... $80.00
WWII AIRBORNE PARA JUMP WING: 2".
PB. Sterling. Avg. cond. $25.00
WWII AIRBORNE PARA JUMP WING: PB.
Sterling 1.5". Bronze arrowhead on
shroud. Above avg. cond. $55.00
WWII AIRBORNE PARA JUMP WING: Pb.
Sterling/J.J.W. marked w/combat star &
arrowhead devices. On British-made
508th A/B para oval w/silk embr. border on
black felt base. Above avg. cond.
.... $100.00

WWII AIRBORNE PARA WING ON OVAL: English made. Sterling wing w/open-catch Pb. J.R. Gaunt, London hmkd. Has 2 combat stars (applied to chute shroud lines & one wing) + arrowhead device. Stitched on black felt 507th para oval. Exc. cond. $185.00

WWII AIRBORNE PARA WING: 1.5" wide. Pb. Sterling hmkd. Above avg. cond. $30.00

WWII AIRBORNE RIGGER PARA WING: Full size. PB. "Ludlow-London" hmkd. Block letter "R" applied to parachute canopy. Above avg. cond. $54.00

WWII ARMY AIRBORNE CHAPLAIN PARA WING: English made. Sterling para wing made by Ludlow, London (well hmkd) w/ open-catch Pb. Has Chaplain's cross design applique on shroud lines & battle star applique on one wing. On black felt 505th para oval. Above avg. cond. $107.00

WWII ARMY AIRBORNE MEDIC JUMP WING: PB. Sterling w/maroon flash. Exc. cond. $82.00

WWII ARMY AIRBORNE PARA WING: full size-stamped silver finish metal-PB-Gaunt hmkd. Near mint cond. $47.00

WWII CHAPLAIN PARA WING: Sterling. PB. "J.J.W." hmkd. Chaplain cross device applied to shroud lines. On British-made 508th A/B oval w/white silk embr. border on black felt backing. Above avg. cond. $100.00

WWII GLIDER TROOP WING: 1.5". Sterling. PB. Glider in center. Above avg. cond. $21.00

WWII NAVAL AVIATOR WING: 2 7/8" wide heavy gold bullion design on uncut 3 1/4x1 3/8" navy blue felt backing. Near mint cond. $31.00

WWII NAVAL AVIATOR WING: 2.75" wide heavy gold bullion design on uncut tan gabardine. Mint cond. $40.00

WWII NAVY COMBAT AIRCREW WING: 2". Multi-piece. PB. Meyer/sterling marked. Above avg. cond. $20.00

WWII NAVY FLIGHT JACKET NAME TAG WING: 50x100mm light brown leather body w/impressed gold leaf likeness of WWI style USN pilot wing over name & "U.S. Navy." Mint cond. $72.00

WWII NAVY FLIGHT SURGEON WING: 2.75". Pb w/"fall-in" catch. Vanguard N.Y./ sterling hmkd. Above avg. cond. $100.00

WWII NAVY FLIGHT SURGEON WING: 3". 2 pc. PB. 'Amico Sterling 10k gold filled' marked. Medical emblem fixed to observer disc in center. Exc. cond. $235.00

WWII NAVY FLIGHT SURGEON WING: 3". 2 pc. PB. 'N.S. Meyer' marked. Medical emblem fixed to the Observer disc in center. Exc. cond. $145.00

WWII NAVY NAVIGATOR WING: Full size gilded sterling. CB w/riveted center. "H&H" hmkd. Near mint cond. $118.00

WWII NAVY NAVIGATOR WING: Pb. 10k gold on sterling. 2 pc. 'Amico' marked. Navigator emblem fixed to center over crossed anchors. Exc. cond. $145.00

WWII NAVY PILOT WING: 1 5/8". Gilt finish. Pb. '12k G.F.' marked. Exc. cond. $32.00

WWII NAVY PILOT WING: 1.75" Sterling silver gold filled. In velvet lined sales box. Exc. cond. $40.00

WWII NAVY PILOT WING: 2 5/8". Gold bullion on aviation green gabardine. Avg. cond. $29.00

WWII NAVY PILOT WING: 2.75". Gold filled. CB. Blackington marked. Near mint cond. $93.00

WWII NAVY PILOT WING: 3". PB. Unmarked sterling. Above avg. cond. $38.00

WWII NAVY PILOT WING: Gold bullion on black wool. Exc. cond. $150.00

WWII NAVY/MARINE PARA WING: 3". Gilt. Pb. & unmarked. Near mint cond. $67.00

WWII SPECIAL FORCES UNOFFICIAL PARA WING: 3.5" in gold wire on OD wool w/gold "S.F." on black circular center. Avg. cond. $350.00

WWII WASP WING: Custom made. 70mm. PB. Unmarked. Above avg. cond. $350.00

B. 1946 - Present

AIRBORNE PARA WING: 1.5". Sterling. CB. Exc. cond. $19.00

AIRBORNE PARA WING: Full size. Jeweler quality in heavy sterling silver. Large human skull in center-gold plated. Extra long clutch prongs, pattern often worn by MACV-SOG personnel in center of beret flash. Near mint cond. $292.00

ARMY AIRBORNE PARA MASTER WING, DIAMOND SET: Full size, sterling CB para wing in master grade. Has approx. 10 point diamond professionally set in the very center of the star in wreath above. Has bronze combat jump star added by drilling hole in risers in the center . Above avg. cond. $160.00

ARMY AIRCREW WING (VIETNAM ERA):
CB. "22/M" & sterling marked. Above avg.
cond. $25.00

ARMY MASTER PILOT WING: 2.5".
Sterling/12 C marked. CB. Above avg.
cond. $23.00

ARMY PILOT WING: 2.5". CB. Exc. cond.
.... $20.00

KOREAN WAR ERA USAF COMMAND
PILOT WING: 3". CB. Sterling Meyer
marked. Exc. cond. $35.00

KOREAN WAR ERA USAF PILOT WING:
3". CB. Sterling. Above avg. cond.
.... $27.00

KOREAN WAR ERA USAF PILOT WING:
3". CB. Unmarked sterling. Exc. cond.
.... $22.00

NAVY ASTRONAUT WING: 2.75". Gilt. Multi-
pc. Cb. '1/20 10k GF/Vanguard/154'
marked. 1960s era. Near mint cond.
.... $55.00

NAVY PHOTOGRAPHER MATE WING:
Unofficial. 2.75" wide wing w/old-style
camera applique in center. Gilt finish. Cb.
Near mint cond. $24.00

NAVY PILOT WING: Meyer marked. Above
avg. cond. $43.00

USAF AIRCREW WING: 3". CB. Meyer/
Sterling marked. Exc. cond. $20.00

USAF AIRCREW WING: 3". CB. Unmarked.
Avg. cond. $20.00

USAF BOMBARDIER WING: 2". CB.
Unmarked. Above avg. cond. $20.00

USAF COMMAND PILOT WING: 2" silver
embossed wing design on black finished
leather. Mint cond. $20.00

USAF COMMAND PILOT WING: 2". CB.
Sterling. "Vanguard" marked. Above avg.
cond. $20.00

USAF COMMAND PILOT WING: 2". Pb.
Meyer/9M marked. Sterling. Exc. cond.
.... $22.50

USAF COMMAND PILOT WING: 3". CB.
Sterling. 'VANGUARD, NY/IV' marked.
Exc. cond. $50.00

USAF COMMAND PILOT WING: 3". Cb.
Meyer/22 M/sterling marked. Above avg.
cond. $25.00

USAF CRASH CREW WING: Unofficial. 3".
PB. Silver finish w/crossed axes over
ladder on center shield. Meyer marked.
Avg. cond. $26.00

USAF MASTER NAVIGATOR WING: 2". CB.
N. S. Meyer marked. 1 pc. Silver finish.
Avg. cond. $20.00

USAF MASTER PILOT WING: 2". CB.
Unmarked. Avg. cond. $20.00

USAF NAVIGATOR WING: 3". CB.
Unmarked. Exc. cond. $28.00

USAF NAVIGATOR WING: 3". PB. NS
Meyers Inc. marked. Silver finish. 1 pc.
Avg. cond. $20.00

USAF NAVIGATOR WING: Japanese made.
3.25". Silver bullion w/great detail. Exc.
cond. $20.00

USAF PILOT WING (1950s): 3". PB. Meyer
9/M pattern. Near mint cond. $50.00

USAF PILOT WING (1960s): 3". CB. Maker
H. Sugerman(SUSCO). Above avg.
cond. $23.00

USAF PILOT WING: 2". CB. Silver finish.
Above avg. cond. $20.00

USAF PILOT WING: 2". CB. Sterling. Meyer
marked. Above avg. cond. $20.00

USAF PILOT WING: 2". Frosted finish. Cb.
Sterling marked. Above avg. cond.
.... $23.00

USAF PILOT WING: 3". CB. 'Josten/Sterling'
marked. Die stamped w/hollowed shield,
star, wreath & upper wings. Above avg.
cond. $95.00

USAF PILOT WING: 3". CB. N. S. Meyer
marked. Silver finish. Above avg. cond.
.... $20.00

USAF PILOT WING: 3". PB. Sterling. LGB
marked. Above avg. cond. $50.00

USAF SERVICE PILOT WING: 3". CB.
Unmarked. Avg. cond. $36.00

USAF SR ASTRONAUT WING: 3". Multi-
piece. Cb. Sterling/G-22 marked. Exc.
cond. $30.00

USAF SR FLIGHT SURGEON WING
(1950s): 3". PB. 'V21' & '1/20th' silver
filled marked. Nice. Above avg. cond.
.... $24.00

USAF SR NAVIGATOR WING: 3". CB.
Sterling. 'LGB' marked. Avg. cond.
.... $25.00

USAF SR PILOT WING: 2". Meyer 9/M
marked. Above avg. cond. $20.00

USAF SR PILOT WING: 3". CB. Sterling.
Vanguard marked. Exc. cond. $60.00

USAF SR PILOT WING: 3". CB. Unmarked
Sterling. Above avg. cond. $50.00

USMC RECON WING: 1.5". CB. Gilt finish.
Exc. cond. $28.00

VIETNAM ERA AIRBORNE MASTER PARA
WING: Vietnamese made. Cb. Exc. cond.
.... $30.00

VIETNAM ERA AIRBORNE PARA WING:
1.5" Vietnamese made. CB. Unmarked.
unmarked. Avg. cond. $40.00

CHAPTER FOUR: HEADGEAR

U.S. VISOR CAPS, SERVICE HATS & CAPS

A. Thru World War I (1919)

1890s PILLBOX VISOR CAP: Black wool top w/cylindrical form, ornate gold wire cap band, black chinstrap & thick visor. Has stamped brass wreath w/nickel-finish "180/LOL" in center. Has domed gilt 1872-style side buttons. Fully lined. Size 7. Above avg. cond. $59.00

1890s PILLBOX VISOR CAP: Navy blue melton wool covered circular crown w/two rows gold wire trim, stamped gilt wreath on front of crown w/nickel "VSE" inside, thin gold wire chinstrap w/1872-style side buttons, black oilcloth visor. Silver embossed New York maker's markings on black cotton lining. Size 6 3/4. W/oilcloth storm cover. Avg. cond. $72.00

1895 PILLBOX VISOR CAP: Navy blue melton wool covered circular top w/black woven band, gold wire chinstrap w/1872-pattern domed side buttons, black visor, maker markings on black cotton lining & leather sweatband. Size 7 1/4. Avg. cond. $60.00

1895 PILLBOX VISOR CAP

1900s VISOR CAP: Navy blue melton wool bell crown top w/black mohair band, stamped wreath w/separate stamped lyre in center insignia on front crown, gold wire chinstrap, lyre side buttons, black visor. Faint markings on black lining. Size 7 1/8. Named on sweatband. Avg. cond.
.... $25.00

ARMY 1902 PATTERN OFFICER VISOR CAP: "bell" shaped crown w/navy blue melton wool cover, black woven mohair band w/direct embr. heavy gold bullion device, gold wire chinstrap (has later-era

eagle side buttons), black visor, black cotton lining w/maker markings & leather sweatband w/impressed man's initials. Avg. cond. $97.00

ARMY 1902 PATTERN OFFICER VISOR CAP: Navy blue melton wool covered "bell" crown w/black woven mohair band, direct embr. heavy gold bullion device into front of crown, gold wire chinstrap w/1872-pattern side buttons, black visor, maker markings on black cotton lining. Lacks sweatband. Bullion still bright. Avg. cond. $68.00

ARMY CAVALRY 1902 PATTERN SHAKO BUSH: Vivid gold color, orig. wrappings intact. Above avg. cond. $23.00

CIVIL WAR ARTILLERY EM HAT CORD: Red woven wool w/knot & two acorns, Near mint cond. $32.00

CIVIL WAR OFFICER HAT CORD: Black & gold pattern w/knot & two acorns. Above avg. cond. $42.00

INDIAN WAR ERA ARMY KEPI: Navy blue wool body w/approx. 5" diam. top & long sloping back. Oilcloth trimmed leather bill w/leather chinstrap w/brass buckle & 1855 style eagle buttons. Horstmann maker marked inside-black cotton bag liner. Has a Bronze 1874 pattern 17/Inf/F device pinned to front. Very poor cond. . $402.00

NAVY OFFICER DRESS CHAPEAU: Purchased at Midshipman's Store-U.S.N.A. Black beaver body trimmed in wide, fancy woven black satin. Heavy bullion tassel on each end w/early gilt eagle button on gold wire panel on side. 7 3/8-USNA marked on satin lining-oilcloth sweatband. Avg. cond. $160.00

NAVY OFFICER DRESS CHAPEAU: Black beaver covered body w/wide, ornate woven satin trim-early gilt eagle button on bullion trim panel on side. Horstmann marked on satin lining-sweatband. Below avg. cond. $187.00

NAVY OFFICER DRESS CHAPEAU

NEW YORK GUARD OFFICER DRESS CHAPEAU: Black beaver body trimmed in wide, ribbed black satin-gold bullion tassel on each end w/heavy bullion eagle crested NY state shield on bullion border, ribbon trimmed oval. Small ostrich plume in crown. Satin lined - size 7. Avg. cond. $196.00

NEW YORK GUARD OFFICER DRESS
CHAPEAU

WWI ARMY AIR SERVICE HAT CORD: for WWI flyers Army Air service hat cord. condition w/apparent black & gray pattern. some wear. Avg. cond. $25.00

WWI ARMY BRIG GENERALS OVERSEAS CAP: from Gen. Evan M Johnson. Handsome OD Wool overseas cap w/ Bullion silver star on left side. Size 6 7/8 on sweatband. Segment of Gen.'s flag, Blue field w/Silver bullion Star, Sterling silver match holder like a pair of pants, NY initials on blue wool, two clip .45 cal. ammo pouch dated 1918, Sterling Masonic ring. Above avg. cond. . $282.00

WWI ARMY DAISY MAE FATIGUE HAT: Brown cotton w/soft crown, stitched brim. Small size. Above avg. cond. $20.00

WWI ARMY EM OVERSEAS CAP: English made. OD wool body w/clean white cotton sweatband very well marked w/broad arrow proof, 7 1/8 size, maker name & 1918 date. Above avg. cond. $35.00

WWI ARMY EM VISOR CAP: Lt. OD wool serge top w/brown visor & chinstrap, dark bronze side buttons. Leather sweatband w/silver embossed London/Chicago maker's markings. Lined in dark tan cotton. Front of crown has dark bronze Med. officer device w/open-catch Pb. Size 7. Near mint cond. $75.00

WWI ARMY EM VISOR CAP: Lt. OD wool serge top w/brown visor & chinstrap, dark bronze eagle side buttons. US markings on dark tan cotton lining. Has Sb. inf. device on front of crown in worn dark bronze finish. Small size. Avg. cond. $55.00

WWI ARMY EM VISOR CAP: OD wool top w/stiffener, brown visor & chinstrap, bronze device & side buttons, lt. OD cotton lining. Leather sweatband. Size 6 7/8. Avg. cond. $75.00

WWI ARMY EM VISOR CAP: Private-purchase in OD whipcord w/dark brown visor & chinstrap, bronze eagle side buttons, quilted tan cotton lining & leather chinstrap. Avg. cond. $37.00

WWI ARMY OFFICER CAMPAIGN HAT: Private purchase in OD fur felt w/ribbed satin band. Has officer hat cord that shows oxidation. Leather sweatband is Meyer maker marked. Size 7. Avg. cond. $35.00

WWI ARMY OFFICER VISOR CAP: Olive gabardine top w/lt. OD woven band, dark bronze eagle device, dark tan visor & chinstrap, side buttons, dark tan cotton lining & leather sweatband. Size 7. Near mint cond. $175.00

WWI ARMY OVERSEAS CAP: English made, British-pattern in OD gabardine w/ 2-button front w/dark bronze eagle button-lacks one, dark tan cotton lining. Has officer of inf. collar device pinned to left front. Avg. cond. $28.00

WWI ARMY OVERSEAS CAP: French-made in lt. OD gabardine w/tall crown + red cotton lining, leather sweatband. Gilt brass AEF pin on front w/"AEF" over design of 2 o/seas stripes. Avg. cond. $20.00

WWI ARMY OVERSEAS CAP: OD wool body similar to US/British pattern but w/"V" cut front. Fully lined in dark tan cotton. Exc. cond. $13.00

WWI ARMY VISOR CAP: Em model w/lt. OD wool top, brown visor & chinstrap, bronze side buttons, leather sweatband & dark tan cotton lining. Size 7 3/4. Fitted w/dark bronze officer cap device. Above avg. cond. $139.00

WWI COLD WEATHER FIELD CAP: Dark tan canvas body w/short bill, OD wool lined fold-down earflaps, forest green wool lining. Has faint 5-point star design inked on bill. Above avg. cond. $20.00

WWI COLD WEATHER FIELD CAP: Pale lt. OD canvas body w/short stitched bill + fold-down earflaps, OD wool lining. Above avg. cond. $25.00

WWI DAISY MAE FATIGUE HAT: Dark tan cotton w/soft crown, stitched brim. Faint markings. Small size. Above avg. cond. $27.00

WWI NAVY AVIATOR CAP: Black wool Tam style w/US NAVAL AVIATION around band. Name written in ink on inside. Above avg. cond. $82.00

WWI NAVY OFFICER CHAPEAU & SHOULDER BOARDS: Cased set. Chapeau in black beaver w/woven silk trim, gold wire tassels, panel w/gilt button & black rosette. Silk lined w/English coat-of-arms. Size 7 1/4. Comes in fitted black lacquered tin carrier w/interior compartment. Has dress boards w/fouled anchor ornamentation. Above avg. cond. $292.00

WWI NAVY OFFICER VISOR CAP: Navy melton wool "bell crown" top w/black woven mohair band w/direct embr. bullion device, gold wire chinstrap, gilt brass side buttons, black visor. Clothier's markings on black cotton lining. Size 6 7/8. Avg. cond. $90.00

WWI NAVY OFFICER VISOR CAP

WWI NAVY SAILOR CAP: Issue navy blue melton wool cap w/stiffener in wide crown + wire woven US Navy ribbon & leather sweatband. Named. Avg. cond. $37.00

WWI NAVY SAILOR CAP: Private-purchase in navy blue melton wool w/stiffener in wide flat crown. Lined in green cotton w/ bag liner & woven Charleston/Newport clothier's label. Has silk woven U.S.S. Florida ribbon. Avg. cond. $68.00

WWI NAVY SAILOR CAP: Private-purchase in navy blue melton wool w/lined in dark blue cotton w/bag liner. "Floppy" form. Has wire woven U.S.S. Mount Vernon ribbon. Avg. cond. $33.00

WWI NAVY SAILOR CAP: Private-purchase in navy blue melton wool w/stiffener in wide crown. Has "U.S.S. S-13" cap ribbon w/wire woven. Avg. cond. $177.00

WWI NAVY SAILOR CAP: W/"U.S. JUNIOR NAVAL GUARD" ribbon. Private purchase in dark blue wool w/stiffener in wide crown, purple-shade lining. Size 6 5/8 marked. Ribbon has wire woven letters. Letters are dark from tarnish. Avg. cond. $36.00

WWI NAVY SUBMARINE SAILOR CAP

WWI NAVY SUBMARINE SAILOR CAP: Navy blue wool body w/stiffener in wide crown. Lined in fine blue/white checkered cotton. Has heavy gold bullion on ribbed black satin "U.S.S. R-26" ribbon. Has another ribbon below that was never removed when man transferred to this submarine. Comes w/small type written card giving short history-had only 29 man crew. Above avg. cond. $186.00

WWI USMC CAMPAIGN HAT: OD fur felt body w/brim edge folded under & double-stitched, ribbed satin band, leather chinstrap, leather sweatband, dark bronze finish EG&A device on front of crown. Size 6 7/8. Above avg. cond. $198.00

B. 1920 - 1945

1920/30s AVIATOR FLIGHT HELMET: brown leather skull cup w/peaked front, has WW1 tan military cloth lining no marks & steel clip buckle. Avg. cond. $50.00

1920/30s AVIATOR FLIGHT HELMET

1930s AIR CADET KHAKI OVERSEAS CAP: AAF piping. Faded union label inside, Air cadet patch on left side of cap. Exc. cond. $60.00

1930s ARMY WINTER SERVICE CAP: 1938 dated from tag. Tan poplin shell w/sewn visor w/wool liner & earflap Mint unissued. Exc. cond. $11.00

ARMY OFFICER VISOR CAP (M1926): Lt. OD whipcord top w/woven band, stiffener in wide crown, dark brown visor & chinstrap, gilt brass device & side buttons. Named. Faint maker markings on cotton lining. Size 7 1/4. Avg. cond. $26.00

ARMY OFFICER VISOR CAP (M1926): OD whipcord top w/stiffener in wide crown, dark tan woven band, gilt brass device & side buttons, dark brown leather visor & chinstrap. Maker marked on lining. Capt.'s name inked on sweatband. Size 7. Avg. cond. $20.00

ARMY OFFICER VISOR CAP (M1938 DRESS WHITE): White cotton top w/ stiffener, woven cap band, Gaunt/London

HEADGEAR

hmkd. device, gold wire chinstrap w/side buttons. Size 7 1/8. Norfolk, Va. maker marked. W/extra white cotton top & comes in hat box. Above avg. cond. $55.00

ARMY OFFICER VISOR CAP
(M1938 DRESS WHITE)

ARMY OFFICER VISOR CAP (M1938 DRESS WHITE): White cotton top w/ woven band & black patent bill. 6 7/8 w/gilt eagle device-gold wire chinstrap. Marked to Langley field tailor shop inside w/ Medical Capt.'s calling card inside. Shows some yellowing. Avg. cond.
.... $40.00

ARMY OFFICER VISOR CAP (M1938): Field grade. "Floppy" navy blue melton wool top w/gilt brass device, gold wire chinstrap w/ribbed cavalry piped insert, gold wire chinstrap w/gilt side buttons, bullion 'scramble eggs' on wool covered visor. Satin lined w/Kansas City/St. Louis maker markings. Full sweat shield. Size 7. Above avg. cond. $53.00

USMC WINTER FIELD CAP

USMC WINTER FIELD CAP: Marine green wool w/ear flaps, wool stitched bill & high front peak. Crown not split. Size tag sewn in 6 7/8. Near mint cond. $75.00

WWII AAF AIR CADET OVERSEAS CAP: Dark-shade OD gabardine body w/AAF piping, OD satin lining & 1941 dated Qm

label. Size 7 1/8. Above avg. cond.
.... $34.00

WWII AAF BILLED CAP (A-3): Type A-3, size 7 1/2 on sewn label. Herring bone twill fatigue material w/crudely stamped AAF logo on back. Near mint cond.
.... $124.00

WWII AAF BILLED CAP (A-3)

WWII AAF BILLED CAP (A-3): Ball cap style w/multi-piece top-printed AAF spec. label w/inspector's stamp & stitched bill. Size 7 1/2. Near mint cond. $54.00

WWII AAF BILLED CAP (A-3): Dark shade OD HBT-size 7 1/2 on printed spec. label inside-large AAF ink stamp on the outside. Has large stitched bill. Near mint cond.
.... $65.00

WWII AAF BILLED CAP (A-3): Lt. OD HBT W/soft crown, stitched bill, 1942 dated/ AAF marked Qm tag. Well marked. Near mint cond. $91.00

WWII AAF BILLED CAP (A-3): Mint-multi piece dark OD HBT construction w/ stitched bill. Has printed oilcloth spec. label inside-size 7 1/2. Large AAF ink stamp on back. Mint cond. $86.00

WWII AAF BILLED CAP (A-3): light OD, HBT w/long, stitched bill-printed spec. label inside-size 7 1/2. shape. Near mint cond.
.... $75.00

WWII AAF BILLED CAP (A-3): light OD/Tan shade HBT cotton in multi-piece construction-stitched bill w/printed AAF spec. tag inside. Has large, dark blue ink AAF stamp inside & out. Near mint cond.
.... $55.00

WWII AAF BILLED CAP (A-3): multi-piece HBT construction w/stitched bill w/oilcloth spec. label inside-size 7 1/2. Large AAF ink stamp on back. Mint cond. $101.00

WWII AAF BILLED CAP (B-1): Lt. OD gabardine soft crown w/covered semi-stiff visor, leather sweatband, AAF marked/ 1942 dated Qm tag. Well marked. Size 6 7/8. Above avg. cond. $151.00

WWII AAF BILLED CAP: OD green herringbone fatigue cloth w/sewn bill. Size

7 1/2 on cloth tab at rear inside. Dated 1942 from specs. Mint cond. $139.00

WWII AAF BILLED CAP: Tan twill w/vented sides & dark brown extended bill Above avg. cond. $59.00

WWII AAF BILLED WINTER CAP (B-2): Brown leather w/sheep skin ear covers & inside lining. Sewn spec tag incl. size 7 1/4. Avg. cond. $100.00

WWII AAF BILLED WINTER CAP (B-2): Dark brown leather body w/semi-soft leather bill, fold-down earflaps. Size 7 1/8. Avg. cond. $103.00

WWII AAF BILLED WINTER CAP (B-2): Dark brown leather w/fleece-lining, fold-down earflaps, semi-soft leather bill, woven AAF marked spec label. Size 7 1/4. Exc. cond. $174.00

WWII AAF BILLED WINTER CAP (B-2): Dark brown leather w/fleece-lining, semi-soft bill, fold-down earflaps, woven AAF spec label. Exc. cond. $150.00

WWII AAF BILLED WINTER CAP (B-2): Leather body. Fleece lined & w/fleece lined earcovers. Type B-2, size 7 1/2. Above avg. cond. $145.00

WWII AAF BILLED WINTER CAP (B-2): Leather body. Fleece lined & w/fleece lined earcovers. Type B-2, size 7 1/4. Near mint cond. $154.00

WWII AAF BILLED WINTER CAP (B-2): Size 7 1/4 in dark brown leather w/fleece lining, semi-soft leather bill, woven AAF marked spec label, fold-down earflaps. Exc. cond. $150.00

WWII AAF BILLED WINTER CAP (B-2): Type B-2 cap in brown leather w/fleece lining-large woven spec. label inside-size 7 1/4-excellent but bill has been neatly removed-worn under flak helmet by an Air Gunner w/the 92nd bomb group. Lot includes a fleece lined leather chincup for flight helmet, pair of black rubber ear pads for set of Aviation headphones. Above avg. cond. $124.00

WWII AAF EM OVERSEAS CAP:Tan cotton-small size w/AAF piping-small cloth winged prop on left front. Avg. cond. $20.00

WWII AAF EM VISOR CAP: Size 7 1/2. Dark olive fur felt top w/stiffener, brown leather visor, front & rear chinstraps, gilt brass device & side buttons, full sweatshield. Above avg. cond. $56.00

WWII AAF FLIGHT HELMET (AN-H-15): Tan twill material size large w/padded leather chin strap & goggle head band restraints. left inner earpiece pad missing. Avg. cond. $34.00

WWII AAF FLIGHT NURSE CAP (K-1): Dark tan cotton w/ribbed sweatband, AAF marked woven spec label, AAF/Knox maker markings on satin lining. Size 22. Near mint cond. $48.00

WWII AAF FLIGHT NURSE CAP (K-1): Size 22 in tan cotton w/ribbed sweatband, Knox/AAF markings on satin lining, woven AAF marked spec label. Near mint cond. $48.00

WWII AAF OFFICER CRUSH VISOR CAP: 7 1/4- in tan worsted wool w/woven band, soft leather visor & chinstrap, original gilt eagle device. Plastic sweat shield in crown is still pliable. Exc. cond. $116.00

WWII AAF OFFICER CRUSH VISOR CAP: soft brown leather bill w/dark olive twill body & chin strap goes completely round & has buckle in the back. Oil cloth lining & a partial leather sweat band. Size tag for 6 7/8, 2 vent holes on either side & gilt metal officers eagle on front. Avg. cond. $121.00

WWII AAF OFFICER CRUSH VISOR CAP: Tan cotton twill top w/OD woven band, gilt brass device & side buttons, semi-soft leather visor, chinstrap. Size 7 1/8. Stitching to visor edge. Above avg. cond. $84.00

WWII AAF OFFICER CRUSH VISOR CAP: soft OD gabardine top w/light OD woven band-glove soft russet brown leather visor, front & rear chinstraps & over-size gilt eagle device. Approx. size 7. "N. Stockman" w/officer's serial # written on the underside of bill. Avg. cond. ... $97.00

WWII ARMY AIRBORNE EM OVERSEAS CAP: "Square-cut" dark OD gabardine body w/if piping, OD satin lining. Leather sweatband inked w/man's name & "101/327 GIR." Patch on left front has white embr. glider design on dark blue twill w/lt. blue border. Avg. cond. $24.00

WWII ARMY AIRBORNE EM OVERSEAS CAP: Dark OD gabardine w/engr. piping, "sharkskin" lining, "82/307 Eng" handwritten in maker on leather sweatband. Has embr. on blue cotton glider patch w/red border on left front. Avg. cond. $40.00

WWII ARMY AIRBORNE EM OVERSEAS CAP: Size 7 1/4 OD wool cap w/inf piping. "82/325 GIR" handwritten in marker on sweatband. Has embr. on blue cotton glider w/lt. blue border patch on left front. Qm label removed. Above avg. cond. $20.00

WWII ARMY AIRBORNE EM OVERSEAS CAP: Size 7 1/8 tan cotton unpiped cap w/ faint Qm tag, embr. on lt. blue cotton Glider Airborne patch on rt. front & sterling Pb. 1st lt. bar. Sweatband handwritten "61

HEADGEAR

G.B. Bn. 17 AB" in black marker. Avg. cond. $25.00

WWII ARMY BILLED CAP (B-3): UBT fatigue cloth & heavily stitched bill. Inside white web reinforced crown & fatigue sweat band. Above avg. cond. $20.00

WWII ARMY CAVALRY CAMPAIGN HAT: OD fur felt body w/ribbed satin band, leather chinstrap, cav. piped hat cord w/ acorns & slides, bronze type I cap device. Faint Qm markings on underside of leather sweatband. Size 7 1/8. Avg. cond. $33.00

WWII ARMY CAVALRY CAMPAIGN HAT: OD fur felt w/ribbed satin band, Pb. 14th Cav. DI on front of crown, cav. piped cord w/acorn & slide, "The Army Store Tucson, Ariz." markings on leather sweatband., dark brown leather chinstrap. Size 7. Avg. cond. $27.00

WWII ARMY COLD WEATHER FIELD CAP: Dark green canvas body w/dark green wool lining, short stitched bill, fold-down earflaps. 1941 dated Qm tag. Size 6 3/4. Above avg. cond. $10.50

WWII ARMY COLD WEATHER FIELD CAP: Dark green canvas w/dark green lining, short stitched brim, fold-down earflaps w/ chinstrap. 1940 dated Qm tag. Still has several paper inspector tags stapled to body. Exc. cond. $25.00

WWII ARMY COLD WEATHER FIELD CAP: Dark green canvas w/dark green wool lining, fold-down earflaps, stitched bill. Size 7 1/8. 1941 dated Qm tag. Exc. cond. $21.00

WWII ARMY COLD WEATHER FIELD CAP: Dark green canvas w/dark green wool lining, short stitched bill, fold-down earflaps. 1940 dated Qm tag. Size 7 1/4. Still has paper inspector tags stapled to body. Exc. cond. $13.00

WWII ARMY DAISY MAE FATIGUE HAT: Dark blue denim body w/soft crown & stitched brim. 1934 dated Qm tag. Named inside. Size 7. Exc. cond. $90.00

WWII ARMY DAISY MAE FATIGUE HAT: Dark blue denim w/"beachball" crown, stitched brim. Qm label. Size 6 5/8. Color dark. Above avg. cond. $25.00

WWII ARMY DAISY MAE FATIGUE HAT: Dark blue denim w/soft crown & stitched brim. Size 6 7/8. Above avg. cond. $30.00

WWII ARMY DOCTOR VISOR CAP: Dark tan cotton top w/crown stiffener, woven band, brown leather visor & chinstrap, gilt brass device & side buttons. Size 7 3/8. Dr.'s name tag inside. Above avg. cond. $60.00

WWII ARMY EM CRUSH VISOR CAP: quality cap w/dark tan gabardine top w/

"floppy" form, gilt brass device & side buttons, dark brown semi-soft visor, mis-matched front & rear chinstraps. Marked "The Crusher" model. Size 7 1/8. Size 7. Above avg. cond. $160.00

WWII ARMY EM CRUSH VISOR CAP

WWII ARMY EM OVERSEAS CAP: Private purchase. Dark OD elastic w/arty piping, green satin lining. Size tag is marked size 7 3/7. Has Sb. Arty DI w/design of two trees above fleur-de-lis design. Above avg. cond. $11.00

WWII ARMY EM VISOR CAP: Brown-shade fur felt top w/"floppy" form, brown leather visor, front & rear chinstraps, gilt brass device & side buttons. Size 7 1/4. Avg. cond. $20.00

WWII ARMY EM VISOR CAP: Dark OD gabardine top w/crown stiffener, brown visor & chinstrap, gilt brass side buttons. "The Gordonia Caps" maker marked on satin lining. Size 7 1/8. form & cond. Above avg. cond. $37.00

WWII ARMY EM VISOR CAP: Dark tan cotton top w/stiffener, gilt brass device & side buttons, dark brown visor & chinstrap. "The Gordonia Caps" marked. About size 7 1/8. form. Above avg. cond. $17.00

WWII ARMY EM VISOR CAP: Dark tan cotton twill top w/crown stiffener, russet brown visor & chinstrap, gilt side buttons. $28.00

WWII ARMY EM VISOR CAP: OD fur felt top w/crush" form, lt. OD cotton lining brown visor & chinstrap, gilt brass device & side buttons. Size 6 3/4. Avg. cond. $20.00

WWII ARMY EM VISOR CAP: OD fur felt top w/stiffener, gilt brass device & side buttons, brown visor & chinstrap. Satin lining marked "U.S. Army All Wool Garrison Cap." Size 7. W/storm cover. Above avg. cond. $16.00

WWII ARMY EM VISOR CAP: OD wool serge top w/crown stiffener, dark brown visor & chinstrap, gilt brass device & side buttons. Lined in lt. green cotton. Patent label underneath sweat diamond. Larger size. Avg. cond. $25.00

WWII ARMY EM VISOR CAP: OD wool serge top w/stiffener, brown visor, front &

rear (slightly mis-matched) chinstraps, gilt brass device & side buttons. Size 7 1/4. Named to man on "Soldier's Service Store" label. Above avg. cond. $14.00

WWII ARMY EM VISOR CAP: OD wool serge top w/stiffener, gilt brass device & side buttons, brown visor & chinstrap, pressed paper sweatband, lt. OD cotton lining. Size 7. Clean. Above avg. cond. $40.00

WWII ARMY EM VISOR CAP: OD wool serge top w/stiffener, gilt brass device & side buttons, brown visor & chinstrap, purple-shade satin lining w/maker's markings. Size 7. Above avg. cond. $23.00

WWII ARMY EM VISOR CAP: Tan cotton top w/"crush" form, brown visor & chinstrap, gilt brass device & side buttons. Satin lined-sweatshield removed. Size 7 1/8. Avg. cond. $20.00

WWII ARMY HBT FATIGUE CAP: Dark OD HBT w/stitched semi-stiff bill + pleated body, 1944 dated Qm tag. Size 7 1/4. Exc. cond. $90.00

WWII ARMY HBT FATIGUE CAP: Size 6 3/4 in dark OD HBT w/pleated body, stitched bill. Exc. cond. $11.50

WWII ARMY JEEP CAP: Lt. OD knit w/fold-down earflaps, cardboard stiffener in short bill, size "M" tag. Above avg. cond. $33.00

WWII ARMY JEEP CAP: Lt. OD knit wool w/ fold-down earflaps, cardboard stiffened short bill. Size "M" tag intact. Above avg. cond. $40.00

WWII ARMY JEEP CAP: Lt. OD knit wool w/ short cardboard stiffened bill & fold down earflap. Size "M" tag intact. Near mint cond. $129.00

WWII ARMY JEEP CAP: Lt. OD woolen knit body w/fold-down earflaps, cardboard stiffener in short bill. Size "M" tag intact. Above avg. cond. $40.00

WWII ARMY JEEP CAP: Lt. OD woolen knit w/fold down earflaps, stiffener in short visor. Medium size. Above avg. cond. $69.00

WWII ARMY M. P. OFFICER VISOR CAP: Tan cotton twill top w/tan woven band + russet brown visor, gilt brass device & side buttons. Fully satin lined w/large plastic sweatshield. Has matching front & rear white leather chinstraps. Size 7 1/8. Exc. cond. $100.00

WWII ARMY NURSE SERVICE CAP: Light creme colored worsted wool w/matching chinstrap, stitched bill, satin lining & ribbed sweatband. Knox maker. Size 21. Gilt brass device. Above avg. cond. $47.50

WWII ARMY OFFICER CAMPAIGN HAT: OD fur felt body w/ribbed satin band, dark

brown leather chinstrap, leather sweatband. Fitted w/officer-grade hatcord w/tassels & slide. Size 7 1/4. Above avg. cond. $56.00

WWII ARMY OFFICER CRUSH VISOR CAP: Dark tan worsted wool body w/ "crush" form, dark tan woven band, soft brown leather visor, front & rear chinstraps, oversize gilt brass device, side buttons. "Flighter" model. Size 7 1/8. Avg. cond. $90.00

WWII ARMY OFFICER CRUSH VISOR CAP

WWII ARMY OFFICER CRUSH VISOR CAP: Dark OD gabardine top w/floppy form, semi-soft brown leather visor & chinstrap, woven band, oversize device, side buttons. Satin lined. Lacks sweatband. Size 7 1/4. Avg. cond. $59.00

WWII ARMY OFFICER CRUSH VISOR CAP: soft brown leather bill & chinstrap w/ gilt eagle device & side buttons. Bancroft "Flighter" brand-small size. Avg. cond. $71.00

WWII ARMY OFFICER CRUSH VISOR CAP: soft leather bill & chinstrap w/gilt eagle device & side buttons. a. size 7- "Flighter" brand by Bancroft. Palm Beach tan top. Avg. cond. $55.00

WWII ARMY OFFICER PINK VISOR CAP: "Pink" gabardine w/ribbed "creme" colored satin lining, leather sweatband. Size 7. Maker's tag inside. Exc. cond. $63.00

WWII ARMY OFFICER VISOR CAP: Dark OD fur felt w/stiffener, woven band, oversize gilt brass device, side buttons, russet brown leather visor & chinstrap. Size 7 1/8. Above avg. cond. $40.00

WWII ARMY OFFICER VISOR CAP: Dark OD gabardine top w/stiffener, woven band, oversize gilt brass device, side buttons, russet brown leather visor & chinstrap, satin lining w/full sweatshield. Size 6 7/8. Mint cond. $48.00

WWII ARMY OFFICER VISOR CAP: OD fur felt top w/"floppy" form, woven band, brown visor & chinstrap, oversize Luxembourg hmkd. device. Yellow satin

HEADGEAR

lined. Size 7 1/8. Above avg. cond.
.... $61.50

WWII ARMY OFFICER VISOR CAP

WWII ARMY OFFICER VISOR CAP: Dark OD gabardine top w/woven band, "floppy" form, brown leather visor, mis-matched front & rear chinstraps, satin lining, gilt brass device & side buttons. Size 7 1/8. Above avg. cond. $25.00

WWII ARMY OFFICER VISOR CAP: Dark tan "palm beach" wool top w/stiffener, woven band, gilt brass device, side buttons, russet brown leather visor & chinstrap. Gold embossed Camp Blanding Exchange markings on leather sweatband. Size 7 1/4. Above avg. cond. $50.00

WWII ARMY OFFICER VISOR CAP: Dark tan worsted wool top w/woven band, gilt brass device & side buttons, brown visor & chinstrap. Size 6 7/8. Avg. cond. . .$45.00

WWII ARMY OFFICER VISOR CAP: Dark tan worsted wool w/"floppy" appearance, woven band, brown visor & chinstrap, gilt brass device & side buttons, paper Reg. Army Officer Serv. Cap tag inside. shape. Size 7 1/8. Above avg. cond. $33.00

WWII ARMY OFFICER VISOR CAP: Issue in dark OD gabardine w/stiffener, woven band, brown leather visor & chinstrap, gilt brass device, side buttons. 1942 dated Qm markings. Reg. U.S. Officer's Service cap marked on sweatband. Still has $5.00 price tag. Satin lining. Size 7 1/8. Above avg. cond. $40.00

WWII ARMY OFFICER VISOR CAP: Lt. OD fur felt top w/stiffener, woven band, brown leather visor & chinstrap, gilt brass device & side buttons. Makers marked on lining. Size 7. Avg. cond. $24.00

WWII ARMY OFFICER VISOR CAP: Med.-shade OD fur felt top w/stiffener, woven band, gilt brass device & side buttons, dark brown leather visor & chinstrap. Size 7 3/8. Above avg. cond. $40.00

WWII ARMY OFFICER VISOR CAP: OD fur felt top w/"floppy" appearance, woven band, gilt brass device & side buttons, russet brown leather visor & chinstrap,

maker markings on satin lining w/full sweatshield. Size 7. Above avg. cond. $82.00

WWII ARMY OFFICER VISOR CAP: OD fur felt top w/OD woven band, brown leather visor, front & rear chinstraps, gilt brass device & side buttons. Luxembourg maker marked. Gold leaf initials on leather sweatband. Size 7 3/8. Couple nips to top. Above avg. cond. $75.00

WWII ARMY OFFICER VISOR CAP

WWII ARMY OFFICER VISOR CAP: OD fur felt top w/stiffener, olive woven band + russet brown leather visor, front & rear chinstrap, oversize gilt brass device & side buttons. Berkshire brand. Lined in satin w/ full sweatshield. Size 7 3/8. Avg. cond. $51.00

WWII ARMY OFFICER VISOR CAP: OD fur felt top w/woven band, gilt brass device & side buttons, brown visor & chinstrap. Lined in lt. OD cotton w/oval sweatshield. Above avg. cond. $65.00

WWII ARMY OFFICER VISOR CAP: OD fur felt top w/woven band, gilt brass device & side buttons, russet brown leather visor & chinstrap, satin lining inked w/officer's name & service #. Size 7 3/8. Some nips to top. Avg. cond. $38.00

WWII ARMY OFFICER VISOR CAP: OD fur felt top w/woven band, oversize gilt brass device, side buttons, brown leather visor & chinstrap. Size 7. Some nips top & tatter to sweatshield. Avg. cond. $35.00

WWII ARMY OFFICER VISOR CAP: Tan cotton top w/stiffener, woven band, gilt brass device & side buttons, russet brown leather visor & chinstrap + full sweatshield. Size 7 3/8. Above avg. cond. $51.50

WWII ARMY OFFICER VISOR CAP: Tan cotton twill top w/crown stiffener, gilt brass device & side buttons, russet brown leather visor & chinstrap. Size 7. 1943 dated Qm markings on sweatband. Avg. cond. $11.00

WWII ARMY OFFICER VISOR CAP: Tan worsted wool top w/"floppy" form, woven band, russet brown leather visor & chinstrap, side buttons. Size 6 7/8. Satin lined w/woven maker's label underneath sweatshield. Above avg. cond. $20.00

WWII ARMY OFFICER VISOR CAP: Tan worsted wool top w/woven band, "floppy" form, brown leather visor & chinstrap, gilt brass device & side buttons. Size 7 1/8. Reg. Army Officer Serv. Cap marked. Named w/service #. Avg. cond. $20.00

WWII COAST GUARD RESERVE CPO VISOR CAP: Tan cotton top w/stiffener in crown, black woven band w/sterling USCG Reserve device, black visor & chinstrap, gilt NAVY side buttons. NAVY authorized markings inside. Size 7 1/8. Some age. Avg. cond. $40.00

WWII MARINE FEMALE DAISY MAE PATTERN UTILITY HAT: Distinctive green cotton w/wide stitched brim, "beachball" crown, Knox maker markings on ribbed green satin sweatband. Named. Size 21 1/2. Has bronze plastic EG&A device on front-eagle. From estate of female Marine. Above avg. cond. $135.00

WWII MARINE FEMALE SERVICE CAP: Forest green wool cargo w/semi stiff visor, scarlet chincord, bronze 1937-pattern EG&A device, side buttons. Satin lined. Size 21 1/2. Above avg. cond. $55.00

WWII MARINE FEMALE SUMMER OVERSEAS CAP: Clean distinctive green cotton twill body w/white piping, dark green satin lining. Size 22 1/2. Name label on sweatband. Exc. cond. $37.00

WWII MARINE FEMALE SUMMER SERVICE CAP: Distinctive green cotton body w/semi-stiff bill, white chincord, gilt 1937-pattern device, side buttons. Knox maker marked on satin lining. Size 21 1/2. From estate of female Marine. Above avg. cond. $47.00

WWII MARINE FEMALE SUMMER SERVICE CAP: Distinctive green cotton twill body w/semi-stiff bill, white cord chinstrap, gilt brass 1937-pattern EG&A device, side buttons. Knox maker markings on satin lining, ribbed satin sweatband. Size 21 1/2. Named. Above avg. cond. $45.00

WWII MARITIME SERVICE OFFICER VISOR CAP: Dark tan cotton top w/ stiffener, multi-piece device on black woven band, gold wire chinstrap w/single NAVY side button (lacks one), black visor. Bancroft maker. Size. 7. Avg. cond. $30.00

WWII MARITIME SERVICE OFFICER VISOR CAP: Navy blue melton wool top w/"floppy" form, sterling device on black woven band, gold wire chinstrap, NAVY

gilt side buttons, black visor. Size 7. Avg. cond. $65.00

WWII MARITIME SERVICE OFFICER VISOR CAP

WWII MERCHANT SHIP OFFICER VISOR CAP: White cotton top w/"floppy" form + black woven band w/direct embr. bullion & enameled applique device, gold wire chinstrap w/USCG side buttons & black visor. Size 7. Above avg. cond. $40.00

WWII NAVY AVIATOR OFFICER VISOR CAP: Av. green gabardine top w/stiffener, sterling device on black woven band, gold wire chinstrap w/gilt side buttons, black visor. Size 7 1/8. Above avg. cond. $88.00

WWII NAVY AVIATOR OFFICER VISOR CAP

WWII NAVY COLD WEATHER HAT: Blue twill w/wool lining & straps to hold goggles in place. Neck flap & chin strap. Exc. cond. $24.00

WWII NAVY DONALD DUCK CAP: Navy blue melton wool body w/silk woven USS San Francisco ribbon. Small size. Avg. cond. $40.00

WWII NAVY DONALD DUCK CAP: Navy blue melton wool w/gold leaf "U.S. Navy" ribbon. Size 7 3/8. Little wear. Above avg. cond. $14.00

WWII NAVY OFFICER VISOR CAP: Clean tan cotton top w/stiffener, direct embr. heavy bullion device on black woven band, gold wire chinstrap, side buttons. Size 6 7/8. Avg. cond. $30.00

WWII NAVY OFFICER VISOR CAP: Navy blue melton wool top w/crown stiffener, black woven band w/sterling device, gold wire chinstrap w/side buttons, black visor.

Clothier's store marked on leather sweatband. Size 7 1/4. Above avg. cond. $35.00

WWII NAVY OFFICER VISOR CAP: Navy blue melton wool top w/stiffener, sterling device on black woven band, gold wire chinstrap, side buttons, black visor. Size 7 1/4. Above avg. cond. $40.00

WWII NAVY OFFICER VISOR CAP: Navy melton blue wool top w/stiffener in crown, black woven band w/sterling device, gold wire chinstrap, gilt side buttons & black visor. Named to a lt. Size 7. W/storm cover. Avg. cond. $50.00

WWII NAVY OFFICER VISOR CAP: White cotton top w/stiffener in crown, multi-piece device on black woven band, gold wire chinstrap, brass side buttons. "All-Bilt Uniforms" maker marked. Size 7 1/8. Above avg. cond. .... ¡$40.00

WWII NAVY WARRANT OFFICER VISOR CAP: White cotton top w/"floppy" appearance, black woven band w/direct embr. gold bullion wreath w/crossed anchor device in center, gold wire chinstrap, side buttons, black visor. Size 7 3/8. Avg. cond. $19.00

WWII NURSE SUMMER CAP: Tan linen Kepi style w/Brass Device centered above bill. Simulated chin strap of same material separates bill from body. Reinforced bill w/ same material covering, multiple rows of stitching. Lined interior w/rayon sweatband & hmkd. Knox of NY. Size 22. Exc. cond. $70.00

WWII RED CROSS FEMALE HAT: Blue gray wool kepi style had w/Metal & enamel emblem on front bow. Lined inside. Above avg. cond. $37.00

WWII USMC EM VISOR CAP: Forest green wool top w/stiffener in wide crown, 1937-pattern device, black visor & chinstrap w/ gilt USMC side buttons. Size 7. Avg. cond. $33.00

WWII USMC EM VISOR CAP: Forest green wool top w/stiffener in wide crown, dark leather visor & chinstrap, 1937-pattern EG&A device & side buttons. Size 7 1/8. Above avg. cond. $30.00

WWII USMC HBT UTILITY CAP: Lt. OD HBT w/stitched bill, pleated body, 1944 dated spec tag. Size small. 1937-pattern EG&A stencil on front of crown. Name inked in white marking pen on sweatband. Exc. cond. $139.00

WWII USMC HBT UTILITY CAP: Lt. OD HBT w/stitched bill, pleated body, stenciled 1937-pattern EG&A device on front of crown. Named. Size 7 3/8. shape w/light soiling. Above avg. cond. .. $53.00

WWII USMC HBT UTILITY CAP: Lt. OD HBT w/pleated body, stitched bill, 1937-

pattern EG&A stencil on crown. Small size. Avg. cond. $25.00

WWII USMC SUMMER VISOR CAP: Dark tan cotton top w/quatrefoil, tan woven band, cordovan leather visor & chinstrap, dark bronze side buttons, Imperial/H-H hmkd. 1937-pattern device. Size 7 1/8. Named. Clean example. Above avg. cond. $110.00

WWII USMC SUMMER VISOR CAP

WWII W.A.V.E. OVERSEAS CAP: Gray seersucker w/woven WAVES label. Named. Above avg. cond. $14.00

WWII WAAC EM SERVICE CAP: OD barathea cylindrical body w/matching chinstrap & OD plastic WAAC buttons, semi-stiff visor, satin lining w/sweatshield, ribbed satin sweatband & WAAC marked/ 1943 dated Qm tag. Size 23. Fitted w/gilt brass Army Em device. Above avg. cond. $72.00

WWII WAAC GARRISON OVERSEAS HAT: dark brown w/yellow green piping, 22 1/2 size & silk lining. Above avg. cond. $40.00

WWII WAAC OFFICER SUMMER SERVICE CAP: Dark tan cotton twill cylindrical body w/covered semi-stiff bill, matching chinstrap w/OD plastic WAAC side buttons, ribbed satin sweatband, lt. OD cotton lining, sweat shield. Size 21. 1943 dated Qm tag. Has gilt WAAC device on front of crown. Above avg. cond. $190.00

WWII WAAC OVERSEAS CAP: Tan. 22 1/2 w/yellow green piping & label & named inside w/#. Above avg. cond. $30.00

WWII WAAC SERVICE CAP: Dark tan cotton w/cylindrical body, semi-stiff visor, matching chinstrap, OD plastic WAAC side buttons, cotton lining, ribbed sweatband, 1943 dated/WAAC marked Qm tag. Has gilt brass Army officer device. Size 21 1/2. Above avg. cond. $32.00

WWII WAAC SUMMER CAP (CLASS "A"): Cylindrical tan cotton w/semi-stiff covered bill, chinstrap, ribbed satin sweatband, OD plastic WAAC side buttons, 1943 dated

Qm tag. Size 23. No device. Exc. cond.
.... $50.00

WWII WAC EM SUMMER SERVICE CAP:
Tan gabardine covered circular top, bill &
chinstrap w/gilt brass device & side
buttons, satin lining w/foil maker's label
under sweatshield, dark OD ribbed satin
sweatband. Size 22 1/2. Above avg. cond.
.... $60.00

WWII WAC OFFICER OVERSEAS CAP:
Size 21 in OD wool serge w/clean dark tan
cotton lining w/US Army Inspector ink
stamp markings, Pb. curve-form 1st lieut.
bar. shape. Above avg. cond. $42.00

WWII WAC OFFICER OVERSEAS CAP:
Size 21 in dark OD barathea w/WAC's
name label stitched to satin lining, Pb.
curve-form 1st lt. bar. Avg. cond. .. $35.00

WWII WAC OFFICER SERVICE CAP: Dark
OD barathea top w/matching chinstrap,
stitched semi-stiff visor, satin lining, ribbed
satin sweatband, gilt brass device. Size
22. WAC's initials stitched inside. Above
avg. cond. $70.00

WWII WAC OFFICER SUMMER SERVICE
CAP

**WWII WAC OFFICER SUMMER SERVICE
CAP:** Cylindrical dark tan gabardine body
w/matching chinstrap, covered visor, gilt
brass device & side buttons, ribbed satin
sweatband. Stetson marked. Size 22.
Above avg. cond. $91.00

**WWII WAC OFFICER SUMMER SERVICE
CAP:** "Creme" colored worsted wool w/
stitched visor, matching chinstrap, gilt
brass device & side buttons, Knox
markings on satin lining, ribbed
sweatband. Size 22. Above avg. cond.
.... $42.00

**WWII WAC OFFICER SUMMER SERVICE
CAP:** Creme colored worsted wool body
w/stitched bill, matching chinstrap, Knox
maker markings on satin lining. Size 22.
No device. Ribbed satin Above avg. cond.
.... $24.00

WWII WAC SUMMER OVERSEAS CAP:
Size 22 in tan cotton twill w/1944 dated
Qm tag. Exc. cond. $20.00

**WWII WAVE OFFICER DRESS SERVICE
CAP:** Visor less cap w/soft white cotton

top, sterling device on black woven band,
black satin lining, woven US Navy Nurse's
Uniform label on ribbed sweatband.
Named. Size 22. Avg. cond. $95.00

WWII WAVE OFFICER DRESS SERVICE
CAP

C. 1946 - Present

ARMY CAMO BALL CAP: Issue in 6-color
desert camo w/stitched brim. Size 7 1/4.
Avg. cond. $23.00

**ARMY FEMALE OFFICER FIELD GRADE
DRESS WHITE HAT:** White cotton
cylindrical body w/stitched brim, hat band
w/gold bullion "scramble eggs", white satin
lining, woven "Ambrose, New York" label
on ribbed white satin sweatband. Size
21 1/2. Comes in matching oval-shaped
heavy pressed paper hat box. Exc. cond.
.... $30.00

**ARMY FEMALE OFFICER FIELD GRADE
SERVICE HAT:** AG wool serge body w/
stitched brim, band w/gilt brass device &
gold bullion "scramble eggs". Size 21 1/2.
Named. Above avg. cond. $30.00

ARMY GREEN BERET: Size seven Near
mint & w/Capt. metal track on yellow flash
w/black trim. Above avg. cond. $20.00

ARMY MUSICIAN OFFICER VISOR CAP

ARMY MUSICIAN OFFICER VISOR CAP:
1950s. Tan cotton top w/soft roll crown
stiffener, woven band, russet brown
leather chinstrap & visor, gilt brass device
of eagle w/lyre design above in place of
star field, side buttons. Size 6 3/4.
Appears unworn. Light age. Above avg.
cond. $50.00

ARMY OFFICER DRESS BLUE VISOR CAP: Navy blue fur felt top w/gold wire band w/green & yellow ribbed insert, gold wire chinstrap, device & side buttons, gold bullion "scramble eggs" on visor. Vans Bro., Taiwan markings. Size 7. Avg. cond. $11.00

ARMY OFFICER DRESS BLUE VISOR CAP: Navy blue worsted wool top w/soft roll crown stiffener, silk woven chinstrap & "scramble eggs" on visor. Bancroft brand. Size 6 5/8. No band or device. Exc. cond. $20.00

ARMY OFFICER FIELD GRADE VISOR CAP: AG fur felt top w/soft roll stiffener. Complete w/device, gold wire chinstrap & gold bullion "scramble eggs" on visor. Named to a major. Size 7 1/8. Quilted satin lining. Above avg. cond. $20.00

ARMY OFFICER FIELD GRADE VISOR CAP: AG fur felt top w/woven band, gilt brass device & side buttons, gold wire chinstrap, heavy gold bullion "scramble eggs" on visor. Flight Ace brand. Size 7. Above avg. cond. $11.00

ARMY OFFICER FIELD GRADE VISOR CAP: Size 7 1/8. Flight Ace brand. Complete w/device, silk woven chinstrap, gold bullion "scramble eggs" on visor. Avg. cond. $19.00

ARMY SPECIAL FORCES BERET: Issue rifle green wool beret w/1979 dated issue markings on black cotton lining, sweatband w/adj. tie in rear. Size 6 7/8. Front has S/F crest over 7th S/F Grp. recognition bar. Some fading & age. Avg. cond. $20.00

ARMY SPECIAL FORCES BERET: issue rifle green wool felt beret w/black sweatband w/tie in rear, fully embr. solid red flash on front w/1st lt. bar. Lining removed. Large size. Avg. cond. $35.00

ARMY SPECIAL FORCES BERET: Issue in rifle green wool w/black leather sweatband w/adj. tie in rear. Black cotton lining removed. S/F DI on front. Also, 40mm dia. 10th Sp. Forces Grp. (Airborne) token mach. engraved on reverse side w/man's name & "Airborne Bug". Avg. cond. $34.00

CAMO TIGER STRIPE BOONIE HAT: Overall stitched cotton w/wide brim that snaps-up on both sides, metal grommet vent holes, lt. blue lining & blue vinyl sweatband. Size 7. Exc. cond. $69.00

COAST GUARD "DONALD DUCK" CAP: White cotton top w/silk woven ribbon. Size 7. Above avg. cond. $28.00

KOREAN WAR ERA ARMY OFFICER OVERSEAS CAP: Private-purchase in dark tan worsted wool w/leather sweatband. Faintly named on satin lining. Has 3rd Inf Regt. ribbed satin ribbon section stitched to rt. front. Size 7 1/4. Above avg. cond. $20.00

KOREAN WAR ERA ARMY OFFICER VISOR CAP: Dark OD gabardine top w/ soft-roll crown stiffener, woven band, brown leather visor & chinstrap, gilt brass device & side buttons. Green stain lined w/sweatshield that has couple tears. Large size. Above avg. cond. $42.00

KOREAN WAR ERA ARMY OFFICER VISOR CAP: OD fur felt top w/soft roll stiffener, woven band, russet brown visor, front & rear chinstraps, gilt brass device, side buttons. Size 7 1/8. Faint Qm markings on sweatband. Avg. cond. $20.00

KOREAN WAR ERA ARMY PILE FIELD CAP (M-Q1): Size 7. Dark OD cotton w/ alpaca lined fold-down earflaps, 1950 dated Qm tag. Has subdued metal s/sgt chevron on front of stitched bill. Solid-all labels intact. Above avg. cond. $19.00

KOREAN WAR ERA USMC EM VISOR CAP: dark tan worsted wool top w/ cordovan visor & chinstrap, side buttons. Size 7 1/8. No device. WWII-era USMC visor cap tops w/stiffeners in wide crowns. Avg. cond. $21.00

NAVY ADMIRAL VISOR CAP: White cotton top w/stiffener in crown, black woven band w/bullion NAVY officer device direct embr. into front, gold wire chinstrap, gilt NAVY side buttons, heavy gold bullion flag officer "scramble eggs" on visor. "Berkshire - Flex" brand. Size 7 1/2. Cap belonged to Adm. Levering "Rosie" Smith commander of NAVY Nuclear Submarine fleet. Above avg. cond. $187.00

NAVY BALL CAP: Navy blue knit body w/adj. back, "scramble eggs" direct embr. on bill, "USS Intrepid" patch on front. Has brass & enamel "Hope" pinion front. Above avg. cond. $17.00

NAVY BALL CAP: USS Sphinx ARL-24. Navy blue knit body. Adj. size. Has patch stitched to front w/dress-size surface warfare badge (frosted silver finish) pinned to front. Exc. cond. $20.00

NAVY BALL CAP: USS Voge FF-1047. Navy blue knit body. Adj. size. Has patch stitched to front w/dress-size surface warfare badge (frosted silver finish) pinned to front. Exc. cond. $20.00

NAVY CPO VISOR CAP: Complete w/white cotton top & CPO device. Size 7 1/8. Bancroft brand. W/extra white & tan gabardine tops. Exc. cond. $22.00

NAVY CPO VISOR CAP: Stay-white vinyl top w/device on black woven band, black visor & chinstrap, gilt side buttons. Size 7. Art Caps maker. Above avg. cond. $24.00

NAVY CPO VISOR CAP: White cotton top w/ crown stiffener, woven band w/CPO device, glossy black visor & chinstrap, side buttons. Bancroft Pak-Cap brand. Size 7 1/8. Exc. cond. $12.00

NAVY EM VISOR CAP: "Stay-white" vinyl top w/black woven band, frosted silver device & side buttons, glossy black visor & chinstrap. Bancroft "Zephyr" brand. Size 7 1/2. Worn only short time. Exc. cond. $24.00

NAVY EM VISOR CAP: Complete w/white cotton top & frosted silver NAVY device on black woven band. Size 6 7/8. Worn only for short time. Exc. cond. $20.00

NAVY OFFICER FLAG GRADE VISOR CAP: 1950s. White cotton top w/sterling device on black woven band, gold wire chinstrap, side buttons, gold bullion "scramble eggs" on visor. Capt.'s calling card inside. Bancroft brand. Size 7. Avg. cond. $40.00

NAVY OFFICER FLAG GRADE VISOR CAP: White cotton top w/stiffener, black woven band w/sterling device, gold wire chinstrap w/side buttons, gold bullion "scramble eggs" on visor. Bancroft "Zephyr" brand. Size 7. Above avg. cond. $34.00

NAVY OFFICER VISOR CAP: 1950s. Size 7 wicker frame w/white cotton top, sterling device on black woven band, gold wire chinstrap, black visor. Named. Above avg. cond. $28.00

NAVY OFFICER VISOR CAP: 1950s. Tan cotton top w/sterling device (some tarnish) on black woven band, gold wire chinstrap, NAVY side buttons, black visor. "The Wolbro" model. Size 6 7/8. Above avg. cond. $45.00

NAVY OFFICER VISOR CAP: 1950s. White cotton top w/device on black woven band, gold wire chinstrap, NAVY side buttons, black visor. Bancroft brand. Size 7 1/2. Avg. cond. $25.00

NAVY OFFICER VISOR CAP: White cotton top w/multi-piece device on black woven band, gold wire chinstrap, gilt side buttons & black visor. Size 7 1/4. Bancroft brand. Sweatband still retains $56.99 price tag. Near mint cond. $45.00

NAVY SEAL CAMO BERET: Large size, in woodland ripstop camo lined in black satin, black vinyl sweatband w/adj. tie. Has full-size gilt NAVY SEAL badge on front. Above avg. cond. $20.00

USAF BRIG GENERAL DRESS VISOR CAP: Flight Ace brand cap w/black worsted top w/soft roll crown stiffener, black woven band, silver wire chinstrap w/ frosted silver side buttons, heavy silver bullion "lightning bolts & clouds" on wool covered visor. Size 7 1/8. Has Luenberg maker hmkd. device. Has Brig Gen. Marion L. Boswell's calling card inside. shape. Above avg. cond. $86.00

USAF BRIG GENERAL DRESS VISOR CAP

USAF FIELD CAP: Size 7 1/4. Sage green cotton w/fold-down earflaps, woven spec label, stitched bill. Has Cb major leaf affixed to front. Above avg. cond. .. $20.00

USAF FLIGHT CAP (D-1A): Dark shade blue wool serge w/dark blue wool lining, woven spec label, fold-down earflaps, leather sweatband. Well marked. Med. size. Above avg. cond. $25.00

USAF OFFICER DRESS VISOR CAP: Black worsted cover w/black woven band, heavy bullion on black felt covered base w/Sb. post, silver wire chinstrap, frosted silver side buttons & black visor. Size 7 1/8. Above avg. cond. $25.00

USAF OFFICER FIELD GRADE DRESS VISOR CAP: Black worsted wool top w/ woven band, frosted silver device & side buttons, silver wire chinstrap, heavy silver bullion "lightning bolts & clouds" on visor. Luxembourg brand. Size 6 7/8. Exc. cond. $22.00

USAF OFFICER FIELD GRADE VISOR CAP: USAF-shade blue knit top w/woven band, frosted silver device & side buttons, black chinstrap, heavy silver bullion "lightning bolts & clouds" on visor. Size 7 1/2. Bancroft brand. Near mint cond. $20.00

USAF OFFICER FIELD GRADE VISOR CAP: USAF-shade blue worsted top w/soft roll stiffener, woven band, frosted silver device & side buttons, black chinstrap, heavy silver bullion "lightning bolts & clouds" on visor. "Flight Ace" brand. Size 7 1/2. Near mint cond. $33.00

USAF OFFICER SENIOR VISOR CAP: AF blue cloth crown w/Blue elastic band. Gray alloy Cap device 2.5" high. Black patent leather chin strap above visor anchored by two USAF buttons on side. Black leather strap w/buckle around back of band also anchored at buttons. Wool lined visor w/ bullion lightning & arrows emitting from clouds. Slight damage to one arrow & lightning bolt. Lined interior w/leather sweatband. Hmkd. Berkshire Deluxe. Above avg. cond. $72.00

USAF OFFICER SENIOR VISOR CAP

USAF OFFICER VISOR CAP: USAF-shade blue worsted top w/soft roll stiffener + woven band, frosted silver device, side buttons, black leather visor & chinstrap. "Flight Ace" brand. Capt.'s typewritten card w/size. Size 7 1/8. In Flight Ace marked bag. Above avg. cond. $20.00
USMC BALL CAP: Blue wool felt body w/ stitched bill, woven Japan maker's label. Has Japanese-made fully embr. sqdn. patch design on front, "'70-'71/VMFA-115/ Iwakuni/Da Nang/Chu Lai" direct embr. around body. Exc. cond. $72.00
USMC BERET: English-made green wool body w/spec label on black cotton lining, black leather sweatband. Size 6 1/2. Has dark bronze 1962-pattern Em visor cap device on front-has been there a while. Avg. cond. $20.00
USMC FEMALE CAP: Uniform soft side kepi style w/EM brass device at front. Red twist cord w/knots for chin strap & visor in matching marine green twill w/crown. Size 22 1/2 & lined interior. Exc. cond. ..$20.00
USMC OFFICER VISOR CAP: Forest green wool gabardine top on wick frame, w/ quatrefoil, woven band, cordovan visor & chinstrap, dark bronze Meyer hmkd. 1937-pattern EG&A device, side buttons & Quantico, Va. maker markings. Size 71/8. W/storm cover. Above avg. cond. ..$23.00
USMC UTILITY CAP: Dark OD HBT w/ pleated body, stitched bill, EG&A device iron-on on front. Size small. Still has several paper Qm inspector tags attached. Mint cond. $12.50
VIETNAM ERA ARMY AVIATOR BALL CAP: Nam made in OD cotton w/black aviator wing & Capt.'s bar direct embr. into the

front of the cap. Small size. Avg. cond. $36.00
VIETNAM ERA ARMY BALL CAP: Black velveteen pleated body w/semi-stiff covered bill. Nylon mesh lined. Sweatband ink stamped "M/A.S." Has "Charlie/D.M.Z./ Manchu" direct mach. embr. in yellow on front of crown & "O'Hara" across back panel. Exc. cond. $70.00
VIETNAM ERA ARMY BALL CAP: Size 7 5/8 in dark OD cotton w/1970 dated spec label. Has Cb lieut. col. leaf affixed to front of crown. Above avg. cond. $11.00
VIETNAM ERA ARMY BOONIE HAT: Issue in OD ripstop. Size 6 3/4. In issue bag. 1972 dated. Mint cond. $10.50
VIETNAM ERA ARMY BOONIE HAT: Issue in OD ripstop. Size 6 3/4. W/insect net. 1969 dated. In issue bag. Mint cond. $11.00
VIETNAM ERA ARMY BOONIE HAT: Issue pattern in OD poplin. W/insect net. Size 6 7/8. 1968 dated. In issue bag. Mint cond. $28.00
VIETNAM ERA ARMY BOONIE HAT: Overall stitched in dark OD poplin w/wide brim that snaps-up on one side, matching chinstrap w/addl. leather slide. W/insect net inside pocket in top of crown. Size 7 1/4. Near mint cond. $90.00
VIETNAM ERA ARMY BOONIE HAT: Overall-stitched brown-shade OD cotton body w/wide brim that snaps up on both sides, 2 nylon mesh covered metal grommet vents on each side. Lined in red cotton w/red vinyl sweatband. Has printed "Thailand" tab stitched to one side of brim. Small size. Above avg. cond. $40.00
VIETNAM ERA ARMY BOONIE HAT: Theater-made in overall stitched olive cotton w/wide brim that snaps-up on one side, large aluminum grommet wire vents, brown vinyl sweatband, chinstrap. Has color Nam made insignia-hand embr. on red cotton "Bien-Hoa/Viet-Nam" tab on brim, "Viet-Nam" patch on front of crown w/design of U.S./SVN flags. Small size. Avg. cond. $45.00
VIETNAM ERA ARMY BOONIE HAT: Vietnamese made multi-piece construction short brim boonie hat made from South Vietnamese National Field Police pattern material. Avg. cond. $49.00
VIETNAM ERA ARMY CAMO BOONIE HAT: Issue in ERDL pattern camo ripstop. Size 6 5/8. 1969 dated. In issue bag. Mint cond. $11.00
VIETNAM ERA ARMY CAMO BOONIE HAT: Issue pattern in ERDL pattern camo ripstop. Size 6 7/8. 1968 dated. Near mint cond. $20.00

VIETNAM ERA ARMY CAMO BOONIE HAT:
Made from spot pattern camo parachute
silk. Overall stitched w/metal grommet
vents, shroud line chinstrap. Has "3-9 Ser.
Bn/Med. Supt." inked on one side of brim
& "Udon Thailand" on other, name inside
crown. Above avg. cond. $56.00

VIETNAM ERA ARMY CAMO BOONIE HAT

VIETNAM ERA ARMY GREEN BERET: Rifle
green wool body w/black leather
sweatband w/tie in rear, black cotton lining
w/1971 dated printed markings. Canadian-
made. Size 7. Exc. cond. $93.00
VIETNAM ERA ARMY GREEN BERET: Rifle
green wool size 6 1/2 & Hmkd. Canadian
Commercial Corp. Beret Flash has black
background w/diagonal red & yellow
stripes. Attached to flash is DI for 46th
Special forces Detachment. Mint cond.
.... $60.00

VIETNAM ERA ARMY GREEN BERET

VIETNAM ERA ARMY OFFICER VISOR
CAP: AG fur felt top w/soft roll crown
stiffener, woven band, gilt brass device,
side buttons, gold wire chinstrap, gold
bullion "scramble eggs" on wool covered
visor, golden satin lining. Large size.
Above avg. cond. $20.00
VIETNAM ERA ARMY SURVIVAL SUN HAT:
Reversible from dark OD to brilliant
orange poplin w/stitched brim, soft crown
& adj. headband. Well marked. Near mint
cond. $30.00
VIETNAM ERA USAF BOONIE HAT: Nam
made hat in overall stitched dark olive
cotton w/wide brim that snaps-up on both
sides, nylon mesh covered brass grommet
vent holes, red vinyl sweatband & pale
orange lining. Has theater mach. made
"Nakhonphanom" tab on one side of brim.
Small size. Above avg. cond. $30.00

VIETNAM ERA USAF COWBOY HAT: OD
cotton w/wide stitched brim that snaps up
on each side-red cotton lined-size 57
marked. Has Scarce Thai/Nam machine
made-color "Nakhon Phanom" tab sewn to
front. Above avg. cond. $53.00
VIETNAM ERA USMC EM VISOR CAP: Tan
worsted wool top w/cordovan visor &
chinstrap + 1962-pattern device & side
buttons. Size 6 7/8. Above avg. cond.
.... $30.00
VIETNAM ERA USO "BOB HOPE" TOUR
HAT: Blue baseball cap with large "3AD"
direct embroidered to the front & palm
tress with "3390 S.W. 4133 BW" to one
side & palm tress with "Anderson AFB
Guam 1969." "Sheryle Uliman" sewn to
rear. Clipped to the side & encased in
plastic is a caricature of Bob Hope with
"Bob Hope Show 1969 Escort." Exc. cond.
.... $36.00

U.S. HELMETS

A. Thru World War I (1919)

1874 ARMY DRESS HELMET: Black felt
covered body w/black trim band, arty side
buttons, leather sweatband, vent at top of
crown. W/fluted spike & oak leaf base.
Above avg. cond. $111.00

1881 ARMY DRESS HELMET

1881 ARMY DRESS HELMET: Canvas
covered body in black finish w/stamped
brass acorn/oak leaf base w/fluted spike,
large stamped brass eagle front plate w/
crossed cannons. Green lining. Remains
of sweatband on cork spacers. No side
buttons or chinstrap. Avg. cond. . $145.00

1881 ARMY HELMET: Black dubbed canvas covered fiber body w/green lining, leather sweatband on cork spacers, vent at top of crown w/acorn & oakleaf base & fluted spike, inf side buttons. Has 1872-pattern stamped brass eagle front plate. Avg. cond. $187.00

1881 ARMY HELMET

1881 ARMY INFANTRY DRESS HELMET: Navy blue wool covered cork body w/gilt brass fittings, 1881 inf/eagle front plate (has holes in shield for numeral but none remains). Satin lined w/leather sweatband. Avg. cond. $132.00

1881 NEW YORK STATE HELMET: White wool covered fiber shell w/stamped brass inf side buttons w/hooks, stamped brass "Excelsior" front plate w/applique "2" numeral, fluted spike at brass vent at top of crown. Avg. cond. $107.00

1881 NEW YORK STATE HELMET: Black felt covered cork body w/green lining, large vent at top of crown w/acorn & oak leaf base w/fluted spike, inf. side buttons w/chinstrap hooks. Union shield w/hook on back of crown, New York "Excelsior" front plate w/applied "1" device. Crack up center of rear brim. Above avg. cond. $85.00

1881 NEW YORK STATE SUMMER DRESS HELMET: White cotton covered cork body w/long rear visor, tall crown, N.Y. State front plate w/"14" applied to shield. Has 1872 spike base w/unusual tapered brass plume holder & long black horse hair plume. Inf side buttons w/hooks. Green cotton lined. Cork spacers on leather sweatband. Size 6 7/8. Avg. cond. $370.00

1881 SUMMER SERVICE HELMET: White cotton covered cork body w/threaded vent cap in crown, green cotton lining, cork spacers on leather sweatband. Size 6 7/8. Hooks for chinstrap but none remains. Above avg. cond. $150.00

1881 SUMMER SERVICE HELMET

1889 ARMY SUMMER PITH HELMET: Canvas covered cork shell w/vent at top. Extended rear for sun protection. Web band were crown blends into brim. Lined interior w/leather sweatband. Avg. cond. $90.00

NEW YORK STATE MILITIA HELMET: 'Tarbucket' style w/wool sides patent leather crown & lower band, parade visor w/crazed leather. Gilded brass device w/ large spread wing eagle w/Italicized cipher Initials on chest & motto banner at bottom reading 'EXCELSIOR.' Small pompom at front top w/two shades of green darker on top. Avg. cond. $118.00

NEW YORK STATE MILITIA HELMET

WWI ARMY 3RD ARMY CAMO HELMET: Semi-smooth sand finish shell w/overall handpainted design of geometric designs in shades of orange, yellow, lt. blue & green, 3rd Army patch design painted on front of crown. Good leather chinstrap intact. Lacks liner. Avg. cond. $91.00

WWI ARMY 5TH DIV. HELMET: Semi-smooth olive sand finish steel shell w/ small dark 5th Div. patch design handpainted on front of crown-red diamond w/thin black border & "5" in center. Fair liner & chinstrap. Avg. cond. $76.00

WWI ARMY 101ST F. A. HELMET: Semi-smooth dark olive sand finish shell w/ handpainted unit design on front of crown, good liner & broken chinstrap. W/matched pair of dog tags on neck cord. Insignia somewhat crude & "101" at top is almost rubbed out. Avg. cond. $60.00

WWI ARMY 103RD M. G. BN. HELMET: OD sand finish shell w/good liner & chinstrap. Has faint unit design painted on front of crown. Avg. cond. $51.00

WWI ARMY 103RD M. G. BN., 26TH DIV. HELMET: Semi-smooth olive sand finish shell w/handpainted design on front of crown. Good liner. Fair chinstrap. Avg. cond. $97.00

WWI ARMY 103RD M. G. BN., 26TH DIV. HELMET

WWI ARMY 27TH DIV. CAMO HELMET: Sand finish shell w/large geometric shape camo pattern in shades of orange, green & dark brown separated by black lines, 27th Div. patch design painted on front of crown. Good liner. No chinstrap. Avg. cond. $60.00

WWI ARMY 27TH DIV. HELMET: Semi-smooth olive sand finish steel shell w/ small 27th Div. patch design handpainted on front of crown. Fair liner. Broken chinstrap. Couple dings to crown & $17.50 price marked on top of crown. Scarce helmet. Avg. cond. $70.00

WWI ARMY 33RD DIV. HELMET: OD sand finish shell w/handpainted 33rd Div. patch design on front of crown, fair liner & chinstrap. Avg. cond. $38.00

WWI ARMY 33RD DIV. HELMET: Dark OD sand finish w/small handpainted 33rd Div.

patch design on front of crown-cross design. No chinstrap. Avg. cond. .. $55.00

WWI ARMY 33RD DIV. HELMET: Coarse OD sand finish shell w/handpainted patch design on front of crown. Good liner. Lacks chinstrap. Above avg. cond. $32.00

WWI ARMY 33RD DIV. HELMET

WWI ARMY 33RD DIV. HELMET: Semi-smooth OD finish shell w/33rd Div. patch design painted on front of crown. Fair chinstrap. No liner. Avg. cond. $35.00

WWI ARMY 35TH DIV. HQ HELMET: has rough dark olive finish with black painted 35th division emblems on both sides, has liner but chin straps are gone. Avg. cond. $28.00

WWI ARMY 35TH DIV. CAMO HELMET: Semi-smooth sand finish shell painted in erratic camo design in shades of dark yellow & lt. blue/green. 35th Div. patch design painted on each side of crown w/all white quadrants & borders. No chinstrap or liner. Avg. cond. $69.00

WWI ARMY 35TH DIV. CAMO HELMET

WWI ARMY 35TH DIV. HELMET: Semi-smooth OD shell. Brim lacks metal band around edge. Rodent damage to liner. Good chinstrap. Has handpainted 35th Div. patch design w/2 black quadrants & border, 2 yellow quadrants. Avg. cond. $27.00

WWI ARMY 42ND "RAINBOW" DIV. "WAR ART" HELMET: OD sand finish shell w/ large 4th Div. patch design painted on front of crown. Has various campaign locations painted in black overall on shell. Fair liner & chinstrap. Avg. cond. $70.00

WWI ARMY 77TH DIV. HELMET: Semi-smooth OD finish shell w/77th Div. patch design neatly painted on front of crown. Avg. cond. $44.00

WWI ARMY 42ND "RAINBOW" DIV. "WAR ART" HELMET

WWI ARMY 78TH DIV. HELMET: OD sand finish shell w/78th Div. patch design neatly painted to one side of crown in area that has been smoothed. Good liner & chinstrap. Above avg. cond. $40.00

WWI ARMY 87TH DIV. CAMO HELMET: OD sand finish shell w/faint erratic camo design in shades of red, brown & lt. green, 87th Div. patch design on front of crown. Good liner, leather chinstrap. Avg. cond. $85.00

WWI ARMY 87TH DIV. CAMO HELMET

WWI ARMY 89TH DIV. HELMET: Dark semi-smooth olive sand finish steel shell w/89th Div. patch design w/red insert w/"A" in center handpainted on each side. No liner. Fair chinstrap. Avg. cond. $50.00

WWI ARMY 89TH DIV. HELMET: OD sand finish shell w/handpainted 89th Div. patch design in black on each side of crown-faint signs of same patch design painted underneath these. Has good liner & broken chinstrap. Avg. cond. $29.00

WWI ARMY 89TH DIV. HELMET: OD sand finish steel shell w/89th Div. patch design w/lt. blue insert handpainted on each side of crown. Fair liner & fair chinstrap-both w/ area of rodent damage. Avg. cond. $65.00

WWI ARMY ADV. SECTOR CAMO HELMET: Sand texture steel shell in erratic camo pattern in shades of green, brown-some shades hard to distinguished by heavy yellowing. Patterns separated by black borders. One side of crown has Adv. Sec. patch design neatly painted. No liner or chinstrap. Avg. cond. $35.00

WWI ARMY ARTY UNIT HELMET: Semi-smooth olive finish steel shell w/large 145th (145 above large crossed cannons) unit design handpainted on front of crown. Fair liner. No chinstrap. Avg. cond. $75.00

WWI ARMY CAMO HELMET: Sand finish shell w/liner & chinstrap. Appears unissued. Shell has interesting overall geometric shapes in shades of yellow, green, white & brown separated by black borders. Above avg. cond. $100.00

WWI ARMY CAMO HELMET

WWI ARMY CAMO HELMET: Sand finish shell w/erratic design in green & dark tan separated by thin black borders. One side of shell has dark rectangular shaped design. Liner & chinstrap removed but no dents or dings. Above avg. cond. ..$80.00

WWI ARMY ENGINEER HELMET: OD sand finish shell has handpainted design of red engr. castle inside segmented white circle on dark blue square field on front of crown. Back of crown has name scratched into surface of paint. Good liner. Broken leather chinstrap. Avg. cond. $49.00

WWI ARMY HELMET: OD finish shell. Pattern w/o rolled brim edge. Fair liner & chinstrap. Has after-the-fact "Keystone" patch design painted on one side w/28 DIV." in center. Avg. cond. $60.00

WWI ARMY HELMET

WWI ARMY HELMET: OD sand finish shell w/liner & leather chinstrap. Exc. cond. $72.00

WWI ARMY HELMET: OD sand finish shell w/fair liner & chinstrap. Avg. cond. $24.00

WWI ARMY HELMET: OD sand finish shell w/good liner & broken chinstrap. Avg. cond. $32.00

WWI ARMY HELMET: OD sand finish shell w/good liner & fair chinstrap. Above avg. cond. $40.00

WWI ARMY HELMET: OD sand finish shell. Fair leather chinstrap. No liner. Avg. cond. $10.00

WWI ARMY HELMET: OD sand texture finish steel shell w/liner & good chinstrap. Above avg. cond. $55.00

WWI ARMY HELMET: Rough OD sand finish shell w/good liner & chinstrap. Fine example. Above avg. cond. $41.00

WWI ARMY WAR ART HELMET: Sand finish shell overall finished in erratic camo pattern in shades of yellow, black & green w/thin orange borders. Has handpainted 225 Inf, France, Worlds War, USA AEF 1918-19, etc. lettering. No liner or chinstrap. Avg. cond. $45.00

WWI ARMY WAR ART HELMET: Sand finish shell w/fair liner. No chinstrap. Shell overall painted in erratic camo pattern in brown-orange & green separated by black lines. Adv. Sector patch design neatly painted on front of crown. Several dents. Avg. cond. $30.00

WWI ARMY WAR ART HELMET: Semi-smooth sand finish shell has camo design in four sections w/erratic thin red borders. Sections in white, red, yellow & blue. Front of crown has simple U.S. flag design & brim painted "Tabone." No liner. Fair chinstrap. Avg. cond. $85.00

WWI ARMY WAR ART HELMET: Semi-smooth sand finish shell refinished in erratic camo pattern in shades of blue, green, white, dark tan & black. Has likeness of French flag painted on one side of crown & U.S. flag on other side of crown. Poor liner & chinstrap. Avg. cond. $118.00

WWI ARMY WAR ART HELMET

WWI AVIATOR FLIGHT HELMET & GOGGLES: Tan leather w/ear cups lace up back for sizing. tabs for goggles. Hole on L. side, outer shell penetrated. Shows wear & staining. No pads on earphone holes. Sewn tag says Type 1-A by Western Electric flannel lined. Amber

lenses in goggles w/fur pad around eyes. Avg. cond. $128.00

WWI AVIATOR FLIGHT HELMET W/ GOGGLES: Very good condition helmet w/soft cloth lining in dark OD green color. Weathered leather exterior is supple including chin strap & restraining strap. 11 pieces of leather used in exterior assembly. Goggles have amber lenses w/ virtually no loss of clarity. Some deterioration of wind screen & face pads. Above avg. cond. $160.00

WWI AVIATOR FLIGHT HELMET: 4 piece brown leather body is chamois lined w/ woven name label inside. Has snap down goggles straps in back. Avg. cond. $50.00

WWI AVIATOR FLIGHT HELMET: Classic pattern in black leather w/multi piece "Beach Ball" crown & side skirts w/ pierced, diamond shaped ear panels & integral chin straps w/snaps. Brown wool lined, has diamond on top of crown w/ small strap for streamer. Avg. cond. $65.00

B. 1920 - 1945

AMERICAN FIELD SERVICE FRENCH MODEL 26 ADRIAN HELMET: OF finish-standard pattern Adrian helmet w/good liner & chinstrap. Has bronze front plate w/ slightly stylized spread wing US eagle atop Union shield. Has "C. G. Jr. France '40". piece from early WWII Europe. Above avg. cond. $588.00

WWII AAF FLAK HELMET (M-3)

WWII AAF FLAK HELMET (M-3): OD flocked finish shell w/pivoting protective earcups-lack felt pads. Clean lt. OD webbing w/ headband, adj. lt. OD web chinstrap. Near mint cond. $65.00

WWII AAF FLAK HELMET (M-3): OD flocked finish shell w/pivoting earcups, lt. OD web chinstrap, lt. OD webbing. Faint Capt. bar design on front of crown. Avg. cond. $49.00

WWII AAF FLAK HELMET (M-4A2): Dark OD cotton covered shell w/dark OD nylon lining, protective ear cups, leather chinstrap, printed spec label. Front of crown is ink stamped "TK. CO. 182d INF." Avg. cond. $48.00

WWII AAF FLIGHT HELMET (A-11)

WWII AAF FLIGHT HELMET (A-11): Dark brown leather w/chamois lining + woven AAF marked spec label, large rubber oval earcups, chinstrap, snaps & clip for oxygen mask, AAF inkstamp markings. Med. size. Avg. cond. $79.00

WWII AAF FLIGHT HELMET (A-11): Modified. Brown leather body is chamois lined w/large black rubber oval ear cups-size large w/woven AAF spec. label inside. Has been modified by installing press snaps in the top edges of the rubber ear cups-this for mounting the type A-1 removable visor. Avg. cond. $145.00

WWII AAF FLIGHT HELMET (A-11): Dark brown leather exterior w/hard rubber mounts for earphones, straps for goggles, snaps for O2 etc. & chin strap. Chamois lined interior w/pads for ears & sewn label w/size (medium) also stamped AAF emblem. Above avg. cond. $65.00

WWII AAF FLIGHT HELMET (A-9): Lt. OD cotton w/fleece earpads, adj. leather chinstrap w/fleece pad, AAF marked woven spec label. Large size. In issue carton. Mint cond. $37.00

WWII AAF FLIGHT HELMET (A-9): OD green twill helmet w/web straps & hooks for mask & goggles etc. Interior has sheepskin pads for ear comfort & sewn label w/size (large). Leather chin strap. AAF emblem on forehead. $20.00

WWII AAF FLIGHT HELMET (A-9): Lt. olive cotton twill body w/lt. OD trim, fleece earpads, leather chinstrap, woven AAF marked spec label. Size Med. Exc. cond. $50.00

WWII AAF FLIGHT HELMET (A-9)

WWII AAF FLIGHT HELMET (A-9): Size large in lt. OD cotton w/woven AAF marked spec label, fleece earpads, adj. leather chinstrap w/fleece pad. Exc. cond. $25.00

WWII AAF FLIGHT HELMET (AN-H-15): Tan Cotton Poplin w/leather straps to hold goggles, mounts for earphones. Snaps for O2 mask & mike. Missing chin strap. Interior has sewn label & chamois lined earpads. Above avg. cond. $20.00

WWII AAF FLIGHT HELMET (AN-H-15): Tan Twill w/leather tabs & snaps for mask & straps for goggles, one strap snap missing. Black hard rubber earphone mounts. Interior has sewn label sized large, chamois covers on ear pads. No chin strap. Above avg. cond. $20.00

WWII AAF FLIGHT HELMET (B-5)

WWII AAF FLIGHT HELMET (B-5): Fleece lined-brown finish body w/fleece covered chinstrap & metal fittings. Size x-large w/ woven spec. label inside. Hole punched in each side at ear for gossport or receiver access but never had ear cups applied. Exc. cond. $196.00

WWII AAF FLIGHT HELMET (B-6): Dark brown leather exterior w/padded chin strap. Sheared sheepskin inner lining & sewn size tab (small) + w/label dated 42. Mint cond. $175.00

WWII AAF FLIGHT HELMET (B-6): Dark brown leather outside & sheared fleece inner lining w/sewn mfg. label. Some insect damage to exterior leather & fleece. Straps for the goggles. Padded chin strap. Avg. cond. $84.00

WWII AAF FLIGHT HELMET (B-6)

WWII AAF FLIGHT HELMET (A-4): Lt. OD gabardine body w/woven AAF marked spec label, fleece earpads, leather chinstrap w/fleece pad. Well marked. Above avg. cond. $20.00

WWII ARMY HELMET (M-1): OD sand finish shell w/dark OD web chinstraps. Fiber M-1 liner w/lt. OD webbing, nape strap, leather sweatband & chinstrap. Front of helmet crown has 2nd Armor design neatly painted. Above avg. cond. $93.00

WWII ARMY HELMET (M-1)

WWII ARMY HELMET (M-1): OD sand finish shell w/lt. OD web chinstraps. W/rare pressed paper liner w/lt. OD cloth covering, clean lt. OD webbing, leather chinstrap. Above avg. cond. $276.00

WWII ARMY HELMET LINER (M-1): Lt. OD cotton covered pressed liner shell w/clean

lt. OD webbing & nape strap, leather sweatband & liner. Has 1st lt. bar neatly painted on front of crown in silver paint. Above avg. cond. $116.00

WWII ARMY HELMET LINER (M-1)

WWII ARMY M. P. HELMET LINER (M-1): lt. OD webbing, neck strap, leather sweatband & chinstrap. In black finish & has white painted metal M. P. letters on front-each letter has twin Sb. post. Above avg. cond. $29.00

WWII ARMY OFFICER SUN HELMET: CBI made. Thick fiber body is covered in tan cotton twill w/several small metal grommet vent holes, matching adj. chinstrap. Underside of brim lined w/green cotton. Fully lined inside crown w/Calcutta's maker label. Has Capt.'s name & serial # inked inside. Size 7. Avg. cond. $32.00

WWII ARMY PARATROOP HELMET LINER (M-1C): Fiber shell in dark olive finish w/lt. OD webbing, nape strap & leather sweatband + riveted dark OD web yoke straps. No chincup. Name & service number painted in white on underside of lip. Avg. cond. $50.00

WWII CAMO HELMET NET: Cord net tied in 2" squares. Laced w/burlap scrim in shades of olive & dark tan. Above avg. cond. $28.00

WWII FLIGHT CAP: Summer tan twill w/chin strap & snap tabs for goggles. Sewn tag inside unreadable. Appears medium sized. Avg. cond. $66.00

WWII FLIGHT CAP: Summer tan twill w/chin strap & snap tabs for goggles. Sewn tag inside w/hmkd. 'BUCO' & size 'Med.' Near mint cond. $66.00

WWII FLIGHT HELMET: Black twill w/chin strap & snap tabs for goggles. Sewn label 'BUCO' & size medium inside. Possible navy skull cap-no mil markings visible. Above avg. cond. $55.00

WWII HELMET (M-1): Dark OD sand finish shell w/lt. OD web chinstraps on fixed bales. Faint white vertical stripe painted on back of shell crown. Also, M-1 liner w/lt. OD webbing, nape strap, leather sweatband. Avg. cond. $82.00

WWII HELMET (M-1): OD sand finish shell w/lt. OD web chinstraps on fixed bales. W/ pressed paper liner w/white webbing, correct leather sweatband, leather chinstrap name penciled on underside of lip. Above avg. cond. $167.00

WWII HELMET (M-1)

WWII HELMET (M-1): Dark OD sand finish shell w/lt. OD web chinstraps on flexible swivels. W/M-1 liner w/lt. OD webbing, nape strap & leather chinstrap- faint traces of once having sgt chevron design on front crown. Avg. cond. $37.00

WWII HELMET (M-1): Dark olive sand finish shell w/dark OD web chinstraps, fiber liner w/dark OD webbing. W/badly tattered USMC HBT spot pattern camo cover. Avg. cond. $35.00

WWII HELMET (M-1): OD sand finish shell w/dark OD web chinstraps. W/fine sand finish shell w/clean lt. OD webbing, leather chinstrap. Above avg. cond. $40.00

WWII HELMET (M-1): OD sand finish shell w/lt. OD web chinstraps on fixed bales, fiber liner w/dark OD webbing, nape strap, leather sweatband & chinstrap. Fitted w/ string net in 2" squares. Avg. cond.
.... $53.00

WWII HELMET (M-1): OD sand finish shell w/lt. OD web chinstraps on fixed bales. W/ pressed paper liner-lt. OD cotton covered shell w/lt. OD webbing, nape strap & leather sweatband & chinstrap. Avg. cond.
.... $116.00

WWII HELMET (M-1): OD sand finish shell w/lt. OD web chinstraps, good M-1 helmet liner w/lt. OD webbing, nape strap, leather chinstrap & sweatband. Fitted w/reversible from green to tan spot pattern camo HBT cover w/large EG&A stencil on front. Above avg. cond. $82.00

WWII HELMET (M-1): OD sand finish shell w/lt. OD web chinstraps. Avg. cond.
.... $25.00

WWII HELMET (M-1): Steel shell in OD sand re-finish w/lt. OD web chinstraps on fixed bales. M-1 liner has lt. OD webbing, nape strap, leather chinstrap & sweatband. Has neatly painted 87th Div. large patch design on front of crown w/smaller s/sgt. chevron painted below. Fitted w/camo net in 1/4" squares. Avg. cond. $124.00

WWII HELMET (M-1917A1 "TRANSITION"): OD sand finish shell w/oiled leather covered sheet metal liner, dark tan web chinstraps. Avg. cond. $27.00

WWII HELMET (M-1917A1 "TRANSITION"): OD sand finish shell. Has dent in top of crown, silver touch-up paint on top of crown. Tan web chinstraps. Leather covered sheet metal liner lacks laces-dark in couple sections. Avg. cond. $30.00

WWII HELMET (M-1917A1 "TRANSITION"): Rough OD sand finish shell w/dark tan web chinstraps, leather covered sheet metal liner. Brim lacks rolled metal lip. Avg. cond. $35.00

WWII HELMET (M-1917A1 "TRANSITION"): Thick OD sand finish shell w/dark tan leather covered sheet metal liner, dark tan web chinstraps. Above avg. cond.
.... $65.00

WWII HELMET NET: British made. Tied in 2" squares w/Dennison marked & 1944 dated tag. Exc. cond. $30.00

WWII NAVAL AVIATOR FLIGHT HELMET (M-450): Summer style w/tan twill shell, goggle straps & leather chinstrap w/cup. Sewn label inside, size tab for 7 1/4. Near mint cond. $72.00

WWII NAVY AVIATOR FLIGHT HELMET (NAF-1092)

WWII NAVY AVIATOR FLIGHT HELMET (NAF-1092): Dark brown leather w/ chamois lining, woven NAF marked spec label, embossed brown leather chinstrap w/embossed fleece-lined chincup. Size 7 1/8. Near mint cond. $133.00

WWII NAVY AVIATOR FLIGHT HELMET (NAF-1092): Dark brown leather w/ chamois lining, woven spec label w/ designation "NAF 1092," nickel finish buckles for chinstrap not included. Size 7 1/8. Above avg. cond. $100.00

WWII NAVY AVIATOR FLIGHT HELMET (NAF-1092W): Brown leather exterior. Fleece lined interior w/no labels. Padded chin strap. Avg. cond. $40.00

WWII NAVY HELMET (M-1917A1 "TRANSITION" "WAR ART"): Smooth dark olive finish domed steel shell w/many neatly handpainted designs of naval life & subjects all around crown-"USN" on front of crown w/stylized crow above, sailor on shore leave, Wildcat fighter plane, "US Navy" life ring, fouled anchor, crow atop skull & crossbones, "Iceland" polar bear, flying tiger design w/"Roaring Rosa" below, firing warship w/"Morton's Raiders", Nazi submarine periscope & more. Underside brim & interior painted in blue-gray, dark tan web chinstraps & leather covered liner in worn gold finish. Avg. cond. $219.00

WWII NAVY HELMET (M-1917A1 "TRANSITION" "WAR ART")

WWII NAVY HELMET (M-2): Large steel shell in blue sand finish w/one-piece foam pad liner. NAVY marked. Above avg. cond. $28.00

WWII PARATROOP HELMET (A-8): OD twill w/leather chinstrap & chin cup. Snaps & bands for goggles. AAF emblem on outside. Sewn inside label & size (large). Near mint cond. $76.00

WWII USMC CAMO HELMET COVER (M-1): Reversible from green to tan spot pattern camo on HBT. Avg. cond. $59.00

WWII USMC CAMO HELMET COVER (M-1): Reversible from green to tan spot pattern camo canvas w/ink stamped EG&A device on front (green side only).

USMC/maker/Australia 1943 marked. Near mint cond. $165.00

WWII PARATROOP HELMET (A-8)

WWII USMC CAMO HELMET COVER (M-1)

WWII USMC OFFICER SUN HELMET: CBI-made helmet-white cotton covered thick cork body w/brown leather chinstrap & trim, vent in top of crown, underside of brim lined in dark green cotton. Reverse side of sweatband named to a lt. w/serial number & "Manila 1940." Has handwritten name label underneath sweatshield. 1937-pattern Em EG&A device affixed to front of crown. Above avg. cond. $93.00

WWII USMC OFFICER SUN HELMET

C. 1946 - Present

ARMY AIRBORNE PARATROOP HELMET:
1950s. Exterior paint job w/white field,
black wing-like shapes on either side &
metal jump wings on center front over
painted name & small heraldic emblem
above all. Open chin cup, web chinstrap.
Air guard labeled head restraint & top
cushion. Avg. cond. $195.00

ARMY AIRBORNE TRAINING HELMET:
Red plastic football pattern fiber shell in
dark olive finish w/"Test Operation"
stenciled in white across front of crown.
White webbing w/tan leather trim. Wilson
marked. Avg. cond. $40.00

ARMY AVIATOR FLIGHT HELMET (APH-1):
Matte black finish on exterior w/dual visor
& boom mike on left side. Padded web
chin strap & floating earpieces w/snaps for
Oxygen mask. Custom black leather
covered fit & comfort pads. Exc. cond.
.... $250.00

ARMY AVIATOR FLIGHT HELMET (APH-1)

ARMY AVIATOR FLIGHT HELMET (SPF-4)

ARMY AVIATOR FLIGHT HELMET (SPF-4):
OD finish shell w/single visor & velcro tabs
on cover + elastic tube across back. Boom
mike on left side. Web chin strap, floating
padded earpieces & web + leather head

restraint. Avionics intact. Exc. cond.
....$160.00

ARMY AVIATOR FLIGHT HELMET (SPH-4):
Single clear visor under shield. OD finish
on exterior. Avionics installed & boom
mike on left side. Padded earphones,
leather head comfort/restraints &
styrofoam pads in shell. Avg. cond.
.... $114.00

ARMY AVIATOR FLIGHT HELMET (SPS-4):
OD finish w/wear. Single center pull clear
visor + cracked shield. Boom mike on left
side. Interior w/comfort pads & head
restraints. Earphones loose in padded
receptacles. Avg. cond. $139.00

ARMY HELMET (KEVLAR FRITZ): Kevlar
shell in OD sand finish w/dark OD nylon
webbing, chinstrap, leather sweatband.
Size small shell. Fitted w/woodland camo
cover w/EG&A stencil on front of crown
area & OD elastic helmet band. Above
avg. cond. $42.00

ARMY HELMET (KEVLAR FRITZ): OD sand
finish shell w/dark OD nylon webbing,
chinstrap, sweatband. Medium size shell.
Woodland camo cover w/subdued metal
pfc rank device on front. Exc. cond.
.... $74.00

ARMY HELMET (KEVLAR FRITZ)

ARMY HELMET (KEVLAR FRITZ): OD sand
finish shell w/dark OD nylon webbing &
chinstrap + leather sweatband. Large size.
1983 dated. Exc. cond. $65.00

ARMY HELMET (KEVLAR FRITZ): OD sand
finish shell w/dark OD nylon webbing,
chinstrap, leather sweatband. Large size
shell. W/woodland camo cover & helmet
band. Above avg. cond. $51.00

ARMY HELMET (KEVLAR FRITZ): OD sand
finish shell w/dark OD nylon webbing,
chinstrap, sweatband & "brain" pad.
Woodland camo cover & OD helmet band.
Incl. instruction booklet. Nice. Near mint
cond. $94.00

ARMY HELMET (KEVLAR FRITZ): OD sand
finish shell w/dark OD webbing &
chinstrap. Incl. sweatband in issue bag,
instruction booklet. 1989 dated. Small size
shell. Near mint cond. $48.00

ARMY HELMET LINER (M-1): Berlin Bde. 6941 Guard Bn. Glossy black finish fiber shell w/wide white band painted around shell. Union shield design w/3-star field decal on front of crown. Lacks most of dark OD webbing. Avg. cond. $27.00

ARMY HELMET LINER (M-1): White finish fiber shell w/dark OD webbing + leather sweatband. Has 95th Div. patch design decal on each side of crown. Tear to nape strap. Avg. cond. $20.00

COAST GUARD AVIATOR FLIGHT HELMET (SPH-3B)

COAST GUARD AVIATOR FLIGHT HELMET (SPH-3B): White exterior w/reflective tape pattern & Coast Guard wings on visor cover. Dual rams horn visors. Boom mike on left side w/complete avionics & chin strap. Floating padded earphones. Leather & web head restraints. Above avg. cond. $177.00

COMBAT VEHICLE CREW HELMET: Gentex model size small & dated 1/88. Original box & inner bag. Near mint cond. $34.00

COMBAT VEHICLE CREW HELMET: Sealed in orig. shipping box by Gentex. Dated 2/86 on box, size small. Near mint cond. $20.00

COMBAT VEHICLE CREW HELMET: Size medium, reinforced plastic w/OD sand textured surface. Ear cut outs & fitted inserts w/padded earphones & boom mike. Electronics incl. Above avg. cond. $35.00

COMBAT VEHICLE CREW HELMET: Size medium. Reinforced plastic w/OD sand textured surface. Ear cut outs & fitted inserts w/padded earphones & boom mike. Electronics incl. Above avg. cond. $20.00

FLIGHT HELMET (HGU-39P): Flyer Chemical Warfare. White exterior. No visor or alligator clips. Green web chin strap w/pad. Ear piece assemblies w/ leather tabs & snaps, leather pad & web comfort fit assembly. Helmet dated 1974 on back. External label & last service dated Oct. 86. Exc. cond. $91.00

FLIGHT HELMET (HGU-39P): Flyer Chemical Warfare. White exterior. No visor or alligator clips. Green web chin strap. Ear piece assemblies w/leather tabs & snaps, leather pad & web comfort fit assembly. Helmet dated 1980 on internal mfg. label & last service dated Sept. 85. Exc. cond. $75.00

FLIGHT HELMET (SPH-4): 1980s. Exterior covered in reflective tape. Dual visors w/ ram's horn controls. Sophisticated electronics w/high security interlocking connectors. Custom fitted black leather covered comfort fit pad. Padded chin & neck strap. Floating padded earpieces/ boom mike/snaps for mask. Exc. cond. $100.00

HELMET (M-1): Experimental model. Non-magnetic metal shell in M-1 shell configuration w/dark OD web chinstraps on metal swivels. Near mint cond. $100.00

HELMET (M-1): OD re-finish shell w/nylon chinstraps on snap-on swivels. Includes Nam era liner w/dark OD webbing, leather sweatband & fitted w/reversible leafy pattern camo cover & 2 OD elastic helmet bands. Lot includes extra Nam era M-1 helmet liner. Avg. cond. $20.00

HELMET LINER (M-1): Nam era fiber liner w/dark OD webbing. Finished in semi-gloss dark olive w/large metal Korean War era s/sgt chevron on front of crown & orange stripe around crown. Left side has "This We'll Defend" decal & 5th "Crusaders/None Finer" unit decal on rt. side. Above avg. cond. $20.00

KOREAN WAR ERA ARMY AIRBORNE GENERAL HELMET LINER (M-1): Fiber shell 1952 dated w/dark OD webbing. Shell in dark green finish w/blue & white bands around shell. Rt. side has 101st patch design decal & left side has regt. crest design of elephant in ancient battle gear. Front has Sb. 1-star gen. star. Avg. cond. $60.00

KOREAN WAR ERA NAVY AVIATOR FLIGHT HELMET (JET): Model H-4 Black finished exterior. No avionics. Mount for boom mike on right side. Interior w/leather & web head restraints. Size large. Above avg. cond. $50.00

KOREAN WAR ERA NAVY AVIATOR FLIGHT HELMET: Ridged top pattern w/ gold finish. Decaled pilot wing on front, gothic initials. Boom mike on right side &

fit adj. straps on outside. Padded leather head band, web restraints & shock pad liners. Gentexite label w/hand written names & 1954 date on ear covers. Avg. cond. $86.00

KOREAN WAR ERA NAVY AVIATOR FLIGHT HELMET (JET)

KOREAN WAR ERA NAVY AVIATOR FLIGHT HELMET

NAVY AVIATOR FLIGHT HELMET (APH-6): w/Horseshoe bayonet fittings. Red & white reflective tape pattern on outside. Hand written VP-92 on one side. Single visor clear. Avionics incl. Padded blue web chin & neck strap. Padded head phones installed. Limited fit/comfort padding. Avg. cond. $145.00
NAVY AVIATOR FLIGHT HELMET (APH-6): w/Horseshoe bayonet fittings. White finish. Navy wing & 'Navy' on visor cover. Single visor, clear. Blue web padded chin & neck strap. Padded earpieces & internal avionics. White styrofoam liner. Exc. cond. $210.00
NAVY AVIATOR FLIGHT HELMET (EXPERIMENTAL): For protection in nuclear environment. White outer shell w/ tear drop shaped panel above face w/ filtered inlet at bottom. Removable double framed goggles w/gold film coated lens & leather padded. Goggles raise & lower on

spring loaded metal hinges. Bayonet receptacles provided. Padded chinstrap, neck strap & earphones. Interior has only styrofoam pads. Above avg. cond. $370.00

NAVY AVIATOR FLIGHT HELMET (EXPERIMENTAL)

NAVY AVIATOR FLIGHT HELMET (HGU-34): W/bronze finish, single visor. Navy wings & 'Navy' on shield. Right side boom mike assembly & avionics. Chin & neck strap. Tabs for mask snaps have snaps missing. Padded earphones, leather wrapped foam comfort/fit pads. Above avg. cond. $158.00

NAVY AVIATOR FLIGHT HELMET (HGU-34)

NAVY AVIATOR FLIGHT HELMET (HGU-34/P): Single visor-center pull. Cover taped w/blue, silver stars. Back hand-painted w/ winged crest. Bayonet grips on each side + chinstrap. Black edge roll & comfort/fit pads. Avionics. Above avg. cond. $91.00
NAVY AVIATOR FLIGHT HELMET (HGU-34/P): White w/white & red reflective tape in random pattern. Single center pull clear visor & bayonet fittings. Left side boom mike & internal avionics. Black edge roll, chin & neck straps. Interior, black comfort/ fit pads & padded earpieces. Above avg. cond. $91.00

NAVY AVIATOR FLIGHT HELMET (JET CREW): 1950s. Ribbed exterior w/white finish & red shape painted at top. WWII type Pioneer one piece goggles w/amber lens. Mike boom mount on right side. Helmet & inner liner both size medium. Helmet interior has leather & web fit/comfort restraints. Green twill skull cap w/ear phone receptacles. Sewn label in back. Chin strap & snaps for mask. Exc. cond. $294.00

NAVY AVIATOR FLIGHT HELMET
(JET CREW)

NAVY AVIATOR FLIGHT HELMET (JET): 1950s. Small Centex football style helmet w/Gold finish & white/orange reflective tape on exterior. Gold NAVY wing decal on center front. One piece goggles w/clear lens rest above forehead. Boom mike attached on right side. Avionics installed. Padded inner lining w/web & leather head restraints. Tan twill helmet liner w/padded earphones & leather snaps for mask. Leather chin strap included. Sewn label. Above avg. cond. $101.00

NAVY AVIATOR FLIGHT HELMET (JET): Gold finish w/day-glo tape pattern. Wings & 'Navy' on shield. Web chin & neck strap, chin mount missing. Avionics & leather tabs w/snaps for mask. Ear pieces w/o pads. Comfort/fit pads installed. Avg. cond. $47.00

NAVY FLIGHT DECK CREW HELMET: Tan cotton w/1975 dated spec label, chinstrap. Size 7 1/4. Green plastic cranial plates painted dark red w/reflective tape sections & red finished earcups. Avg. cond. $20.00

NAVY FLIGHT DECK CREW HELMET.: Two piece impact resistant shell w/head set mounted between. Deep sound padded ear cups + Goggles. Incl. Kelly green. High visibility deck vest. Above avg. cond. $50.00

NAVY FLIGHT DECK CREW HELMET

NAVY FLIGHT HELMET (APH-6): White fiberglass shell w/NAVY decal on front. Army style foam pads glued inside. W/ cloth inner helmet. Avg. cond. $158.00

NAVY FLIGHT HELMET (APH-6/A): White w/single visor & navy wing decal in front. Mfg. label at back. Chin & neck straps, padded. Oxygen mask (P22001 No hose) connected by alligator clips. Padded interior. Avionics. Above avg. cond. $129.50

U.S. ADVISOR HELMET (M-1C): To ARVN Rangers. Standard U.S. issue. Semi-smooth sand finish steel shell w/metal mounted, dark OD web chin straps in M-1C airborne configuration. Shell has been over-painted in 3 tone color scheme utilizing the OD base color. 3 rank blossoms painted low across rear. Large rendition of black panther's head on star in front-red, white, black & yellow. Name written in white grease pencil inside. Lacks liner. Above avg. cond. $538.00

USAF FLIGHT HELMET (HGU-2A/P)
& MASK

USAF FLIGHT HELMET (HGU-2A/P) & MASK: Exterior covered w/camo tape. Center pull single visor, tinted. Bayonet receptacles. Padded chin & neck strap.

Thin tan edge roll. Interior w/gray plastic padded ear pieces & custom padded black leather comfort/fit pads. MBU-5/P mask-80 dated, w/complete avionics, & offset bayonets. Hose has single QR. connector. Exc. cond. $256.00

USAF FLIGHT HELMET (HGU-39/P): White exterior, no visor. Vehicular use disclaimer on back, x-large tag on eyebrow. O2 mask bayonet receptacles on both sides. Padded earphone assemblies on each side + internal avionics. Green nylon web chinstrap. Neck restraint, leather & web head restraint & comfort fit. Exc. cond. $85.00

USAF FLIGHT HELMET
(HI ALT PRESSURE)

USAF FLIGHT HELMET (HI ALT PRESSURE): Custom fitted green fiberglass shell w/AF emblem over face plate latch. Integrated avionics incl. mike at left side of face plate opening. Special K1 hood to mate to suit. Full face latch plate (missing). Chamois lined padded face frame, earpieces & head restraints. Avg. cond. $578.00

USAF FLIGHT HELMET (P-1B): Personal helmet of named Msgt. White finish. US Air Force emblem decal & spring actuated tinted visor. White web chin strap. Net covers over earpieces. Web & leather head restraint & comfort set. AF emblem at top of inside. Exc. cond. $525.00

USAF FLIGHT HELMET (P-1B)

USAF HELMET (M-1): OD sand finish shell w/shield-shaped unit patch design decal on each side. Lacks chinstraps. Includes WWII era M-1 liner w/lt. OD webbing. Name painted in white inside. Avg. cond. $10.00

VIETNAM ERA ARMY ARMOR CREWMAN HELMET: Domed fiber shell in OD sand finish w/dark OD webbing, padded earcups wired w/receivers, "boom" mike w/lead wire & plug. Avg. cond. $24.00

VIETNAM ERA ARMY HELICOPTER AVIATOR FLIGHT HELMET (SPS-5): Exterior painted in blue w/gold & white pattern. Over each ear is dark blue star & name 'BLUE STAR.' Single center pull visor w/cover. List of names & units in Nam apparently supported by pilot. Left side boom mike & floating padded earpieces. Leather & web head restraint/ comfort pads. Sized regular. Above avg. cond. $244.00

VIETNAM ERA ARMY HELICOPTER
AVIATOR FLIGHT HELMET (SPS-5)

VIETNAM ERA ARMY PARATROOPER HELMET (M-1C): Lt. OD sand finish shell w/dark OD web chin straps on metal swivels. Incl. thick fiber M-1C liner w/dark OD webbing, yoke straps, chincup, nape strap & sweatband. Shell has faint signs of removed "7" taped numerals. Above avg. cond. $20.00

VIETNAM ERA SUN HELMET: Tan cotton covered fiber shell w/green lining, adj. sweatband & web chinstrap. Metal grommet vents. DSA contract markings. Mint cond. $12.50

VIETNAM ERA USAF FLIGHT HELMET (HGU-7/P): W/detachable white visor, White plastic helmet w/notches at sides for earphones & boom mike. Safety warning label at back. White nylon padded chin strap. Ear phones suspended by white nylon webbing & right side supports mike. Compression pads front & rear, no other head restraints. Exc. cond. .. $93.00

U.S. GI FIELD GEAR/ INDIVIDUAL EQUIPMENT

A. Thru World War I (1919)

AMMO BELT (1910 MILLS 10 POCKET): Lt. olive web w/rimless eagle snap on each pocket flap. Brass fittings. Faint date. Mills marked. One-half of front has replacement section of 1943 dated OD web riveted in place. Avg. cond. $75.00

AMMO BELT (45/70): Dark tan web w/50 stitched loops that have three thin rows of black horizontal stripes. Brass fittings. Avg. cond. $133.00

AMMO BELT (M1910 9 POCKET): Dark tan web w/rimless bronze eagle snap closure on flaps & bronze colored fittings. Name stenciled on reverse side. Above avg. cond. $69.00

AMMO BELT (MILLS 9 POCKET): Mills marked-tan canvas & web w/brass fittings. Above avg. cond. $35.00

ARMY BACK PACK (1916): Lt. OD canvas body w/lt. OD web straps & matching mess kit carrier. US//9 marked on flap. Lot includes RIA marked/1914 dated mess kit w/stamped markings on handle. Avg. cond. $27.00

ARMY ENGINEER COMPASS (1917) IN WATCH STYLE CASE: Hanging ring, nickel silver 2" hinged watch case w/ working compass & marked on case. Avg. cond. $28.00

ARMY HAVERSACK (1904): Dark tan canvas body w/tan trim. Brass hooks for sling but not included. US/RIA marked. Flap approx. 14x14". Stencil marked "C/ Inf/3/Ore" & "2." Avg. cond. $24.00

ARMY HAVERSACK W/AERO SQDN. MARKINGS: Tan canvas body w/several pockets & approx. 14x13.5" flap. W/adj. dark tan web shoulder strap. US/RIA marked. Flap has hand inked name & stenciled "17th./Aero/Sqdn./116." Avg. cond. $38.00

BLANKET STRAPS (M1912): Brown leather. Buckles, straps & center hook strap. Near mint cond. $36.00

CANTEEN (1919) W/WHITE CLOTH SIDES: 12" dia. 3.5" wide, 4 metal strap loops on the side & WW1 patent date Jan 16, 1917 & July 29, 1919. White canvas covers rope mounted on both sides w/black stenciled sides. Stopper is same white canvas w/leather strip. Avg. cond. $35.00

CANTEEN RIG: 1917 dated cover in lt. OD canvas w/dark tan trim & wire belt hanger. Initials inked on front. Also, 1942 dated canteen cup & good 1943 dated canteen. Above avg. cond. $37.00

CARTRIDGE BELT (1903 MILLS 9 POCKET): Tan canvas w/9 pouches sewn into the belt. Leather saber strap w/metal loop. Avg. cond. $20.00

CARTRIDGE BELT (MILLS 1903 MODEL 9 POCKET): Post 1906 Mfg. w/reinforced puckers at pocket bottom. hmkd. each end w/Mills inside bullet & patent dates. Above avg. cond. $120.00

CARTRIDGE BELT (MILLS 1903 MODEL 9 POCKET): Post 1906 Mfg. w/reinforced puckers at pocket bottom. hmkd. each end w/Mills inside bullet & patent dates. Above avg. cond. $60.00

CARTRIDGE BELT (MILLS 1903 PATTERN 9 POCKET): 9 pouch belt. Back labeled '2nd 10 105/10-2-105.' Below avg. cond. $60.00

CARTRIDGE BELT (MILLS VARIATION 40 ROUND): 2.5" wide tan web body w/brass T-closure, stamped brass adjustments 'Mills etc..May18.15.' 1 3/8" tall loops w/ black border stripes for .30 cal. Near mint cond. $69.00

CARTRIDGE BELT: Mills hmkd. on brass tip, 1910 model for marines. Has US bronze button on right side of buckle. Avg. cond. $103.00

CARTRIDGE BOX (1874 MCKEEVER 20 ROUND PISTOL): Black leather. Serviceable. Avg. cond. $28.00

CARTRIDGE BOX (FRAIZER 1872 PATENTED): Black finished leather w/top latch & lower hinged front. Brass oval w/ NY in italic style. Wood holder has 18 round capacity. Above avg. cond. $150.00

CARTRIDGE POUCH (MCKEEVER 30-40 KRAG) Dark brown leather pouch w/US embossed in oval on flap w/brass stud closure strap. Stitched leather belt loops on back & 20 stitched tan web ammo loops inside. RIA/1904 marked. Includes 14 live rounds. Avg. cond. $50.00

CARTRIDGE POUCH (MCKEEVER 30/40 KRAG): Dark brown leather w/US embossed in oval on body. 20 stitched dark tan web loops for 30/40 Krag ammo & brass stud closure flap. RIA marked & 1909 dated. Avg. cond. $26.00

CARTRIDGE POUCH (MCKEEVER 45/70): Dark brown leather w/"US" in oval on front. Waterville arsenal marked. Canvas loops for 45/70 inside. Above avg. cond. $47.00

CARTRIDGE POUCH (MCKEEVER STYLE 34/40): Rock Island Arsenal made & 1909 dated. Leather w/US in oval on front & canvas ammo loops inside for .34-40 Ammo. Avg. cond. $33.00

CAVALRY BRIDLE ASSEMBLY: Pre-WWI. Dark stiff leather w/brass & steel fittings. Two 1.5" brass discs on sides w/raised US national emblems. Avg. cond. $66.00

CAVALRY CARBINE SCABBARD (M1895): Saddle mounted & hmkd. Rock Island Arsenal. Dark leather w/curved brass plate at top. Straps for securing incl. Exc. cond. $198.00

CAVALRY CARBINE SCABBARD (M1895)

CAVALRY HORSE BIT: 5x7" "H" shaped iron body. RIA marked w/"N.S." inspector's initials. Fixed rings on 1 end & flexible rings on the other end. Above avg. cond. $30.00

CAVALRY HORSE GAS MASK CARRIER: Dark tan web body w/heavy webstrap & metal fittings. US marked. Above avg. cond. $34.00

CAVALRY PISTOL BELT (M1912): Dark tan web w/dark bronze finish fittings & saber "D" ring. Above avg. cond. $65.00

CAVALRY PISTOL BELT (M1912): Lt. OD web w/brass fittings & saber ring. Avg. cond. $16.00

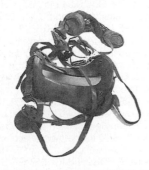

CAVALRY SADDLE (MCCLELLAN)

CAVALRY SADDLE (MCCLELLAN): Pre-WWI. 12" seat, brass fittings, woven hemp cinch, leather adj., side pads & metal stirrups, pair of stamped brass US eagles w/loops from rigging. Avg. cond. $160.00

CAVALRY SADDLE (MCCLELLAN): Pre-WWI. Basic saddle w/o straps & accessories, for 12" seat. Near mint cond. $145.00

CAVALRY SADDLE (MORGAN): Post Civil War. Russet leather w/accessories. One covered stirrup & straps. Woven horsehair cinch w/3 leather positioning disks. Mounting straps. Avg. cond. $180.00

CAVALRY SADDLE RIFLE BOOT FOR MCCLELLAN SADDLE (M1912): Marked Rock Island Arsenal, 1918. Heavy leather cup for rifle butt & leather pad to protect horse & strap to secure to saddle. Above avg. cond. $347.00

CAVALRY SPURS: Pre-WWI. Army cavalry spurs, nickel steel w/solid rowel. hmkd. 'RIA 1912' at back. Leather boot strap. Avg. cond. $101.00

CHINA EXPEDITIONARY SERVICE SWORD BELT AND HANGER: 1901. Brown russet leather belt with darkened brass clips, hooks for sword. Single claw matching belt buckle. Maker is Ridabocker, N.Y. Worn between 1901-03 in China service. Above avg. cond. $76.00

CIVIL WAR AMMO POUCH DEVICE (6TH CORPS): Unofficial device made of curved brass plate w/cross device fixed on face. Mounted by loop & lug. Above avg. cond. $75.00

CIVIL WAR BINOCULARS: French made & marked on eyepiece. "Army Navy Extra Powerful" on tube. Black finished brass tubes. Leather on barrels. Lenses good. Below avg. cond. $45.00

CIVIL WAR BINOCULARS: Gray metal body with black wrinkle finish on entire body & steel lens frames & black hard rubber eye lenses. 2 hanging loops on side. 4.5x8" extended. Avg. cond. $66.00

CIVIL WAR CAMP INDIV. COOK STOVE: Coffee pot style w/lid, pot & tin stove. Stove has two vents & covered fire place. Lamp incl. Above avg. cond. $145.00

CIVIL WAR CANTEEN: Tin const., cylindrical, 6" dia & 2" wide. Soldered seams & 3 soldered strap loops. Man's leather belt used as strap. Avg. cond. $72.00

CIVIL WAR CARBINE BRUSH & CORD: Brass brush w/fiber bristles & leather cord w/brass connector. Exc. cond. $27.00

CIVIL WAR CARTRIDGE BOX (PERCUSSION REVOLVER): Cavalry issued. Flap cover secures at bottom, two belt loops in back. Single chamber for rounds. No marks apparent. Black finish. Above avg. cond. $95.00

CIVIL WAR CAVALRY CARBINE SOCKET: Dark leather cylindrical tube 3" high w/ strap for cavalry saddle. Holds carbine, barrel down. Above avg. cond. $48.00

CIVIL WAR CLAY PIPE: 6" white clay. Bowl w/design of cannon & crossed rifles on either side. Avg. cond. $30.00

CIVIL WAR CLOTH KNAPSACK W/ STRAPS: Black treated cloth & black leather straps. Below avg. cond. $131.00

CIVIL WAR CLOTH KNAPSACK
W/STRAPS

CIVIL WAR DOCTOR INSTRUMENT: Small bronze disk w/spring loaded blade & lever on side. Fully operational & intended for cuts to promote bleeding. Above avg. cond. $79.00

CIVIL WAR DOCTOR TOOLS: Set of glass drawing cups for bleeding patients & wood gripped veining knife. Exc. cond. .. $80.00

CIVIL WAR DOCUMENT CARRIER: 16x2" tin cylinder w/cap for carrying documents. Black finish. Above avg. cond. $35.00

CIVIL WAR FLAG POLE TOP: Gilded tin eagle pole cap. Exc. cond. $244.00

CIVIL WAR FLUTED POWDER FLASK: Hmkd. on top. Thumb operated dispenser. Brass casing w/polished flutes & darkened areas between. Light leather cords thru carry rings. Above avg. cond. $55.00

CIVIL WAR FOLDING DISH: 4x8" metal dish w/4 folding sides & black lacquer finish. Functions normally & folds to easily stored size. Avg. cond. $76.00

CIVIL WAR KEYED FLUTE (PICCOLO): Wood w/nickel silver keys & bands. 1862 dated. Near mint cond. $147.00

CIVIL WAR MESS PLATE & UTENSILS: 8" dia. shallow bowl & dish of steel w/rolled edges. Fork & spoon w/US stamped on handles. Avg. cond. $91.00

CIVIL WAR MESS TIN CUP W/WIRE HANDLES: Lid & bottom show signs of heating. Avg. cond. $49.00

CIVIL WAR MINIATURE BRASS TELESCOPE IN ORIGINAL CASE: 3" folded & 6" extended 3 section brass & black case body, screw out lenses & excellent optics. Comes in 2 piece paper board cylinder & shows very little use. Probably used by officer, for compact carrying. Very rare. Above avg. cond. $160.00

CIVIL WAR POCKET COMPASS IN CASE: 8 pt az. ring w/floating pointer & locking lever. Glass cover, brass case. Kept in octagonal box w/blue velour lining & blue satin interior padded top. Above avg. cond. $164.00

CIVIL WAR SPURS: Brass. W/rowels, one rowel missing some teeth. Avg. cond. $145.00

CIVIL WAR STOVE: Nice tin stove w/ refillable kerosene burner & ventilated cook tower. 6" high, metal base & folding wire handles. Above avg. cond. $90.00

CIVIL WAR TABLE FORK: Narrow 3 tine design in steel w/pewter fittings on slab type bone grips. Above avg. cond. $11.00

CIVIL WAR TIN BOX: Silvered lid, decorated w/space for initials. Darkened sides. 3.5x2x2". Above avg. cond. $65.00

CIVIL WAR UNION BAND BASS DRUM STICK: Oak drum stick w/leather padded tip & marked US/1861 near grip. Exc. cond. $87.00

DISPATCH CASE (1914): Tan canvas folding body w/plastic grid covers for maps, pen/ pencil slots & detachable sling. Exc. cond. $28.00

ENTRENCHING TOOL (1880): Bright metal blade inset to reinforced metal hilt. Turned-ribbed oak handle w/'US' stamped at guard end. Hard leather scabbard w/ brass throat & belt ring. Stamped US near throat. Exc. cond. $275.50

ENTRENCHING TOOL (1880)

INDIAN WAR ERA ARMY BLANKET ROLL:
1884 blue-gray coarse wool blanket, dark
blue stripe on one side. Above avg. cond.
.... $93.00

INDIAN WAR ERA ARMY BLANKET ROLL

INDIAN WAR ERA ARMY CANTEEN: Has
US on one side & Signal corps emblem on
the other w/13 above & USV below & 54
at bottom of side. Exc. cond. $120.00

INDIAN WAR ERA ARMY CANTEEN

INDIAN WAR ERA BEDROLL BLANKET:
M1884 Blue/gray w/stripes. Above avg.
cond. $72.00
INDIAN WAR ERA CAVALRY LINK STRAP
FOR BRIDLE (1892): Dark brown leather
w/metal snap hook at one end & brass
fittings. RIA marked. Above avg. cond.
.... $20.00
INDIAN WAR ERA PICKET PIN SHOVEL:
Breakdown shovel head w/picket pin for
handle. Handle has hammer end w/claws

& shovel head is curved point spade type.
dated on back '1845 USA.' Exc. cond.
.... $70.00

INDIAN WAR ERA PICKET PIN SHOVEL

INDIAN WARS ERA BINOCULARS: French
made field glasses w/hmkd. on lens
frame. Extension tubes marked "Field/
Marine extra powerful." Leather covered
optic tubes. Below avg. cond. $40.00
LEATHER CASE FOR MODEL 1915 B. C.
SCOPE: Leather case w/interior wooden
supports for scope, leather lens cups &
metal brackets for accessories. Two
leather straps to secure case lid in transit.
Wide flap at one end w/strap & notch for
hanging on saddle. Faded stenciling on
top. Exc. cond. $32.00
MEDICAL INSTRUMENT/SUPPLY ROLL:
Orangish-dark tan canvas body w/lt. OD
trim & olive web straps. Inside has several
stitched olive web loops for instruments
(none included) & snap pockets covered
by flap w/rimless dark bronze eagle
snaps. US/Med. Dept. marked. Above
avg. cond. $20.00
MESS KIT (M1906): Traces of silver finish to
magnetic gray metal body & cover.
Handle marked 'U.S.' Avg. cond. .. $20.00
MILITARY EQUIPMENT PADLOCK: Pre-
1900. Thick sheet metal body w/pivoting
brass "U.S." marked key hole & safety
chain. Avg. cond. $34.00
NAVY BINOCULARS (6x30): Black finish
metal bodies covered in brown grain
leather. Eyepieces can be rotated to
amber tint. USN/Bureau of Navigation/
U.S. Naval Gun Factory marked. Serial
numbered. Includes fitted leather carrying
case. Avg. cond. $45.00
NAVY CARTRIDGE POUCH (M1889): Dark
leather w/USN embossed in oval on flap,
fitted wooden block insert, 2 leather belt
loops on back. Below avg. cond. .. $35.00
NAVY CARTRIDGE POUCH (MILLS):
Stenciled w/navy emblem on back. Light
green canvas pouch for two .45 auto pistol
clips. Above avg. cond. $37.00

NEW YORK STATE BUCKLE & BELT: Stamped brass buckle w/'SNY.' 2" wide black leather body. Avg. cond. $125.00

PISTOL HOLSTER (MILLS 1909 USN COLT MODEL .45 CAL.): Stitched & riveted lt. olive web body w/stud closure flap w/large brass snap & Mills marked riveted brass tip & brass belt hanger device. Faint Mills markings on web. Above avg. cond. $300.00

REVOLVER HOLSTER (M1897 .38 COLT): Dark brown leather w/riveted leather belt loop & brass stud closure half-flap. Brass ring at bottom w/rawhide leg thong. 1917 dated. US embossed in oval on body. Above avg. cond. $47.00

REVOLVER HOLSTER (M1897 .38 COLT): RIA marked & 1909 dated. Dark brown leather riveted belt loop & brass stud closure half-flap. US embossed in oval on body. Avg. cond. $30.00

REVOLVER HOLSTER (M1897 COLT): Folded & stitched brown leather w/brass stud closure half-flap, riveted belt loop. US embossed in oval on body & brass ring for leg thong. RIA marked & 1910 dated. Above avg. cond. $47.00

RIFLE SLING (1904) W/KRAG RIFLE BARREL BAND STILL ATTACHED: Dark oiled brown leather. RIA marked & 1904 dated. Barrel band w/sling swivel is "U" hmkd. Avg. cond. $40.00

RIFLE SLING (M1917 KERR): Tan web w/ metal fittings. Well marked. Incl. copy of info. sheet on this sling. Above avg. cond. $25.00

SPANISH AMERICAN WAR 3RD US VOL. HAVERSACK: Tan canvas w/straps & stenciled crossed rifles w/3/H at cross & VOL. over US. Avg. cond. $47.50

SPANISH AMERICAN WAR ARMY CANTEEN

SPANISH AMERICAN WAR ARMY CANTEEN: Tan canvas covered circular

tin body w/cork stopper on safety chain. U.S. marked. Includes correct pattern dark leather sling w/brass hooks at each end. Avg. cond. $101.00

SPANISH AMERICAN WAR ARMY CANTEEN W/UNIT MARKINGS: Tan canvas covered circular metal body w/cork stopper on safety chain & shoulder strap attachment loop on each side of body. US marked. Other side is stenciled "US VOL/ K/Inf/44/93." Avg. cond. $60.00

SPANISH AMERICAN WAR ARMY HAVERSACK: Dark tan canvas. Flap measures approx. 14x14". US/RIA marked. Brass loops for sling. Above avg. cond. $24.00

SPANISH AMERICAN WAR BACK PACK: Tan canvas w/US on front & pouch on underside of flap. Avg. cond. $30.00

SPANISH AMERICAN WAR CANTEEN: Canvas covered canteen w/stopper top on chain. Faint marks of coast Arty unit incl. crossed cannon show on side. Avg. cond. $53.00

SPANISH AMERICAN WAR CARTRIDGE BELT (MILLS 45/70): 50 loops & 6 handgun ammo loops. Unit mark on back of belt. Brass fittings. Above avg. cond. $244.00

SPANISH AMERICAN WAR CARTRIDGE BELT (MILLS STYLE 45/70): 3" wide black web belt w/45 stitched web ammo loops & brass fittings. Above avg. cond. $56.00

SPANISH AMERICAN WAR HAVERSACK: Tan canvas w/straps. Marked on outside of flap 'TROOP C, 55" & hand written name. 3 storage pouches on under side of flap & two side pouches under main storage area. Above avg. cond. $55.00

SPANISH AMERICAN WAR KANSAS NATIONAL GUARD UNIT CANTEEN: Circular tin body w/dark tan canvas cover. Front side has faint unit stencil over "U.S." & "K.N.G." below & "17/32" stenciled on opposite. Avg. cond. $56.50

SPANISH AMERICAN WAR CARTRIDGE BELT AMMO BELT: Rifle ammo loops, brass fittings & brass 'US' buckle plate. Above avg. cond. $98.00

TRENCH PERISCOPE CASE (M1917): Stitched brown leather body w/stud closure, hinged lid & stitched belt loop on back. Inspector marked. Above avg. cond. $35.00

WWI AMMO BELT (10 POCKET): 10 pouch belt tan canvas w/'LONG 5-18' marked on back side. Above avg. cond. $25.00

WWI AMMO BELT (9-POCKET): In olive web & canvas w/brass fittings. Small for attachment of pistol ammo pouch. Avg. cond. $25.00

WWI AMMO BELT (9-POCKET): Tan canvas & web w/brass fittings. Well marked & 1918 dated. .45 clip pouch. Above avg. cond. $38.00

WWI AMMO BELT (B.A.R. GUNNER 4-POCKET): Dark tan canvas & web w/ riveted metal butt cup & built-in .45 clip pouch & metal fittings. 1918 dated. Above avg. cond. $27.00

WWI AMMO BELT (M1914 MILLS) W/ HOLSTER: Mills M1914 mounted cartridge belt set w/1918 date on back & brass cavalry tag marked 2B36. 9 cartridge pouches. Model 1912 US .45 cal. auto pistol holster. US in large oval on flap. Swivel frog hmkd. 'Rock Island/1913' on back. Leather strap wrapped around base. Above avg. cond. $200.00

WWI AMMO BELT (M1914 MILLS)
W/HOLSTER

WWI AMMO BELT (MILLS 10 POCKET): Dark tan web w/Mills markings & 1918 date w/dark bronze colored fittings also Mills marked. Above avg. cond. $20.00

WWI AMMO BELT (MILLS 10 POCKET): Dark tan web w/Mills markings & 1918 date w/dark bronze colored fittings also Mills marked. Above avg. cond. $38.00

WWI AMMO BELT (MILLS 9 POCKET): Tan canvas w/Navy buttons on the pouches & Mills hmkd. on ends of belt. Avg. cond. $129.00

WWI AMMO BELT (MILLS 9 POUCH): Blackened brass fittings & Mills hmkd. on brass tips. Stenciled on inside, '56/ (crossed cannons)/ E/US.' Exc. cond. $68.00

WWI AMMO VEST (11 POCKET): Dark tan & lt. OD canvas. Well marked & 1918 dated. Near mint cond. $11.00

WWI ARMY CORPS SIGNAL FLAG KIT: Tan canvas carrier w/straps & labeled w/SC emblem/"US ARMY/FLAG KIT" Two flags

w/wooden rods & red/white panels. Above avg. cond. $20.00

WWI ARMY FENCING OUTFIT: Incl. Well padded wire mesh helmet w/full face & neck cover & reinforced open weave at eye level. Adj. leather restraint. Right handed gauntlet w/rigid leather & padded soft leather at fingers. Padded neck piece & padded chest protector. Avg. cond. $150.00

WWI ARMY FIRST AID INSTRUCTION PACKET: 2.5x4x4.5" sealed carton labeled to contain the first aid instruction packet-1917 dated. Above avg. cond. $45.00

WWI ARMY GUIDON COVER: Dark tan canvas body w/rope closure opening at one end. Above avg. cond. $34.00

WWI ARMY INDIVIDUAL DRESSING PACKET: Wrapped in original paper. Well marked & 1917 dated. Exc. cond. $17.00

WWI ARMY MEDICAL KIT: Forceps kit in canvas carrier, has forceps & scissors in fold up pouch. User's name, Service number & unit (88th Div.) printed on inside. Above avg. cond. $27.00

WWI ARMY SADDLE BLANKET: Black wool horse-side lining w/heavy gold cloth trim & quilted brown saddle-side cover w/gold felt stars on corners. Incl. mfg. cloth tag. Avg. cond. $80.00

WWI ARMY WOOL BLANKET: Lt. OD wool w/brown-shade stripe at either end. Avg. cond. $35.00

WWI ARMY WOOL BLANKET: Dark gray wool w/green stripe at either end. Marked U.S. & also has woven maker's label. Above avg. cond. $38.00

WWI ARMY WOOL BLANKET: Lt. OD wool w/OD stripe at either end. US in center & dark tan stitch reinforced edges. Above avg. cond. $72.00

WWI AVIATOR GOGGLES: Tear drop shaped lenses w/pale green tint. Spring held wind shields around eyes. Leather bridge at nose & headband. Above avg. cond. $45.00

WWI BACK PACK: Dark tan canvas body w/ dark tan web straps & dark metal fittings & matching mess kit carrier. US marked & 1918 dated. Includes tan canvas lower half that is "B.2nd/65" unit marked. Avg. cond. $11.50

WWI BACK PACK: Tan canvas w/tan web straps & brass fittings. US/RIA marked & 1918 dated. Above avg. cond. $12.00

WWI BAR CLIP BELT: Tan 3 pouch carrier w/ web strap. Dated on rear 7-18. Snap locked flaps. Near mint cond. $27.00

WWI BELT POUCHES: Two tan canvas pouches w/flap tops & belt loop. Above avg. cond. $20.00

WWI BINOCULARS (WAR DONATION): 8.25" long brass bodies w/Paris maker marked eye-pieces. Covered in black leather. Optics are clear. Comes in matching fitted leather case. Attached oval dog tag reads "Donated to U.S. Navy...." Avg. cond. $102.00

WWI BINOCULARS (WAR DONATION)

WWI BINOCULARS: Marked "France" on grommet at view end, Marked "Aviation" on each adj. barrel. 4 1/2 x power. Leather covered brass barrels. Black leather case w/purple velvet lining. Leather carry strap. Avg. cond. $70.00

WWI BINOCULARS

WWI BROWNING AMMO BELT FILLING MACHINE IN PORTABLE BOX: Heavy metal construction w/hand cranked feed control. Rotating grips to grasp & place shells on belt. Accessories stored below & Marked 'BROWNING BELT FILLING MACHINE MODEL OF 1918.' OD green box w/latches & leather carry strap. Exc. cond. $124.00

WWI CANTEEN & COVER: Dark tan canvas cover w/wire belt hanger. US marked & 1918 dated. Includes 1918 dated canteen. Above avg. cond. $11.00

WWI CANTEEN & COVER: dated 1915/RIA on inside of cover. Cover is stenciled NA (national army) on side. Avg. cond. $38.00

WWI CANTEEN COVER W/UNIT MARKINGS & CANTEEN: 1917 dated tan canvas cover w/wire belt hanger. US marked 1917 dated. Stenciled "63/Inf/C" markings. Incl. 1917 dated canteen. Above avg. cond. $20.00

WWI CANTEEN COVER: Lt. olive canvas w/ rimless bronze finish eagle snaps & wire belt hanger. US marked. Above avg. cond. $87.00

WWI CANTEEN COVER: Tan canvas w/wire belt hanger. 1918 dated. Avg. cond. $25.00

WWI CANTEEN COVER: Lt. OD canvas w/ dark tan bottom panel & trim & wire belt hanger. US/RIA/1917 marked. Above avg. cond. $40.00

WWI CANTEEN RIG: 1918 dated canteen & cup in 1918 dated tan canvas cover. Avg. cond. $11.00

WWI CANTEEN RIG: Aluminum canteen & cup w/stamped markings on bottom in 1918 dated tan canvas cover. Above avg. cond. $20.00

WWI CANTEEN RIG: Clean 1918 dated canteen & cup marked "2 D/16" on handle & 1918 dated canvas cover w/US/Inf equip ID disc. Above avg. cond. ... $33.00

WWI CANTEEN W/CAVALRY COVER: US marked & 1918 dated. Includes 1918 dated tan canvas cover. Above avg. cond. $20.00

WWI CANTEEN, CUP & COVER: 1918 dated canteen w/cup. Dark tan canvas cover US/RIA marked & 1917 dated. Canteen & cup rate Above avg. cond. Cover Exc. cond. $97.00

WWI CARLISLE BANDAGE POUCH: Dark tan canvas w/wire belt hanger & 2 snap closure flap. 1918 dated. Exc. cond. $32.00

WWI CARLISLE BANDAGE: Olive finish sealed tin. Well marked & 1918 dated. Avg. cond. $40.00

WWI CARRIER FOR SPRINGFIELD 1903 RIFLE: Tan canvas w/heavy leather flap top. Carry strap of web w/dark metal fittings. Above avg. cond. $75.00

WWI CARRIER: Leather. Semi-diamond shaped w/hinged rigid lid & brass stud & buckle latch. Marked Rock Island Arsenal/ 1917 on side. Three leather loops for strap on sides. Avg. cond. $20.00

WWI CARTRIDGE BELT (10-POCKET) W/ CARLISLE BANDAGE POUCH: Dark tan web & canvas w/dark bronze colored fittings. 1918 dated. Dark tan canvas pouch is 1918 dated. Exc. cond. .. $34.00

WWI CARTRIDGE BELT: Non-Mills variant of the 9 pouch ammo belt. Tan canvas web. Exc. cond. $87.00

WWI CAVALRY DISPATCH CASE: Leather case w/inner pouches for dispatches & heavy straps for fixing to saddle. Additional straps incl. web clip pouch for .45 auto dated 1918. Below avg. cond. $75.00

WWI CAVALRY HORSE RONDEL: Brass rondel from harness. Intertwined USA in center. Brass w/lead fill. Avg. cond. $25.00

WWI CAVALRY SADDLE BAG SET: Military saddle bags w/oval & raised US on flap of each pouch. Three strap security. Pebble grain leather exterior & removable white canvas liner. 1917 dated on cross shoulder band. Above avg. cond. $295.00

WWI CAVALRY SADDLE BAG SET

WWI CAVALRY SADDLE BAGS: Russet leather. Stiff pattern with cross leather strap. Buckle down tops. Named to owner. Avg. cond. $93.00

WWI CAVALRY BUGLE: Mouthpiece & double loop to horn. Below avg. cond. $100.00

WWI CAVALRY HORSE GAS MASK CARRIER: 2 compartment dark tan web body w/dark OD web straps & dark bronze metal fittings. US marked. Above avg. cond. $40.00

WWI CAVALRY SADDLE BLANKET: Dark blue wool w/yellow trim & yellow star on each forward corner. Exc. cond. ... $20.00

WWI CAVALRY SPURS: Nickel plated & marked US at back. Leather straps. Solid rowel. Avg. cond. $31.50

WWI CAVALRY SPURS: Nickel plated metal spurs marked US on underside & leather

boot strap & pad. Above avg. cond. $40.00

WWI COLLAPSIBLE FIELD WATER BUCKET: 11.5" dia. Tan canvas w/covered rope "bale" handle. US marked & 1918 dated. Above avg. cond. $11.00

WWI COMPASS IN POUCH: Alloy case in pocket watch form w/Wittnaur hmkd. on face. Black leather pouch. Avg. cond. $37.00

WWI COMPOUND WIRE CUTTERS.: Marked on one arm & dated 1918. Wood grips. Above avg. cond. $93.00

WWI DISPATCH CASE: All leather w/brass fittings. Stamped 'SERVICE CO/113TH INF.' Avg. cond. $35.00

WWI DISPATCH CASE: Leather w/OD wool blanket material as finish. Leather strap & metal hooks for carrying & single chamber w/full length flap on front. "Horstmann Co, Philadelphia" hmkd. embossed on inside of flap. Mint cond. $78.00

WWI DOCTOR HYPODERMIC KIT: Small, hinged lid alum. container marked "Med. Dept. U.S.A." on lid. Contains nickel finish syringe, 2 glass vials w/tiny pills inside, extra needles, etc. In OD felt pouch. Above avg. cond. $34.00

WWI ENGINEER LENSATIC COMPASS: Brass case w/windowed lid & index line. Sight & compass inside. Safety ring for carrying. Avg. cond. $35.00

WWI EQUIPMENT TRIPOD (M5): Brass body w/adj. legs & adj. mount. OD finish. Avg. cond. $133.00

WWI FIELD TELEPHONE (EE-3B): Wooden case w/metal top & phone inside w/ terminal mounts & wires. On back side is power crank. Above avg. cond. $44.00

WWI FIELD TOILETRY KIT: Dark tan cotton roll-up case w/several pockets. Contains field mirror, package of sewing needles, leather razor strop, small olive finish canister w/thimble & buttons, 2 soap dishes w/lift-off lids, 2 "Handy Grip" shaving sticks in metal canisters & pocket size sewing kit w/contents. Avg. cond. $65.00

WWI FIRST AID KIT: Canvas bi-fold case w/ snap lid. Marked faintly on front. Contents complete. Above avg. cond. $55.00

WWI FLARE CARTRIDGE POUCH: Dark tan web w/many stitched loops inside for cartridges. Lift-dot closure flap. Rings on back for sling. Avg. cond. $145.00

WWI FLARE PISTOL HOLDER: Tan canvas web holster w/full flap & snap closure. Leather tip. Avg. cond. $25.00

WWI FOLDING MAP CASE: Light OD canvas construction w/celluloid protected map pocket, pencil slots & carry case. Has actual map of trench fortifications for training in Spartanburg SC at Camp Wadsworth. Exc. cond. $82.00

WWI FOOT LOCKER (100TH AERO SQDN. OFFICER): 13x17x31" fiberboard foot locker in regulation pattern w/metal trim & triple hasps on lid. Handpainted w/2nd Army & Air Service cockade motifs & "Lt. R.S. Barker/Air Service/American E.F." & large rendition of 100th Aero Sqdn. insignia-devil riding downward falling bomb. Complete w/inner tray. Above avg. cond. $440.00

WWI GAS ALARM: Manually operated by swinging green painted wood handle. Copper plated steel bell w/clapper & 'GAS' painted on two sides. Avg. cond. .. $50.00

WWI GAS ALARM: Multi-piece wooden constr. Has handle that acts as a rachet & when turned against body makes sharp "clicking" sound. Avg. cond. $34.00

WWI GAS MASK (103RD M. G. BN., 26TH DIV.): Dark tan canvas carrier bag w/dark tan web straps, large unit insignia design painted on one side. Includes plaster repair envelope. Avg. cond. $118.00

WWI GAS MASK: 3x4x1.5" yellow painted tin box body w/perforations in back. Mouth piece on metal spout in top w/rubber tip. Nose clip attached w/short piece of string. Above avg. cond. $34.00

WWI GAS MASK: In dark tan canvas carrier w/name inked on body. Plastic lenses & soft connector tube. Incl. anti-dimstick & plaster repair envelope. Avg. cond. $28.00

WWI GAS MASK: Tan canvas carrier w/tan web straps. Mask is soft w/"butterfly" valve. Incl. anti-dim stick & plaster repair envelope. Faint ink markings on side of carrier. Above avg. cond. $82.00

WWI GAS MASK: W/good lenses & intact "butterfly" valve & soft flexible hose. In canvas carrier name to a pvt. in HQ Co. 69th Arty CAC AEF. Avg. cond. $34.00

WWI GAS SIREN FOR TRENCHES: Hand held & blown. Black oxide finish w/chain & pocket hook. Exc. cond. $53.50

WWI GRENADE POUCH (11-POCKET): Dark tan canvas w/web straps. Exc. cond. $20.00

WWI HAVERSACK W/AERO SQDN. UNIT MARKINGS: Lt. OD canvas body w/ 12x12" flap & metal snap hooks for sling. RIA marked & 1914 dated. Flap stenciled "24th/Aero. Sqdn./KANS. Inside also stenciled w/unit. Avg. cond. $30.00

WWI MACHINE GUN SHOULDER STOCK (M1919A6): Gray parkerized metal stock.

For Browning M1919A6 weapon. Avg. cond. $20.00

WWI MARCH COMPASS (MARK VII MOD. E.): By Sperry Gyroscope Co. Olive finish metal body. Well marked. Brown leather carrying case w/wire belt hanger device. Above avg. cond. $45.00

WWI MARKING KIT: Complete set of dies & brass anvil w/hammer for marking tags, tools etc. Stored in wood box-OD finish, stenciled & w/1st Sgt tag for Co. C, 74th inf. Above avg. cond. $118.00

WWI MEDIC BELT (10-POCKET): Dark tan canvas w/dark tan web pocket flaps w/ rimmed eagle snap closures & dark bronze colored metal fittings. Mills marked. Above avg. cond. $112.00

WWI MEDICAL BELT (MILLS M1910 ENLISTED): Dark tan canvas & web w/ dark bronze metal fittings. Mills marked. Eagle snap closure flaps. Above avg. cond. $40.00

WWI MEDICAL BELT (MILLS M1910 OFFICER): Dark tan canvas web adj. belt w/one large & one small pocket on each side & dark bronze colored fittings. Lieut.'s name inked on back. Mills marked. Above avg. cond. $101.00

WWI MEDICAL KIT: Tan canvas pouch w/ snap flap. Complete contents. Marked US on front & dated 10-18 inside. Webstrap & belt clip. Above avg. cond. $40.00

WWI MUSICIAN POUCH: OD wool over leather w/leather strap. Full flap lid w/ leather latch tab. Handwritten name & 'AEFU' Band. Avg. cond. $30.00

WWI N.Y. GUARD CANTEEN COVER: Dark tan canvas body w/wire belt hanger. Stenciled "N.Y.G." on front. Above avg. cond. $28.00

WWI NAVAL BINOCULARS: Brass tubes w/ partial leather wrap. hmkd. on left eyepiece pivot arm & Navy marked at tube bell end. Black finish on metal parts. Avg. cond. $35.00

WWI NAVY BINOCULARS: Black finish brass bodies Bausch & Lomb/U.S. Navy marked. Serial numbered. 6 power. Brown crinkle texture leather covered. Includes leather neck strap. Adj. eyepieces w/ filters. Above avg. cond. $40.00

WWI NAVY DOG TAG: Oval-shaped. Man's name, 1917 dated & USN marked on front w/thumb print on reverse side. Clean. Above avg. cond. $28.00

WWI OFFICER SWAGGER STICK: Rosewood. Has brass butt from rifle cartridge & metal point from brass casing & jacketed bullet. Exc. cond. $50.00

WWI PANORAMIC SIGHT: Brass & steel const. w/two prismatic lenses. Multiple calibrations. hmkd. Warner Swazey Co. & dated 1917. Exc. cond. $125.00

WWI PISTOL BELT (MILLS): W/stenciled unit markings. Tan web w/brass fittings. Mills marked. Faint arty unit markings. Avg. cond. $23.00

WWI PISTOL BELT & CARLISLE BANDAGE POUCH: Tan web belt w/Mills marked brass fittings & 1918 dated tan web pouch. Above avg. cond. $26.00

WWI PISTOL HOLSTER (.45): Dark brown leather w/US embossed in oval on flap & wire belt hanger device. 1918 dated. Avg. cond. $36.00

WWI PISTOL HOLSTER (.45): Dark brown leather w/US embossed in oval on flap & wire belt hanger. Boyt/inspector marked. Above avg. cond. $28.00

WWI PISTOL HOLSTER (.45): Dark brown leather w/US embossed in oval on stud closure flap & wire belt hanger device. Inspector marked. Avg. cond. $45.00

WWI PISTOL HOLSTER (.45): Dark brown leather w/US embossed in oval on stud closure flap & wire belt hanger. 1918 dated. Above avg. cond. $45.00

WWI PISTOL LANYARD: Dark tan cord w/ metal slide & snap hook. Exc. cond. $13.00

WWI POCKET COMPASS: Brass case w/ floating needle & fixed az. ring. Removable lid. Avg. cond. $20.00

WWI POCKET COMPASS: Dull nickel finish body. "Eng. Dept./U.S.A. 1918" marked on hinged lid. Face "USA Nite" marked. Above avg. cond. $30.00

WWI RED CROSS BAG: OD tan twill w/red crosses in front & back & red silk lining. One piece w/handle. Multi-purpose utility bag. Avg. cond. $12.00

WWI REVOLVER HOLSTER (M1897 .38 COLT): Folded & stitched brown leather body w/US embossed in oval on body & brass stud closure half-flap & riveted belt loop & brass lanyard ring. 1918 dated. Above avg. cond. $49.00

WWI REVOLVER HOLSTER (M1897 COLT): Dark brown leather w/US embossed in oval on body & brass stud closure half-flap. 1918 dated. Avg. cond...........$35.00

WWI RIFLE SCABBARD (M1904): Dark leather body. RIA marked. Other faint markings. $45.00

WWI RIFLE SLING: Brown leather w/metal fittings. Well marked & 1918 dated. Above avg. cond. $23.00

WWI SHORT JAWED PLIERS: Has US on one arm. Operable. Avg. cond. $23.00

WWI SHOTGUN SHELL BELT: Heavy canvas web w/darkened metal fittings & cotton loops for shells. Near mint cond. $80.00

WWI SHOULDER CARRIED MUSETTE STYLE BAG.: Marked 'US/682' on flap & Rock Island Arsenal inside. Three storage pouches on underside of flap & five storage pouches inside main area. Tan canvas. Exc. cond. $55.00

WWI SHOVEL (T HANDLE) W/COVER: Metal throat of spade & wooden handle U.S. marked. Olive finish. Lt. OD & dark tan canvas/web cover w/wire belt hanger. US marked & 1918 dated. Above avg. cond. $76.00

WWI SHOVEL (T HANDLE): Entrenching tool w/spade blade & t-handle. Marked US on shaft. Shovel painted dark red w/black grip. Avg. cond. $35.00

WWI SHOVEL COVER (T HANDLE): Dark tan web w/wire belt hanger. US marked & 1918 dated. Exc. cond. $29.00

WWI SIGNAL CORPS SIGNAL FLAG KIT: Two flags on wood poles, each red/white & stored in tan canvas type m-113 case w/ straps & printed signal corps label. Above avg. cond. $24.00

WWI SIGNAL CORPS SIGNAL FLAGS IN CANVAS CASE: Std R/W flags on wood rods. Canvas case w/stamped emblem & US ARMY/FLAG Kit below. Carry Strap included. Above avg. cond. $23.00

WWI SIGNAL CORPS SIGNAL FLAGS: 9 flags w/42" wood rods. Avg. cond. $20.00

WWI SIGNAL TRAINING CARDS: Complete set in orig. box. Playing card size. Avg. cond. $25.00

WWI SQUAD LEADER POUCH: Dark tan canvas w/twin lift-dot fasteners on flap. Web carrying strap. US marked & 1918 dated. Exc. cond. $23.00

WWI TELEGRAPHY/BUZZER SYSTEM: Signal corps system w/battery powered telegraphy key & buzzer circuit w/control switch. Portable leather case w/stenciled legend on lid. Instructions inside lid. Model 1914. Exc. cond. $65.00

WWI TELESCOPE (M1915A1) W/CASE: Binocular viewing w/prismatic lenses & adjustments for elev. & azimuth. Leather case w/accessories & spares. Above avg. cond. $145.00

WWI TRENCH BINOCULARS: Leather carrier & tripod. OD finish w/leather covers for eyepieces. Accessories included in carrier. Labeled on face. Orig. straps incl. Tripod has wood legs w/metal extensions & pivoting/swiveling base for binoculars.

Lockable az. ring. Adjustable for height & stability. Exc. cond. $211.00

WWI TRENCH PERISCOPE CASE: Leather case w/leather hinged flip lid, loops for carry strap & belt loop on back. Marked near top B. T. & CO/ 14. Good. Above avg. cond. $21.00

WWI TRENCH PERISCOPE: Wood box w/ mirrors at each end & adj. stake for stability. 7 wire bands for additional strength. OD finish. Avg. cond. $61.00

WWI TRENCH SHOTGUN BELT: 18 round capacity in tan light canvas & elastic belt. Above avg. cond. $66.00

WWI UNIT MESS CONTAINER: Tin box 16.5x10x8" w/snap on lid labeled USQMC & hmkd. Avg. cond. $25.00

WWI USMC .45 PISTOL CLIP POUCH: Dark tan canvas & web w/twin lift-dot closure flap that is U.S.M.C. marked. 1918 dated. R. H. Long maker. Exc. cond. $50.00

WWI USMC .45 PISTOL CLIP POUCH: Tan canvas & web w/twin lift-dot closure flap that is U.S.M.C. marked & 1918 dated. Above avg. cond. $50.00

WWI USMC AMMO POUCH (3-POCKET): Dark tan canvas w/lift-dot closure flaps. USMC marked & 1918 dated. Exc. cond. $71.00

WWI USMC AMMO POUCH (3-POCKET)

WWI USMC BACK PACK LOWER-HALF: Dark tan canvas w/web straps & leather connector. Faint U.S.M.C. markings. Above avg. cond. $27.00

WWI USMC FIRST-AID BANDAGE: Paper wrapped bandage w/printed EG&A design

on front & 1917 dated USMC QM markings. Avg. cond. $72.00

WWI USMC PISTOL BELT (MILLS): Dark tan web w/brass fittings. Mills marked. Has USMC button snap for pistol clip pouch. Stenciled markings on back side. Avg. cond. $86.00

WWI USMC PISTOL BELT RIG: Dark tan web belt w/brass fittings w/U.S.M.C. marked dark tan canvas & web .45 clip pouch, 1918 dated & U.S.M.C. marked Carlisle bandage pouch, 1918 dated & U.S. marked tan canvas canteen cover, 1918 dated w/canteen & cup. Avg. cond. $145.00

WWI USMC PISTOL BELT RIG

WWI WATER BAG: Portable w/canvas strap & crossed ropes on bottom. hmkd. & dated 1918 on bottom & 'CO G/131st Inf' & commanders name. Above avg. cond. $20.00

WWI WEB BELT W/8 POUCHES: Long mfg. 1917 dated. Two wide sections w/4 pouches each & std width web interconnect. Ea. side has two regular sized pouches & two large clip sized pouches. Above avg. cond. $25.00

WWI WIRE CUTTER: Compound cutter w/ heavy rubber insulated grips & 5000 volt limit stamped on cutting head. Avg. cond. $90.00

WWI WRISTWATCH: Stem wound, black face radium treated night glow numerals w/hmkd. (Leonard West) on face. Nickel plated case. Exc. cond. $108.00

B. 1920 - 1945

1920s ARMY OFFICER MAP CASE: 5.5x11" lt. brown fold-up leather case. Stitched slots for pens/pencils on one side. Other unfolds to show plastic grid. QM & 1921 marked. Includes adj. leather shoulder strap. Exc. cond. $63.00

1930s ARMY BLANKET: OD brown wool w/ US in center & Phila. QM depot tag on side. Dated on tag 8-12-35. Above avg. cond. $23.00

1930s ARMY BLANKET: Stenciled Artillery unit on center (5th ARTY) & dated 1935 on mfg. tag. OD brown. Above avg. cond. $45.00

1930s CAVALRY CANTEEN COVER W/ CANTEEN: US marked canvas cover has adj. brown leather strap w/heavy metal snap hook at top. 1934 dated. Includes WWI design aluminum canteen & cup. Avg. cond. $75.00

1930s CAVALRY CANTEEN COVER: Dark tan canvas cover w/adj. leather strap w/ metal snap hook at top. US marked & 1935 dated. Includes 1918 dated canteen. Above avg. cond. $39.00

CARTRIDGE BELT (M1923): US inked pocket w/9-others & faint 1943/maker. Snap straps inside each pocket. Avg. cond. $20.00

GOGGLES (M1938 RESISTOL): Nickel frames w/clear glass lenses & rubber face pad & black elastic headband. Left lens shows clouding. Come in Strauss & Buegeleisen marked oval aluminum case w/hinged lid. Avg. cond. $72.00

HAVERSACK: Pre-WWII. Tan canvas w/ leather bottom & canvas strap. Buttoned back pouch & roomy front pouch w/divider. Flap w/strap. Avg. cond. $11.00

MORTAR SIGHT (60MM): Black metal case w/mounting flange & two calibration knobs & two bubble levels. Above avg. cond. $37.00

NAVY LANDING PARTY PISTOL CLIP POUCH (MILLS .45 CAL.): Dark tan web body w/outer surfaces painted in black & twin lift-dot closures on flap. Mills marked & 1919 dated. Above avg. cond. .. $30.00

USMC PADLOCK: Brass construction w/ labeled key incl. Etched oval w/USMC stamped in middle. Exc. cond. $45.00

WWII AAF AIRCREW HEADSET: Twin spring metal head bands w/russet leather covers support two padded earphones. Boom mike mount on exterior of one earphone. Twist wire cord w/male connector. Above avg. cond. $40.00

WWII AAF AIRCREW SURVIVAL WHISTLE: Nickel plated. English marked. On hanger ring. Avg. cond. $23.00

WWII AAF AIRCREW SURVIVAL WHISTLE: Small size police style in nickel plated brass. English maker marked. Above avg. cond. $36.00

WWII AAF AIRCREW THROAT MIKE: Black elastic strap to hold against vocal cords & 2 mikes on flex strap to press against throat. Exc. cond. $20.00

WWII AAF ANTI-FLAK GOGGLES: OD finish & elastic head band. No lens, just slots in the metal to allow adequate vision while protecting eye area. Still wrapped in protective paper. Exc. cond. $100.00

WWII AAF ANTI-FLAK GOGGLES: OD steel w/visibility slots & contoured to fit face. Padded for comfort & has elastic headband. Near mint cond. $200.00

WWII AAF AVIATOR KIT BAG (AN-6505-1): Dark tan canvas w/zippered opening & lt. OD web grab handles. Well marked. Includes circular aluminum ID number tag. Avg. cond. $30.00

WWII AAF AVIATOR KIT BAG (AN-6505-1): Lt. OD canvas body w/zipper closure & dual web carry handles. Well marked. Has AAF patch design ink stamp markings. Avg. cond. $61.00

WWII AAF AVIATOR SUNGLASSES: Thin metal wire frames w/dark tinted lenses & plastic coated wrap-around ear pieces. In brown leather case, cotton lined. Avg. cond. $20.00

WWII AAF AVIATOR SUNGLASSES: Green tint to lenses, bridge & forehead pads, wire frame. Lined leather case w/snap flap. Exc. cond. $50.00

WWII AAF B-17 GUNNER KNEE PADS: Leather exteriors & sheepskin interiors w/ padded strap. Above avg. cond. $212.00

WWII AAF BOMBARDIER STOP WATCH: Black face, sweep second hand, inner dial for 5/10 min. times. Specs on back & dated 44. Pocket watch style w/stem wind. Above avg. cond. $50.00

WWII AAF BOMBARDIER/NAVIGATORS MASTER WATCH: Elgin model. Black face w/dual dial 24 hr ability & sweep second hand. Stem wound pocket watch style. Nickel plated case. Exc. cond. $165.00

WWII AAF BOMBER CREWMAN FLAK VEST: 3 piece. Brown canvas w/white velveteen lining. Front panel, back panel & apron. Red break-away handle for dropping armor quickly in case of bail-out. Avg. cond. $328.00

WWII AAF CLOTH AVIATION CHART: 2-sided. Color on rayon. Includes Sheet A (43/A) France, Belgium & Holland & Sheet B (43/B) German-Swiss Frontier/France & Spain. Folded. Near mint cond. .. $105.00

WWII AAF CLOTH AVIATION CHART: Color printed on white rayon. 2-sided. No. 4, Tyrol & No. 6, Balkans. 1943 dated. Some fraying to edges. Above avg. cond. $133.00

WWII AAF CLOTH AVIATION CHART: Color.
2-sided on white rayon. Includes Peking
NJ 50 & Ryojun NJ 51. 1944 dated. Above
avg. cond. $13.00

WWII AAF CLOTH AVIATION CHART:
Large-size. Printed on white rayon.
Includes North & South Burma. Scale
1:1,000,000. Marked "Printed at the
Survey of India Officers (P.L.O.). Avg.
cond. $82.00

WWII AAF CLOTH AVIATION CHART: Multi-
color on white rayon. 2-sided. Cyrenaica &
Anglo-Egyptian-Sudan. Above avg. cond.
.... $100.00

WWII AAF CLOTH AVIATION CHART: No.
30, South Burma & No. 31, North Burma.
2-sided. Color on white rayon. Avg. cond.
.... $23.00

WWII AAF CLOTH AVIATION CHART:
No.133-K'Un-Ming, Yunnan, China to
Chabua, Assam, India Western & Eastern
portions. Colorful. 2-sided on white rayon.
1944 dated. Folded. Exc. cond. .. $184.00

WWII AAF COLD WEATHER FIELD
SHELTER AIR MATTRESS (A-2): Cold
weather Field shelter air mattress type A-
2. Marked US Air Corps. Dated November
1941, Tan cotton body w/black rubberized
underside. Incl. inflation instr. 36x75" plus
attachment. Documentation. Exc. cond
.... $50.00

WWII AAF COMPASS (ARMY TYPE D-12
FLOATING AZ): 6.5" in Dia & 5" high w/
floating az. indicator showing all four
cardinal directions at once. Rotatable az.
ring on outside w/N-S axis emphasized w/
parallel lines. Three mounting points on
sides. Exc. cond. $80.00

WWII AAF COMPASS IN BOX: Pocket
watch style in alloy case w/slip cover &
box. Box labeled 'COMPASS ASSEMBLY
POCKET TYPE' w/specs & hmkd.
'Longines-Wittnaur Watch Co.' 1941. Near
mint cond. $129.00

WWII AAF CRASH AX: Marked RP-4 on
head, green w/pick end & ax end.
Insulated grip to 20,000 volts. Above avg.
cond. $39.50

WWII AAF ESCAPE COMPASS (BRITISH
MADE): 15mm dia. Exc. cond. $36.00

WWII AAF FIGHTER PILOT SEAT PACK W/
LIFE RAFT: Canvas case w/zipper
enclosure holding raft & bottle. Heavy
steel clips to attach the pack to the chute
harness. Avg. cond. $72.00

WWII AAF FIRST AID KIT W/CONTENTS:
Dark tan canvas impregnated body w/
zippered sides, pockets & snaps for
bulkhead. Well marked w/painted red
cross design. Includes several contents:
bandages, gauze, tourniquet & more.
Above avg. cond. $37.00

WWII AAF FIRST AID KIT: OD green canvas
w/zipper closures & title. US medical
emblem on front, Red Cross emblem at
one end. Most contents intact. Above avg.
cond. $24.00

WWII AAF FLIGHT BAG: Leather. Brief case
style w/two straps & brass latch. Gilt label
on front reads 'AIRCRAFT INSPECTORS
KIT/AIR FORCE/UNITED STATES ARMY.'
Multiple compartments inside. Above avg.
cond. $177.00

WWII AAF FLIGHT GOGGLES (AN-6530):
Tinted green lenses in metal frames w/
HMKD. 'AN-6530' on bridge hinge. One
piece rubber cushion surrounds frame.
Black elastic band. Exc. cond. $201.00

WWII AAF FLIGHT GOGGLES (E-1 DARK
ADAPTATION): Folding bodies w/red
tinted plastic lenses. In Am. Optical maker
box w/AF contract markings. Exc. cond.
.... $11.00

WWII AAF FLIGHT GOGGLES LENS SET
(B-8): 8 plastic lenses in various tints in
cotton carrier w/AAF markings. Exc. cond.
.... $11.00

WWII AAF FLIGHT HELMET EARCUPS:
Molded black rubber oval-shaped bodies
w/thick chamois padding. NAF marked.
Exc. cond $27.00

WWII AAF FLIGHT SUNGLASSES (SP1-
111): Model SP1-111 w/green tinted
lenses, cushion wire earpieces & nose &
forehead pads. Brown cardboard case w/
gilt AAF emblem & name & specs, paper
guarantee & snap closure. Above avg.
cond. $96.00

WWII AAF FLIGHT SUNGLASSES
(SP1-111)

WWII AAF HEADSET (TH-37): Web covered head bands & chamois covered earpads. Above avg. cond. $37.00

WWII AAF INDIVIDUAL PARACHUTE: By Hayes Mfg. Chute case w/all retaining straps & wires in place but no chute or shrouds. D-ring & cable mounted. Harness intact. Inspection record shows use 1944-1949. Avg. cond. $475.00

WWII AAF LIFE RAFT RADAR REFLECTOR KIT: Mint unissued & in orig. box-sealed. dated June 22, 1945. By Vendo Co. KCMO. Exc. cond. $20.00

WWII AAF MAE WEST LIFE PRESERVER (AN-6519-1): Yellow cotton body w/yellow web straps & rubber inflation tubes. 1944 dated. Above avg. cond. $38.00

WWII AAF MAE WEST LIFE PRESERVER (AN-6519-1): Yellow. Dated Feb. 14, 1945. hmkd. Firestone Co. Auto & manual inflation & straps to secure. Exc. cond. $165.00

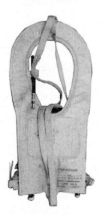

WWII AAF MAE WEST LIFE PRESERVER
(AN-6519-1)

WWII AAF MAE WEST LIFE PRESERVER (B-3): Yellow cotton body w/yellow web straps & leather panel in front of body. 1941 dated QM markings. Above avg. cond. $145.00

WWII AAF MAE WEST LIFE PRESERVER (B-4): Bright yellow cotton body w/yellow web straps & manual inflation tubes. AAF marked & 1943 dated. Inspection dates stenciled on front. Above avg. cond. $139.00

WWII AAF MAE WEST LIFE PRESERVER (B-4): Yellow fabric over rubber bladders w/straps. Type B-4 dated 1942. Above avg. cond. $59.00

WWII AAF MAE WEST LIFE PRESERVER (B-5): Dated Oct. 1944. Yellow waterproof canvas over bladders. Auto & self inflation capability. Web straps & rings to secure. Exc. cond. $180.00

WWII AAF MAE WEST LIFE PRESERVER
(B-4)

WWII AAF MAE WEST LIFE PRESERVER (B-5): Dated Oct. 1945. Yellow waterproof canvas over bladders. Auto & self inflation capability. Web straps & rings to secure. Exc. cond. $91.00

WWII AAF MAE WEST LIFE PRESERVER
(B-5)

WWII AAF MECHANIC APRON (B-1): Dark olive canvas body w/stitched pockets & web straps. Well marked w/AAF ink stamp markings. Exc. cond. $40.00

WWII AAF MECHANIC APRON (B-1): Olive canvas w/several pockets & web straps. Well marked. Above avg. cond. $25.00

WWII AAF NAVIGATOR MASTER WATCH: Pocket style w/specs on back. hmkd.

"Hamilton Watch Co." & dated 42. 24 hr. dial w/sweep second hand, stem set & wind. Above avg. cond. $163.00

WWII AAF NAVIGATOR STOP WATCH (A-8): Elgin brand. Nickel case is well marked on back. Crystal in nice shape. Works. Comes in worn issue carton w/1943 dated & A. C. marked spec. label. Above avg. cond. $135.00

WWII AAF NAVIGATOR STOP WATCH (A-8): Elgin brand, Nickel case is well marked on reserve 1944 contract markings. Nice crystal. Black dial. Works. Markings on back somewhat faint. Above avg. cond. $95.00

WWII AAF NAVIGATOR STOP WATCH (A-8): Pocket style hmkd. 'Elgin' on specs. Ten sec dial & 5 min. inner dial. Stem wound. Hinged rear for maintenance. 1944. Above avg. cond. $76.00

WWII AAF NAVIGATOR WATCH (A-7A): 12/24 hr dial, sweep sec hand & stem set & wound. Two piece band. Avg. cond. $223.00

WWII AAF NAVIGATOR WATCH (A-17): Nickel body is very well marked on reverse. Number on black face. Waltham maker. On black leather wristband. Avg. cond. $145.00

WWII AAF NAVIGATOR WATCH (A-17): Waltham. Nickel case is well marked on reverse w/contract markings & U.S. Property. Crystal clean. Black dial. Comes on brown leather wristband w/gold leaf "Genuine Leather." Works. Above avg. cond. $196.00

WWII AAF NAVIGATOR WATCH (A-17A): Nickel case is U.S. Property/contract marked on back. Nice crystal w/only couple minor scratches w/numbers on black dial. Works. Above avg. cond. $159.00

WWII AAF NAVIGATOR WATCH CARRY CASE: Gray metal case w/shock mounting inside for watch & window in top to view. Brass spec plate. Near mint cond. $86.00

WWII AAF NAVIGATOR WATCH CASE IN ORIGINAL BOX: Shock-proof carrying case for the master navigation watches (watch not included) utilized by navigators of bombing aircraft in World War Above avg. cond. The case is a cylindrical two-piece "can" with a window in the top so the watch could be observed without removing it from its shock-proof mounting. Manufactured by the Geo. H. Adamson Co. Mint cond. $75.00

WWII AAF OFFICER FOOTLOCKER: GI footlocker in OD finish plywood. Maker marked & 1942 dated inside lid. "U.S."

marked outside. All metal fittings. Above avg. cond. $40.00

WWII AAF OXYGEN MASK (A-10): 1942 dated rubber mask w/web straps & attaching rings for helmet & hose w/connector for oxygen. Size small. Above avg. cond. $126.00

WWII AAF OXYGEN MASK (A-10): Mfg. date 4/43. Imprinted spec disk at front. Mask in generally good cond. but some cracking on edges & inside. Complete set of web straps & snaps to mount. Hose shows age & brittleness but still intact. Above avg. cond. $61.00

WWII AAF OXYGEN MASK (A-14): Molded green rubber mask w/molded-in AAF markings, flexible rubber hose & dark OD web straps. W/instructions & accessories. In issue pressed paper carton w/1944 dated & AC marked spec label. Above avg. cond. $101.00

WWII AAF OXYGEN MASK (A-14)

WWII AAF OXYGEN MASK (A-14): 1944 dated w/soft rubber, avionics, web straps & ribbed hose w/connector. Above avg. cond. $47.00

WWII AAF OXYGEN MASK (A-14): In box. Dated 4-45, size medium. Web straps for mounting. Two other connector options inside box. Above avg. cond. $57.00

WWII AAF OXYGEN MASK (A-14): Medium size w/soft supple rubber & full avionics. Web straps mate to helmet. Ribbed hose complete w/connector. Orig. issue box. Nov. 44 date. Exc. cond. $107.00

WWII AAF OXYGEN MASK (A-9): Soft rubber w/gray web mounting straps. 1-42 dated on front & sized as short. Ribbed flex hose w/connector. Above avg. cond. $135.00

WWII AAF SEWING KIT: Light OD cotton roll-up pouch contains thread, safety pins. Above avg. cond. $26.00

WWII AAF SEXTANT (A-10): Optical sextant, battery powered, drum recording, celestial observation device. Orig. wood box w/accessories & spares. Dated 1942 & last

inspection 1945. Above avg. cond.
.... $60.00

WWII AAF SEXTANT (A-10)

WWII AAF SEXTANT (A-10A): Bubble
collimator, optics, elevation control &
power supply all in single unit. Case
stores spares & dome hanger. Exc. cond.
.... $96.00
WWII AAF SEXTANT (AN-5851-1):
10x10x11" hinged lid, black bakelite case
w/instruction & nomenclature plates on lid.
Massive, hand held unit. Includes hanger
bracket for inside the aircraft. Avg. cond.
.... $38.00
WWII AAF WRIST COMPASS (L-1): 47mm
dia. Bakelite/plastic body. Well marked.
Exc. cond. $31.00
WWII AAF WRIST WATCH (A-1): Nickel
body is very well marked on reverse w/
AAF contract markings. Black dial. Elgin
brand. On nice dark OD poplin wristband.
Above avg. cond. $107.00
WWII AAF WRIST WATCH (A-11): Elgin
brand. Nickel body is AAF marked on
reverse. Works. Nice crystal. On dark OD
poplin adj. wrist band. Gov't. inspection
.... $223.00
WWII AAF WRIST WATCH (A-11): Elgin
brand. Nickel body is well marked on
reverse w/AF contract markings. White
numbers on black dial. Crystal has no
major scratches. Comes on dark tan
ribbed nylon wristband. Avg. cond.
.... $93.00
WWII AAF WRIST WATCH (A-11): Elgin
brand. Nickel case is AAF marked on
reverse. Nice crystal. Runs. No band.
Gov't. inspection tag still attached. Non-
hacking type. Near mint cond.
.... $222.00
WWII AAF WRIST WATCH (A-11): Nickel
body is well marked on reverse w/USAAF
contract markings. Black dial. Crystal
good. On OD poplin wrist band. Above
avg. cond. $185.00
WWII AAF WRIST WATCH (A-17A): Small
faced dial w/black background, 24 hr. dial,

sweep second hand. Stem wound &
luminescent face. Specs on back. Tan one
piece wrist band. Exc. cond. $175.00
WWII AIRBORNE HELMET FIRST-AID KIT
POUCH: Dark OD cotton body is rubber
lined & has 4 dark tan web ties. Near mint
cond. $80.00
WWII AIRBORNE NIGHT SPOTTER DISKS:
Circular disks w/glow in dark center, worn
on helmets for night ID. Plastic encased &
drilled for attaching cord. Above avg.
cond. $55.00
WWII AIRBORNE NIGHT SPOTTER DISKS:
Rare night visibility device attached to
helmets by pathfinders & other night
operations types. Cloth storage case.
Above avg. cond. $177.00

WWII AIRBORNE NIGHT SPOTTER DISKS

WWII AMMO BAG: British made canvas
ammo bag for Thompson gun clips. Dark
green w/straps. Used mostly by
paratroops. Exc. cond. $35.00
WWII AMMO BELT (10 POCKET): Dark OD
web w/metal fittings. US marked & 1944
dated. Nice shape. Above avg. cond.
.... $30.00
WWII AMMO BELT (10 POCKET): Dark OD
web w/metal fittings. US marked. Above
avg. cond. $17.00
WWII AMMO BELT (10 POCKET): Lt. OD &
dark tan web w/metal fittings. US marked
& 1942 dated. Above avg. cond. .. $20.00
WWII AMMO BELT (10 POCKET): Lt. OD
web w/metal fittings. US/Boyt marked &
1942 dated. Avg. cond. $30.00
WWII AMMO BELT (BAR 6 POCKET): Lt.
OD canvas & web w/dark finish metal
fittings. US marked, 1942 dated. Exc.
cond. $30.00
WWII AMMO BELT (BAR 6 POCKET): Lt.
OD canvas & web w/metal fittings. US/
Boyt marked & 1942 dated. Above avg.
cond. $28.00

WWII AMMO BOX: Wire band reinforced, heavy wood box w/metal handles on each side. Stenciled w/load data, 210 cartridges cal. .50, Ordnance emblem, TAIFW. Avg. cond. $40.00

WWII AMMO CLIP POUCH (THOMPSON S.M.G.): 5-pocket lt. OD web body w/large belt loop on back, lift-dot closure flaps. US marked & 1942 dated. Avg. cond. $28.00

WWII AMMUNITION BAG (M-2): Dark OD canvas body w/hole for placing over head & large carrying pocket on each side. Well marked. Avg. cond. $23.00

WWII AMMUNITION BAG (M-2): Lt. OD canvas body w/dark OD trim that slips over head w/large pocket on front & back. Well marked. Exc. cond. $20.00

WWII AMMUNITION BAG: Combination dark tan/OD canvas & web. US marked, 1943 dated. Above avg. cond. $20.00

WWII AMMUNITION BAG: Dark OD canvas body. Divided internally. OD web straps. US marked & 1945 dated. Exc. cond. $30.00

WWII ARMY BACK PACK: Lt. OD canvas body w/lt. OD web straps & dark metal fittings & mess kit carrier. US marked & 1942 dated. Little use. Above avg. cond. $29.00

WWII ARMY BACK PACK: Lt. OD canvas body w/matching mess kit carrier & lt. OD web straps & metal fittings. US marked & 1942 dated. Nice one. Exc. cond. $27.00

WWII ARMY BLANKET: Australian made. 1942 dated on mfg. tag, Gray green color w/some variations. Avg. cond. $40.00

WWII ARMY BLANKET: OD wool w/sewn edges. Above avg. cond. $12.00

WWII ARMY BLANKET: Single bed blanket, US in center & OD wool construction. Exc. cond. $28.00

WWII ARMY BUGLE: Brass w/nickel plated mouthpiece. Const. w/two loops before the bell. Marked "US REGULATION" on throat of horn. Avg. cond. $50.00

WWII ARMY BUGLE: hmkd. "SLINGERLAND/USA" on bell. All metal fitted mouthpiece & double loop pipe w/ spit valve. Avg. cond. $35.00

WWII ARMY C RATION UNIT B: Biscuit, confection & beverage. 3" x 3.5" cylindrical can w/opener on bottom. Top labeled in black. Dated 5-43 on top of can. Above avg. cond. $80.00

WWII ARMY CAMO JUNGLE BACK PACK: Spot pattern camo on lt. green background canvas w/lt. OD web straps &

brass fittings. US marked & 1943 dated. Nice shape. Above avg. cond. $145.00

WWII ARMY CHEMICAL CORPS GAS MASK: In canvas carrier w/CC emblem under 'US.' Above avg. cond. $40.00

WWII ARMY CAMO JUNGLE BACK PACK

WWII ARMY CIPHER CONVERTER: Model M-209-B fully operational w/paper tape & code discs. TM-11-380 (marked restricted) accompanies the equipment. OD canvas carry case w/multipurpose webstrap incl. Case has utility pouch on outside for small parts. Converter in metal case w/6 resettable key wheels & alphabet wheel, tape drum in lid & feeder to print head. Manually operated internal components can be exposed & reset according to manual procedures. Servicing tools stored in lid. Near mint cond. $1,106.00

WWII ARMY FIELD DESK: 20.5x16x14.5" size. Plywood body w/riveted metal corner plates & frame. 1944 dated metal spec tag riveted to top. Leather carrying handle on each side. Lift down cover w/dual latch closure & hasp lock. Inside has several sliding drawers. In olive re-finish. Above avg. cond. $282.00

WWII ARMY FLASHLIGHT: OD green plastic case. Model MX944/U. Uses 3 D cell batteries. Near mint cond. $29.00

WWII ARMY FLASHLIGHT: TL-122-B w/OD Plastic body & metal belt clip. Avg. cond. $28.00

WWII ARMY JUNGLE BACK PACK: Lt. OD canvas body w/lt. OD web straps & metal fittings. US marked & 1942 dated. Above avg. cond. $61.00

WWII ARMY MEDICAL KIT: Complete medical kit in metal box w/labeled lid & Army med. logo. Contents appear complete. Above avg. cond. $44.00

WWII ARMY MEDICAL SERVICE STOVE: Coleman type white gas two burner stove in stainless steel case w/Med service emblem on lid. Avg. cond. $69.00

WWII ARMY MESS KIT: 1944 dated. Contains fork & spoon. Above avg. cond. $20.00

EQUIP. & FLD. GR.

WWII ARMY MOTORCYCLIST BELT: Custom belt for member of 36th Armored Infantry Div. Wide tanned leather w/three buckles. Unit no., name & crossed rifles. Incl. map of Europe. Above avg. cond. $75.00

WWII ARMY NURSE DOG TAGS: matched pair on an odd chain-has secondary hooks for detaching tags. Near mint cond. $37.00

WWII ARMY OFFICER FOOT LOCKER: 30.5x16x12" dark olive finish fiber body w/ riveted metal edges & corner plates & leather carrying handles & dual latch closure hinged lid w/hasp lock (no key included but not locked). Stenciled w/ lieut.'s info. & has Alaskan Def. Cmd. patch design decal on lid (some chipping to design). No inner tray. Avg. cond. $26.00

WWII ARMY OFFICER SWAGGER STICK: For 1st Lieut. in Armor. Nickel plated w/ enameled emblem on end & tank on crossed sabers on side above Lieut.'s bar. Metal tip bullet shaped. Wood between. Exc. cond. $28.50

WWII ARMY ORDNANCE DEPT. WATCH: Wrist watch by Bulova w/black face, glo dial, 12 hr dial, sweep second hand & stem wound & set. Two piece band & specs on back. Operable. Exc. cond. $145.00

WWII ARMY ORDNANCE WRIST WATCH: Bulova. Nickel body well marked on reverse. Works. On ribbed dark OD nylon wrist band. Above avg. cond. $93.00

WWII ARMY ORDNANCE WRIST WATCH: Bulova. Nickel case is Ord. Dept. marked on back. Crystal nice. Black face. On nice OD poplin wristband w/nickel buckle. Above avg. cond. $65.00

WWII ARMY ORDNANCE WRIST WATCH: Nickel case is "ORD. DEPT./U.S.A." hmkd. on back w/nice crystal & numbers on white face. On ribbed gray nylon band. Above avg. cond. $70.00

WWII ARMY PARATROOP CLIP POUCHES FOR M1A1 CARBINE: Hold four 15 round clips per/pouch. OD green canvas w/ printed ID on ea. Exc. cond. $177.00

WWII ARMY PARATROOPER EQUIPMENT DROP BAG: Felt padded & canvas covered zipper closed bag w/reinforced web straps & hangers. For delivering Radios w/paratroops. Avg. cond. .. $19.00

WWII ARMY PERSONNEL WATCH: Wrist watch by Bulova w/black face, glo dial, 12 hr dial, sweep second hand & stem wound & set. Two piece leather band, specs on back & Clear crystal. Operating. Exc. cond. $139.00

WWII ARMY SEWING KIT: Dark OD cotton folding pouch w/several button, needles & thread. Above avg. cond. $11.00

WWII ARMY SIGNAL CORPS FIELD TELEPHONE (EE-8-B): Black bakelite handset & side handcrank in heavy dark OD web carrier w/dark OD web carrying straps. Well marked. Issue carton w/1945 mfg. date & 1951 repacking date. 1945 dated TM manual. Exc. cond. $70.00

WWII ARMY SIGNAL CORPS POUCH (DS-34): Leather w/single long flap covering two small pouches. Above avg. cond. $20.00

WWII ARMY SIGNAL CORPS TRANSMITTER (BC-604-DM): Signal corps issue w/1943 Date. Incl. TM-11-600 dated 1943 w/instr. on machine. Enclosed metal case w/exterior controls & 4 spring actuated locks for mounting. Above avg. cond. $50.00

WWII ARMY SKI POLES: Alum poles w/fold up tips & leather wrist straps. Avg. cond. $20.00

WWII ARMY SLEEPING BAG LINER: OD brown wool w/ties. Avg. cond. $10.00

WWII ARMY SLEEPING BAG: Down filled. Tan cloth cover, zipper. Above avg. cond. $30.00

WWII ARMY SLEEPING BAG: OD wool w/ zipper entry & light web ties. Above avg. cond. $100.00

WWII ARMY TRAINING BB GUN (DAISY LEVER ACTION): Used by army for marksmanship training. Marked on receiver 'PROPERTY OF US ARMY/5A TRAINING AIDS CENTER' & on stock 'PROPERTY OF US GOVERNMENT / WPNS, DEPT., USATS.' Weighted to M1 scale. Avg. cond. $145.00

WWII ARMY WALKIE-TALKIE (BC-611-F): Smooth OD finish metal body w/ telescoping antenna, waterproofed talk button & 1945 dated metal spec plate. Avg. cond. $55.00

WWII ARTILLERY CLINOMETER: Blackened brass & metal w/bubble level, attachable accessory. Scaled angulation indicators. Wood & leather box w/strap. Near mint cond. $60.00

WWII ARTILLERY GRAPHIC TABLE SLIDE RUN (M-23): For Arty calcs. In orig. box dated May 18,1945 w/carry case of canvas. Two rules w/supporting materials. Exc. cond. $25.00

WWII AVIATOR GOGGLES ("DEVELOPMENT DEPARTMENT" CONTROLLED SAMPLE): Similar to AN6530 type. Hinged nickel frames, curved glass lenses w/1 piece gray rubber face pad. Chamois lined white elastic headband. Has lead sealed "Development Department" test sample tag, 43 dated w/ handwritten specs. Tag reads "Similar to 3402-6." In carton marked w/hand written label. Above avg. cond. $425.00

WWII AVIATOR GOGGLES (B-8): w/green lens & full set of replacements in cloth container. Chamois liner. Exc. cond. $43.00

WWII AVIATOR STYLE SUN GLASSES: Amber lenses in wire frames w/flex wire earpieces & padded nose brace. Avg. cond. $29.00

WWII AVIATOR SUNGLASSES IN CASE: Green tint lenses & brass plated wire frame. Padded nose & forehead. Brown leatherette case w/gilt wing & 'AVIATION' on flap. Avg. cond. $28.00

WWII AVIATOR SUNGLASSES IN CASE: Green tinted lenses & wire earpieces. Pads for forehead & nose. Avg. cond. $65.00

WWII AVIATOR SUNGLASSES: Rose Brown tinted lenses in wire frames w/cushioned forehead & nose. Leather case w/snap lid & paper label inside w/specification & order numbers. Above avg. cond. $100.00

WWII AVIATOR SUNGLASSES

WWII BACK PACK TYPE PARACHUTE (AN-6512-1): Dated on canopy case 1943. Case is OD brown canvas & harness of white canvas webbing. D-ring on left shoulder strap. Mfg. National Automotive Fibers Inc. Avg. cond. $480.00

WWII BACK PACK: British made. Lt. OD canvas body w/dark tan trim, dark tan web straps & matching mess kit carrier. US/British made marked. Above avg. cond. $39.00

WWII BACK PACK: Lt. OD canvas body w/lt. OD web straps & metal fittings. US marked & 1942 dated. Includes mess kit carrier & lower half. Above avg. cond. $20.00

WWII BACK PACK: Lt. OD canvas body w/lt. OD web straps, mess kit carrier & dark finish fittings. Exc. cond. $55.00

WWII BACK PACK: Lt. OD canvas body w/ matching mess kit carrier & lt. OD web straps & dark finish fittings. US marked & 1942 dated. Exc. cond. $28.00

WWII BANDSMAN POUCH: Lt. OD wool covered brown leather body w/stud closure flap. Horstmann maker hmkd. Includes matching leather sling. Exc. cond. $30.00

WWII BAROMETER IN CASE: Type ML-316/TM w/sealed case & dual calibrated dial. hmkd. on dial & dated 1944. Padded waterproof case w/5 snap rigid lid & web carry strap. Exc. cond. $66.00

WWII BARRACKS BAG: Lt. OD cotton body w/rope draw closure opening & 1942 dated QM tag. Above avg. cond. .. $21.00

WWII BAZOOKA BAG: Army/Marine camo bag w/carry strap for two piece bazooka weapon. Mint cond. $279.29

WWII BAZOOKA ROUND BAG: Dark OD canvas body w/dark OD web straps. US marked & 1945 dated. Exc. cond. $28.00

WWII BINOCULARS (AMERICAN MADE CONTRACT): hmkd. on barrel & 6x30 power. British broad arrow marked on barrel end. Cloth neck strap. Avg. cond. $40.00

WWII BINOCULARS (M-15A1): w/M24 case. OD color, coated optics & conventional design. 7x50 power. Leather carry case. Avg. cond. $51.00

WWII CAMO JUNGLE BACK PACK: Spot pattern camo on green background canvas body w/lt. OD web straps & metal fittings. US marked & 1943 dated. Above avg. cond. $145.00

WWII CAMO MOSQUITO HEADNET: Cotton & fine mesh constr. w/camo SPOT pattern on lt. green background & stitched bullet loop band. Designed to fit over M-1 helmet. Near mint cond. $26.00

WWII CAMO PARACHUTE: Complete w/ canopy, shrouds, risers & harness. 1945 dated. QR on harness chest straps. Exc. cond. $893.00

WWII CAMO SHELTER-HALF: Reversible from green to tan spot pattern camo canvas w/OD finish ribbed metal buttons & 1944 dated spec tag. Avg. cond. .. $94.00

WWII CAMO TENT-SIZE MOSQUITO NET: Spot pattern camo on lt. green background fine mesh & cotton. Above avg. cond. $25.00

WWII CANTEEN (BRITISH MADE): Lt. olive canvas w/dark tan trim & wire belt hanger.

US/British made & broad arrow marked & 1944 dated. Avg. cond. $25.00

WWII CANTEEN (EXPERIMENTAL): Black porcelain body w/threaded cap. 1944 dated canteen cup. 1942 dated lt. OD canvas cover. Avg. cond. $17.50

WWII CANTEEN CUP: Dark blue porcelain over metal. Metal handle hinged. Avg. cond. $75.00

WWII CANTEEN IN PROTECTIVE PAPER WRAPPING: Canteen w/threaded cap on safety chain. US marked & 1945 dated. Paper wrapping w/contract markings. Near mint cond. $34.00

WWII CANTEEN RIG: 1944 dated canteen & cup in lt. OD canvas cover. Above avg. cond. $13.00

WWII CANTEEN RIG: 1945 dated canteen & cup in 1943 dated lt. OD canvas cover. Above avg. cond. $20.00

WWII CANTEEN RIG: Canteen & cup US marked & 1942 dated. In 1942 dated lt. OD canvas cover. Above avg. cond. $37.00

WWII CARBINE CARRIER (FOLDING STOCK): OD green canvas paratroop carrier w/belt loop, leg strap & padded interior Dated 1944 inside flap, secured w/ snaps. US marked. Exc. cond. ... $107.00

WWII CARBINE SCABBARD (M-1A1): Padded lt. OD canvas body w/twin lift-dot closure flap & lt. OD web straps. US marked & 1943 dated. Near mint cond. $151.00

WWII CARBINE SCABBARD (M-1A1)

WWII CARBINE CARRIER (M-1): Canvas carrier w/zipper closure & web straps. 1945 dated. Above avg. cond. $82.00

WWII CARBINE CARRIER (M-1): OD green canvas w/zipper. Avg. cond. $41.00

WWII CARBINE CARRIER (M-1): OD green canvas, zipper, sling. US marked outside & dated 1944 inside. Exc. cond. . $200.00

WWII CARBINE SCABBARD (M-1): Dark OD web & canvas body is approx. 21" in o/a length. US marked. Unissued condition. Exc. cond. $75.00

WWII CARBINE SLING (M-1): Green web w/ metal fittings & dated 1944. Above avg. cond. $23.00

WWII CARLISLE BANDAGE LOT: Includes 3 bandages in OD finish sealed tins & unissued dark tan web British-made belt pouch-well marked. Near mint cond. $19.00

WWII CARLISLE FIRST AID PACKETS: In delivery box, camo metal covered units. Specs on pkg. end. Exc. cond. $23.00

WWII CARRIER PIGEON MESSAGE TUBE: Clear plastic body marked PG-67 w/snap black webstrapfor attachment to leg. Exc. cond. $28.00

WWII CAVALRY PACK/SADDLE COVERS: Tan canvas w/US at bottom & dated 1942, trimmed in heavy leather. Avg. cond. $59.00

WWII CHEMICAL CORPS GAS MASK BAG: Black rubberized material w/green webstraps. No stenciled Chem. corps emblem or words 'GAS MASK.' Unused. Exc. cond. $20.00

WWII CHEST PACK PARACHUTE CASE: Model A-4, 12/44 dated canvas case w/ elastic cords. hmkd. Switlik Parachute Co. Above avg. cond. $32.00

WWII CHEST PACK PARACHUTE: AN-6513-1A model 24 ft canopy. Mfg. May 44, last insp. Apr. 45. Complete. OD colored canvas case w/rigid back & metal connectors. Avg. cond. $175.00

WWII CHEST PARACHUTE AND HARNESS ASSEMBLY W/BACK PAD: Chest pack is shell w/D-ring & Filler padding (no chute). Dated 1944 w/bungees, clip rings & handles. Harness of white canvas web w/ clips for chute pack & shoulder & leg straps. Twist to lock, push to release latch. OD back pad secured to harness. Exc. cond. $330.00

WWII CHEST TYPE PARACHUTE PACK FRAME (AN-6511-1): Dated Oct. 29 1943. All accessories to allow immediate rigging. Light green/tan canvas material. Exc. cond. $30.00

WWII CIGARETTE CASE: Transparent yellow-tinted plastic body w/lift-off lid. Exc. cond. $12.00

WWII CIGARETTE CASE: Transparent green-tinted plastic body w/lift-off lid. Above avg. cond. $11.00

WWII CLEANING KIT (SMALL ARMS): 3.5" cylindrical metal tube w/threaded cap & materials for cleaning weapon. Avg. cond. $20.00

WWII COMBAT CARGO PACK: Dark OD canvas w/waterproof liner & dark OD web

straps. US marked. Above avg. cond.
.... $28.00

WWII COMBAT PACK RIG (M1944): Dark OD canvas pack is US marked & 1944 dated. Rigged w/suspenders & 1944 dated dark OD canvas shovel cover & US/Ames/1944 marked folding shovel. Pieces in good shape. Above avg. cond.
.... $48.00

WWII COMBAT SUSPENDERS (M1936): British made. Dark OD web w/dark finish metal fittings. British made/broad arrow proof marked & 1943 dated. Above avg. cond. $37.00

WWII COMBAT SUSPENDERS (M1936): Lt. OD web w/metal fittings. US marked & 1942 dated. Exc. cond. $49.00

WWII COMPASS (UNIVERSAL SUN): Encased. Supplement to magnetic compass. Uses sun or north star to accurately fix directions. Metal az. ring w/adj. bar for year, month & day calibrations. Instruction book TM5-9422, bubble levels & shadow bars. OD wood box w/latches. Exc. cond. $100.00

WWII COMPASS BELT POUCH: Dark OD canvas w/lt. OD trim & twin lift-dot closures on flap & wire belt hanger device. Above avg. cond. $23.00

WWII COMPASS IN CASE: Army engineer (lensatic) compass in black metal case dated 5-45 & in canvas belt carrier. Above avg. cond. $80.00

WWII CROSSBOW BOLT/ARROW ("WILLIAM TELL") 10" long w/alum. shaft, turned steel point & flat alum. flechettes. Fletchettes painted yellow. Above avg. cond. $140.00

WWII D RATION BAR: Orig. pkg. Eating instructions on side. Above avg. cond.
.... $80.00

WWII D-DAY GAS BRASSARD: British made mustard colored paper gas detector with white cloth ribbon attachments intact. Near mint cond. $244.00

WWII D-DAY LANDING ARMBAND: Reflective material w/US Flag. Pins on. Exc. cond. $72.00

WWII DALTON AIR NAVIGATION COMPUTER: Circular slide rule w/sliding grid for wind calc. Instruction book. E-6B. Mfg. by Weems. Above avg. cond.
.... $35.00

WWII DOG GAS MASK: Black rubberized material w/elongated face mask to accommodate snout & special curved eyepieces. Two side filter canister mounts & lower exhalator valve. Straps. Exc. cond. $328.00

WWII DUFFEL BAG: Dark OD canvas. US marked & 1943 dated. Above avg. cond.
.... $11.00

WWII ENGINEER COMPASS (M-2): Steel case w/brass fittings. Mirror under lid & sighting hole at bottom. Plastic belt mounted case. Avg. cond. $40.00

WWII ENTRENCHING TOOL CARRIER: OD green canvas w/flap & snap. US marked on front, hmkd. & date(1943) inside. Exc. cond. $20.00

WWII ENTRENCHING TOOL: Dated 1945 on blade. Solid wood handle. Above avg. cond. $25.00

WWII ENTRENCHING TOOL: T-handled tool w/US on metal reinforcing strap. OD finish is worn. Tan canvas belt carrier dated 1943. Avg. cond. $49.00

WWII EQUIPMENT STRAP: Heavy web. 2" wide OD body w/large hook to each end, 2-brass adjustment buckles, inked 'U.S. Mautner Bros. 1942' & about 7' long. Near mint cond. $20.00

WWII FIELD STOVE: Large OD finish cylindrical fuel tank w/black enamel framework & 2 separate burners. Instructional label intact. US marked & 1945 dated. Comes w/US marked & 1944 dated aluminum carrying case w/hinged lid & carrying handle. Avg. cond.
.... $105.00

WWII FIELD STOVE: US marked & 1945 dated unit w/folding metal legs & instructional label. Cylindrical aluminum carrier. Gas. Avg. cond. $42.00

WWII FIRST AID KIT: Metal box w/stenciled ID on top & Med. Svc. emblem in center. Incl. tourniquet, compresses & bandages. Avg. cond. $17.00

WWII FIRST AID KIT: Red cross on white field on front. Small misc. pouch in front & main pouch. Camo bandage incl. Case designed for aircraft & ground use. Avg. cond. $40.00

WWII FIRST AID POUCH: Small OD cotton design. Well marked. Avg. cond.
.... $30.00

WWII FLARE FIRING DEVICE: Steel one shot tube for small survival flares. Removable barrel for load & spring loaded pull bar to shoot. Above avg. cond.
.... $72.00

WWII FLARE GUN HOLSTER (M-8): Brown leather w/snap retaining strap & metal fittings. Made in Canada ink stamped on body. Exc. cond. $19.00

WWII FLASHLIGHT (TL-112-B): OD plastic body w/anglehead. Includes spare bulb. Avg. cond. $20.00

WWII FLASHLIGHT: Elbow style. OD plastic case w/darkened brass fittings, hooded light & battery. Avg. cond. $11.00

WWII FLIGHT GOGGLES (NIGHT ADAPTATION): Black leather w/dark red lenses mounted in metal rings attached to the leather. Elastic wire head band. Used to stimulate night vision. Above avg. cond. $30.00

WWII FLIGHT GOGGLES (POLAROID M1944): One piece green tinted lens w/ chamois lined face pad & head band. Above avg. cond. $27.00

WWII FLIGHT GOGGLES (POLAROID M1944): One piece red tinted lens w/ chamois lined face pad & head band. Above avg. cond. $28.00

WWII FLIGHT GOGGLES (VARIABLE DENSITY): In tin case w/spares & instructions. Amber lenses installed & red flip down lens on outside. Exc. cond. $30.00

WWII GAS ALARM GONG: U shaped steel pipe that is struck by wooden bar to sound gas alarm. Incl. cotter key & chain. Avg. cond. $34.00

WWII GAS DETECTION BRASSARD: Vesicant paper body w/lt. OD web tie at top. Above avg. cond. $350.00

WWII GAS MASK (M-1): Dark tan cloth covered molded rubber mask w/good lenses & elastic harness & rectangular metal filter. Lacks butterfly valve but good overall shape. In tan canvas carrier w/lt. OD web straps-well marked. Avg. cond. $20.00

WWII GAS MASK (M-2A1): 1942 mold dated rubber mask w/elastic harness, rectangular metal filter unit. OD canvas carrier w/anti-dim stick. Above avg. cond. $33.00

WWII GAS MASK (M-2A1): 1943 mold dated mask w/rectangular metal filter unit. Above avg. cond. $37.00

WWII GAS MASK (M3 DIAPHRAGM): 1941 mold dated rubber mask w/"butterfly" valve & rectangular metal filter unit. In well marked dark tan canvas carrier w/anti-dim stick. Above avg. cond. $34.00

WWII GOGGLES (B-8): Black rubber frame w/green tinted lens. Extra lenses in pouch. Issue box w/specs on lid. Dated 1945. Above avg. cond. $42.00

WWII GOGGLES (B-8): Orig. fiber box w/ accessories & spare lenses. Exc. cond. $112.00

WWII GOGGLES (POLAROID ALL-PURPOSE): One-piece gray rubber frame w/plastic lens & black elastic headband. Oilcloth case w/spare lens. Avg. cond. $20.00

WWII GOGGLES (POLAROID B-8): Amber lens & dark rubber frame. Exc. cond. $82.00

WWII GOGGLES (POLAROID M1944): In N-2 goggle box. Avg. cond. $28.00

WWII GOGGLES (SINGLE AXIS ROTATABLE): Vented rubber face piece w/two lenses w/variable color gradient. Lever over eyes can be pulled to change the color in front of the eyes. Near mint cond. $61.00

WWII GRENADE LAUNCHER ADAPTER (M-1A2): dated 1945 & 3-69. OD finish w/ spring clips to hold grenade Above avg. cond. $20.00

WWII GRENADE LAUNCHER LOT: M1 rifle adapter, black metal w/align pin, latch & barrel extension. Grenade adapter 1945 mod 3-69 w/practice grenade & WWII sight assembly in canvas belt pouch. Above avg. cond. $80.00

WWII GRENADE LAUNCHER SIGHT (M-15): Original protective wrapping. Instructional/firing table sheet & 1944 dated dark OD canvas belt pouch. Near mint cond. $14.00

WWII GRENADE LAUNCHER SIGHT (M-15): Parts still wrapped in protective wax paper. Includes instruction sheet. In dark OD canvas carrying case, 1944 dated. Near mint cond. $20.00

WWII GRENADE POUCH (2 POCKET): Lt. OD canvas. 1944 dated paper QM inspector tag. Near mint cond. $20.00

WWII GRENADE POUCH (3 POCKET): Lt. OD canvas bodies. Lt. OD web flaps in same design as those on Carlisle bandage pouches. Lt. OD web straps & wire belt hanger device. US marked & 1944 dated. Near mint cond. $38.00

WWII HATCHET: Metal US marked & 1945 dated. Wooden handle US marked & 1945 dated. Dark OD canvas cover w/wire belt hanger device. Above avg. cond. ..$45.00

WWII HEAD PHONE SET: ANB-H-1 by Utah-Chicago w/leather padding on head band & soft rubber on earpieces. Male connector & Orig. storage box. Exc. cond. $150.00

WWII HEAD SET W/BOOM MIKE: Leather pads for head bands & chamois on earpieces. Avionics incl. Avg. cond. $25.00

WWII HEADSET & CHEST MIKE SET: Padded headset & avionics & straps & Chest mike assembly. For use on aircraft or ground support. Above avg. cond. $72.00

WWII HOWITZER ARTILLERY SLIDE RULE: Three boards w/scales for range, elev. & fuse settings & slide rule assembly to run calcs. Green canvas carry case. Above avg. cond. $25.00

WWII JOINT SERVICE BINOCULARS: Army Signal corps & Naval Gun Factory marked. 6x30 power Tan leatherette cover on tubes & carry strap. Adj. prismatic lenses, right lens inoper. Avg. cond. $30.00

WWII JUNGLE BACK PACK: Lt. olive canvas body w/lt. OD web straps, metal fittings. US marked. Date faint. Above avg. cond. $63.00

WWII JUNGLE BACK PACK: Medium-shade OD canvas body w/lt. OD web straps, metal fittings. US marked & 1942 dated. Above avg. cond. $59.00

WWII K RATION MEAL: Breakfast unit in storage box. Above avg. cond. $76.00

WWII K RATION MEAL: Supper unit in storage box. Above avg. cond. $76.00

WWII K RATION: Pressed paper carton w/ maroon printing w/contents list & malaria warning. Wax sealed inner sleeve. Avg. cond. $86.00

WWII KNAPSACK: W/all straps. 1942. hmkd. "Boyt." US on front flap. Tan canvas & Exc. cond. $45.00

WWII LIFE PRESERVER BELT: USN marked & 1943 dated. W/inflatable chambers & metal clamps. Manual inflation tubes. Above avg. cond. $28.00

WWII LIFE RAFT ANTENNA: Radar reflective antenna. Extendible folding pole w/umbrella-like ribs that extend to support wire mesh antenna. Passive tuned to reflect radar signals. Instructions. Above avg. cond. $20.00

WWII LIFE RAFT EMERGENCY LIGHT: Battery powered w/red & white lens, cord w/safety clip. Above avg. cond. $27.00

WWII LIFE RAFT RADIO (GIBSON GIRL): T-74/CRT-3 survival radio for 5/20 man life rafts. Crank arm & wrench on back. Avg. cond. $66.00

WWII LIFE RAFT SAIL: Sail rolled & fitted in red storage bag w/instructions. Above avg. cond. $25.00

WWII LINEMAN TOOL POUCH: WWII nice leather two pocket vertical pouch w/TL-29 knife & lineman's pliers. Used but clean & undamaged. Above avg. cond. $79.00

WWII M. P. WEB PISTOL BELT: WWI-era belt w/brass fittings has been painted white. Avg. cond. $25.00

WWII MACHINE GUN CARRIER (REISING): Canvas carrier w/leather cup tip & leather carry strap. Case has 4 pockets for clips. Avg. cond. $101.00

WWII MACHINE GUN LINKER/DELINKER KIT (.50 CAL.): In orig. box w/outside label incl. part nos. Exc. cond. $20.00

WWII MAP CASE: Dark tan canvas w/lt. OD trim. US/Boyt marked & 1943 dated. Stenciled "14th Signal Center" on flap. Avg. cond. $20.00

WWII MAP CASE: Lt. OD canvas w/several pockets & stitched pencil/pen slots & detachable lt. OD web sling. Includes plastic map grid protective cover. US marked & 1942 dated. Marked "HOW Co. 107." Above avg. cond. $40.00

WWII MEDICAL DEPT. BLANKET: Hospital blanket in white wool w/maroon details. Stamped 1944 on blanket & 1943 on insp. tag. Above avg. cond. $12.00

WWII MEDICAL KIT: OD canvas case w/ white cross on top & title in front. Web sling carrier. Zipper enclosed w/full complement of dressings, bandages & accessories Above avg. cond. $26.00

WWII MESS HALL TRAY: Six-compartment design. US marked & 1943 dated. Avg. cond. $20.00

WWII MESS KIT: W/utensils. Dated 1944 on handle. Exc. cond. $15.00

WWII MORTAR AMMO BOX: Wood box w/4 rd capacity for 81mm mortar rounds. Dated 9-44, stenciled comments on 3 sides. Rope handle & metal latches. Avg. cond. $40.00

WWII MORTAR BASE PLATE (M2 60MM): Heavy metal unit in OD finish. Avg. cond. $282.00

WWII MORTAR SIGHT (M-4): Sight w/ calibrations & mount. Black metal. 1941. Avg. cond. $34.00

WWII M. P. WHISTLE: OD plastic whistle w/ US Army & 1944 on side. Black lanyard. Above avg. cond. $19.00

WWII MUSETTE BAG (BRITISH MADE): Lt. olive canvas w/tan trim & straps & metal fittings. US/British made marked. 1944 dated & broad arrow proofed. Avg. cond. $45.00

WWII MUSETTE BAG: Lt. OD canvas body w/web straps & sling. US marked & 1943 dated. Avg. cond. $25.00

WWII MUSETTE BAG: Lt. OD canvas w/lt. OD web straps. US marked & 1940 dated. Includes web sling. Above avg. cond. $59.00

WWII NAVY AVIATOR SUNGLASSES: Cushion wire glasses w/green tinted windows, nose & forehead pads. Exc. cond. $54.00

WWII NAVY AVIATOR SURVIVAL MIRROR (M-580A): Sealed in issue package w/ printed instructions. Exc. cond. $90.00

WWII NAVY BAROMETER: Brass case w/ hanging ring, glass face over exposed works & dial. Indicator has adjustment. $24.00

WWII NAVY BINOCULARS (BUREAU MARK 21 7X50) W/CASE: Black crackle finish on optic tubes, Specs & hmkd. (SARD) on base plates. Adj. focus lenses w/soft rubber formed eyepieces. Black leather case. Exc. cond. $120.00

WWII NAVY BLANKET: White wool w/blue stripe & embr. US Navy at either end. Above avg. cond. $27.00

WWII NAVY CARTRIDGE BELT (MK-I): Lt. OD web belt w/two thin black lines running length of body & many stitched web loops & metal fittings. USN marked & 1943 dated. Above avg. cond. $37.00

WWII NAVY CORPSMAN MEDICAL BAG: Dark tan canvas body w/lt. OD web straps. Red cross printed on flap & "U.S.N." below. Above avg. cond. $30.00

WWII NAVY DAISEY MAE LIFE PRESERVER VEST: Dark blue-gray cotton body w/matching web straps & manual inflation tubes. USN marked & 1944 dated. Above avg. cond. $88.00

WWII NAVY FIELD PACK: USMC pattern. Lt. OD canvas body w/lt. OD web straps & sliding pads on shoulder straps. USN marked. Incl. dark tan cotton bag marked "Shipping Documents War Dept. Only." Avg. cond. $22.00

WWII NAVY FLARE CARTRIDGE BELT (MK-I) & SIGNAL PISTOL HOLSTER (MK-5): Dark tan web w/stitched web cart. loops & metal fittings. Includes dark tan web holster w/wire belt hanger & lift-dot closure flap. Both well marked. Above avg. cond. $34.00

WWII NAVY FLARE GUN (BRITISH MADE): Break breech model for loading & single shot. hmkd. on side & USN on each grip. Above avg. cond. $32.00

WWII NAVY GAS MASK (MARK III) IN BAG: Mask, hose & canister in canvas bag w/ carry straps. Avg. cond. $20.00

WWII NAVY HAND HELD RANGE FINDER: Black plastic w/center viewer & adj. vert. calibration wires. Positioned 24" from eye, placing wires on wing tips of approaching aircraft will give range to target. Multiple scales covers most WWII enemy fighters. Spec plate on rear & dated 1943. Exc. cond. $44.00

WWII NAVY ID CARD GAME "WEFTUP": 54 cards w/various aircraft & instructions. In box. Avg. cond. $24.00

WWII NAVY LIFE BELT (B-P-6 PNEUMATIC): Dark tan cotton body w/ manual inflation tube. Well marked. Exc. cond. $35.00

WWII NAVY LIFE PRESERVER: Yellow waterproofed material in Mae West Design. Manual & gas operated inflation means. Yellow webbing straps for wear. Last inspection date- 1945. Avg. cond. $59.00

WWII NAVY PORTABLE SIGNAL LIGHT: Type A-Incl. Gun type signal lamp w/ switches & filters & mount bracket assembly & two sets of cables & some accessories. Electrical assembly chart included. Avg. cond. $25.00

WWII NAVY SEXTANT (MARK I MOD 0 BALL RECORDING) W/STORAGE CASE.: Calibrated at US Naval Observatory & dated Oct. 27, 1944. Mergenthaler made in black & brass. Wooden carry case. Exc. cond. $192.00

WWII NAVY SIGNAL CARD SET: 70 card flag set for Navy & International code. Orig. box. Above avg. cond. $25.00

WWII NAVY SIGNAL FLARE GUN (MARK 5): 1942. Break front loading, single shot. USN on checkered grips. Black finish. Above avg. cond. $65.00

WWII NAVY SIGNAL LIGHT: Hi intensity light, hand held w/cabling & accessories in metal storage box w/USN stamped into lid. Avg. cond. $28.00

WWII NAVY SPYGLASS: 16 power quartermaster spyglass 32" long w/black leatherette covering on metal tube & adj. optics. 1942 dated at viewing end. In oak box w/felt padded braces inside, metal spec plate. Exc. cond. $250.00

WWII NAVY STOP WATCH (TYPE B CLASS 7): Elgin brand. Nickel body is BuOrd & serial numbered on reverse. Black numbers on white faced dial that is "Elgin Timer" marked. Bezel loose but included. Comes in protective cotton bag & in thick pressed paper box w/USN spec. label. Works. Above avg. cond. $133.00

WWII NAVY SURVIVAL E & E GOLD COIN KIT: COMNAVAIRLANT, Norfolk, VA. Heavy black rubber two part case w/ provisions for eight items. Contains 5 foreign gold coins, various denominations & three gold rings. Serial Number 1739 on tag inside & inscribed on outside. Exc. cond. $1,300.00

WWII OFFICER BARRACK BAG: Lt. OD cotton w/rope draw closure opening. 1942 dated QM tag. Above avg. cond. .. $10.00

WWII OFFICER FIELD MESS CHEST:
Reinforced trunk style chest w/lid storage
for assorted knives/spoons & kitchen
ware. Main storage holds enameled metal
dishes, bowls, coffee maker & serving
pieces. Avg. cond. $40.00

WWII OFFICER KIT BAG: Dark tan canvas
w/leather carrying handle. Above avg.
cond. $34.00

WWII ORDNANCE AMMO BOX LOCK:
Brass. Heavy duty hasp lock w/key entry
on bottom & crossed cannon emblem on
face. Avg. cond. $45.00

WWII ORDNANCE DEPT. PAD LOCK:
Heavy brass body w/Ord. Dept. branch
design & maker markings w/nickel hinged
ring riveted to one side. Avg. cond.
.... $20.00

WWII ORDNANCE WRIST WATCH: Bulova
made, 12 hr dial & small second dial.
Stem set & wound. One piece band.
Above avg. $250.00

WWII OSS TIRE SPIKE: 2-piece tubular
metal body w/formed spikes at each end.
Designed to puncture tires of vehicles &
airplanes when run over. W/photocopy of
info. on item. Avg. cond. $143.00

WWII PACK SADDLE BAGS FOR MULE OR
HORSE.: Two tan canvas bags w/
strapping for mounting to pack animal.
Above avg. cond. $27.00

WWII PARACHUTE (B-10): By Pioneer
Parachute Company. Harness set w/
canvas case for canopy, shrouds &
supporting accessories. Shrouds, risers &
wires. 1945. Above avg. cond. ... $520.00

WWII PARACHUTE FLARE GUN: gray
metal body w/tip-over barrel & integral
checkered grips. "Sklar Signal Pistol"
marked. Above avg. cond. $67.00

WWII PARATROOP EQUIPMENT DROP
CASE

WWII PARATROOP EQUIPMENT DROP
CASE: Heavily padded canvas covered
body approx. 13" in dia. & 26" tall. Strap

closure opening & heavy tan web carry
handle. Avg. cond. $265.00

WWII PARATROOP MEDICAL BACK PACK:
W/straps, center pouch, two side pouches.
Some orig. medicines. Green w/green
webbing. Exc. cond. $147.00

WWII PARATROOP PATHFINDER RADIO:
Eureka-beacon, Airborne Beacon T/R unit.
Model PPN-RT37 in A/B drop bag. Exc.
cond. $1,250.00

WWII PARATROOP RESERVE CHUTE:
Trainer version, w/24 ft white silk canopy,
shrouds etc. Normal markings. Avg. cond.
.... $133.00

WWII PARATROOP WALKIE TALKIE: In
drop bag. Reinforced canvas w/heavy
duty zipper. Interior lined w/shock pads w/
radio encased. Exc. cond. $301.00

WWII PARATROOP WALKIE TALKIE

WWII PARATROOP WEAPON BAG: Quilt
padded canvas bag w/zipper closure &
alum clip. For Carbine or Tommy gun.
Labeled on one side. Exc. cond.
.... $203.00

WWII PARATROOPER NORMANDY D-9
MANNEQUIN: Metal dummy paratrooper
dropped at Normandy. 18.5" tall w/many
uniform details displayed, incl. boots
jacket, hood/helmet & facial features. A
real parachute pack featuring chute, waist
harness risers clipped to shoulder rings,
ripcord & static cord assembly. Above avg.
cond. $2,481.00

WWII PERISCOPE (M-70H): 30" steel tube.
Direct optic coated lens scope used on
tanks. Rubber goggle style viewer w/
monocular vision allowed. Above avg.
cond. $56.00

WWII PERSONAL RAZOR KIT: Gillette razor
kit. Appears to be stainless steel w/razor,
blade holder & mirror inside. Ornate lid

includes Army & Navy symbols & American eagle image in center. Above avg. cond. $40.00

WWII PICK AX IN CARRIER: Short handle. OD wood handle w/metal pick & hoe head in canvas carrier w/belt clip. Carrier marked US. Avg. cond. $20.00

WWII PILOT NAVIGATION KIT: Brown leather exterior w/gilt lettering. Brass zipper w/flex web panels. Interior compartment w/multiple document & equip pockets. Above avg. cond. $93.00

WWII PISTOL BELT (BRITISH MADE): Dark tab web w/brass fittings. US marked. Above avg. cond. $76.00

WWII PISTOL BELT RIG W/HOLSTER: Brown leather .45 holster w/wire belt hanger. US embossed on flap. Boyt/1944 marked. Dark OD web pistol belt w/metal fittings, dark OD web Carlisle bandage carrier w/bandage in sealed orange-finish tin. Avg. cond. $42.00

WWII PISTOL BELT RIG: Dark OD web belt w/brass fittings & 1942 dated lt. OD web Carlisle bandage pouch & 1943 dated canteen & cup in dark OD canvas cover. Avg. cond. $20.00

WWII PISTOL BELT RIG: Dark tan web belt w/metal fittings & Boyt/1942 marked brown leather .45 hip holster w/US on flap, wire belt hanger & Carlisle bandage carrier. Avg. cond. $53.00

WWII PISTOL BELT RIG: Includes WWI-era dark tan web pistol belt w/"D"-shaped saber ring & brass fittings. Fitted w/1942 dated Carlisle bandage pouch w/bandage in sealed orange-finish tin & 1943 dated lt. OD canvas canteen cover w/good 1943 dated canteen. Above avg. cond. $33.00

WWII PISTOL BELT: Dark tan web w/metal fittings. US marked & 1942 dated. Above avg. cond. $23.00

WWII PISTOL BELT: Lt. OD web w/metal fittings. US marked & 1943 dated. Above avg. cond. $48.00

WWII PISTOL HOLSTER (.45 CAL.): Hip style. Brown leather w/US embossed in oval on stud closure flap & wire belt hanger. Boyt/42 marked. Nice shape. Above avg. cond. $129.00

WWII PISTOL HOLSTER (.45 CAL.): Hip style. Brown leather w/matching straps, US embossed in oval on body. US/Enger-Kress marked. Above avg. cond. ..$53.00

WWII PISTOL HOLSTER (.45 CAL.): Dark tan leather w/US embossed in oval on

press stud closure flap & wire belt hanger. Sears/1942 marked. Exc. cond. ... $95.00

WWII PISTOL HOLSTER (.45 CAL.)

WWII PISTOL HOLSTER (.45 CAL.): Brown leather w/US embossed in oval on body, matching shoulder strap. US/maker/1943 marked. Above avg. cond. $74.00

WWII PISTOL HOLSTER (.45 CAL.)

WWII PISTOL HOLSTER (.45 CAL.): Hip style. Brown leather w/US embossed in oval on brass stud closure flap & wire belt hanger & rawhide thong. Boyt/44 marked. Nice shape-light age. Above avg. cond. $84.00

WWII PISTOL HOLSTER (.45 CAL.): Shoulder style. Brown leather w/US embossed in oval on body, matching shoulder strap. US/Sears/1943 marked. Above avg. cond. $95.00

WWII PISTOL LANYARD: Dark tan cord w/ brown leather trim & dark finish metal hook. 1943 dated. Exc. cond. $34.00

WWII PISTOL LANYARD: Maker marked & 1943 dated. Cord body w/leather trim & brass fittings. Exc. cond. $33.00

WWII POCKET COMPASS (WALTHAM): Brass body w/flip cover. Face Waltham hmkd. Jeweled bearing & actuating safety lever. U.S. marked. Dark blue pressed paper box w/label. Above avg. cond. $145.00

WWII PUP TENT: Treated green cloth w/ poles, wrapped & tied w/parachute shroud line. Avg. cond. $30.00

WWII RADIO COMMUNICATION OUTFIT: Box w/BC-746-A tuning unit. Chest speaker unit T-39-B w/straps & connectors. Antenna base assembly w/ electronics & connection for antenna. POGO antenna unit, dated 1944. Exc. cond. $300.00

WWII RADIO EQUIPMENT CARRY ALL: OD green canvas w/multiple pockets on both sides of center hanger. Web straps on underside. Most pockets have snap fastened flaps. Avg. cond. $24.00

WWII RADIO GEAR PACK W/STRAPS: OD. About 3.5x11x12" body w/flap, two closure straps, web shoulder strap & web fittings inside divided pouch. Avg. cond. .. $20.00

WWII RADIO KEY: Dated Dec. 26, 1944. Key set for Morse transmissions. Near mint cond. $17.00

WWII RANGE FINDER: 90 degree optics w/ rubber cushioned eyepiece & adjustable focus. 4 pos. light control & mounting holes on base. Above avg. cond. ..$28.00

WWII RED CROSS NURSE WRIST WATCH: White face/black numbers. Black nylon thin band. Stem wound & set. Hinged case. Avg. cond. $145.00

WWII REVOLVER HOLSTER (VICTORY MODEL): Brown leather w/US embossed in oval on body, lift-dot closure half-flap & wire belt hanger device. US/maker marked & 1943 dated. Above avg. cond. $100.00

WWII REVOLVER HOLSTER (VICTORY MODEL)

WWII RIFLE BAG (SPRINGFIELD 1903-A3): Dark OD canvas body w/dark OD webstrap& brown leather trim. US marked & 1943 dated. Above avg. cond. .. $82.00

WWII RIFLE CLEANING KIT: In metal tube w/removable ends. Above avg. cond. $19.00

WWII RIFLE SCABBARD: Folded & stitched brown leather w/matching leather straps & riveted metal bolt cover. US marked & 1943 dated. Above avg. cond. $101.00

WWII RIFLE SCABBARD: Folded & stitched brown leather w/riveted black finish metal bolt cover. US/maker/1943 marked. Incl. one matching strap. Above avg. cond. $84.00

WWII RIFLE SCABBARD

WWII RIFLE SCOPE (M-7): Black metal tube. Leather lens caps. Avg. cond. $29.00

WWII RIFLE SCOPE (M-84 SNIPER): Orig. M-1D mount. Rubber shade ring on viewing end. Above avg. cond. $280.00

WWII RIFLE SLING: Dark tan leather w/dark fittings. 1943 dated. Above avg. cond. $49.00

WWII RUCKSACK (FRAMED): Commonly referred to as mountain back pack. Lt. OD canvas body is US marked & 1943 dated w/lt. OD web & green leather straps & green leather trim. On OD finish tubular metal frame. Unissued example. Exc. cond. $60.00

WWII SAW: Disston made & dated 1943. Case includes two handles, file & chisel. Black pebble grain leather. Avg. cond. $25.00

WWII SEWING KIT: Roll up type in OD twill. Complete contents. Above avg. cond. $30.00

WWII SHARK REPELLENT KIT: Black pack w/water soluble repellent. Exc. cond. $24.00

WWII SHAVING KIT & SOAP: Mint items, Gem razor kit in orig. box w/instr. & bar of soap w/discussion of options of use. Above avg. cond. $24.00

WWII SHOE POLISH (TIN OF GRIFFIN A*B*C WAX BRAND): Brown finish tin w/ white printing. Contains 3 1/2 oz. of brown polish. Above avg. cond. $10.00

WWII SHOTGUN AMMUNITION BELT POUCH: Lt. OD canvas body w/twin lift dot closure flap, stitched web shell loops & stitched web loops on back. US marked & 1942 dated. Avg. cond. $177.00

WWII SHOVEL (FOLDING) W/COVER: Dark OD finish. US/Ames/1945 marked on blade. Lt. OD canvas cover w/dark OD trim & wire belt hanger. US marked & 1945 dated. Above avg. cond. $30.00

WWII SHOVEL (FOLDING) W/COVER: US/ Wood/1944 marked. OD finish. 1945 dated dark OD canvas cover w/wire belt hanger. Avg. cond. $24.00

WWII SHOVEL (T HANDLE) W/COVER: US marked. Lt. OD web cover w/wire belt hanger-US marked & 1942 dated. Above avg. cond. $72.00

WWII SHOVEL (T HANDLE) W/COVER: US marked. Olive finish. W/1943 dated lt. OD canvas cover w/dark OD trim. Avg. cond. $40.00

WWII SHOVEL (T HANDLE): Metal throat of spade & wooden handle are U.S. marked. Olive finish. Avg. cond. $41.00

WWII SIGHT (M-14) IN LEATHER CARRYING CASE: M-14 mortar sight w/ az. & elev. controls in leather case w/ metal belt clip & rings for carry strap & securing strap. Above avg. cond. ..$71.00

WWII SIGNAL CORPS REPAIR KIT: CY-684/GR repair kit in metal case w/labels. W/full set of tubes, fuses, vibrator & lamps. Exc. cond. $20.00

WWII SIGNAL CORPS SATCHEL BAG: 4x8x10: soft light OD canvas body w/box-style top & adjustable shoulder strap. Top stenciled "Satchel Signal." Near mint cond. $50.00

WWII SIGNAL CORPS TRANSMITTING KEY (J-38): Black bakelite base w/multi-piece metal key. 1943 dated pressed paper issue carton. Above avg. cond. $25.00

WWII SIGNAL CORPS VOLT-OHMMETER: Meter w/leads inside labeled metal box. Multiple inputs & selections & zero adj. control. Carry strap. Above avg. cond. $20.00

WWII SIGNAL FLAG KIT: OD green CS-16 canvas case w/carry strap & two red/white flags on short poles. Exc. cond. ... $20.00

WWII SIGNAL LAMP EQUIPMENT SET (SE-11): Canvas two pouch carrier for all parts, Lamp M-227 & M-341 shoulder stock & tripod. Can be shoulder aimed or mounted, trigger lighted or Morse keyed. Powered by 5 'D' cell batteries. Red tint hood or clear light. Includes manual TM

11-392. Complete set plus instructions, Exc. cond. $200.00

WWII SIGNAL LAMP EQUIPMENT SET (SE-11)

WWII SIGNAL MIRROR: ESM-2 survival signal mirror in paper envelope. W/ lanyard. Above avg. cond. $14.00

WWII SKI GOGGLES: Dark lenses, fur trimmed cloth eye protectors & narrow head band. Leatherette pouch. Exc. cond. $20.00

WWII SKI GOGGLES: Green tinted laminated lenses w/metal frames & padded lt. OD surrounds & elastic headband. Above avg. cond. $10.00

WWII SKIS: 74" long, wooden, w/"Stratos" maker marked metal bindings. Avg. cond. $65.00

WWII SLEEPING BAG (M1942): Lt. OD cotton shell w/down & feather filled "pink" satin lining. 1942 dated. US marked. Above avg. cond. $90.00

WWII SOAP TIN: OD 1.5x3x4" hinged w/ scrip lettering across top. Original finish. Mint cond. $42.00

WWII STENCIL OUTFIT: Contains dry ink, brush, metal letter & symbol forms. In wood box w/sliding lid. Above avg. cond. $90.00

WWII STEREOSCOPE: In Orig. box. Folding device w/focusable lenses & head rest. Model CF-8. Above avg. cond. $12.00

WWII SURGICAL INSTRUMENTS: From field medical kit. Incl. probes, tweezers, clamps, cutters & more. Avg. cond. $20.00

WWII SURVIVAL COMPASS: E & E compass, 18mm across, easily hidden. Avg. cond. $26.00

WWII SURVIVAL FISHING KIT: Dark OD HBT material cloth roll-up case w/many stitched pockets for various lines, hooks &

fishing accessories & instruction sheet. Exc. cond. $45.00

WWII SURVIVAL KIT CONTAINER: Multi-purpose plastic container w/instr. on side. When contents removed, used as water bottle. Above avg. cond. $20.00

WWII SURVIVAL PARACHUTE RATIONS: Single can from flight survival kit. Gold tone tin unopened w/contents listed on top. Packed by Charms Inc. Avg. cond. $166.00

WWII SURVIVAL RADIO (GIBSON GIRL): AN-CRT-3. Found in 20 man rafts & survival dories. Padded case w/antenna segments & accessories. Waterproof exterior w/straps & clips. Exc. cond. $187.00

WWII SURVIVAL RADIO (GIBSON GIRL): In yellow canvas case w/carry straps. Radio in yellow metal case w/all switches etc. on top & accessible. Heavy webstrapfor securing while cranking. Generator powered. Continuous signal or hand keyed. Exc. cond. $124.00

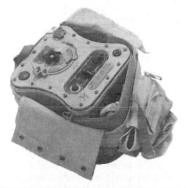

WWII SURVIVAL RADIO (GIBSON GIRL)

WWII SURVIVAL VEST FISHING KIT (C-1): Clear plastic case w/instructions, lures & line. Exc. cond. $90.00

WWII TANK PERISCOPE (M5): 7" x 11" x 2" w/handle for removal. Metal case w/ compression springs for snug fit & wide viewing angle. Bakelite case around prism. Above avg. cond. $20.00

WWII TANK TELESCOPE (M-38): Black case. Mirrored optics w/floating reticle in center. Mounted on brass base w/spring controlled positioning. Avg. cond. $20.00

WWII TELESCOPE (M-17): 1943 dated w/ view lens & focus ring & sight lens w/clear, neutral, red & amber lenses. Spec plate on side. Pedestal mount. OD finish. Avg. cond. $45.00

WWII TELESCOPE (M-17): Elbow style. Prismatic optics in OD finished metal telescope. Specs. 4 position lens selection, power input & rubber eyepiece. Mounted to 6.25" wood disk w/6.5" x 3/4" rod. Above avg. cond. $223.00

WWII TELESCOPE (M-38A2): Brass case w/ black finish, prismatic optics, mounting studs. Above avg. cond. $26.00

WWII TELESCOPE (M-46): 1943 dated w/ full optics in metal tube. Exc. cond. $25.00

WWII TELESCOPE (M-86F): OD finished metal tube w/optics & scale on one lens. Two brackets for mounting clamps & M76 carrying case. Above avg. cond. .. $23.00

WWII TELESCOPE (M-120 HORIZONTAL): Orig. packing. Rubber eye piece, OD finish & specs plate. Near mint cond. $85.00

WWII TENT-SIZE MOSQUITO NET: Lt. OD cotton & dark tan mesh constr. Exc. cond. $22.00

WWII THOMPSON S.M.G. COVER: Dark OD canvas w/leather trim & zippered opening. Well marked. Exc. cond. $91.00

WWII THOMPSON S.M.G. COVER

WWII THOMPSON S.M.G. COVER: Heavy dark OD canvas body w/zippered opening, leather trim. Well marked. Exc. cond. $53.00

WWII THOMPSON S.M.G. LEATHER SCABBARD: Folded & stitched dark brown leather body w/brass attachment loop & short strap. US marked. Leather has been treated w/paraffin. Avg. cond. $223.00

WWII TRAINING AID FOR M1903 RIFLE: Small gray sheet metal unit w/angled glass lens. In issue box. Designed to teach how to line-up sights. Exc. cond. $30.00

WWII THOMPSON S.M.G. LEATHER SCABBARD

WWII TRAINING RIFLE: Springfield 03 model W/functioning receiver, fixed trigger, plugged barrel. Sling swivels. Avg. cond. $37.00

WWII USMC AMMO CLIP POUCH (THOMPSON S.M.G.): For .45 cal. stick clips, 3 to a pouch. Indiv. flap cover w/ snap. Belt loop for ammo belt & marked USMC & 1944. Exc. cond. $38.00

WWII USMC AMMO CLIP POUCH (THOMPSON S.M.G. 5 POCKET): Dark tan web w/lift dot closures on indiv. flaps & wide belt loop on back. USMC marked & 1942 dated. Avg. cond. $29.00

WWII USMC AMMO POUCH (THOMPSON S.M.G. 3 POCKET): .45 cal. SMG clip carrier w/snap flaps. belt loop & dated 1944. Unused, well marked & Mint. Near mint cond. $42.00

WWII USMC BLANKET: Forest green wool w/black stripe at either end & USMC embr. in center. Avg. cond. $45.00

WWII USMC CAMO PONCHO/SHELTER-HALF: Reversible from green to tan spot pattern camo canvas w/metal snaps. Above avg. cond. $90.00

WWII USMC CANTEEN COVER & EXPERIMENTAL CANTEEN: Lt. OD canvas cover w/criss-cross straps, wire belt hanger. Model w/o hole in bottom. Black porcelain canteen, US marked, 1942 dated. Avg. cond. $30.00

WWII USMC CANTEEN COVER: Dark tan canvas w/wire belt hanger device stitched near top of body. Includes 1918 dated canteen w/1918 dated cup. Avg. cond. $40.00

WWII USMC CANTEEN COVER: Lt. OD canvas body w/criss-cross straps, wire belt hanger & stitch grommet hole in bottom. Includes 1943 dated canteen & cup. Above avg. cond. $23.00

WWII USMC CARBINE CLIP POUCH (M-1): Lt. OD web. USMC/Boyt marked & 1945 dated. Exc. cond. $27.00

WWII USMC CARBINE CLIP POUCH BELT (M-1) W/POUCHES & CLIPS: OD web trouser-design belt w/dark metal tip & open-face buckle & 5 female snaps for attachment of pouches. W/5 lt. OD web M-1 Carbine clip pouches, USMC/Boyt marked & 1945 dated. Also, 10 carbine clips. Exc. cond. $147.00

WWII USMC CHAPLAIN FLAG: 1943/44 dated on bunting. Pennant style 5' long w/ blue cross on white field. Near mint cond. $75.00

WWII USMC COMBAT SUSPENDERS: Dark green web straps w/black metal buckles & spring snaps. Exc. cond. $20.00

WWII USMC COMBAT SUSPENDERS: Dark OD & lt. OD web w/brass fittings. Above avg. cond. $13.00

WWII USMC FIELD BAG: Dark tan canvas body w/lt. OD web straps & sliding shoulder pads. USMC/Boyt marked & 1943 dated. Above avg. cond. $33.00

WWII USMC FIELD PACK & MESS KIT: Dark tan canvas body w/lt. OD trim & web straps w/sliding shoulder pads. USMC/ Boyt marked & 1943 dated. Also, 1945 dated canteen. Avg. cond. $29.00

WWII USMC KNAPSACK: Lt. OD canvas body w/different shade lt. OD trim & web straps. 1942-1943 dated. Above avg. cond. $27.00

WWII USMC MAP CASE: Lt. OD canvas w/ dark tan trim. Several pockets, plastic grid map cover & sling. US marked & 1941 dated. EG&A design. Avg. cond. .. $32.00

WWII USMC MAP CASE: Tan canvas w/web strap, snap fittings & zippered fold out panel w/glassine protectors for maps. Green felt pad. Outer lined pouch for documents. Avg. cond. $85.00

WWII USMC MEDIC BACKPACK: OD green canvas w/light trim & white web straps. Pouches & pockets for medical gear. Folds into musette style pack when empty. Avg. cond. $90.00

WWII USMC PISTOL HOLSTER (.45 CAL.): Shoulder style. Dark brown leather body w/US, matching straps including shoulder strap w/sliding pad. USMC/Boyt/44 marked. Above avg. cond. $177.00

WWII USMC SEA BAG: Heavy dark tan canvas body. Above avg. cond. $20.00

WWII USMC STRAIGHT RAZOR: Marked 'USMC' on shank of blade. Black plastic cover for blade & mfg. box for storage. Very sharp & very nice. Exc. cond. $59.00

WWII USMC SWAGGER STICK: 22" long. High quality brown wooden body w/nickel tip & handle w/EG&A applique . Exc. cond. $66.00

WWII USMC WATER BAG (3 GAL): White canvas covered. Marked USMC & 1944. Dispensing cap & sealing or travel cap. Avg. cond. $25.00

WWII USMC OFFICERS VALISE: 28x19" Tan canvas & pouched on both sides. Canvas web straps w/blackened brass fittings. Uniform storage area. Avg. cond. $60.00

WWII USMC OFFICERS VALISE

WWII USMC WRIST WATCH BAND: On board In cellophane. Nylon cordovan color & one piece. Exc. cond. $19.00

WWII WALKIE TALKIE RADIO (BC-611-F): Smooth dark OD finish metal body w/ telescoping antenna, rubber covered talk push button. Signal Corps marked/1945 dated. Dark OD web strap. Avg. cond. $51.00

WWII WALKIE-TALKIE RADIO (BC-611-F): OD crinkle finish unit w/telescoping antenna, waterproofed push button, 1945 dated spec label & dark OD web strap. Above avg. cond. $60.00

WWII WEAPON CLEANING KIT: In metal case w/handle. Two oilers, cleaning rods & brushes. Assorted sizes copper brushes & special lubricants. Avg. cond. $32.00

WWII WIRE CUTTERS IN CARRIER: 1945 dated cutters in canvas carrier w/snap closure. Above avg. cond. $35.00

WWII WRIST COMPASS: Fluid filled. Brown plastic case w/az. ring on outside & pointers inside. Brown leather strap. Hmkd. & in orig. box. Exc. cond. $53.00

WWII WRIST COMPASS: Taylor model, liquid filled. OD bakelite body well marked on reverse. Leather wristband. Above avg. cond. $55.00

WWII WRIST COMPASS: Taylor model. Brown bakelite body. Well marked on back. Leather adj. wrist band. Above avg. cond. $42.00

WWII WRIST COMPASS: Taylor. Fluid filled. Brown bakelite body. Well marked. Above avg. cond. $35.00

WWII WRISTWATCH (BULOVA A-7A): 12/24 hr dial w/sweep second hand & stem set & wound. 1938 date. One piece nylon band. Exc. cond. $217.00

WWII WRISTWATCH: Bulova wrist watch w/ black face, 12 hr dial, sweep second hand. Two piece nylon band. Near mint cond. $135.00

WWII WRISTWATCH (A-11): Contract date 43 from specs on back. Black face & 12 hr dial & sweep second hand. Leatherette expansion band. Above avg. cond. $165.00

WWII WRISTWATCH (A-11): Black face w/ sweep second hand, 12 hr dial, specs on back & dated 43. Green nylon band. Above avg. cond. $160.00

WWII WRISTWATCH (ELGIN): Nickel finish case w/white face dial-2nd hand dial-15 jewel movement. Pale cotton band. Avg. cond. $35.00

C. 1946 - Present

AIRCRAFT CRASH AX: Netherlands made RP-4 w/pick head & ax head. Insulated grip to 20,000 volts. Avg. cond. $20.00

AIRCRAFT CRASH AX: Large metal head w/ notched curved ax blade & extended pick head. Insulated handle. Marked Aircraft/ Escape. Avg. cond. $33.00

AIRCRAFT PICK HEAD CRASH AX: Heavy gray metal unit w/combination pick/cutting edge head & black rubber insulated handle. Comes in issue carton. Current issue item. Exc. cond. $82.00

ANTI-TANK WEAPON (AT-4): Swedish made. 39" long shoulder fired missile launcher w/instructions on tube, carry strap & wire stand. Exc. cond. $105.00

ANTI-TANK WEAPON (AT-4): 40" long, 3.4" tube dia. shoulder fired weapon. All controls are external & Instructions, both written & graphic are fixed to outside. Green web carry strap. Above avg. cond. $273.00

ARMY HELICOPTER HEADSET SYSTEM: Headset w/unpadded earphones & left side boom mike, chest controller & web straps & cabling. Avg. cond. $40.00

ARMY RADIO (RT-175/PRC-9): OD metal case w/electronics, Hand held telephone type receiver, whip antenna & magnesium battery in separate pack. Last inspection $117.00

ARMY WRIST COMPASS: Dry type. Dated 1949 & hmkd. 'Waltham Watch Co.' OD plastic case w/full hinged cover & green web strap. Avg. cond. $39.00

AVIATOR KIT BAG: Sage green canvas w/web carry handles & zipper. Well marked & 1981 dated. Avg. cond. $25.00

BACKPACK PARACHUTE: 1952. 24 ft. day-glo & white paneled canopy. Avg. cond. $200.00

BREAD TYPE RATION: 1951 dated. Large tin can in dark OD finish w/black printed markings. Key on bottom. Above avg. cond. $30.00

CAMO GREASE PAINT: White & loam colorant, OD metal tube. Exc. cond. $20.00

CANTEEN COVER (EXPERIMENTAL): Belt-carried 1 QT rubberized cover. Exc. cond. $20.00

CANTEEN: OD Plastic. 1964 dated. Avg. cond. $11.00

CAVALRY SOLDIER DUFFEL BAG: Dark OD canvas body w/built-in nylon shoulder straps. Bottom panel red/white & stenciled in blue "M-1354/D TRAP/1/10 CAVE/194TH SBA." Avg. cond. $20.00

CBR OXYGEN MASK SYSTEM: Clear Plastic shield w/flex fitting O2 mask w/mike & avionics. Headband assembly w/padded earphones. O2 hose has screw fitting at end. 1979. Exc. cond. $68.00

COLLAPSIBLE CANTEEN/FLOATATION BLADDER (5 QT): Comes in sealed cardboard carton that has 1968 date. Near mint cond. $48.00

COMPASS (M-2) IN PLASTIC CARRIER: Engineering type w/two bubble levels on face & reflective image when sighting. Above avg. cond. $28.00

DOD GENERAL PURPOSE WATCH: Westclox made, Black face, sweep second hand, 12/24 hr & glo dial, clear crystal, stem set & wound. Plastic case w/black nylon one piece band. Above avg. cond. $60.00

EMERGENCY DISTRESS LIGHT: Nam era strobe type signal light. Orange plastic case, battery powered & stored in green nylon pouch. Above avg. cond. $27.00

EMERGENCY/RESERVE CHEST PACK PARACHUTE FRAME & COVER: OD green light canvas cover w/accessories. Above avg. cond. $20.00

ENGINEER COMPASS: Heavy brass case w/liquid compass & rotating az. ring. Two

point sighting bar also used to cover glass when closed. Black finish & marked on bottom WFS L1A1. Avg. cond. $85.00

FIRING DEVICE (M-57): For detonating claymore mines. Plastic lever presses sealed switch to complete electric circuit. Metal bar for safety lever. Above avg. cond. $21.00

FLASH SUPPRESSOR: For MG, .50 cal. Serial number. 4 hole mount to weapon. Exc. cond. $11.00

GOGGLES: One piece clear lens & one piece frame & conformal face mask w/head band. 1988. Exc. cond. $21.50

INTELLIGENCE SERVICE STEREO VIEWING GLASSES: Post WWII. Black plastic frame & legs w/two piece adjustable viewing lenses. Stored in Plastic case & marked Abrams Inst. Corp. Exc. cond. $55.00

JUNGLE HAMMOCK: 1962 dated. W/rigging lines & instructional tag still attached. Nice. Exc. cond. $31.00

KOREAN WAR AIRBORNE WRIST COMPASS: Brass case w/plastic rotatable lens w/compass rose & fixed indices. Floating pointer. Leather wrist strap. Near mint cond. $40.00

KOREAN WAR AMMO BELT (BAR 6 POCKET): Dark OD canvas & web w/metal fittings. US marked & 1952 dated. Above avg. cond. $24.00

KOREAN WAR AMMO BELT (10 POCKET): Dark OD web w/brass fittings. Includes 2 dark OD web Carlisle bandage pouches, 1952 & 1945 dated. Above avg. cond. $20.00

KOREAN WAR BACKPACK STYLE PARACHUTE: Green nylon case w/web straps & alum buckles. Chute in back pack, D-ring on left shoulder harness. Quick release fittings on each shoulder harness. Dated Nov. 1952. Switler Parachute Mfg. Co. Above avg. cond. $100.00

KOREAN WAR ERA PARACHUTIST INDIVIDUAL WEAPON CASE (M1950): Padded dark OD canvas w/zipper. US marked & 1951 dated. Above avg. cond. $34.00

KOREAN WAR FIELD RADIO (RT-176): Radio & battery pack latched together as unit w/independent labels. 1963. Accessory pack, canvas w/two pouches, contains head set/mike & antenna sections. Avg. cond. $40.00

KOREAN WAR LENSATIC COMPASS: Folding OD finish body is US/1952 marked. Above avg. cond. $40.00

KOREAN WAR PARATROOP RIFLE CASE: Padded OD green case w/zipper. Rings & straps. Above avg. cond. $50.00

KOREAN WAR RUCKSACK (FRAMED): Dark OD canvas body w/dark tan leather trim & dark OD web straps. On OD finish tubular metal frame. US marked, 1951 dated. Includes slip-over white cover. Above avg. cond. $72.00

KOREAN WAR USMC AMMO BELT (10 POCKET): OD web w/brass fittings. USMC marked. Above avg. cond. $30.00

KOREAN WAR USMC DOG TAGS: Matched pair oval-shaped tags. 1/50 Tetnus shot date. On beaded neckchain. Above avg. cond. $69.00

KOREAN WAR WRIST COMPASS (M1949): OD finish metal body w/clear plastic dial w/directional markings & OD plastic hinged cover on dark OD web wrist strap. US marked & 1942 dated. Avg. cond. $59.00

LIFE PRESERVER (LPU-21B/P): Sage green w/two inflatable bladders at waist & one at neck. Adj. straps & waist buckles. Above avg. cond. $35.00

LIFE RAFT ACCESSORY KIT: Orig. box. Jan 1974 revised notice. Complete, includes repair kit. Exc. cond. $45.00

LIFE RAFT SURVIVAL KIT FISHING SET: Post WWII. Stored in a clear plastic container w/instructions & an assorted lot of tackle, lines & accessories. Shipping sleeve is in place w/mfg. address. Exc. cond. $30.00

M. P. SIDEARM HOLSTER & AMMO CLIP POUCH: Both in black leather. Holster is US/Bianchi/#99A-RH P marked. Clip pouch is US marked & 1979 dated. Avg. cond. $31.00

M. P./SHORE PATROL NIGHTSTICK: 22" long turned wood body. US marked on handle endcap. Rawhide thong. Near mint cond. $20.00

MAE WEST LIFE PRESERVER (LPP-1A): Mae West style vest w/signal light, whistle, manual inflation tube, auto inflation, dye marker & battery pack. Stored in day-glo orange nylon packet w/wear instr. on side. Near mint cond. $45.00

M. P. ARMBAND: Black leather armband w/ shoulder flange & White leather letters for DMZ, M. P. & Korean characters. Avg. cond. $20.00

NAVIGATION WRIST WATCH (A-17A): hmkd. "Bulova." Black face w/12/24 hr dial & sweep second hand. Nylon wrist bands. Above avg. cond. $95.00

NAVIGATION WRIST WATCH: USAF contract to Hamilton Watch Co. Dated 1980. 12/24 hr dial w/sweep second hand & stem wound. Nylon strap. Exc. cond. $72.00

NAVY AIRCREW COMPUTER (MARK 8 HAND HELD): Circular slide rule format for time, speed & distance computations etc. White plastic & black lettering. Marked G. Felsenthal & Sons. Avg. cond. .. $20.00

NAVY AVIATOR CLIP BOARD (MARK 2A LEG TYPE): Molded gray plastic w/spring clip on each end. Contains several grid sheets w/written entries-circa 1960s. Has wide elastic leg strap. Light unit is incomplete. Avg. cond. $20.00

NAVY AVIATOR THIGH DESK & CHECKLIST: Gray plastic w/light & clip for papers & leg straps. Checklist for TA-7C aircraft dated 15 January 1979. Above avg. cond. $24.00

NAVY BACK PACK PARACHUTE: Complete w/harness & seat pad. Switlik hmkd. on chute case. Record card attached. All components. Avg. cond. $100.00

NAVY DISTRESS MARKER LIGHT (SDU-30): Molded orange plastic body w/cord lanyard & velcro attachment panel. Well marked. 1984 dated. Exc. cond. ... $20.00

NAVY LIFE PRESERVER VEST (MARK 2): Bright yellow cotton body w/yellow nylon straps & manual inflation tube. 1958 dated. Includes USN marked distress marker light & several dye markers & OD plastic whistle. Avg. cond. $72.00

NAVY LIFE PRESERVER: 1969 dated in gray rubberized bag, Day-glo orange Mae West style vest & shoulder/chest straps for securing. Above avg. cond. $25.00

NAVY LIFE PRESERVER: Dark gray nylon covered bladders w/manual & auto inflation. Contract dated May 1984. Waist belt & pouch for survival gear. Above avg. cond. $20.00

NAVY SEAL SPECIAL OPERATIONS WATERPROOF GEAR BAG: Sage green nylon body w/diagonal zippered opening w/rubber covering. Sage green nylon straps. Unmarked. Above avg. cond. $48.00

NAVY SURVIVAL VEST (SV2-A): 1970s. Nylon w/nylon & web straps. Includes sheath for knife, holster for gun in zippered pouch & extensive use of velcro. Above avg. cond. $37.00

OXYGEN MASK (MBU-5/P): Soft face mask & full plastic sleeve frame w/straps & offset bayonets. Dated 1977 on mask & maintenance tag. Hose w/single connector. Exc. cond. $50.00

OXYGEN MASK (A-14B): 1958. Complete. Hose w/dual connector & web straps w/ snap connectors. Avg. cond. $35.00

OXYGEN MASK (A-14B): Size medium, no avionics, Soft rubber showing signs of age. White web head band attached to masks web connectors. Flex rubber hose w/dual connector. Avg. cond. $50.00

OXYGEN MASK (EXPERIMENTAL): Complete avionics. Gray plastic frame w/ green webbing & bayonet fittings. Soft dark gray conformal mask for lower face coverage, mike & valve inside. Conventional hose & single QR fitting. Exc. cond. $205.00

OXYGEN MASK (MS-22001): Rigid plastic brace over nose piece w/bayonet fittings. Avionics. Hose has dual QR fitting. 1956. Above avg. cond. $89.00

OXYGEN MASK (MS-22001): Dated 1974. Offset bayonet mounts Avg. cond. $40.00

OXYGEN MASK (MS-22001-5): 1968. Soft plastic cheeks. Mike & valves. Nylon covered hose. Avg. cond. $55.00

OXYGEN MASK (PL-291): No other usable marks. Could fit masks from A-14 forward. Near mint cond. $12.50

PARACHUTE CONTAINER: Backpack style. Contoured rigid back w/4 flaps that close to contain chute & risers. Mfg. date 1978, MOD date 10-80. Above avg. cond. $30.00

PARACHUTE SEAT PACK.: Incl. all straps, back & seat pads & seat pack. Back pad has written inst. on adjusting straps. D-ring on left shoulder strap. Pack dated Oct. 1958. Above avg. cond. $116.00

PARACHUTIST MEDICAL POUCH: 1949. Dark OD canvas folding body w/web straps. Above avg. cond. $30.00

PERISCOPE SIGHT (T-42): 14.25" tall metal housing w/metal spec plate. Section of housing w/eyepiece in interior white finish-rest in dark OD. Some wear to finish but optics are clear. Above avg. cond. $35.00

PILOT CLIP BOARD: Stored in shipping container from mfg. Type MXU-5/P, straps to thigh & contains small light, clip for papers & storage for pencils. Mil specs on each end of box. Exc. cond. $28.00

PILOT KNEE DESK: Made by North American Aviation. Clips at each end. Web strap. Avg. cond. $28.00

PISTOL HOLSTER (.45 CAL.): Shoulder style. Black leather w/US. Matching shoulder strap w/sliding leather shoulder pad. Above avg. cond. $45.00

PROTECTIVE FIELD MASK (M-9A1): 1952 mold dated rubber mask w/"cheek" filter unit & elastic head harness. Dark OD canvas carrier w/tubes of atropine & pralidoxime chloride injections. Above avg. cond. $20.00

RADIO BEACON SET (AN-URT-33B-1): Unit in OD finish w/large 1984 dated spec/ instruction decal. Includes power unit-both in issue heavy plastic bags. Mint cond. $72.00

REVOLVER HOLSTER FOR MESH AVIATOR SURVIVAL VEST: Black leather. In issue package. Mint cond. $10.50

SLEEPING BAG (M1949 TYPE I MOUNTAIN): Feather filled lt. OD w/ zipper & spec/instructional label. Above avg. cond. $30.00

SLEEPING BAG: 1953. Down filled w/wolf fur trim & waterproof liner. In waterproof clothing bag. Exc. cond. $145.00

SLEEPING BAG: Down bag in sealed fiberglass 13" sq./1" deep container w/ center wing nut lock & wire lanyard to open seam. Fits in ejection seat survival kit. Unopened & labeled. Exc. cond. $59.00

STARS & STRIPES DELIVERY BAG: White canvas bag for newspaper delivery. Has Pacific Stars & stripes red stencil on flap cover. Adj. straps & shows soiling from use. Avg. cond. $30.00

SURVIVAL EQUIP HOLDER: One man kit that can be converted to canteen when items are removed. Instructions stenciled on back. Above avg. cond. $12.50

SURVIVAL KIT: Plastic container, well marked on all sides, w/contents & instructions. Above avg. cond. $32.00

TELEPHONE SET (TA-312/PT): OD finish metal unit w/side power handcrank & 1962 dated spec tag & handset. Avg. cond. $20.00

TELESCOPE (M-65 B.C.): Massive metal body in OD finish w/adj. "rabbit" ear optics. Various adj. knobs w/light filters. Metal spec plate. Leather retainer tabs for protective lens covers. Fitted OD finish wooden case w/hinged lid. 21x10.25x9.5". Avg. cond. $139.00

TELESCOPE (M-84) W/CASE: Optics clear. Black finish metal tubular body w/rubber eye pad & adj. dials & mount. Dark OD canvas carrying case. Exc. cond. $400.00

TOOL POUCH (CS-34): Lineman double pocket pouch in issue box & dated Oct.

52. Tan leather w/long flap covering two pockets, belt loop. Near mint cond. $20.00

TRAINING RIFLE (M-16): Non-firing training device w/black composition & metal structure. ID'd as TASO-FG/D-9-1109 on stock. W/clip, grip & trigger, all levers & buttons to simulate sighting & firing. Above avg. cond. $223.00

U.D.T. MODEL "DUCK" SWIM KICK FINS: Molded black rubber. Voit marked. Stenciled w/yellow "13." Avg. cond. $23.00

USAF AIRCREW WATCH (A-17): Aircrew wrist watch by Waltham w/black face, glo dial, 12/24 dial, sweep second hand & stem wound & set. Two piece band & specs on back. Operable. Exc. cond. $189.00

USAF BACK PACK PARACHUTE: 1953 dated heavy green web harness w/alum fittings. Green Nylon pack for chute materials. Risers in place but shrouds cut & chute not present. Pack components present. Dated Apr. 53. Harness well marked. Above avg. cond. $100.00

USAF BAILOUT OXYGEN BOTTLE: 100 PSI emergency oxygen supply in green steel bottle w/indicator meter & flow control valve. Kept in canvas pouch w/ straps to attach to flyer. Famous green apple on wire for initiation. Above avg. cond. $30.00

USAF CPU-26A/P AIR NAVIGATION COMPUTER: Aluminum circular slide rule w/window on back & alum. slide wind/ groundspeed grid. Brown plastic case. Avg. cond. $20.00

USAF CREW MEMBERS WATCH: 1967 dated wristwatch w/steel case, black face 12/24 hr dial & sweep second hand. Stem wound w/specs on back. No hmkd. Nylon band. Exc. cond. $45.00

USAF FIRE FIGHTERS OXYGEN MASK: Soft conformal inner liner w/large one piece view plate & O2 assembly. Earphones attached to head band assembly, avionics pass thru & around hose. Maint. insp. card. Exc. cond. $68.00

USAF FLASH PROTECTOR GOGGLES (EDU-2/P): Mint goggles w/special flash suppresser lenses in front & side. Soft gray conforming rubber pads around frames. Electric operation & worn w/mask & helmet. For flight crew use only. Stored in padded environmentally stable case. Rare. Near mint cond. $188.00

USAF FLIGHT CREW HEAD SET W/BOOM MIKE ON LEFT SIDE. BOTH EAR

COVER CASES: hand marked. Camo (leaf pattern) helmet cover, Viet era dated 1969. Above avg. cond. $28.00

USAF FLIGHT CREW WATCH: Type A-17 wrist watch w/black face, glo & 12/14 dial, sweep second hand, Clear crystal, stem set & wound & specs in rear. Two piece leather band (stained). Operational. Above avg. cond. $164.00

USAF FLIGHT SUNGLASSES: green glass lenses in nickel frames-in fitted blue vinyl pouch. Above avg. cond. $20.00

USAF HELMET BAG: Sage green w/zipper closure & padded interior. AF emblem on side & web Handles. Hand written comments on side. Few stains. Avg. cond. $90.00

USAF LIFE PRESERVER (PU-10/P): Sage green nylon covers & webbing. Day glo red bladders Specs on cloth tag on back pad. Dated 5/73. Exc. cond. $29.00

USAF MAE WEST LIFE PRESERVER: Yellow Mae West style dated 1967 from Dover AFB, Del. Web straps & emer. whistle on outside. Shows little use. Above avg. cond. $20.00

USAF NAVIGATION COMPUTER (MB-4): Aluminum circular slide rule w/wind, drift & air/ground speed calculator using plastic sliding scale. Brown plastic carry case. Avg. cond. $20.00

USAF NAVIGATOR WATCH (A-8): Waltham Watch Co. made & hmkd. 1952. Black face dial w/10 sec face & 10 min. inner dial. Stem wound. Exc. cond. $60.00

USAF NAVIGATOR WATCH (A-17): Metal case w/specs on back & 12/24 hr dial & sweep second hand & leather wrist band, stem set & wound & dated 56 on specs. Operational. Above avg. cond. $93.00

USAF NAVIGATOR WATCH (A-17A): Hmkd. "Bulova watch co" & dated 59. 12/24 hr dial & sweep second hand & stem set & wind. Unofficial expansion band for wrist. Specs on back. Operational. Above avg. cond. $145.00

USAF OXYGEN MASK (MBU-4/P): 1966 dated. Hose has single connector. Avg. cond. $45.00

USAF OXYGEN MASK (MBU-4/P): 66 Dated w/black metal clips to attach mask to helmet. No avionics, specs on cheek flaps. Single connector hose. Shows some surface cracking & has flat spot near fitting. Avg. cond. $24.00

USAF OXYGEN MASK (MBU-5/P) 1961. Plastic shell w/nylon web & bayonet catches, soft rubber mask w/all components & mike & avionics. Flex hose w/wrap-a-round mike cord & single QR fitting. Exc. cond. $92.00

USAF OXYGEN MASK (MBU-12P): USAF mask, Orig. packing bag. Gray plastic soft mask w/hard plastic cover. Black nylon web straps & metal clips to mount. Ribbed flex hose. Mike mounted. Near mint cond. $145.00

USAF OXYGEN MASK (MS-22001): Has avionics but no other accessories to make it functional. Clean & very good for build up to ops. configuration. Avg. cond. $37.00

USAF OXYGEN MASK (QUICK DONNING CREWMEMBER): Oxygen mask w/blue alum padded brackets. Allows rapid donning of mask, securing to head immediately & the bracket feature will clear the head set. Exc. cond. $55.00

USAF RADIO CARRIER VEST: Blue nylon w/zipper front & two pockets for portable units. In orig. shipping box w/specs. Mint cond. $100.00

USAF REMOVE BEFORE FLIGHT STREAMER: Red canvas w/title in white. This one is from a North American Aviation aircraft. Above avg. cond. $20.00

USAF SURVIVAL KIT FISHING KIT: 1960s era. Clear plastic case 1 x 2.75 x 4.5" w/ written instructions & a selection of lures, lines & hooks. Above avg. cond. $20.00

USAF SURVIVAL KIT: Includes, Emergency water, mosquito net, flash guard, bandages, nylon cord, markers, first aid materials & more. Above avg. cond. $30.00

USMC AMMO CLIP BELT (M-14): Web w/7 pouches for M-14 rifle clips, shows wear. Avg. cond. $22.00

USMC DUFFEL BAG: Olive canvas bag is stenciled w/heavy tank design & "-7th Tank Bn.-A Co." above & "7/TK" below. Other side stenciled w/3rd Mar. Div. patch design w/"A-Co. 3d Tk Bn." above & "3d Mar. Brig. F.M.F." below. Above avg. cond. $24.00

USMC PISTOL BELT AND BELT PLATE: large plate with USMC logo on soiled white woven belt. Above avg. cond. $11.00

USMC PISTOL HOLSTER (.45 CAL.): Shoulder style. Black leather w/US embossed in oval on body & matching straps. USMC marked on reverse. Shows little age. Exc. cond. $55.00

USN LIFE PRESERVER VEST: Yoke type. Orange nylon body w/manual inflation tube. Well marked & 1969 dated. Includes US marked/1966 dated plastic whistle.

Comes in gray vinyl waist pouch w/web straps. Above avg. cond. $22.00

VIETNAM ERA "DOG DOO" TRANSMITTER: 4.25" long body molded to resemble solid excrement of dog or similar size animal. Designed to send homing beacon to monitoring aircraft. Comes w/photocopy of spec/info. sheet. Mint cond. $100.00

VIETNAM ERA AIRBORNE PARACHUTE PACK: Canopy & shrouds missing from back pack, replaced with large foam pad. Chest pack hand labeled "NAM" a peace symbol "66-67" "T. Jones." All webbing & quick release intact. Above avg. cond. $128.00

VIETNAM ERA ARMY ARTY FUSE SETTER: Model XM63-battery powered w/finger switch & view screen. Two handed use. Avg. cond. $20.00

VIETNAM ERA ARMY TRANSMITTER RECEIVER SYSTEM: AN/PRT-4 transmitter. Handy-talkie style & AN/prt-9 helmet mounted receiver system. PRT-9 uses 9v battery. Avg. cond. $59.00

VIETNAM ERA AVIATOR EJECTION SEAT MINI SURVIVAL PACK: Sage green nylon seat pack w/cutout for control stick w/ zipper enclosed survival items. Includes canned water, medical & gen. survival items in indiv. pouches. Above avg. cond. $40.00

VIETNAM ERA AVIATOR FLARE PEN: 4" long milled alum. device w/spring loaded firing pin. Has pivoting eye screw for lanyard in 1 end-includes spent flare casing-67 dated. Above avg. cond. $16.00

VIETNAM ERA AVIATOR SURVIVAL KIT: Includes packet No. 1 & 2 in dark green pouches. Exc. cond. $59.00

VIETNAM ERA BODY BAG

VIETNAM ERA BODY BAG: Large OD rubberized body w/6 reinforced integral carry handles w/heavy OD web straps. US marked. 1965 dated. Zipper opening. Above avg. cond. $85.00

VIETNAM ERA CANTEEN & COVER: Vietnamese made SVN QM item patterned after U.S. issue plastic canteen. Molded in dark olive plastic. "Chi De Dung Nuoc Tranh Ngon Lua Va Vi Lo Nong/Q/ .L.V.N.C.H./Dai Dong 1969" marked. OD canvas cover, Viet. made & patterned after US. Snap flaps & wire belt hanger. Above avg. cond. $84.00

VIETNAM ERA CAPTURED EQUIPMENT TAG: Brass & stamped w/data-'5th SFG (ABN)/NHA TRAN/rel. to CONUS/ 120.' Avg. cond. $40.00

VIETNAM ERA CBR MASK SYSTEM: M25A1 in case, w/mask & single faceplate, mike, straps & hose, canister & accessories. Green canvas bag. Exc. cond. $55.00

VIETNAM ERA DOG MUZZLE: Multi-piece riveted tan leather body is US marked, 1968 dated. Exc. cond. $22.00

VIETNAM ERA DUFFEL BAG: Dark OD canvas w/dark OD web straps. US marked & 1972 dated. About as good as they come. Mint cond. $30.00

VIETNAM ERA ENGINEER COMPASS: 1966 dated army topographical compass w/map x-ref. capability. Lanyard incl. Avg. cond. $33.00

VIETNAM ERA EQUIPMENT BELT RIG: Dark OD web belt w/metal fittings & female snap ends for attachment of pouches & 3 M-14 clip pouches. M8 scabbard & 1944 dated canteen w/cup in dark OD canvas carrier. 1968 dated USMC combat suspenders. Avg. cond. $82.00

VIETNAM ERA FIELD BUTT PACK: Dark OD canvas w/dark OD web straps. US marked & 1970 dated. Includes original load bearing equip. assembly sheet. Near mint cond. $12.00

VIETNAM ERA FIELD PACK: Dark OD canvas body in assault pack design. DSA contract marked. Named. Above avg. cond. $25.00

VIETNAM ERA FIELD RATION ACCESSORY PACKET: Sealed brown package that contains various items including cigarettes. Near mint cond. $34.00

VIETNAM ERA FIELD RATION: For long range patrol units. Gray envelope sealed for all conditions w/contents identified on sides. Menu #4 beef with rice. Above avg. cond. $40.00

VIETNAM ERA FIELD TELEPHONE: In Green canvas case w/strap. Labeled

CY127/B/P1. External crank, internal headset, controls & batteries. Above avg. cond. $45.00

VIETNAM ERA FIRST AID KIT: Nylon pouch w/plastic container inside, all contents. Belt clips on back & hmkd. inside flap. Exc. cond. $40.00

VIETNAM ERA FIRST AID KIT: Squad size. OD Brown plastic case w/red cross. X-ref. list in lid. Above avg. cond. $40.00

VIETNAM ERA FLIGHT HELMET BAG: Padded sage green nylon w/1967 spec label & cord draw closure. Avg. cond. $53.00

VIETNAM ERA FUSE SETTER HANDLE M63: Battery powered w/thumb control & small view screen. Two hand use, all metal. Avg. cond. $20.00

VIETNAM ERA GUN COVER: In 1967 dated issue package. Near mint cond. ... $13.00

VIETNAM ERA HELICOPTER GUNNER SAFETY VEST: Nylon web mesh w/straps & metal clips to secure gunner in open door. Exc. cond. $84.00

VIETNAM ERA HELMET CARRYING BAG: Dark OD nylon w/quilted OD nylon lining, zipper & dual "grip" handles. 1974 dated. Above avg. cond. $48.00

VIETNAM ERA INTRUSION DETECTING SET (AN-PSR-1A): Dark OD finish control set w/operating instruction plate inside hinged lid & panel w/many knobs & attachment posts. Also, 4 seismometers & headset & ground rod. Comes in correct dark OD canvas carrying case w/heavy web straps & 1968 dated USMC tech. manual set. Exc. cond. $177.00

VIETNAM ERA JUNGLE HAMMOCK: Dark OD mesh, cotton & rubberized constr. w/ rigging lines. Above avg. cond. $28.00

VIETNAM ERA LIFE VEST (AV-5): Bright yellow nylon w/1969 dated markings & white nylon web straps. Above avg. cond. $30.00

VIETNAM ERA LOAD BINDERS: Lot of 6 1967 dated binders. For securing & tensioning cargo loads on aircraft. Exc. cond. $20.00

VIETNAM ERA MEDICAL KIT: Nylon pouch w/plastic container inside, all contents. Belt clips on back. Exc. cond. $40.00

VIETNAM ERA NAVY LIFE PRESERVER (MARK 2): Bright orange nylon w/orange nylon straps & manual inflation tube. Well marked & 1968 dated. Accessories incl. Navy marked MOD. 761-1 strobe light, 2 smoke & illumination flares & 2 sea dye markers & plastic whistle on cord & shark repellent. Avg. cond. $63.00

VIETNAM ERA PONCHO/SHELTER-HALF: Dark OD rubberized materiel w/metal snaps & 1968 spec markings. Above avg. cond. $23.00

VIETNAM ERA PONCHO: OD coated nylon twill w/1967 markings. Exc. cond. . .$25.00

VIETNAM ERA PUGILS STICKS: Pr. 44" long w/padded cylinders at each end. Molded plastic bar. Avg. cond. $40.00

VIETNAM ERA RUCKSACK FRAME: OD finish tubular metal body. No straps, etc. Exc. cond. $25.00

VIETNAM ERA RUCKSACK: OD nylon body is US marked. Instruction label. OD finish tubular metal frame. Avg. cond. $60.00

VIETNAM ERA RUCKSACK: OD nylon pack US marked & 1968 dated. OD finish tubular frame w/nylon shoulder straps. Avg. cond. $82.00

VIETNAM ERA RUCKSACK: Dark OD nylon body w/several storage pockets. On OD finish tubular metal frame complete w/ shoulder straps & kidney pad. US marked. 1968 dated. Above avg. cond. ... $263.00

VIETNAM ERA RUCKSACK

VIETNAM ERA SEAT PACK SURVIVAL GEAR (A-7): Padded seat from ejection survival pack w/emergency oxygen bottle & release valve & actuating lanyard. Seat lid w/specs. Sage green nylon pack w/ lanyard for attaching to seat & 11 survival items in pouch at bottom, mostly medical & cord & whistle. Above avg. cond. $177.00

VIETNAM ERA SURVIVAL KIT FISHING PACK: Clear plastic case w/contents list. Components & fishing instr. inside. Sealed w/green tape. Exc. cond. $20.00

VIETNAM ERA SURVIVAL KIT: For HOT-WET climates. OD plastic container w/ printed instructions. Above avg. cond. $37.00

VIETNAM ERA SURVIVAL PLANT ID CARDS: Box of photo studies of SEA plants with written details. In orig. Box. Above avg. cond. $20.00

VIETNAM ERA SURVIVAL SALT WALTER DISTILLATION KIT: From life raft kit. 1966. Exc. cond. $30.00

VIETNAM ERA TENT-SIZE MOSQUITO NET: Dark OD nylon mesh w/1971 dated spec tag. Near mint cond. $40.00

VIETNAM ERA TRAIL SENSOR ANTENNA: Camo antenna that looks like low plant w/o leaves, 21" tall. Above avg. cond. $45.00

VIETNAM ERA USAF GUU-1/P HOLSTER ASSEMBLY: Black leather body w/snap closure retainer strap & wire belt hanger on swivel mount. Nickel fittings. Well marked, 1964 dated. Exc. cond. ... $32.00

VIETNAM ERA USAF SECURITY POLICE AMMO CLIP POUCHES (M-16) W/CLIPS: OD/gray canvas 2-pocket pouches w/lift-dot closure flaps. Includes 2 well marked clip pouches. Above avg. cond. $20.00

VIETNAM ERA USAF TYPE LIFE PRESERVER (LPU-10/P): 1968. Bright fluorescent orange nylon. Above avg. cond. $40.00

VIETNAM ERA USMC CARGO FIELD PACK (M1941): Dark OD canvas w/dark OD web straps & metal equip. clips & fittings. Well marked & 1972 dated. Above avg. cond. $23.50

VIETNAM ERA WHITE PANEL MARKER: 12 x 2.3' w/grommets at corners. Type AL-121. Exc. cond. $20.00

VIETNAM ERA WRIST WATCH: Dated Aug. 1965 Type DTU 2A/P w/black face, 24 hr dial & sweep second hand. Stem wound & sealed case. Exc. cond. $115.00

WALKIE-TALKIE (RT-196/PRC-6): OD finish metal body w/riveted spec tag & antenna & dark OD web wrist strap. Some wear to finish. Avg. cond. $28.00

U.S. KNIVES

A. Thru World War I (1919)

ARKANSAS TOOTHPICK (CIVIL WAR CONFEDERATE): 10.5" long w/tip. Small guard w/forward pointing tips. Wood grip. Below avg. cond. $387.00

ARKANSAS TOOTHPICK (CIVIL WAR CONFEDERATE)

BOLO KNIFE (MODEL 1909): 14" bright steel blade marked 'SA/(ord bomb)/1910' & 'US/5688.' 2-pc wood grip. Brass pommel. Above avg. cond. $98.00

BOLO KNIFE (MODEL 1909): 14" polished steel blade hmkd 'US/15378' & 'SA/(ord bomb)/1912' on ricasso. Black finished guard. Walnut grips held by 3 brass rivets w/brass pommel. Leather sheath w/ blackened brass throat & latch pin. Hmkd 'LADEW//HJB.' Exc. cond. $255.00

BOLO KNIFE (MODEL 1909): 14" steel blade hmkd 'US/55758' & 'Plumb/PHila/ (ord bomb)/1917' on ricasso. Black finished steel guard. Walnut grip held by 3 rivets. Brass pommel. Russet leather scabbard w/blackened brass throat & catch. Brass swivel ring at tip. Belt loop on back & hmkd ' Rock Island Arsenal/1911/ HEK.' Near mint cond. $191.00

BOLO KNIFE (MODEL 1909)

BOLO KNIFE (MODEL 1917 CT): Dark blade hmkd 'US MOD 1917/CT' & 'AC CO. 1918.' Wood ribbed grips. 1918 dated scabbard. Exc. cond. $118.00

BOLO KNIFE (MODEL 1917 CT): Polished steel blade etched w/'Plumb' name & 'Double Life' in box on side. Steel guard & 2-pc wood grips held by 2 screws.

Pommel in birds head style. Above avg. cond. $130.00

BOLO KNIFE (MODEL 1917): Hmkd on ricasso 'Plumb/Phila./1918' & 'US MOD 1917.' Blade is pitted & scratched. Grip in good shape for age. Scabbard is canvas over wood & is dated 1918 on leather tip. Avg. cond. $45.00

BOLO KNIFE (MODEL 1917): Hmkd 'Plumb/ Phila 1918' & 'US/Mod 1917.' Blued blade. Type II scabbard. Above avg. cond. $100.00

BOWIE KNIFE (CIVIL WAR CONFEDERATE): 15.5" blade. 1-pc brass D guard w/2-pc walnut grip w/hand cut checker pattern. Avg. cond. $333.00

BOWIE KNIFE (CIVIL WAR CONFEDERATE): Battlefield recovery. 12.5" blade w/pointed oval steel guard. Above avg. cond. $500.00

BOWIE KNIFE (CIVIL WAR CONFEDERATE): Battlefield recovery. 17.5" length. Home made, w/steel guard & round wood grip. Bowie tip classic. Guard is oval w/pointed top & curved forward. Below avg. cond. $750.00

BOWIE KNIFE (CIVIL WAR): 15" blade w/ 'William/W S/Swlft.' '12' at rlcasso. Tln 'D' guard w/knuckle bow. Stag grip. Above avg. cond. $527.00

BOWIE KNIFE (CIVIL WAR)

DAGGER, DRESS, GENERAL ULYSSES S. GRANT'S: 11.5" plated dagger blade, engraved for 1/2 the length. Brass hilt begins w/a brass cap for scabbard before the filigree guard. The guard has quillons w/upswept & downswept curves. Ferrule w/interlocking ring design & brass backstraps w/leaf design bracket the grips. Large brass knights head pommel is secured w/slotted metal screw. Leather scabbard w/plain brass tip & ornate brass throat w/combined lattice & open sunburst design showing leather through the open areas. One suspension ring attached to throat brass. Avg. cond. $3,685.00

ENTRENCHING KNIFE: Dated 1892 on brass guard. Polished steel blade. Brass guard w/extensions to secure blade. Turned wood grip. Hmkd Springfield Armory. Dark leather scabbard w/brass throat & belt clip. Hmkd Watervlet Arsenal. Near mint cond. $2,638.00

FIGHTING KNIFE (CIVIL WAR ERA CONVERSION): Blade cut down to 10.75". 'Ames Co./Chicopee, Ms' marked ricasso. Brass guard & muzzle ring retained but grip modified & wrapped leather strips. Cutdown scabbard included. Above avg. cond. $295.00

FIGHTING KNIFE
(CIVIL WAR ERA CONVERSION)

HOSPITAL CORP KNIFE (MODEL 1887): 12" polished steel blade w/'Hospital Corps/US Army' monogrammed on side. Initials 'N J' at ricasso. Steel guard & ribbed wood grip w/steel ferrule & pommel. Black leather scabbard w/brass throat & belt clip, marked Rock Island Arsenal on back. Exc. cond. $1,026.00

HOSPITAL CORP KNIFE (MODEL 1904): 12" blade, blunt end & hmkd 'SA/ord emb/ 1914' & 'US/38188' at ricasso. Brass guard & notched wood grip. Scabbard of leather over wood, brass throat & belt loop. Avg. cond. $65.00

HOSPITAL CORP KNIFE (MODEL 1904): Bright steel blade. Hmkd 'SA/1910' w/'ord bomb.' Serial # '15032' under 'US.' S curved brass guard & wood grips. Leather scabbard w/1912-Rock Island Arsenal marks & metal belt clip. Exc. cond
.... $221.00

HOSPITAL CORP KNIFE (MODEL 1908): 12" steel blade w/hmkd 'SA/bomb symbol/ 1908' on ricasso. Brass guard w/S curved quillons & contoured, notched wood grip w/brass rivets. Black leather sheath w/ steel throat, metal belt loop & marked Rock Island Arsenal-1912. Exc. cond.
.... $154.00

RIFLEMAN KNIFE (1849): By Ames Mfg. Co. of Cabotville, Mass. Hmkd on ricasso. 12" steel blade. Insp. initials on reverse of ricasso & edge of guard. Brass guard. Short ferrule & wood grip held by 3 rivets w/lanyard hole. Black leather sheath w/ brass tip & throat. 1st U.S. issue knife. Avg. cond. $2,500.00

TRENCH KNIFE (MODEL 1917 LF&C): Blued triangular blade. Pyramidal knuckles on sheet metal crossguard, marked LF&C & dated 1917. Black walnut grip has 'VK' carved in 1 side. Green

leather scabbard w/blued metal fittings. Above avg. cond. $150.00

TRENCH KNIFE (MODEL 1917 LF&C): Blued triangular blade. Walnut grip. Steel guard & knuckle bar w/7 knobs incl. skull cracker. Hmkd on guard 'LF&Co./1917.' Below avg. $175.00

TRENCH KNIFE (MODEL 1917 LF&C): Blued triangular blade. Heavy sheet metal D shaped knuckle bow w/pyramidal knuckle flares, marked 'U.S. L.F.&C. 1917.' Finger notched black walnut grip. Olive drab finished leather scabbard, maker marked & dated 1918, w/blued metal tip & throat. Exc. cond. $269.00

TRENCH KNIFE (MODEL 1917 LF&C): Hmkd 'US/LF&C/1917' on guard. Wood grip. Leather scabbard. Avg. cond.
.... $60.00

TRENCH KNIFE (MODEL 1917 LF&C): Blued triangular blade. 7 bumps on knuckleguard & skull cracker. Hmkd on guard 'US/ LF & CO/1917.' Leather scabbard w/black metal fitting. Near mint cond. $500.00

TRENCH KNIFE (MODEL 1917 OCL): Blued triangular blade. Dark steel guard & knuckle bow w/double row of 5 knobs each. Walnut grip w/cross hatching. Hmkd on face of guard 'US/OCL/1918.' Custom leather sheath. Exc. cond. $450.00

TRENCH KNIFE (MODEL 1917) Blued triangular blade. Hmkd on guard 'US /LF & C / 1917.' Wood grip. Avg. cond. .. $66.00

TRENCH KNIFE (MODEL 1917): Blued triangular blade, unmarked. Walnut grip. Hmkd on knuckle guard 'AC Co. 1917.' Double row of knobs & skull cracker. Green finished leather scabbard w/metal fittings. Exc. cond. $200.00

TRENCH KNIFE (MODEL 1917): Blued triangular blade. 2 rows of 5 knobs & skull cracker on knuckle guard. Hmkd on inside of bar 'AC Co. USA 1917.' Exc. cond. $181.00

TRENCH KNIFE (MODEL 1917)

TRENCH KNIFE (MODEL 1918 MK I): 'HD&S' model from 1918. 8" DE style blade. 1-pc brass hilt w/4 hole knuckle guard & skull cracker. Hmkd on side 'US 1918/HD&S.' Avg. cond. $315.00

TRENCH KNIFE (MODEL 1918 MK I): 6.5"
DE blade. 1-pc brass hilt has 4 hole
knuckle guard w/4 bumps & skull cracker.
Hmkd 'US 1918/LF&C 1918.' Scabbard
dated 1918. Above avg. $213.00

TRENCH KNIFE (MODEL 1918 MK I): Blued
blade w/'Au Lion' hallmark on ricasso. 1-
pc brass grip w/4 finger knuckle grip & 'US
1918' on side. Skull cracker at rear. Black
finished metal scabbard. Exc. cond.
.... $282.00

TRENCH KNIFE (MODEL 1918 MK I): Brass
grip, hmkd 'LF&C' & dated 1918. Sheet
metal scabbard is complete w/belt hooks
& is also marked 'LF&C' & dated 1918.
Exc. cond. $245.00

TRENCH KNIFE (MODEL 1918 MK I):
Modified w/non-std blade. 8" DE steel
blade w/all brass hilt. Marked on side 'US
1918/O. C. L. 1918.' Knuckle spines are
sharply pointed. Oval guard. Avg. cond.
.... $420.00

TRENCH KNIFE (MODEL 1918 MK I)

TRENCH KNIFE (MODEL 1918 MK I): Steel
blade. 1-pc brass knuckle guard hilt
marked on side 'LF&C CO. 1918' & 'US
1918.' 4 hole guard w/spikes & skull
cracker. Metal scabbard. Below avg.
cond. $163.00

TRENCH KNIFE (WWI 1918 MK I): French
made & Marked Au Lion on ricasso. Bright
steel DE blade w/1-pc brass knuckle
guard hilt. 4 hole w/skull cracker & marked
US 1918 on side. Blackened metal
scabbard w/belt clips. Exc. cond.
.... $263.00

B. 1920 - 1945

FIGHTING KNIFE (AUSTRALIAN MADE): 6"
steel blade, Hmkd 'East Bros/Sidney' on
ricasso. Hmkd 'US/1944' on blade side of
guard. Wood grips w/Broad arrow insp.
mark. Leather sheath. Exc. cond.
.... $533.00

FIGHTING KNIFE (AUSTRALIAN MADE):
Hmkd on blade 'Gregsteel/US 1944.' Steel
guard. Wood grips. Leather sheath. Above
avg. cond. $301.00

FIGHTING KNIFE (AUSTRALIAN MADE):
Hmkd on guard 'Whittingslove' & 'US
1944.' 5.75" blade. Wood grip. Leather

sheath Hmkd on neck & dated 'Sydney
1944.' Avg. cond. $196.00

FIGHTING KNIFE (CASE): WWII era. 6.85"
parkerized blade. Slightly curved steel
guard. Polished leather washer grip. Black
plastic pommel. Tan leather sheath. Mint
cond. $750.00

FIGHTING KNIFE (CASE): WWII era. 6.9"
polished DE blade. Hmkd 'CASE' on
ricasso. Steel guard curved toward point.
Washer grip. Black plastic pommel.
Sheath has brown frog & black finished
cover. Avg. cond. $448.00

FIGHTING KNIFE (CASE 'PIG STICKER'):
WWII era. 6.5" polished steel DE dagger
blade w/unusual ricasso marked 'CASE.'
Tang runs length of hilt & is covered by 2-
pc wood grip w/3 rivets. Stamped 'US' on
side of grip. Leather sheath w/metal belt
clip. Above avg. cond. $255.00

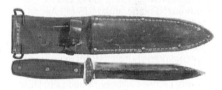

FIGHTING KNIFE (CASE 'PIG STICKER')

FIGHTING KNIFE (CASE 'PIG STICKER'):
WWII era. Chrome plated blade. Marked
'CASE XX' at ricasso. 2-pc wood grip w/
rivets. Exc. cond. $250.00

FIGHTING KNIFE (CASE XX): Nickle plated
blade, hmkd 'CASE-XX' & '337-6" Q.'
Half guard w/ribbed leather grip. Tan
leather sheath. Name & service # hand
printed on frog. Exc. cond. $106.00

FIGHTING KNIFE (CASE XX): WWII era.
The '337-6"Q model w/bright blade &
ricasso hmkd w/'337-6" Q' + rev w/'CASE'.
Ribbed leather washer grip & heavy steel
pommel w/checkered butt. Tan leather
sheath. Near mint cond. $263.00

FIGHTING KNIFE (EGW): WWII era. 6.25"
steel blade w/trade bottle opener &
sawback feature. Marked 'EGW/Knife' on
ricasso. Steel half guard. Contoured
leather grip. Tang extends beyond
pommel & drilled for ring. Leather sheath.
Avg. cond. $34.00

FIGHTING KNIFE (EGW): WWII era. Steel
blade. Hmkd on ricasso 'EGW/KNIFE.' 1/2
guard. Leather sheath. Avg. cond.
.... $38.00

FIGHTING KNIFE (GERBER): 6.75" steel
DE blade w/sawback on both edges.
Hmkd on ricasso. 1-pc black textured
finish hilt, drilled at pommel for lanyard.

Black leather sheath w/lanyard at tip & guard strap. Above avg. cond. $97.00

FIGHTING KNIFE (JOHN EK): WWII era. Variant on the commando knife, 6.75" DE blade w/John Ek signature & address on blade & '2/L274' on ricasso. Guardless wood grip w/trademark pattern & 3 steel rivets. Tang extends beyond grip & grip is drilled for lanyard. Leather sheath w/hand stamped pattern on face. Above avg. cond. $270.00

FIGHTING KNIFE (KABAR): WWII era. 6" plated steel blade patterned after Mark II. Steel disc for pommel. Tan leather sheath. Marked on guard. Above avg. cond. $76.00

FIGHTING KNIFE (LANGBEIN): WWII era. Hmkd on ricasso 'Langbein/New York.' Polished steel blade. Hilt drilled for lanyard at pommel. Leather sheath similar to M6. Above avg. cond. $387.00

FIGHTING KNIFE (M3): WWII era. Parkerized blade hmkd 'US M3 Aerial/ Marinette, Wisc.' Polished ribbed leather grip. US M8 scabbard & web frog. Near mint cond. $360.00

FIGHTING KNIFE (M3): WWII era. Parkerized blade. Hmkd 'US M3 Boker' on guard. Leather washer ribbed grip. USM8 scabbard. Exc. cond. $275.00

FIGHTING KNIFE (M3): WWII era. Blued blade, guard & pommel. Guard hmkd 'US M3/Camillus.' Polished grooved leather grip. USM8 scabbard. Near mint cond. $238.00

FIGHTING KNIFE (M3)

FIGHTING KNIFE (M3): WWII era. Dark blued blade hmkd 'Case.' Contoured leather grip. M6 sheath. Above average cond. $173.00

FIGHTING KNIFE (M3): WWII era. Parkerized blade. Hmkd 'US M3/CASE' on guard. M6 sheath dated 1943. Avg. cond. $201.00

FIGHTING KNIFE (M3): Anodized blade. Hmkd 'US M3/Imperial' on guard. Scabbard stenciled w/a name & USM8 on throat. Avg. cond. $76.00

FIGHTING KNIFE (M3): WWII era. Blued blade hmkd 'Imperial.' Leather washer grip. Dark leather M6 sheath hmkd 'Milsco' & dated 1943. Avg. cond. $99.00

FIGHTING KNIFE (M3): WWII era. Parkerized blade, 'US M3 Imperial 1943' engraved on side of blade. Polished ribbed leather washer grip. M6 sheath dated 1943. Near mint cond. ... $1,420.00

FIGHTING KNIFE (M3): WWII era. Parkerized blade. Hmkd 'US M3 IMPERIAL.' Leather grip. USM8 scabbard. Above avg. cond. $100.00

FIGHTING KNIFE (M3): Hmkd 'US M3 Kinfolks Inc.' Blued blade. Grooved leather washer grip. M6 tan leather scabbard. Exc. cond. $565.00

FIGHTING KNIFE (M3)

FIGHTING KNIFE (M3): WWII era. Blued blade & Hmkd 'PAL.' Leather washer ribbed grip. Milsco M6 sheath w/belt loop dated 1943. Avg. cond. $99.00

FIGHTING KNIFE (M3): WWII era. Grey blade hmkd 'Pal 1943.' Oval leather grip shows. M6 sheath Hmkd 'US M6/LEC/ 1943/FUA.' Above avg. cond. $222.00

FIGHTING KNIFE (M3): WWII era. Blued blade hmkd 'R.C.Co.' Leather grip. Dark brown leather M6 sheath hmkd 'Milsco/ 1943.' Avg. cond. $249.00

FIGHTING KNIFE (M3): Anodized blade. Hmkd 'M3-Utica' on blade & 'US' on ricasso. Grooved leather washer grip. USM8 model scabbard. Avg. cond. $125.00

FIGHTING KNIFE (M3): WWII era. Grey blade hmkd 'US M3 Utica.' Avg. cond. $100.00

FIGHTING KNIFE (M3): WWII era. Parkerized blade hmkd 'US M3 Utica.' Leather grip. USM8 scabbard w/web frog. Near mint cond. $198.00

FIGHTING KNIFE (MK I USN): WWII era. Hmkd 'H Boker & Co/USA' on ricasso. Blued blade. Black plastic pommel. Leather grip. Leather scabbard. Above avg. cond. $65.00

FIGHTING KNIFE (MK I USN): WWII era. Blued blade. 'Camillus' marked on ricasso. Leather grip. USN Mk 2 scabbard. Exc. cond. $62.00

FIGHTING KNIFE (MK I USN): WWII era. Hmkd 'Geneva Forge' on ricasso under 'Mark 1.' Smooth leather grip. Alum pommel. Mark 1 scabbard. Avg. cond. $49.00

FIGHTING KNIFE (MK I USN): WWII era. Grey unfullered blade marked 'USN/

Colonial/ Prov. R. I.' on ricasso. Solid
rubber composition half guard, grip &
pommel. Grip is grooved for traction. Avg.
cond. $20.00
FIGHTING KNIFE (MK I USN): WWII era.
Hmkd on ricasso 'Geneva Forge.' Blued
blade. Half guard. Leather grip. Alum
pommel. Riveted sheath w/USN at throat.
Exc. cond. $65.00
FIGHTING KNIFE (MK I USN): WWII era.
Hmkd on ricasso 'KaBar, Olean NY.' Blued
blade. Half guard. Leather fold over style
sheath w/USN on throat. Avg. cond.
.... $75.00
FIGHTING KNIFE (MK I USN): WWII era.
Parkerized blade. Hmkd 'Camillus/NY' on
ricasso. Leather grips bound by black
plastic washers. Near mint cond.
.... $160.00

FIGHTING KNIFE (MK I USN)

FIGHTING KNIFE (MK I USN): Hmkd on
ricasso 'KaBar/Olean, NY.' Half guard.
Leather grip. Leather sheath of roll over
design & USN marked at throat. Exc.
cond. $76.00
FIGHTING KNIFE (MK I USN): Hmkd 'Pal
RH35' on ricasso. Mark I canvas
scabbard. Above avg. cond. $65.00
FIGHTING KNIFE (MK I USN): WWII era.
Parkerized blade. Hmkd 'PAL RH-35' &
'USN/MK I' on ricasso. MK1 scabbard.
Avg. cond. $40.00
FIGHTING KNIFE (MK I USN): WWII era.
'Schrade' marked on ricasso. Leather
sheath. Exc. cond. $33.00
FIGHTING KNIFE (MK I USN): WWII era.
Blued blade. Hmkd 'ROBESON
SHUREDGE/NO. 20' & 'USN/M.K.1.' on
ricasso. Polished aluminum pommel. Fold
over leather sheath w/USN at throat.
Above avg. cond. $63.00

FIGHTING KNIFE (MK I USN)

FIGHTING KNIFE (MK I USN UDT
VERSION): WWII era. Special rust
resistant bright blade. Hmkd on ricasso

'USN/MK2' w/Mfg struck over. Smooth
leather grip. Green plastic scabbard w/
nylon web frog & hilt strap. Near mint.
.... $282.00
FIGHTING KNIFE (MK II USN): Blued blade.
Hmkd 'US/Camillus' at ricasso. Above
avg. cond. $16.00
FIGHTING KNIFE (MK II USN): WWII Era.
Blued blade. Hmkd 'CAMILLUS, NY' &
'USN/MARK2.' Leather grip. Mark 2 model
scabbard. Exc. cond. $110.00
FIGHTING KNIFE (MK II USN): WWII era.
'Camillus' hmkd on guard. Parkerized
blade. Tan leather USN sheath. Avg. cond.
.... $30.00
FIGHTING KNIFE (MK II USN): WWII era. In
protective paper with protective wrap on
throat of scabbard. Parkerized blade w/
'Camillus' on ricasso. Near mint cond.
.... $177.00
FIGHTING KNIFE (MK II STYLE):
Parkerized blade. Hmkd 'US/Conetta.'
Leather washer grip. Dark leather sheath
w/hilt strap. Exc. cond. $35.00
FIGHTING KNIFE (MK II USMC): WWII era.
Parkerized blade hmkd 'KA-BAR.' Smooth
grooved leather grip. Tan leather sheath.
Exc. cond. $102.00

FIGHTING KNIFE (MK II USMC)

FIGHTING KNIFE (MK II USN): WWII era.
Dark parkerized blade. KaBar marked on
guard. Polished ribbed leather grip. MKII
scabbard. Mint cond. $110.00
FIGHTING KNIFE (MK II USN): WWII era.
Hmkd 'KABAR' on ricasso. Blued blade.
Guard hmkd 'US' & 'USN.' Polished ribbed
leather grip. Russet leather sheath w/USN
at throat. Near mint cond. $121.00
FIGHTING KNIFE (MK II USN): WWII era.
Parkerized blade. Hmkd 'KA-BAR/OLEAN
NY' on ricasso. Polished ribbed leather
grip. Leather sheath. Above avg. cond.
.... $160.00
FIGHTING KNIFE (MK II USN): WWII era.
Parkerized blade hmkd 'US NAVY' & 'RH
(PAL IN CIRCLE) 37.' Fold over leather
scabbard w/USN at throat & hilt strap.
Near mint cond. $175.00
FIGHTING KNIFE (MK II USN): WWII era.
Bright blade hmkd 'US NAVY' & 'PAL RH-
37' on ricasso. Grooved leather washer
grip. Russet leather sheath w/USN at
throat. Avg. cond. $49.00

FIGHTING KNIFE (MK II USN): WWII era.
Parkerized blade. Hmkd 'USN/MARK 2' &
'ROBESON SHUREDGE' on ricasso.
Leather grip. Tan leather roll over sheath
w/'USN' at throat. Near mint cond.
.... $151.00

FIGHTING KNIFE (MK II USN)

FIGHTING KNIFE (MK II USN): WWII era.
Parkerized blade hmkd 'UTICA CUT CO.'
Russet leather sheath. Near mint
.... $68.00
FIGHTING KNIFE (MK II USN): WWII era.
Anodized blade. Hmkd 'UTICA CUT. CO.'
on ricasso. Curved guard. Avg. cond.
.... $35.00
FIGHTING KNIFE (MURPHY): WWII era. 6"
bright blade. 1-pc cast alum grip, hmkd
'Murphy Combat' on one side & 'USA'
other. Green leather sheath. Exc. cond.
.... $300.00
FIGHTING KNIFE (MURPHY): WWII era. All
metal. Fullerless steel blade. 1-pc alum
grip, Simulated stag surface. Hmkd
'Murphy Combat Knive' on one side &
'USA' on other. Leather sheath. Exc. cond.
.... $381.00
FIGHTING KNIFE (NEW ZEALAND MADE):
6" DE blued blade & one piece alum. hilt.
Ribbed grip w/knobbed knuckle guard &
skull cracker. Leather sheath w/guard
strap. Belt loop on back. Handwritten
JMD/Guam/1944 on back. Exc. cond.
.... $225.00
FIGHTING KNIFE (NEW ZEALAND MADE):
WWII era. Done for US Marines. 5.75"
long steel blade w/'N Z/CUTLERS CO/
AUKLAND' on side. One piece aluminum
ribbed grip. Above average cond.
.... $263.00
FIGHTING KNIFE (PAL RH-36): WWII era.
Bright 6" blade. Marked on ricasso. Steel
crossguard. Leather washer grip. Oval
gray metal pommel. Brown leather sheath.
Avg. cond. $30.00
FIGHTING KNIFE (USMC): WWII era. Blued
blade. Marked 'KABAR' on ricasso. Dark
ribbed leather washer grip. Tan leather
sheath. Above average cond. $118.00
FIGHTING KNIFE (USMC): WWII era. Dark
anodized blade. Hmkd 'Camillus' &
'USMC' on ricasso. Leather sheath. Avg.
cond. $62.00

FIGHTING KNIFE (USMC): WWII era. Hmkd
'Camillus' on guard. Parkerized blade.
Leather sheath. Average condition.
.... $28.00
HOSPITAL CORP KNIFE (WWII USMC):
11.5" heavy metal blade Hmkd 'USMC/
Chatillon, NY.' 2-pc wood grip w/brass
rivets. Leather scabbard, hmkd 'Boyt/43.'
Avg. cond. $82.00
HOSPITAL CORP KNIFE (WWII USMC):
Bright blade hmkd 'USMC.' Wood grips
held by 4 steel rivets. Black leather
scabbard by 'Boyt 42'. Above avg. cond.
.... $85.00
MEDICAL CORP KNIFE (WWII USMC):
Hmkd 'USMC/CHATILLON, NY' on blade.
Wood grip held by 3 brass rivets. Russet
leather scabbard w/brass throat, leather
lanyard & hmkd 'BOYT/44' on belt loop.
Above avg. cond. $76.00
SMATCHET (OSS): 11" parkerized blade w/
steel guard & pommel. 2-pc wood grip
held by steel rivets. Leather lanyard
attached at pommel. Brown leather sheath
w/guard strap & belt loop. Exc. cond.
.... $538.00
SMATCHET (OSS): Chrome plated 11"
blade w/oval steel guard. 2-pc black
plastic grip held by 3 steel rivets. Black
dyed leather over wood sheath w/belt loop
& guard strap. Exc. cond. $460.00

SMATCHET (OSS)

SMATCHET (WWII OSS): Unmarked.
Parkerized blade. Black plastic grip w/3
rivets. Black leather covered wood
scabbard. Exc. cond. $410.00
STILETTO (ANDERSON): WWII era. 8.35"
DE steel stiletto blade made from tip of
1913 Patton saber. Short fuller extends to
grip. 1-pc molded marbleized black plastic
grip w/'Made in USA' on one side & hmkd
on other. Custom leather sheath. Exc.
cond. $288.00
STILETTO (ANDERSON): WWII era. Made
from M1913 Patton saber section.
Polished steel blade. Grey plastic grip w/
raised 'Anderson Glendale,calif' & 'Made
in USA' on other side. Leather sheath.
Above avg. cond. $433.00
STILETTO (CASE): WWII era. Less common
variant w/blued blade & card. Hmkd on

ricasso 'CASE.' DE dagger blade. Steel guard. Contoured smooth leather grip. Marked black plastic pommel. Tan leather sheath. Exc. cond. $658.00

STILETTO (CASE): WWII era. Marked on ricasso 'CASE.' Chrome plated, DE dagger style blade. Smooth leather contoured grip. Black plastic pommel is trademarked. Dark leather sheath. Exc. condition. $500.00

STILETTO (OSS): WWII era. 7" DE blade. Knurled grip. Unmarked. OD metal pancake flapper scabbard w/leather sheath in metal tip. Avg. cond.. $1,500.00

STILETTO (USMC): Entire knife finished in black. 7" DE blade. 1-pc metal hilt w/oval guard & checkered grip. Type III tan leather sheath. Above avg. cond. $750.00

STILETTO (USMC): Hmkd on blade 'Camillus/Cutlery Co/Camillus, NY.' 7.25" polished steel blade. 1-pc cast metal hilt w/oval guard & checkered grip. Type I sheath w/10 staples at throat & lanyard at tip. Above avg. cond. $588.00

STILETTO (USMC)

STILETTO (V-42 CASE): Polished steel blade w/thumb groove just above the 'CASE' hallmark. Steel guard w/leather back & leather washer grip. Steel pointed skull cracker pommel. V-42 sheath. Near mint. $1,903.00

STILETTO (V-42 CASE): WWII era. Blued blade w/ribbed thumb rest. Hmkd 'CASE' on ricasso below thumb rest. Forward curved guard, ribbed metal grip + skull cracker. Dark leather sheath. Exc. cond. $1,500.00

STILETTO (V-42 CASE): WWII era. Prototype model - bright 7.25" blade w/grooved thumb rest. Marked 'CASE' on ricasso. Leather backed steel guard. Polished smooth leather grip w/polished domed pommel. V-42 leather scabbard variation w/o staples at throat. Exc. cond. $1,250.00

STILETTO (WESTERN): WWII era. Polished steel blade. Hmkd on ricasso. Brass guard. Leather grip w/multicolored spacers at each end. Brown leather sheath. Mint cond. $1,062.00

SURVIVAL KIT KNIFE (USN): WWII era. Cutting blade hmkd 'Colonial/Prov RI.'

Saw blade. Black plastic grips. Above avg. cond. $62.00

SURVIVAL KNIFE (AIR-DROP KIT): WWII era. Found on 10 man Pacific raft kits & land/air drop kits. 14.5" parkerized blade. Black checkered plastic grip. Unmarked. Mint cond. $225.00

SURVIVAL KNIFE (AIR-DROP KIT)

SURVIVAL KNIFE (CASE): WWII era. Based on USN Mark 1. 5" bright blade. Marked 'CASE' on ricasso. Steel half guard. Smooth leather grip. Spec. circular pommel w/screw out butt reveals small chamber for matches etc. Dark leather sheath. Exc. cond. $536.00

SURVIVAL KNIFE (CASE XX): WWII era. Bright steel 4.75" blade. 'CASE/Tested XX' marked on ricasso. Grip covered in OD paint & diamond design between rivets. Threaded but w/waterproof chamber. OD finished leather sheath w/ 'YORK' stenciled on front. Exc. cond. $301.00

SURVIVAL KNIFE (M2): WWII era. Single blade. Marked 'Presto/Pat Jan 30-40' & 'Geo Schrade/Knife Co Inc' on ricasso. Simulated bone grips. OD green nylon lanyard tied to bail. Blade lock & rel button on side. Mint cond. $712.00

SURVIVAL KNIFE (V-44): WWII era. 9" chromed steel blade w/'WESTERN' stamped near ricasso. Brass guard. 2-pc molded black plastic grip held by 3 brass rivets. Tan sheath w/belt loop & hilt strap. Exc. cond. $500.00

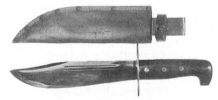

SURVIVAL KNIFE (V-44)

SURVIVAL KNIFE (V-44): Australian made version w/9.25" bowie style blade & wide oval steel guard. 2-pc wood grip held by 3 rivets. Grip stamped '112.' Black leather sheath w/belt loop. Exc. cond. $370.00

SURVIVAL KNIFE (V-44): WWII era. Hmkd on blade 'CASE XX.' 9.25" polished steel blade w/two thin fullers on each side. Brass guard w/ball quillons. Black plastic grip held by 3 steel rivets. Black leather sheath. Near mint cond. $191.00

TRENCH KNIFE (WWII 1ST RANGERS): 9" broad steel blade. Unmarked. 1-pc brass hilt w/knuckle guard. Guard equipped w/7 gear type bumps. Dark leather sheath. Above avg. cond. $500.00

TRENCH KNIFE (WWII EVERETT): Black finish. 6.75" center fullered DE blade. Green finished 1-pc knuckle guard grip. Marked on knuckle guard. Tan leather sheath w/6 staples on throat. Near mint. $875.00

TRENCH KNIFE (WWII EVERETT): Black finished. 6.75" DE dagger blade. 1-pc alum hilt. 4 hole knuckle guard w/studs. Smooth upper grip & marked on side below grip-both sides. Tan leather sheath, patterned after M6, 6 staples at throat & grommet at tip. Exc. cond. $501.00

TRENCH KNIFE (WWII EXPERIMENTAL): Patent applied for (#1193) & marked on grip. Owners name also marked on grip. 9" dagger style blade w/blue-green preservative finish. Steel guard & knuckle bow w/two rows of 5 sharp knobs on bow. Wood & alum sandwich grip w/alum on outside. Heavy leather sheath w/ reinforced hilt strap. Above average condition. $1,078.00

TRENCH KNIFE (WWII EXPERIMENTAL)

TRENCH KNIFE (WWII NEW ZEALAND MADE): Steel DE blade & 1-pc alum grip w/ribbed knucks guard. Unmarked. Dark brown leather sheath w/restraining strap for guard. Angled belt loop in back. Above avg. cond. $300.00

TRENCH KNIFE (OSS): Made from cut down 1873 socket bayonet. Metal knucks guard w/five bumps & black rubber hose grip. Blade extends to form skull cracker. Leather frog w/straps & metal 1873 scabbard. Above average cond. $349.00

TRENCH KNIFE (WWII RANGER STYLE): 8.5" bowie style anodized blade. 1-pc cast alum hilt w/knuck guard & 3 ribs. Leather

sheath designed after ranger sheath. Avg. cond. $390.00

TRENCH KNIFE (WWII): Alum hilt, Knuckle style 4 hole grip. 6" blued DE dagger style blade. Hmkd on side of grip 'PARSONS.' Leather sheath. Exc. condition. .. $328.00

UTILITY KNIFE (NAVY): Camillus marked on ricasso of cutting blade. Incl can opener blade & over sized bail w/simulated wood grips. Cotton cord lanyard. Exc. cond. $21.00

UTILITY KNIFE (T-29): WWII era. Knife blade hmkd 'Boker.' Screw driver blade w/ cutting edge. Bail on large end. Above avg. cond. $14.00

UTILITY KNIFE (USMC): WWII era. Checkered metal grips w/'U S MARINE CORPS' on side. Cutting blade, punch can, bottle openers & bail. Above average cond. $50.00

UTILITY KNIFE (USN WWII): Pocket style, single blade w/'Camillus/cutlery' on ricasso. Wood grips. Oversize bail. Exc. cond. $43.00

C. 1946 - Present

BOLO KNIFE (VIETNAM ERA SPECIAL FORCES): 9.5" thick blade w/blunt end & sharp cutting edge. Steel ferrule w/black finish. 1-pc curved wood grip. OD alum covered wood scabbard w/leather belt loop. Exc. cond. $451.00

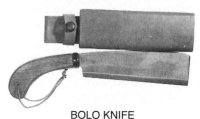

BOLO KNIFE
(VIETNAM ERA SPECIAL FORCES)

BOLO KNIFE (VIETNAM ERA SPECIAL FORCES): Copied after 1917 CT pattern. Black finished blade & hilt. Dark wood grips held by 3 brass rivets. Exc. condition. $250.00

BOLO KNIFE (VIETNAM ERA SPECIAL FORCES): Rectangular blade. Light colored wood grip held by ferrule. Wood scabbard w/alum wrap. Average condition. $294.00

FIGHTING KNIFE (DESERT STORM): M4 bayonet. Steel guard w/o muzzle ring. Black checkered plastic grip on 1 side & black cast metal grip & knucks assembly on the other. Single hole for first finger. Steel pommel. Scabbard black plastic marked 'M10.' Multiple maker marks on scabbard. Black webbing belt loop. Near mint. $71.50

FIGHTING KNIFE (KABAR MODEL 1205): 5 7/8" parkerized blade. Kabar marked on ricasso. Contoured black plastic grip framed by matching spacers & black metal pommel. Black finished leather roll over style sheath. Near mint condition .. $35.00

FIGHTING KNIFE (M2): Modern version. Hmkd 'Camillus' on ricasso of parkerized blade. Near mint. $20.00

FIGHTING KNIFE (M2): Modern version. Hmkd 'Camillus' on ricasso of parkerized blade. Near mint. $20.00

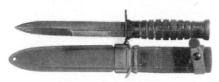

FIGHTING KNIFE (M2)

FIGHTING KNIFE (M2): Vietnam Era. 'Camillus' marked on ricasso. Camo leather sheath w/metal unit on front below throat & green woven lanyard at bottom. Above avg. cond. $23.00

FIGHTING KNIFE (MK III USN): 6" long dark finish blade w/clip point & serrated back edge. Well marked. Straight crossguard. Checkered black plastic grips. Steel pommel. USN marked. Wrist thong. Black plastic sheath. Near mint condition. $23.00

FIGHTING KNIFE (MK III USN): 5.75" long dark finish blade has serrated edge & clip point. Straight crossguard. Checkered black plastic grips. Metal pommel. Web wrist thong. Black plastic sheath. USN marked. Type used by SEALS. Mint condition. $38.00

FIGHTING KNIFE (VIETNAM ERA KABAR MODEL 1207): Popular Vietnam knife w/ 5.75" nickle plated blade, brass guard & alum pommel. Notched washer grip w/ colored washers at each end. Hmkd 'Kabar/1207 USA.' Tan leather sheath w/ logo on front. Exc. cond. $75.00

FIGHTING KNIFE
(VIETNAM ERA KABAR MODEL 1207)

FIGHTING KNIFE (VIETNAM ERA KABAR MODEL 1207): Polished steel blade, narrow fuller & hmkd on ricasso. Leather washer grip notched along bottom. Tan leather roll over style sheath w/logo at throat. Near mint. $108.00

FIGHTING KNIFE (VIETNAM ERA KABAR MODEL 1207): Polished 6" blade & Hmkd on ricasso. Brass guard. Leather washer grip & alum pommel. Leather sheath hmkd. Above avg. cond. $28.00

SURVIVAL KNIFE (MC-1): Hmkd 'Camillus' on ricasso. Dayglo orange plastic grips, brass blade lock assembly. Near mint condition. $45.00

SURVIVAL KNIFE (MC-1): Dayglo grips w/ brass blade lock & release. Hmkd 'LOGAN SMYTHE Venice Fla.' Exc. cond. $35.00

SURVIVAL KNIFE (MC-1): Used for cutting parachute shroud lines. USAF issue. W/ switch cutting blade & shroud cutter. Hmkd on ricasso. Controls on side. Dayglo grips. Exc. cond. $28.00

SURVIVAL KNIFE (JET PILOT): 6" blade. Version hmkd 'Camillius'. Dark steel blade & grooved leather grip. Leather sheath w/stone pouch. Above average condition. $86.00

SURVIVAL KNIFE (JET PILOT): Early version by Camillus w/6" parkerized blade. Hmkd on ricasso. Leather sheath w/stone pocket & stone. Avg. cond. $87.00

SURVIVAL KNIFE (JET PILOT): Hmkd on pommel 'Camillus/1967.' Bright blade. Sheath has stone. Avg. condition .. $35.00

SURVIVAL KNIFE (JET PILOT): Hmkd on pommel 'ONTARIO/1-73.' Parkerized blade. Leather sheath w/stone pouch w/ stone & metal reinforced tip. Near mint condition. $45.00

SURVIVAL KNIFE (VIETNAM ERA USN SEAL): All black w/clip point blade & sawtooth back. Checkered rubber grips. Black plastic & webbing scabbard. Marked 'Mk3 modo.' Exc. condition. $35.00

TRENCH KNIFE
(VIETNAM ERA PROTOTYPE)

TRENCH KNIFE (VIETNAM ERA PROTOTYPE): Developed from M6 bayonet by Milpar. Parkerized blade. Hmkd on guard. Knuckle bow welded to guard & mated to pommel & has 3 wide ribs on under side. Checkered black grips. US M8A1 scabbard. Above average cond. $144.00

UTILITY KNIFE (SEAL SWITCH BLADE): Modern made. 5.75" folded w/4" parkerized blade. Single release/latch pin & black plastic ribbed grips. Mint condition. $135.00

UTILITY KNIFE (USMC): Hmkd 'Camillus' w/ 1994 date on ricasso. Checkered metal grips w/'USMC' on one side. 4 jack knife blades + bail. Exc. condition. $13.00

U.S. BAYONETS & MACHETES

A. Thru World War I (1919)

BAYONET (1790S COMMITTEE OF SAFETY): Blued triangular blade & muzzle ring. 17.25" blade. In post Civil War leather scabbard w/pivoting belt loop. Avg. cond. $68.00

BAYONET (CIVIL WAR ROBBINS & LAWRENCE 'WINDSOR'): Musket socket bayonet. Marked w/emblem at base of top flute. Operable compression ring. Avg. cond. $45.00

BAYONET (KRAG): All metal w/chrome plating. Wood grips. Scabbard w/belt clip & black leather pad. Near mint cond. $41.51

BAYONET (KRAG): Bright steel blade. "US" on obv, 1908 on rev of ricasso. Wood grips. Avg. cond. $40.00

BAYONET (KRAG): Dated 1898 on ricasso & "US" marked. Bright steel blade. Steel guard & pommel. Wood grips. Steel scabbard. Above average condition. $76.00

BAYONET (KRAG)

BAYONET (KRAG): Dated 1898 on ricasso, "US" on rev. Bright steel blade. Wood grips. Blued scabbard. Above average condition. $74.00

BAYONET (MODEL 1812 MUSKET) Variant on basic bayonet. Triangular blade. No retaining ring or compression ring. Avg. cond. $44.00

BAYONET (MODEL 1812 MUSKET): Triangular blade w/mark near base. Narrow fuller on top flute. Above average condition. $87.00

BAYONET (MODEL 1816 SOCKET): No latch or ridge at end of muzzle ring. Avg. cond. $40.00

BAYONET (MODEL 1816 SOCKET): No latch or ridge at end of muzzle ring. Below avg. cond. $29.00

BAYONET (MODEL 1855 ROBBINS & LAWRENCE): The 'Windsor' Rifle-Musket bayonet, Initials & hallmark on ricasso. Functional compression ring. Avg. cond. $55.00

BAYONET (MODEL 1855 SOCKET): Hmkd "US" at base of top flute. Compression ring, operable. Below average condition. $34.00

BAYONET (MODEL 1866/1869 CADET MUSKET): Hmkd 'LH' at base of top flute. Blued steel blade. Below average condition. $35.00

BAYONET (MODEL 1870 PERIOD PEABODY MARTINI RIFLE): Socket bayonet w/cruciform blade & 'L78' on socket. Working compression ring. Avg. cond. $17.00

BAYONET (MODEL 1873 CADET SOCKET): "US" at base of blade. Steel scabbard. Leather frog w/brass disc 'US' in center, pivots & brass belt hanger. Above avg. cond. $65.00

BAYONET (MODEL 1873 SOCKET): 18" blade w/US stamped on face flute. 3" socket w/functional compression ring. Avg. cond. $35.00

BAYONET (MODEL 1873 SOCKET): Marked "US" at base of top flute. Blued finish. Leather scabbard w/metal tip & '4355 1887' on side. White leather throat & tab. Avg. cond. $72.00

BAYONET (MODEL 1873 SOCKET)

BAYONET (MODEL 1895 EXPORT): By Winchester Arms Co. Bright blade. Marked on Guard, Solid wood grips & birds head pommel. Above average condition. $145.00

BAYONET (MODEL 1905): Blued blade. Hmkd 'SA/bomb symbol/1906' on ricasso. Above avg. cond. $60.00

BAYONET (MODEL 1905)

BAYONET (MODEL 1905): Bright blade. Ricasso hmkd 'SA/(ord bomb sym)/1909' & US 385423. Canvas covered scabbard w/RIA marked leather tip & wire belt loop. Exc. cond. $195.00

BAYONET (MODEL 1905): Steel blade. Hmkd 'SA/bomb emblem/1907' & ser# 227087. Wood grips. Tan canvas covered wood scabbard w/leather tip. Average condition. $68.00

BAYONET (MODEL 1917): Grey blade. Ricasso hmkd 1918 & Remington stamp. Grips w/well defined twin vertical notches. Green leather sheath w/metal tip & throat. Heavy leather frog for wire belt loop. Exc. cond. $107.00

BAYONET (MODEL 1917): Ricasso obv w/ '1917' over circled W, Rev w/Ord bomb/ 'US.' II-.. .... $51.00

BAYONET (REVOLUTION ERA): 'L' slot on muzzle ring & triangular blade. Below avg. cond. $83.00

BAYONET (SPRINGFIELD RIFLE): Bolo style. Bright metal blade. 'US/14517' on ricasso. Steel guard w/muzzle ring & pommel. Wood grips. Exc. condition. $280.00

MACHETE (WWI ARMY "COLLINS & SON #1005"): Heavy coarse blade. Hmkd near hilt. Tan leather scabbard w/brass throat & tip. Embossed decorations on one side & Collins & Co. is embossed just below the throat. Near mint. $128.00

MACHETE (WWI ARMY ENGINEER): 15.5" blade. Coco bolo handle held by four brass rivets. Leather scabbard w/brass throat & tip. Marked 'DCFF' on front. Avg. cond. $42.00

MACHETE (WWI ARMY ENGINEER): Bright curved blade, marked w/partially stamped mfg logo and 'No. 1005.' Tang tapers toward butt of green horn grips, copper rivets. Regulation sheath. Above avg. cond. $48.00

B. 1920 - 1945

BAYONET (M1): WWII era. Anodized blade. Hmkd 'AFH/U (ORD BOMB)S' on ricasso. Steel guard & pomel. Average cond. $40.00

BAYONET (M1): WWII era. Hmkd 'AFH/U ord bomb S' on ricasso. Bright blade. Ribbed brown plastic grips. Green fibre scabbard. Avg. cond. $34.00

BAYONET (M1): WWII era. Hmkd 'UC/US' w/ord bomb. Excellent condition $66.00

BAYONET (M1)

BAYONET (M1): WWII era. Hmkd 'UFH/U ord bomb S' on ricasso. Blued blade. Green fibre scabbard. Excellent condition. $82.00

BAYONET (M1905E1): WWII era. 10" parkerized spear point blade, hmkd 'AFH' & dated 1942. Black plastic ribbed grip. Green fiber scabbard w/metal throat. Avg. cond. $42.00

BAYONET (M4): 'Imperial' hmkd on guard. Anodized blade. Brown leather sheath. Exc. cond. $100.00

BAYONET (M4): Blued blade. Hmkd on guard 'US M4/Camillus.' Polished leather grip. USM8A1 scabbard. Exc. condition. $75.00

BAYONET (M4): Blued blade. Hmkd 'US M4/ IMPERIAL' on guard. USM8 scabbard. Above avg. cond. $50.00

BAYONET (M4): Marked 'Camillus' on guard. Parkerized blade. Grooved leather washer grip. Dark metal hilt. Near mint cond. $48.00

BAYONET (M4): Parkerized blade. Hmkd on guard 'US M4/Imperial.' Ribbed leather grip. USM8A1 scabbard w/lanyard. Above avg. cond. $65.00

BAYONET (MODEL 1942): Anodized blade. "PAL 1942" hmkd on ricasso. Black plastic ribbed grips. Model 1917 scabbard w/ metal tip & throat. Average condition. $58.00

BAYONET (MODEL 1942): Steel blade. Hmkd on ricasso 'UC/ord bomb + US/ 1942.' Brown fiber scabbard. Average condition. $55.00

CRASH AXE (WWII AIRCRAFT): Green painted metal head w/spiked & conventional ends. Black rubber composition high voltage resistant handle w/checkered grip. Marked RP4 on head. Average condition. $72.00

CRASH AXE
(WWII AIRCRAFT)

CRASH AXE (WWII AIRCRAFT): Metal head has pick end & trade axe end. Handle is metal covered w/dense rubberized material capable of withstanding up to 20,000 volts of electricity. Above average condition. $39.00

MACHETE (18" COLLINS): U.S. marked w/ Collins Logo-1942 dated. Black composition grips. Remains of paper label on 1 side of blade. In US/Boyt/44 marked OD canvas sheath. Average condition. $66.00

MACHETE (18"): WWII era. Hmkd 'Collins' and dated 1944. Plastic grip. Canvas scabbard. Exc. cond. $24.00

MACHETE (18"): WWII era. Hmkd 'DISSTON/US/1943' at ricasso. Black plastic grips held by 4 rivets. Green canvas sheath, pistol style w/internal stone pocket & stone. Above average condition. $164.00

MACHETE (26" USN): WWII era. Hmkd 'collins & co' on ricasso & 'USN MK1/ 1942.' Canvas scabbard w/'USN/MK1' at throat. Above average condition. .. $33.00

MACHETE (WOODMAN PAL): Blued blade. Hmk 'WOODMAN'S PAL/284' on side of blade. Knuckle guard. Average condition. $45.00

MACHETE (WOODMAN PAL): WWII era. Black finished machete style blade w/ brush hook. Hmkd 'WOODMAN'S PAL/ 784' on side of blade. Black finished steel knuckle guard & leather grip. Canvas sheath w/sharpening stone & zipper closure. Exc. cond. $112.00

MACHETE (WOODMAN PAL): WWII era. Hmkd on blade 'Victor Tool Co.' Leather grip. Canvas sheath w/instructions & sharpening stone. Above avg. cond. $120.00

MACHETE
(WOODMAN PAL)

MACHETE (WWII AAF SURVIVAL): Case XX non folding version. Has blued 10" blade. Dark stained wood grips w/4 rivets. Above avg. cond. $50.00

MACHETE (WWII CAMILLUS FOLDING): Black plastic grip & modified blade - cut down to 1" longer than grip. Camillus marked. Avg. cond. $28.00

C. 1946 - Present

BAYONET (M5): Gray parkerized finish on all metal-Imperial maker marked. Black checkered bakelite grips. Exc. condition. $31.00

BAYONET (M5A1): Blued blade. Hmkd guard 'USM5A1/ IMPERIAL.' USM8A1 scabbard. Above avg. cond. $34.00

BAYONET (M16 RIFLE EXPERIMENTAL): Parkerized 'USN MK II' blade. M7 bayonet guard & pommel latch. 'Connetta' hmkd ricasso. Leather sheath same as USN MK II. Near mint. $100.00

BAYONET
(M16 RIFLE EXPERIMENTAL)

BAYONET (M6): Anodized blade. Hmkd on guard 'US M6/AERIAL.' Black plastic checkered grips. US M8A1 scabbard. Exc. cond. $34.00

BAYONET (M6): Parkerized blade. Hmkd on guard 'Milpar.' Checkered black plastic grips. Green fiber scabbard. Above avg. cond. $37.00

BAYONET (M6): Sealed in metallic lined moisture proof delivery pouch dated 1/71. Mint cond. $49.00

BAYONET (M6): Vietnam era. Sealed delivery pouch w/bayonet & scabbard inside. Dated Apr 1962. Hmkd Milpar. Mint cond. $53.00

BAYONET (M7): Parkerized blade. Hmkd on guard 'BOC.' Black checkered plastic grips held by 2 screws. US M8A1 scabbard. Exc. cond. $20.00

BAYONET (M7): Sealed in delivery wrap. Dated 12/89 w/fed specs & bar code on outer cover. Mint cond. $25.00

BAYONET (M9): Latest version of Bayonet-Knife concept. 7" steel anodized blade w/ sawback & slot for wire cutting duties. Hmkd 'M9/LANCAY/USA' on ricasso. Steel guard/muzzle ring. Slotted, ribbed & checkered OD plastic grip. OD plastic scabbard w/black metal wire cut assembly at tip. Nylon web frog w/grip strap, plastic

QR buckle & metal belt loop. Sharpening stone on back of scabbard. Mint cond.
.... $136.00

U.S. SWORDS

A. All Periods

ARMY SWORD (MODEL 1840 EM) 40" OA size with iron dbl. ring scabbard having throat and drag of iron. Brass D knuckle guard with leather and brass wire wrapped grip. Brass pommel cap. Above avg. cond.
.... $350.00

ARMY SWORD (MODEL 1840 NCO): Straight blade. 'PH' hmkd on ricasso. Brass hilt w/fixed langets on guard, single strand bow & ball pommel. Grip is ribbed. Steel scabbard. Average condition.
.... $214.00

ARMY SWORD
(MODEL 1840 NCO)

ARMY SWORD (MODEL 1902 OFFICER): Blade engraved & personalized. Luxemburg hmkd on ricasso. Basket guard. Notched black plastic grip. Leather woven cord w/knot. Steel scabbard w/ engraved presentation 'PRESENTED BY/ H Q DET/2ND CA.' Near mint. ... $250.00

ARMY SWORD (MODEL 1902 OFFICER): Curved blade w/patriotic etchings on upper 1/3. 4 strand knuckle basket from guard to pommel. Black finished notched wood grip nested into back strap. Woven leather cord & knot fixed to cord slot in knuckle bow. Polished scabbard w/two suspension rings & decorated red yarn knotted to rings. Exc. cond. $120.00

ARMY SWORD (MODEL 1902 OFFICER): Engraved bright blade. 3 strand knuckle basket & backstrap blending into pommel. Ferrule secures notched wood grip. Scabbard w/grip & two ring bands. Avg. cond. $65.50

ARMY SWORD (MODEL 1902 OFFICER): German made version w/damascus steel blade. Nicely engraved & named. Hmkd 'Weyersburg & Kirschbaum, Solingen.' Hilt is dulled nickel finished metal. Notched

black finished wood grip. Polished steel scabbard w/2 ring bands & drag. Exc. cond. $450.00

ARMY SWORD (MODEL 1902 OFFICER): Nickle plated engraved blade. Hmkd 'The Ames co.' on ricasso. Alloy 3 strand basket knuckle guard w/slot for knot. Formed grip w/notches under back strap. Hooked quillon. Metal Scabbard w/two ring bands & drag. Avg. cond. 95.00

ARMY SWORD (MODEL 1902 OFFICER): Slight curved blade, engraved & personalized. Steel guard & basket. Metal backstrap frames notched bakelite handle. Leather cord w/knot. Steel scabbard. Avg. cond. $350.00

ARMY SWORD
(MODEL 1902 OFFICER)

CAVALRY SABER (MODEL 1840 DRAGOON): Curved blade. Hmkd on ricasso. Brass guard w/2 strand knuckle basket & bow. Phrygian helmet pommel. Wood grip. Steel scabbard w/two ring bands. Avg. cond. $339.00

CAVALRY SABER (MODEL 1840 DRAGOON): Nickle plated steel blade w/ US on obv. Hmkd on reverse at ricasso. Brass hilt w/oval guard, three strand knuckle basket & bow, Phrygian helmet pommel & Wood grip w/leather & wire wrap. Nickle plated steel scabbard w/drag & two ring bands. Above average cond. $260.00

CAVALRY SABER (MODEL 1840): Heavy blade. Ames maker marked & 1850 dated. Brass hilt w/leather wrapped grip. Heavy scabbard. Average condition. $345.00

CAVALRY SABER (MODEL 1860 EM LIGHT CAV): Brass guard & knuckle basket. Wire wound enameled wood grip. Hmkd on ricasso, obv w/AmesCo./Chicopee/Mass & rev w/US/DS/1863. Average condition.
.... $327.00

CAVALRY SABER (MODEL 1860 LIGHT CAV): Curved steel blade. Hmkd 'Ames Co, chickapee, Mass' & 'US/J T/1861' on ricasso. Polished brass hilt. Leather covered & wire wrapped contoured wood grip. Polished steel scabbard w/two ringbands. Exc. cond. $125.00

CAVALRY SABER
(MODEL 1860 LIGHT CAV)

CAVALRY SABER (MODEL 1860 LIGHT CAV): French made version done by contract. Bright curved blade. Hmkd 'Manufacture Francis/Saintietienne.' All brass hilt w/2 strand knuckle guard & phrygian Helmet pommel. Wood grip is wire wound. Average condition. .. $289.00

CAVALRY SABER (MODEL 1872 OFFICER): Bright curved blade w/ engraved pattern on 1st 1/3rd. HM Shannon, Miller & Crane of NY. Brass hilt w/oval guard & Eagle on arrows on side toward pommel. Phrygian helmet pommel. Wood grip, fishskin wrapped & wire bound. Steel scabbard w/brass throat, drag & suspension rings. Above avg. cond. $450.00

CAVALRY SABER (MODEL 1872): Steel blade. German hmkd & initials 'DES' on ricasso. Brass hilt. Steel scabbard. Above avg. cond. $286.00

CAVALRY SABER (MODEL 1912 'PATTON'): Bright steel DE fullered blade. Springfield arsenal emblem/1917 hmkd on obverse & US/32694 on reverse of ricasso. Deep curved guard & knuckle basket. Checkered composition grip, backstrap & thumb rest. Leather cord & knot. Steel scabbard w/tan canvas cover. Exc. condition. $265.00

CAVALRY SABER (MODEL 1912 'PATTON'): Steel DE fullered blade. Springfield arsenal emblem/1913 hmkd on obverse & US/4134 on reverse of ricasso. Cutlass style knuckle basket. Checkered composition grip, backstrap & thumb rest. Steel scabbard w/canvas cover. Above avg. cond. $150.00

CAVALRY SABER (STARR CONTRACT OF 1812-13): Curved blade full Starr hallmark 'P/LS/N STARR/US' w/Luther Sage the inspector. Steel guard w/reverse P-style knuckle bow & back strap. Black leather wrapped wood grip. Above avg. cond. $280.00

FOOT SWORD (MODEL 1850 OFFICERS): Curved etched blade. Hmkd at ricasso. Brass hilt w/wood grip wrapped in fishskin & gilt brass wire. Part of guard is open pattern w/floral design. Pommel is of Phrygian helmet design. Above avg. cond. $200.00

NAVAL SWORD (MODEL 1852 OFFICER): 31.5" polished blade w/etched embellishments. Marked on ricasso 'made USA.' Brass guard with floral knuckle basket labeled USN on face. Knuckle guard extends to pommel w/dolphins head. Pommel is of phrygian helmet style & has 13 stars around eagle. Quillon is in dolphins head form. Grip is wire wound white fishskin over wood. Black leather scabbard has brass throat & tip. Suspensions rings are done in knotted hawser design & tip drag is in dolphin design. Exc. cond. $225.00

NAVY SWORD (MODEL 1852): Nearly straight blade, nickel plated & engraved on both sides, named to officer. Proved emblem on ricasso. Guard has USN on floral pattern. Grip is wood w/fishskin & gilt wire wrapped. Brocade ribbon & sword knot looped at pommel. Scabbard is black leather w/brass fittings using the knotted hawser pattern on ring bands. Above avg. cond. $200.00

SPANISH-AMERICA-WAR SHORT SWORD: Unmarked 20" steel blade w/ brass guard & bone grips. Elaborate leather scabbard w/wrapped leather thong. Average cond. $40.00

CAVALRY SABER
(MODEL 1912 'PATTON')

U.S. AWARD & QUALIFICATION BADGES

A. Thru World War II (1945)

ARMY PRE WWII OFFICER RESERVE CORPS BREAST BADGE: 1930s pocket badge for Officers reserve corps. Enamel on sterling. Pb. Said to be first unit oriented pocket badge in Army. Exc. cond. $60.00

CIVIL WAR BREAST BADGE "IX CORPS": Bronze brooch w/ribbon & bronze pendant. Exc. cond. $236.00

CIVIL WAR BREAST BADGE "XXII CORPS": Brass 5 arm cross forming pentagon shape w/disc in center w/ crossed cannon over stacked cannon balls. Pb. Exc. cond. $236.00

COMBAT INFANTRYMAN BADGE: Cast body w/blue painted inset. Reverse has 2 small Sb. fastening posts. Above avg. cond. $21.00

COMBAT INFANTRYMAN BADGE: Cb. Sterling marked. Above avg. cond. $12.00

COMBAT INFANTRYMAN BADGE: English made. 76mm. Pb. Enameled blue center. "J&J.B'Harn." marked. Avg. cond. $50.00

DEFENSE AGENT AWARD BADGE: Pb. Bronze w/Minute man on shield & second award + honor award bars & tank emblem at bottom. Above avg. cond. $20.00

MARKSMAN BADGE "1900s ARMY FIELD ARTY 1st CLASS CANNONEER": Pb. Gilded brass w/Arty piece over '1st class Gunner.' Marked "D Battery, 5th Field Arty #65." Exc. cond. $281.00

MARKSMAN BADGE "PRE WWI COAST ARTILLERY CORPS 1ST CLASS GUNNER": Brass Pb. brooch suspending crossed cannons w/etched target buoy. Marked 36th Company Coast Art #65. Exc. cond. $96.00

MARKSMAN BADGE "PRE WWII ARMY PISTOL EXPERT": Pb. bar reads 'Pistol Expert' w/pendant w/wreath w/crossed revolvers inside. Above avg. cond. $51.00

MARKSMAN BADGE "PRE WWII ARMY SHARPSHOOTER": Sterling bar & pendant.' Above avg. cond. $20.00

MARKSMAN BADGE "WWI USMC": Large "Distinguished" brooch w/"Sharpshooter" suspender & sharpshooter grade pendant. Pb. Avg. cond. $45.00

MARKSMAN BADGE "WWII ARMY": W/"81-MM Mortar" bar. Pb. Sterling marked. Above avg. cond. $45.00

MARKSMAN BADGE "WWII USMC SHOOTING": Pb. brooch. 3 bars - 'Hand Grenade', 'Ex-Small Bore' & 'SS-Pistol.' Most sterling marked. Avg. cond. ..$20.00

MARKSMAN BADGE 1892 "22ND N.Y. INF REGT.": 25mm wide. Tarnished base w/ black enameled design & lettering. Prong back. Above avg. cond. $20.00

MARKSMAN BADGE 1900 "22ND REGT. N.Y. N.G.": 27mm wide. Black enamel detail. Prong back. Avg. cond. $20.00

MARKSMAN BAR "WWI ARMY": Pb. gilt bar w/'Marksman' in center & target symbols at each end. Above avg. cond. $20.00

MARKSMAN BAR "WWII ARMY": Pb. Sterling. Above avg. cond. $20.00

MARKSMAN MEDAL "WWI SHARPSHOOTER": Pb. Target centered in Patee cross + 1906-07-08 bar. Sterling. Avg. cond. $20.00

NAVY SHIPYARD BADGE "SAN FRANCISCO": 75mm wide 7-point star design w/great nation eagle design clutching anchor in center. Pb. Avg. cond. $100.00

NAVY AVIATION CADET SOLO BAR: PB. Gilt w/silver anchor on oval design in center. On N.S. Meyer card. Near mint cond. $20.00

NAVY BADGE 1930S WWII "C AND R INSPECTOR USN '407'": Stamped white metal w/black enameled lettering. PB. Maker marked. 2.5"x1.75". Near mint cond. $26.00

NAVY MASTER-AT-ARMS VR-4 BADGE: 45x66mm. Nickel finish. Black detailed lettering. Pb. Marked. Avg. cond. ..$75.00

NAVY MASTER-AT-ARMS VR-4 BADGE

NAVY SHIPYARD BADGE "WWI 'WAR SERVICE': 43x57mm. Stamped eagle, anchor & ship design in gold & silver finish. Above avg. cond. $32.00

NAVY SHORE PATROL BADGE "CHIEF, 3RD NAVAL DIST.": 43x61mm. Nickel finish w/black detailed lettering. Pb. Hmkd. Above avg. cond. $95.00

NAVY SHORE PATROL BADGE "CHIEF, 3RD NAVAL DIST."

NAVY SR SANITARY INSPECTOR BADGE: PB. Fouled anchor in center, 'Senior Sanitary/TINS' above, 'Inspector' below & blue star at bottom. Exc. cond. $45.00

SECT. OF DEF. AIDE BREAST BADGE: 3-prong back. Silver & gilded finish. Enameled details. In Meyer box. Above avg. cond. $32.00

WWI STRETCHER BEARER BADGE: Pb. 1.5" w/wreath around stretcher w/cross over medic emblem. Above avg. cond. $30.00

WWI WAR SERVICE BADGE: SB. Bronze 1" pin w/crossed cannons & ord. bomb at cross w/ring reading 'War Service/Eddystone Rifle Plant.' Above avg. cond. $35.00

WWII AAF TECHNICIAN BADGE: 2 bars for Radio Operator and Radio Mechanic. PB. Exc. cond. $26.00

WWII AAF TECHNICIAN BADGE: 4-blade prop with Radio Mech. & Radio Operator bars. PB. Exc. cond. $20.00

WWII AAF TECHNICIAN BADGE: Pb. Sterling. Above avg. cond. $23.00

WWII AAF TECHNICIAN BADGE: W/ "Mechanic" bar. Pb. Sterling marked. Above avg. cond. $25.00

WWII ARMY CORPS AREA BADGE: Sterling. Design of crossed arrows over bow in center of wreath. On Pb. "U.S. Army" brooch. Marked. Exc. cond. $25.00

WWII ARMY DRIVER BADGE: W/'Driver-W' bar. Jostens/sterling marked. Exc. cond. $20.00

WWII ARMY SERVICE CLUB PIN: For Employee ID. CB. Blue triangle w/US in center. Army/Service Club at top-bottom. Above avg. cond. $20.00

WWII COMBAT INFANTRYMAN BADGE: Unmarked. PB. Enameled face. Avg. cond. $30.00

WWII COMBAT MEDIC BADGE: Pb. Unmarked. Above avg. cond. $20.00

WWII DEFENSE AWARD: Merit award from Treasury Dept. to US Defense agent. National shield w/2nd award & honor award bars w/bronze medal showing tank & star. PB. Above avg. cond. $27.00

WWII DIVER BADGE 1ST CLASS: Gold bullion on tan twill. Mint cond. $20.00

WWII GLIDER BADGE "CHEMICAL MORTAR UNIT": Standard design. Sterling marked. Applied copper-colored Chemical Corps branch design w/ arrowhead device. Pb. Above avg. cond. $81.00

WWII GLIDER INF TROOP BADGE: English made. PB. Maker/sterling marked. Bronze 5-point star applique in center of wreath. Above avg. cond. $39.00

WWII GLIDER INF TROOP BADGE: English made. Pb. Unmarked sterling. Above avg. cond. $31.00

WWII NAVY BREAST BADGE "RESERVE MERCHANT MARINE": 2.75" wide. Gilt. Pb. Amico marked. Exc. cond. $34.00

WWII NAVY INSTRUCTOR BADGE: Pb. 2.5" oval w/white background w/ 'Instructor' at top & 'Naval Training School/Naval Armory/Michigan City Indiana.' Avg. cond. $20.00

WWII NAVY MASTER-AT-ARMS BADGE: PB. 'Master at arms of USS Sandoval.' Naval emblem centered inside ring of comments. Above avg. cond. $59.00

WWII NAVY PT BOAT BADGE: 64mm. Sterling marked. Pb. Above avg. cond. $75.00

WWII NAVY PT BOAT BADGE: PB. Sterling. Exc. cond. $100.00

WWII NAVY SECURITY BADGE "BANGOR SUB BASE": Nickel plated w/blue lettering. 'Naval Sub Base/Bangor' over No. '127' & 'Security/Police.' PB. 3". Exc. cond. $34.00

WWII NAVY SECURITY BADGE: Navy emblem in center w/'NAS Lemoore/ Security' above & 'Patrolman' below. Silver finish. Exc. cond. $35.00

WWII NAVY SUBMARINE COMBAT
BADGE: Stamped silver. 1 pc. No holes in
scroll. "Sheridan-Perth-Silver" marked.
PB. Above avg. cond. $244.00

WWII NAVY SUBMARINE QUALIFICATION
BADGE OFFICER GRADE: Full size. Pb.
Meyer marked. Above avg. cond. .. $45.00

WWII NAVY SUBMARINE QUALIFICATION
BADGE: 2.75". Pb. Brass finish. Meyer
marked. Avg. cond. $31.00

B. 1946 - Present

AID TO PRESIDENT BREAST BADGE:
50mm. Multi-pc. Cb. Mint cond. ... $166.00

ALLIED AIR FORCES CENTRAL EUROPE
POCKET BADGE: Cb. 1.75" disc w/flags
of involved nations displayed in color &
'Allied Air Forces Central Europe -
Headquarters' Above avg. cond. . $115.00

ALLIED LAND FORCES, CENTRAL
EUROPE BADGE: 33x42mm. Multi-piece.
Nickel & blue enamel. Cb. Near mint cond.
.... $20.00

ARMY MISSILE BADGE: Cb. Red enamel
field w/gray metal missile. Marked US
Army. Exc. cond. $20.00

ARMY NUCLEAR REACTOR QUAL.
BADGE: 29mm. Frosted. 'Sterling/S21'
marked. Cb. In maker packaging. Near
mint cond. $25.00

ARMY RECRUITER BADGE: Cb. 2.5" dia.
Gray metal w/recruiter emblem on front.
Avg. cond. $20.00

ARMY RECRUITER BREAST BADGE: Full
size. Frosted silver w/dark green enamel
detail. Cb. 3 applied star devices to
bottom. Above avg. cond. $16.00

COMBAT INFANTRYMAN BADGE 3rd
AWARD: Full size. Cb. Sterling. 'Simon-
Ster' marked. Exc. cond. $34.00

COMBAT INFANTRYMAN BADGE:
Vietnamese made. Hand embr. color
design on OD sateen. Above avg. cond.
.... $30.00

COMBAT MEDIC BADGE: Cb. Simon GI/
sterling marked. Above avg. cond.
.... $25.00

DEPT. OF ARMY GENERAL STAFF ID
BREAST BADGE: Full size. Cb. Gilt brass
w/enameled design. Above avg. cond.
.... $55.00

DEPT. OF ARMY GENERAL STAFF ID
BREAST BADGE: Full size. Cb. Multi-pc.
Gilt & enamel finish. "G-22" marked. Mint
cond. $20.00

JOINT CHIEFS OF STAFF BREAST
BADGE: Dress size. Multi-pc. Cb. Meyer
marked. Mint cond. $16.00

JOINT CHIEFS OF STAFF BREAST
BADGE: Full size. Multi-pc. Cb. Meyer
marked. Mint cond. $20.00

JOINT CHIEFS OF STAFF BREAST
BADGE: Gold filled. Crossed 4 swords
with enameled flag shield & black lettering
over sterling marked wreath. Maker
marked. CB. 2". Above avg. cond.
.... $36.00

NAVY SUBMARINE QUALIFICATION
BADGE: 3". Sterling. Pb. Meyer marked.
Exc. cond. $60.00

NAVY SUBMARINE QUALIFICATION
BADGE

NAVY SUBMARINE QUALIFICATION
BADGE: Gilded brass. Pb. Marked. Near
mint cond. $20.00

NAVY UDT ENLISTED GRADE BREAST
BADGE: 53mm. Frosted silver finish. Cb.
'Antaya-A26-1/20 Silver Filled' marked.
Exc. cond. $40.00

TOMB OF THE UNKNOWN SOLDIER
HONOR GUARD BREAST BADGE:
Frosted silver finish. Cb. Exc. cond.
.... $19.00

USAF COMBAT CREW QUALIFICATION
BADGE: Full size. Frosted silver w/enamel
detail. Cb. Meyer/sterling marked. Exc.
cond. $25.00

USAF CRASH & RESCUE BOAT
CREWMEMBER BADGE: PB. Model craft
w/waves at rear. Exc. cond. $45.00

USAF FIRE PROTECTION BADGE: PB.
Frosted w/eagle at top & gilt center w/3
crossed early hose nozzles. Rim reads
'Fire Protection' & 'USAF.' Exc. cond.
.... $30.00

USAF MISSILEMAN BADGE: 63mm. CB.
Near mint cond. $20.00

USAF MISSILEMAN BADGE: Cb. Gray alloy
finish. Avg. cond. $20.00

USAF MISSILEMAN BADGE: Fully embr. in
white & black. 3.25". Near mint cond.
.... $20.00

USAF PARA RESCUE BADGE: 39mm. Cb.
Marked 'Antaya/G1/Silver Filled/1/20
Sterling.' On 1968 dated issue card. Exc.
cond. $25.00

USAF PARA RESCUE BADGE: 40mm. Cb.
Antaya/GI/Silver Filled/1/20 Sterling
marked. Above avg. cond. $20.00

USAF SECURITY POLICE BADGE: PB. Stamped badge No. Above avg. cond. $34.00

USAF SR MISSILEMAN BADGE: 55mm. Frosted silver finish. CB. Above avg. cond. $20.00

USAF SR MISSILEMAN BADGE: 77mm. Vanguard marked. CB. Frosted silver finish. Avg. cond. $20.00

USMC CRASH CREW SECTION, K-BAY BADGE: 46x63mm. Multi-piece. Nickel finish w/Navy blue lettering & badge #. Pb. Exc. cond. $334.00

USMC MILITARY POLICE BADGE: 53x78mm. Gilt finish w/black lettering & badge #, gilt & enamel USMC EG&A applique design in center. Pb. Near mint cond. $175.00

USMC MILITARY POLICE CID BADGE: 53x71mm size. Gilt finish w/blue enamel lettering, gilt & enamel USMC EG&A applique design in center. Pb. Marked. Near mint cond. $370.00

U.S. MEDALS

A. Thru World War I (1919)

ARMY PHILIPPINE INSURRECTION MEDAL (1899): Ring suspender. numbered on rim. Avg. cond. $143.00

ARMY PHILIPPINE INSURRECTION MEDAL: Ring suspender. Numbered on rim. Wrap brooch mtd. ribbon. Above avg. cond. $61.00

ARMY-NAVY VETERAN UNION MEDAL: Ornate gilt brass pendant on multi-striped ribbon mtd. on "Auxiliary" brooch. Marked. W/matching lapel pin. Above avg. cond. $20.00

CIVIL WAR CAMPAIGN MEDAL: Thick bronze pendant w/ring suspender. Numbered on rim. Mtd. wrap brooch w/ "fall-in" catch. Exc. cond. $297.00

CIVIL WAR SERVICE MEDAL: numbered. Thick bronze finish pendant w/ring suspender. Obverse w/bust design of Lincoln & reads "With Malice Toward None With Charity For All." Reverse side reads "The Civil War 1861-1865" inside wreath design. Red, white & blue striped ribbon drape mtd. on wrap brooch. Exc. cond. $748.00

CIVIL WAR SOUTHERN CROSS OF HONOR: 34mm bronze cross on pin mounted brooch. Crankshaw of Atlanta marked. Plain in front for engraving. Above avg. cond. $184.00

CIVIL WAR VETERAN SOUTHERN CROSS OF HONOR: Bronze cross pendant on

screw-back brooch. Marked. Above avg. cond. $285.00

MARKSMANSHIP MEDAL "1880-1890S ARMY THIRD CLASS PRIZE": Brass. 48mm. Design of kneeling soldier in spiked cork helmet firing rifle w/design of Sibley tent in background. Above avg. cond. $28.00

MARKSMANSHIP MEDAL "1914 2ND REGT.": 31mm dia bronze finish pendant w/enameled shooting target applique & reads "CNG/2nd Regt.." On "General Ford Medal." Pb. brooch w/"Marksman Badge 1914" suspender bar. Maker marked. Above avg. cond. $20.00

MEXICAN BORDER SERVICE MEDAL "PENNSYLVANIA N.G.": Mtd. ribbon. W/ Pb. ribbon bar. In pressed paper maker's box. Exc. cond. $32.00

MEXICAN BORDER SERVICE MEDAL: numbered on rim. Ring suspender on wrap brooch mtd. ribbon. Above avg. cond. $91.00

MEXICAN EXPEDITION MEDAL (1916): Pb. brooch w/enameled US & Mexican tri-color bars & title. Brass patee cross w/light blue enameled arms & crossed rifles in center. Avg. cond. $60.00

NAVAL WEST INDIES CAMPAIGN SAMPSON MEDAL: 38mm dia thick bronze pendant w/ring suspender. Engraved to Wardroom Steward's name on rim. Short drape ribbon mtd. on "USS Puritan" brooch w/open-catch Pb. Rare. Above avg. cond. $1,000.00

NAVAL WEST INDIES CAMPAIGN
SAMPSON MEDAL

NAVY CROSS "BLACK WIDOW": 63x120mm Navy blue leatherette covered "Coffin" style case has white silk & blue velvet lined interior. Dark bronze Navy cross on dark bronze split brooch mtd. ribbon. W/ribbon bar. Rare. Mint cond. $710.00

NAVY MEXICAN SERVICE MEDAL (1911-1917): numbered. Exc. cond. $145.00

NAVY MEXICAN SERVICE MEDAL (1911-1917): numbered. Avg. cond.
.... $223.00

PHILIPPINE INSURRECTION SERVICE MEDAL: Sterling. Red/white/blue ribbon sewn to brass Pb. bar w/eagle over 'First Montan/US Vol.' 1.75" pendant w/soldier accepting wreath of peace all bordered by campaigns, dates & patriotic phrase. Back has Montana scene & unit assignment. Above avg. cond. $328.00

PUERTO RICO OCCUPATION MEDAL: Avg. cond. $59.00

S.A.W. ARMY 1898 MEDAL: Ring suspender. numbered on rim. Wrap brooch mtd. ribbon. W/ribbon bar. In 1936 dated issue box. Exc. cond. $75.00

S.A.W. MEDAL: 37mm. Multi-pc brass body w/design of telephone poles & landscape in background. Border in design of buckled belt & engraved "Special Correspondent" + linked suspender bar engraved "L.F.D." on spread wing eagle brooch engraved "War With Spain" w/open-catch Pb. Avg. cond. $180.00

S.A.W. NEW JERSEY MEDAL: Bronze pendant w/Pb. brooch & 'New Jersey Volunteer' on face. Linked chain supports the bronze patee cross pendant w/wreath circling center. Reads 'SPANISH AMERICAN WAR 1898.' Above avg. cond. $75.00

S.A.W. SERVICE MEDAL "MISSOURI STATE VOLUNTEER 1898": Bronze finish w/official MO seal design on front. Ring suspender. Avg. cond. $27.00

S.A.W. SERVICE MEDAL: 42mm wide dark bronze finish thick 5-sided pendant w/design of soldier in uniform of that war on front & reads "Santiago July 10-17 1898." Reverse reads "From the Citizens of the District of Columbia/First District of Columbia Regiment U.S.V." On "Presented to" open-catch Pb. brooch. Above avg. cond. $210.00

S.A.W. SERVICE MEDAL: Bronze satin finish pendant w/ring suspender on crimp brooch mtd. ribbon. Rim numbered. Above avg. cond. $72.00

S.A.W. SERVICE MEDAL: Rim numbered. Wrap brooch mtd. ribbon. In pressed blue paper issue carton. Above avg. cond.
.... $82.00

USMC PHILIPPINE CAMPAIGN MEDAL: (1899-1903). Thick pendant in nice bronze satin finish w/ring suspender on wrap brooch mtd. ribbon. Above avg. cond.
.... $51.00

WAR MANEUVERS MEDAL "1908 PINE CAMP, N.Y.": 36mm dia. w/"Com I Pany" &

"Regi 2 Ment" bars on Pb. brooch. Avg. cond. $14.00

WWI CAVALRY MEDAL: Blue ribbon. Brass pendant showing train passing guard Cattle cars show horses & men of cavalry. Avg. cond. $42.00

WWI MARINE MEDAL GROUP: Marine Good Conduct Medal w/ribbon w/bar 'US MARINE CORPS' w/rifle suspender for pendant. numbered. WWI Victory Medal w/France bar. Battle Star & Maltese Cross. Incl. ribbon bar. Sharpshooter Badge. Relative in Service pin. Avg. cond.
.... $177.00

WWI PURPLE HEART (VETERAN ISSUE): WWII vintage-cased Purple heart on lot brooch mtd. ribbon. Pendant engraved "Samuel F. Murdock." Comes w/ribbon bar & lapel device + copy of file card stating man was wounded March 17, 1918 + 3 different newspaper clippings stating medals were awarded on Victory day celebration anniversary of war w/Japan. Near mint cond. $74.00

WWI PURPLE HEART: Enamel pendant w/numbered rim is hand engraved w/name on reverse. Split brooch mtd. ribbon. W/original carton numbered to match medal. Incl.'s. brief research for man WIA w/59th Inf. Sept. 28, 1918. Near mint cond.
.... $150.00

WWI PURPLE HEART: Wrap mtd. ribbon to split brooch & suspending pendant. Enameled heart behind Washington's profile. Serial numbered & named. W/ribbon bar & WWI veterans pin. Avg. cond.
.... $83.00

WWI VICTORY MEDAL NAVY W/"TRANSPORT" CLASP: Bronze pendant on wrap brooch mtd. ribbon w/"Transport" clasp affixed. Above avg. cond. $25.00

WWI VICTORY MEDAL W/"FRANCE" CLASP: On long drape wrap brooch mtd. ribbon. Above avg. cond. $11.00

WWI VICTORY MEDAL W/"FRANCE" CLASP:: On wrap brooch mtd. ribbon. In 1920 issue box. Above avg. cond.
.... $20.00

WWI VICTORY MEDAL W/2 CLASPS: Pb. brooch. 2 bars - Meuse Argonne & Defensive sector. Avg. cond. $27.00

WWI VICTORY MEDAL W/5 CLASPS: On long drape ribbon mtd. on wrap brooch. W/Def. Sec, Champagne-Marne, Aisne-Marne, St. Mihiel & Meuse-Argonne clasps. Avg. cond. $32.00

WWI VICTORY MEDAL W/CLASP: Pb. brooch. Naval Battery clasp. Avg. cond.
.... $30.00

WWI VICTORY MEDAL W/CLASP: Wrap brooch. Naval pattern "Overseas" clasp. Avg. cond. $40.00

WWI VICTORY MEDAL W/CLASP: Wrap brooch. Naval pattern "Patrol" clasp. Above avg. cond. $66.00

WWI VICTORY MEDAL W/CLASP: Wrap brooch. Naval pattern Atlantic Fleet clasp. Above avg. cond. $40.00

WWI VICTORY MEDAL W/SALVAGE CLASP: Pb. brooch. Avg. cond. . $145.00

WWI VICTORY MEDAL: On wrap brooch mtd. ribbon w/"France" clasp. Exc. cond. $10.00

WWI VICTORY MEDAL: On wrap brooch mtd. ribbon w/Def. Sec. clasp. Near mint cond. $23.00

WWI VICTORY MEDAL: Ribbon sewn to Pb. brooch & holds brass 'Siberia' bar. Above avg. cond. $106.00

B. 1920 - 1945

AIR MEDAL: Issue box dated 7/24/43: Avg. cond. $60.00

AIR MEDAL

AIR MEDAL: Machined engraved for named Capt. of 38th Bomb group. Exc. cond. $93.00

AIR MEDAL: Named. Bronze pendant on wrap brooch mtd. ribbon. In case w/ribbon bar & LP. Near mint cond. $50.00

AIR MEDAL: Slot brooch. Above avg. cond. $16.00

AIR MEDAL: W/presentation case w/ribbon bar & LP. Above avg. cond. $25.00

AIR MEDAL: Wrap brooch ribbon. W/ribbon bar. In WWII leatherette case. Above avg. cond. $30.00

AMERICAN DEFENSE MEDAL: W/'Foreign Service' bar. Above avg. cond. $24.00

ARMY COMMENDATION MEDAL: On card w/ribbon bar & lapel pin. Avg. cond. $16.00

ARMY DISTINGUISHED SERVICE CROSS: Bronze satin finish. Slot brooch. Above avg. cond. $59.00

ARMY GOOD CONDUCT MEDAL: Machine engraved name on reverse in block letters. On slot brooch mtd. ribbon. Above avg. cond. $20.00

ARMY GOOD CONDUCT MEDAL: On slot brooch mtd. ribbon. Named on reverse in mach. engraved block letters. Above avg. cond. $11.00

ARMY GOOD CONDUCT MEDAL: Slot brooch mtd. ribbon. In 1945 dated issue box w/ribbon bar & LP. Reverse of medal is mach. engraved w/name. Above avg. cond. $11.00

ARMY GOOD CONDUCT MEDAL: Slot brooch mtd. ribbon. Named on reverse in mach. engraved block letters. Exc. cond. $20.00

ARMY OCCUPATION MEDAL W/"JAPAN" CLASP: Crimp brooch. Exc. cond. $13.00

BRONZE STAR: Bronze star pendant on slot brooch mounted ribbon w/machine engraved name to back in block capitals. Exc. cond. $27.00

BRONZE STAR: Machine engraved. W/case w/ribbon bar & LP. Exc. cond. $34.00

COAST GUARD GOOD CONDUCT MEDAL: Pb. brooch. Bar reads 'US COAST GUARD.' Avg. cond. $36.00

COMBAT AIR MEDAL: Bronze toned pendant. Pb. brooch. Reverse privately machine engraved & reads 'S/SGT/ (name)/AC.' W/lapel pin & ribbon bar. Cased. Above avg. cond. $100.00

DISTINGUISHED FLYING CROSS Slot brooch. Avg. cond. $24.00

DISTINGUISHED FLYING CROSS: Bronze pendant on brooch mtd. ribbon-w/ribbon bar. Cased. Near mint cond. $20.00

DISTINGUISHED FLYING CROSS: Bronze pendant on brooch mtd. ribbon. Name impressed in block letters on reverse. Avg. cond. $49.00

DISTINGUISHED FLYING CROSS: Bronze satin finish. Slot brooch. In leatherette presentation case w/ribbon bar & LP. Above avg. cond. $35.00

DISTINGUISHED FLYING CROSS: Deep bronze finish on SB mtd. ribbon. Rev privately machine engraved "1st Lt./ (Name)/USAAC." W/lapel pin & ribbon bar. Cased. Above avg. cond. $150.00

DISTINGUISHED FLYING CROSS

DISTINGUISHED FLYING CROSS: On slot brooch mtd. ribbon. In WWII-era leatherette presentation case. Above avg. cond. $27.00

DISTINGUISHED FLYING CROSS: On slot brooch mtd. ribbon. In WWII-style leatherette presentation case. Above avg. cond. $30.00

DISTINGUISHED SERVICE CROSS. numbered. Bronze pendant stamped. Above avg. cond. $65.00

EUROPEAN AFRICAN MED CAMPAIGN MEDAL: In original issue box, bronze pendant on crimp brooch mounted ribbon. Ribbon bar. Mint cond. $28.00

MERCHANT MARINE MEDITERRANEAN-MIDDLE EAST WAR ZONE MEDAL: Crimp brooch. Mint cond. $20.00

MERCHANT MARINE WWII VICTORY MEDAL: Crimp brooch. Avg. cond. $20.00

NAVY CHINA SERVICE MEDAL: Crimp brooch. Avg. cond. $20.00

NAVY GOOD CONDUCT MEDAL: Medal mach. engraved in block letters w/man's full name & 1940 dated. On slot brooch mtd. ribbon. Avg. cond. $27.00

NAVY GOOD CONDUCT MEDAL: Named on reverse in mach. engraved block letters w/name & 1945 date. Slot brooch. Above avg. cond. $20.00

NAVY GOOD CONDUCT MEDAL: Named on reverse in mach. engraved block letters. Slot brooch. Exc. cond. $20.00

NAVY GOOD CONDUCT MEDAL: Ribbon mtd. on slot brooch. Mach. engraved on reverse in block letters w/man's name & 1945 dated. Above avg. cond. $13.00

NAVY GOOD CONDUCT MEDAL: Ribbon sewn to brooch & holding three brass bars for 1933, 1937, 1940 awards. Rev of pendant is machine engraved w/Name & 1928 date. Avg. cond. $164.00

PHILIPPINE LIBERATION MEDAL: Gilt & enamel. Crimp brooch. Mint cond. $11.00

PRISONER-OF-WAR MEDAL: Crimp brooch. W/ribbon bar. In 1991 dated issue plastic carton. Mint cond. $10.00

PURPLE HEART (2 TO SAME MAN): Both case & engraved on back, no serial number on side. Two styles of engraving used. Above avg. cond. $150.00

PURPLE HEART: numbered. Gilt & enamel. Mtd. slot brooch. W/lapel pin. In WWII-style presentation case. Above avg. cond. $31.00

PURPLE HEART: numbered. Mtd. on slot brooch. W/ribbon bar & lapel pin. In leatherette presentation case. Above avg. cond. $38.00

PURPLE HEART: numbered. Mtd. on slot brooch. W/ribbon bar & lapel pin. In leatherette presentation case. Above avg. cond. $39.00

PURPLE HEART: numbered. Mtd. on slot brooch. W/ribbon bar. In leatherette case. $38.00

PURPLE HEART: numbered. Slot brooch Exc. cond. $28.00

PURPLE HEART: numbered. Slot brooch. Above avg. cond. $28.00

PURPLE HEART: Gilt & enamel on slot brooch mtd. ribbon. Avg. cond. $21.00

PURPLE HEART: Gilt & enamel. Slot brooch mtd. ribbon. W/lapel pin & ribbon bar. In leatherette presentation case. Above avg. cond. $35.00

PURPLE HEART: Gilt pendant w/plastic insert. Named in block letters. W/ribbon bar. Cased. Mint cond. $47.00

PURPLE HEART: Hand engraved pendant. numbered. W/case w/lapel pin & ribbon bar. Avg. cond. $100.00

PURPLE HEART: In presentation case w/ lapel pin & ribbon bar. Slot back mounted to Pb. brooch. Enameled pendant. numbered & named. Near mint cond. $72.00

PURPLE HEART: Multi-pc. pendant on slot brooch mtd. ribbon. numbered. Above avg. cond. $37.00

PURPLE HEART: Name in small block letters on reverse. In carton w/ribbon bar. Above avg. cond. $55.00

PURPLE HEART: Slot brooch. Reverse hand engraved "Lt. General." Near mint cond. $25.00

PURPLE HEART: W/case w/ribbon bar & LP. Exc. cond. $45.00

PURPLE HEART: WWII blue leatherette case. Named. Slot brooch W/ribbon bar & lapel pin. Near mint cond. $76.00

SELECTIVE SERVICE MEDAL: Slot brooch. W/case w/lapel pin & ribbon bar. Above avg. cond. $11.00

SELECTIVE SERVICE SYSTEM MEDAL: Black leatherette case w/gold title. Heavy bronze with mounted ribbon & bar. Near mint cond. $20.00

SILVER STAR: Slot brooch. 1942 dated box, numbered. Above avg. cond. $29.00

SOLDIER MEDAL: Slot brooch mtd. ribbon. W/ribbon bar & lapel pin. In leatherette presentation case. Above avg. cond. $37.00

SOLDIER MEDAL: Slot brooch. Numbered. Above avg. cond. $137.00

USMC GOOD CONDUCT MEDAL: numbered. "US Marine Corps" brooch. Above avg. cond. $80.00

USMC GOOD CONDUCT MEDAL: Pb. bar. Above avg. cond. $20.00

USMC GOOD CONDUCT MEDAL

USMC GOOD CONDUCT MEDAL: Pendant is mach. engraved on reverse "No.15826/ (name)/1st Enlistment/1918-1922." On short-drape ribbon on rope trimmed "U.S. Marine Corps" Pb. brooch. Above avg. cond. $68.00

USMC GOOD CONDUCT MEDAL: W/"U.S. Marine Corps" brooch. Above avg. cond. $22.00

USMC GOOD CONDUCT MEDAL: W/rifle suspender bar on "U.S. Marine Corps" brooch. Above avg. cond. $27.00

WAC MEDAL: Crimp brooch. Near mint cond. $20.00

WAC MEDAL: Slot brooch. Above avg. cond. $16.00

WAC MEDAL: Slot brooch. Above avg. cond. $20.00

C. 1946 - Present

AIR FORCE CROSS: Bronze satin finish multi-piece pendant w/enamel detail on crimp brooch mtd. ribbon. Near mint cond. $25.00

AIR FORCE CROSS: Bronze satin finish multi-piece pendant w/enamel detail on crimp brooch mtd. ribbon. Older strike. Near mint cond. $40.00

AIR FORCE CROSS: Bronze satin finish multi-piece pendant w/enameled detailed wreath on crimp brooch mtd. ribbon. Near mint cond. $38.00

AIR MEDAL W/CERTIFICATE: Vietnam. 1967 dated award certificate named to 1st lt. Framed. Air Medal on crimp brooch mtd. ribbon w/ribbon & lapel pin. 1967 dated issue box w/fitted interior. Above avg. cond. $112.00

AIR MEDAL W/CERTIFICATE

AIR MEDAL: On crimp brooch mtd. ribbon. Mint cond. $20.00

AIR MEDAL: W/older style case. Pendant on crimp brooch mounted ribbon. Above avg. cond. $20.00

ARMED FORCES RESERVE MEDAL: On crimp brooch mtd. ribbon. "Minuteman" design on back. Near mint cond. .. $20.00

ARMY COMMAND & GENERAL STAFF COLLEGE TABLE MEDAL: Honor Graduate award - 3" brass table medal called the 'General George C Marshall Award.' Exc. cond. $40.00

ARMY COMMENDATION MEDAL: Crimp brooch mtd. ribbon. Above avg. cond. $20.00

ARMY DISTINGUISHED SERVICE CROSS: Bronze satin finish pendant on crimp brooch mtd. ribbon. Mint cond. $22.00

ARMY DISTINGUISHED SERVICE CROSS: Bronze satin finish pendant on crimp brooch mtd. ribbon. Mint cond. $22.00

ARMY DISTINGUISHED SERVICE CROSS: Nice bronze satin finish cross on crimp brooch mtd. ribbon. Near mint cond. $35.00

ARMY DISTINGUISHED SERVICE CROSS: On crimp brooch mtd. ribbon. Mint cond. $24.00

BRONZE STAR: Slot brooch mtd. ribbon. In full size Arrow presentation case w/ribbon bar & lapel pin. Exc. cond. $20.00

COAST GUARD COMMENDATION MEDAL: Full size on crimp brooch mtd. ribbon. In 'Arrow' case w/mini medal, ribbon bar & lapel pin. Exc. cond. $20.00

COAST GUARD DISTINGUISHED SERVICE MEDAL: Full size & mini on crimp brooch mtd. ribbons. Near mint cond. $65.00

COAST GUARD DISTINGUISHED SERVICE MEDAL: On crimp brooch mtd. ribbon. Exc. cond. $50.00

COAST GUARD EXPERT PISTOL SHOT MEDAL: On crimp brooch mtd. ribbon. Near mint cond. $20.00

COAST GUARD GOOD CONDUCT MEDAL: On crimp brooch mtd. ribbon. Mint cond. $20.00

DEPT. OF THE ARMY SUPERIOR CIVILIAN SERVICE MEDAL: On crimp brooch mtd. ribbon. Exc. cond. $21.00

DEPT. OF THE NAVY DISTINGUISHED CIVILIAN SERVICE MEDAL: Gilt & enamel pendant on crimp brooch mtd. ribbon. Near mint cond. $108.00

DISTINGUISHED FLYING CROSS: Bronze satin finish pendant on crimp brooch mtd. ribbon. Mint cond. $20.00

DISTINGUISHED FLYING CROSS: On crimp brooch mtd. ribbon. In plastic case. Mint cond. $11.00

DISTINGUISHED FLYING CROSS: On crimp brooch. In plastic case. Mint cond. $20.00

DISTINGUISHED SERVICE CROSS: Bronze satin finish pendant on crimp

brooch mtd. ribbon. W/ribbon bar & lapel pin. Exc. cond. $55.00

DISTINGUISHED SERVICE MEDAL: Cased w/mini, ribbon bar, lapel pin. Mint cond. $60.00

DISTINGUISHED SERVICE MEDAL

HUMANE ACTION MEDAL (BERLIN AIRLIFT): On slot brooch mtd. ribbon. W/ribbon bar. In pressed blue paper box. Exc. cond. $11.00

JOINT SERVICE COMM. MEDAL: Multi-pc. on crimp brooch mtd. ribbon. Exc. cond. $20.00

JOINT SERVICE COMMENDATION MEDAL: Above avg. cond. $12.00

KUWAIT LIBERATION KUWAIT MEDAL: Multi-piece gilt & nickel pendant on unmounted ribbon. In green finish presentation case w/hinged lid. Exc. cond. $13.00

KUWAIT LIBERATION: Multi-pc. gilt & nickel pendant on unmounted ribbon. W/ribbon bar w/device. In green issue case w/ hinged lid & fitted interior. Near mint cond. $25.00

LEGION OF MERIT CHIEF COMMANDER: Breast medal. Enameled in white, red & green w/center of 13 stars on blue field. Mint cond. $226.00

LEGION OF MERIT MEDAL: Enameled details on crimp brooch mtd. ribbon. Near mint cond. $20.00

LEGION OF MERIT OFFICER GRADE: Gilt & enameled pendant on crimp brooch mtd. ribbon. W/mini medal, ribbon bar & lapel pin. All w/officer device. Exc. cond. $48.00

LEGION OF MERIT: Enamel finish pendant. Ribbon mtd. on crimp brooch. W/ribbon bar & Lapel pin. In 'Arrow' medal case. Near mint cond. $20.00

LEGION OF MERIT: Enameled details w/Pb. brooch. W/presentation case w/lapel pin & ribbon bar. Near mint cond.

.... $22.00

MEDAL OF HONOR ARMY: W/full neck ribbon. Mint cond. $318.00

MEDAL OF HONOR ARMY

MEDAL OF HONOR ARMY: Light blue neck ribbon w/snaps, throat knot w/13 stars & brass suspender in Army emblem likeness holding 5 pt star pendent w/enameled green wreath. Mint cond. $150.00

MEDAL OF HONOR ARMY

MEDAL OF HONOR NAVY/USMC: W/neck ribbon. Mint cond. $289.00

MEDAL OF HONOR NAVY/USMC

MEDAL OF HONOR USAF: Light blue neck ribbon w/snaps, throat knot w/13 stars & brass suspender w/Valor bar & AF emblem holding 5 pt star pendent w/ enameled green wreath. Mint cond.

.... $263.00

MEDAL OF HONOR USAF: W/full neck ribbon. Mint cond. $250.00

MEDAL OF HONOR USAF

MERCHANT MARINE KOREAN SERVICE MEDAL: On crimp brooch mtd. ribbon. Mint cond. $31.00

MERCHANT MARINE VIETNAM SERVICE MEDAL: On crimp brooch mtd. ribbon. Mint cond. $13.00

MERITORIOUS SERVICE MEDAL: On crimp brooch mtd. ribbon. Mint cond. $20.00

MERITORIOUS SERVICE MEDAL: W/ribbon bar & LP. Near mint cond. $25.00

MINI DEFENSE DISTINGUISHED SERVICE MEDAL: On crimp brooch mtd. ribbon. Mint cond. $10.00

MINI NAVY MEDAL OF HONOR: Unmounted ribbon w/13 star cluster near pendant. Anchor suspends the 5 star pendant w/center showing liberty vanquishing the enemy. Above avg. cond. $40.00

MINI USAF DISTINGUISHED SERVICE MEDAL: On crimp brooch mtd. ribbon. Mint cond. $10.00

MORTAR COMPETITION TABLE MEDAL: 50mm diam. Silver finish w/U.S. Helmet, rifle & oak leaf spray on obverse. "Top 4.2 Mortar" engraved on reverse. Above avg. cond. $11.00

NATIONAL DEFENSE MEDAL: Bronze pendant on crimp brooch mounted ribbon. W/ribbon bar. In box. Near mint cond. $28.00

NATIONAL SECURITY MEDAL: Blue ribbon w/unique yellow ladder down center. Pendant has eagle perched on 1.5" oval wreath around blue star burst. Mint cond. $540.00

NAVY / MARINE CORPS MEDAL FOR HEROISM: Crimp brooch mtd. ribbon. Mint cond. $20.00

NAVY / MARINE CORPS MEDAL: On crimp brooch mtd. ribbon. In original plastic. Mint cond. $10.00

NAVY CHINA SERVICE MEDAL: On crimp brooch mtd. ribbon. Above avg. cond. $20.00

NAVY COMMENDATION MEDAL: On crimp brooch mtd. ribbon. Near mint cond. $20.00

NAVY CROSS (KOREAN ERA): Wrap mtd. ribbon on Pb. brooch suspending pendant. Reverse w/name engraved (unofficial). Above avg. cond. $343.00

NAVY CROSS: Bronze finish. On issue card. Mint cond. $54.00

NAVY CROSS: Satin finished bronze cross pendant on crimp brooch mounted ribbon. Near mint cond. $55.00

NAVY DISTINGUISHED SERVICE MEDAL: On crimp brooch mtd. ribbon. Near mint cond. $49.00

NAVY DISTINGUISHED SERVICE MEDAL: On crimp brooch mtd. ribbon. Near mint cond. $55.00

NAVY EXPEDITION MEDAL: On crimp brooch mtd. ribbon. Mint cond. $20.00

NAVY EXPERT PISTOL SHOT QUAL. MEDAL: On crimp brooch mtd. ribbon. In

1989 dated issue envelope. Near mint cond. $10.00

NAVY CROSS (KOREAN ERA)

NAVY EXPERT RIFLEMAN SHOT QUAL. MEDAL: On crimp brooch mtd. ribbon. In 1988 dated issue envelope. Near mint cond. $92.00

NAVY GOOD CONDUCT MEDAL: On crimp brooch mtd. ribbon. Mint cond. $20.00

NAVY GOOD CONDUCT MEDAL: Pendant mach. engraved in block letters w/man's name & 1947 dated. On slot brooch mtd. ribbon. Avg. cond. $30.00

NAVY GOOD CONDUCT MEDAL: Slot brooch. Named & 1951 dated in mach. engraved block letters. Avg. cond. $20.00

NAVY RESERVE MERITORIOUS SERVICE MEDAL: On crimp brooch mtd. ribbon. Near mint cond. $20.00

POW MEDAL: On crimp brooch mtd. ribbon. Mint cond. $10.00

POW MEDAL: On crimp brooch mtd. ribbon. Mint cond. 20.00

PURPLE HEART (USMC KOREAN WAR ERA): Full size on slot brooch mtd. ribbon. Machine engraved in block letters w/ "U.S.M.C." below man's name. W/3 place ribbon bar. 2 USMC EM Collar Devices. 2 lapel pins. Avg. cond. $177.00

SILVER STAR: Crimp style brooch. W/lapel pin. Near mint cond. $22.00

SILVER STAR: On crimp brooch mtd. ribbon. Mint cond. $12.00

SILVER STAR: On crimp brooch mtd. ribbon. Exc. cond. $13.00

SILVER STAR: On crimp brooch mtd. ribbon. Named in private machine engraved style. Mint cond. $40.00

UN KOREA MEDAL: Gilt bronze pendant on Korea hanger bar on crimp brooch mounted ribbon. Exc. cond. $28.00

UN KOREA SERVICE MEDAL: On crimp brooch mtd. ribbon. Near mint cond. $20.00

USAF AIRMAN MEDAL: Bronze satin finish pendant on crimp brooch mtd. ribbon. W/ ribbon bar & lapel pin. In 'Arrow' presentation case & 1990 dated gov't. issue carton. Mint cond. $20.00

USAF AIRMAN MEDAL: On crimp brooch mtd. ribbon. W/ribbon bar & lapel pin. In 'Arrow' medal case & 1969 dated issue box. Near mint cond. $26.50

USMC CHINA SERVICE MEDAL: Dark bronze finish pendant on slot brooch mtd. ribbon. Exc. cond. $37.00

USMC CHINA SERVICE MEDAL: On crimp brooch mtd. ribbon. Mint cond. $20.00

USMC CHINA SERVICE MEDAL: On crimp brooch mtd. ribbon. Above avg. cond. $28.00

USMC EXPEDITION MEDAL: On crimp brooch mtd. ribbon. In plastic case & 1981 dated issue box. Mint cond. $20.00

VIETNAM SERVICE MEDAL: Japanese made. Above avg. cond. $22.00

U.S. MILITARY RELATED BOOKS & MANUALS

A. Thru World War I (1919)

BOOK "107TH FIELD ARTILLERY USNG": 1918. Sb, large format, 100 pgs. with photo roster, cover page is water damaged. Avg. cond. $22.00

BOOK "108TH INFANTRY": WWI. Sb, magazine format, 150 pgs. of captioned photo roster of all soldiers. Tearing to cover. 1918 Avg. cond. $22.00

BOOK "1ST BN. 406TH TELEGRAPH BN.": WWI. Hb, large format, 300+ pgs. of photos & roster in back, gold embossed cover of US line man & plane passes. Avg. cond. $22.00

BOOK "28TH DIVISION PENNSYLVANIA'S GUARD IN WWI": History of Keystone or Iron Div. Also Penn. Guard & predecessor Penn. Militia. Hb, large format, 558 pgs., w/roster & ills. 1924 dated. Cover shows wear & some water damage. Avg. cond. $69.00

BOOK "2ND DIV.- SUMMARY OF OPERATIONS IN THE WORLD WAR" WWI: 1944. Sb, med. format, 126 pgs. with 6 large folded battle maps in sleeve on front cover. Pub. By American Battle Monuments Commission. Avg. cond. $17.00

BOOK "32ND DIV.": WWI. 1920 hb, large format, 315 pgs. with lots of photos & roster in back. Avg. cond. $50.00

BOOK "351ST INFANTRY": WWI. Hb, large format, 1919, 117 pgs. Many photos. Color patch design embossed on cover. Exc. cond. $61.00

BOOK "55TH FIELD ARTILLERY BRIGADE" ED. BACON: WWI. 1920 hb, 330 pgs. with detail history of the company with lots of photos & rosters Avg. cond. $30.00

BOOK "89TH DIV.": WWI. Hb, large, 500+ pgs. of photos & maps. Sound shape w/ flaking to binder cover Avg. cond. $36.00

BOOK "90TH DIV.": WWI. Hb, 259 pgs. with photos, fold out maps & roster. Has 1 pg. loose in center. Avg. cond. $25.00

BOOK "A GUIDE TO THE AMERICAN BATTLE FIELDS IN EUROPE" AMERICAN BATTLE: 1927. Monuments Commission. 281 pgs. w/lots of period photos of the war & foldout maps + back cover sleeve w/folded maps. Great WWI battle ref. Avg. cond. $23.00

BOOK "A HISTORY OF THE MOTOR TRANSPORT CORPS

RECONSTRUCTION PARK 772": Sb, med. format, 46 pgs. Illus. & description from May 1917 to Dec. 1917. Above avg. cond. $20.00

BOOK "AIR SERVICE BOYS FLYING FOR FRANCE": by Charles Armory Beach. Story of the young heroes of the Lafayette Escadrille. Hb, med. format, 1919, 218 pgs. Shows some age. Above avg. cond. $25.50

BOOK "AMERICAN ARMIES & BATTLEFIELDS IN EUROPE" WWI: Hb. med. format, 545 pgs. 1938. History, guide & reference book about operations in WWI. Lots of b/w photos, colored strategic maps of operations. Pocket for 3 maps on hardcover of book. Avg. cond. $21.00

BOOK "ANECDOTES POETRY & INCIDENTS OF THE WAR" NORTH & SOUTH 1861-65: 1866. Hb, med. size, 560 pgs. on the Civil War history & w/ engravings of Lincoln, Lee Grant & other officers of both sides. Good period book. Avg. cond. $29.00

BOOK "BEDFORD FORREST & CRITTER COMPANY": Confederate General. 1931. Hb, mod. format, 102 pgs. on the Civil War history of the great General. Avg. cond. $34.00

BOOK "BEFORE ENDEAVORS FADE" WWI BATTLEFIELDS: Sb, 164 pgs. with 100s of present day photos of the area & museums around them. Avg. cond. $24.00

BOOK "CADILLAC MOTOR COMPANY HISTORY OF WWI". 1939 hb, 78 pgs. with detail history of the company with lots of photos of the production during the war & with roster & records of the employees that serve. Avg. cond. $18.50

BOOK "CIVIL WAR COLLECTOR'S ENCYCLOPEDIA": Hb, large format, 356 pgs., dj., 1963, w/photos & illustrations on arms, uniforms & equipment of the Union & CSA. Avg. cond. $25.00

BOOK "FIGHTING THE FLYING CIRCUS" BY RICKENBACKER: Signed copy "With every best wish to Wm. Sears" signed by Capt. Eddie Rickenbacker. Hb, med. format, 1919, 371 pgs. by Commanding officer 94th Pursuit Squadron US Air Service. Near mint cond. $150.00

BOOK "FORTIETH DIVISION-1917/1919": Hb, large format, 1920 dated, 179 pgs. Many photos, w/personnel roster & charts. Cover shows some age. Above avg. cond. $88.00

BOOK "FROM HARLEM TO THE RHINE" BY ARTHUR W. LITTLE: The Story of

New York's colored volunteers. All Black WWI unit. Hb, med. format, 382 pgs. 1936, 1st ed. Exc. cond. $60.00

BOOK "GUIDE TO EXCAVATED COLONIAL & REVOLUTIONARY WAR ARTIFACTS" + PHOTOS: Sb, large format, 1988 by Deborah A. Sprouse 129 pgs. Many photos. + 2-12x12" approx. size oval shaped photos depicting Generals of the South & Fallen Brave. Exc. cond. $23.00

BOOK "HISTORY & ROSTER 417TH TELEGRAPH BATTALION SIGNAL CORPS": United States Army American 1918-1919, sb, med. format, 23 pgs. Cover illus. insignia. Above avg. cond. $40.00

BOOK "HISTORY OF THE 77TH DIVISION": Hb, large format, 1919, 225 pgs. Many photos, roster & citation list. Also incl. cartoons & battle songs. Color embossed design on cover. Above avg. cond. $35.00

BOOK "HONOR ROLL BUREAU COUNTY, ILL. 1917-19": Hb, large format, 300 pgs. with photos & bios. on the doughboys that fought Avg. cond. $32.00

BOOK "HOW THE MIGHTY HAVE FALLEN": Souvenir program US Government War Exposition lake front Chicago, Sept. 2 to 15. Avg. cond. $21.00

BOOK "LIVINGSTON COUNTRY ILL. IN THE WORLD WAR": Hb, large format, 655 pgs. on the war history with lots a photos & roster Avg. cond. $32.00

BOOK "MEMOIRS OF FRANCE & THE 88TH DIVISION": WWI. Hb, large format, 1920, 172 pgs. Many photos, charts & personnel roster. Above avg. cond. $30.00

BOOK "MICHIGAN VOLUNTEERS OF '98": Hb, large format, 1898 dated, 50+ pgs. A complete photographic record of Michigan's part in the Spanish-American War of 1898. Many photos & muster roll of volunteers. Patriotic design of American flag & soldier on cover. Exc. cond. $101.00

BOOK "MICHIGAN VOLUNTEERS OF 98": Hb, large, 80 pgs. of b/w photo record of the states part in the war. Has roster & roster photos. Avg. cond. $20.00

BOOK "MILITARY SCIENCE & TACTICS": 1890. Sb, pocket size, 665 pgs., Prepared for Military Students & profusely illustrated. Exc. cond. $40.00

BOOK "NEW ENGLAND AVIATORS 1914-1918 - THEIR PORTRAITS & THEIR RECORDS": vol. 1 Hb. 1919 dated with 472 pgs. of great reference photos of uniforms wings & insignia of individual aviators. Includes Army & Naval aviators.

Rare book w/nice uniform study. Avg. cond. $187.00

BOOK "MICHIGAN VOLUNTEERS OF '98"

BOOK "NEW TESTAMENT U.S. ARMY": distributed by the Pocket Testament League. Brown cover has WAAC imprinted & PTL emblem Shows slight age. Above avg. cond. $25.00

BOOK "NEW YORK & THE WAR WITH SPAIN" 1903: Hb, med. format, 500 pgs. History of the Empire State Regiments with b/w photos, with correspondence relating to the regiments, index of the diff. regiments of N.Y. State Volunteers & military history of the State of New York. Fold-out photo of the First Regiment-Evening Parade Book of the Mayville, N.Y. Library, with book slip showing name & date. Avg. cond. $40.00

BOOK "NOTES ON MILITARY EXPLOSIVES" WEAVER 1917: Hb, 380 pgs. with text & diagrams. Avg. cond. $27.00

BOOK "PICTORIAL ATLAS ILLUSTRATING THE SPANISH-AMERICAN WAR": Hb, large format, 1898 dated, 189 pgs. Many photos, drawings & color printed maps. Lot incl. newspaper dated Sept. 10, 1898 from the Saturday Globe. Shows slight age. Above avg. cond. $27.00

BOOK "REGIMENTAL BIOGRAPHY OF THE 21ST ENGINEERS LIGHT RAILWAY AEF": Hb, large format, black cover, gold print, 235 pgs. 1919 dated. Picture biography w/roster of 21st. Exc. cond. $44.00

BOOK "REGIMENTAL HISTORY OF THE 316TH INFANTRY" 1930: Hb, small format, 100 pgs. Above avg. cond. $20.00

BOOK "REPORT OF THE GETTYSBURG MONUMENT COMMITTEE": of the 121st

N.Y. Volunteers hb, med. format, 83 pgs. supplemented w/names of contributors & sketch of regiment. Has unit photos. Late 1890s dated. Above avg. cond. $36.00

BOOK "SOLDIERS & SAILORS IN THE CIVIL WAR 1861-66": 1898. Hb, med. format, 167 pgs., red linen w/gold embossing, w/register of Manchester Men in the Civil War. Above avg. cond. $34.00

BOOK "SOLDIERS OF THE GREAT WAR": 3 Volume set. all hb, large format, 450 + pgs. each with names & photos of the soldiers who lost their lives in WWI. Great reference books & hard to find a complete set in good condition. Avg. cond. $185.00

BOOK "THE .45-70 SPRINGFIELD": Hb, large format, 1980 dated. 381 pgs. Dark red cover w/gold lettering. This copy is #36 of Special First Edition of 1000 copies & autographed by the authors. History & development of Springfield arms. Near mint cond. $90.00

BOOK "THE 32ND DIVISION IN THE WORLD WAR": issued by the Joint War History Commissions of Michigan & Wisconsin. Hb, large format, 319 pgs., 1920 dated. W/picture history of 32nd & honor roll & Distinguished Service Decorations. Avg. cond. $29.00

BOOK "THE 37TH DIVISION IN THE WW" HISTORY 1917-1918: Medium format, hb, 1926, 404 pgs. w/b&w photos of the division. 1st ed., very good condition. Avg. cond. $20.00

BOOK "THE 88TH DIVISION IN THE WW OF 1914-1918": Hb, large format, 1919, 236 pgs. w/photos & roster. Above avg. cond. $48.00

BOOK "THE AEROPLANE SPEAKS" BARBER: 1917. Hb, med. format, 156 pgs. on the aspects of flying & working on airplanes. Has lots of illus. of all airplanes of the period. Interesting reference. Avg. cond. $29.00

BOOK "THE BOAT BOOK OF THE US NAVY" STAMPED TO USS TEXAS: 1927. Hb, small format, 266 pgs. published by Navy Dept. w/lots of illus. color flags & codes. Avg. cond. $24.00

BOOK "THE BREVET MEDAL" 1988, HISTORY OF THE BREVET MEDAL: Sb, med. format, 175 pgs. book deals with the history of the Brevet Medal. Photos & documents from the US Marine Corps. Good reference book. Above avg. cond. $24.00

BOOK "THE COMPLETE STARS & STRIPES NEWSPAPER": A remarkable compilation in book form of one copy of each overseas issue From Feb. 8th 1918 to June 13th 1919. 24x18" HB w/ reinforced spine. Spine is worn & cracked from use, cover is clean but slightly discolored. Avg. cond. $70.00

BOOK "THE FOURTH DIVISION" BY CHRISTIAN A. BACH: Its Services & Achievements in the World War. Hb, med. format, 1920, 368 pgs., some photos. Avg. cond. $20.00

BOOK "THE HORSE SOLDIER 1776-1943": 4 Volume set. Vol. I-"The Revolution, The War of 1812, the Early Frontier 1776-1859" Vol. II-"Frontier, Mexican War, Civil War, Indian Wars 1851-1880" Vol. III-"Indian Wars, Spanish American War, Brink of Great War 1881-1916" Vol. IV-"WWI, Peacetime Army, WWII 1917-1943" All hb, large format, dj., 133+ pgs 1978 dated. Above avg. cond. $90.00

BOOK "THE NORTHERN BARRAGE-MINE FORCE 1918": 1919 hb, large format, 127 pgs. almost all photos & roster photos. Rare unit history. Avg. cond. $30.00

BOOK "THE NOVELTIES OF THE NEW WORLD" 1860, NAMED TO THE OFFICERS & CREW US GUNBOAT WACHUSETT IN 1862: Hb, small format, 324 pgs. by Bandyard & has been named twice to the gunboat above on inside cover. Embossed cover & carrier on the ship in the Civil War. Avg. cond. ... $86.00

BOOK "THE OFFICIAL RECORD OF THE UNITED STATES' PART IN THE GREAT WAR" 1920s: Hb. med. format, 310 pgs. Government account of thirteen American battles in WWI. Illustrated with 85 diagrams, maps & tables, official register of awards of the DSC & DSM, bibliography of the Great War. Avg. cond. $34.00

BOOK "THE PEOPLE'S WAR BOOK & ATLAS": WWI. Pictorial War History, Cyclopaedia Chronology & Atlas of the World. Autographed Edition by Lt. Colonel W. A. Bishop known as the World's Ace of Aces. Incl. Official War Reports & Authentic Articles. W/war maps, charts & diagrams, nearly 500 ills. & colored plates. Hb, black cover, large format, 1920 dated, 550+ pgs. Exc. cond. $61.00

BOOK "THE SECOND DIVISION AMERICAN EXPEDITIONARY FORCES-1917/1919": Sb, med. format, 1919, 31 pgs. Publication of General Orders, Bulletins & Newspaper Articles will illustrate the great part the 2nd Division played in the Great World War. Exc. cond. $30.00

BOOK "THE STORY OF THE 91ST DIVISION": Medium format, hb, 1919, 177 pgs. w/b&w photos & maps. WWI history. Avg. cond. $48.00

BOOK "THEY'RE FROM KANSAS-HISTORY OF THE 353 INFANTRY-1917/1918": Hb, med. format, 1921 dated, 315 pgs. History of 353 Infantry Regiment 89th Division National Army, w/Regimental Directory, American Expeditionary Forces. Above avg. cond. $34.00

BOOK "TRAIL OF THE 61ST": 1919. Hb, med. format, 230 pgs. with some photos. Avg. cond. $51.50

BOOK "TWELFTH U.S. INFANTRY 1798-1919 - ITS STORY BY ITS MEN" BOOK: Hb. 1919 dated. 425 pages w/some illus. Includes rosters. Name inked on inside cover page. Avg. cond. $20.00

BOOK "US ARMIES & BATTLEFIELDS IN EUROPE" WWI: 1938 US Government guide. Hb, med. format, 546 pgs. w/lots of b/w photos, maps & large folded map section on envelope back cover. Great ref. to the battlefields & history. Avg. cond. $15.50

BOOK "WAR OF THE REBELLION": Compilation of the official Records of the Union & Confederate Armies. Series II, Vol. VIII. Washington Government Printing Office 1899 dated. Hb, med. format, 1059 pgs. Exc. cond. $27.00

BOOK "WAR OF THE REBELLION": Official Records of the Union & Confederate Armies. Hb, med. format, 1887 dated, 1200+pgs. Series I, Vol. XIX. by Lt. Col. Robert N. Scott. Shows slight age. Above avg. cond. $23.00

BOOK "WHAT SAMMY'S DOING" COL. MOSS US ARMY: 1917. Sb, med. format, 141 pgs. w/100s of captioned photos of Doughboy boy training in WWI. Avg. cond. $28.00

BOOK "WITH THE 308TH ENGINEERS FROM OHIO TO THE RHINE & BACK": 1923. Sb, large format 243 pgs. with photos & roster. Binder is loose but comes in original shipping box. Above avg. cond. $24.00

BOOKLET "CAROLINA & THE SOUTHERN CROSS": 1914. Sb, large format, 20 pgs. July, 1914 dated. published by Official Organ of North Carolina, United Daughters of the Confederacy. Above avg. cond. $24.00

BOOKLET "GENERAL PERSHING OFFICIAL STORY OF THE AEF IN FRANCE": 1919. Sb, med. format, 38 pgs. w/some illus. Avg. cond. $20.00

BOOKLET "THE FIRST IRON CLAD NAVAL ENGAGEMENT IN THE WORLD": hb med. format, ills. 1906 dated. History of facts of the great Naval battle between the Merrimac & Monitor. Above avg. cond. $27.00

MANUAL "AIR SERVICE MEDICAL MANUAL": 1918. Hb, large format, 36 pgs. with lots of photos & illus. of the WWI aviator & plane. Hard to find. Avg. cond. $18.00

MANUAL "DESCRIPTION & RULES FOR THE US RIFLE": WWI. by Washington Government Printing Office 1917, hb, med. format, 79 pgs. Management of caliber .30, model of 1903 rifle, w/photos, illus., & charts. Shows some age. Above avg. cond. $38.00

MANUAL "EQUIP. MANUAL FOR SERVICE IN EUROPE -PIONEER REGIMENT OF THE INFANTRY": Sb, small format, 35 pgs. of information & states on cover Confidential & is not to be taken into front line trenches. GHQ of AEF Aug. 1918. Red cover. Avg. cond. $45.00

MANUAL "FRENCH-ENGLISH MILITARY TECHNICAL DICTIONARY": 1917 US Government. Hb, med. format, 581 pgs. w/up to date WWI supplement on the latest French terms Avg. cond. $12.00

MANUAL "INFANTRY DRILL REGULATIONS" SPURGIN: Catechism edition. small format, 269 pgs. of illus. of training of SAW soldiers. Very good condition for period. Above avg. cond. $18.00

MANUAL "INFANTRY DRILL REGULATIONS- MANUAL OF ARMS CAL. .45 & .30": 1898 SAW Manual. Hb, small format, 400 pgs. published by war dept. w/lots of illus. & other. Avg. cond. $28.00

MANUAL "PAYMASTER'S DEPARTMENT US MARINE CORPS 1917": Hb, large format, 1917, 319 pgs. Unique since amendments & revision are glued in separately. Cloth cover shows slight wear. Above avg. cond. $90.00

MANUAL "REVISED US ARMY REGULATIONS 1861": Hb, med. format, 1861, 558 pgs. has ills. charts, tables, etc. Shows age. Above avg. cond. $135.00

MANUAL "UNITED STATES RIFLE CAL .30 MODEL OF 1917": 1918. Sb, med. format, 78 pgs. w/fold outs & great illus. Rare manual for era. Avg. cond. $21.00

MANUAL "US NAVY REGULATIONS 1920": by Navy Dept., Bureau of Navigation hb,

med. format, 830+ pgs. 1920 dated. In
interesting steel binder. Above avg. cond.
.... $40.00
MANUAL "NOTEBOOK FOR THE
GENERAL STAFF OFFICER": 1918
French printed. dark green folder cover w/
150 + pgs. & cell map overlays, not used
& unusual manual. Avg. cond. $17.00
SOUVENIR PHOTO BOOK "1898 SAW 2D
MISSOURI VOL. INFANTRY CAMP IN
TENN.": Sb, small with 58 b/w photos
plates of the soldiers, camp, the CW battle
field. Cover is off but remains w/book. Has
roster in back Avg. cond. $21.00
SOUVENIR PHOTO BOOK "1898 SAW
CAMP THOMAS (CHICKAMAUGA
CHATTANOOGA AREA)": 1898. Sb, small
with 69 b/w photos of the soldiers, camp,
the CW battle field & other. 4 of the back
pgs. are coming loose from staples. Avg.
cond. $19.00

B. 1920 - 1945

"25 MISSIONS-STORY OF THE MEMPHIS
BELLE": Sb, small format, 36 pgs., 1943
w/crew photo Exc. cond. $20.00
BOOK "100 CENTURY DIVISION 1944": Hb,
large format, 1940s, 150+ pgs., w/photos
& roster. Above avg. cond............. $50.00
BOOK "103RD INFANTRY, 43RD
INFANTRY DIVISION": Hb, large format,
1942, 107 pgs. History & picture account
of unit in WWII, plus roster of personnel in
Camp Shelby 1942. Above avg.
cond. $30.00
BOOK "12TH ARMORED DIVISION
HELLCATS": Hb, large format, 1947, 90+
pgs. Exc. cond. $49.00
BOOK "12TH BOMBER GRP THE
EARTHQUAKERS IN ETO": 1948,
embossed cover, large format, 150 pgs. w/
photos. Above avg. cond. $150.00
BOOK "13TH AIRBORNE DIVISION-FORT
BRAGG, NORTH CAROLINA": Hb, large
format, 200+ pgs. 1945 dated. Editorial &
pictorial history of Division, w/roster.
Padded leatherette cover w/Division
Insignia. Autograph, Lt. General Lesley J.
McNair, Exc. cond. $132.00
BOOK "13TH AIRBORNE": 1946 1st ed. Hb,
large format, 350 pgs. Above avg. cond.
.... $160.00
BOOK "13TH AIRFORCE FROM FIJI
THROUGH THE PHILIPPINES": Hb, large
format, 190 pgs. w/art, illus. & history. Avg.
cond. $72.00

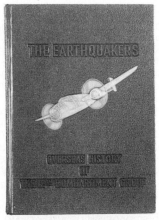

BOOK "12TH BOMBER GRP THE
EARTHQUAKERS IN ETO"

BOOK "14TH ARMORED DIV.": Hb, large
format, 200 pgs. Avg. cond. $75.00
BOOK "14TH ARMORED DIVISION": Hb,
large format, 200+ pgs. Exc. cond.
.... $55.00

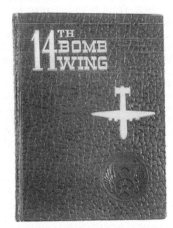

BOOK "14TH BOMBER WING 8TH AAF IN
ETO"

BOOK "14TH BOMBER WING 8TH AAF IN
ETO": 1945. Large format, 150 pgs., b/w
photos. Avg. cond. $244.00
BOOK "1936 CRUISE LOG OF USS
COLORADO INTO THE DOMAIN OF
NEPTUNUS REX": Sb, med. mag. format,

45 pgs. of photos & history of the ship, has roster & lots of penned in captions to the ceremony & crews autographs. Avg. cond. $51.50

BOOK "1ST CAVALRY DIVISION": Sb, large format, 2nd print 1947 250 pgs. w/photos. Avg. cond. $45.00

BOOK "207TH COAST ARTILLERY (AA) CAMP STEWART 1941": Hb. 114 pages w/illus. Some autographs in back. 1941 dated. Avg. cond. $26.00

BOOK "2ND ENGINEER SPECIAL BRIGADE": Hb, large format, WWII, 261 pgs. Above avg. cond. $40.00

BOOK "305TH INFANTRY SECOND TO NONE" 1949 1ST EDITION: Hb, med. 243 pgs. w/roster & photos Avg. cond. . . $63.00

BOOK "32D INFANTRY DIVISION WORLD WAR II": Hb, dj., med. format, 416 pgs., w/ many photos & maps. Exc. cond.
.... $135.00

BOOK "33 DIVISION US ARMY-CAMP FORREST 1941-1942": Pictorial History. Hb, large format, 429 pgs. w/roster. Above avg. cond. $55.00

BOOK "345TH INFANTRY REGIMENT-87TH INFANTRY DIVISION": Hb, large format, 1946, 195 pgs. Exc. cond.
.... $74.00

BOOK "347TH FIGHTER SQUADRON 350 FIGHTER GROUP 12TH AF": Hb, large format, 159 Exc. cond. $150.00

BOOK "355TH AAA SLT BN.": 1946. Hb, large format, 276 pgs. Avg. cond.
.... $65.00

BOOK "35TH DIVISION-CAMP ROBINSON, ARKANSAS 1941": Medium format-SB w/ large division insignia on the cover. Photos pre-war equipment in use, "General" Harry Truman in uniform, etc. Near mint cond. $59.00

BOOK "35TH INFANTRY DIV. SANTA FE": Hb, large format, 200 pgs. w/photos. Avg. cond. $55.00

BOOK "376TH INFANTRY REGIMENT 1921-1945": Hb, large format, 1945 dated, 202+ pgs. Pictorial & editorial history of 376th in France & Germany. Incl. Awards & Decoration roster. Above avg. cond.
.... $75.00

BOOK "397TH BOMB GRP. M 'BRIDGE BUSTER': Hb, 1946, large format, 100 pgs. Near mint cond. $125.00

BOOK "3RD ARMOR DIV. SPEARHEAD IN THE WEST 1941-45": Hb. 260 pages w/ illus. Avg. cond. $65.00

BOOK "413TH INFANTRY REGIMENT": Hb, large format, 1946, 170 pgs. Near mint cond. $82.00

BOOK "42ND DIV. 242D INFANTRY REGT.": 1944. Hb/large format, 132 pgs. w/b&w photos. Avg. cond. $30.00

BOOK "42ND RAINBOW INF DIV.": Hb, annual size, 200 pgs. w/photos. Avg. cond. $37.00

BOOK "42ND RAINBOW INFANTRY DIVISION": Hb, large format, 100+ pgs., 1946. Above avg. cond. $54.00

BOOK "43RD INFANTRY DIVISION 1941-5 WINGED VICTORY": Sb, med. format, 39 pgs. Maps. Avg. cond. $20.00

BOOK "444TH BOMB GROUP VERY HEAVY SPECIAL": Hb, large format, 1947, 100+ pages. Exc. cond. $177.00

BOOK "76TH INFANTRY DIVISION": Hb, large format, 243 pgs. 1946. Above avg. cond. $60.00

BOOK "452ND BOMBARDMENT GROUP": AAF. Hb, large format, approx. 60 pgs., printed in England circa 1945. Photos & illus. Artwork on flight jackets. Info. on Medal of Honor winners. Original wartime printing. Color printed squadron insignia on back. Exc. cond. $150.00

BOOK "456TH BOMBER GRP. 1944-45 IN ITALY": Sb, large format, 120 pgs. Sqdn. insignia cover. Avg. cond. $150.00

BOOK "458TH BOMBARDMENT GROUP (HEAVY)": Reynolds, 1979, hb, large format, 72 pgs. Avg. cond. $35.00

BOOK "45TH AAA GROUP- 45 DAYS": Hb, 89 pgs. with all b/w captioned cartoon graphics. Avg. cond. $45.00

BOOK "45TH INFANTRY DIVISION": Hb, large format, 1946 200 pgs. Avg. cond.
.... $87.00

BOOK "487TH BOMBER GRP. SEPT. 1943-NOV. 45 IN THE ETO": Large format, 150 pgs., b&w photos. Avg. cond. $300.00

BOOK "4TH CAV. RECON. SQDN. FIGHTIN' FOURTH": Paper covers w/stapled format. 35 pages w/maps, some illus. & roster of KIA. Comes in original mailing sleeve w/ 1945 dated postal cancellation stamp. Above avg. cond. $70.00

BOOK "506TH PARACHUTE INFANTRY REGIMENT 6.20 42-6.4.45": Hb, large format, 150 pgs. Avg. cond. $142.00

BOOK "50TH ARMOR INFANTRY BN": Hb, med. format, color cover 110 pgs. w/ photos. Binder cover. Avg. cond.
.... $40.00

BOOK "557TH BOMBARDMENT SQUADRON (M)": Hb, large format, 154 pgs., 1945. Above avg. cond. $187.00

BOOK "487TH BOMBER GRP. SEPT. 1943-NOV. 45 IN THE ETO"

BOOK "5TH MARINE DIVISION IN WWII-THE SPEARHEAD": Hb, dj., large format, 325 pgs. 1946 dated. The WWII history in word & picture of the 5th Marine Division from Camp Pendleton to Japan. Incl. appendix w/list of casualties, KIA, Wounded, Awards & Decorations & personnel roster. Exc. cond. $97.00

BOOK "64TH FIGHTER WING 1942-45": Hb, large format, 200 pgs. w/photos. Avg. cond. $110.00

BOOK "67TH TROOP CARRIER SQDN. FEB. 43-AUG. 1944": Hb, large format, 250 pgs. w/war photos & roster. Color insignia on cover. Avg. cond. $100.00

BOOK "6TH ARMOR DIV.": Sb, med. format, color cover 175 pgs. w/photos. Avg. cond. $44.00

BOOK "726TH RAILWAY OPERATING BATTALION-CLOVIS, NEW MEXICO": Hb, large format, blue cover w/gold imprint. 1943 dated. W/roster of staff & companies. Avg. cond. $49.00

BOOK "727TH RAILWAY OPERATING BN": Hb, large format, 102 pgs. w/photos & roster. Avg. cond. $90.00

BOOK "73RD BOMB WING IN ATO": 1945. Large format, 150 pgs. Above avg. cond. $150.00

BOOK "76TH INFANTRY DIV.": 1946 1st ed. Hb, large format, 248 pgs. Avg. cond. $93.00

BOOK "81ST INFANTRY WILDCAT DIVISION IN WWII": Hb, large format,

1948, 307 pgs. Above avg. cond. $72.00

BOOK "860TH ENGINEERING AVIATION BATTALION": Hb. Large format. Avg. cond. $59.00

BOOK "873RD BOMB WING OD 20TH AAF IN ATO SUPERFORT SAGA": 1945, large format, 96 pgs. Avg. cond. $177.00

BOOK "88TH DIV. THE BLUE DEVILS IN ITALY": 1st edition. Medium format. Hb. 360 pages w/illus. + rosters. 1947 dated. Above avg. cond. $55.00

BOOK "88TH DIV. THE BLUE DEVILS IN ITALY"

BOOK "8TH AAF TARGET GERMANY". Hb, large format, 118 pgs. w/photos. Avg. cond. $18.00

BOOK "933D ENGINEER AVIATION REGT. IN PACIFIC": 1945 sb, large format, 76 pgs. Avg. cond. $61.00

BOOK "94TH ARMORED FIELD ARTILLERY BATTALION IN THE EUROPEAN THEATER": Editorial & pictorial history dating 29 Dec. 1943 to 9 May 1945. Hb, large format, 128 pgs., Info. on Medal of Honor Winners & personnel roster & group photos. Avg. cond. $55.00

BOOK "95TH INFANTRY DIV. 1918-1946": Hb, med. format, 300 pgs. w/photos Avg. cond. $89.50

BOOK "960TH ENGINEERS-EIGHT SCORE & A WAR": Sb, med. format, 20 pgs. Above avg. cond. $40.00

BOOK "A PICTORIAL HISTORY U.S.S. MASSACHUSETTS": large format. Hb. Avg. cond. $59.00

BOOK "AAF 5TH BOMBARDMENT GRP.": Boxed hb, large format, 100 pgs. Above avg. cond. $68.00

BOOK "AAF PILOT TRAINING SCHOOL SMYRNA TENN": Hb, large format, 50+ pgs. Avg. cond. $40.00

BOOK "AAF TECHNICAL TRAINING COMMAND BUCKLEY FIELD DENVER CO.": Hb, large format, 172 pgs. Avg. cond. $30.00

BOOK "AIRBORNE ETO 1940-1945 MTO": Sb, large format, 285 pgs. numbered 793 copy out of 1000 & signature. English & French. Near mint cond. $46.00

BOOK "AIRBORNE FIVE ELEVEN": 1943. Pictorial & editorial review of the 511th Parachute Infantry, Camp Machall, North Carolina. W/Who's Who in the regiment & portrait roster. Wartime print. Exc. cond. $75.00

BOOK "ALL AMERICAN" STORY OF 82ND AIRBORNE DIVISION: Small, sb, 32 pgs., picture history of unit after invasion in Europe. Avg. cond. $32.00

BOOK "ALLIED MILITARY FIGHTING KNIVES & MEN WHO MADE THEM FAMOUS": Buerlein 1984. Hb, dj.., 183 pgs. w/hundreds of photos. Signed by author. Mint cond. $33.00

BOOK "AMERICAN GUERRILLA FIGHTING BEHIND ENEMY LINES" FRENCH FOREIGN LEGION: 1943. Hb, dj., med. format, 316 pgs. Avg. cond. $34.00

BOOK "ARMY & NAVY LEGION OF VALOR": Medium format, hb, 1944, 110 pgs. color plates & b&w photos. Hb with spiral spine. Avg. cond. $40.00

BOOK "AVIATION BADGES & INSIGNIA OF THE US ARMY 1913-46" CAMPBELL: 1977. Hb, large format, 103 pgs. Signed by author. Mint cond. $35.00

BOOK "BATTLE ROUTE 30TH INFANTRY DIVISION 1944": Hb, med. format, 1946, 356 pgs. Above avg. cond. $49.00

BOOK "BILLETS & BULLETS OF 37 DIVISION": Cartoons & Ragtime, SB, small format, 79 pgs. 1919 dated. Contains Chronology of 37th Division. String bound. Exc. cond. $25.00

BOOK "BORN IN BATTLE": 513th bombardment squadron. Hb, med. format, 1944 dated, 367 pgs. Above avg. cond. $35.00

BOOK "CARRIER WAR" HISTORY OF TASK FORCE 58: Jensen, medium format, hb 1945, 173 pgs. Above avg. cond. $24.00

BOOK "CARTHAGINIANS ROMANS & AMERICANS": 355th AAA SLT BN. Hb, large format, 1946, 274 pgs. Exc. cond. $72.00

BOOK "CHENNAULT'S FLYING TIGERS 1941-1945": WWII History. 1982. Hb, large format, 396 pgs. with 100s of photos. Mint cond. $89.00

BOOK "CLASS OF 43-G 304TH AAFFTD COLEMAN TX": Hb, large format, 56 pgs., men wearing A-2 jackets. Photos. Avg. cond. $29.00

BOOK "CLASS OF 44-H CAVU" GOODFELLOW TX.: Hb, large format, 56 pgs., photos & autographs Avg. cond. $37.00

BOOK "CLEAR THE BRIDGE-WAR PATROLS OF THE USS TANG": Hb, dj., med. format, 4th printing 1979, 480 pgs., True story of WWII submarine. Exc. cond. $82.00

BOOK "COMBAT NARRATIVE 10TH INFANTRY REGIMENT 1944-1945": Hb, med. format, 165 pgs. 1946. Exc. cond. $55.00

BOOK "COMBAT RECORD 504TH PARACHUTE INFANTRY REGIMENT": Sb, large format, 1945, 50+ pgs. Above avg. cond. $276.00

BOOK "DANGER FORWARD-1ST DIVISION": Hb, large format, 1947, 428+ pgs. Exc. cond. $101.00

BOOK "EDGED WEAPONS" WILKINSON: Hb, dj., med. 260 pgs. w/illus. & photos + information from flint to the dress daggers of WWII Germany. Avg. cond. $40.00

BOOK "EIGHT STARS TO VICTORY- NINTH INFANTRY DIVISION": Hb, large format, 1948, 401 pgs. Exc. cond. $42.00

BOOK "EIGHT STARS TO VICTORY-9TH INFANTRY DIVISION": Hb, large format, 406 pgs. 1948 dated. Exc. cond. .. $59.00

BOOK "EIGHTH US ARMY-UP TO NOW!!": Hb, large format, 30 pgs. 1940s. Exc. cond. $40.00

BOOK "FIELD GUIDE TO SLOTTED BAYONETS OF THE WORLD" ROSS: 1994 sb, large format 1st ed. signed. 200 pgs. dealing with bayonets of the world w/ lots of illus. Mint cond. $32.00

BOOK "FIELD MUSIC US MARINE CORPS": Hb, med. format, 1935 dated, 194 pgs. W/notes & lyrics. Exc. cond. $24.00

BOOK "FIGHTING ON GUADALCANAL": Sb, pocket size, 1943 issue, 69 pgs. Personal notes of the fighting men in the Solomon Islands. Above avg. cond. $25.00

BOOK "FLYING FORTRESS" JABLONSKI: 1965 hb, med., 368 pgs. Avg. cond. $37.00

BOOK "FLYING TIGERS": By Larry M. Pistole. Hb, dj., large format, 1981, 260+

pgs. Signed by author. Above avg. cond. $40.00

BOOK "FOLLOW ME - 2ND MARINE DIVISION IN WWII": Hb, large format, 293 pgs. Above avg. cond. $61.00

BOOK "FOLLOW ME" 2ND MARINE DIV.: Medium format, hb, 305 pgs. w/b&w photos, maps, etc. Avg. cond. $45.00

BOOK "FOLLOW THRU-TESTIMONIAL 60TH INFANTRY REGIMENT": Hb, small format, 110+ pgs. by Morton J. Stussman, 1st Lt. Inf. Above avg. cond. $30.00

BOOK "FORTY FIFTH INFANTRY DIVISION": Large format, HB, 1946, 195 pgs. Avg. cond. $72.00

BOOK "GUADALCANAL CAMPAIGN": Sb, med. format, 1947, 188 pgs. by C. B. Cates. Photos & fold out battle maps. Above avg. cond. $50.00

BOOK "HELLS ANGELS BOMBER GRP. IN ENGLAND": Sb, large format, 31 pgs. Avg. cond. $143.00

BOOK "HISTORY 31ST INFANTRY DIVISION IN TRAINING & COMBAT": Large format. Hb. 200 pages. 1946. Above avg. cond. $76.00

BOOK "HISTORY 363TH INFANTRY": Hb, med. format, 354 pgs. Above avg. cond. $40.00

BOOK "HISTORY ELEVENTH AIR FORCE": Sb, large format, 20+ pgs. Avg. cond. $38.00

BOOK "HISTORY OF 3RD INFANTRY DIVISION IN WWII": Hb, large format, 1945, 573 pgs. W/roster. Avg. cond. $46.00

BOOK "HISTORY OF THE 87TH INFANTRY DIVISION: 1946. Hb, large format, 500+ pgs. Avg. cond. $229.00

BOOK "HISTORY OF THE FIFTH BOMB GROUP": Hb, large format, 1946, 40+ pgs. Photos. Exc. cond. $55.00

BOOK "HISTORY OF THE OHIO NATIONAL GUARD & NAVAL MILITIA": 1938. Hb, large format, 475 pgs. with 100s of photos & group roster photos. Above avg. cond. $55.00

BOOK "HISTORY OF THE US NAVAL OPERATIONS IN WWII": 13 volume set. all Hb, dj., 1975, 300-500 pgs. ea. book w/photos. Both fronts. Above avg. cond. $133.00

BOOK "HISTORY OF WAC DETACHMENT * 9TH AIR FORCE": Hb, 198 pgs. w/ narrative & photos. Cover has color 9th AF emblem. Personalized autograph on fly leaf. Very good condition. Above avg. cond. $139.00

BOOK "IN COMBAT W/HQ COMPANY, 3RD BATTALION, 232ND INF RAINBOW

DIVISION": Hb, med. format, 1946, 97 pgs. by Bert McNeil, Jr. Above avg. cond. $54.00

BOOK "IN MEMORIAM GEORGE S. PATTON, JR. GENERAL US ARMY": Sb, med. format, 29 pgs. Prepared at 3rd Army HQ Bad Tolz, Germany, March 1946 to commemorate the death of this great general. Booklet has pictorial & historical account of his great battles, other achievements. Exc. cond. $40.00

BOOK "IWO JIMA-AMPHIBIOUS EPIC": Hb, large format, 249 pgs. 1954 by Lt. Col. Whitman S. Bartley USMC. Exc. cond. $41.00

BOOK "JANE'S ALL THE WORLD'S AIRCRAFT": 1942. Hb, large format, 400 pgs. w/b/w photos. Avg. cond. $49.00

BOOK "JOLLY ROGERS BOMBER GRP. 1942-44 IN THE ATO": Sb, large format, 120 pgs. Avg. cond. $187.00

BOOK "JOLLY ROGERS BOMBER GRP. 1942-44 IN THE ATO"

BOOK "JUNGLE CAMP": Spiral bound, large paperback book published by 33rd Division. Exc. cond. $59.00

BOOK "MARINE CORPS UNIFORMS & EQUIPMENT IN WWII" MORAN: 1992 hb, dj., large format, 138 pgs. w/lots of photos & captioned ID's on the uniforms. Mint cond. $40.00

BOOK "MARINES IN THE CENTRAL SOLOMONS": Official USMC battle history. 1952 hb, med. format, 184 pgs. Avg. cond. $35.00

BOOK "MIGHTY MONTY": Hb, med. format, 1945, 30+ pgs. USS Montpelier. Above avg. cond. $55.00

BOOK "MISSION 13-DEMING ARMY AIR FIELD, SEPT. 11, 1943": Hb, large format. Exc. cond. $35.00

BOOK "MISSION ACCOMPLISHED" 29TH TACTICAL AIR COMMAND: Sb, small format, 31 pgs. w/photos. Part of 9th AAF. Avg. cond. $20.00

BOOK "MISSION COMPLETED": 854th Aviation Engineers from Jan 1, 1943 to Sept. 2, 1945. Dated 1945, hb, large format., 130 pgs. w/numerous photos. Avg. cond. $59.00

BOOK "NAVAJO CODE TALKERS" NATHAN ASSENG: Hb med. format, 1992. 114 pgs. w/photos on history of WWII Navajo language USMC code that was unbreakable by the Japanese. Avg. cond. $23.00

BOOK "NAVY WAVES ANNUAL OF THE HYDROGRAPHIC OFFICE": Sb large format, 61 pgs. 1944. Above avg. cond. $35.00

BOOK "NAZI CONSPIRACY & AGGRESSION - INTERNATIONAL MILITARY TRIALS, NUREMBERG": 10 Volume set. Hb, med. format, 1000 Pgs. by Office of United States Chief of Counsel for Prosecution of Axis Criminality 1946-47 Exc. cond. $171.00

BOOK "NEW JERSEY NATIONAL GUARD 1940": Hb, large format, 331 pgs. Above avg. cond. $37.00

BOOK "ONE DAMNED ISLAND AFTER ANOTHER": WWII AAF. Howard & Whitley, medium format, Hb, 1946, 403 pgs. w/b&w photos. Above avg. cond. $90.00

BOOK "OPERATION CROSSROADS": 1946. Official pictorial record-Office of the Historian Joint Task Force One. Hb, med. format, 224, pgs. Exc. cond. $50.00

BOOK "ORANGE TAILS-358TH FIGHTER GROUP & ANCILLARY UNITS": Hb, large format, 214 pgs., Dec. 1945 dated. WWII story of the 358th Fighter Group in picture w/squadron roster. Brown cover w/gold imprint. Exc. cond. $247.00

BOOK "OSS SPECIAL WEAPONS & EQUIPMENT": Spy Devices of WWII by H. Keith Melton. Hb, dj., large format, 1991, 127 pgs. w/photos & ills. Exc. cond. $40.00

BOOK "OUR LEAVE IN SWITZERLAND": Visit of American soldiers to Switzerland 1945/46. Hb, dj., large format, 178 pgs., 1940s, w/photos. Above avg. cond. $39.00

BOOK "OUR PATRIOTS OF AMERICA NORTH CAROLINA WWII": Hb, large format, 1944, by National Patriotic Publ. NC w/roster. Avg. cond. $55.00

BOOK "PELELIU": Official USMC battle history. 1950 sb, large format, 209 pgs. w/ Photos & fold out maps. Avg. cond. $40.00

BOOK "PICTORIAL HANDBOOK OF MILITARY TRANSPORTATION" ETO UNIT: Sb, large format, 80 pgs. of photos & captions. 1945 Avg. cond. $18.00

BOOK "PICTORIAL HISTORY HARBOR DEFENSES OF BOSTON 1941": Large format. 130 pages w/illus. Avg. cond. $28.00

BOOK "PICTORIAL HISTORY SECOND WORLD WAR": 8 Volume set. Hb, med. format, 500+ pgs. Volumes issued 1944 thru 1948. Exc. cond. $80.00

BOOK "PICTORIAL MANUAL AIRCRAFT & SURFACE CRAFT ONI 41-42": Sb, med. format, 1942 by Naval Intelligence. Silhouettes of Japanese warships. Exc. cond. $55.00

BOOK "RAKKASAN - 187TH AIRBORNE REGIMENTAL COMBAT TEAM": Sb, large format, 1950s. 30+ pgs. Exc. cond. $24.00

BOOK "REGIMENT OF THE CENTURY-397TH INFANTRY REGIMENT": 1945 dated, 307 pgs., picture history of regiment Exc. cond. $75.00

BOOK "RENDEZVOUS W/DESTINY": 101st Airborne Div. 1948, hb, med. fmt., 810 pgs., some photos & maps. Above avg. cond. $70.00

BOOK "ROLL OF HONOR-BATTLE OF ARNHEM 1944": By Soc. of Airborne Museum, compiled by J. A. Hey. Sb, large format, spiral bound, 1986, Photos, list of KIA & casualties, names of glider pilots, roster. Exc. cond. $38.00

BOOK "ROSTER OF OFFICERS & ENLISTED MEN 84TH INFANTRY DIVISION ETO-WWII": Sb, med. format, 1946 dated, 140 pgs. Near mint cond. $35.00

BOOK "SAGA OF THE ALL AMERICAN": WWII 82nd airborne history. Hb, large format, 1946. 250+ pages. Many photos. Above avg. cond. $276.00

BOOK "SAGA OF THE USS ESSEX CV-9": Hb, large format, 1946, 141+ pgs., Picture history of war operations. Exc. cond. $133.00

BOOK "SAIPAN": Official USMC battle history. 1950 sb large format, 287 pgs. w/ photos & fold out maps. Avg. cond. $40.00

BOOK "SCOTT FIELD AAF TECHNICAL TRAINING COMMAND": Hb, large format. Plastic binder. 70 pgs. Avg. cond. $26.00

BOOK "SECOND BATTALION 333RD INFANTRY IN THE ETO-OCT. 1944/ SEPT. 1945": Sb, med. format, 55 pgs. 1945 dated. Historical account of combat operations during this period incl. maps. Above avg. cond. $30.00

BOOK "SECOND ENGINEER SPECIAL BRIGADE": Hb, large format, 1946, 255+ pgs. Above avg. cond. $95.00

BOOK "SHEPHERD OF THE SEAS" 8TH AAF AIR RESCUE: Sb. Stapled large format. 130 pages w/illus. & photos. Avg. cond. $114.00

BOOK "SIXTH INFANTRY DIVISION US ARMY": Hb, large format, 1941, 305 pgs. Above avg. cond. $40.00

BOOK "SPECIAL & ATTACHED UNITS 2ND CAVALRY DIVISION": Hb, large format, 1941, 100 pgs. Exc. cond.
.... $72.00

BOOK "STORY OF 305TH INF.-SECOND TO NONE": Hb, med. format, 1949, dated 1st ed. 242 pgs. Above avg. cond.
.... $42.00

BOOK "SWORDS & DAGGERS": By R. Wilkinson. Hb, med. format, 1967, 256 pgs. W/clear detailed photos of weapons w/description. Above avg. cond. ... $37.00

BOOK "TARAWA TO TOKYO-1943-46": Story of the USS Lexington CV-16. Hb, large format. Exc. cond. $85.00

BOOK "TARAWA": Official USMC battle history. 1947 sb large format, 87 pgs. w/ photos & fold out maps. Avg. cond.
.... $40.00

BOOK "THE 304TH INFANTRY REGIMENT": Hb, dj., large format, 1946, 349 pgs. Exc. cond. $55.00

BOOK "THE 304TH INFANTRY": 1946. Hb, large format, 350 pgs. Avg. cond.
.... $48.00

BOOK "THE 4TH MARINE DIVISION IN WWII": Hb, large format, 1946 dated, 225 pgs. Exc. cond. $60.00

BOOK "THE 56TH FIGHTER GROUP IN WWII": Hb, large format, 1948, 221 pgs. Near mint cond. $150.00

BOOK "THE 6TH INFANTRY DIVISION 1939-1945": Hb, large format, 179 pgs. 1947. Above avg. cond. $72.00

BOOK "THE 81ST INFANTRY WILDCAT DIVISION IN WORLD WAR II": Hb. Large format. 1948 dated-1st edition. Approx. 370 pages w/illus. Avg. cond. $53.00

BOOK "THE 81ST INFANTRY WILDCAT DIVISION IN WWII": Hb, dj., large format, 305+ pgs. 1948. Exc. cond. $111.00

BOOK "THE AIRCRAFT YEAR BOOK 1939": Hb, med. format, 580 pgs. illus. libr. book from Grumman Aircraft Corp. Above avg. cond. $30.00

BOOK "THE AIRCRAFT YEAR BOOK FOR 1935": Hb, med. format, 528 pgs. illus. libr.

book from Grumman Aircraft Corp. Above avg. cond. $40.00

BOOK "THE AIRCRAFT YEARBOOK FOR 1944": Hb, med. format ills. 727 pgs. Libr. book from Grumman Aircraft Corp. Above avg. cond. $38.00

BOOK "THE ARMED FORCES OF WWII": Hb, large format, 312 pgs., dj., 1981, w/ photos of uniforms, insignia & organization. Colorful, good reference. Avg. cond. $32.00

BOOK "THE EARTHQUAKERS": Overseas history of the 12th Bomb. Gp. Hb. Medium format. 147 pages w/illus. 1947 dated. Above avg. cond. $100.00

BOOK "THE ELEVENTH CAVALRY FROM THE ROER TO THE ELBE-1944/1945": Sb, small format, 1945 dated illustrates the story of participation in WWII. + Camp Hood, Texas "Tank Destroyer Center" brochure. Above avg. cond. $75.00

BOOK "THE FIFTH INFANTRY DIVISION IN THE ETO": Hb, large format, 1945 dated, 150+ pgs. Exc. cond. $65.00

BOOK "THE FIFTH INFANTRY DIVISION IN THE ETO"

BOOK "THE FIGHTING 36TH": Hb, large format, 150 pgs. Above avg. cond.
.... $49.00

BOOK "THE FOURTH ARMORED DIVISION - FROM THE BEACH TO BAVARIA": Hb. by Capt. Kenneth Koyen. 295 pages w/ line drawing illus. & photo illus. section. 1946. Above avg. cond. $118.00

WWII "82ND AIRBORNE DIVISION": Hb, dj. large format, 400 pgs. Avg. cond.
.... $101.00

PRINTED MILITARIA

BOOK "THE HISTORY OF THE 446TH BOMB GROUP H 1943-1945": Hb, dj., large format, limited edition of 2000 copies. Near mint cond. $71.00

BOOK "THE HISTORY OF THE 71ST INFANTRY DIVISION": Hb, large format, 117 pgs. WWII. Exc. cond. $50.00

BOOK "THE JUNGLEERS": Hb, large format, 208 pgs., Picture history of the 41st infantry division in WWII Exc. cond. $40.00

BOOK "THE LUCKY BASTARD CLUB" FLETCHER: 1992 hb, dj., 500 pgs. w/ photos. Above avg. cond. $30.00

BOOK "THE MARSHALL CAVENDISH ILLUSTRATED ENCYCLOPEDIA OF WWII": 25 Volume set. Hb, large format, 1972, 100+ pgs. by Brigadier General James L. Collins, Jr. Chief of Military History, Dept. of the Army. Exc. cond. $66.00

BOOK "THE NAVY AT WAR": by Hanson W. Baldwin. Paintings & drawings by combat artists. Hb, large format, dj., 147 pgs. 1943, Above avg. cond. $20.00

BOOK "THE RECAPTURE OF GUAM": By Major O. R. Lodge, USMC. Hb. 214 pages w/illus. & fold-out maps. 1954 dated. Above avg. cond. $35.00

BOOK "THE REPUBLIC THUNDERBOLT": by Republic Aviation Corp. 1943. Sb, large format, 22 pgs. Story of Corp. & Thunderbolt in word & picture. Above avg. cond. $26.00

BOOK "THE ROUGH RIDERS" BY THEODORE ROOSEVELT: Hb, med. format, 1922 dated, 320 pgs., w/some illus. Avg. cond. $24.00

BOOK "THE SHOWBOAT" U.S.S. CAROLINA BB-55: Large format. Hb. Above avg. cond. $135.00

BOOK "THE SKY LANCER 417TH BOMB GROUP": Hb, dj., large format, 1946 dated, 100+ pages. Exc. cond. ... $175.00

BOOK "THE SKY LANCER-417TH BOMB GROUP": Hb, large format, 1946. 250 pages. Official history of A-20 bomber group composed of 672nd, 673rd, 674th & 675th Bomb Squadrons. Lot also incl. program from the 1978 417th BG reunion. Above avg. cond. $160.00

BOOK "THE SPEARHEAD 5TH MARINE DIVISION": Hb, large format, 324 pgs. Exc. cond. $59.00

BOOK "THE STORY OF THE 390TH BOMBARDMENT GROUP (H)": 11x13" format, hb, dark blue cover w/gold imprint, 472 pgs. 1947 dated. From date of activation at Geiger Field, April 1943, until the departure from England in June & July 1945. Shows bombardments over German cities, battles over France, etc. Tabulation of Combat Mission. Incl. group photos, in training & life on Framlingham base. Also has Roster of 380th & attached Units. Exc. cond. $381.00

BOOK "THE STORY OF THE CENTURY - 100TH INFANTRY DIVISION": Hb, large format, 413 pgs., 1946. Exc. cond. $100.00

BOOK "THE THIRD MARINE DIVISION" 1ST EDITION: Medium format, hb, 1948, approx. 350 pgs. w/numerous b&w photos. Above avg. cond. $38.00

BOOK "THE THIRD MARINE DIVISION" 1ST EDITION: WWII History. By 1st lieut.'s R. A. Aurthur & K. Cohlmia. Hb. 1948 dated. 260 pages w/illus. Above avg. cond. $32.00

BOOK "THE THIRD MARINE DIVISION": Hb, med. format, 1948. 300 pages. Exc. cond. $76.00

BOOK "THE WEST POINT ATLAS OF AMERICAN WARS": Vol. 1- years 1689-1900. Vol. 2-years 1900-1953. issued by Dept. of Military Art & Eng. US Military Academy, West Point. Hb, large format, 2nd Printing 1960, 150+ pgs. Exc. cond. $50.00

BOOK "THEY CALLED ME DIXIE": American fighter ace, former member, Eagle Squadron. Hb, dj., med. format, 270 pgs. photo illus. by Captain Rich. L. Alexander USAAF. Above avg. cond. $24.00

BOOK "THIRD MARINE DIVISION": Hb, med. format, 335 pgs. Above avg. cond. $34.00

BOOK "THIS DAMN TREE LEAKS-A COLLECTION OF WAR CARTOONS FROM MEDITERRANEAN: 1945. Stars & Stripes, Sgt. Bill Mauldin. Sb med. format, 117 pgs. with all WWII cartoons by a GI. Avg. cond. $20.00

BOOK "THUNDERBOLT ACROSS EUROPE": 83rd div. unit history. Large format, HB, 1945. 118 pages. Avg. cond. $40.00

BOOK "TINIAN": Official USMC battle history. 1951 hb, med. format, 165 pgs. w/ photos & fold out maps. Avg. cond. $38.00

BOOK "TYNDALL FIELD FLEXIBLE GUNNERY CLASS 43-20": AAF. Sb, med. format, photos, 16 pgs. Above avg. cond. $26.00

BOOK "U.S.S. NEVADA": Large format. Hb. 195 pages. Avg. cond. $76.00

BOOK "UNIFORMS & INSIGNIA OF THE NAVIES OF WWII": Hb, dj., large format, 1991, 112 pgs. by Andrew Mollo. Near mint cond. $37.00

BOOK "US ARMY IN WORLD WAR II-A PICTORIAL RECORD": 3 Volume set. All volumes hb, large format. 1990. Compiled by the Center for Military History of the US Army. Volumes average 450 pgs. Near mint cond. $34.00

BOOK "US SUBMARINE LOSSES WWII": Medium format, hb, 1963, 243 pgs. of rosters for the various subs & the location of the losses. Above avg. cond. ... $38.00

BOOK "USAAF NINTH AIR FORCE": Hb, large format, 20+ pgs. Book consists of collection of color action paintings. All are captioned. Signed copy. Color printed patch design on cover. Above avg. cond. $55.00

BOOK "USS ADMIRAL W. S. BENSON (AP 120)" SHIP HISTORY: Hb, large format, 75 pgs. Avg. cond. $26.00

BOOK "USS AUGUSTA UNDER FIRE" SINO-JAPANESE INCIDENT: 1937-38. Hb, med. format, 136 pgs. with photos on the action in Shanghai China. Ship history. Above avg. cond. $51.00

BOOK "USS AUGUSTA UNDER FIRE" SINO-JAPANESE INCIDENT: 1937-38

BOOK "V-CORPS OPERATIONS IN THE ETO, 6 JAN 1942-9 MAY 1945": Hb, large format, 511 pgs. Book is based on official reports & records, unit histories & After Action Reports & personal interviews.

Book contains photos & situation maps of operation. Above avg. cond. $90.00

BOOK "WAR DIARY USS ALABAMA 1942-1944": Hb, large format, 20+ pgs. Exc. cond. $55.00

BOOK "WIDE WING" AN ANNUAL FOR THE AIR TECH COMMAND SUPPORT GROUP: Medium format, hb, approx. 150 pgs. w/b&w photos. This is annual from occupied Europe presenting the various sections of the support group w/photos & rosters of the members. Avg. cond. $25.00

BOOK "WITH THE 114TH IN THE ETO": Hb, med. format, 192 pgs. Exc. cond. $40.00

BOOK "WWII COMBAT SQUADRONS OF THE USAF": Hb, dj., large format, 1992, 833 pgs. Official military record of every active squadron. Near mint cond. $145.00

BOOK "XX CORPS": Hb, large format, 1984, 406 pgs. Near mint cond. $32.00

BOOK. "HUMP PILOT ASSOCIATION CHINA-BURMA-INDIA HISTORY": 1979. Hb, large format, 596 pgs. w/100s of war photos. Mint cond. $82.00

BOOKLET "3RD US ARMY IN EUROPE 1944-1945": Sb, large format, Aug. 1945 dated. Booklet records activities of 3rd from its arrival in UK Jan. 1944 until 9 May 1945 in Germany. Above avg. cond. $65.00

BOOKLET "BOMBARDIERS' INFORMATION FILE": Sb, med. format, 1945, w/9 different sections. Photos, illus., & charts. Exc. cond. $118.00

BOOKLET "MERRILL'S MARAUDERS-FEB./MAY 1944": Sb, med. format, 117 pgs., History & pictorial account of 5307th Composite Unit in Burma. Fold-out map. Annex lists casualties, decorations. American Forces in Action Series published by Historical Division, War Dept. + "Marauders" patch, curved, yellow letters on red background & gray edging. approx. 3" long. Exc. cond. $315.00

MANUAL "AAF SERVICE TRAINING SCHOOL MANUAL": In black binder, large format, 1942 dated & publ. by Glenn L. Martin Co. W/illus., charts & data. Above avg. cond. $85.00

MANUAL "AIRCREWMAN'S GUNNERY MANUAL": issued by US Navy & US Army. Sb, black binder. 1944 dated. W/ technical & pictorial descriptions. Avg. cond. $49.00

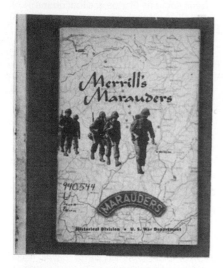

BOOKLET "MERRILL'S MARAUDERS-
FEB./MAY 1944"

MANUAL "AMMUNITION": Instructions for
the Naval Service May 1943. Sb, large
format, 158 pgs. Ordnance Pamphlet No
4. Above avg. cond. $45.00
MANUAL "AN01-60FE-1": Handbook Flight
Operating Instructions USAFT-6C Navy
Model SNJ-4 Aircraft. Sb, large format, 40
pgs. 1945 dated. Revised 24 November
1950. Exc. cond. $81.00
MANUAL "ARMAMENT B-24D AIRPLANE":
Hb, large format, 1943, 184 pgs. Prepared
by Consolidated Aircraft Corp. W/illus. &
data. Exc. cond. $40.00
MANUAL "ARMY AIR FORCES RADIO
DATA & FLIGHT INFOR.": 1943. Sb, large
format, 38 pgs. w/illus. & charts Avg. cond.
.... $34.00
MANUAL "ARMY MODEL C-47A, NAVY
R4D-5 BRITISH MODEL DAKOTA III
AIRPLANES": published by AAF,
Aeronautics & Air Council of UK, 15 May
1945. Punch holed for binder, 200+ pgs.
Parts catalog for above models. Near mint
cond. $50.00
MANUAL "ARMY MODELS C-54A,B,D,E, +
NAVY MODELS R5D-1,2,3,4
AIRPLANES": for Erection & Maintenance
Instructions. 20 Nov. 1944, Rev. 10 Mar
1945. Published jointly AAF & Air Council
of UK. Punch holes, 200+ pgs. W/
drawings, technical information, fold out
diagrams, etc. of aircraft. Exc. cond.
.... $60.00
MANUAL "B-29 GUNNER'S INFORMATION
FILE": Sb, small format, red leatherette w/
two snaps for closure, spiral bound, 30

pgs. Duties & responsibilities of B-29
Gunner. Above avg. cond. $35.00
MANUAL "ARMY VEHICLES GUIDE": 1946,
sb, med. format, 415 pgs. w/photos &
exact specs. Avg. cond. $177.00
MANUAL "AT-6C/D-SNJ-5 OR HARVARD
IIA/III": 1944. Loose leaf manual for
binder. Above avg. cond. $51.50
MANUAL "BROWNING MG CAL. .50 HB.
M2 MOUNTED IN COMBAT VEH": 1942.
Sb, small format, 141 pgs. b/w photos of
the gun in tank & armor truck & on tripod.
Avg. cond. $25.00
MANUAL "EMPLOYEES BOEING
AIRCRAFT COMPANY": small format, sb,
28 pgs. 5th Ed. Dec. 1942. W/list of
Benefits + Rules. Avg. cond. $31.00
MANUAL "ENGINE CHANGE MANUAL
BOEING B-29": Hb, small format, w/two
snaps for closing, 1944 dated, 326 pgs.
Exc. cond. $40.00
MANUAL "ERECTION & MAINTENANCE
INSTRUCTIONS AVENGER 1": Model
TBF-1, TBM-1 Airplane Released by
Bureau of Aeronautics Navy Dept. July 12,
1943 dated. In 3 ring binder, 524 pgs. w/
illus., technical data & charts. Grumman
Aircraft Engineering Corp. Shows use.
Above avg. cond. $292.00

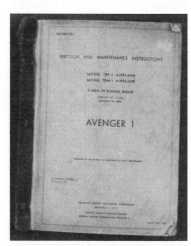

MANUAL "ERECTION & MAINTENANCE
INSTRUCTIONS AVENGER 1

MANUAL "EXPLOSIVES & DEMOLITIONS":
Sb, 1945 dated, med. format, photo illus.
hole punched, 147 pgs. Above avg. cond.
.... $36.00
MANUAL "FLIGHT MANUAL B-24D": by
Consolidated Aircraft Corporation. Hb,
large format, 1942, 180+ pgs. Photos, ills.
& charts. Exc. cond. $50.00

MANUAL "FLIGHT MANUAL B-25C/D AIRPLANE": In orig. loose leaf binder, 8x7". Produced by North American Aviation & distributed by AAF. 326 pgs. separated into flight ops sections & amendable for currency. B/W, photo-diagrams & text. Above avg. cond. $161.00

MANUAL "FLIGHT MANUAL PB4Y-2 AIRPLANE": 1945. Hb, Large Format, 86 pgs. Photos & illus. Above avg. cond. $33.00

MANUAL "FLIGHT OPERATING INSTRUCTIONS USAF F-89C AIRCRAFT": 1951. Sb, large format, for 3-ring binder, 157 pgs. Exc. cond. ... $90.00

MANUAL "FLIGHT THRU INSTRUMENTS": Hb, med. format, 143 pgs., 1945 dated. Issued by Aviation Training Div. US NAVY. Exc. cond. $38.00

MANUAL "FM 21-150, UNARMED DEFENSE FOR THE AMERICAN SOLDIER JUNE 30, 1942": Sb, small format, 315 pgs., 1942 dated, by War Dept. w/ills. Exc. cond. $20.00

MANUAL "GENERAL SERVICE NOTES PB4Y-1 BOMBARDMENT AIRPLANE": by Consolidated Vultee Aircraft Corp. Sb, med. format, 1944, 305 pgs. W/charts, diagrams & ills. Exc. cond. $36.00

MANUAL "GERMAN 88MM ANTIAIRCRAFT TME9-369A: 29 June 1943. sb, med. format, 183 pgs. Near mint cond. $139.00

MANUAL "GERMAN INFANTRY WEAPONS": German infantry Weapons, Special Series, No. 14. issued by War dept., May 25, 1943. Sb, med. format, 182 pgs. w/illus. & figures, receiving stamp HQ San Antonio ASF Depot. Exc. cond. $50.00

MANUAL "GET TOUGH" 1943 ISSUE: Sb, small format, 120 pgs., w/ills. Avg. cond. $75.00

MANUAL "GET TOUGH": How to win in hand-to-hand fighting as taught to the British commandos & US Armed forces. Sb, med. format, 1942 dated. 120 pgs. & illustrations. Above avg. cond. $26.00

MANUAL "HANDBOOK FOR COMBAT AIR INTELLIGENCE OFFICERS": by AAF Air Intelligence School, Harrisburg, Pa. Jan. 1944. hb. large format, 159 pgs. Near mint cond. $93.00

MANUAL "HANDBOOK ON GERMAN MILITARY FORCES": TM-E 30-451. 1943 dated. Hb covers w/string tie binding. 372 pages covering wide aspect of German military forces-many color plates of uniforms. Above avg. cond. $65.00

MANUAL "HARRIS EC INSTRUCTION MANUAL OF THE JOHNSON LIGHT MACHINE GUN": Sb, med. format, 1st Ed. Horizontal Feed Model, 88 pgs. W/fold out drawing of Johnson Light Machine Gun. Above avg. cond. $72.00

MANUAL "ID US GOVERNMENT AIRCRAFT": 1942. Sb, small format, 150 pgs. of photos & lots of profiles of the early WWII military planes. Very good period reference. Above avg. cond. $12.00

MANUAL "INDIVIDUAL SCORE BOOK FOR THE US RIFLE" GOVERNMENT PRINTING OFFICE: 1935. Sb, small format, 100 pgs. with unissued charts & target pgs. Above avg. cond. $10.00

MANUAL "INSTRUCTION BOOK WRIGHT CYCLONE 14 AIRCRAFT ENGINES": Publ. by Wright Aeronautical Corp. 1940. Second Edition. Sb, large format, 100+ pgs. Contains installation, operation & maintenance information supported by illus. diagrams, charts, etc. Above avg. cond. $50.00

MANUAL "INSTRUCTION BOOK WRIGHT CYCLONE 9 AIRCRAFT ENGINES": Publ. by Wright Aeronautical Corp. 1940. First Edition. Sb, large format, 100+ pgs. Contains installation, operation & maintenance information supported by illus., diagrams, charts, etc. Above avg. cond. $50.00

MANUAL "INSTRUCTION MANUAL FOR PRATT & WHITNEY ENGINES R1830-43-& 65": Hb, large format, 1943 dated, 377 pgs. Used in Consolidated Vultee Liberators prepared by Buick Motor GMC. Exc. cond. $30.00

MANUAL "LANGUAGE GUIDE": Foreign language manuals issued by War Dept. in 1943. Incl. Norwegian, German, French & Portuguese. Sb, small, 90+ pgs. Above avg. cond. $45.00

MANUAL "MAINTENANCE MANUAL AN01-60GD-2 AIRCRAFT": Sb, large format, for 3-ring binder, 604 pgs. Exc. cond. $139.00

MANUAL "MAINTENANCE MANUAL AT6C & SNJ-4 AIRPLANES": Sb, large format, for 3-ring binder, 564 pgs. T.O. 01-60FE-4. Exc. cond. $93.00

MANUAL "MAINTENANCE MANUAL B-17 BOMBER": Sb, large format, for 3-ring binder, 481 pgs. T.O. No. 01-20ef-2. Exc. cond. $177.00

MANUAL "MAINTENANCE MANUAL B-29 AIRPLANE: Sb, large format, for 3-ring binder, 600+ pgs. T.O. No. 01-20EJ-2. Exc. cond. $196.00

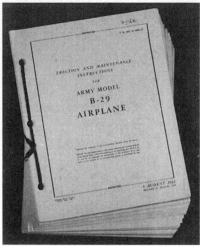

MANUAL "MAINTENANCE MANUAL B-29 AIRPLANE

MANUAL "MED. TANK M4A3 75MM OR 76MM GUN 105MM HOWITZER: 1944. Sb, med. format, TB 9-759-10" 238 pgs. Avg. cond. $81.00

MANUAL "MILITARY INTELLIGENCE ID OF US GOVERNMENT AIRCRAFT": 1942. Sb, 151 pgs. with 100s of photos & profiles of all US planes during the start of the war. Feb. 21 1942, small format, Above avg. cond. $12.00

MANUAL "MODEL BC-1A, AT-6, AT-6A,SNJ-3 MADE BY NORTH AMERICAN AVIATION": Sb, large format, for 3-ring binder, 177 pgs. T.O. No. 01-60FC-2 Exc. cond. $72.00

MANUAL "MOUNTAIN OPERATIONS" FM 70-10: 1944. Sb, small format, 247 pgs. b/w illus. Avg. cond. $37.00

MANUAL "ONI 229-JMSTI, JWR": issued by Div. Naval Intelligence for reporting Japanese merchant & naval vessels. W/silhouettes of vessels. Sb, med. format, punch holed for binder, Exc. cond. $40.00

MANUAL "PILOT'S INFORMATION FILE": AAF WWII. "Pilots' Information File" hb, large format, 1943, Above avg. cond. $49.00

MANUAL "PILOTS' INFORMATION FILE" 1944: Sb, large format, binder bound w/ 250 pgs. illus. Avg. cond. $35.00

MANUAL "PRATT & WHITNEY OVERHAUL": For B-24D engines. Red Covered loose leaf manual. 1310 pgs.

text, photos & diagrams. Exc. cond. $66.00

MANUAL "PREFLIGHT STUDY MANUAL FOR CIVIL AIR PATROL CADETS": Sb, large format, 100+ pgs. 1940s + Civil Air Patrol US Cadet Patch. Above avg. cond. $34.00

MANUAL "PROPOSED CONVERSION FROM MILITARY TO COMMERCIAL AIRPLANES": 1943. Hb, 52 pgs. binder with illus. & complete study on C47, C53, C54A. Above avg. cond. $37.00

MANUAL "RECOGNITION PICTORIAL MANUAL" 1943 AIRCRAFT ID: Sb, 50 pgs. Avg. cond. $20.00

MANUAL "RECOGNITION-PICTORIAL MANUAL": Contains silhouette & description of US Army, US Navy, British, German, Japanese, Italy, USSR & Misc. Aircraft. Sb, string bound, issued by War Dept. & Navy. 1940s. Above avg. cond. $55.00

MANUAL "REPAIR FOR ARMY MODELS C-46,C-46A,C-46D, NAVY MODEL R5C-1 AIRPLANES": Sb, large format, punch holed for binder, 25 March 1944, Rev. 5 may 1945 w/illus. by AAF. Exc. cond. $40.00

MANUAL "SHOTGUNS ALL TYPES" TM 9-285: 1942. Sb, med. format, 257 pgs. w/ photos & illus. of break downs of all models & makes used in WWII. Exc. ref. Avg. cond. $19.00

MANUAL "SUBMARINE SAFETY RESPIRATION & RESCUE DEVICES": issued by Navy Dept. 1938, sb, 135 pgs. Exc. cond. $32.00

MANUAL "THOMPSON SUBMACHINE GUN, CAL. .45 M1928A1": 1941. Sb, 80 pgs. with photos & illus. Avg. cond. $30.00

MANUAL "TM1-440- PARACHUTES & AIRCRAFT CLOTHING": Sb, med. format, Jun. 1945 dated, 154 pgs. issued by War Dept. Exc. cond. $59.00

MANUAL "US NAVY UNIFORM": Hb, med. format, 1927, 60 pgs. Photos & illus. Avg. cond. $53.00

MANUAL FM23-36 REVOLVER": Colt, Caliber .45, M1917 & revolver, Smith & Wesson, Caliber .45, M1917, issued by War Department, October 20, 1941. Sb, small format, Near mint cond. $34.00

PHOTO ALBUM WWII AAF: 11.5x15" album, Photographs embossed in cover, string bound w/approx. 100 b/w photos. Many shots of planes, as B-29, B-24, B-17. Shots of docks, supplies & vehicles & troops. Some captioned. Exc. cond. $90.00

SOUVENIR PROGRAM "HOLLYWOOD VICTORY CARAVAN": Proceeds of program given to Army Emergency Relief & Navy Relief Society. Sb, large format, 35 pgs. In red, white & blue colors, w/ads inside. Above avg. cond. $37.00

C. 1946 - Present

BOOK "101ST AIRBORNE DIV. 1968 VIETNAM YEAR BOOK": Large format. Hb. 144 pages. In original mailing sleeve. Above avg. cond. $96.00
BOOK "1958 CRUISE HISTORY CARRIER USS SHANGRI LA": Hb, 150 pgs. Avg. cond. $34.00
BOOK "1958 USMC 2-2-2 REINFORCED 2ND MAR. DIV. MED. CRUISE": HB. B&W illus. including landing in Lebanon. Above avg. cond. $68.00
BOOK "1964/5 CRUISE HISTORY OF PATROL SQDN. 47 ON WESTPAC CRUISE": Hb, embossed cover 70 pgs. Avg. cond. $30.00
BOOK "25 YEARS USS YORKTOWN CVS 10-SILVER ANNIVERSARY": Hb, large format, 294 pgs. Exc. cond. $30.00
BOOK "27TH INFANTRY DIV. 1948 YEARBOOK": Hb, annual size, 150 pgs. w/photos. Avg. cond. $35.00
BOOK "406TH FIGHTER-INTERCEPTOR WING 1955 ANNUAL": Manston England, hb, large format, Picture History. Avg. cond. $75.00
BOOK "5TH SPECIAL FORCES GROUP (AIRBORNE) DESERT SHIELD/DESERT STORM HISTORY": Hb. 196 pages. Mint cond. $76.00
BOOK "5TH SPECIAL FORCES GROUP (AIRBORNE) DESERT STORM HISTORY": Hb, large format, 200 pgs. Mint cond. $75.00
BOOK "THE 25TH'S 25TH...IN COMBAT": Hb. 400 pages. Avg. cond. $51.00
BOOK "82ND AIRBORNE DIV., 3RD BDE. 1969 VIETNAM II": Large format. Hb. 143 pages. Above avg. cond. $60.00
BOOK "82ND AIRBORNE DIV., 3RD BDE. FEB. 1968 TO MARCH 1969 HISTORY "VIETNAM": Large format. Hb. 67 pages. Above avg. cond. $84.00
BOOK "82ND AIRBORNE DIVISION POWER PACK": Dominican Republic 1965-1966. Hb, large format, 96 pgs. Exc. cond. $20.00
BOOK "AMERICAN BAYONET 1776-1964" HARDIN: Hb, dj., large format, 1964 234 pgs. Avg. cond. $84.00

BOOK "AMERICAN BRITISH & CONTINENTAL PEPPERBOX FIREARMS": By Jack Dunlap. Hb, dj., large format, 1964, 279 pgs. Above avg. cond. $26.00
BOOK "BLT 1/6 MARINES LANDING FORCE MEDITERRANEAN 1967 ANNUAL": Hb, large format, 140 pgs. Avg. cond. $34.00
BOOK "CARRIER USS FORRESTAL 1967 ANNUAL": Hb, large format, 359 pgs. Above avg. cond. $51.00
BOOK "CRUISE BOOK MOVIN' WEST MIDWAY '74": Hb, large format, 368 pgs. Exc. cond. $27.00
BOOK "CRUISE HISTORY 25TH ANNIVERSARY FIGHTING I USS INTREPID (CVS-11) 1943-1968": Hb, large format, 336 pgs. Exc. cond. ... $42.00
BOOK "CRUISE HISTORY CARRIER USS RANGER 1983/84": Hb, large format, 389 pgs. Avg. cond. $30.00
BOOK "CRUISE HISTORY OF CARRIER USS YORKTOWN 1969": Hb, large format, 357 pgs. 5" jacket patch of the Yorktown. Avg. cond. $82.00
BOOK "FIRST AIR CAVALRY DIVISION IN VIETNAM": Hb w/Dj. By Edward Hymoff. 153 pages. 1967 dated. Above avg. cond. $87.00
BOOK "HISTORY 844TH ENGINEER AVIATION BATTALION": Sb, large format, 1953, 130+ pgs. Above avg. cond. $28.00
BOOK "INDIANA NATIONAL GUARD 38TH INFANTRY DIV. 1949 ANNUAL": Hb, large format, 200 pgs. Avg. cond. $25.00
BOOK "KENTUCKY RIFLE PATCHBOXES & BARREL MARKS": by Roy F. Chandler. Hb, large format, 1972, 400 pgs. Above avg. cond. $35.00
BOOK "MILITARY INSIGNIA 20TH CENTURY": Hb, dj., large format, 1986, 223 pgs. By Rosignoli. Exc. cond. $34.00
BOOK "NAVAL SUPPORT ACTIVITY, DANANG 1969 ANNUAL": Hb. Large format. Approx. 300 pages. Above avg. cond. $60.00
BOOK "OCCUPATION DIARY FIRST CAVALRY DIVISION": Sb, med. format, 57 pgs. by First Cavalry Division in Japan 1945-1950. Exc. cond. $26.00
BOOK "PACIFIC DIARY II USS MANCHESTER": June 1951 - 1952. Hb, large fmt., lots of photos. Near mint cond. $72.00
BOOK "TANK BATTALIONS US ARMY" SAWICKI: Hb, dj., 1983, 420 pgs. Mint cond. $30.00

BOOK "THE CALL OF DUTY-MILITARY AWARDS & DECORATIONS OF US": Hb, large format, 1994, 383 pgs., by Strandberg & Bender. Color ills. guide. Near mint $48.00

BOOK "THE GATHERING OF EAGLES" 1985 US ACES WWI-NAM: Autographed edition. Sb, large format, 40 pgs. color art of 16 aces from all wars, 1 WWI, 11 WWII, 2 Korean & 2 Nam era aces all with signatures over photos. Boyington, Yeager, Gabreski & others. Near mint cond. $256.50

BOOK "THE HOWITZER" US MILITARY 1951 ANNUAL FOR WEST POINT: Hb, large format, 486 pgs. Avg. cond. $28.00

BOOK "THE P.38 PISTOL, THE WALTHER PISTOLS 1930-1945": Hb, large format, 1978, Vol. I, 327 pgs. by Warren H. Buxton. Near mint cond. $81.00

BOOK "THE USS ESSEX & CARRIER AIR TASK GROUP TWO": Hb, large format, 143 pgs. Second Korean Cruise 1952/ 1953. Exc. cond. $124.00

BOOK "THIS IS WAR!" DUNCAN: Korean war. Hb, dj., large format, 1980s 200 pgs. w/lots of photos on the history of the forgotten war. Still shrink wrapped. Mint cond. $30.00

BOOK "US SPECIAL FORCES SHOULDER & POCKET INSIGNIA" PUGH: Sb, 327 pgs. Mint cond. $30.00

BOOK "US AIRBORNE 1940-1990 50TH ANNIVERSARY": Hb, large format, 512 pgs. Mint cond. $45.00

BOOK "USS BOXER FAR EAST CRUISE 1956-1957": Hb, large format, 260 pgs. Above avg. cond. $30.00

BOOK "USS RANGER CVA-61 CRUISE": Hb, large format, 303 pgs. Exc. cond. $31.00

BOOK "VIETNAM II 3D BRIGADE, 82ND AIRBORNE DIV. JAN. TO DEC. 1969": Hb, large format, 140 pgs. Near mint cond. $38.00

BOOK "THE GRIM REAPERS" UNIT HISTORY 3RD BOMB GROUP 1918-1985: Hb, large format, 104 pgs. w/lots of photos. Near mint cond. $32.00

MANUAL "ARMY MODEL UH-1D/H HELICOPTERS": TM 55-1520-210-20. issued by Dept. Army, 1971, sb, med. format, 300+ pgs. Exc. cond. $32.00

MANUAL "BLUE BOOK OF COASTAL VESSELS SOUTH VIETNAM": 1967 dated. Hb. Medium format. 556 pages w/ illus. & data. Avg. cond. $87.00

MANUAL "F-102A USAF SERIES AIRCRAFT TO 1F-102A-1": 1960 dated. In binder. Exc. cond. $59.00

MANUAL "FLIGHT MANUAL BASIC-USAF SERIES C-130B, C-130E, C-130H AIRCRAFT": Hb, large format, 1986. Above avg. cond. $34.00

MANUAL "SURVIVAL TRAINING & PERSONAL EQUIP PERSONNEL": 1954 USAF. Sb, med. format, 312 pgs. w/100s of illus. & photos of the Korean war era. Avg. cond. $82.00

U.S. MILITARY RELATED PHOTOS, POSTCARDS & TRADE CARDS

A. All Periods

AAF RECOGNITION TRAINING SLIDES: Revised Naval Vessel Supplement No. 1. 4x12" size box containing approx. 350 slides. Above avg. cond. $91.00

BLACK UNIT PHOTO: 1929. 8x20" b/w rolled photo. Shows soldiers wearing 1926 style uniform. No sleeve insg. Could be a pioneer unit. Shows water stains. Avg. cond. $129.00

CASED CIVIL WAR IMAGE ON TIN: simulated gutta-percha style case. Image of seated Union soldier in shell jacket-holds musket across his chest-wearing belt w/oval "US" plate, large ammo pouch & socket bayonet attached. Above avg. cond. $180.00

CIVIL WAR 6TH PLATE TINTYPE OF YOUNG SOLDIER: Studio portrait in gilt frame, part of folding frame (cover missing). Shows young man in dress uniform w/kepi & 4 button colored sleeve tabs. Tabs & collar buttons suggest he may be West Point cadet. Above avg. cond. $80.00

CIVIL WAR CDV LINCOLN MOURNING: 1865. 3.5x4.5" card art of Washington holding Lincoln & putting wreath on head of great leader. Has been professionally framed. Avg. cond. $50.00

CIVIL WAR CDV OF CONFEDERATE SOLDIER: 70x100mm, chest up shot a man in light gray Northern Virginia Depot Jacket stand up collar w/single button done & other not. Avg. cond. $125.00

CIVIL WAR CDV OF ENLISTED TROOP: Fed artillery man enlisted & holding cap in hand. Avg. cond. $25.00

CIVIL WAR 6TH PLATE TINTYPE OF
YOUNG SOLDIER

CIVIL WAR CDV LINCOLN MOURNING:
1865

CIVIL WAR CDV OF GEN. BEN BUTLER:
2.5 x 4" partial right profile showing dress
collar, epaulettes & two rows of buttons on
tunic. Above avg. $72.00

CIVIL WAR CDV OF GEN. MCCLELLAN:
2.25x4" w/nice portrait head pose &
autograph of General at bottom. Above
avg. cond. $45.00

CIVIL WAR CDV ON TIN: 2.5x3.75" full
standing shot of 2 men in dark overcoats
w/light color tunics & kepis. Probably a
state unit. Good clear detail & same unit
as above lot. Above avg. cond. $93.00

CIVIL WAR CDV ON TIN: 2.5x3.75" full
standing shot of 7 men in dark overcoats
w/light color tunics & kepis. Probably a
state unit. Good clear detail. Above avg.
cond. $100.00

CIVIL WAR IMAGE ON TIN: Cased. 3x4"
image of young, seated union soldier.
Photo back drop of camp scene in back w/
waving US flag. In brass framette w/glass.
Avg. cond. $125.00

CIVIL WAR IMAGE ON TIN: Cased.
70x80mm full length shot of Union soldier
in frock coat & kepi-oval US belt plate &
Eagle cross strap plate have been gold
toned. Avg. cond. $125.00

CIVIL WAR IMAGE ON TIN: Cased.
70x80mm waist up image of young man in
dark shell jacket, lighter shade kepi. In
brass framette w/glass-in gutta-percha
style, hinged lid case. Above avg. cond.
.... $125.00

CIVIL WAR IMAGE ON TIN

CIVIL WAR POSTCARD PHOTO OF E. E.
ELLSWORTH: Photo ills. soldier of N.Y.
Fire zouaves. 1st soldier killed in the war
Was Col. of Regiment. Above avg. cond.
.... $25.00

CIVIL WAR SOLDIER LETTER &
ENVELOPE: is a letter from a man on the
US Ship of Release off Beaufort NC & are
dated Oct. 12,1864. This one talks of
Admiral Farragut taking command & of
Admiral Lee & yellow fever out break &
the Steamer Bat" captured off Wilmington
& also mention "The Owl" & the Rebels
are expecting a attack at Wilmington by
Farragut. The 2 1/2 pgs. folded letter is in
ink & very easy to read script. Part of
address side has stamp size section cut
out. Going to New Bedford Mass, Avg.
cond. $52.00

CIVIL WAR UNION SOLDIER PHOTO:
12x17" size, sepia color print depicting
young Union soldier, standing position in
frock coat & cap. Above avg. cond.
.... $93.00

CONFEDERATE GENERAL JOSEPH JOHNSTON COMMEMORATIVE POSTCARD: Early 1900s w/3 color flags of army above photo of man w/birth & death dates & poem written for him. Unused nice w/gilt outline of flags. Out of Louisville. Above avg. cond. $25.00

PHOTO OF MEDAL OF HONOR WINNER: 2- 5x7" photos of Capt. Lance Sijan first AF Academy graduate to win Medal of Honor. One in full position as drawing. Exc. cond. $40.00

PHOTO OF MEDAL OF HONOR WINNER: 5x7" b/w press released & signed photo of Joe Foss, 1943 USMCR VMF-121. Exc. cond. $37.00

PHOTO OF MEDAL OF HONOR WINNER: 8x10" b/w autographed photo of medal winner David McCampbell. Good details of ribbons, medal & uniform. Exc. cond. $45.00

PHOTOGRAPH SIGNED BY CLAIRE CHENNAULT: 8x10" size, framed. A head & shoulders portrait of Chennault dressed in full military attire. Following the Japanese invasion of China in 1937, he became Chiang Kai-Shek's air adviser & formed a volunteer air corps "The Flying Tigers" to aid China in the war against Japan. Near mint cond. $433.00

BOOK "MILITARY POSTCARDS 1870-1945" SMITH: Sb, large format, 240 pgs. dealing w/US & German Imperial & Nazi period British & others countries cards. Very good photo ref. Above avg. cond. $25.00

STEREO VIEWING CARDS "WORLD WAR THROUGH THE STEREOSCOPE" VOL. 1 & 2 IN BOOK SHAPED BOX: 105 cards. B&W photos. Keystone View co. Box in shape of two books. Avg. cond. $240.00

STEREO VIEWING CARDS ON THE AMERICAN FLEET CIRCA 1900: 25 cards. Color tinted w/several on USS Maine & on US subs. Very hard to find. In original box. Above avg. cond. $38.00

TRAINING CARDS: approx. 35 - cards, 5x8" b/w showing tanks & vehicles w/tech. description. Exc. cond. $40.00

UNIT PHOTO 449TH FTR. SQDN. (A. W.): 1949. 10x59" b/w rolled photo of off. & em. standing in front of hanger w/P-82 aircraft in background. Taken at Ladd AFB, Alaska. Above avg. cond. $30.00

WWI BLACK BAND IN FRANCE PHOTO: Official signal corps photo. 5x7". WWI black officer leading all black army band in the street under the sign of Hotel Tunis. Rare to see a black officer in any photo. Mint cond. $145.00

WWI STEREO VIEWING CARDS: Complete boxed set of WWI Keystone Division. Cards are numbered 1-50 & come in the orig. "book" case. These are in perfect condition, b & w photos of suprisingly grisly scenes in some instances - wounded, dead & the aftermath of battle. Avg. cond. $96.00

WWI USMC COLOR TINTED PHOTO INK BLOTTER: 4x9" w/photo of Marines on ship board in full gear & titled "Uncle Sam's Fighting Marines Dreadnought New York" Has July 1917 calendar & some fading to blotter but unused. Above avg. cond. $35.00

WWII HALLMARK'S COMIC SOLDIER CARDS IN ORIGINAL ENVELOPE: 9 card some dupl. & 12 envelops/ large envelope can be folded & sent to the soldier to write. Avg. cond. $16.00

WWII OFFICIAL WOMEN'S RESERVE ACTIVITIES PHOTO SET NO. 24: 20 B&W photos showing Woman Marines in various activities. In original envelope. Exc. cond. $28.00

U.S.MILITARY RELATED POSTERS, MAPS & CHARTS

A. All Periods

KOREAN WAR MAP: Orig. battle map for combat jump. Used by named officer in subsequent ground activity. Has homemade carrier & map has been covered w/plastic film. Officer part of 187th Parachute RCT. Above avg. cond. $34.00

POSTER "3RD WAR LOAN BACK THE ATTACK": 10x14" never folded, color graphics of paratroopers coming down in back ground while a GI w/Tommy gun is on the ground. 1943. Mint cond. ... $45.00

POSTER "BUY US DEFENSE BONDS": 15.5x17" approx. size color poster showing worker "I'm Buying Bonds Are You?" published by Bethlehem Steel Co. Rolled. Above avg. cond. $36.00

POSTER "DOOLITTLE TOKYO RAIDERS": 18x27" color printed art poster of "0820 18 April 1942" by Robert Moak. Depicts aircraft carrier in rolling sea waters & twin engine plane in air. Limited edition art poster & signed by Doolittle & artist. Ready for framing. Exc. cond. $95.00

POSTER "OUR CARELESSNESS THEIR SECRET WEAPON PREVENT FOREST FIRES": 1943. State Forest Service. 28x22". Graphics in color of Hitler & Tojo w/forest fire in back ground. Reads "Our Carelessness Their Secret Weapon Prevent Forest Fires." Rolled. Near mint cond. $143.00

POSTER "OUR CARELESSNESS THEIR SECRET WEAPON PREVENT FOREST FIRES"

POSTER "POLAND WAR AID": WWII. 11x16". white paperboard w/red lettering "To Poland The Armies Bought Death! Nature: Cold & Hunger but America Sends Hope & Life. Maryland address, never folded. Above avg. cond. $20.00

POSTER GRUMMAN F4F - 4 WILDCAT: 17x26 poster w/4 inch blue border. Color print depicts F4F-4 Wildcat Flown by Capt. Joe Foss 26 victories, Marine Fighter Squadron 121, Guadalcanal Island 1942. Limited Edition & signed by pilot & artist. Ready for framing. Near mint cond.
.... $75.00

POSTER POLICE ACTION AT YALU RIVER: 20x24" color printed poster depicting North American F-86E-10 Flown by Maj. Frederick C. Blesse-10 victories, 334th Fighter Interceptor Squadron, North Korea, Fall 1952. Limited Edition & signed by artist & pilot. Printed 1989, placed on cardboard in plastic cover. Ready for framing. Near mint cond.
.... $76.00

POSTER US TREASURY: 10x14" color print sketch depicting face of fighting man w/ camouflage helmet "Next" in center. Island of Japan in background "6th War Loan" printed in lower right hand corner. Published by US Government Printing Office 1944. Exc. cond. $45.00

POSTER US TREASURY: 10x14" color print sketch depicting fighting man ready to throw a hand grenade. "Let'em Have It" printed on top. "Buy Extra Bonds 4th War Loan" printed across bottom. 1943. Exc. cond. $38.00

POSTER USMC RECRUITING: 8x10.5" heavy card stock w/design of young Marine in dress blues w/background scene of helicopters & attacking Marines & reads "Teamwork...Join the Marines." 1961 dated. Avg. cond. $30.00

POSTER "UNDER THE SHADOW OF THEIR WINGS OUR LAND SHALL DWELL SECURE": 27x37", color print, 1944 dated, General Cable. From the imfamous "Fight Talk" series. Vivid color. Near mint condition. $159.00

POSTER "UNDER THE SHADOW OF THEIR WINGS OUR LAND SHALL DWELL SECURE"

POSTER WAR BOND 7TH WAR LOAN POSTER-THEY ALSO SERVE, WHO BUY WAR BONDS: 9x20". Long folded, color graphics of GI w/carbine, in battle. Has a civilian holding a $100 & $50 saving bond & dated 1945. Shrink wrapped on cardboard Avg. cond. $20.00

PRINT COVER ART FOR WWII LIBERTY MAGAZINE: Shrink wrapped on artist board. Hand painted color & black & white. Signed by R. Douglass. Rare. Avg. cond. $125.00

PRINT COVER ART FOR WWII LIBERTY MAGAZINE

PRINT "EMKE'S WOLF PACK" LIMITED EDITION-NUMBERED & SIGNED: 24x32" color print depicts P47s providing cover for a lone B17. Print is signed by Col. Hub Zemke, Gabby Gabreski, Robert Johnson & Col. Bud Mahurin. Certificate of Authenticity enclosed. Rolled & ready for framing. Mint cond. $350.00

PRINT "HOME AT DUSK" LIMITED EDITION-SIGNED & NUMBERED: 24x32" color print by Robert Taylor depicts P-51s returning to England on Christmas 1944. Signed by 6 famous P51 pilots, Col. C. E. 'Bud' Anderson, Capt. Jim Brooks, Col. Bob Goebel, Col. James Goodson, Col. Herschel Green, Col. Walker 'Bud' Mahurin. Sold out print. Rolled. Certificate of Authenticity enclosed. Ready for framing. Mint cond. $375.00

PRINT "HOT PURSUIT" LIMITED EDITION-SIGNED & NUMBERED PRINT: 24x32" color print. This sold out Nickolas Trudgian print depicts P51s & ME109s in air combat with B17s in background on a mission. Signed by P51 pilots Maj. 'Kit' Carson,

Maj. Richard 'Bud' Peterson & ME109 pilots Capt. Ernst Reinert, Maj. Erich Rudorffer. Rolled. Certificate of Authenticity enclosed. Ready for framing. Mint cond. $175.00

PRINT "MIDWAY-THE TURNING TIDE" LIMITED EDITION-SIGNED & FRAMED: 24x32" color print depicts SBD Dauntlesses from carrier Enterprise preparing to attack Japanese fleet. This Robert Taylor print is signed by Capt. Edward Anderson, Commander Richard Best, Commander Don L Ely & Rear Adm. Wilber Roberts. Sold out prints Rolled. Certificate of Authenticity enclosed. Ready for framing. Mint cond. $375.00

VIETNAM ERA POSTER "KNOW YOUR ENEMY" 1967 MACV COMMAND: 16x25" color poster of 4 diff. soldiers of the N. Vietnamese armies, Viet Cong officer & soldier, NVA soldier & medic & with the flags of each, captioned. Avg. cond. $223.00

VIETNAM ERA SURVIVAL CHART: DOD evasion chart in waterproof plastic & dated Jan 1966. Covers SEA section of central SVN, DMZ & Laos. Back side for southern NVN & Laos. Avg. cond. $85.00

WWI POSTER "HALT THE HUN": 20x29" approx. size, color printed poster "Halt the Hun- Buy US Government Bonds, Third Liberty Loan" Depicts group of soldiers, red flaming battle front. Rolled. Exc. cond. $40.00

WWI POSTER "HUN OR HOME?": Approx. 20x30" in size, color printed illustration of German soldier w/his spiked helmet in pursuit of a woman & child. Big letters on top read "Hun or Home? Buy More Liberty Bonds" Above avg. cond. $66.00

WWI POSTER "VICTORIOUS ALLIES": 16x20" color graphics of a battle scene with the 3 flags of the Allies w/tanks & planes, shows US & French troops fighting together as a long line of German POWs are led through trenches. 1918 dated. Above avg. cond. $49.00

WWI POSTER "VICTORY & PEACE": 16x20" color graphics of a peaceful country side scene over 3 flags of the Allies draping over 2 color art of a Army soldier & other of a sailor telling the tales of the great war deeds. Avg. cond. $40.00

WWI POSTER NAVY RECRUITING: 10x14" size color print "Gee I Wish I Were A Man, I'D Join The Navy" Depicts pretty girl in Navy attire. Above avg. cond. $55.00

WWI POSTER RED CROSS: 20x30" size color printed Red Cross Roll Call poster. Rolled. exc. cond. $55.00

WWI POSTER RED CROSS: 29x39" approx. size color printed poster of Red Cross nurse depicting "I summon you to comradeship in the Red Cross" 1918 dated. Rolled. Exc. cond. $72.00

WWI POSTER VICTORY LIBERTY LOAN POSTER "BUY ANOTHER JOIN THE YD (YANKEE DIVISION): 20x25" red/white/blue graphics. Avg. cond. $76.00

WWI POSTER WAR SAVING STAMP "YOUR WAR SAVING PLEDGE": 21x32" color graphics of doughboy/Uncle Sam/civilian "Our Boys Make Good Their Pledge Are You Keeping Yours?" Avg. cond. $28.00

WWII AAF CLOTH CHART: approx. 20x25" size, color printed, double printed escape map of Asiatic Series, No. 34 + No. 35. 1944 US Army Map Service, Near mint cond. $20.00

WWII AAF CLOTH CHART: approx. 23.5x24" size, color printed, double printed escape map of Otomari, Sea of Japan + Vladomiro, USSR. First Edition 1942, 2nd Edition 1943 Was reproduced under the direction of the Commanding General US AAF. Folded. Ready for framing. Near mint cond. $20.00

WWII AAF SURVIVAL CHART & CARRIER: #34 & #35 for China 1941. Life raft plastic waterproof container. Above avg. cond. $70.00

WWII ARMY NURSE RECRUITING POSTER: Framed. poster is 20x32" color photo of army nurse in full uniform "You are Needed Now Join the Army Nurse Corps" Avg. cond. $97.00

WWII POSTER "I'M COUNTING ON YOU": 20x28" with 1943 plead with color art of Uncle Sam with finger to lips & not to discuss troop movement. Avg. cond. $45.00

WWII POSTER "THIS IS THE ENEMY": 20X28", color litho of a arm with a swastika on sleeve & w/bayonet struck through a bible, "This is the Enemy." Above avg. cond. $91.00

WWII POSTER "BUDGET TO BUY VICTORY BONDS & BUILD YOUR BANK ACCOUNT": 21x31" shows attractive woman working on household-expenses. Above avg. cond. $45.00

WWII POSTER AAF AIRCRAFT SAFETY: 17x22" size color printed depicting "Check Brakes While You Taxi" "Line Up With

Runway" "Don't Fly Too Low" & "Always Fasten Safety" Near mint cond. ... $177.00

WWII ARMY NURSE RECRUITING POSTER

WWII POSTER ARMY: 26x36" red, white & blue poster. w/dead American Soldier Shown Where He Fell-in center. This Happens Every 3 Minutes-on top on red. Stay On The Job & Get It Over-on blue at bottom. US Government Printing Office 1945, Official Signal Corps Photograph. Folded. Exc. cond. $53.00

WWII POSTER FRAMED LINEN ARTIST PROOF FOR WOMEN TO JOIN THE SERVICES: 20x30" frame w/smaller poster w/beautiful color graphics of 4 lovely women in all 4 uniforms of each of the services, "For Your Country's Sake Today-For Your Sake Tomorrow" done by Steele Savage & has union mark. 1944. Above avg. cond. $184.00

WWII POSTER NAVY IN MEMORY OF USS DORADO: 20x28" color print published by US Government Printing Office 1944. Print depicts U-boat w/two seamen on look out. W/message "Fire Away" in center. At bottom Buy Extra Bonds. Exc. cond. $66.00

WWII POSTER OWI 1943: 2.5 x 3.5' color printed poster Has red background with 5 US Navy soldiers in black & 5 blue stars on top. Reads: "The five Sullivan brothers 'missing in action' off the Solomons They did their part." Exc. cond. $82.00

WWII POSTER OWI: approx. 2.5 x 3.5 color printed poster, black background w/ likeness of battleship in flames in corner & foreground soldier raising his fist. "Avenge December 7" printed in bold orange letters. 1942. Exc. cond. $90.00

WWII POSTER TORPEDO SQUADRON EIGHT POSTER-THE TURNING POINT: 17x26 poster w/4 inch blue border. Color print depicts Torpedo Sq. Eight, Battle of Midway, June 3-5 1942. Limited Edition & signed by Ens. George Gay, Sole Survivor & artist. Ready for framing. Near mint cond. $90.00

WWII POSTER WOMEN ARMY CORPS "MINE EYES HAVE SEEN THE GLORY": 20x30" frame w/color graphics of shadow profiles of GIs in combat while a woman in Army uniform looks up. Has WAC & Women's Army Corps + emblem on both sides. Avg. cond. $94.00

WWII POSTER WOMEN ARMY CORPS "MINE EYES HAVE SEEN THE GLORY"

WWII PRINT PROMO FROM ELECTRIC BOAT COMPANY: 20x24" size, 3 posters, captioned "The Green Dragon's Lair" "Reward of Victory" + print of PT Boat, torpedo + ghostly rider on horse back. Near mint cond. $145.00

U.S. NEWSPAPERS, MAGAZINES & BROADSIDES PERIODICALS

MAGAZINE "LEATHERNECK": 1950 issue on the 175th Anniversary of the Marine Corps. Above avg. cond. $30.00

MAGAZINES "YANK THE ARMY WEEKLY": (11) May/Dec. 1945 issues. Reporting on Freedom & Food, Washington Faces the Peace, etc. Exc. cond. $21.00

MAGAZINES "YANK THE ARMY WEEKLY": Jan-July 1945 issues. European Edition. W/headlines such as "How German Killed American Prisoners of War," "Normandy Invasion Beach," "One Year After. 7th Division Veterans Compare Three Campaigns," etc. Above avg. cond. $30.00

NEWSPAPER "THE WORLD" WITH THE HEADLINE ON THE SINKING LUSITANIA: New York paper dated May 9 1915. Has partial list of the famous Americans killed in the torpedoing of the ocean liner. Folded & a complete paper. Above avg. cond. $38.00

NEWSPAPER "US ORDERS KAISER TO EXPLAIN DEATHS OF 136 AMERICANS": New York paper dated May 8 1915. "The Evening Telegram" extra edition with total killed in the torpedoing of the ocean liner. Folded & complete paper with no tears. Avg. cond. $32.00

WWI MAGAZINE "THE INDIAN" 2ND DIV. NEWS: 8 issues. Titled 'The Indian', Published by 2nd Div. occupation forces. Size 11.5x9" sb, some color. Under 20 pgs. Each copy sealed in plastic & cover assorted vols. & issues. Above avg. cond. $60.00

WWI SHEET MUSIC "MOTOR TRANSPORT CORPS": cover has graphics of army trucks convoy. March for the piano. Above avg. cond. $11.00

WWII PERIODICAL "PRISONERS OF WAR BULLETIN": 3 issues dated 1944 + 1945 publ. by the American National Red Cross w/reports on Japanese + German camps. Exc. cond. $55.00

WWII PERIODICAL "THE FORWARD OBSERVER": Publication by 492 Armored Field Artillery Battalion at Camp Cooke, Cal. dated 5 August 1944, 29 July 1944. Avg. cond. $12.00

WWII SHEET MUSIC "DER FUEHRER'S FACE": 1942 from Walt Disney's motion Picture "Donald Duck in Nutzi Land" 3 pgs., large format. Exc. cond. $25.00

U.S. MILITARY RELATED DOCUMENTS, ASSORTED PAPER ITEMS & FRAMED ITEMS

A. All Periods

AMERICAN REVOLUTIONARY WAR DOCUMENT: Treated w/preservative & sealed in Acetate. Handwritten authorization from State of Pennsylvania Treasury to pay a Capt. Robert Craig the sum of One thousand, one hundred & seven pds., 4 shillings for clothing his troops. Signed by appropriate officials & Capt. Craig. Above avg. cond. $125.00

CALLING CARD AIR SERVICE OFFICER: White pressed paper w/design of aircraft. Reads "(Name)/270th Aero Squadron A.E.F./Air Service U.S.A./(address) Minneapolis, Minn." Avg. cond. $33.00

CIVIL WAR DOCUMENT APPOINTMENT FOR SOLDIER IN OHIO MILITIA: 1863. 10x12" document. Soldier was appointed as third corporal in Co. D. 15 Regiment. Avg. cond. $60.00

CIVIL WAR DOCUMENT NCO COMMISSION.: Made out to Thermon W. Seane, First Wisc. Cavalry, March 15th, 1862 in Kenosha, Wis. Signed by commanding off. & Adj. Exc. cond. $100.00

CIVIL WAR DOCUMENT NCO COMMISSION

CIVIL WAR DOCUMENT NCO COMMISSION: 114th Reg. Ill. Inf. Vols. promoting him to Sergeant on Sept. 18, 1862 at Camp Butler. Signed by Col. & Adj. Folded. Exc. cond. $50.00

CIVIL WAR DOCUMENT PAY VOUCHER RECORD.: #193 to Capt. C. J. Baily 17th Maine Inf. Feb. 6, 1864. Large fold out w/ many signatures of people he mustered into service & ranks. Exc. cond. ... $75.00

CIVIL WAR DOCUMENT NCO COMMISSION

CIVIL WAR LETTER SOLDIER OF 14TH REG. NEW HAMPSHIRE VOL.: Nov. 1862. has letterhead & envelope named to unit 4 pgs. & tells father of returning from picket duty & finding tent burned to ground & loss of personal items including a armor vest which cost $8 & tells of his girlfriend. Avg. cond. $45.00

CIVIL WAR LETTER: Folded 8x12" from the HQ of the 16th Ohio Battery at New Orleans Aug. 3, 1864 to Washington with info of stores lost or destroyed in the field for the 3rd quarter of 1863. Signed by Commanding captain & all handwritten. Avg. cond. $21.00

CIVIL WAR PERSONAL ACCOUNT SHEETS.: Showing payment for clothing allowance w/many dates. 4 large ledger sized sheets w/diff. person listed on ea. side. All men enlisted in 143rd Penn Vols., in Wyoming Co. Penn. August 1862. One transferred to invalid corps, one deserted, one can only make his mark X. Many signatures of men & witnesses. Folded & a few tiny stains. Exc. cond. $135.00

CIVIL WAR UNION INVOICE LIST OF STORES & ORDNANCE FROM OFFICERS: 9x10" official abstract dated Sept. 1863 & named to 16th Ohio Bat. Completely filled in w/number & all weapons & ammo for a artillery unit. Avg. cond. $35.00

COMMISSION DOCUMENT: 1839. Matted, 14x18" document from the State of Maine w/seal. Commission to the rank of Lieut., Co. B, 2nd Bde, 1st Div. Artillery Battalion. Avg. cond. $40.00

CONNECTICUT APPOINTMENT DOCUMENT + MUSTER ROLL: 13x16" Warrant dated 16 October 1793 appointing Moses Seymour "Serjeant" in the First Light Infantry Company, 29th Regiment of Connecticut Militia. + Muster role of the "Serjeant's" Third Division, undated. 8x13" Handwritten in ink. Above avg. cond. $90.00

DESERT SHIELD DEATH CARD: Original Bicycle "808" Ace of Spades death card that states "Desert Shield" at bottom. These 808's were only manufactured twice. One for Desert Shield (marked) & Vietnam Phoenix (unmarked). Near mint cond. $16.00

DESERT STORM LEAFLETS: 10-3x6.5" color printed leaflets w/Saddam Hussain portrait on one side & Safe Conduct Pass on other as distributed during Gulf war by UN. to encourage surrender. Near mint cond. $21.00

DESERT STORM PROPAGANDA LEAFLETS USMC: 10. Dollar bill size, shows stealth attacking Iraqi forces, USMC emblem & several rows of characters. Mint cond. $30.00

DOCUMENT ENLISTMENT RECORD: WWI enlistment for named soldier in 12x9.5" black finished wood frame w/glass. Dated Mar 10, 1919 on official stamp. Describes enlistment of soldier from Sept. 9,1918 until release. Completed by hand in ink. Above avg. cond. $20.00

DOCUMENT HONORABLE DISCHARGE: 1865. 8.75x11" document discharges sergeant from 2nd Regiment United States. in 1865. Document is hand captioned w/several signatures. Reverse side has an official stamp. Exc. cond. $45.00

LETTER SIGNED BY ANDREW HIGGINS-PT BOAT MANUFACTURER IN NEW ORLEANS: letter head shows landing crafts & PT boats. Nov. 20 1945. Also a 3x4" b/w photo of several PT boats being readied to ship Avg. cond. $40.00

PAY & CLOTHING VOUCHER FOR OHIO VOL. CAPT.: State of Ohio vouchers totaling $554.00 for pay & clothing allowances + Activation papers, all signed & stamped. No. 2784 voucher #3 for period 1 Nov. 1862 thru 28 Feb. 1863. Above avg. cond. $30.00

SPANISH AMERICAN WAR DOCUMENT: 9x11" Honorable Discharge Document from 7th Regiment of Cavalry in year 1899. Has signature of Captain. Reverse side of document contains his Military Record. Above avg. cond. $35.00

VIETNAM ERA DEATH CARDS: Bicycle "808" Ace of Spades death card made only for the Phoenix Program in Vietnam during 1967-68. The other card is for the 101st Airborne. Shows a winged skull & chute with 101st patches & "Quan Sat Viet Cong." Above avg. cond $45.00

WWI ARMY MEMORIAM: 10.5X14.5". WWI document w/Pershing's signature & hand written entries on deceased. Memorializes death of soldier in heroic terms on formal Army document. Wood frame. Avg. cond. $135.00

WWII ARMY OFFICER'S ID CARD: early tri-fold pattern issued by the war department-has ID "Mug Shot" photo in the center-finger prints on 1 side & data on the other. Serial number is also printed on the outside of the card. Issued to a 2nd lieut. in the signal corps-November 20, 1942-has official embossed seal over-lapping photo. Above avg. cond. $20.00

WWII DOCUMENT AWARD OF COMBAT INFANTRYMAN BADGE: 8 x 10" official Document copy issued to PFC 255th Inf. US Army 1945 & Combat Infantryman Badge. 1x3" in size, depicting rifle on blue back- ground w/oak leaves. Above avg. cond. $38.00

WWII ID WHEEL ON ARMY/NAVY INSIGNIA BY WONDER BREAD: 4x5" paperboard w/b/w graphics of the rank & insignia of the military of US during WWII. Avg. cond. $20.00

U.S. ORDNANCE & FIREARM RELATED PARTS & EQUIPMENT

A. All Periods

AMMO CLIP (.45 CAL.): Nice shape. Above avg. cond. $33.00

ARMY CARTRIDGE BOX (1905 .38 CAL PISTOL): Brown leather w/embossed US in oval on front. Holds 12 rounds in wooden insert. Back is marked 'ROCK ISLAND/ARSENAL/1905.' Some wear where leather bends. Avg. cond. $40.00

ARMY DUMMY LAW WEAPON: Covers on firing tube. Some wear signs but definitely a display quality piece. Above avg. cond. $45.00

ARTY DUMMY TRAINING ROUND (105MM): 1969 dated. Designated Comp-B, Heat-T for Gun M68. In black cardboard transport container. Exc. cond. $60.00

ARTY DUMMY TRAINING ROUND
(105MM)

ARTY FUSE SETTER (M-26): massive circular body w/rotating numeral grids &

heavy folding grip. Well marked. Exc. cond. $21.00

ARTY ROUND (.50 CAL.): Marked on base, T67 - typical brass case & projectile. Avg. cond. $28.00

ARTY ROUND (37MM): 1899 dated Winchester made 8.5" tall round w/ polished brass case & polished projectile w/wide copper drive band. Above avg. cond. $20.00

ARTY ROUND (40MM MK 25 SALUTING SHELL): 8.75" length. Brass casing. 1944 dated. Well marked. Above avg. cond. $10.00

ARTY ROUND (40MM MK 2 MOD 1): 40mm Mk. 2 Mod 1 brass shell 12.5" tall & needing polish & Dummy training fuse for arty shell. Model M44A2. Avg. cond. $20.00

ARTY ROUND (75MM COMMEMORATIVE): Shell has 3" round plaque commemorating the 25,000,000th shell produced by Bridgeport Brass Co. & dated October 27th 1941. Avg. cond. $75.00

CARBINE BARREL (M-1): Shiny bore & good parkerized finish. Exc. cond. $40.00

CIVIL WAR CANNON BALL: 10" dia. cast iron, 4" dia. with surface rust & cast marks. Good example Avg. cond. $40.00

CIVIL WAR CANNON BALL: Battlefield retrieval, 3.25" dia. w/pitted surface & mounted on 6.75x8" wood base. Above avg. cond. $40.00

CIVIL WAR CARTRIDGE POUCH: Likely 1855 model - 9x7x2.5 w/large inner chamber for cartridges & smaller flap covered pouch. Two buckles on bottom, (one missing) & undated dictionary in cartridge chamber(likely to help keep shape). Leather shows wear & surface erosion in spots. Some straps missing. Below avg. cond. $125.00

CIVIL WAR MUSKET HAMMER: Steel w/ light wear & rust signs. Some marks on inside of pivot arm. Avg. cond. $10.00

CIVIL WAR PISTOL CARTRIDGES

CIVIL WAR PISTOL CARTRIDGES: Blue pressed paper carton w/label that reads

"R. Bartholow's Solid Water Proof Cartridge for Army Holster Pistol/Patented, May 21st, 1861". Contents remain. Above avg. cond. $205.00

CIVIL WAR POWDER FLASK: Dixon & Sons patent. Brass dispenser & cap & flattened style copper bow. Hmkd. on top of cap. Typical tarnish & minor stains. Avg. cond. $50.00

DUMMY LAND MINE: Artillery delivered mine dummy test & training device. Blue w/metal vanes all around. Avg. cond. $25.00

MINE (ANTI PERSONNEL) IN CARRY ALL: M18A1 mine carry bag w/cord on winder & 1966 dated detonator & instr. Two pouch canvas bag w/flap & strap. Clean. Above avg. cond. $76.00

MISSILE LAUNCHER (M-222 SURFACE ATTACK GUIDED): 40" long, 5" dia. Kevlar tubular body. Has 1985 dated spec. plate on side. Has folding stand assembly, etc. intact. Includes 1979 dated manual for M74 model. Shows some age. Above avg. cond. $95.00

MORTAR ROUND (60MM): OD body w/ black warhead & alum impact fuse. No propellant in motor section. No marks visible. Exc. cond. $69.00

MORTAR ROUND (60MM)

MORTAR ROUND (60MM): Wired fuse w/ black band, yellow shell & brown painted

fins. Details printed on sides. Above avg. cond. $55.00

MORTAR ROUND: Stokes. Yellow case & motor. Bronze fuse w/safety pin. Marked inert. Above avg. cond. $132.00

MUSKET LOCK PLATE: 1864 Springfield musket lock plate. Some normal scratches. Above avg. cond. $25.00

NAVY HUDSON GUN 1.1 ROUND: Fused projectile over brass shell, inert w/ marked bottom. Avg. cond. $35.00

PISTOL GRIPS (.45): one pair of brown plastic checkered grips pre-drilled & notched for frame. Above avg. cond. $24.00

PISTOL HOLSTER (.45 CAL.): Shoulder style. 1962 dated Boyt built. Embossed 'US' on front, Leather & web straps for support. Tan leather shows some wear. Exc. cond. $76.00

PRACTICE BOMB: Silver finish, has single lug suspension, provision for nose fuse (not present) & four fins (one bent slightly). Avg. cond. $48.00

RIFLE GRENADE LAUNCHER (M-16 40MM): Black finish w/ribbed section in front of trigger housing. Metal mounting loops on top. Above avg. cond. $145.00

ROCKET LAUNCHER (AT-4): 40" long w/ instructions on outside, Web carry strap & Fire/safe controls. No weapon internally & port covers missing. Above avg. cond. $80.00

ROCKET LAUNCHER TUBE (DRAGON): 40" long tube in OD finish. Has endcaps & OD web sling & trigger. Well marked. Above avg. cond. $78.00

SMOKE GRENADE (M-18): Green smoke grenade w/light green painted top & pin in fuse. Bottom drilled out. Above avg. cond. $20.00

SPANISH AMERICAN WAR ARTY PROJECTILE: Safed, appears 37mm- solid w/copper compression band. dated 1898 Above avg. cond. $20.00

SPANISH AMERICAN WAR PISTOL SHOULDER STOCK: For Stephens Pistol; Metal shoulder stock-frame style w/screw type latch. All metal, plated but rust very evident Avg. cond. $35.00

SUB CALIBER ADAPTER FOR 57MM RECOILLESS: Special training aid for system to allow practice w/small arms ammo. One adapter allows using .22 cal. ammo indoors for simulation training. the .30 adapter will give realistic noise & recoil effect when used outside. Official govt. issue but so little known, it is not in manuals. Stored in wood case w/hasp

lock. Incl. documentation. Exc. cond.
.... $125.00
TRAINING GRENADE: Incl. Mint, in pouch
grenade sight for M1 rifle & Labeled
training grenade. Some finish missing.
Avg. cond. $24.00
TRAINING PISTOL: 9mm Beretta Cast hard
rubber w/all details complete, no moving
parts but same size as real weapon. Exc.
cond. $40.00
TRAINING PISTOL: M1911A .45 Auto pistol
in cast hard rubber. All details complete,
some of casting is crude around butt &
rear of grip. Avg. cond. $72.00
VIETNAM ERA AMMO CLIP (9MM): for
Swedish MB45 weapon, used by some
US special forces units. Avg. cond.
.... $26.00
VIETNAM ERA DUMMY BOMBLET (BDU-
28/B): Day glo red case w/para fins tied
down & labeled on bottom. Avg. cond.
.... $10.00
VIETNAM ERA DUMMY SMOKE GRENADE
(M-18): Dummy grenade w/all
components present. Painted red at top
below fuse. Labeled on side M18/Smoke/
red. Exc. cond. $22.00
VIETNAM ERA GRENADE: Dated 1973
from fuse assy. Complete w/pin & arm.
Smoothcase. OD finish. Above avg. cond.
.... $12.00
VIETNAM ERA GRENADE: Smooth dark-
finish iron body w/plug in bottom. Includes
OD finish M204A2 fuse w/spoon, handle &
safety ring. 1968 dated. Above avg. cond.
.... $25.00
VIETNAM ERA ROCKET LAUNCHER
(LAW) W/INERT ROCKET: Recaptured
from NVA, 1972 dated weapon shows
wear, some abrasion to finish & lack of
care. US instr. are readable on sides.
Rocket has black finished warhead &
brass engine exhaust. Avg. cond.
.... $82.00
VIETNAM ERA TRAINER RIFLE (M-16A1):
Life-size in molded hard rubber w/metal
barrel. Good details. Avg. cond.
.... $250.00
VIETNAM ERA VULCAN ROUND (30MM):
Nicely finished in OD tan paint w/brown
fused tip & base. Exc. cond. $22.00
WINCHESTER BULLET MOLD: Cal. .32
WCF, orig. mold w/wood handles & hmkd.
on metal. Above avg. cond. $25.00
WWI AIRCRAFT BOMB: Aerodynamic shape
w/four fins for control. Appears to have
fused nose & used 3 suspension lugs for
hanging from aircraft (2 are missing). Avg.
cond. $100.00
WWI ARTY ROUND (13MM): Safed round
w/brass case & copper jacketed projectile.

Base indicates 1918 production date
otherwise unremarkable. Minor tarnish.
Above avg. cond. $38.00
WWI ARTY ROUND (37MM): ID's & dated 5-
17 on base. Good brass & complete w/
copper compression ring. Above avg.
cond. $12.00
WWI ARTY ROUND (37MM): W/solid
projectile. 1916 date on bottom. Safed.
Avg. cond. $20.00
WWI ARTY ROUND (75MM): Brass shell w/
projectile & adj. fuse in nose. Fuse is
taped in place. Good driving band of
copper & light tarnish on case. Avg.
cond. $38.00
WWI GRENADE: Safed, intact w/arm, fuse &
safing pin. Case marked MO. Above avg.
cond. $127.50
WWI PRACTICE GRENADE: Fragmentation
grenade case w/arm & pin. Well rusted.
Avg. cond. $61.00
WWI TRAINING 18 POUNDER ROUND: 22"
tall w/fused projectile, all from brass &
light weight. Can be separated for study.
Bottom has specs. Avg. cond. $66.00
WWII AIRCRAFT ROUND (20MM): 1944
dated MK4 w/solid projectile. Safety'd
case. Avg. cond. $20.00

WWII BOMB (250 LB)

MISC. MILITARIA

WWII AMMO CLIP (20 RD THOMPSON): Black metal. Hmkd. on side. Light use. Above avg. cond. $20.00

WWII AMMO CLIP (40MM AUTO CANNON 4 ROUND): dated 1945 on shells. Clip w/ spring loaded latches holds four rounds (with out projectiles) Clip marked 40mm Ammunition Clip MK 7 MOD 0. Avg. cond. $21.00

WWII AMMO CLIP (THOMPSON 30 RD): 30 rd stick clip mint in orig. box & paper wrapper. Exc. cond. $25.00

WWII ARTY DUMMY ROUND: Laminated wood dummy shell for loading training. Above avg. cond. $20.00

WWII ARTY ROUND (37MM): Fuse is gray steel tip. Above avg. cond. $37.00

WWII BOMB (250 LB): Std configuration w/ boxed fin at rear & provisions for nose & tail fuse. Either two or one lug suspension. Dark green finish. Avg. cond. $250.00

WWII DUMMY ARTY ROUND (37MM MK III-A2): 5.75" tall brass casing is 1940 dated. Has M50 'dummy' projectile w/1941 dated driving band. Avg. cond. $23.00

WWII 57MM DRILL ROUND: 23" overall length w/drill cartridge warhead, some polish remaining. Above avg. cond. $20.00

WWII DUMMY GRENADE: Silver finished fragmentation grenade w/pin & arm in place on fuse. Bottom drilled out. Above avg. cond. $20.00

WWII FLARE PISTOL (M-8) W/HOLSTER: Single shot, break barrel loading & Black plastic grips. Includes a used flare shell in chamber. Metal parts show some rust patina. Holster of tan leather w/alum plate on side & hmkd. 'Made in Canada.' Above avg. cond. $70.00

WWII FLASH HIDER FOR M-2 BROWNING .50 M. G. BARREL: Unit is complete w/all mounting hardware. Exc. cond. $27.00

WWII GRENADE: Complete w/Pin, arm & fuse case. Some rust in spots. Avg. cond. $20.00

WWII GRENADE: Safe grenade but complete w/arm, pin & fuse assembly. Some residual pale green paint remains. Avg. cond. $63.00

WWII GRENADE: complete w/arm, fuse & safety pin. Case is serrated & shows finishing in OD green paint. Exc. cond. $87.00

WWII GRENADE: complete w/arm, fuse & safety pin. Case is serrated & shows some residual paint signs. Above avg. cond. $50.00

WWII HIGH WOOD FOR FOLDING STOCK CARBINE: Complete 3 piece set, stock, pistol grip & handguard for M1A1 model.

In unissued condition. Near mint cond. $200.00

WWII MORTAR ROUND (60MM): Dummied but complete. Fused nose w/safing wire. Label printed on side & date 1943 stamped in case. Above avg. cond. $37.00

WWII NAVY DUMMY ROUND (3"): 34" tall-turned oak & gray metal unit-well marked & 1943 dated on metal base plate-has simulated fuse assembly w/metal base ring. Above avg. cond. $30.00

WWII OSS CROSSBOW BOLT: 9.75" alum w/steel point & alum fins. Fins canted slightly to impart spinning motion to bolt in flight. Mint cond. $179.00

WWII PENLIGHT FLARE GUN: Black metal tube w/lanyard & thumb operated trigger. Incl. two red mini flares. Above avg. cond. $25.00

WWII PISTOL HOLSTER: Shoulder type. Embossed natural leather holster w/ leather shoulder strap & canvas web body strap. Marked S35 on shoulder strap. Avg. cond. $22.50

WWII REVOLVER HOLSTER (.38 CAL.): Shoulder style. Brown leather intended for .38 cal. revolver likely 3" barrel. No marks evident. Alum buckles on shoulder harness. Exc. cond. $45.00

WWII RIFLE GRENADE LAUNCHER (M-1 M-7): Well marked. Avg. cond. $20.00

WWII RIFLE GRENADE LAUNCHER SIGHT (M-15): Parts still in protective wrapping. Includes instruction sheet. In 1944 dated dark OD canvas carrying case. Some soiling to case. Exc. cond. $20.00

WWII RIFLE GRENADE LAUNCHER SIGHT (M-7): 8" long gray metal body. Well marked. Above avg. cond. $20.00

WWII THOMPSON M1928A1 .45 CAL. FINNED BARREL: Still in original protective wrapping. Near mint cond. $57.00

WWII WATERPROOF FUSE IGNITER: Pyrotechnic charge in waterproof container & safed w/grenade style pull pin. Metal parts show some corrosion. Avg. cond. $20.00

U.S. MILITARY VEHICLE & AIRCRAFT RELATED ACCESSORIES

A. All Periods

AAF AIRCRAFT BANKING INDICATION GAUGE DISPLAY (B-17 I-101-C): Unit w/ black finish. Well marked. Mounted in nicely made wooden display frame for table top/desk display & engraved "B-17 Flying Fortress" plate at bottom. Exc. cond. $72.00

AAF AIRCRAFT DIRECTION GAUGE DISPLAY (B-17): Unit w/black finish. Well marked. Mounted in nicely made wooden display frame for tabletop/desk display & engraved "B-17 Flying Fortress" plate at bottom. Exc. cond. $66.00

AAF AIRCRAFT FUEL PRESSURE GAUGE DISPLAY (B-17 C-14A): Unit w/black crinkle finish & metal spec. plate. Well marked. Mounted in nicely made wooden display frame for tabletop/desk display & engraved "B-17 Flying Fortress" plate at bottom. Exc. cond. $50.00

AIRCRAFT ANTENNA FIN (F-15): For F-15 aircraft, w/mounting base & recessed coupler. 14" above surface. Exc. cond. $20.00

AIRCRAFT COCKPIT LIGHT & EXTENSION CORD (B-47): Black cylindrical case w/ recessed bulb & removable red tinted lens cover. Socket mount permits relocation to several positions in cockpit. Exc. cond. $20.00

AIRCRAFT CONTROL STICK (B-8): Thumb operated flight controls & firing switch & disconnects. Black finished wood display stand incl. Orig. used in F-100, F-101 aircraft. Above avg. cond. $145.00

AIRCRAFT EJECTION SEAT SURVIVAL PACK: Modern. From Navy A-6 aircraft, Green plastic container w/survival pack, raft & lanyard to deploy pack prior to landing. Seat pad in place as are oxygen lines. Includes beacon radio & a lot of survival items from kit, all stored inside. This model dated 4-74. Exc. cond. $221.00

AIRCRAFT GAUGE FOR INCHES OF MERCURY: Black plastic case w/3" white dual dials. Calibration knob on side. Avg. cond. $20.00

AIRCRAFT GYRO HORIZON INDICATOR (AN-5736-1): 1943 dated from spec. plate. Black dial w/white indicators. Displays degrees of bank angle left or right. Avg. cond. $20.00

AIRCRAFT HORIZONTAL CONTROL GYRO (P-1 AUTO PILOT): Visual display gives horizon & bank angles to 90 degrees. Can be caged when not in operation. Has adj. horizon indicator. Operational. Exc. cond. $20.00

AIRCRAFT INERTIAL SWITCH (SA-3/A): Used on most fighters. Side panel mounted w/clear dome up. Sensitive metal bar inside sensed motion changes & reacted. Above avg. cond. $20.00

AIRCRAFT KOLLSMAN PRESSURE ALTIMETER: Black face w/0 to 1000 feet on dial & both 1000 ft & 10,000 ft indicators Adj. Kollsman window is functional. Connecting plug on back has been cut. Exc. cond. $55.00

AIRCRAFT LOAD ADJUSTER IN CASE: 1950s era. Slide rule style w/instructions & leather carry case. For AT-7 type aircraft (Believe Army Caribou light transport). Nice piece. Exc. cond. $28.00

AIRCRAFT MOUNTED RPM INDICATOR DISPLAY (B-17): Solid oak display w/mint RPM gauge center mounted w/red fuel shut off knob set above. Engraved plate below ID's aircraft & nickname. Near mint cond. $93.00

AIRCRAFT NAVIGATOR FLASH CURTAINS KC-135): Cold War. Heavy duty aluminized canvas curtain to prevent nuclear flash from blinding the crew navigator. Tie down cords & braces supplied. Above avg. cond. $24.00

AIRCRAFT OCTANT (A-7) IN CARRYING CASE: 1941 dated. Battery powered optical sighting celestial observation device. Hand held or suspended, allowed time controlled observations w/collimation & preserved readouts. Stored in wooden box w/accessories & spares. Above avg. cond. $34.00

WWII BUBBLE SEXTANT (AN-5854-1): Very nice example of 1944 dated navigational tool. Battery powered & stored in well equipped wood case. Incl. Batteries, battery pack & other accessories. Mil spec. plate on side. Above avg. cond. $45.00

AIRCRAFT SEXTANT (A-10A) IN CASE: 1943 dated sextant w/collimating optics, adj. bubble & battery powered. Stored in wood case w/provisions for power supply & other accessories. Case in wood w/ padded braces in lid. Incl. maintenance & surplus disposal. tags. Exc. cond. $125.00

AIRCRAFT TACTICAL FIGHTER CONTROL STICK.: Black plastic contoured to fit hand, has trim button, autopilot disengage, fire button & two other buttons for aircraft control. Wire bundle extends out bottom. $55.00

ANTENNA CONTROL ASSEMBLY (LRU-13): Black finish metal body w/riveted spec. plate. Well marked. Includes controlling stick w/operation devices. Avg. cond. $188.00

FLIGHT MANUAL SET (B-24D): Set of 7 hb Consolidated Vultee logoed manuals covering complete flight ops. for aircraft. Std size w/text, photos & diagrams & each vol. covers different area of flight regime i.e., power plants, fuel systems, Hydraulics, radio maintenance etc. Two related documents & a pilot flight training test are also incl. In a company provided pilots brief case in brown leather w/double carrystrap & brass latch. Exc. cond. $355.00

NAVY SHIP COMPASS: Eclipse-Pioneer built floating liquid compass w/powered lighting & adj. Mounted to wood base & supplied w/small screw driver for fine calibration. Spec. plate & naval emblem on side. Above avg. cond. $118.00

NAVY SHIP COMPASS

USAF AIRCRAFT COCKPIT LAMP: Mint type C-4A w/mount bracket & cord. Gives white or red light, movable & focusable. Near mint cond. $25.00

VIETNAM ERA AIRCRAFT LOAD ADJUSTER (B-57B): In Leather carrier. Slide rule style w/payloads. Avg. cond. $23.50

WWI AIRCRAFT PROP BLADE & HUB: Wood blade w/metal reinforced leading edge, black finish w/yellow tip & 10% missing. Avg. cond. $54.00

WWII AAF AIRCRAFT AERIAL CAMERA (K-20 HAND HELD): adj. lens settings, Magazine film, manually operated. Hmkd. Fairchild aircraft & dated 1942 from spec.

plate. Stored w/accessories in reinforced fiber box. Box exterior shows age & wear but contents are in very good condition. Exc. cond. $250.00

WWII AAF AIRCRAFT BLACKOUT LAMP ASSEMBLY (SCR-573/SRC-643-A): In issue box w/AAF marked spec. label. Above avg. cond. $28.00

WWII AAF AIRCRAFT CABIN/COCKPIT LIGHT: Type A-8 adj. fluorescent lamp w/ mating bracket. Stenciled spec. plate on one end. Above avg. cond. $12.00

WWII AAF AIRCRAFT DIRECTIONAL GYRO INDICATOR GAUGE (AN-5735-1): 4.5" deep black finish housing w/3" dia. dial & adj. knob below. Riveted metal spec. plates on back w/1943 AC contract markings. Decal on top w/1964 overhaul date. Above avg. cond. $20.00

WWII AAF AIRCRAFT DRIFTMETER (B-3): By Bendix Corp. Gyro stabilized optics for determining wind drift affect. Used rectangular reticule grid on viewplate to observe rate of drift. A 360 degree az. ring allowed accurate measurement. Timing device, solar shade, spare lens all with orig. equip. 67" long & mounted through aircraft floor at navigator station. Exc. cond. $200.00

WWII AAF AIRCRAFT DRIFTMETER EXTERNAL PERISCOPE: The fuselage mounted periscope & optics for the driftmeter at the navigator station. At one end is gearing for motors & mounting plate, at the other is glass dome over prismatic mirror system to pass view to navigator. Black metal tube protects the components. Above avg. cond. .. $150.00

WWII AAF AIRCRAFT FIRST AID KIT: Tan canvas container w/red cross emblem & title. Zipper & snap closures & full set of first aid gear for airborne emergencies. Avg. cond. $25.00

WWII AAF AIRCRAFT GYRO HORIZON INDICATOR AIRCRAFT GAUGE (AN-5736): 7.25" deep black crinkle finish housing w/3.5" dia. dial face. 2 riveted metal spec. plates on reverse w/AC contract markings. Above avg. cond. $50.00

WWII AAF AIRCRAFT LOAD ADJUSTER (A-26C): Slide rule device in leather case used for determining weight distribution & aircraft center of gravity for take off & inflight operations. Above avg. cond. $20.00

WWII AAF AIRCRAFT LOAD ADJUSTER RULER: Slide rule is marked for use w/ CG-4A LRW-1 aircraft. Comes in fitted russet brown leather case w/gold embossed lettering to same aircraft. Near mint cond. $26.00

WWII AAF AIRCRAFT TURRET GUN SAFETY BELT (C-1): Heavy dark OD web strap w/zinc chromate finish metal buckle & fittings. Well marked. Good shape. Type M4 "Valves Regulating Jet Engine Operated Pressurized Suit" w/1948 dated AF contract marked spec. tag. Avg. cond. $25.00

WWII AIRCRAFT BEAM GAUGE (IN-4A): Bendix. For Air navigation & some bombing techniques. Allows for radio homing to signal by following arrow indicator. Exc. cond. $20.00

WWII AIRCRAFT BOMB RELEASE INTERVAL CONTROL: Last insp. on 9-5-45. Used in all WWII & later bombers. Has weapons select switch & No. of weapons to release switch & Interval control. Select/train light. 9x5x4" size for internal components. Above avg. cond. $51.00

WWII AIRCRAFT CLOCK (8 DAY): Hmkd. Wittnaur on back. Black face w/12 hr dial & sweep second hand. Fully operational. Avg. cond. $38.00

WWII AIRCRAFT CLOCK (8 DAY): Unmarkcd. Black facc w/12 hr dial & sweep second hand. Fully operable. Avg. cond. $49.00

WWII AIRCRAFT CLOCK (8-DAY): Elgin brand. Black dial. Black bakelite body. Above avg. cond. $74.00

WWII AIRCRAFT COCKPIT LIGHT (B-7): Control/power box w/toggle on off switch & multipurpose light on extendible cord. Mint cond. $20.00

WWII AIRCRAFT COCKPIT LIGHT: Light mount & cord & red night vision lens. Avg. cond. $20.00

WWII AIRCRAFT COMPENSATING SIGHT (K-11): Designed for B-24 nose guns. Fore & Aft pip sights w/refracting mirror between. Tinted lens available to control light. Presets for alt & air speed all on metal box containing a targeting solution computer. Bore sight instructions on side. Sperry made. Exc. cond. $177.00

WWII AIRCRAFT CONTROL PANEL: Panel for Aircraft recognition lights. Box has 4 toggle switches for white/red/green/amber & light upper or lower lights & indicator light & keying switch. 3.5x3.5x1.5 dims. Above avg. cond. $25.00

WWII AIRCRAFT CYLINDER HEAD TEMP INDICATOR GAUGE: Allows monitoring of two cylinders from single gauge. Temp range -50 to & 150 in centigrade. Above avg. cond. $26.00

WWII AIRCRAFT COMPENSATING SIGHT

WWII AIRCRAFT ENGINE OIL TEMP GAUGE: Includes line & transducer. 2" dia. gauge w/100 to 250 degrees range. Above avg. cond. $20.00

WWII AIRCRAFT ENGINE RPM & HOURS GAUGE: Very Clean gauge w/RPM dial indicator trom 0 to 4000 rpm. Has hours operations window w/six position indicator. Appears fully operational. No indication for type of engine or craft. Above avg. cond. $30.00

WWII AIRCRAFT FUEL QUANTITY GAUGE: Dial range from 0 to 300 gals & reads from right to left descending. Some minor wear on dial. Above avg. cond. $20.00

WWII AIRCRAFT GROUND FLOW CHECK METER: In case w/instructions. Used for ground check of oxygen pressure & flow rate on aircraft. Near mint cond. ... $45.00

WWII AIRCRAFT GUN CAMERA: Bell & Howell. 1942 dated & mountable to aircraft frame. 35mm lens w/presetable values based on mission. Film cartridges used. Avg. cond. $72.00

WWII AIRCRAFT GUN CAMERA: Fairchild. Cartridge fed w/preset lens values. Incl. several feet of cable & connector All contained in torn canvas carrier. Avg. cond. $25.00

WWII AIRCRAFT GUN SIGHT: Model N-6A elec. powered Target imaging sight. Black case, optics & power receptacle. Has 1943 dated parts tag attached. Stored in orig. box w/label. Above avg. cond. $75.00

WWII AIRCRAFT HIGH PRESSURE
HYDRAULIC GAUGE: 2" face w/range 0
to 2000 psi. 1942 dated on specs at rear.
Above avg. cond. $20.00

WWII AIRCRAFT LOAD ADJUSTER (A-26)
IN CASE: Slide rule style w/colored
graphics. Stored in leather case w/Class
30d annotated under lid. Exc. cond.
.... $26.00

WWII AIRCRAFT PSI. GAUGE: Black case
& face. Luminescent dial from 0 to 35 PSI.
(could be in x 100). Some dial info.
blacked out. Above avg. cond. $20.00

WWII AIRCRAFT RADIO ALTIMETER:
Model ID 14/APN-1 w/center pivot dial &
dual settings, one for under 500 ft & one
for over 500 feet. Setting controlled by
range knob on front. Above avg. cond.
.... $56.00

WWII AIRCRAFT RATE OF CLIMB
INDICATOR: This item is rated only for
ground trainer/simulator use only (see tag
on back). Single dial shows Climb or
Descent limits reads to 2000 fpm.
Indicator pivots on center. Connector on
back w/power cord cut. Exc. cond.
.... $36.00

WWII AIRCRAFT RECIPROCATING
ENGINE CARTRIDGE STARTER UNIT:
Mfg. by Breeze Corps Inc. Has metal gun
tube for cartridge accessed by lever action
to move receiver chamber to side.
Pressure relief valve at top. Sample
cartridge supplied. Exc. cond. $182.00

WWII AIRCRAFT RF LOOP ANTENNA: OD
painted loop antenna on aerodynamic
base & cable tubing for installation on
aircraft. Yellow danger labels. Exc. cond.
.... $34.00

WWII AIRCRAFT STANDBY MAGNETIC
COMPASS (MB-1): Whiskey compass w/
floating az. indicator & window w/etched
read line. Glass is milky from chemical
reaction. Spec. plate on back. Avg. cond.
.... $20.00

WWII AIRCRAFT TURN & BANK
INDICATOR: Standardized presentation
w/yellow on all indicators. Adj. horizon &
floating wing. No marks or specs. Avg.
cond. $20.00

WWII AIRCRAFT TWO BOMB RELEASE
SIGNAL LAMPS: Installed on bombers to
signal formation. Metal, aircraft powered,
focus beam. Brackets present- no bulbs.
Need cleaning. Avg. cond. $20.00

WWII AIRCRAFT WING MOUNTED AMMO
BINS: OD finished alum cans w/loader
door & feeder door & carry handle. Avg.
cond. $20.00

WWII ARMY SIGNAL CORPS RADIO
COMPASS: Fairchild Aviation built w/gray
crinkle finish box & 4.5" dial w/var. adj.

know. aircraft 400 cycle powered &
connector at back. Above avg. cond.
.... $40.00

WWII AUTOSYN COMPASS TESTER:
Wood case w/accessories inside &
Compass rose w/adj. pointer. Dated 1943
from specs. Avg. cond. $25.00

WWII BUBBLE SEXTANT (AN-5851-1):
Celestial sighting device w/Automatic
collimator to give accurate read outs.
Presetable & capable of multiple shots w/o
leaving station. Stored in black bakelite
case w/hanger, battery pack &
accessories. Leather carry strap broken.
Avg. cond. $75.00

WWII IFF CONTROL BOX: Code select
switch, gain control (output power) &
signal interrogation switch. Black crinkle
finish on box. Above avg. cond. $20.00

WWII JEEP TACHOMETER: 4" dia. w/dash
chrome trim. Incl. odometer function &
hmkd. on rear. Above avg. cond.
.... $27.00

WWII MAIN 'J' BOX FOR TURBO
SUPERCHARGER REGULATOR TYPE
B: Still sealed in Mfg. shipping container &
all seams have been reinforced w/tape.
spec. tag in place & shows 8/9/45 date.
Exc. cond. $40.00

WWII MARK II ASTRO COMPASS: Gray
metal pedestal w/compass upon it.
Compass has double bubble level & az.,
Latitude & elev. scales & sighting
aperture & instruction booklet. Black
plastic storage box w/metal tag on lid &
carry strap. Exc. cond. $150.00

WWII NAVY AIRCRAFT ANTENNA MAST
(CORSAIR): 30" with 8" wood base & dark
blue painted copper top, has all fitting &
along with the gull wings was a trade mark
of the famous fighter in WWII. Avg. cond.
.... $65.00

WWII NAVY AIRCRAFT CAMERA (F-8):
Hmkd. Keystone Mfg. Co., Magazine
loaded & preset lens values & 15" focal
length. Aircraft powered. Stored w/
accessories in reinforced box w/labels.
Exc. cond. $250.00

WWII NAVY AIRCRAFT CODED HOMING
DEVICE: Aircraft components only, Pilots
control box w/3 control switches & remote
relay switch box & remote power supply &
antenna frequency control box. Has equip
spares & code sheets included. dated Mar
1941. Exc. cond.
.... $100.00

WWII NAVY CAMERA (K-25B) CAMERA IN
CASE: Powered by 28V aircraft power,
uses removable film magazines, preset
lens values. Stores in reinforced fiber case
w/accessories. Case labeled on lid. Above
avg. cond. $250.00

WWII NAVY CAMERA (K-25B) CAMERA
IN CASE

WWII NAVY SEXTANT: AN-5851-1 model w/
auto avg., day-night operation & battery
powered. Prismatic type optics & black
crinkle finish case. Stored in bowling ball
style padded bag w/accessories incl. &
secured in pockets. Appears operational.
Bag is generously labeled w/instr. &
warnings. Above avg. cond. $90.00

WWII NAVY SHIP BINNACLE COMPASS:
Gimbaled brass frame w/white compass
face-fully operable. Hmkd. Lionel Corp. &
dated 1942. 9.25" across face & 12" on
frame. Lacks pedestal. Exc. cond.
.... $171.00

WWII SEXTANT (A-10A): Std sextant w/
prism optics, bubble sight & recording
drum. Stored in weathered but tight box.
Accessories incl. additional disc for
recording, battery power pack & cord &
spare lens. spec. plate on lid. Avg. cond.
.... $50.00

U.S. TRENCH ART ITEMS

A. All Periods

DESK SET FROM ALUMINUM: Privately
done, gives 13x5" base w/knobs at each
end + two lidded urns for cigarettes &
ashtray in center w/replica of mortar in
center that conceals lighter. Exc. cond.
.... $125.00

DESK SET FROM ALUMINUM

DISPLAY SET FOR 75MM RECOILLESS
ROUND: Wooden base w/felt padded
supports holding immaculate 75MM
recoilless round. Perforated casing is
lacquered & base has detonator removed.
projectile has open tip & pre-grooved
compression band. Black finish shows
minor spotting. Exc. cond. $150.00

FAREWELL GIFT TO NAVAL OFFICER IN
BRONZE: 4x5" bronze plate w/Shinto
shrine gate mounted on it & Japanese
writing on each side. In front is Name +
(SC) USN/AUGUST 1955/NAVAL
SUPPLY DEPOT/ YOKOSUKA, JAPAN.
Nice piece. Exc. cond. $31.00

NAVY SOUVENIR ASHTRAY: Nickel plated
w/mounted .50 cal. round converted to
lighter + DI style flags on each side of
alum plaque for USS Roosevelt Med.
cruise 1959. Avg. cond. $45.00

TORPEDO MODEL ON MARBLE LIKE
BASE: Brass blunt nosed warhead section
& nickel plated center & aft. 12.5" long
incl. dual 4 blade props & spinner. 3
moveable brass fins. Supported on two
struts & provision for a border of brass
stanchions to hold a chain or rope. Only
two remain. This is a very handsome
display piece & deserves serious
attention. Avg. cond. $295.00

TRENCH ART BRASS TUBE AS VASE

TRENCH ART BRASS TUBE AS VASE: 13" tall w/wood plug at base & art work w/owl & butterfly on peened background. Needs some polish. Above avg. cond. $70.00

TRENCH ART CANDLE STICKS FROM HELMET PLUME SOCKET: Brass Plume socket from Army dress parade helmet (1870-90) w/brass leaf base added & attached to walnut base. Brass Candle holder attached to top. Handsome candlestick + documentation on bottom. Exc. cond. $66.00

TRENCH ART DESK PEN SET: alum base & accessories incl. ink well, paper clip well & two pen holders + two brass posts & .50 cal. round in horizontal display. Nicely done & interesting appearance. Above avg. cond. $30.00

TRENCH ART PAIR OF LAMPS FROM MORTAR SHELLS: 81 mm mortars inverted & attached to nickel plated metal bases, drilled for wiring & sockets installed in motor exhaust outlet. Shells & fins are nickel plated. Wiring & sockets should be replaced for safety. Avg. cond. $70.00

TRENCH ART WIND CHIMES: From brass shells, hanger is base of 75mm & chimes are cut down 20mm shells w/length selected for sound. Avg. cond. $35.00

TRENCH ART FROM 57MM SHELL: Two tiered wood base w/nickel plated cartridges on each corner + silver plated eagle on rifle round w/'US CARTRIDGE CO' on it. Center is plated 57mm arty shell w/miniature hat & Army shield. Three looped candlestick bulb holders w/ simulated candle extensions. Sides of main piece have attached by screws, tall torches w/3 wreaths. Avg. cond.
.... $150.00

VIETNAM ERA TRENCH ART URN FROM 105MM SHELL: Beautiful brass urn from 1943 dated 105mm shell. Polished brass w/fluted top & inscribed for name indiv. from Da Nang Viet Nam/Nov. 66/Nov. 67. Avg. cond. $30.00

TRENCH ART PAIR OF LAMPS FROM MORTAR SHELLS

TRENCH ART PAIR OF SHELL VASES: Two 13.5" 75mm shells fluted & engraved in flower pattern w/roses & star pattern background. Avg. cond. $85.00

TRENCH ART SALT & PEPPER SHAKERS FROM 20MM PROJECTILES: Teak base w nickel plated carrier hook + two salt/ pepper holders from projectiles. Nickel plated w/lead tops. Above avg. cond.
.... $20.00

WWI COMMEMORATIVE DECORATOR TO THE 12TH AERO SQUADRON

WWI COMMEMORATIVE DECORATOR TO THE 12TH AERO SQUADRON: Wood stand w/mahogany finish & Metal + enamel American shield w/upswept wings. In center of shield is number '12.' A 37mm round is mounted in center w/ornate rose decoration on brass shell portion. At top of shell is engraved 'meuse argonne - 12th

Aerospace Sqdn./meuse argonne Sept. Oct. 1918. Projectile has mfg. marks on side & top has nice brass open emblem of aircraft in flight. Above avg. cond. $229.00

WWI PLASTER DOUGHBOY LAMP: Features antiqued statuette of Fully equiped doughboy climbing the sandbags. AT side is well w/elec fixture in bottom. Amber glass globe covers bulb. Wiring damaged. Above avg. cond.
.... $75.00

WWI PLASTER DOUGHBOY LAMP

1918.' Brass St. Mihiel coat of arms on side. Above avg. cond. $45.00

WWI TRENCH ART 75MM SHELL AS DECORATOR PIECE: Polished brass naval shell w/Greek oriented etched artwork. Features Liberty standing by English & greek flags + crown & naval anchor w/greek phrases. Shows dates 1914 thru 1919 over Crossed cannon & grenade emblem. Below liberty is date 1-4-19. Above avg. cond. $70.00

WWI TRENCH ART 75MM SHELL AS VASE: Brass shell 14" tall w/elaborate peened decoration showing VERDUN & oak branches. Nice polished finish. Above avg. cond. $72.00

WWI TRENCH ART 75MM SHELL AS VASE

WWI TRENCH ART 75MM SHELL AS DECORATOR PIECE

WWI TRENCH ART 1ST AERO SQDN. NAPKIN RING: Made from brass shell & etched w/'1ST AERO SQ/SEPT 12-14,

WWI TRENCH ART ASHTRAY IN BRONZE

WWI TRENCH ART ASHTRAY IN BRONZE: Contains small mini ball & rifle bullet on each side w/cast pig holding german helmet in hand. French saying on side 'DE YSER AU PHIN.' Avg. cond. $135.00

WWI TRENCH ART CIGARETTE LIGHTER: 57mm dia. brass body w/convex sides & striking wheel. Avg. cond. $59.00

WWI TRENCH ART LAMP FROM SHELL: 22.5" tall w/base from large cal. shell & column from 40mm round drilled for wire. Three .50 cal. rounds mounted about 1/2 way up column. Assembly for two lights & harp for shade at top. Shade is WWI helmet w/orig. hand painted unit designator for 21st Engineers, 1st Army & a likely anti aircraft emblem. Needs rewiring. Avg. cond. $69.00

WWI TRENCH ART LAMP FROM SHELL

WWI TRENCH ART LAMP FROM SHELL: 12" dia. wood base w/23" high mounted shell & projectile. Three hooped down facing sockets w/bullets on end of chains. All metal has gray finish. Shell decorated w/cartoon characters from period incl. Jiggs, Andy Gump & Katzenjammer kids. Above avg. cond. $132.00

WWI TRENCH ART LAMP: metal base has 75mm arty shell projectile as body w/OD sand finish Army helmet shell as shade. Complete w/on & off pull chain + wire w/ bakelite wall plug. Above avg. cond. $84.00

WWI TRENCH ART LIGHTER FROM BULLET: Brass 'SOUVENIR D ALLIMAGNE' w/doves, flowers, ships &

geese in decor. Bottom screws out to reveal lighter materials. Avg. cond. $65.00

WWI TRENCH ART LAMP

WWI TRENCH ART PAIR OF FOREIGN 75MM SHELLS: 14" tall & formed as vases w/deep fluted lower portions & decorated uppers. Branches w/leaves & 'REIMS' on each. Fluted top for effect. Avg. cond. $112.00

WWI TRENCH ART PAIR OF FOREIGN 75MM SHELLS

WWI TRENCH ART PAIR OF VASES FROM SHELL CASINGS.: From 75mm shells American issue. Lower 1/3 fluted + decor art at top & Argonne Meuse on one - St. Mihiel on the other. Well polished. Above avg. cond. $141.00

WWI TRENCH ART PAIR OF VASES FROM SHELL CASINGS

WWI TRENCH ART SALT & PEPPER SHAKERS: Made from silver plated brass casing & bullet shaped top w/holes. Both Engraved 'CAMP STANLEY' & 'R. H. / MOTHER.' Minor dents & tarnish. Avg. cond. $12.00

WWI TRENCH ART SHELL: 4" short 37mm shell, highly polished, engraved to show hunting scene all around shell. Above avg. cond. $65.00

WWI TRENCH ART SHELL: 4" tall 37mm shell dated 1917 w/hand engraved record of indivs. part in war. Name at top w/ battles listed below, incl. Chateau Theirry, Meuse-Argonne, St. Mihiel & army of occupation. Date at bottom. Avg. cond. $66.00

WWI TRENCH ART SHELL: 75mm shell 13.5" tall w/twisted flutes at bottom half & decorated for remainder. Reads 'VERDUN' + 1918 w/old Indian good luck symbol in middle. Avg. cond. $38.00

WWI TRENCH ART SHELL: 75mm shell cut down to 10" height & decorated w/raised profile of Gen. Pershing w/name below & crossed American & French flags w/dates 1914 to 1918 above & below cross. Star pattern textured background. Above avg. cond. $115.00

WWI TRENCH ART SHELL

WWI TRENCH ART SOUVENIR 75MM VASES: Brass shells w/fluted bases & nicely decorated upper sections. Shows flower pattern w/one reading 'ARGONNE/ 1918,' the other 'VERDUN/1918' in raised relief. Decorative pattern in background. These have been polished & lacquered. Above avg. cond. $129.00

WWI TRENCH ART TABLE SETTING: Brass Knife, fork & spoon w/.30 rounds as grips & brass tines, blade & spoon. All marked souvenir of France & each handle has Different crest. Exc. cond. $32.00

WWI TRENCH ART VASE FROM 75MM SHELL

WWI TRENCH ART VASE FROM 75MM SHELL: 13.75" high w/plain top, Middle third decorated. For Lorraine-Toul sector w/flowers & oak leaves. At bottom has Signals corps emblem w/30th above & FSB/July 4, 1918 at bottom. Avg. cond. $80.00

WWI TRENCH ART VASES: Designed to carry a messge on both vases. Each 14" tall, fully decorated w/oak leaves & branches, Both have 'WORLD WAR' on upper part of vase, one has 'MEUSE' & the other has 'ARGONNE' at the bottom. Well polished. Above avg. cond. $143.00

WWI TRENCH ART VASE FROM 75MM SHELL

WWI TRENCH ART VASE

WWI TRENCH ART VASE FROM 75MM SHELL: Foreign shell-American art. Uncommon copper color to brass, fluted bottom 1/3. Arrowhead design w/ 'CHATEAU THIERRY' on rim + Unit shield in center & 'Souvenir' over shield & '1918' below. Avg. cond. $55.00

WWI TRENCH ART VASE: From 75MM shell, 13.5" tall w/fluted bottom 1/3 & artistically treated upper Features raised letters 'ST MIHIEL' & attractive raised image of Grecian nude seated & leaning forward. Above avg. cond. $55.00

WWI TRENCH ART VASES

WWI TRENCH ART VASES

WWI TRENCH ART VASES: 12" & 9" tall, each representing a different battle. The 12" shell is ornately decorated to commemorate the Argonne Battle while the 9" shows tree & leaves to commemorate the Verdun battle. Avg. cond. $90.00

WWI TRENCH ART VERDUN MEMORIAL SHELL VASE: US 75mm shell w/flutes near base & etched flowers + 'VERDUN' & '1919' on side. 13.5" tall. Avg. cond. $34.00

WWII 7TH WAR LOAN AWARD: Impressive 22" tall mounted 57MM shell & projectile w/award plaque on base. Antique finished wood base w/polished brass shell & chromed projectile (compression ring still copper). Plaque is chromed & states '7th war loan, first class award/class B., Banner w/'INSPECTION DIVISION' + 1945 'INDEPENDENCE DAY'/US NAVY YARD, WASHINGTON, DC.' Few minor nicks on wood finish & brass showing some darkening. Exc. cond. $175.00

WWII DISPLAY OF SMALL ARMS & ARTY SHELLS: Nicely done arrangement of 7 arty shells cut down & stacked in decreasing size to form tower. Nickel plated 20mm shells w/gilded .50 cal. rounds surround the base. .30 cal. rifle & carbine rounds form a ring around the 37mm round that crowns the piece. Crossed cannons & a DI of an Arty unit are on the side. Above avg. cond. $120.00

WWII TRENCH ART 20MM ROUND DISPLAY ON PEDESTAL: 20mm round displayed w/nickel plated projectile + brass case on brass pedestal. Round set at about 40 degrees off vertical for effect. Above avg. cond. $20.00

WWII TRENCH ART ASHTRAY FROM 105MM HOWITZER SHELL & FRENCH COINS: Shell cut down to base for ashtray + Match holder in center from .30 cal. rifle round + 3 cigarette holders made from French coins. Above avg. cond. ... $34.00

WWII TRENCH ART ASHTRAY FROM 105MM SHELL: Brass 105mm shell from 1944 cut down to 2" high for ashtray. Four rifle rounds act as pedestals for center & 50 cal. round in center for decor. Above avg. cond. $25.00

WWII TRENCH ART ASHTRAY FROM 75MM SHELL: Cut down & w/circular handle installed. Handle engraved '1944-1945' & around base is 'Germany,' 'England', 'Belgium', 'France.' Above avg. cond. $28.00

WWII TRENCH ART ASHTRAY FROM JAPANESE ARTILLERY SHELL: Center (detonator area inside) has metal

engraved w/Japanese emblems. Base has ordnance marks in Japanese. Avg. cond. $23.00

WWII TRENCH ART ASHTRAY FROM SHELL: British 3" mark II shell cut down w/two Half penny's bent & soldered in as holders. Above avg. cond. $11.00

WWII TRENCH ART CHESS SET: A truly remarkable craft effort using 37mm & 40mm shells cut down for a container & small ammo to build a complete chess set w/all pieces clearly identifiable. Built during or shortly after the war, large ammo is dated 42 & 43. Includes brown leatherette backed paper chess board & one stenciled on coarse cotton cloth. Exc. cond. $400.00

WWII TRENCH ART GRENADE LAMP: 4" dia. turned alum base w/grenade mounted in center. Frag. type w/lever & pin in place. Socket above fuse. Wiring is vintage WWII. Above avg. cond. $45.00

WWII TRENCH ART LAMP BASE: Metal 3 tiered base w/mounted Japanese 75MM shell & projectile. Polished brass base w/ chromed plaque w/Japanese characters at top & 'JAPANESE 75MM SHELL /FIRED AT AMERICAN TROOPS/ GUADALCANAL 1942' at bottom. Nickel plated projectile w/harp & socket mount at tip. Channeled for wiring. This is a superior piece Near mint cond. $175.00

WWII TRENCH ART LIGHTER: Lighter made from projectile of German 25MM round. Avg. cond. $35.00

WWII TRENCH ART PISTOL LIGHTER: Made from brass scrap & two .45 cal. shells. Looks like auto pistol, grip & trigger pull away to expose lighter. Avg. cond. $97.00

WWII TRENCH ART SHELL: 1941 dated 37mm shell 8.5" tall w/decor from top to bottom in tropic theme. No writing or dates on sides. Above avg. cond. $21.00

WWII TRENCH ART SHELL: 20mm cannon shell w/fused projectile & converted into cigarette lighter. On marbleized base + waterproof compass topped match carrier. Avg. cond. $20.00

WWII TRENCH ART TABLE LAMPS FROM 37MM SHELLS: 75mm bases w/37mm mounted. Electric cord threaded to base from lamp socket No decor. Appear complete & functional. Avg. cond. $34.00

WWII TRENCH ART V FOR VICTORY: Constructed from 2" Aerial gunners Pb sterling wing w/two halves of a .50 cal. MG bullet mounted to form a 'V' for victory below. Nicely done but shows light tarnish. Above avg. cond. $53.00

U.S. MILITARY PLAQUES & TROPHIES

A. All Periods

AVIATION DEPOT SQUADRON PLAQUE: 12th Aviation. painted design of eagle claw & atom energy on disc at center with gold lettering on black painted wooden shield. 10" wide & 13" high. 50s & 60s. Hanger to back. Mint cond. $20.00

CIVIL WAR ERA UNION GENERAL PLAQUE: Cast iron w/black paint finish showing bust profile of general in dress blouse. 12" oval presentation. Above avg. cond. $28.00

KOREAN WAR ARMY REMEMBRANCE PLAQUE: 15x13" rectangle w/13x11" metal presentation display for named CPL. Framed in Army branch & division emblems + image of forces landing. Presentation gives Cpl.'s name enlist date (1/16/1951), assigned units & service number. Saw Combat in Korea & display includes CIB & ribbon bar. Above avg. cond. $30.00

KOREAN WAR USAF 5TH AIR FORCE PLAQUE: Oak. Hand painted emblem in center w/'5th AIR FORCE' above & 'KOREA' below. Above avg. cond. $53.00

NAVY AVIATION PLAQUE: 11x9" wood shield w/painted metal 6" disc in upper center. Shows black bat over earth rise w/ sun & moon in sky. Rim reads- 'AIR DEVELOPMENT SQUADRON FIVE / VX5.' Avg. cond. $19.00

NAVY AVIATION PLAQUE: Ceramic. Mounted on wooden base ceramic shows clouds & sea w/'AIR FORCE' at top & gold Navy wings against black w/'PACIFIC FLEET/NAMED INDIV' below. Avg. cond. $20.00

NAVY USS HELENA CA 75 - PROUD & FEARLESS PLAQUE: 10.5x12" thick wood shield-shaped body is varnished. Has cast 7.5" wide applique w/painted details. Hanger device on back. Above avg. cond. $80.00

NAVY USS SAMUEL B. ROBERTS DD 823 PLAQUE: 9x12" shield-shaped wood body in varnished. Has 7" dia. cast applique w/ painted details. Avg. cond. $80.00

USAF TACTICAL FIGHTER SQUADRON PLAQUE: 8x6" Wood shield w/3" painted disc of angry bee in boxing gloves +

banner '22ND TACTICAL FIGHTER SQUADRON.' Avg. cond. $20.00

USMC PLAQUE: 15" dia. plastic cast of marine emblem, painted in full color. Emblem in center w/maroon background & rim reads in gold, 'DEPARTMENT OF THE NAVY/UNITED STATES MARINES.' Near mint cond. $50.00

VIETNAM ERA FAREWELL MUG: Polished alloy mug-4.5" high, flared base & handle. Enameled metal DI for 19th TASS w/ Snoopy flying his house + 'VIETNAM' in center & 'CURSE YOU CHARLIE' in bottom banner. For outstanding support by named indiv. Above avg. cond. $49.00

VIETNAM ERA NAVY NC-4 COMMEMORATIVE PLAQUE: Presented to RADM WS Guest on 10 May 1969. 10x12" wood rectangle w large brass display showing route of the NC-4 & its sister seaplanes + comments about the ship & mission problems. Above avg. cond. $27.00

VIETNAM ERA NAVY PLAQUE: Wood plaque 8x7" w/enameled 5" metal disc showing Viking like profile banner reads 'VMA9AW0 225.' Brass plate reads 'TO/ THE MAD RUSSIAN/BIG BIG THANKS/ VIETNAM 1966-1967.' Above avg. cond. $34.00

VIETNAM ERA NAVY SHIP PLAQUE

VIETNAM ERA NAVY SHIP PLAQUE: Rare 7.7" wood shield shaped plaque with heavy 5" cast aluminum Vietnamese made plaque piece for the "USS BRULE AKL-23" in Vietnam. Also states in Vietnamese "Kip Thoi Day Du Lien-Tuc Yem Tro." Above avg. cond. $95.00

VIETNAM ERA TROPHY MUG: 7" high nickel plated 105MM shell from C-130

Specter bird w/20mm nickel plated shell for a handle. Wood bullet completes. Engraved. Above avg. cond. $45.00

VIETNAM ERA USAF TROPHY MUG: Silver plated. Named mug w/Etched candlestick over indiv. name & 'IN APPRECIATION FOR FLYING/OVER 160 NIGHT COMBAT MISSIONS/OVER THE TRAIL WITH THE/ CANDLESTICKS.' Light tarnish patina & dark spotting. Avg. cond. $61.00

VIETNAM ERA USMC 1ST MARINE DIV. PLAQUE: 8x12" painted wood plaque w/ Raised wood 1st Marine Div. logo & Viet Nam banner. Brass plaque at bottom is generalized presentation by Gen. Wheeler USMC Commander. Avg. cond. $28.00

VIETNAM ERA USMC AVIATOR PLAQUE: Vietnam made. Black finished 11x9" shield w/1st Marine air wing decal in upper center covered w/Plexiglas. Exc. cond. $42.00

WWI 88TH DIV. COMMEMORATION PLAQUE: Bronze. 3.5" diamond plate w/ clover like design & centering on standing soldier. Background typifies the war & France appears at top. 'EIGHTY EIGHTH/ INFANTRY DIVISION' is on a wall nearby. Exc. cond. $100.00

WWI NAVY PLAQUE: Gunnery trophy presented by USS Texas in 1916 to RED-E after Battle efficiency exercises. 3.5x6" solid cast brass w/impression of part of Texas Super structure. Back has comments incl. fact that Secy. Navy & Naval board witness activities. Incl. are photos & documentation. Exc. cond. $212.00

WWI VICTORY PLAQUE: "A TRIBUTE TO ONE WHO SERVED 1917-18." 8X10" wooden base with brass front, with color flags of the Allies & Marshal Foch's Victory Message to the troops. Named to a Sgt. in the 35th Division Engineers. Above avg. cond. $28.00

WWII AAF PRESENTATION PLAQUE: 15x13" wood plaque w/decorated & enameled brass plate 13x11". For named 1st Lieut., has aircrew wing & navigator wing decal, unit (870th BS, 497th BG) 20th AF emblem & ribbon decals (incl. air medal & army GC). Exc. cond. $34.00

WWII AAF UNIT PLAQUE: 7" square wood base w/low black diamond centered. Bright yellow bird carrying bomb mounted on diamond. Represents 513th bombardment Squadron (Heavy). Above avg. cond. $105.00

WWII ARMY QUARTERMASTER PLAQUE: Brass. 12" dia. w/wheel showing 13 stars (one missing) & crossed sword & key above hub. Eagle w/spread wings at top. Hanger incl. Above avg. cond. $40.00

WWII NAVY CONSTRUCTION UNIT COMMEMORATIVE PLAQUE: 16x15" Walnut plaque in US shield outline w/ painted image of Star & bars shield for background of bare chested Navy man w/ sledge hammer. Motto reads 'CONSTRIMUS/BATUIMUS/USN.' FLAWLESS. Near mint cond. $90.00

WWII NAVY SEABEE PLAQUE

WWII NAVY SEABEE PLAQUE: Wooden base w/beveled sides & mounted metal plate w/'SEABEES CAN DO.' Mounted to plate is alum bar supporting brass 7" long Seabee in full regalia w/machine gun, wrench, bulldog face & DD hat cocked back on head. On side of base is plate listing locations Seabees fought at, incl. Tulagi, Kawajalein, Iwo Jima. Exc. cond. $244.00

WWII NAVY USS DUPAGE PLAQUE: 16x10" w/carved dates (44-45) & dragon wrapped around a 5. over 'USS DUPAGE APA41.' W/list of engagements from Marshalls to Luzon w/dates & type of activity. Above avg. cond. $65.00

WWII USMC IWO JIMA PLAQUE: 17x13" wood w/3 dim carved portrayal of the Flag raising on Surabachi. Excellent detail & strong emotional presence. In upper right, across from flag, is full color USMC emblem w/title & motto on rim. Exc. cond. $164.00

U.S. MILITARY RELATED ARTWORK

A. All Periods

BUST OF GENERAL PERSHING: 4.5" high desk size cast metal bust of Pershing in full dress w/medals. Has bronze tone, fair

features + name on base. Avg. cond.
.... $30.00
CAVALRY DISPLAY FRAMED: Nice glassed
display of 1st, 2nd & 3rd cavalry embr.
patches on black field w/'CAVALRY'
spelled at bottom. Limed oak frame. Exc.
cond. $200.00
CIVIL WAR CONFEDERATE VETERAN
8TH TEXAS CARTOUCHE BOX: Veteran
item. Hand formed leather. Approx. 5x3x1"
in size. Tan leather with Star on front &
around it, '8th Texas Cavalry Regiment.'
Above are battle honors, 'Shiloh,
Murfeesboro, Chickamauga.' Lid opens to
show photo of owner in civilian attire.
Made for a veteran of the CSA cavalry.
Near mint cond. $282.00

SPANISH AMERICAN WAR BUST OF
ADMIRAL SAMPSON

SPANISH AMERICAN WAR BUST OF
ADMIRAL SAMPSON: Bronze. 4' disc w/
raised profile of Adm. Sampson's left side,
titled & signed by Artist in lower right.
Above avg. cond. $76.00
TANK DESTROYER FORCES
DECORATOR: 15x13.25" wood frame w/
OD painted inset. Top has painted design
of 4-cog Tank Destroyer Forces patch
design, Texas state flag & crossed cav.
sabers & reads "Texas" over arrow &
"7,300 Miles/11,680 KM" below. Provision
on back for hanging on wall. Above avg.
cond. $69.00
USAF LOS ALAMOS PATCH FRAMED
DISPLAY: 19x11" limed oak frame w/black
field & single Manhattan project patch in
center + disclaimer stating the patch was
worn by the commanding Officer at the
time of the first Atomic bomb test. Exc.
cond. $20.00
USMC COMBAT MARINE RELIEF
SCULPTURE: 20x13" wood frame of 12"

tall 3d sculpture of Nam era marine in flak
jacket & carrying M16 stepping over sand
bags & enemy weapon. USMC emblem in
lower left of sculpture. Copper back
ground. Above avg. cond. $59.00
USMC SGT. JIGGS MASCOT ASHTRAY:
4x8" cast plaster base w/3 dimensional
likeness of Bull Dog wearing campaign
hat-master Sgt. chevrons on his blanket
w/USMC device & "Sergt. Jiggs-USMC."
Avg. cond. $36.00
WWI DOUGHBOY STATUETTE: 9" tall cast
metal w/copper tone finish showing
doughboy standing resolutely with rifle.
Much of uniform & equipment is well
detailed from his leg wraps to the pouches
on his cartridge belt. Above avg. cond.
.... $56.00
WWII COLOR LITHO OF CHANCE
VOUGHT F4U-1 CORSAIR BY THE
MANUFACTURER: 11x15" shows a
unmarked Corsair attacking a Japanese
ship. Avg. cond. $24.00
WWII IWO JIMA FLAG RAISING DESK
STATUETTE: Cast metal w/bronze finish
showing replica of famed photo. Shows 6
men raising flag on Suribachi. Avg. cond.
.... $58.00
WWII NAVY SUBMARINE REMEMBRANCE
TRAY: 15x21" wooden serving tray w/litho.
has wooden frame & handles. B/w litho of
submarine with label of man name &
service on USS Sea Cat. Glass front.
Some yellow staining to litho Avg. cond.
.... $24.00
WWII AAF AVIATOR STATUE: 9.5" tall white
plaster statue w/Army aviator figure in
flight helmet & goggles, coat w/large
collar, flight trousers & A-9 style boots.
Has large aircraft tire design behind him.
Overall copper finish. Felt lined base.
1943 dated. Above avg. cond. $40.00

U.S. MILITARY RELATED GLASSWARE

A. All Periods

1900S S.A.W MILK GLASS DISH "THE
AMERICAN HEN"

1900s S.A.W MILK GLASS DISH "THE AMERICAN HEN": 4x6" w/lid of of US eagle w/3 eggs "Porto Rica" "Cuba" "Philippines" on each. The oval base pattern as a nest w/"The American Hen" on both sides. Has Pat. Applied for on base. Near mint cond. $65.00

ARMY AAA BEER MUG: German made. Tan ceramic 5" beer mug style w/"BATTERY C, 440TH AAA AW BN/ YANKEE CLUB/ON THE RHEIN IN 1945'. NOTE: YANKEE CLUB is highlighted with color. Above avg. cond. $90.00

ARMY INF CERAMIC MUG FOR ARMY UNIT: 8" beer stein w/emblem of 1st Bn., 26Th. INF & nick name 'Blue Spaders.' Regt. & 1st Div. emblems in mini size incl. Nice one. Above avg. cond. $20.00

ARMY MEDICAL DEPT. CHINA GRAVY BOAT: White china gravy boat w/maroon Army Medical department emblem on one side. Avg. cond. $16.00

ARMY MEDICAL SERVICE CHINA: large creamer & two small bowls, saucers & salad plates. All have Logo dishes have maroon band also. Above avg. cond. $28.00

ARMY MEDICAL SERVICE COFFEE CUP: Single coffee cup w/maroon US Army Medical Service emblem on side. Above avg. cond. $11.00

ARMY TANK UNIT COMMEMORATIVE STEIN: German made. To commemorate 1st European units to receive the M1 Abrams tank in Jan 82. White ceramic w/ silver trimmed base. Spectacular imagery incl. the tank, emblems for 3rd Div., Sheaf & Forces in Germany. Pewter like hinged lid. Near mint cond. $59.00

ARMY UNIT PRESENTATION STEIN

ARMY UNIT PRESENTATION STEIN: 7" tall white porcelain body w/gilt trim + heavy Self Propelled gun, regt. crest design w/ motto "Fulfill Your Mission" & Kitaingen/ Main Falterturm designs. Silver-colored ornate flip-top & relief design of sitting nude woman at bottom. Presented to Capt. in 3d Div. Arty. in 1967. Above avg. cond. $65.00

INDIVIDUAL'S UNIT MUG: German stein in white w/gold trim & Pewter like metal lid w/ matador/mace missile on top. color picture of missile on side & unit emblem on other. For 'Lutz' of 587th Tactical Missile Group, Sembach AFB Germany. Above avg. cond. $80.00

NAVY USS NIMITZ COFFEE MUG: Handled mug w/ships logo on side. Above avg. cond. $13.00

SGT 2ND ACR COFFEE CUP: A cut above in quality in presence. Well done green & gold emblem w/motto & 1st Squadron 2nd ACR above. Sgt rank shown in gold leaf + Name over crossed sabers w/2/1 in center & 'BORDER OPERATIONS NCO' below. Exc. cond. $12.50

USAF 22ND TROOP CARRIER SQDN. COFFEE MUG: China. Full color sqdn. emblem on one side featuring burro w/ pack & neat portrayal of C-124 Globemaster on the other. Some light crazing on finish. Above avg. cond. $93.00

WEST POINT CADET MESS SAUCER: Expressly made for the Cadet mess & so marked on bottom. White china w/blue border & West Point emblem on side. Avg. cond. $21.00

WWII ARMY OFFICER VISOR CAP GLASS CANDY DISH: Molded in shape of Officers visor cap w/removable crown. Device painted w/gilt. Above avg. cond. $20.00

WWII PATRIOTIC GLASSES: Set of 8. Nice glassware w/double gold band at top. Tumbler sized w/decaled V for victory r/w/ b colors w/pinup in 'V' & job title at bottom Incl.: Air raid warden, Medical aide, aux. fireman etc. Each has a different pinup. Exc. cond. $45.00

U.S. MILITARY SPOTTER MODELS & CARDS & PROMO MODELS & KITS

A. All periods

AIRCRAFT B-1 MODEL: 1/150 scale model w/wings in full sweep & mounted on wood pylon. 8" W.S. & 11.5" fuselage. Stand has Titles. Above avg. cond. $30.00

AIRCRAFT BUILDER DISPLAY MODEL: North American F-86 Sabre jet, one piece cast plastic w/gray finish, brown radome & decals. 5" W.S. & mounted on bronze finished weighted globe w/rod passing thru Palmdale CA. Ring around globe carries company & aircraft name. Exc. cond. $195.00

AIRCRAFT CONTRACT DISPLAY MODEL: B-2. Northrop Corp. supplied solid model w/stand. II" W.S. few features & dated 1989 on underside. Near mint cond. $86.00

AIRCRAFT CONTRACTOR DISPLAY
MODEL: ARMY MOHAWK

AIRCRAFT CONTRACTOR DISPLAY MODEL: Army Mohawk. Well done model of twin turboprop recce craft. Great details incl. triple tail, turbo pods & high visibility cockpit w/two pilots. Decals excellent & show very slight wear. Clear Acrylic base w/strut & labeled w/Grumman & Mohawk names. Exc. cond. $225.00

AIRCRAFT CONTRACTOR DISPLAY MODEL: F-105. One piece cast plastic w/ sharp camo finish & decals, mounted on white plastic stand w/builder name/F-105/ Thunderchief on arrow shaped base. Exc. cond. $65.00

AIRCRAFT CONTRACTOR DISPLAY MODEL: F-9F Cougar Recce variant w/ 10" W.S. light toned underside & gray top. Decals incl. camera bay windows. Clear acrylic base w/title & logo. Exc. cond. $125.00

AIRCRAFT CONTRACTOR DISPLAY
MODEL: F-9F COUGAR

AIRCRAFT CONTRACTOR DISPLAY MODEL: Grumman F-14. 7" W.S. in full sweep, can be positioned as desired. Desert camo upper & light lower w/4 missiles on fuselage. Israeli decals in place. No stand. Exc. cond. $50.00

AIRCRAFT CONTRACTOR DISPLAY MODEL: Grumman supplied model of F9F-8T Cougar jet fighter. 10" W.S. & decked out in safety white & day glo red. Two seat trainer version of combat craft. Nice decaling Incl. use of Marine on aft fuselage. Acrylic stand w/title & logo. Exc. cond. $135.00

AIRCRAFT CONTRACTOR DISPLAY MODEL: McDonnell-Douglas F-15 Eagle. Blue-green finish w/full complement of USAF decals. Full set of air to air missiles w/one damaged. Clear acrylic stand w/ Company F-15 logo. 7" wingspan & positioned in climbing attitude. Above avg. cond. $20.00

AIRCRAFT CONTRACTOR DISPLAY MODEL: Navy F-4H w/stand. 7" W.S. w/ gray Navy finish, 4 sidewinder missiles on underside & great detail for model size. Acrylic stand has McDonnell ID on front. Exc. cond. $72.00

AIRCRAFT CONTRACTOR DISPLAY MODEL: Navy version F-111B. Swing wing fighter w/6" W.S. at full swing. Externally identical to AF version except for shortened nose. Model decaled as navy carrier fighter. Stand supplied. Above avg. cond. $50.00

AIRCRAFT CONTRACTOR DISPLAY MODEL: T-39 Sabreliner staff transport & proficiency aircraft. Silver underside & white top w/day-glo red safety bands on wingtips, aft fuselsage, vert stabilzer & under nose. Full complement of decals. Minor chipping on paint. Blue plastic stand w/clear arch for aircraft mount. Above avg. cond. $69.00

AIRCRAFT CONTRACTOR DISPLAY
MODEL: T-39 SABRELINER

AIRCRAFT CONTRACTOR DISPLAY MODEL: Nice USN F-11F fighter. White finish w/decals & 9.75" W.S. Nice example of famous fighter that shot itself down in a weapons test. Acrylic stand w/title & logo. Above avg. cond. $95.00

AIRCRAFT CONTRACTOR DISPLAY MODEL: Rockwell International B-1 Bomber. Nicely portrayed with wings in full sweep, the 14.7" model is white w/a full complement of USAF decals including the SAC star band across the nose. A plastic & alum stand w/the Corporate logo in front holds the model about 6" above the table. Exc. cond. $100.00

AIRCRAFT CONTRACTOR DISPLAY MODEL: USAF B-2 Bomber. Northrop contracted 11" plastic molded model w/ command emblems on fuselage Wood stand provided. Mint cond. $79.00

AIRCRAFT CONTRACTOR DISPLAY MODEL: YF-23 Consortium Entry for ATF Competition. 16" long & 10" W.S. Gray plastic w/excellent detail on tactical features. Black stand w/'YF-23/ 'NORTHROP-MCDONNEL DOUGLAS.' Above avg. cond. $40.00

AIRCRAFT CONTRACTOR MODEL: Bell X-1A Test Rock Powered Plane. Gray plastic model w/8.5" W.S. & all needed decals. Blue plastic stand w/Description & Contractor logo. Right horizontal stabilizer broken but saved in bag & repairable. Includes Nice picture of X-1A's launch team & equipment incl. B-29, F-86 chase & ground equip. Pilot in picture appears to be Chuck Yeager. Silver plate award dish w/engraved center from Bell Aircraft to '52/ TRAINERS/BELL X-1A. Above avg. cond. $263.00

AIRCRAFT CONTRACTOR MODEL: McDonnell-Douglas F-4 Phantom Above avg. cond. Nam era camouflage finish on 10" OA model. Great detail & configured w/four sparrow missiles & chin cannon. Plastic stand w/Mfg. logo. Exc. cond. $58.00

AIRCRAFT F-94 MODEL ON STAND: Balsa wood model painted in Late 50s color scheme + decals. Avg. constr. quality & damaged decals. Avg. cond. $24.00

AIRCRAFT SPOTTER MODEL US P-39: Black composition molded w/good detail & 5.5" W.S. & hmkd. 'P-39/June 42.' Good example of the type. Exc. cond. ... $50.00

AIRCRAFT SPOTTER MODEL US T-38 JET FIGHTER IN ORIGINAL SHIPPING BOX: 13" length. 7.5" W.S. Plastic body in white finish w/USAF markings. Nice detail. Includes stand. Comes in original cardboard shipping box that is Northrop marked. Mint cond. $125.00

AIRCRAFT SPOTTER MODEL USN SB2U-3 DIVE BOMBER: 7.25x5.5" black molded composition model of single engine, crew of two dive bomber. Feature details excellent-cowling & cockpit particularly. Marked USN SB2U-3 & dated 6-43. Exc. cond. $43.00

AIRCRAFT SPOTTER MODEL USSR BARGE BOMBER: Molded plastic body in gray finish. 1:144 scale. U.S. Property marked & 1955 dated. Tip of vertical tail surface broken-off. Avg. cond. $25.00

ARMY TANK TRAINING MODEL: Ft Knox training model of ZSU 2/4. Black composition material cast & marked on bottom. Moveable turret & nice details incl. 4 barrels at front (slightly bent) 3x7x3.5" dimensions. Avg. cond. $30.00

CONTRACTOR DISPLAY MODEL OF US SUBMARINE: USS Dolphin (AGSS 555) 9" long stand mounted black composition model w/brass prop (broken). Shows unique design features. Labeled wood stand. Avg. cond. $45.00

FRENCH H39 TANK MODEL: Hand crafted scale model. French H39, crafted in wood w/rubberized tread, movable outer bogies & turret, Impressive detail & artfully done camo paint job. 8.25x 3.75x4" dimensions. Hmkd on bottom & dated 1994. This is an excellent example of scratch modeler skill & armor knowledge. Mint cond. $65.50

FRENCH H39 TANK MODEL

NAVY SHIP MODEL: USS Sandlance. SSN-660, an attack submarine modeled in molded black material w/modest but accurate detail incl. brass single silent run prop. Mounted on wood w/metal posts. Exc. cond. $57.00

SPOTTER MODEL BRITISH DD WARSHIP: 4" cast lead model of British DD J-class. Gray finish-good details. By Superior models. Mint in box. Exc. cond. $10.00

SPOTTER MODEL BRITISH DD WARSHIP: 4" cast lead model of British DD L/M class. Gray finish-good details. By Superior models. In box. Exc. cond. $10.00

SPOTTER MODEL BRITISH DD WARSHIP: 4" cast lead model of British DD S/Z class, Gray finish-good details. By Superior models. In box. Exc. cond. $17.00

SPOTTER MODEL BRITISH FRIGATE: 3" cast lead model of British Frigate, River class, Gray finish w/nice details. Exc. cond. $10.00

SPOTTER MODEL GERMAN DD WARSHIP: 4" gray metal cast model w/ excellent detail. Exc. cond. $11.00

SPOTTER MODEL GERMAN TORPEDO BOAT: 4" gray metal cast model w/ excellent detail. Exc. cond. $16.00

TRAINING MODELS OF TANKS (MODERN): Ft. Knox training center set of 16 scaled tank & APC models in molded black composition material. Incl. common Soviet & European tanks -Leopard II, Chieftain, T-64 & T72, M1 & BMP. Stored in partitioned wood box. Above avg. cond. $264.00

USAF COLONEL AWARD MODEL: Gray plastic model of F-86D w/brown nose radar & appropriate decals. 5" W.S. Large wood base w/angled pipe that fits tail pipe of model. Award plate under Plexiglas at Front. 'COL THOMAS B. WHITEHOUSE/ 1955 USAF FIGHTER GUNNERY & WEAPONS MEET/YUMA AFB, YUMA ARIZ/NORTH AMERICAN AVIATION F-86D SABRE JET.' Exc. cond. $95.00

WWII AAF SPOTTER MODEL BRITISH BLACKBURN SKUA: 7.75" W.S., 6" length in molded black plastic. Marked & 1942 dated on bottom. Avg. cond. $55.00

WWII AAF SPOTTER MODEL OF JAPANESE ZERO: Dated 9-42 & modeled in Black composition material, 7"W.S. + good details. Exc. cond. $53.00

WWII AAF SPOTTER MODEL TRAINING SET

WWII AAF SPOTTER MODEL TRAINING SET: For Identification of categories of non-combatant naval vessels, Incl. 13 gray painted models of varying sizes. Three models missing. Paper list of categories on inside. Two ships have minor missing parts. Stenciled on top by handle w/particulars incl. date-2/45. Many penciled comments on exterior. Ships secured for travel & case folds closed & latches. Rope handles. Avg. cond. $137.00

WWII ARMY SPOTTER MODEL GERMAN TANK: 3.5x8" slush metal cast OD painted of unusual tank w/MG turret on the front & back & small cannon turret w/2 barrel both missing. Labeled in the mold "GERM HVY TANK PZ K.W.6." Avg. cond. $51.00

WWII SPOTTER MODEL GERMAN FOCKE WOLF FW-200: 4 engine bomber. Molded black composition w/18.5" W.S. & solid details. dated 9-42. Above avg. cond. $160.00

WWII SPOTTER MODEL GERMAN HEINKEL 115K: two engine seaplane. Molded black composition w/great details incl. ladders to pontoons. 12" W.S. model. Above avg. cond. $154.00

WWII SPOTTER MODEL GERMAN HEINKEL HE 177: two engine bomber. Molded black composition w/17" W.S. & good detail. Dated 9-43. Above avg. cond. $143.00

WWII SPOTTER MODEL US B-17: 4 engine bomber. Molded black composition W/ 17.5" W.S. & good details. Dated July 42. Early fortress design. Above avg. cond. $129.00

WWII SPOTTER MODEL US B-24: 4 engine bomber. Molded black composition w/ 18.5" W.S. & good details. Dated July 42. Avg. cond. $95.00

WWII SPOTTER MODEL US BATTLESHIP U.S.S. MISSOURI: 21" long. Wood & lead constr. Lacks a secondary turret & crane. Avg. cond. $114.00

WWII TRAINING PHOTO STAND-UPS OF MILITARY PILOTS OF BRANCHES OF ARMED FORCES: 9.5x13" paperboard w/ 8 color photos of pilots in flight gear & dress uniforms. Marine/Navy/Army. Tear out like paper dolls & fold over 6" stand ups. Great detail. Unusual. Mint cond. $61.00

U.S. MILITARY JEWELRY, SWEETHEART ITEMS, CIGARETTE LIGHTERS/CASES

A. All Periods

ADMINISTRATIVE SUPPORT UNIT ZIPPO LIGHTER: Nickel finish case w/flip top. One side engraved w/design & "Administrative Support Unit." Near mint cond. $30.00

AIRBORNE SIGNET RING: S/S w/airborne eagles on each side & blue stone in crest. 'AIRBORNE/ U S ARMY' around stone. Above avg. cond. $48.00

AIRCRAFT CONTRACTOR LAPEL PIN.: Metal wings on shield. Shield has blue enamel field w/'1' in center. across top of wing is 'CHANCE VOUGHT.' Pb displayed in plastic box w/clear top. Exc. cond. $11.00

ALLIED LAPEL PIN: Post WWII. Pb shows German, British, French & White flag w/ diagonal crossed blue bands. Banner at bottom says 'ALLIES.' Above avg. cond. $35.00

ARMY 24TH CORPS CIGARETTE CASE: Silver plated w/corps emblem on front w/ XXIV Corps below. Back has 'rendezvous/ Seoul Korea/1948.' Avg. cond. $23.00

ARMY 44TH DIV. WATCH FOB: Brass. reads 'Co/A/114 INF/44th Div.' in raised letters + cowhide strap w/hair still on. Above avg. cond. $27.00

ARMY 69TH DIV. CIGARETTE CASE: WWII Occupation force 4.5x3.5" case. Has gold plated occupation zone map on lid + 'US OCCUPATION ZONE' at top w/Div. emblem & '1946' at bottom. Gold plated. Exc. cond. $25.00

ARMY AIRBORNE SIGNET RING: Army Airborne w/red stone in face. Airborne emblems on sides & 'AIRBORNE U. S. ARMY' around stone. Sterling. Above avg. cond. $46.00

ARMY AIRBORNE SIGNET RING: Sterling. Red stone in face w/airborne images on sides & 'AIRBORNE U. S. ARMY' around stone. Miniature jump wings fixed on stone. Some light patina. Above avg. cond. $46.00

ARMY INFANTRY CIGARETTE CASE: Sterling w/national emblem w/colored shield. Beneath emblem is nicely detailed large crossed rifle infantry emblem. Interior clean & typical. Dark gray tarnish patina throughout. Color on eagle has faded & some chipping evident. Above avg. cond. $48.00

ARMY LADY COMPACT.: 3.5" brass w/snap lid & still containing powder puff, powder & mirror. top is blue enamel w/raised Army brass emblem in center of lid. Some tarnish on brass. Avg. cond. $55.00

ARMY NCO RETIREMENT GOLD WATCH: Mounted to heavy woven fob. Hmkd. 'Waltham premier' & works fine. Engraved on back 'PRESENTED TO/1ST SERGT H H WILBUR/BY OFFICERS & MEN OF/A CO. 66TH INFANTRY LT/30 YEARS SERVICE/SEPT 24TH 1938.' Near mint cond. $209.00

CURTIS WRIGHT PRODUCTION PIN: S/B Winged disk w/company name in center & production/soldier around rim + 100% in tab below. Above avg. cond. $20.00

CIVIL WAR CANTEEN PIN: Pb. silvered eagle pin w/looped chain to miniture canteen complete w/stopper, cover & band. Body covered in nice floral pattern. Exc. cond. $75.00

GERMAN OCCUPATION LIGHTER & CASE: Lighter has s/s case w/engraved outline map of US occupation zone in Germany. Age & tarnishing has partially obscured map. Nickel silver case w/nice enameled SHAEF emblem in one corner & partly colored US occupation zone map. Avg. cond. $60.00

GERMAN OCCUPATION SOUVENIR BRACELET: Shop made slip on alum bracelet engraved 1946 souvenir of Bremerhaven Germany. Nice. Avg. cond. $25.00

CIVIL WAR CANTEEN PIN

ILLINOIS NAT GUARD SWEETHEART PIN: 1902. Pb w/'Co G' on bar & metal heart w/ unit & location. Above avg. cond. $45.00

JAPAN OCCUPATION LIGHTER: Penguin Zippo Style Flip Top. From Yokota Japan w/Nice 5th AF DI style emblem on lid & 6102nd Air Base Wing emblem on body + 'SAYONARA/1958-9 / OFFICERS OPEN MESS/ YOKOTA AIR BASE/JAPAN. Avg. cond. $30.00

KOREA ERA AAA UNIT LIGHTER: Japanese-made. Brushed silver finish case w/flip-top. Has "26th AAA AW Bn./ (SP)" & crest design applique on one side + "Korea 1956" & "26/Arty/A" on other. Above avg. cond. $30.00

KOREA ERA SOUVENIR LIGHTER: Korean maker marked. Brushed silver finish case w/flip-top. Has engraved & painted design of Japan/Korea w/locations & small S. Korea, UN & Japan flag designs. Above avg. cond. $20.00

KOREAN ERA M. P. LIGHTER: Lid reads 'Company D/728th M. P. BN. Emblem on Face & back reads '58-KOREA-59' over crossed pistols w/728 over D. Avg. cond. $32.00

NAVY 7TH FLEET LIGHTER: Zippo slimline style w/'UNITED STATES' over Metal & enamel 3 star blue flag + 'SEVENTH FLEET' at bottom. On other side is nice Seventh fleet Metal & enamel emblem as DI. Exc. cond. $20.00

NAVY 7TH FLEET PRESENTATION ZIPPO LIGHTER: Brushed silver finish w/flip-top. One side has engraved & painted 7th US Fleet patch design. Other has design of V. Adm. flag & "Presented By Vam Robert B. Baldwin COMSEVENTHFLT." Near mint cond. $56.00

NAVY ACADEMY GRADUATION PIN: Gold w/naval emblems: wings, sabers, ships & seahorses + 1948 grad year. Exc. cond. $54.00

NAVY BUCKLE PIN: Silvered Pb brooch w/ 1900 navy buckle disk. Exc. cond. $30.00

NAVY CORAL SEA CV-43 ZIPPO LIGHTER: Nickel finish case w/flip-top. Engraved w/ design of ship & ship's crest. Comes w/ Zippo maker box. Light surface scratches to case. Avg. cond. $34.00

NAVY FINGER RING: Sterling/Jostens hmkd. Ornate R.T.C. Great Lakes designs w/lt. blue "starburst" stone. Large finger size. In ring box. Exc. cond. $28.00

NAVY SHIP ZIPPO LIGHTER: USS DONNER

NAVY SHIP ZIPPO LIGHTER: For 57-58 Med cruise emblem w/ship in center &

'USS DONNER LSD 20.' Continents filled w/brass. Above avg. cond. $59.00

NAVY SHIP ZIPPO LIGHTER: Early 1950s. For escort destroyer, etched on side is picture of ship & title, 'USS DE LONG/DD 884.' Initials scratched on back. Avg. cond. $90.00

NAVY SHIP ZIPPO LIGHTER: USS DELONG

NAVY SHIP ZIPPO LIGHTER: Early Post WWII. Has color enhanced etching of USS Leyte w/'USS LEYTE/CV-32', Faint outline of Sgt & name on lid. Avg. cond. $100.00

NAVY SHIP ZIPPO LIGHTER: USS LEYTE

NAVY SHIP ZIPPO LIGHTER: 1963 model. Flip top slim. Polished nickel finish w/ enameled etched picture of carrier against the glob & 'USS ENTERPRISE/CVAN 65.' Above avg. cond. $20.00

NAVY SHIP ZIPPO LIGHTER: 1976. Has USS Dwight D. Eisenhower emblem on front. Exc. cond. 45.00

NAVY SHIP ZIPPO LIGHTER: Early Post WWII. Has etched picture of ship & labeled 'USS LST 551.' Note: no ships name. Avg. cond. $75.00

NAVY SHIP LIGHTER: for USS CARP, lid w/ colored submariners badge + Novelty enameled emblem on body + handsome raised, engraved photo of sub under 'USS CARP/ SS338.' Exc. cond. $28.00

NAVY SHIP ZIPPO LIGHTER: Late 1950s. USS Lake Champlain cvs-39. Brushed silver finish case w/flip-top. Has engraved design of carrier & name on one side. Avg. cond. $40.00

NAVY SHIP ZIPPO LIGHTER: Slim-Line. Has etched & colored picture of USS Albany, CG-10 on polished metal case. Displayed in Zippo box. Exc. cond. $40.00

NAVY SWEETHEART PIN: Sterling Pb shield w/enameled 'NAVY' at top & navy wings below & 'V-5' at bottom. Avg. cond. $24.00

NAVY TABLE LIGHTER: Ronson. Holiday commemorative w/'MERRY CHRISTMAS/ 1955' on one side & 'CPO CLUB USN' over etched USN anchor + 'SASEBO JAPAN.' Above avg. cond. $35.00

NAVY USS ENDURANCE MSO-435 LIGHTER: Brushed silver finish case w/ flip-top. Super-Ace, Japan maker. Has enameled USS Endurance patch-design applique on one side & engraved "'Trawler Killers' A Wooden Ship With Iron Man, Vietnam 1970" on other. Exc. cond. $52.00

NAVY USS MINNEAPOLIS-ST. PAUL SSN-708 ZIPPO LIGHTER: "Slim-line" model w/nickel plated case w/flip top. Top engraved w/likeness of submarine "dolphin" badge + boat's patch design below. Details are enameled. Exc. cond. $20.00

NAVY WAVES PURSE COMPACT: Brass 2" compact w/inside mirror & Wave logo on lid. Logo is loose. Avg. cond. $75.00

OFFICER PRESENTATION STERLING CIGARETTE CASE: 3x4.5" ribbed body w/hinged lid-has diamond shaped monogram-sterling marked inside w/ engraved presentation from colonel to a Capt-1919 dated. Nice. Above avg. cond. $93.00

USAF 2792D USAF HOSPITAL ZIPPO LIGHTER: Brushed silver finish case w/ flip-top. Has enameled crest design applique on one side. Nice shape-appears unused. Above avg. cond. $20.00

USAF 436TH MIL AIRLIFT WING LIGHTER: brush finished lighter has small enameled & gilt design mini DI device applied to front. Back is plain. Mint cond. $20.00

USAF 98TH BOMB WING LIGHTER: Zippo style, sterling flip top case w/engraved map of Korea on one side + unit insignia & "98th Bomb Wings 1951 Japan" on the other side. Above avg. cond. $100.00

USAF CIGARETTE LIGHTER: 1950s. Zippo style-flip top in brushed steel case. Has applied enamel pin with design for the 2nd Radio Relay Sqdn. of a mountain goat on a tight rope over the mountains. Comical. Avg. cond. $20.00

USAF SAC ZIPPO LIGHTER: Well marked Zippo flip top w/Sac emblem etched on face. Shows wear on lid & near etching. Marks an era. Avg. cond. $82.00

USAF STRATEGIC AIR COMMAND LIGHTER: Brushed silver finish case w/ flip-top. 'Penguin,' Japan maker hmkd. Has gilt brass & enamel SAC patch-design applique on one side. In maker box. Exc. cond. $25.00

USMC 2ND MARINE DIV. NECKLACE: 15x22mm gilt & enamel 2nd Mar. Div. patch design pendant on fine lined gold neckchain. Exc. cond. $31.50

USMC CHINA SERVICE CIGARETTE LIGHTER: Silver case w/built in lighter. Front has marine emblem w/'US Marines' above & 'TSINGTAO CHINA' below. Back has twin dragons & Owners Initials. Some wear. Avg. cond. $93.00

USMC LAPEL PIN: 10 kt. Gold w/S/B mint. Near mint cond. $20.00

USMC LIGHTER: Named for Capt. + Silvered metal Corps emblem on side. Above avg. cond. $25.00

USMC ZIPPO LIGHTER: Brushed silver finish case w/flip-top. Has small EG&A applique w/"Bronx Platoon/November 10, 1953" engraved on one side & initials engraved on others. Above avg. cond. $177.00

USNA LADIES HAIR CLIP: Sterling & Hmkd. Bowed clip w/PB & short spike on inside of bow. Applied to outside is emblem for USNA & is dated 1911 on emblem. Exc. cond. $42.00

VIETNAM SERVICE LIGHTER: Brushed silver finish case w/flip-top. Interesting domed "windproof" design. Zenith brand. One side engraved w/design of bamboo shoort & "1962 NSAPAC." Above avg. cond. $25.00

VIETNAM SERVICE LIGHTER: Lid engraved w/sgt's name, Body engraved as follows: 'CO A 1ST /ENGR BN/ QUAN-LOI/VIETNAM/ 66-67-68.' Other side has 1st div emblem. Above avg. cond. $45.00

VIETNAM SERVICE ZIPPO LIGHTER: 1968 dted & showing nearly all finish removed to brass base. Lid reads 'KHE SANH/ 67-68.' MACV EMBLEM below & verse on back side. Avg. cond. $55.00

VIETNAM SERVICE ZIPPO LIGHTER: 1968 dted, has 'VIET-NAM/CAM-RANH/68-69.'

Etched is 1st MAW tab over 1st MAW emblem. Back is combat verse. Avg. cond. $60.00

VIETNAM SERVICE ZIPPO LIGHTER: 1968 dted, has 'VIET-NAM/PHU-CAT/68-69' on lid. Etched emblem showing cobra by chopper. On back is vulgar verse. Avg. cond. $30.00

WESTPOINT GRADUATE STERLING SWORD PIN: 1935. 50mm likeness of Westpoint cadet's sword in sterling-pin back w/early style saftey catch. Has Westpoint eagle on shield crest affixed to blade w/"1935" on shield. Near mint cond. $42.00

WWI LIGHTER FROM BULLET: Brass 'SOUVENIR D ALLIMAGNE' W/doves flowers ships & geese in decor. Bottom screws out to reveal lighter materials. Avg. cond. $65.00

WWI LIGHTER FROM BULLET

WWI SIGNAL CORP MEMORIAL SIGNET RING: Signal corps memorial ring for WWI. Sterling silver w/signal corps crest & war dates on rim. Military emblems on each side. Some wear on raised features. Avg. cond. $77.00

WWII AAF 8TH AF SOUVENIR CIGARETTE CASE: 3x5" hinged aircraft alum. body crafted by hand w/concealed hinge & latch. Has etched 8th AF patch design on one side + odd likeness of 4 engine airplane that appears to be a cross between a B-17 & a B-24 on the other side. Inside has two comical images of "Sad Sack" character. Well done. Above avg. cond. $118.00

WWII AAF 8TH AIR FORCE SOUVENIR BRACELET: Bright nickel plated brass band w/incised, short wing 8th Air force patch design in center-"England-ETO-1945-USAAF" on band. Generic inscription inside "With Love." Near mint cond. $48.00

WWII AAF ID BRACELET: S/S w/ID bar & name + Ser no of indiv + second bar w/ AAF Winged prop logo. Lite tarnish but nice looking. Avg. cond. $55.00

WWII AAF ID BRACELET: Sterling w/AAF emblem on side & Initials in script. Odd link chain. Above avg. cond. $41.00

WWII AAF LIGHTER

WWII AAF LIGHTER: 31x44x16mm milled aluminum block w/fine relief design of winged star in circular depression in one side. Has small flip cover for wick. Very nicely done. Supposed to be type produced by Italian POWs. Above avg. cond. $105.00

WWII AAF RING: Sterling w/AAF emblem on crest. Some wear. Avg. cond. $56.00

WWII AAF SIGNET RING: 10 kt G/F w/AAF emblems(winged props) on both side & forms the crest. Reads around crest 'UNITED STATES AIR CORPS.' Some wear. Above avg. cond. $117.00

WWII AAF SIGNET RING: S/S w/nice looking eagles on sides + AAF emblem (winged prop) for crest. Plus, crest swings away to expose a picture pocket like a locket. Above avg. cond. $91.00

WWII AAF SIGNET RING

WWII AAF SWEETHEART PILOT WING: Sterling 1/20th 10k marked. Pb w/saftey catch. 1 1/8" size. Hmkd. Above avg. cond. $20.00

WWII AAF SWEETHEART PIN: P/B stamped polished metal-looks like fighter w/AAF stars on wings. Above avg. cond. $20.00

WWII AAF SWEETHEART PIN: Small gilt & enamel ferry command patch chain linked to small USA pin. Near mint cond. $20.00

WWII AAF SWEETHEART WING: 1.5" PB S/S pilot wing w/enameled stars & bars in centr + bow across tip to tip w/'CRIDER FIELD.' Avg. cond. $70.00

WWII AAF SWEETHEART WING: Pilot style wing, PB w/gilded center disc & army emblem surrounded by jewel chips. Exc. cond. $22.00

WWII AAF SWEETHEART WINGS: 1.5" PB sterling gilt Wings w/nice detail & good color. Above avg. cond. $20.00

WWII AAF SWEETHEART WINGS: 14 kt gold P/b AAF winged prop sweetheart wings on orig cards (2). Exc. cond. $33.00

WWII AIBORNE SIGNET RING: Has chute on signet w/copper inserts on each side spelling '82,' chute has airborne on the canopy. Avg. cond. $40.00

WWII AIRBORNE SWEETHEART BRACELET: Features Airborne wings on crest & 'love, Joe' on back. link chain & chute worn smooth. Avg. cond. $28.00

WWII ARMY 100TH DIV CIGARETTE CASE: WWII alloy case w/brass & enamel DI of 100th div emblem in center. Avg. cond. $20.00

WWII ARMY 174TH INF. FINGER RING: Unkd. Appears sterling. Engraved designs w/enameled regt. crest design at top. Small finger size. Above avg. cond. $45.00

WWII ARMY EM VISOR CAP SWEETHEART COMPACT: 75mm dia top. Plastic body in OD finish for top, brown visor & chinstrap & gold painted device. Top is hinged & opens to reveal mirror (some chips to reflective back) & application pad. Above avg. cond. $45.00

WWII ARMY NURSE ID BRACELET: 12x40mm curve formed sterling body hand engraved in beautiful script to "Lt. Florence A. Blair / N-721310." Avg. cond. $53.00

WWII ARMY SIGNET RING: Man's signet ring w/enameled crest for 5th Inf Regt US Army HM & S/S mrked inside. Eagle over national shield on each side. Above avg. cond. $90.00

WWII BRACELET WITH EMBARKATION ID PHOTO: 2x3" clear plastic w/LA port of embarkation & photo w/thumb print & pb nickeled brass w/same name & alum chain & w/catch. Avg. cond. $37.00

WWII CBI BRACELET: chain link w/clasp + large oval metal disk in center. Sunburst around CBI emblem w/'MARY' at top, dates (1942,43,44) on sides + Burma, India & China & BCI at bottom. Back reads 'ALL MY LOVE FROM/FLORIN' INDIA. Avg. cond. $114.00

WWII CBI BRACELET: enameled CBI & AAF emblems w/US flag in center & banners w/china, india, burma included. Near mint cond. $265.00

WWII CHRISTMAS BRACELET: S/S 1.5" wide slave bracelet w/size adj & interesting paralell patterns of hatching on face. Inscribed on inside 'Louise 'Mom' Barrett/Love Hank Xmas England 1944'. Needs light polishing. Above avg. cond. $95.00

WWII CIGARETTE BOX: Chest style w/hinged lid & aromatic wood lining. HM 'Gorham 314' sterling. Lid engraved w/emblem (DI style) of 696th AFA BN & title below. Above avg. cond. $100.00

WWII CIGARETTE CASE: Alum case w/engraving in & outside. Front-Med emblem (name) & US Army. Back-Bathing beauty on couch. Inside, Army emblem & initials 'PE' + star in cigarette chamber. Avg. cond. $60.00

WWII DUNHILL SERVICE LIGHTER: Dark brownish-red painted metal body w/hinged cover for wick. Well marked. In pressed paper maker's carton. Exc. cond. $40.00

WWII DUNHILL SERVICE LIGHTER: In orig box Lipstick style metal finish w/wind screen & flip up cover on striker wheel. Above avg. cond. $12.00

WWII ID BRACELET: Classic heavy link bracelet w/Bombardiers wing on bar & name + Ser. # on back. Some wear on wing. Sterling. Avg. cond. $49.00

WWII ID BRACELET: Has Gilt Navy pilot wing in center, reinforce links & signs of wear on pilot wing. Avg. cond. $44.00

WWII LIGHTER: Looks like 1943 Zippo, w/black crinkle finish. Exc. cond. $34.00

WWII LIGHTER: Milled aluminum block in design of boot w/small circular amber inset details & simulated lace front + hinged wick cover. Approx. 46x45x15mm size. These items supposedly made by Italian POWs. Above avg. cond. ... $72.00

WWII NAVY OFFICER ID BRACELET: 36xx33 oval-shaped flat body (appears sterling) engraved to man (full name), "169341/LT.USNR/T 7/42 O." Body only-no wrist chain. Avg. cond. $25.00

WWII NAVY SUBMARINE SERVICE CIGARETTE CASE: 5x3.25x1.5" brass body w/lift-off lid. Has 3" brass likeness of fleet boat on lid. Avg. cond. $65.00

WWII NAVY SWEETHEART PIN: 46mm wide visor cap design in simulated mother-of-pearl w/mini mini USN fouled

anchor applique. Above avg. cond.
.... $29.00

WWII NAVY SWEETHEART SHOULDER BOARD PIN

WWII NAVY SWEETHEART SHOULDER
BOARD PIN: 46x20mm black crinkle finish
sterling silver body w/brass appliques of
lieut. rank, line officer stars & USN button.
Pb. Vanguard, N.Y./sterling hmkd. Above
avg. cond. $76.00

WWII REMEMBER PEARL HARBOR
LAPEL PIN: 63mm wide pierced cast
"Remeber Pearl" body w/applique
simulated pearl. pb. Above avg. cond.
.... $21.00

WWII REMEMBER PEARL HARBOR PIN:
Pb metal spelling out "Remember" &
"Harbor" w/mounted pearl between. Avg.
cond. $23.00

WWII SEABEE BRACELET: Nice enameled
emblem on brass disc fixed to dark stone.
Gilt links for bracelet. Above avg. cond.
.... $65.00

WWII SEABEE BRACELET

WWII SON-IN-SERVICE PIN: Gilt & enamel
Pb brooch w/Great Nat. Seal design
attached by small lined chain. In maker
carton w/sliding lid. Above avg. cond.
.... $20.00

WWII SWEETHEART BRACELET: Womans
bracelet w/brass & enamel Army emblem
in center. Remainder appears silver
plated. Scissors latch. Above avg. cond.
.... $35.00

WWII SWEETHEART PIN: 13mm 2nd lieut.
bar design attached to "U.S." design by
small linked chain. Both pieces are 10k
hmkd & Pb w/"fall-in" catch. Exc. cond.
.... $45.00

WWII SWEETHEART PIN: Hand painted
eagle w/'IN SERVICE' on chest & open
Sweetheart banner in talons. Avg. cond.
.... $20.00

WWII SWEETHEART PIN: Pb s/s Qm pin w/
'US' fixed at bottom. Good detail. Above
avg. cond. $20.00

WWII SWEETHEART RING: Sterling from
Lieut. Col.'s leaf. Above avg. cond.
.... $32.00

WWII USAF BRACELET: Likely english
made, nickel or chrome plated metal w/
AAF emblem in center & ETO/1945 on
each side + England & USAAF on each
arm. Engraved 'With Love' on back. Exc.
cond. $34.00

WWII USMC SILVER ID BRACELET: 2" oval
with worn emblem with name & home
town. Chain with clasp. Avg. cond.
.... $36.00

WWII USMC SWEETHEART HEART
SHAPED LOCKET: gold finished heart
locket has EGA device on the front. Has
loop for wear on chain. Mint cond.
.... $20.00

WWII ZIPPO LIGHTEER: 1943/44 period
black crinkle finish w/HM on bottom &
inside on inner sleeve. This is a 4 hinge
model. Avg. cond. $213.00

WWII ZIPPO LIGHTER IN BOX: Black
crinkle finish case w/flip-top. Zippo
marked. Comes in Zippo box in good
shape. Above avg. cond. $225.00

WWII ZIPPO LIGHTER: Black crackle finish
+ 3 part hinge for lid & HM inside & on
bottom. Avg. cond. $160.50

WWII ZIPPO LIGHTER: Full size marked on
inside. All the black crinkled finish
remains. Near mint cond. $450.00

WWII ZIPPO LIGHTER: Scarce-original w/
black crinkle finish-has small likeness of
USN officer's device applied to 1 side.
Exc. cond. $200.00

ZIPPO LIGHTER: 1953. Color enhanced
etching of USS Worchester, a light cruiser.
Below picture is 'USS WORCHESTER/
CL-144.' Above avg. cond. $97.00

ZIPPO LIGHTER

ZIPPO LIGHTER: 1958 dated has nice diagram for GE Aircraft Nuclear propulsion program. Avg. cond. $35.00

ZIPPO LIGHTER

ZIPPO LIGHTER: Has Aberdeen proving ground etched on face under etched & colored ordance bomb. Light wear. Above avg. cond. $72.00

ZIPPO LIGHTER: 1961 dated Has 1st div logo etched on side inside a gold colored wreath. Above avg. cond. $40.00

ZIPPO LIGHTER: 1967. Good case w/ bronze mini USMC emblem soldered on side. Exc. cond. $35.00

U.S. MILITARY RELATED PILLOWCASES & SOUVENIR ITEMS

A. All Periods

ASHTRAY FOR NATIONAL WAR COLLEGE: Heavy glass w/feet & pewtered top surface. College logo in bottom. Above avg. cond. $20.00

CIVIL WAR CONFEDERATE VETERANS CONVENTION BUTTON: Nicely preserved celluloid image of stars & bars centered on button w/'RALEIGH, MAY 20, 1895.' Designed for lapel wear. Exc. cond. $116.00

CIVIL WAR VETERAN CELULOID BUTTON: 32mm dia. Design of crossed US & CSA flags & reads "Presented by Courier-Journal." Stickpin back. Maker marked. Exc. cond. $95.00

CIVIL WAR WOOD DECORATED BOX: Oak box w/chambered interior & green velvet lining. Lid has decals of 9th Corps. Initials FJR (RFJ?) & US/Potomac Flags bracketing portrait of Union Capt. Ornate chinese-style plate & handle w/matching swing latches. Nicely preserved & attractive. Exc. cond. $110.00

DEPARTURE SOUVENIR FOR NAMED SGT: Two layered silk embr. farewell banner. Embr w/US flag- Japan Logistics cmd emblem. Named Sgt + dates 51-52/ USAH 8166 AUPX. Includes Commanders name & embr first names of members of the unit, some in pink others in grey. Hmkd. 'Yamashita.' Above avg. cond. $34.00

GAR 49TH NAT'L ENCAMPMENT AT WASHINGTON D.C., 1915 SOUVENIR: 28mm wide gilt brass pendant in shape of heart on Pb "Souvenir" brooch w/painted details. Hmkd. Above avg. cond. $38.00

GAR CONVENTION SOUVENIR WHISKEY BOTTLE: Small bottle patterned after CW canteen w/U S on back. Handsome full color label promoting 33rd annual encampment at Philadelphia, PA. 1899. Great shape. Exc. cond. $250.00

GAR ENCAMPMENT SPOON: 104mm tall. Handle in in design of GAR membership medal. Spoon reads "26th National Encampment/GAR/Washington DC 1892." Sterling hmkd. Above avg. cond. $45.00

GAR SOUVENIR CANTEEN: Clay ceramic 4" canteen w/details of June 1900 encampment by dept of Iowa at Davenport. One side has GAR medal & compliments of Aug Wentz post #1, Davenport. Missing one strap handle. Above avg. cond. $118.00

GAR SOUVENIR CANTEEN

GAR SOUVENIR WHISKEY BOTTLE: 1902. Clear glass 1/2 pint bottle w/'PBW' on bottom & gold leaf writing on side 'GAR/ 36TH/ENCAMPMENT/1902.' Stopper style bottle & no stopper. Avg. cond. $93.00

GRANT PROFILE TABLE MEDAL: Bronze 3" two sided issued by act of Congress. Grant's profile on one side & Grecian scene on other. Exc. cond. $25.00

KOREA REMEMBRANCE PILLOW CASE: 11TH EVAC HOSPITAL - PUSAN KOREA: 17x17" red cotton body w/large color machine embr. 8th army patch design in center-yellow machine embr. "11th Evac Hospital Pusan Korea." Near mint cond. $30.00

KOREAN WAR SILK SCARF: Dated on scarf 1953, Has Map of Korea, a border of flags involved in Korea & verses from Korean songs. Hand painted on nylon. Exc. cond. $28.00

KOREAN WAR SOUVENIR SCARF: small green scarf in silk w/embr dragon pattern in many colors & 'SEOUL KOREA/1952' above dragon. Avg. cond. $11.00

KOREAN WAR SOUVENIR SHIELD: Korean made. 210mm x 180mm blue cloth shield w/paper backing. Hand stiched features American, U. N. & Korean flags over multi-colored dragon. Text at top & bottom, reads 'RETURNED FROM HELL / 1951 KOREA 1952.' Avg. cond. $21.00

NAVY COOKIE TIN: Metal tin w/swing handle & nicely painted pictures of US Naval vessels. On lid is USS Idaho also inclued are USS Guam, USS Chicago, USS Raleigh & more. All Pre WWII ships. Special note: both USS Arizona & Lexington shown on side. Above avg. cond. $50.00

NAVY TABLE MEDAL, 1960 COMMEMORATIVE FOR LAUNCHING OF USS ENTERPRISE. 64mm brass medal w/bronze finish, displays particulars of Launch on front & back. Above avg. cond. $20.00

OCCUPIED JAPAN-MADE 1ST CAV. DIV. SCARF: Cavalry yellow silk body is approx. 42.5x8.75" w/fringe at each end. One side has nice hand quilted 1st Cav. Div. patch design w/likeness of Japanese isnald below w/location "Sapporo" & "Kokkaido" below. Above avg. cond. $55.00

SPANISH AMERICAN WAR ADMIRAL DEWEY CELEBRATION CELULOID MEDALLION: 54mm dia metal trimmed body w/design of Dewey & Battleship Olympia on front. Reads "New York Celebration To America's Hero Sept. 29 & 30, 1899." Reverse has rotating calendar of events. Above avg. cond. $55.00

SPANISH AMERICAN WAR ADMIRAL DEWEY SOUVENIR: 31x35mm gilt brass shield-shaped pendant w/bust design of Dewey & reads "Return of Admiral Dewey New York Sep. 28, 1899." On painted "Souvenir" brooch. Avg. cond. $25.00

SPANISH AMERICAN WAR SINKING OF BATTLESHIP U.S.S. MAINE SOUVENIR PAPER WEIGHT: Thick clear glass body measures approx. 4x2.5x.75". Bottom has image of the Maine exploding. Above avg. cond. $37.00

UCV LAPEL PIN

UCV LAPEL PIN: Sb enameled Union of Confederate Veterans pin for dues paid on 1914 convention. Good job on flag. Exc. cond. $118.00

USMC SHANGHAI 1947 SOUVENIR FLYING SCARF: 8x30" soft white silk body w/fringes on each end-fine silk embr. dargon on 1 side w/intials "R.D.B." & "Shanghai China 1947." Near mint cond. $32.00

VIETNAM ERA SOUVENIR ASHTRAY: Beautiful 6" diameter black lacquered ashtray with extensive mother-of- pearl inlay in the form of flowers. Brass inner tray. High quality GI souvenir South Vietnam ashtray. Exc. cond. $27.00

VIETNAM ERA SOUVENIR ASHTRAY: Two piece green ceramic w/Embasssy Hotel Saigon on side + Bird logo. Above avg. cond. $48.00

WWII AAF AVIATOR SCARF: White rayon. Has stamped black Army Air Forces on one side. Above avg. cond. $40.00

WWII ENGLAND SOUVENIR: WWII 15" sq maroon cloth w/chain stitched blue & white border + Impressive chain stitched 8th AF emblem on upper two thirds. At bottom is 'GREETINGS FROM ENGLAND' in chain stitch. Near mint cond. $35.00

WWII NAVY TRAINING STATION AT BRONX, N.Y. STUFFED MASCOT: Approx 12x9" suffed likeness of USN mascot in yellow & purple-blue felt. Printed likeness of USN officer device & lettering on each side. Some fading to color. Avg. cond. $20.00

WWII P-38 ASHTRAY

WWII P-38 ASHTRAY: All metal w/tear dropped shaped ash bin & graceful pylon fro model. 7" wing span, plated all metal model w/one prop missing (taped in bottom of bin.) Lockheed emblem missing from front. Avg. cond. $297.00

WWII PILLOW COVER: CAMP MACKALL, N.C. AIRBORNE. Ribbed satin body w/ flocked design of decending paratroopers & Troop Carrier Cmd patch design. Yellow fringe. Avg. cond. $20.00

WWII PILLOW SHAM: Blue field w/red-gold border & red fringe. AAF emblem in center w/US ARMY AIR FORCES above. At bottom, Larado Army Air field, Texas. Liberal use of gold flock letters. Above avg. cond. $35.00

WWII PROPELLAR LETTER OPENER: 9" long, 3 dimensional likeness of 2 blade propeller w/1.5" tall domed hub in center- "Keep 'Em Buying - WSAN Allentown, Penna." Avg. cond. $25.00

WWII RANK WHEEL SCARF: Full color 24" sq w/tri-service EM & Officer rank wheel in center. Outer block is army, middle is marine & inner is navy. Cap devices in corners. Above avg. cond. $30.00

WWII REMEMBER PEARL HARBOR PIN: PB brass w/tri color paint-shows airplane circling globe pulling banners w/theme. Avg. cond. $55.00

WWII SOUVENIR COMPACT

WWII SOUVENIR COMPACT: Designed like enlisted visor cap. Crown lifts to expose mirror & powder. Painted metal. Above avg. cond. $75.00

WWII SOUVENIR FROM ENGLAND: Rayon hankie w/english lace trim. Peach colored w/embr flowers in each corner & 8th AF patch in center & 'GREETINGS FROM ENGLAND' embr. below. Above avg. cond. $20.00

WWII SOUVENIR HANDKERCHIEF: Silk, colored trim & printed airborne wing in corner w/'11th Airborne Divison/188th/ paraglider infantry/the Philippines/1945.' Avg. cond. $20.00

U.S. MILITARY FLAGS, STREAMERS, GUIDONS, PENNANTS & BANNERS

A. All Periods

20 STAR US FLAG: 32x52" of sewn construction w/bunting & ties. Bunting hand marked 'Jackman' in ink. Minor repairs near bunting. Good color definition. Above avg. cond. $275.00

36 STAR US FLAG: 2x3' w/cord on bunting & all printed two sided image. Minor wear. Above avg. cond. $139.00

42 STAR US FLAG: 12x17" printed, two sided issued 1889 for Washington State statehood but never officially issued. Avg. cond. $82.00

44 STAR US FLAG: 12x17" printed, two sided showing some wear & tear. Issued in 1890 for Wyoming state hood. Avg. cond. $90.00

45 STAR US FLAG: Sewn construction, two sided, 3x4' issued in 1896 for Utah statehood. Some color fading. Above avg. cond. $140.00

45 STAR US FLAG: Spanish American War Era. Sewn silk w/multiple tears at end. Star embr. in white thread. Bunting w/ leather tabs & reinforced loops. Gold fringe on three sides. Below avg. cond. $98.00

46 STAR US FLAG: 32x56" printed flag two sided, issued 1907 for Oklahoma statehood. Some wear on bunting & darkening of color. Above avg. cond. $85.00

46 STAR US FLAG: 3x5' sewn const w/ printed stars & two sided. Shows age, few minor stains. Avg. cond. $40.00

48 STAR US FLAG: 5x8' wool blend sewn stars & stripes w/bunting & rope. Some wear evident on star field near bunting. Avg. cond. $11.50

50 STAR US FLAG: 5x9' Nylon multi piece const. w/embr. stars. Shows soiling & use, formerly of US Governent. Above avg. cond. $28.00

50 STAR US FLAG: 5x9' Postal dept flag, Nylon multipiece constr & sewn-on stars, light soiling. Above avg. cond. $35.00

AIR COMMANDO BANNER: 22x16" OD velour w/ember. '56TH AIR COMMANDO WING' over embr O-2 birdog acft & 'NAKHON PHANOM.' A few minor spots but really sharp. Exc. cond. $45.00

ANTI AIRCRAFT ARTILLERY UNIT GUIDON.: Swallowtail guidone 26 x 15" in red w/gold charactors for Battery A 1st Battalion, 42nd Regiment. Center emblem shows crossed cannons w/vertical missile. Near mint cond. $12.00

ARMED FORCES RABBI FLAG: 4x6' nylon w/blue field & sewn images for Jewish faith. Two sided w/white fringe. Near mint Exc. cond. $59.00

ARMY AIR DEFENSE ARTILLERY GUIDON: Scarlet nylon/wool swallow tail guidon w/ Gold Air Defense emblem sewn-on both sides. Mint condition & 2.5x1.5 size. Near mint cond. $20.00

ARMY AVIATION GUIDON: Nam era Swallow tail guidon in blue blended wool w/yellow army wings in center, two sided. 28x19" w/bunting. Mint. Near mint cond. $35.00

ARMY GUIDON: Swallow tail design in wool blend w/red & white panels forming guidon. Red panel has white numbers '107' & white panel has red letter 'F' Lite wear. Above avg. cond. $34.00

ARMY MEDICAL CORPS SWALLOW TAIL GUIDON: Dark maroon Poly Blend 28" long w/sewn on white medical emblem for both sides. Near mint cond. $13.00

ARMY QUARTERMASTER SWALLOWTAIL GUIDON: 29.5x20" buff coored cotton body w/applique design. 1961 dated Qm label. Above avg. cond. $30.00

ARMY UNIT FLAG: Beige nylon flag w/ multipiece construction & embr. Unit emblem for 319th Quartermaster in center w/blue banner below carrying '319TH QUARTERMASTER.' Unit metal DI attached at corner. Two sided flag 3x4" w/ bunting. Some lite stains. Above avg. cond. $150.00

ARTILLERY GUIDON: Scarlett field w/yellow crossed cannons. Swallowtail design 29x18". Two sided sewn const. Exc. cond. $20.00

ARTILLERY GUIDON: Swallow tail design 29x18" w/sewn yellow crossed cannon on each side. Wool blend fabric. Near mint cond. $30.00

ARTILLERY SWALLOW TAIL GUIDON: Red blended cloth w/reinforced bunting & sewn two-sided crossed cannon emblems in yellow gold. Exc. cond. $13.00

CAVALRY GUIDON: Swallow tail design 29x18" w/Horizontal scarlet over white panels. Sewn const + some darkening of white at bunting. Exc. cond. $20.00

CHAIRMAN JCS-CAR FLAG: 1x2' Nylon w/ embr National emblem bracketed by two blue & two white stars. Two sided + JCS breast badge, Cb. 2.3" brass disc w/ scalloped edges & white enamel center + silvered metal JCS emblem. Rare Exc. cond. $538.00

CIVIL WAR CONFEDERATE FLAG: CW era flag from family that claims to have flown it over home during conflict. Above avg. cond. $187.00

DEPUTY CHIEF OF STAFF FLAG: 66x51" beautiful flag w/US eagle on large star & four smaller stars. Outstanding detail. Exc. cond. $1,115.00

ENGINERS SWALLOW TAIL GUIDON: Red poly blend cloth 28" long w/reinforced bunting & two sided sewn white engineers castle emblem. Near mint cond. ... $14.00

HAND PAINTED WAR LOAN BANNER: White cotton w/red & yellow fringe & Blue & red images for the Sixth War loan/Buy Bonds campaign. Above avg. cond. $339.00

MILITARY GUIDON: Blue wool blend field in swallowtail design. Two sided sewn constr. Yellow emblems. At top, '24th' over spread wing eagle & 'AIR DEFENSE SQ' at bottom. Near mint cond. $30.00

NAVY ADMIRAL 3 STAR COMMAND FLAG: WWII dark blue 5x8' wool blend w/bunting. Three white hand sewn stars. Minor soiling at edge. Exc. cond. $45.00

NAVY COMMISSIONING PENNANT: Seven star pennant about 4' in length. WWI era. Avg. cond. $21.00

NAVY PENNENT: 29" blue felt w/yellow letters spelling US Navy. Above avg. cond. $28.00

NAVY REAR ADMIRAL FLAG: 3x4" rayon w/ gold fringe, leather hangers at bunting. Near mint cond. $55.00

RANGER F/INF/75 UNIT "SWALLOW-TAIL" GUIDON: 27x20" black cotton body w/ applied golden-yellow applique panels. 2 sided. Leather tabs in bunting. Exc. cond. $82.00

SECRETARY OF DEFENSE FLAG: 4x6'
white nylon w/crimson fringe & heavily
embroidered DOD emblem in center, two
sided. Near mint cond. $691.00

SIGNAL CORPS SWALLOW TAIL GUIDON:
Orange Poly blend cloth 28" long w/
reinforced bunting & two-sided sewn
signal corps emblem in center. Mint
condition. Near mint cond. $11.00

USAF BRIG GENERAL FLAG: 3x4" w/gold
fringe on blue rayon field. Leather hangers
on bunting. Mint condition. Near mint
cond. $50.00

USAF GENERAL 3 STAR FLAG: Yellow
fringe around blue nylon field. Stars are
sewn on & two sided. Size 3x4'. Near mint
cond. $50.00

USAF GENERAL 4 STAR FLAG: 3x4' sewn
construction w/gold fringe & blue field w/4
white stars. Near mint cond. $70.00

USMC FIELD MEDICAL SERVICES
SCHOOL FLAG: 1974 issue. 2x3' Red
background & double sided. USMC
emblem in center & school title at bottom.
Avg. cond. $48.00

USMC FIRST SERVICE REGIMENT FMF
STANDARD: Measures approx. 67x51"
size. Scarlet nylon body w/golden-yellow
fringe + beautiful applied panel & chain-
stitched EG&A design & unit scroll on both
sides. Leather tabs in bunting. Tag reads
"Made by Dettra Flag Products/Made in
U.S.A." These standards used from 1940
thru 1955. Above avg. cond. $1,075.00

USMC FLAG: 1930s. 4x5' flag that was used
in the China service of 1930s & retained
by Marine NCO when he retired. Wool
blend w/dark blue panel & colored USMC
emblem. Two sided w/reinforced bunting.
Documentation included. Above avg.
cond. $641.00

USMC FLAG: Type flown at HQ's. Large flag
w/applied E.G.A. & scroll. Avg. cond.
.... $290.00

USMC LT. GEN. FLAG: 3x4' red rayon w/
gold fringe + leather hangers on bunting.
Near mint cond. $72.00

WWI NAVY PENNANT: Blue 29" wool
pennant w/painted picture of Naval ship &
'Christening' & 'USS SAN DIEGO SEPT
16TH 1914.' Avg. cond. $45.00

WWI RELATIVE IN SERVICE BANNER FOR
TANK CORPS: Red felt w/white field &
blue star. 'TANK CORPS' above & picture
of tank at bottom. Above avg. cond.$40.00

WWI RELATIVE IN SERVICE BANNER:
Brown felt w/embr. 'SIGNAL CORPS' at
top & embr. rel. serving banner in center &
signal corps embr. emblem at bottom. One
edge discolored. Avg. cond. $25.00

WWII IN SERVICE WINDOW BANNER: Red
border w/white center & blue star over

AAF winged star. Says 'OUR SON' at top
& 'IS IN THE/ARMY AIR FORCE.' Some
fading of velour finish. Avg. cond.
.... $30.00

WWII INFANTRY GUIDON: Dark blue knit
body is "swallow-tail" design. Approx
28x19" size w/applied white cotton "139/
Inf/C" design. 2-sided w/undated Qm label
in button. Above avg. cond. $64.00

WWII MARINE UNIT HQ GUIDON FLAG:
Heavy red cotton flag w/two sided multi
piece construction. Has Marine emblem in
center w/'FMF' above & '3/11   HQ' below.
Reinforced bunting. Exc. cond. $79.00

WWII NAVY REAR ADM FLAG: Dark blue
wool blend w/two white vertical stars sewn
on. Two sided w/bunting & grommets.
Avg. cond. $20.00

WWII NAVY SUBMARINE GUIDON: 18x26"
swallow tail guidon in red wool w/heavy
canvas bunting & anchor w/fish entwined.
Avg. cond. $30.00

WWII OCCUPATION OF JAPAN FLAG:
Japanese meatball flag w/added phrases
by Occupation forces. Reads 'ALLIED
OCCUPATION FORCES/21ST RCT/24TH
DIV/ OKAYAMA JAPAN/NOV 45' All
American words have Japanese
counterpart beneath. 2x3' size in silk. Avg.
cond. $50.00

WWII RELATIVE IN SERVICE WINDOW
BANNER: 11x15" w/black wood post &
gold cord. Red w/white field & blue star
center Some fading. Avg. cond. ... $28.00

WWII RELATIVE SERVING IN MARINES
BANNER: On wooden pole w/gold cord.
Narrow red border w/bottom gold fringe.
White center w/USMC emblem in middle
& 'SERVING IN THE' above + 'US/
MARINES' at bottom. Avg. cond.
.... $14.00

WWII THEATER MADE STREAMER: 4' long
white silk of french or italian origin. Black
embr 'COMBAT INFANTRY REGIMENT.'
Exc. cond. $25.00

WWII UNIT CAMPAIGN STREAMER: In
EAME colors, 3x45' w/Yellow embr 'AIR
OFFENSIVE, EUROPE 1942 - 1944. Exc.
cond. $105.00

WWII UNIT CAMPAIGN STREAMER: In
EAME colors, 3 x45" w/Yellow embr
'EGYPT LIBYA 1942 - 1943.' Plated snap
provided. Exc. cond. $35.00

WWII UNIT CAMPAIGN STREAMER: In
EAME colors, 3x45" w/Yellow embr
'NORMANDY 1944.' Exc. cond. ... $90.00

WWII USMC COMMANDANTS FLAG:
4' 8"x6' 8" in size. Machine sewn from
individual pieces & shows red field w/
USMC emblem surrounded by 4 white
stars. Above avg. cond. $338.00

ABBREVIATIONS

AAC: Army Air Corp
AAF: Army Air Forces
Abn: Airborne
Adv: Advanced
AF: Air Force
AFB: Air Force Base
AG: Army Green
AN: Army-Navy (Standardization Program)
ANG: Air National Guard
Arty: Artillery

BAR: Browning Automatic Rifle
Bde: Brigade
BDU: Battle Dress Uniform
BMR: Bomber
Bn: Battalion

CAC: Coastal Artillery Corps
CAL: Caliber
Camo: Camouflage
Cav: Cavalry
Cb: Clasp Back
CBI: China-Burma-India
CBR: Chemical, Biological, Radiological
col: Colonel
cond: Condition
CPO: Chief Petty Officer
CW: Civil War

DI: Distinctive Insignia
Div: Division
DOD: Department of Defense

EG&A: Eagle, Globe, and Anchor, Marine Corps Emblem
EM: Enlisted Man
Embr: Embroidered
Engr: Engineer
ERDL: Engineer Research and Development Laboratory
ETO: European Theater of Operations

FIG: Fighter Interceptor Group
FTR: Fighter
GAR: Grand Army of the Republic
GRP: Group

hb: Hard Bound
HBT: Herringbone twill
hmkd: Hallmarked
Inf: Infantry
INTCP: Interceptor

Lieut: Lieutenant
Lt: Light

M: Model
MG: Machine Gun
MK: Mark
MM: Millimeters
MP: Military Police
Msgt: Master Sergeant
mtd: Mounted

NCO: Noncommisioned Officer

OD: Olive Drab
OG: Olive Green
OSS: Office of Strategic Studies
OWI: Office of War Information

Pb: Pin Back
Pfc: Private First Class
PO: Petty Officer

Qm: Quartermaster
QR: Quick Release

RCT: Regimental Combat Team
rect: Rectangular
Regt: Regiment
RIA: Rock Island Arsenal
Rt: Right

SAC: Strategic Air Command
SAW: Spanish American War

Sb: Screw Back
sb: Soft Bound
sgt: Sergeant
SMG: Sub Machine Gun
Spec: Specification
SQDN: Squadron

T-sgt: Technical Sergeant
TAC: Tactical Air Command

UCV: Union of Confederate Veterans
USA: United States Army
USAF: United States Air Force
USMA: United States Military Academy
USMC: United States Marine Corps
USN: United States Navy
USNA: United States Naval Academy

WAAC: Women's Army Auxiliary Corps
WAC: Woman's Army Corps
WAF: Women in Air Force
WASP: Women's Airforce Service Pilots
WAVES: Women Accepted for Volunteer Emergency Service
WO: Warrant Officer
WWI: World War One
WWII: World War Two

GLOSSARY

Aiguillette: A decorative cord (usually gold color) worn over the shoulder by designated aides to senior level officers.

Alpaca: The wool of llama like mammal (an Alpaca) that was widely used as the lining for cold weather and flight clothing during the WWII period.

Blood Chit: A note or message carried by aircrews (usually) to be used in the event of a crash or bailout over hostile territory. It usually identified the nationality of the crewman and had messages of assistance in the local languages. Often a monetary reward was offered for the safe return of the crewman.

Brassard: A cloth armband usually worn for identification purposes.

Breeches: A style of pants worn by Army personnel in the interwar period which were characterized by a baggy or loose fit around the thighs and a tight fit below the knees.

Browning Automatic Rifle (BAR): A light machine gun first developed in 1917 and used widely in Army service from WWI into the 1960's.

BuAero: U.S. Navy Bureau of Aeronautics. Responsible for design and testing of aviation related equipment and vessels.

Bullion: Gold or silver lace, thread, or braid used as decoration on military uniforms.

Crossguard: Part of a knife or bayonet that separates the blade from the handle and protects the hand of the person holding the weapon.

Epaulettes: Ornamental fringed shoulder pads worn as part of a uniform.

ERDL Camouflage: A four color, random pattern camouflage designed in 1948 by the Army Engineer Research and Development Laboratory and widely used in Vietnam.

Frog: A loop or other device used to attach a knife scabbard or sheath to a belt.

Fuller: A groove or indentation found on the blade of many types of edged weapons.

Garand M1: A semiautomatic .30 cal rifle adopted by the Army in 1936. It was the standard infantryman's weapon in WWII and Korea.

Grand Army of the Republic (GAR): An organization of Union veterans of the Civil War.

Guidon: A small flag or pennant carried by military organizations to identify individual units.

Hallmarked (Hmkd): A mark or method of identification used to indicate the source or manufacturer of an item.

Herringbone Twill (HBT): A special weaving pattern used with various fabrics known for its strength and durability. Widely used in uniforms in the WWII era.

Kepi: A style of military hat identified by a round flat top which slopes toward the front visor.

Krag: Officially the Krag Jorgensen M1896 .30 cal. rifle. Widely used in the Spanish American War.

Kevlar: Special fiber developed by DuPont in 1965. Widely used for bullet proof vests and other types protective clothing.

LAW: Tube launched light antitank weapon widely used by the U.S. Army in Vietnam and later.

Leggings: Cloth or leather covering worn as part of military uniforms. It usually covers from the top of the shoes to about the bottom of the knee. Worn widely thru WWII.

Nomex: A special fire resistant polyamide fiber developed by DuPont. Widely used in aviation related clothing.

Pommel: The knob found on the hilt of a sword or on the end of the handle or grip of a knife or bayonet.

Puttees: Similar to leggings (see above).

Quatrefoil: An elaborate decoration found on uniforms which is in the form of a flower with four petals or set of four leaves.

Quartermaster Corps: The branch of the Army that has responsibility for the design, testing, procurement, and supply of clothing, food, and other items needed by the Army for its soldiers.

Quillions: An extended crossguard (see above) found on many types of swords. Often straight or S-shaped they are used to protect the hand of the person holding the weapon or to entangle an opponents blade.

Shako: A style of military hat identified by a high crown, stiff construction, and often is decorated with a plume.

Smatchet: A multipurpose edged weapon that combined the characteristics of a fighting knife and machete into one.

Springfield M1903: The standard infantry rifle used by American troops in WWI. It was a .30 cal. design that was adopted for use prior to WWI and remained in limited service until 1945 as a sniper weapon.

Ricasso: The area of the blade of an edged weapon that is below the crossguard or quillions.

This resource directory focuses on clubs, associations, and periodicals that specialize in some category of American militaria. The following list is a sample of some of these resources.

Clubs / Associations

American Society of Military History
Los Angeles Patriotic Hall
1816 S. Figueroa
Los Angeles, CA 90015
Phone: 213-746-1776

American Society of Military Insignia
Collectors
526 Lafayette Ave.
Palmerton, PA 18071
Newsletter: *Trading Post*

Association of American Military
Uniform Collectors
P.O. Box 1876
Elyrie, OH 44036
Phone: 316-365-5321
Newsletter: *Footlocker*

Association of American Sword
Collectors
P.O. Box 288
Parsonsburg, MD 21849

Civil War Roundtable, The
357 W. Chicago Ave.
Chicago, IL 60610
Phone: 312-944-3085
Newsletter: *Civil War Roundtable
Newsletter*

Civil War Society, The
P.O. Box 770
Berryville, VA 22611
Phone: 800-247-6253
Magazine: *Civil War Magazine*
Frequency: Bimonthly

Company of Military Historians
North Main St.
Westbrook, CT 06498
Phone: 203-399-9460
Newsletter: *Military Collector and
Historian*

Dare Blade Collector's Society
3938 Pineway Dr.
Kittyhawk, NC 27949
Phone: 919-261-1149

Military Knife and Bayonet Club
1142 West Grace St.
Richmond, VA 23220
Magazine: *The Military Blade
Journal*
Frequency: Quarterly

Military & Police Uniform
Association
P.O. Box 69A04
West Hollywood, CA 90069
Phone: 213-650-5112
Newsletter: *Military & Police
Uniform Association Newsletter*

Military Vehicle Preservation
Association, Dallas/Ft. Worth
Arrowhead Chapter
P.O. Box 921
Keller, TX 76248
Phone: 817-379-6875
Newsletter: *Pintlehook*

National Knife Collectors
Association
P.O. Box 21070
Chattanooga, TN 37421
Phone: 800-548-1442
Magazine: *National Knife Magazine*
Frequency: Monthly

Orders & Medals Society of
America
P.O. Box 484
Glassboro, NJ 08028
Newsletter: *The Medal Collector*

South Florida Militaria Collectors
Society
14481 S.W. 2898 Terrace
Leisure City, FL 33033
Phone: 305-246-5431

Periodicals

*American Militaria Sourcebook &
Directory*
Type: Directory
Phoenix Militaria, Inc.
P.O. Box 245
Lyons Station, PA 19536-9986
Phone: 215-682-1010

America's Civil War
Type: Magazine
Frequency: Bimonthly
Cowles Magazines, Inc.
6405 Flank Dr.
Harrisburg, PA 17112
Phone: 717-657-9555

Artilleryman, The
Type: Magazine
Frequency: Quarterly
4 Water Street
P.O. Box C
Arlington, MA 02174
Phone: 617-646-2010

Civil War News, The
Type: Newspaper
Frequency: 10 Times per Year
4 Water Street
P.O. Box C
Arlington, MA 02174
Phone: 617-646-2010

Civil War Times Illustrated
Type: Magazine
Frequency: Bimonthly
Cowles Magazines, Inc.
6405 Flank Dr.
Harrisburg, PA 17112
Phone: 717-657-9555

Great Battles
Type: Magazine
Frequency: Bimonthly
Cowles Magazines, Inc.
6405 Flank Dr.
Harrisburg, PA 17112
Phone: 717-657-9555

Historic Weapons & Relics
Type: Newspaper
2650 Palmyra Rd.
Palmyra, TN 37142
Phone: 615-326-5454

Journal of Confederate History
Type: Journal
P.O. Box 1615
Murfreesboro, TN 37133-1615

Knife World
Type: Newspaper
P.O. Box 3395
Knoxville, TN 37927
Phone: 615-523-3339

Man at Arms
Type: Magazine
Andrew Mowbray, Pub.
1525 Old Louisquisset Pike
P.O. Box 460
Lincoln, RI 02865
Phone: 401-726-8011

Military Collector Magazine
Type: Magazine
Frequency: Quarterly
Phoenix Militaria, Inc.
P.O. Box 245
Lyons Station, PA 19536-9986
Phone: 215-682-1010

Militaria Directory
Type: Directory
David C. Williams
2237 Brookhollow Dr.
Abilene, TX 79605

Military History
Type: Magazine
Frequency: Bimonthly
Cowles Magazines, Inc.
6405 Flank Dr.
Harrisburg, PA 17112
Phone: 717-657-9555

Military Trader
Type: Newspaper
Frequency: Monthly
Antique Trader Publications
100 Bryant St.
Dubuque, IA 52003
Phone: 800-334-7165

North South Trader's Civil War Magazine
Type: Magazine
Stephen W. Sylvia, Pub.
P.O. Drawer 631
Orange, VA 22960
Phone: 703-672-4845

Wings and Things
Type: Journal
Frequency: Quarterly
Russ Huff
P.O. Box 17276
Sarasota, FL 34276
Phone: 813-923-3600

MUSEUM / LIBRARY DIRECTORY

There are many locations around the country where collectors of American militaria can research and view the objects of interest to them. Some of these facilities are both museums and research libraries. Federal facilities may require special advance permission in order to gain access to their holdings. The following list is a sampling of these facilities.

Museums / Libraries

III Corps & Fort Hood Museum
Bldg. 418
Battalion Ave. & 27th St.
Fort Hood, TX 76546
Phone: 817-287-8811

Air Force Armament Museum
100 Museum Drive
Eglin AFB, FL 32542-5000
Phone: 904-872-5371

American Armored Foundation
2383 5th Ave.
Ronkonkoma, NY 11779
Phone: 516-588-0033

American Military Museum
40 Pinckney St.
Charleston, SC 29401
Phone: 803-723-9620

American Military Museum
Whittier Narrows Rec. Area
1918 North Rosemead Blvd.
El Monte, CA 91732
Phone: 818-442-1776

Antietam National Battlefield
P.O. Box 158
Sharpsburg, MD 21782
Phone: 301-432-5124

Confederate Research Center
P.O. Box 619
Hillsboro, TX 76645
Phone: 817-582-2555

Fort Sam Houston Museum
Bldg. 123
Fort Sam Houston, TX 78234
Phone: 512-221-1886

Fort Ticonderoga Museum
P.O. Box 390
Ticonderoga, NY 12883
Phone: 518-585-2821

Frontier Army Museum
Reynolds & Gibbons Ave.
Fort Leavenworth, KS 66027
Phone: 913-684-3191

Gettysburg National Military Park
Taneytown Road
Gettysburg, PA 17325

Higgins Armory Museum
100 Barber Ave.
Worcester, MA 01606
Phone: 508-853-6015

Historical Military Armour Museum
2330 Crystal St.
Anderson, IN 46012
Phone: 317-649-8265

Library of Congress
10 First St. SE
Washington, DC 20540
Phone: 202-707-5000

Military Medal Museum and
Research Center
448 N. San Pedro St.
San Jose, CA 95110-1100
Phone: 408-298-1100

Museum of the American
Numismatic Association
818 N. Cascade Ave.
Colorado Springs, CO 80903-3279
Phone: 719-632-2646

Museum of the Confederacy, The
1201 East Clay St.
Richmond, VA 23219
Phone: 804-649-1861

National Archives & Records
Administration
7th & Pennsylvania Ave. NW
Washington, DC 20420

National Firearms Museum
1600 Rhode Island Ave.
Washington, DC 20036
Phone: 202-828-6194

National Knife Collectors Museum
P.O. Box 21070
Chattanooga, TN 37421
Phone 800-548-1442

National Infantry Museum
U.S. Army Infantry Center
Fort Benning, GA 31905
Phone: 405-544-4762

National Museum of Naval Aviation
U.S. Naval Air Station
Pensacola, FL 32508
Phone: 904-452-3604

Patton Museum of Cavalry & Armor
P.O. Box 208
Fort Knox, KY 40121-0208
Phone: 502-624-3812

Remington Gun Museum
P.O. Box 179
Ilion, NY 13357
Phone: 315-895-9961

Rock Island Arsenal Museum
Rock Island Arsenal
SMCRI-PCA-M
Rock Island, IL 61299-5000
Phone: 309-782-5021

Springfield Armory National Historic
Site
1 Armory Square
Springfield, MA 01105
Phone: 413-734-6477

U.S. Air Force Historical Research
Center
Maxwell AFB
Montgomery, AL 36112

U.S. Air Force Museum
Wright-Patterson AFB, OH 45433-
6518
Phone: 513-255-3286

U.S. Army Air Defense Artillery
Museum
Bldg. 5000
Pleasanton Road
Fort Bliss, TX 79916
Phone: 915-568-5412

U.S. Army Aviation Museum
P.O. Box 610
Fort Rucker, AL 36362
Phone: 205-255-4507

U.S. Army Center of Military History,
Museum Division
20 Massachusetts Ave. NW
Washington, DC 20314
Phone: 202-272-0310

U.S. Army Library
The Pentagon
Room 1A518
Washington, DC 20310

U.S. Army Medical Department
Museum
Bldg. 1046
Harry Wurzbach & Stanley Roads
Fort Sam Houston, TX 78234
Phone: 512-221-6277

U.S. Army Ordnance Museum
c/o U.S. Army Ordnance Center and
School
Aberdeen Proving Ground, MD
21005
Phone: 410-278-3602

U.S. Army Quartermaster Museum
Fort Lee, VA 23801
Phone: 804-734-4203

U.S. Army Transport Museum
Besson Hall, Bldg. 300
Fort Eustis, VA 23604
Phone: 804-878-1182

U.S. Horse Cavalry Association &
Museum
P.O. Box 2325
Fort Riley, KS 66442-0325
Phone: 913-784-5759

U.S. Marine Corps Air-Ground
Museum
Bldg. 2014
Quantico, VA 22134
Phone: 703-640-2606

U.S. Marine Corps Museum /Library
Marine Corps Historical Center
Washington Navy Yard
Washington, DC 20374
Phone: 202-433-3534

U.S. Military History Institute
Carlisle Barracks
Carlisle, PA 17013
Phone: 717-245-3152

U.S. Navy Museum
Bldg. 76
Washington Navy Yard
Washington, DC 20374
Phone: 202-433-4882

War Memorial Museum of Virginia
9285 Warwick Blvd.
Newport News, VA 23607
Phone: 804-247-8523

West Point Museum
U.S. Military Academy
Bldg. 2110
West Point, NY 10996
Phone: 914-938-2203

INDEX

Awards & Qualification Badges. 203
   Thru WWII. 203
   1946-Present. 205

Banners. 272
Bayonets and Machetes. 198
   Thru WWI. 198
   1920-1945. 199
   1946-Present. 200
Books and Manuals. 215
   Thru WWI. 215
   1920-1945. 219
   1946-Present. 231

Caps, Service Hats, Visor Caps. 123
   Thru WWI. 123
   1920-1945. 125
   1946-Present. 133
   Chapeaus. 123
   Post WWII Army. 133
   Post WWII Navy. 134
   USAF. 135
   Vietnam Era. 136
   WWI Army. 124
   WWI Navy. 124
   WWI USMC. 125
   WWII AAF. 126
   WWII Army. 127
   WWII Marine Female. 131
   WWII Navy. 131
   WWII USMC. 132
   WWII WAAC. 132
   WWII WAC. 133
Cigarette Lighters and Cases. 263
Cloth Insignia, U.S. Air Force. 91
   1947-Present. 91
   Korean War Era. 91
   Vietnam Era. 96
Cloth Insignia, U.S. Army. 55
   Thru WWI. 55
   1920-1945. 60
   1946-Present. 80
   Civil War Era. 56
   Korean War Era. 82
   SAW. 57
   Vietnam Era. 83
   WWI Era. 57
   WWII Era. 68
   WWII Era AAF. 63
Cloth Insignia, U.S. Navy and Marine
Corps. 97
   Civil War Era. 97
   Coast Guard. 97
   Navy. 98
   USMC. 100
   Vietnam Era. 101
   WWII Era. 103

Documents, Paper Items, and Framed
Items. 239

Flags. 272

Glassware. 259
Guidons. 272

Helmets. 137
   Thru WWI. 137
   1920-1945. 141
   1946-Present. 146
   Army Dress. 137
   Korean War Navy Aviator. 147
   Post WWII Army. 146
   Post WWII Army Aviator. 146
   Post WWII Navy Aviator. 148
   Post WWII Navy. 149
   USAF Flight Helmets. 149
   Vietnam Era Air Force. 150
   Vietnam Era Army. 150
   WWI Army. 138
   WWI Aviator. 141
   WWII AAF Flak. 141
   WWII AAF Flight. 142
   WWII Army. 143
   WWII Naval Aviator. 144
   WWII Navy. 145
   WWII USMC. 145

Individual Equipment and Field Gear. . 151
   Thru WWI. 151
   1920-1945. 161
   1946-Present. 181
   Ammo Belts. 151
   Cartridge Belts. 151
   Cavalry. 152
   Civil War Era. 152
   Indian War Era. 154
   SAW Era. 155
   WWI, Army. **155**
   Ammo Belts. 156
   Canteens. 157
   Cavalry. 158
   Gas Masks. 159
   Pistol Holster. 160
   Shovels. 160
   WWI, USMC. 161
   WWII, AAF. **162**
   Aviator Anti-Flak Goggles. 162
   Aviator Sunglasses. 162
   Cloth Aviator Chart. 162
   Flight Goggles. 163
   Mae Wests. 164
   Navigator Watches. 164
   Oxygen Mask. 165
   Wrist Watches. 166

WWII, Army. **167**
　Back Pack. 169
　Canteens. 170
　Carbine Covers. 170
　Cipher Converter. 167
　Compasses. 171
　Entrenching Tool. 171
　Gas Masks. 172
　Goggles. 172
　Life Raft Equip. 173
　Ordnance. 168
　Paratrooper Equip. 175
　Pistol Equip. 175
　Radio Equip. 176
　Rifle Equip. 177
　Shovels. 178
　Signal Corps. 168,178
　Survival Equip. 179
　Walkie Talkie. 181
WWII, Navy. **174**
　Aviator Equip. 174
　Flare Gun. 174
　Life Preserver. 174
　Signal Light. 174
WWII, USMC. **180**
　Ammo Pouch. 180
　Canteen. 180
　Field Pack. 180
Post WWII. **181**
　Aircraft Ax. 181
　Army Radio. 180,181
　Canteen. 181
　Korean War Era. 181
　Life Raft Equip. 183
　Navy. 183
　Oxygen Mask. 184
　Telescopes. 184
　USAF. 185
　USMC. 186
　Vietnam Era. 186

Jewelry. **263**

Knives. **189**
　Thru WWI. 189
　1920-1945. 191
　1946-Present. 196
　Bolo Knife. 189,196
　Fighting Knife. 190, 191, 196
　Hospital Corp Knife. 190,194
　Smatchet. 194
　Stiletto. 194
　Survival Knife. 195, 197
　Trench Knife. 190,196

Medals. **206**
　Thru WWI. 206

　1920-1945. 208
　1946-Present. 210
Metal Insignia, U.S. Army. **105**
　Thru WWI. 105
　1920-1945. 110
　1946-Present. 114
　Civil War Era. 106
　Indian Wars Era. 107
　SAW. 108
　Vietnam Era. 115
　WWI Era. 108
　WWII Era. 112
　WWII Era AAF. 111
Metal Insignia, U.S. Navy and Marine Corps. **115**
　Coast Guard. 115
　Navy. 115
　USMC. 116
　WWI. 116
　WWII Era. 116
Military Related Artwork. **258**
Military Vehicle and Aircraft Related Accessories. **244**
Models, Spotter and Promotional. **260**

Newspapers, Magazines, Broadsides, and Periodicals. **238**

Ordnance and Firearm Parts and Equipment. **241**

Photos, Postcards, & Trade Cards. **232**
Pillowcases. **269**
Plaques and Trophies. **256**
Postcards, Maps, Charts. **234**

Souvenir. **269**
Streamers. **272**
Sweathearts. **263**
Swords. **201**

Trench Art. **249**

Uniforms, Thru WWI. **7**
　Blouse. 7
　Breeches. 8
　Field Boots. 8
　Frock Coat. 8
　Leggings. 8
　Overcoat. 9
　Sack Coat. 9
　Sam Brown Belt. 10
　Shell Jacket. 10
　Uniforms. 11
Uniforms, 1920-1945. .... **12**
　Blouse. 12
　Boots. 13
　Breeches. 14

Capes. 14
Coat. 14
Coveralls. 14
Flight Suits. 14
Gloves. 16
Jackets. 16
Mackinaw. 21
Overcoat. 21
Parka. 22
Shirts. 23
Shoes. 24
Trousers. 25
Uniforms. 26
Uniforms, 1946-Present. 28
Blouse. 28
Boots. 29
Flak Vest. 29
Jackets. 30
Korean War Era. 33
Navy Aviator. 34
Navy Various. 37
Shirts. 39
Uniforms. 40
USAF. 41
USMC. 47
Vietnam Era. 48

Wings, U.S. 117
1913-1945. 117
1946-Present. 121
WWI. 117
WWII AAF Aerial Gunner. 117
WWII AAF Aircrew. 118
WWII AAF Bombardier. 118
WWII AAF Command Pilot. 118
WWII AAF Navigator. 119
WWII AAF Observer. 119
WWII AAF Pilot. 119
WWII Airborne. 120
WWII Navy Pilot. 121
USAF. 122
Vietnam Era. 122

THE LEADING PUBLICATION FOR MILITARIA COLLECTIBLES

Every issue of *Military Trader* has thousands of items for sale and wanted, show listings and editorial features on the field of Militaria Collectibles.

Use the coupon below, or call toll free 1-800 334-7165 to subscribe today at a *special low rate of only $15 (a 40% savings off the regular price.)*

☐ **YES!** Start my subscription to Military Trader. One Year (12 issues) for only $15.

SAVE 40%

Name _____

Address _____

City _____ Sate _____ Zip _____

E very issue of *Military Trader* has thousands of items for sale and wanted, show listings and editorial features on the field of Militaria Collectibles.

Use the coupon below, or call toll free 1-800 334-7165 to subscribe today at a

special low rate of only $15 (a 40% savings off the regular price.)

SAVE

40%